THE 900 DAYS

The Siege of Leningrad

Harrison E. Salisbury

THE **900** DAYS

The Siege of Leningrad

NEW INTRODUCTION BY THE AUTHOR

A DA CAPO PAPERBACK

Library of Congress Cataloging in Publication Data

Salisbury, Harrison Evans, 1908–
  The 900 days.

  (A Da Capo paperback)
  Reprint. Originally published: New York: Harper &
Row, 1969.
    Bibliography: p.
    Includes index.
    1. Leningrad (R.S.F.S.R.)—Siege, 1941–1944.
  I. Title. II. Title: Nine hundred days.
  D764.3.L4S2   1985   940.54′21   85-11712
  ISBN 0-306-80253-8

Maps by Daniel Brownstein and Andrew Sabbatini
of *The New York Times*

Portions of this book first appeared in *The Reader's Digest* in somewhat different form.

The lines on each of the six part-title pages in this book were drawn from a poem by
Yuri Voronov, "Blockade Jottings." They were translated by Harrison E. Salisbury.

Published by Da Capo Press, Inc.
A Subsidiary of Plenum Publishing Corporation
233 Spring Street, New York, N.Y. 10013

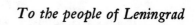

To the people of Leningrad

Introduction

EACH PASSING YEAR DEEPENS OUR REALIZATION OF THE triumph of man's spirit marked by the survival of the great city of Leningrad under the 900-day siege imposed by Hitler's legions in World War II.

Nothing can diminish the achievement of the men and women who fought on despite hunger, cold, disease, bombs, shells, lack of heat or transportation in a city that seemed given over to death. The story of those days is an epic which will stir human hearts as long as mankind exists on earth.

This narrative has itself come to play a role in the Leningrad drama. Published on the 25th anniversary of the lifting of the siege, it has been printed in translation in almost every country around the world. It has been hailed in America, in Europe, and in Asia for its celebration of the extraordinary heroism of the people of Leningrad, whose conduct shines like a beacon in a world which is often murky and not precisely heroic.

Only in one great country has *The 900 Days* not been published. That country is the Soviet Union. True, a Russian-language paperback edition was published—but in the United States. True, there are few citizens of Leningrad who are not aware of *The 900 Days* and tens of thousands of them have read its words and treasure them. Nowhere has *The 900 Days* been read more avidly and with deeper insight and appreciation than in Leningrad. But it has not been published there. Instead it was instantly attacked by the official Soviet propaganda agencies. *Pravda* published a full-page attack, charging that *The 900 Days* besmirched the heroism of Leningrad and demeaned the role of the Communist Party in the city's defense. It was, Pravda declared, one more volley in America's cold-war attack on the Soviet. The name of the venerable Marshal Georgi K. Zhukov was signed to these words—an ironic touch since Zhukov himself had been one of the most savage critics of the blunders and misjudgments (of Stalin and the Party) which led to Leningrad being subjected to the terrible siege.

The drumfire of fatuous polemics was kept on for several years in article after article. In fact, with the 40th anniversary of the end of World War II this theme reappeared in several Soviet commentaries on American "distortions" and "disinformation" about the war on the Eastern Front in World War II. For many years the author was unable to obtain a visa to return to the Soviet Union, and Leningrad specifically. He was for practical purposes declared "persona non grata."

This, as *Pravda* itself would say, "was not accidental." Although the great bulk of information in *The 900 Days* is drawn directly from Soviet sources, supplemented by the author's personal observations of Leningrad when he went there in the days of the lifting of the siege and from interviews of survivors, the valuable and often surprisingly frank reminiscences of military figures published in Moscow and Leningrad at the end of the 1950s and early 1960s quickly dried up.

That source of accurate and revealing information about the siege was a by-product of the relative liberalism of the regime of Nikita S. Khrushchev. When he was supplanted in 1964 by Leonid Brezhnev, it halted. The lid was hammered down. From that day forward the revelations about what happened at Leningrad were suppressed. The story was tidied up. No more blunders. No more intrigue. No more stupidity by Stalin and his generals. Death tolls and suffering were soft-pedaled. In fact, for a long time nothing of consequence was published about Leningrad. Leningrad writers who wanted to write about the heroic event found endless difficulties with their own literary censors. Several Leningraders who assisted with materials for *The 900 Days* encountered special handicaps. One elderly historian found his own work held up until a rival writer published a potboiler on the same subject. A prescription for medicines to treat his heart condition was blocked until he was near death.

Copies of *The 900 Days* sent to residents in Leningrad who helped with the book were seized by customs. American tourists who brought it in their baggage found it again and again confiscated. When I congratulated a young Soviet diplomat who proudly said he possessed a copy, I asked him how he got it. "Oh," he said, "I have a friend in customs." One Leningrader who had contributed time and material to *The 900 Days* first saw the finished book in the hands of an American tourist walking down Nevsky Prospekt. He shyly asked if he could look at the book and then asked the tourist if he would part with it. Unfortunately the tourist, not understanding what was at stake, declined to part with it even when the elderly Leningrad man said: "I'm in that book."

After all these years no work like *The 900 Days* has been published in Leningrad. There was a flurry of reminiscences, some very touching, a fine collection of interviews of individuals, some sensitive poetry – but the best historical and personal accounts came out twenty-five years ago and are drawn on in this volume.

Leningrad did not fit the propaganda picture of the war. Its epic was *sui generis*. The people played more of a role than the Party (this was one of the major criticisms of *The 900 Days* in Moscow). It suffered not only from poor planning and conflicts among high military and party figures but also from Stalin's prejudice against or even fear of Leningrad. Historically, Stalin seems to have felt that because Leningrad (under the name of Petrograd) gave birth to the 1917 Revolution, the city might ultimately rise against him. In a sense, this reflected an historic prejudice of Moscow against the new capital which Peter the Great built to be his "window on the west."

Nor has Moscow's antagonism toward Leningrad declined with the death of Stalin, the fall of Khrushchev, and a succession of lesser Soviet leaders. There is considerable evidence that it exists to this time. During the regime of Politburo member G. V. Romanov as Party Secretary of Leningrad, extraordinary hostility toward the survivors of the 900 Days began to be manifest. It was widely believed in Leningrad that Romanov hoped to remove from the city its very large number of invalids, disabled, and prematurely retired citizens—the victims and survivors of the blockade. They were regarded as an economic drag on the city, unable to take their places at the work benches and on the assembly lines—costing the city heavily, moreover, in medical expenses and pensions.

At the same time hundreds of millions of rubles were spent in restoration and rehabilitation operations of the great palaces and structures destroyed by the Germans. None of these restorations was more impressive than the extraordinary work carried out at Peterhof. This magnificent palace and its grounds had been almost totally demolished. The wrecked palace was still burning when the writer first saw it in the early days of February, 1944. Today it is hard to believe that it had ever been touched by Nazi hands. Not only has the facade been put back just as it was in the heyday of the Czarist regime, but the gutted interior has been done over as nearly as possible, even down to the bric-a-brac. Many Americans and Russians who saw the burning palace in 1944 felt it should be left in ruins as a monument to Nazi brutality.

Peterhof is not alone. Work still goes forward in a program which obviously has as its goal the restoration of Leningrad to its past beauty and glory—but this time only as a kind of living museum. The important governmental, party, artistic, and scientific functions have for the most part (except for the Palace and Hermitage collections) long since been transferred to Moscow. Even the famous Kirov ballet has become kind of a feeder station for the Bolshoi in Moscow.

Historically speaking, no really new revelations have been turned up about Leningrad and the siege. Details have slipped out here and there, but nothing of even secondary consequence. The story as told here is complete. Of course, the details of human suffering and sacrifice can never be collected in toto. Many Leningrad survivors have come forward with their stories since the original publication of *The 900 Days*. Some day there may be a revised edition which will take account of these.

There has been one major development. The great Piskarevsky cemetery, with its hundreds of thousands of Leningraders buried in the mass grave, has become a place of genuine national popular pilgrimage. And a new popular custom has come into being. Young couples with their wedding parties come straight from the marriage "palaces" in their bridal gowns and formal dress to lay wreaths in tribute to the dead. Thus, the living generation pays tribute to the dead. And so the generations go on. Leningrad and the siege will not be forgotten. As Olga Berggolts cautioned, "Let no one forget; let nothing be forgotten." And nothing will. The stones of Piskarevsky make that certain and, in the words of one man born in Leningrad and a survivor of the siege: "Your book is destined to be a monument to our dead, more fine and durable than the stone statues in Piskarevsky Cemetery." That is a tribute which to this author is finer than any prize in the world.

HARRISON E. SALISBURY
New York City
April, 1985

Contents

Maps

A section of photographs follows p. 304.

Principal Personages

AKHMATOVA, ANNA: Leningrad poetess, victim of oppression after World War II.

BERGGOLTS, OLGA: Leningrad poetess and vivid diarist, survivor of the blockade.

BERIA, LAVRENTI P.: Stalin's chief of secret police.

BUDYONNY, MARSHAL SEMYON: Early Red Army cavalry commander, named to head "Reserve Army" the night the Nazis attacked Russia.

BYCHEVSKY, COLONEL B. V.: Chief of Army Engineers in Leningrad.

DUKHANOV, GENERAL MIKHAIL: Former Leningrad staff commander, chief of Sixty-seventh Army.

FEDYUNINSKY, MARSHAL IVAN I.: Commander of important Leningrad front operations.

GOVOROV, MARSHAL LEONID: Artillery specialist and commander of Leningrad front from April, 1942.

INBER, VERA: Moscow writer who spent the blockade in Leningrad, diarist.

KETLINSKAYA, VERA: Leningrad writer, close friend of Olga Berggolts.

KOCHETOV, VSEVOLOD: Cub reporter on *Leningradskaya Pravda* at start of war, diarist.

KUZNETSOV, ALEKSEI A.: Party Secretary in Leningrad, No. 2 to Leningrad's Party boss, Andrei A. Zhdanov.

KUZNETSOV, GENERAL F. I.: Commander of Special Baltic Military District (Northwest Front) at start of war.

KUZNETSOV, ADMIRAL N. G.: Naval Commissar at start of war, prolific writer of memoirs.

LUKNITSKY, PAVEL: Leningrad correspondent of Tass news agency, diarist.

MALENKOV, GEORGI M.: Member of Communist Party Secretariat, alternate member of Politburo, bitter rival of Leningrad Party leader Andrei A. Zhdanov.

MERETSKOV, MARSHAL KIRILL A.: Leading commander on Leningrad front.

MIKHAILOVSKY, NIKOLAI: War correspondent attached to Baltic Fleet.

MOLOTOV, VYACHESLAV M.: Member of Politburo, close associate of Stalin.

PANTELEYEV, L. (ALEXEI): Resident of Leningrad, writer, diarist.

PANTELEYEV, ADMIRAL YURI A.: Chief of Staff of Baltic Fleet.

PAVLOV, DMITRI V.: Leningrad food chief, chronicler of the blockade.

POPKOV, PETER S.: Mayor of Leningrad, associate of Zhdanov.

ROZEN, ALEKSANDR: Writer, diarist.

SAYANOV, VISSARION: Leningrad writer, diarist.

SHTEIN, ALEKSANDR: Leningrad playwright, diarist.

STALIN, IOSIF: Soviet dictator.

TARASENKOV, A. K.: Soviet war correspondent, Leningrad diarist.

TIMOSHENKO, MARSHAL SEMYON K.: Soviet Defense Commissar at war's start.

TRIBUTS, ADMIRAL VLADIMIR F.: Commander of Baltic Fleet.

VISHNEVSKY, VSEVOLOD: Naval correspondent, playwright, diarist.

VORONOV, MARSHAL NIKOLAI N.: Soviet chief of artillery, adviser on Leningrad front.

VOROSHILOV, MARSHAL KLIMENT: Associate of Stalin's, commander of the Leningrad front until September 11, 1941.

ZHDANOV, ANDREI A.: Party Secretary and boss of Leningrad, leading candidate to succeed Stalin.

ZHUKOV, MARSHAL GEORGI K.: Leading Soviet commander, in charge of Leningrad front September 12–October 7, 1941.

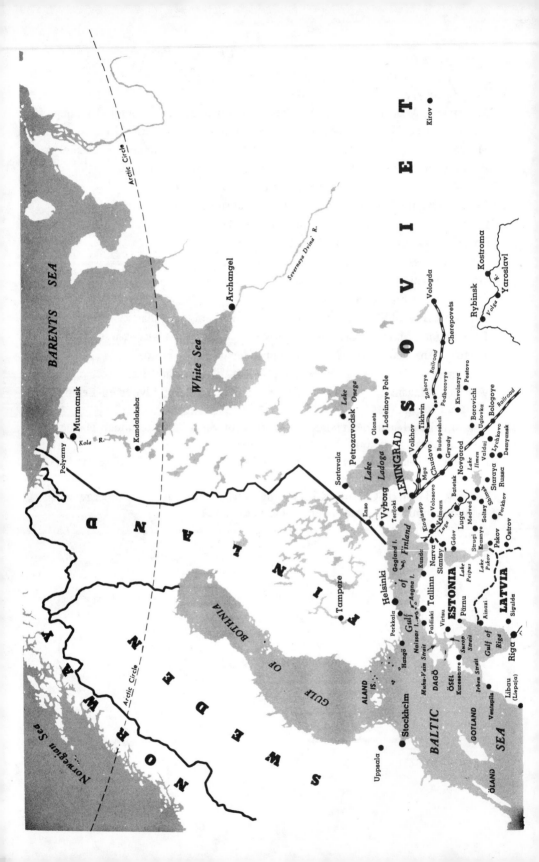

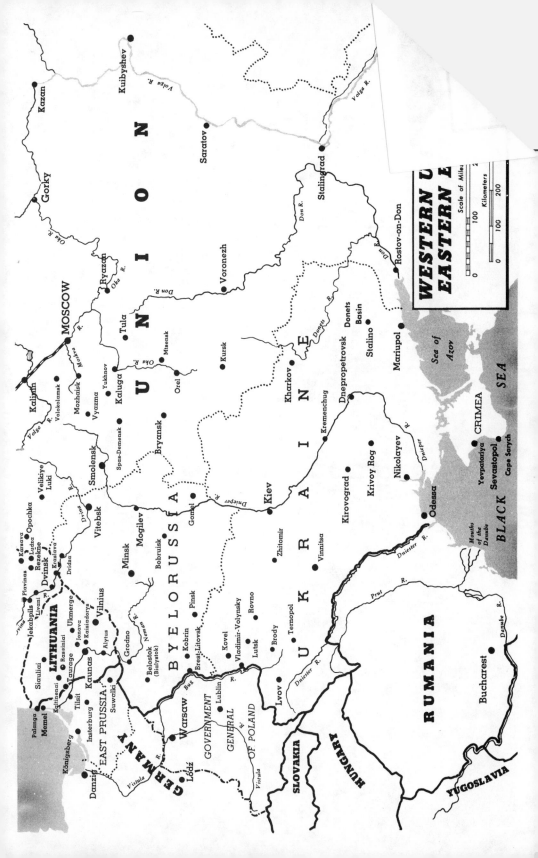

Let no one forget;
Let nothing be forgotten.

—Olga Berggolts

PART I

The Night Without End

Let this tale live forever
In our hearts, forever heard!
Let its memory be our conscience.

1 . *The White Nights*

COLD AND WIND, COLD AND WIND—THIS WAS SPRING 1941 in Leningrad. There had been snow as late as May Day, and the sodden demonstrators slogged past the Winter Palace in wet boots and soaking coats. The cold persisted into June, and it seemed that the Baltic fogs would never lift. Not that this was unusual. Peter the Great did not found his brooding capital on the Neva marshes with any concern for climate or comfort in mind.

The weather began to change with thunderstorms on Thursday, June 19, and again the next day. Finally on the summer solstice, June 21, the sun broke through and sudden bright blue skies blessed the city. Leningrad lived by Pushkin's aphorism that "our northern summer is a caricature of a southern winter," and the solstice by tradition was a special day—the year's longest day, a day which had no end, the whitest of "white nights," when midnight is less than dusk and night never falls.

The shift in the winds, the soft warmth of the sun, the alchemy which transformed the Neva from gray to sparkling blue, the flowering of the limes, the forsythia, the jasmine, brought a holiday mood to the city. In the cream and yellow eighteenth-century buildings of the old university, examinations were finished on the twenty-first of June and classes dismissed. Youngsters in pressed blue suits and girls in white voile flowed across the Palace Bridge from the University Embankment for their *gulyaniye*, the promenade of the White Nights, the singing to *bayans* and guitars, the rendezvous at cafés along the Nevsky Prospekt, the meetings at the Café Ice Cream at eleven, at the Green Frog at midnight, at the corner by Eliseyev's store at 1 A.M. All evening long there were lines outside the Astoria Hotel and the Europa. Within youngsters fox-trotted to the current hit, "We'll Meet Again in Lvov, My Love and I," a song which Eddie Rozner and his Metropole Hotel Jazz Band had made popular.

It had been an uncertain spring in Leningrad—not only because of the weather. Precarious peace prevailed in the Soviet Union, but with World

3

War II deep into its second year who could say how long the peace might last? The government assured Leningrad (and the rest of Russia) that the Nazi-Soviet pact, signed on the war's eve in August, 1939, would guarantee the country against attack. At the meetings of Party cells in the Leningrad factories Communist propagandists stressed again and again that under the treaty each nation pledged itself to carry out no aggression against the other. Any suggestion to the contrary, they hinted, was almost tantamount to treason. *Pravda* editorials hailed the unprecedented era of collaboration in which Russia shipped wheat and oil to the Third Reich in exchange for machinery (and war materials). But the men and women of Leningrad still worried. They harbored a gnawing distrust of the Nazis. Nothing in the course of the war had indicated they could put real confidence in the pledges of Adolf Hitler, no matter what Stalin said. After Poland had been partitioned between Germany and Russia in the autumn of 1939 they had watched the Nazi Panzers quickly overrun Denmark, Norway and France in 1940, and they had been stunned by the savage blitz of the Luftwaffe on England. These demonstrations of Nazi power brought consternation to ordinary Russians.

What made the spring of 1941 more nervous for Leningrad was the new campaign of the Wehrmacht—the quick, successful war against Yugoslavia, the swift conquest of Greece, the occupation of Crete, the threat to the Suez by Rommel's fast-moving desert forces.

Now that they had mastered the continent of Europe, where would the Nazis strike next? England was the obvious answer, but from time to time Leningrad heard rumors that Russia was next on Hitler's list. Moscow denied these reports (the most recent denial had been only a week ago), and no one was likely publicly to challenge Stalin's confident assurances about the pact with Berlin. Far safer to accept the Party line and bury deep within one's consciousness any reservations. Yet the concern persisted in many minds. If—contrary to all pledges, promises and assurances—Hitler did attack Russia, Leningrad would not escape. The city was military by history and military by tradition, founded by Peter the Great in 1703 as a bastion against the Swedes, the Poles, the Lithuanians, the Finns and the Germans, who century after century had fought to breach the gateway to the Russian lands.

But few of those who began their vacation exodus to resorts in the islands of the Gulf of Finland, to the new seashore and lakes that had been won from Finland in the winter war of 1939–40, were giving serious thought at that moment to the Nazi menace. The day was too lovely, the portents reassuring. To most Leningraders it seemed that their city was more secure than it had been for many years, more secure than it had been since Lenin was compelled "temporarily" to transfer the Russian capital back to Moscow in 1918 in the face of a threat that the Germans would overrun it. The "temporary" transfer had become permanent when Finland, Latvia, Estonia and

Lithuania split off from Russia after 1917, leaving the Finnish-Soviet frontier hardly twenty miles from Leningrad and exposing the city to easy conquest.

Now, thanks to the winter war with Finland, Leningrad had a little room for maneuver. Indeed, that room had been the objective of the brutal Soviet attack on her small northern neighbor. The frontier had been pushed back many miles, and when Stalin forced the Baltic states to return to the Soviet Union in the summer of 1940, Leningrad had been given a new protective shield along the Baltic coast.

With the perfect weather of the summer solstice the city rapidly emptied. The staff of the newspaper, *Leningradskaya Pravda,* had acquired a villa at Fox's Bridge on the Gulf of Finland about twenty miles north of Leningrad. They had their material for the Sunday morning issue of June 22 well in hand by Saturday afternoon—nothing of consequence was going on—and most of the staff managed to get away early in the afternoon for the resort.

Not everyone was able to leave Leningrad. Iosif Orbeli, director of the great Hermitage Museum, a man whose Jovian beard made his friends think of an Old Testament prophet, spent the day at his desk in the vast galleries on Palace Square. A dozen problems concerned him. There was his new Department of Russian Culture, just established May 26, after a long effort. Packing cases with at least 250,000 exhibits for the new section jammed the storage area and blocked the emergency exits. There were expeditions preparing for a summer in the field, and at the museum a painters' crew had put up a scaffolding after the May 1 holiday but work had not yet begun. Now, the year's busiest season was at hand, and Orbeli was angry at the delay. He telephoned the Construction Trust. They tried to put him off, promising to start painting at the "earliest possible moment," but he did not hang up until he got a firm date. The work was to start Monday, June 23.

Orbeli left his office late. He expected a large crowd on Sunday. Everything had to be in order. On his desk, marked in blue pencil, was a copy of Saturday's *Leningradskaya Pravda.* The item Orbeli had encircled was headlined: "Tamerlane and the Timurids at the Hermitage." It described two halls devoted to artifacts of the Mongol era. That would bring extra visitors on Sunday, Orbeli knew. Interest in Tamerlane was running high in Leningrad. A week ago a scientific expedition had arrived in Samarkand to examine the Gur Emir mausoleum where Tamerlane was buried. It was gathering material for the celebration of the five hundredth anniversary of Alisher Navoi, the great poet of the Tamerlane epoch. Each day *Leningradskaya Pravda* had printed a dispatch from Samarkand, telling of the progress of the work. On Wednesday the Tass correspondent described the lifting of the slab of green nephrite from Tamerlane's sarcophagus. "Popular legend, persisting to this day," wrote the Tass man, "holds that under this stone lies the source of terrible war. . . ." The story brought chuckles to many readers. Such a fantastic superstition—to believe that by moving an ancient stone war could be unleashed in the world. On Friday *Leningrad-*

The City of
LENINGRAD

Scale of Miles
0   1   2

Kilometers
0   1   2   3

━━━ Railroad   ∿∿∿ Canal

GULF

OF

FINLAND

Piskarevsky
Cemetery

VYBORG

SECTION

Kamenny
Ostrov Bridge

APTEKARSKY I.

Erisman
Hospital

PETROGRAD   SIDE

Lenfilm
Movie Studio

Peter and
Paul Fortress

FINLAND
STATION

Voinova St.

Summer
Gardens

Smolny
Institute

University

Hermitage

Champs de Mars

Okhta
Bridge

VASILEVSKY ISLAND

Admiralty

General Staff Bldg.

Europa Hotel

Astoria
Hotel

Nevsky Prospekt

MOSCOW
STATION

Mariinsky
Theatre

Haymarket

Yusupov
Gardens

Gostiny Dvor

VITEBSK
STATION

Passenger
Freight
Port

Obvodny Canal

BALTIC
STATION

WARSAW
STATION

Badayev
Warehouses

Narva
Gates

Kirov
Works

Moscow
Gates

Freight Yards

Avtovo

MOSCOW
SECTION

Neva River

Neva River

Fontanka Canal

Griboyedov

Sea Canal

Stachek Prospekt

Malaya

Malaya Neva

Nevka

Kirov Prospekt

Troitsky Bridge

Liteiny Br.

Palace Br.

Trubetskoy Bridge

Lt. Schmidt Bridge

Bolshaya Neva

skaya Pravda reported that Tamerlane's coffin had been opened. Examination of the skeleton showed that one leg was shorter than the other. This verified the tradition that Tamerlane was lame.

There was no story from Samarkand in the Saturday paper. Perhaps, mused Orbeli, that is why they printed the item about the exhibit at the museum. He locked his office, bade good night to the guard at the service entrance and walked out into Palace Square. It was, Orbeli thought, the most imposing architectural ensemble in the world—the magnificent Winter Palace and the Hermitage along the Neva embankment, the massive General Staff building and arch across the square and in the center the column commemorating Alexander I. It echoed empire. It had echoed empire since the day when Peter began to sink massive piles into the morass of the Neva estuary at the cost of tens of thousands of lives, to build first his fortress, the gravelin and bastion hulk of Peter and Paul, then the Kronstadt naval base on one of the hundred islands of the Neva Delta and finally to erect the palaces, the boulevards, the grandiose squares which evoked such flamboyant comparatives—the second Paris, the Venice of the North. Just as Petersburg came to call Catherine II the Northern Semiramis, ultimately her capital acquired the denominative which Orbeli most treasured—the Northern Palmyra; Semiramis and Palmyra—the ancient romance and mystery of Asia Minor transmuted into the ice and winter of the Russian north. St. Petersburg, Petrograd, Leningrad, Palmyra—whatever its name, surely there was no city its equal even though at the moment the view from Peter's "window on the West" might be somewhat obscured by Stalin's tyranny.

Orbeli strolled toward the Admiralty with its graceful spire. Across the Neva rose the answering spire of the Peter and Paul Fortress and the façade of the university buildings on the Petrograd side of the river. He turned toward the Nevsky Prospekt, the great boulevard which the poet Aleksandr Blok thought "the most lyric street, the most poetic in the world," where as nowhere else there was a mystery to the women, a dark handsomeness in their appearance, a ghostliness in their promise. Always the city had deeply moved those who saw it. To some it was oppressive, mystical, tragic; to others ethereal, magical, miraculous. To Lenin it was a sweated slum, ripe for agitation, intrigue, revolution. To the Romanovs it was the capital of the world, the seat of absolute authority, the mandate anointed by the blessing of the Orthodox faith.

Always the city evoked superlatives, swaying the beholder by the majesty of its spaces, the richness of its planes, the interplay of water and stone, of granite piles and slender bridges, lowering skies and the endless cold and snow of winter. It was Russia's workshop, Russia's laboratory, the cradle of Russian scholarship and art. Here Mendeleyev discovered the periodic table of the elements. Here Pavlov worked with his dogs on conditioned reflexes. Here Mussorgsky wrote his wild, dark music, Pavlova's fairy feet won the hearts of the grand dukes and the Imperial Ballet spawned Bakst, Diaghilev, Fokine and Nijinsky.

Leningrad was the capital of Russian creative life. On this Saturday, June 21, work went on all day in the rehearsal rooms of the State Ballet School on Alexandrinsky Square. The *grande dame* of Russian ballet, Agrippina Vaganova, was a strict taskmistress. On Sunday the twenty-second the corps was presenting a program at the Mariinsky Theater to mark the thirtieth anniversary of the debut of the ballerina Ye. M. Lukom. The graduation performance by Madame Vaganova's 1941 class of the ballet *Bela* was scheduled for Wednesday the twenty-fifth. All day Saturday work at the barre went on, hour after hour. Madame Vaganova was sixty-three, but she had lost none of her vigor and, as one of her ballerinas noted, "Madame Vaganova was strict as ever."

Karl Eliasberg, director of the Leningrad Radio Committee Symphony, returned to his apartment on Vasilevsky Island rather late that Saturday. He, too, was busy all afternoon with rehearsals. Now he sat down to read the paper and noticed that an exhibition was opening on Sunday in the Catherine Palace at Pushkin to mark the one hundredth anniversary of the death of the poet Lermontov. He decided to attend it. Another musical figure, the composer Dmitri Shostakovich, had quite different plans. Shostakovich was a football fan. Saturday afternoon he bought tickets for the Sunday, June 22, game at Dynamo Stadium.

There was much activity on Saturday at the rambling studios of Lenfilm across the Neva on the Petrograd side. There at No. 10 Kirov Prospekt on the site of the old Aquarium Gardens (where an ice palace had delighted generations of Petersburg youngsters) a film about the composer Glinka was about to get under way. Lyudmila, wife of the playwright Aleksandr Shtein, spent the day making beards for patriarchical boyars, fitting costumes for *Chernomor, Ruslan and Lyudmila,* putting into shape the delicate old Russian headdresses, called *kokoshniki.* Shooting would begin on Monday. Shtein was not with his wife. As an officer in the army reserves he had been called up in early spring for three months' service. He had finished his tour of duty a few days earlier and had gone to relax at a new writers' resort in the formerly Finnish section of Karelia, a few miles north of Leningrad. He spent Saturday night sitting on a rambling wooden porch, talking through the endless twilight with a fellow playwright, Boris Lavrenyov. The evening was tranquil, but later Shtein remembered seeing rockets on the distant horizon and, as he was going to bed about 4 A.M., he thought he heard the drone of airplane engines out over the Gulf of Finland.

All day Saturday there had been comings and goings at Smolny, the rambling complex of classic Russian buildings along the Neva River, once a school for noble gentlewomen, but since 1917 a symbol of revolution. It was here that Lenin and his Bolsheviks set up their command post for the November, 1917, *coup d'état,* and here, since that time, the Leningrad Communist Party apparatus had had its headquarters.

On this Saturday the Leningrad City Party was holding what was called an enlarged plenary session—a general meeting at which secretaries of the city organization, factory directors, economic specialists, labor union representatives and city officials were discussing several important questions—the carrying out of directives which had been approved at the Eighteenth All-Union Party Conference and new plans for industrial construction.

The meeting in the Smolny Assembly Hall, the room in which Lenin proclaimed the victory of the Bolshevik Revolution, did not end until evening. Some delegates headed home. Others joined the casual strollers on the city's broad boulevards, sauntering idly in the filtered midnight light. They paused to stare in curiosity at posters plastered on lamp posts advertising *Romeo and Juliet*, the Prokofyev ballet in which Galina Ulanova was dancing at the Mariinsky Theater the next day. Other posters read: "Anton Ivanovich is Angry . . . Anton Ivanovich is Angry." Not all the delegates recognized this as a teaser for a new movie which was to open soon at the leading houses. They shook their heads in puzzlement and wandered on to peer into the bright shop windows of Nevsky Prospekt.

The top personnel at the meeting did no strolling. They went straight to their offices and waited beside telephones in case of a call. Just before they left Smolny the word had quietly been passed: "Don't get too far away. There may be something coming up tonight."

They had been offered no clue as to what might be happening. Disciplined to carry out Party orders meticulously and without question, they now sat by their telephones, smoking cigarettes, poring over the mountains of paper that perpetually overwhelmed them and wondering what was in the air. Not all went to their offices. Mikhail Kozin, Party organizer for the great Kirov steel works, drove to his summer cottage at Mill Stream, a few miles outside Leningrad, to spend the night with his family. He had no telephone in the country, but his chauffeur went back to the factory, ready to alert him if anything happened.

In the suburb of Pushkin, the old imperial village of Tsarskoye Selo, the soft air and pale light attracted scores of young couples to the linden alleys and stately parks surrounding Rastrelli's exquisite Catherine Palace. Here where the poets Alexander Pushkin and Aleksandr Blok once lived, a new generation of Russian youngsters, many of them fresh from graduation exercises, strolled through the long night. As they passed the squat buildings known as the Half-Moon near the gates of the palace they paused. From the open windows of the Half-Moon came the haunting sounds of a Skryabin sonata. It was the composer Gavriil Popov and his wife, playing two grand pianos in adjoining rooms, separated only by curtains. Popov's opera, *Alexander Nevsky*, was at that moment on the rehearsal schedule of the Mariinsky Theater, being prepared for an autumn premiere.

The Catherine Park was a nest of creative artists. Nearby the composer, Boris Asafyev, was at work, instrumentalizing his opera *The Slav Beauty*, commissioned by the Baku Opera Theater for the forthcoming Nizami festival. In an adjacent apartment the novelist Vyacheslav Shishkov, back a day or two from a vacation in the Crimea, sat at his desk, correcting proofs of a long historical novel.

All winter the young writer Pavel Luknitsky had worked in the same house with Shishkov—it was Alexei Tolstoy's old villa, now a writers' rest home. On June 16 Luknitsky, thin, dark, handsome, intense and as yet unmarried, finished his novel and sent it off to the publisher. Now he was in Leningrad, wondering what to do with his summer. Possibly he would go to the new writers' resort in Karelia. There were lovely grounds there and a beach. In any event he thought he would accept an invitation he had received in the mail the day before. The writers' organization was sponsoring a tour of the old Mannerheim fortified line across Karelia which had lain in Soviet hands since the winter war. Special buses would leave promptly at 7:30 A.M., June 24.

In a big house at No. 9 Griboyedov Canal, not far from the Nevsky Prospekt, the poet Vissarion Sayanov talked through Saturday night with an old friend, a factory worker whom he had met during the winter war with Finland. Sayanov had been a war correspondent, his friend a political officer with a reconnaissance unit. Over a bottle of vodka they recalled the bitter cold in the Finnish forests, comrades who had survived and some who hadn't. It was a leisurely, reminiscent evening, and they did not separate until long past midnight.

Sayanov, a middle-aged poet with a round face and gold-rimmed spectacles, walked a bit with his friend before turning back to go to bed. The city was quiet in the hours before morning—quiet but lighted by a refracted luminosity which flattened the colors, melted out the shadows and washed the great stone buildings with eggshell tints. From a distance came the sound of young voices. They were singing a popular Soviet song: "*Daleko . . . daleko . . .* Far away . . . far away," a plaintive song of a lover far from his sweetheart and home. The chant rose clear and fresh, and down the street appeared a band of students, the girls' dresses white against the darkness of the pavement, the boys in light shirts and navy-blue trousers. Their arms were linked and they slowly walked, singing with a beauty that was rare and unearthly.

For the most part Leningrad now slept, except for wandering youngsters. Over on the Petrograd side the writer Vera Ketlinskaya, walking home along the Kirov Prospekt, watched a slim young boy pause and lift a girl to his shoulders so she could pick a spray of jasmine from an overhanging limb. The boy and girl came up to the Kamenny Ostrov Bridge over the Malaya Neva River. The draw was raised and they waited at the embankment, the girl shivering in the coolness of the night. When the boy tried to put his arm around her, she pulled away willfully and said: "One thing I would never be so stupid as to do is to marry you!"

"Why not?" the boy asked in despair. "Why not?"

"That's what I'm trying to understand myself," the girl said.

Finally, the drawbridge was let down. The boy and girl silently crossed over, the girl still holding the sprig of jasmine. They parted at the corner; then the girl called back: "Fedya!"

"What?" the boy replied.

"Nothing. Come by day after tomorrow. I'll give you back your books."

"All right," the boy said. "Leave them with your mother if you're not home. I'll drop in during the afternoon."

The young couple vanished. Now the avenue stretched empty and quiet. Leningrad was sleeping through the night that was no night . . . the longest of the white nights.

2 . *Not All Slept*

NOT EVERYONE SLEPT THAT NIGHT.

Not Army General Kirill A. Meretskov, Deputy Commissar of Defense, who boarded the Red Arrow express in Moscow at midnight, June 21, on an urgent mission to Leningrad. Hour after hour he stood looking out the window of his polished-mahogany compartment with its heavy brass fittings, its Brussels carpet, its French plumbing. He was riding in an old International car of the French Wagon-Lits Company, a heritage of the imperial past. North of Moscow the searchlight of the Red Arrow's locomotive cut through the dusk and, then, as the train hurtled down the straight course laid out by the engineers of Czar Nicholas I, the horizon slowly lightened. Meretskov knew this country well. During the years 1939–40 he had headed the Leningrad Military District. It was he who commanded the Soviet troops in the winter war on Finland. He had known Leningrad since the days of the Revolution. Almost every mile of broken birch and fir forest between Moscow and Leningrad was familiar to him.

As the landscape spread out in the cool light, he stared from the window, watching the sun rise in a pale-blue sky. The train plunged through the deep green of the forest and then out across watery marshes. Suddenly he heard the wheels echo hollowly on a bridge, and before him appeared the quiet waters of the Volkhov River. Then again swamps, more fir forests, more swamps.

General Meretskov felt a sense of mounting excitement as he saw the Leningrad land again, excitement and a sense of concern, a sense of pride and a sense of history. Pushkin's line ran through his mind:

> Show your colors, City of Peter,
> And stand steadfast like Russia. . . .

He watched silently at the window, his face tense and thoughtful as the train sped on toward Peter's capital. There was much to be done as soon as he arrived.

In the barnlike Leningrad offices of the Baltic Merchant Fleet beside the Neva passenger-freight port a conviction grew on Saturday, June 21, that something strange was afoot. Exactly what no one was certain. Most disturbing was the silence in Moscow, the silence of the People's Commissariat.

It had begun on Friday. When Nikolai Pavlenko, deputy chief of the Political Department, came to his office Friday morning, he found a cryptic radiogram on his desk signed "Yuri." The message—sent in the clear—had been received just before dawn. It said: "Being held. Can't leave port. Don't send other ships. . . . Yuri . . . Yuri . . . German ports holding Soviet ships. . . . Protest. . . . Yuri . . . Yuri . . ."

The message almost certainly had been transmitted from a Soviet freighter, the *Magnitogorsk*, which was unloading cargo in the German port of Danzig. The radio operator of the *Magnitogorsk* was Yuri Stasov, and the message center recognized his characteristic sending style.

What did it mean? What should be done? The *Magnitogorsk* did not respond to wireless messages. There were five other Soviet ships in German ports. No word from them either. The "Yuri" message was relayed to Moscow. No reaction.

Pavlenko didn't leave the matter there. He telephoned Aleksei A. Kuznetsov, secretary of the Leningrad Regional Party Committee, and asked for guidance. Kuznetsov suggested that precautions be taken but warned that "the question evidently is being dealt with in Moscow." For the moment nothing could be done about ships already in German waters, but the fleet authorities decided not to send any more to the west until they knew what was going on. The motor ship *Vtoraya Pyatiletka* and the steamer *Lunacharsky*, bound for German ports, were told to stand by in the Gulf of Finland and be prepared to put into Riga or Tallinn.

All day Saturday the Merchant Fleet waited for instructions from Moscow. None came. Pavlenko consulted Secretary Kuznetsov again. He agreed that the *Vtoraya Pyatiletka* be diverted to Riga and the *Lunacharsky* returned to Leningrad. It was an unusual demonstration of initiative for Soviet bureaucrats—to act without orders from Moscow. Meanwhile, ships in Baltic waters were told to keep in constant communication with Leningrad.

Toward evening the chiefs of the Merchant Fleet met. Sunday was a free day, but they decided that top personnel should come to work. The others would stay in town, ready for a quick call in an emergency. The chief administrative and political officers and their deputies, including Pavlenko, remained at their desks most of the evening, then went home.

The Leningrad Military Command embraced a vast area. In event of war it would become the command center for the region extending from the Baltic Sea to the Arctic reaches of the Kola Peninsula. Subordinate to it, so far as land operations were concerned, was Admiral Arseny G. Golovko, commanding the Northern Fleet at Polyarny on the Murmansk shore. Admiral Golovko had been reporting more and more alarming intelligence. For the past week flights of German reconnaissance planes had been observed over Soviet installations. What should he do? The response was: "Avoid provocation. Don't fire at great altitudes."

Golovko grew increasingly restive. On the previous Wednesday, June 18, Lieutenant General Markian M. Popov, commander of the Leningrad Military District and Golovko's immediate superior under the interlocking Soviet command system, had arrived in Murmansk. Golovko hoped for enlightenment, but none was forthcoming. Popov confined himself to questions of construction of fortifications, new airdromes, supply depots and barracks. If he had any intelligence on the current situation, he did not divulge it.

"Apparently he knows no more than we," Golovko noted in his diary on June 18.

> Sad. Such vagueness is not a very pleasant perspective in case of sudden attack. In the evening Popov left for Leningrad. I accompanied him to Kola. He treated us to a farewell beer in his special car and that ended our meeting.
>
> From Moscow nothing definite either. The situation remains unclear.

It got no clearer on Thursday, June 19. There were more German overflights. Nothing on Friday. On Saturday Moscow's Stanislavsky Musical Theater, starting its summer tour of the provinces, was presenting Offenbach's *La Périchole* in Murmansk. Golovko decided to attend. He took his Military Council member, A. A. Nikolayev, and his Chief of Staff, Vice Admiral S. G. Kucherov, with him. The theater was filled. There were standees.

Golovko relaxed and let the music push his worries out of his mind. So, he thought, judging by their expressions, did his aides.

The audience seemed at ease, possibly because Golovko and his staff were present. "The situation can't be so bad—the chiefs are here." This is what he read in the faces of the spectators as they promenaded in the lobby between the acts.

All the way back to headquarters he, Nikolayev and Kucherov talked about the operetta. Arriving at headquarters a little before midnight, he ordered tea and sat down for the late-evening situation report.

At the Leningrad defense command installations at Kingisepp, on the Moonzund Archipelago of the Estonian Baltic coast, Major Mikhail Pavlovsky spent Saturday, June 21, at Coastal Defense Headquarters. He had been receiving reports of unusual German activity for days, but nothing new came in on Saturday. As he was leaving the office, a friend in the 10th Border Regiment, Major Sergei Skorodumov, telephoned.

"How about getting your better half and coming to the theater? The NKVD song-and-dance ensemble is giving a concert and I've got tickets."

Pavlovsky said he would have to check with his wife.

"Any incidents today?" he asked.

"Absolutely quiet," Skorodumov replied.

The two couples went to the concert. Afterward they walked home. The city was still. Most people had already retired for the night although it was still full daylight on the Baltic.

Pavlovsky and his wife were undressing and talking about an excursion to the country on Sunday when the telephone rang. It was headquarters calling Pavlovsky back to his post.

"What is it?" Pavlovsky's wife asked.

"I don't know, Klavdiya," he replied. "I don't know anything at all. Maybe it's a training maneuver."

He kissed his wife and, opening the door carefully so as not to disturb the sleeping children, walked out of the house. The hour was just before midnight.

What was happening in the Leningrad area was duplicated in other frontier regions.

June 21 found Army General Ivan I. Fedyuninsky in command of the 15th Rifle Corps, based on Kovel and defending the Bug River sector of the Central Front. His concern had mounted since Wednesday the eighteenth, when a German soldier deserted to his lines and reported that the Nazis were preparing to attack Russia at 4 A.M., June 22.[1] When Fedyuninsky reported this information to his chief, Fifth Army General M. I. Potapov, he was curtly told: "Don't believe in provocations." But on Friday, returning from regional maneuvers, Fedyuninsky encountered General Konstantin Rokossovsky. Rokossovsky, commander of a mechanized corps attached to the

---

[1] An extensive literature has grown up around this incident, and there is controversy as to precisely when the deserter made his way to the Soviet lines. The operational journal of the 90th Border Guards unit reports that at 9 P.M., June 21, its fourth unit detained a German who had come across the lines. He gave his name as Alfred Liskof, member of the 222nd Infantry Regiment of the 74th Infantry Division. He surrendered himself at Vladimir-Volynsky, declaring the Germans had been ordered to attack at 4 A.M. He had heard this from his superior, a Lieutenant Schultz, and also had observed troops being disposed for the attack. The information was transmitted by direct wire by a Major Bychevsky to the chief of the Ukraine Border Command at Kiev and was relayed to the Army Command of the Fifth Army at Lutsk. The information was also passed to the commanders of the 87th Infantry Division and the 41st Tank Division at Vladimir-Volynsky. A. B. Kladt, writing in *Istoriya SSSR*, No. 3, 1965, suggests Fedyuninsky was referring to this deserter and that he mistakes the date. Nikita Khrushchev in his "secret speech" of February 25, 1956, mentions a deserter who brought over information on the night of the attack (probably the same Liskof). He says the information was relayed to Stalin on the evening of June 21 but that Stalin ignored it. Liskof became famous in the early days of the war. He was made to issue a statement calling on German soldiers to overturn the Hitler regime. Great posters were plastered up bearing his portrait on one side and the legend: "A mood of depression rules among German soldiers." Dmitri Shcheglov saw the posters on the Leningrad streets June 28. (Dmitri Shcheglov, *V Opolchenii*, Moscow, 1960, p. 8.)

Fifth Army, did not shrug off the signs of imminent Nazi attack. Indeed, he shared Fedyuninsky's concern.[2]

It was late Saturday night before Fedyuninsky retired, but he could not sleep. He got up and smoked a cigarette at an open window. He looked at his watch. The time was 1:30 A.M. Would the Germans attack tonight? All seemed quiet. The city slept. The stars sparkled in a deep azure sky. "Can this be the last night of peace?" Fedyuninsky asked himself. "Will the morning bring something else?"

He was still pondering this question when the telephone rang. It was his chief, General Potapov. "Where are you?" Potapov demanded. "In my quarters," Fedyuninsky replied.

Potapov told him to go immediately to staff headquarters to stand by for a call over the special high-security line—the so-called VC telephone.

Fedyuninsky did not wait for a car. He threw a coat over his shoulders and ran to staff headquarters. He found the VC line out of order. He got through on the ordinary phone, and Potapov ordered him to put his division on alert. "But don't respond to provocations," Potapov insisted. As Fedyuninsky put down the receiver he heard a fusillade of pistol shots—the car which had been sent to bring him to staff headquarters was being fired on by Nazi diversionists who had slipped across the frontier.[3]

Vice Admiral Vladimir Tributs, commander in chief of the Baltic Fleet, charged with the defense of Leningrad's sea approaches, had watched events through the dismal spring of 1941 with unconcealed apprehension. More, perhaps, than any other single Soviet officer, Tributs was apprised of the activity of German planes, German submarines, German transports, German agents and German sympathizers. Somewhat against his inclinations (because of security problems and the difficulty of constructing a new fleet base), Tributs had advanced Baltic Fleet headquarters from its historic seat at the Kronstadt fortress in Leningrad to the port of Tallinn, two hundred miles to the west. The shift had taken place when the Soviets took over the Baltic states in the summer of 1940. It gave Admiral Tributs an observation post within the newly acquired, only partially assimilated Baltic areas. He began to report the arrival of German troops at Memel, just across the new Soviet Baltic border, as early as March, 1941. In the same month German over-flights became a daily phenomenon at most Baltic bases. By June, Admiral

[2] Rokossovsky's concern was not deep enough to keep him from planning a fishing trip on the weekend of June 21-22. At the last minute a concert was scheduled for Saturday night at his headquarters in Novograd-Volynsky, so that instead of being away he was on hand to alert his commanders. But they were ordered to go to their units only "after the concert." (N. V. Kalinin, *Eto v Serdtse Moyem Navsegda*, Moscow, 1967, pp. 8–9.)

[3] A number of similar attacks were reported, including another in Fedyuninsky's command. Grigori Baklanov describes such an incident, probably based on Fedyuninsky, in his novel, *Iul 41 goda*, but makes it occur on the night of June 21, rather than in the early hours of June 22. (Grigori Baklanov' *Iul 41 goda*, Moscow, 1965, pp. 114-115.)

Tributs estimated at least four hundred German tanks had been concentrated just a few miles from the Soviet Baltic border.

Even more suggestive was the conduct of German engineers engaged in work for the Soviet Navy. The Russians had purchased from Germany late in 1939 an unfinished cruiser, the *Lützow*. The Russians towed it to Leningrad in the spring of 1940 for completion in the great Baltic shipyards. Several hundred German specialists were working on the *Lützow*. In April parts and supplies failed to arrive on schedule from Germany, although the Germans previously had been remarkably punctual. Tributs mentioned the delay to Admiral N. G. Kuznetsov, the Naval Commissar, who talked to Stalin about it. But Stalin merely suggested keeping an eye on the situation.

A little later the German engineers began to return home on one pretext or another. By the end of May only twenty remained in Leningrad, and by June 15 the last had vanished.

Simultaneously, German ships disappeared from Soviet waters. By June 16 not one remained.

Tributs was so worried that on Thursday, June 19, he convened his Military Council and decided to order a No. 2 Combat Alert for the Baltic Fleet. Chief of Staff, Vice Admiral Yuri A. Panteleyev, started to scribble out the orders while Tributs telephoned Admiral Kuznetsov in Moscow.

"Comrade Commissar," Tributs told Admiral Kuznetsov, "we have arrived at the view that an attack by Germany is possible at any moment. We must begin laying down our mine barrages or it will be too late. And I think it essential to raise the operational readiness of the fleet."

Tributs listened to Kuznetsov a moment, then hung up.

"He agrees to the alert," Tributs told Panteleyev, "but orders us to be careful and avoid provocation. And we will have to wait on the mine laying. Now, let's get to work. . . ."[4]

On the evening of June 21 Leningrad's sea frontiers—the Baltic Fleet, the shore bases, the coastal artillery as far west as Libau (Lipaja), the island sentries in the Baltic, the new leased-area fortress of Hangö, the submarines, the patrol craft and other sea-borne units—all were on a No. 2 Alert, just a step below all-out readiness for action. Live ammunition had been distributed. Leaves had been canceled. Full crews stood at their posts.

Tributs himself and his staff had left the Old City and moved into their

---

[4] Kuznetsov's memoirs imply that the initiative for the No. 2 Alert came from him. In any event, Kuznetsov did issue orders June 19 for a No. 2 Alert not only for the Baltic Fleet but also for the Northern Fleet and the Black Sea Fleet. The order was issued by the Military Council of the Baltic Fleet, according to K. L. Orlov, *Borba Za Sovetskuyu Pribaltiku v Velikoi Otechestvennoi Voine, 1941–1945*, Vol. I, Riga, 1966. (N. G. Kuznetsov, *Nakanune*, Moscow, 1966, p. 109; Orlov, p. 52.) The Germans had already begun to lay mines in the Gulf of Finland, but this was not detected by the Baltic Fleet patrols. Vice Admiral N. K. Smirnov blames the delay in establishing a Soviet mine barrage for the loss of the mine layer *Gnevny* and the damaging of the cruiser *Maxim Gorky* by German mines in the Gulf of Finland. (N. K. Smirnov, *Matrosy Zashchishchayut Rodinu*, Moscow, 1968, p. 18.)

war command post, an underground shelter outside Tallinn. Tributs got one more alarming report. This came from a sentry ship, the submarine *M-96*, on duty near the entrance of the Gulf of Finland. Captain A. I. Marinesko reported sighting a convoy of thirty-two transports, many under the German flag, near the Bengtsher lighthouse around 4 A.M., June 21.

That evening Tributs was in constant touch with Admiral Kuznetsov in Moscow. The Naval Commissar was an experienced military man. He had served in the navy since boyhood, and in the mid-1930's he went to Spain to advise the Spanish Navy in the Civil War. He shared Tributs' alarm but felt powerless to act in absence of instructions from the Supreme Command. He had put the fleets on the No. 2 Alert on his own responsibility, technically calling it a "training" maneuver. In fact, it was a precaution against sudden war.

Tributs and Kuznetsov conferred after the evening situation report by Deputy Naval Chief of Staff V. A. Alafuzov (Chief of Staff Admiral I. S. Isakov had gone to Sevastopol for the Black Sea maneuvers).

Tributs told Kuznetsov he considered the situation so grave he and his staff proposed to stay at their command post through the night. Kuznetsov repeated that his hands were tied as far as further action was concerned. The two officers concluded their talk in a mood of frustration.

Kuznetsov's worry grew during the evening as he talked with the Black Sea Command at Sevastopol and the Northern Command at Polyarny, and he, too, decided to stay at his post all night. Again he telephoned the fleet commanders, cautioning them to be on the alert.

"At the High Command until late in the evening of June 21," Kuznetsov noted in his memoirs, "all was quiet. No one called me and no one expressed any interest in the preparedness of the fleet."

Sometime between 10:30 and 11 P.M. Kuznetsov got a call from Marshal Semyon K. Timoshenko, the Defense Commissar, who said: "I have some very important information. Come over here."[5]

Together with his deputy, Alafuzov (who was considerably worried because his uniform was badly rumpled and there was no time to change), Kuznetsov hurried out of his office. The Defense Command was just down Frunze Street from naval headquarters, and the two men walked to Timoshenko's office, located in a small building across from entrance No. 5 of the Defense Commissariat.

"After a muggy hot day," Kuznetsov recalls, "there had been a short brisk shower and now it was a bit fresher."

---

[5] Kuznetsov has written several versions of this evening. He gives the time of this call as 10:30 in one version and 11 P.M. in another. Probably it was closer to 11 P.M. Kuznetsov spent only a few minutes with Timoshenko and was back in his own office and on the phone to Tributs by about 11:30 P.M. (N. G. Kuznetsov, "*Pered Voinoi*," *Oktyabr*, No. 11, November, 1965; N. G. Kuznetsov, "*Pered Velikim Ispytaniyem*," *Neva*, No. 11, November, 1965; N. G. Kuznetsov, "*Stranitsy Bylogo*," *Voprosy Istorii*, No. 4, April, 1965; N. G. Kuznetsov, "*Osazhdenny Leningrad i Baltiiskii Flot*," *Voprosy Istorii*, No. 8, August, 1965; N. G. Kuznetsov, *Nakanune*.)

Young couples were strolling, two by two, on the boulevard, and some-where nearby a dance was in progress. The sound of a phonograph came from an open window.

The two men bounded up the staircase to the second floor of the Defense Commissariat. A breeze rustled the heavy magenta curtains, but it was so stifling that Kuznetsov unbuttoned his jacket as he strode into Timoshenko's office. At the table sat General Georgi K. Zhukov, Chief of the General Staff. Marshal Timoshenko was dictating a telegram and Zhukov was filling out a telegraph blank. He had a pad of blanks in front of him and had already used up more than half of them. Obviously, the two had been at work for some hours.

"It is possible that the Germans will attack, and it is necessary that the fleet be in readiness," Timoshenko said.

"I was alarmed by the words," Kuznetsov recalls, "but they were not in any way unexpected. I reported that the fleet was already in a state of the highest military readiness and awaited further orders. I stayed for some minutes to get the situation precisely, but Alafuzov ran back to his office in order to send urgent radiograms to the fleet.

"Only let them be on time, I thought, as I returned to my quarters."

Kuznetsov immediately telephoned Tributs.

"Not more than three minutes passed," Kuznetsov writes, "when I heard on the telephone the voice of Vladimir Filippovich Tributs.

" 'Don't wait until you receive the telegrams which are on the way. Put the fleet on Operative Alert No. 1—combat alert. I repeat—combat alert.'

"Exactly when the Defense Commissariat had received the order, 'Be ready to repel the enemy,' I do not know," Kuznetsov reports. "But I remained without information until 11 P.M., June 21. At 11:35 P.M. I concluded my conversation by telephone with the commander of the Baltic Fleet. And at 11:37, as is recorded in the operational journal, the Combat Alert No. 1 had been announced—that is, precisely within two minutes all units of the fleet began to receive the order to 'repel possible attack.' "[6]

[6] Apparently Kuznetsov transmitted two telegrams. He gives the text of the first, a simple, urgent order, as: "SF KBF CHF PVF DRF Combat Alert No. 1 urgent Kuznetzov." The initials designate the Northern, Baltic and Black Sea fleets and the Pinsk and Danube River flotillas. The second message was fuller. It said: "In the course of 22 and 23 June sudden attack by Germans is possible. German attack may begin with provocational action. Our task not to give rise to any provocation which might increase complications. Simultaneously fleets and flotillas must be in full combat readiness to meet sudden blows by Germans or their allies. I order: transfer to Combat Alert No. 1, carefully camouflaged. Carrying out of reconnaissance in alien territorial waters is categorically forbidden. No other actions are to be taken without special permission."
According to Panteleyev, whose task it was to transmit the Combat Alert to all units of the Baltic Fleet, the No. 1 Alert had been acknowledged by all commands by 1:40 A.M., Sunday, June 22. Kuznetsov says that the Combat Alert No. 1 was announced within twenty minutes of his telephone conversation with Tributs at Hangö, the Baltic bases and other installations. (Kuznetsov, *Oktyabr,* No. 11, November, 1965, p. 167.) Another reference by Kuznetsov says all the fleets were on No. 1 Alert by 4 A.M. (Kuznetsov, *Voprosy Istorii,* No. 8, August, 1965, p. 110.) The individual reports indicate that Libau and Ventspils went on No. 1 alert at 2:40 A.M. Admiral Golovko reported that

The night that was no night wore on.

Later Kuznetsov was to write:

"There are events that cannot be erased from memory. Today, a quarter of a century has passed and I precisely remember the experiences of that tragic evening of June 21–22."

---

all his Northern Fleet units had been alerted by 4:25 A.M. The Black Sea Fleet reported Sevastopol on No. 1 Alert by 1:15 A.M. and all units by 2 A.M. The Danube Flotilla reported itself on No. 1 Alert at 2:22 A.M.

One account, that of the official Soviet history of the war in the Baltic, suggests the No. 1 Alert was issued by Kuznetsov at the strenuous urging of Admiral Tributs, who was said to have telephoned Kuznetsov repeatedly on the night of June 21 requesting such a measure. This same account asserts (possibly mistakenly) that the longer telegram from Kuznetsov was not received until 2:30 A.M. and that its text read: " . . . on Monday 23 June a sudden attack by Fascist Germany is possible but it is also possible that it will be only a provocation." (I. I. Azarov, *Osazhdennaya Odessa*, Moscow, 1962, p. 12; N. Rybalko, *Voyenno-Istoricheskii Zhurnal*, No. 6, June, 1963, p. 63; Kuznetsov, *Neva*, No. 11, November, 1965, p. 157; V. Achkasov, *Voyenno-Istoricheskii Zhurnal*, No. 5, May, 1963, p. 104; I. I. Loktionov, *Dunaiskaya Flotiliya v Velikoi Otechestvennoi Voine*, Moscow, 1962, p. 15; G. F. Godlevskii, N. M. Grechanyuk, V. M. Kononenko, *Pokhody Boyevye*, Moscow, 1966, p. 81; Orlov, *op. cit.*, p. 52.)

3 ٠ *The Fateful Saturday*

TWENTY-FIVE YEARS AFTER THE SATURDAY OF JUNE 21, 1941, Admiral Kuznetsov was still trying to reconstruct what was happening behind the scenes in the Kremlin, in the Defense Commissariat, in the highest circles of the Soviet Government.

He recalled the day as an unusually quiet one. Ordinarily his telephone was busy with calls from commissars and high officials, especially from those whom he liked to call the "fidgety ones," Vyacheslav A. Malyshev and Ivan I. Nosenko, the chiefs of the defense industries. The calls would come in a steady stream until about 6 P.M., when the top officials usually went home for dinner and a little rest before returning to their offices. They were in the habit of staying on duty until 2 or 3 A.M. in the event of a call from Stalin, who worked through most of the night. A commissar who was not at his desk when a call from the *khozyain*,[1] or boss, came through was not likely to be a commissar the following morning.

But Saturday was quiet. Neither Malyshev nor Nosenko called. It was Kuznetsov's impression that since it was Saturday, normally a half-holiday, and moreover a fine day, warm and summery, most of the chiefs had taken the afternoon off and gone to the country. In late afternoon he telephoned Defense Commissar Timoshenko. "The Commissar has left," his office said. The Chief of Staff, General Zhukov, was not in his office either.

Was anything happening in Moscow? Did the whole glorious June day drift by without the Kremlin paying heed to what was afoot?

In one government office there was no quiet. This was the Foreign Commissariat, located in a rambling group of decaying buildings on Lubyanka Hill, across a small square from the red-stone headquarters of the NKVD. Since he had relinquished the premiership to Stalin on May 6 Foreign Commissar Molotov had concentrated on diplomatic duties. However, he retained

---

[1] *Khozyain* is the old Russian word for "master" or "landlord." This is what serfs called their owner. It was customary for bureaucrats to use this term in referring to Stalin.

a suite in the Kremlin, as Deputy Premier, and divided his time between the two establishments, usually working days in the Narkomindel (Foreign Office) and evenings in the Kremlin.

Some time on Friday night, or early Saturday morning, Molotov, acting on orders from Stalin himself (very probably after a long and heated argument within the Politburo), had drafted careful instructions which were telegraphed in cipher to the Soviet Ambassador in Berlin, Vladimir G. Dekanozov.[2]

Dekanozov was instructed to request an immediate meeting with Foreign Minister Joachim von Ribbentrop to present a *note verbale*, protesting the increasing German overflights of Soviet territory. These were said to have numbered 180 in the period between April 19 and June 19, some of them penetrating to a depth of sixty-five to a hundred miles.[3]

Dekanozov was then supposed to draw von Ribbentrop into a discussion of the general state of Soviet-German relations, expressing concern over their apparent deterioration, noting the rumors of possible war and voicing hope that conflict might be avoided. Dekanozov was to assure von Ribbentrop that Moscow was ready for conversations to ease the situation.

The coded instructions to Dekanozov were received in the Berlin Embassy early Saturday morning. In Berlin, as in Moscow, the weather was fine. Berliners were preparing to leave town by afternoon. Many were heading for the Potsdam parks or the Wannsee, where the bathing season was getting under way.

The atmosphere in the Soviet Embassy was serene. I. F. Filippov, the Tass correspondent in Berlin, dropped in after attending the usual dull Saturday morning press conference at the Nazi Foreign Office. He found Dekanozov listening to a report from the Soviet press attaché on the contents of the morning German press. Filippov told the Ambassador that the foreign newsmen had questioned him about rumors of a German attack on Russia. He said that some were considering staying in Berlin for the weekend because of the possibility of news.

"It didn't seem to me that the Ambassador took my news very seriously," Filippov recalled in his memoirs. Dekanozov did detain him after the others had left, however. He asked Filippov what he thought of the rumors. Filippov told the Ambassador that the many facts which the embassy already had in its possession required that the rumors be taken seriously. But the

---

[2] Dekanozov, for many years an official of the Soviet Security Service and close associate of Lavrenti P. Beria, Soviet security chief, was named Soviet Ambassador in Berlin after accompanying Molotov to Berlin for the conference with Hitler and Ribbentrop in November, 1940. Dekanozov was executed with Beria on December 23, 1953.

[3] The figure of 152 violations of the Soviet air frontier from January 1, 1941, to the beginning of the war is given in the official Soviet military history. (P. N. Pospelov, *Istoriya Velikoi Otechestvennoi Voiny Sovetskogo Soyuza, 1941–1945*, Moscow, 1961, Vol. I, p. 479.) The Ukrainian and Byelorussian commands reported 324 overflights from January 1 to June 20, 1941. (V. V. Platonov, *Eto Bylo Na Buge*, Moscow, 1966, quoting *Krasnaya Zvezda*, April 14, 1965.)

Ambassador assured him: "There's no need for a panicky mood. That is just what our enemies want. You must distinguish between truth and propaganda."

Filippov left the Ambassador after telling him he was planning a trip to the Rostok area on Sunday. The Ambassador thought that was a fine idea, and he said he hoped to go for a drive as well.

If Dekanozov was disturbed by Moscow's instructions that he seek an urgent conference with Ribbentrop, he betrayed no sign of it in talking with Filippov.[4]

Valentin Berezhkov, first secretary of the embassy, was instructed to call the Wilhelmstrasse and arrange for the meeting with Ribbentrop. However, the duty officer at the Wilhelmstrasse advised him that Ribbentrop was out of town. Berezhkov then tried to reach Baron Ernst von Weizsäcker, State Secretary of the Foreign Office. He was also unavailable. Berezhkov called a little later. No one in a responsible position could be found. He kept calling at intervals. Finally, about noon, he got Dr. Ernst Wörmann, head of the Political Division of the Foreign Office. Wörmann was no help.

"It seems to me," Wörmann said, "that the Führer must be having some important meeting. Evidently, they are all there. If your matter is urgent, turn it over to me and I'll try and get in touch with the chiefs."

Berezhkov replied that Dekanozov had instructions to talk to Ribbentrop and no one else.

Meanwhile, Moscow began to place urgent calls to the Soviet Embassy in Berlin. Molotov was demanding action. All that Berezhkov could report was that every effort was being made to reach Ribbentrop—without result.

The afternoon wore on in an atmosphere of growing nervousness. Evening fell—and still no Ribbentrop. The rest of the embassy personnel went home. Berezhkov stayed on. Mechanically, every thirty minutes he telephoned the Wilhelmstrasse.

The windows of the Soviet Embassy gave onto the Unter den Linden. Berezhkov sat by his telephone and gazed out on the boulevard, where, as on all Saturdays, the Berliners paraded under their beloved lime trees—girls and women in bright summer prints; men, mostly middle-aged, in dark, rather old-fashioned suits (the youngsters were all in the army); the inevitable policeman in his ugly *Schutzmann* helmet leaning against the wall at the embassy gate.

On Berezhkov's desk lay Saturday's copy of the *Völkischer Beobachter*. In it was an article by Otto Dietrich, Hitler's press chief, expounding on the "threat" which still overhung Hitler's plans to create a thousand-year Reich.

"It was hard," Berezhkov recalls, "to keep from thinking of the rumors

<hr/>

[4] According to Izmail Akhmedov, a Soviet security agent assigned to the Berlin Embassy in May, Dekanozov got a report from an agent on Saturday naming the next day, Sunday, as the time of attack but told his staff to forget it and go on a picnic Sunday. (David Dallin, *Soviet Espionage*, New Haven, 1955, p. 134.)

flying through Berlin and that the latest date given for the attack on the Soviet Union—the twenty-second of June—might this time turn out to be correct."

He thought it more and more strange that in the course of the whole day it had not been possible to get in touch with either Ribbentrop or Weizsäcker, who ordinarily was quick to receive the Soviet Ambassador when the Minister was out of town.

Berezhkov continued his telephoning. Each time the duty officer repeated: "I still have not been able to reach the Reich Minister. But I have your request in mind and am taking steps. . . ."

Finally at 9:30 P.M. Dekanozov was received by Weizsäcker.[5] The Soviet Ambassador presented his complaint about the Nazi overflights. Weizsäcker replied briefly that he would refer the *note verbale* to the appropriate authorities and added that he had been informed of wholesale overflights by Soviet, rather than German, planes, and that "it was therefore the German and not the Russian Government that had cause for complaint."

Dekanozov attempted to broaden the conversation and bring up the general subject of Moscow's anxiety over the course of Soviet-German relations. He was not successful.

Von Weizsäcker's terse minute to von Ribbentrop conveys the measure of Dekanozov's failure:

> When Herr Dekanozov tried to prolong the conversation somewhat, I told him that since I had an entirely different opinion than he and had to await the opinion of my government, it would be better not to go more deeply into the matter just now. The reply would be forthcoming later.
>
> The Ambassador agreed to the procedure and left me.

Saturday, June 21, was a fine day in London. It was both sunny and warm, a combination that is "not very frequent" in London, as Ivan M. Maisky, Russia's Ambassador to the Court of St. James's, noted in his memoirs.

Maisky hurried through his work in the Soviet Embassy at No. 18 Kensington Palace Gardens and by 1 P.M. was on his way with his wife to the Bovington home of Juan Negrin, Premier of the Spanish Republic from 1937 to 1939. For the last year Maisky and his wife had spent almost every weekend at Negrin's house, about forty miles outside London.

The Maiskys got to Bovington a little after two.

"What's the news?" Negrin asked as they shook hands.

Maisky shrugged his shoulders.

"Nothing special, but the atmosphere is threatening and at any moment we can expect something," he replied. He had in mind, of course, an attack by Germany on Russia.

---

[5] Berezhkov omits any mention of Dekanozov's name or of the Dekanozov-Weizsäcker meeting. Because of his execution in 1953 Dekanozov apparently has become an unperson.

Trying not to think of the many reports he had sent to Moscow warning of the likelihood of a German attack, Maisky changed his diplomat's dark pin stripes for summer flannels and went for a stroll in the gardens. He sat on a bench in the green lawn and put his head back to soak in the warm sunshine. The air was filled with the intoxicating scents of summer, but try as he would he could not get out of his mind the dangers of the moment. Suddenly he was summoned to the telephone. The embassy secretary in London told him that Sir Stafford Cripps, the British Ambassador in Moscow who was then home on leave, wanted to see him immediately.

Maisky got into his car and was back in London within the hour. Cripps, in some excitement, was waiting for him in the embassy.

"You recall," Cripps said, "that I have repeatedly warned the Soviet Government of the nearness of a German attack?[6] Well, we now have reliable evidence that the attack will be made tomorrow, on the twenty-second of June, or in an extreme case on the twenty-ninth of June. I wanted to inform you of this."

Maisky dispatched an urgent cable to the Foreign Commissariat. The time was about 4 P.M. (7 P.M. Moscow time). Then he went back to Bovington, to the quiet country, to the tennis courts, to the scents of summer, there to spend an almost sleepless night.

In view of the three-hour difference in time between London and Moscow, Maisky's urgent cable could not have been decoded by the Foreign Commissariat earlier than 8 P.M., possibly not until after 9 P.M., Moscow time. At that hour Molotov still had no word from Berlin concerning Dekanozov's effort to talk to von Ribbentrop.[7]

Possibly stimulated by Maisky's cablegram or, more probably, despairing at Dekanozov's lack of success in getting through to von Ribbentrop, Molotov called the German Ambassador, Count Friedrich Werner von der Schulenburg, to come to his Kremlin office at 9:30 P.M.

Molotov and von der Schulenburg had had frequent meetings during the heyday of the Nazi-Soviet pact. Now talks had become more rare and contacts between the Russians and the Germans were being carried on at lower levels. The summons to the Kremlin came as a surprise to Schulenburg.

Molotov opened the conversation by registering his complaint about aircraft violating the Soviet frontiers. But this, von der Schulenburg quickly realized, was only a pretext for a general discussion of relations, particu-

[6] His most recent warning had been on Wednesday, June 18.

[7] Dekanozov's interview with von Weizsäcker did not occur until 9:30 P.M. Berlin time (11:30 P.M. Moscow time). Dekanozov reported the results of his talk by urgent cable, which could hardly have been transmitted and decoded before 1 or 1:30 A.M. Telephone connections between Moscow and Berlin normally were very fast—not more than ten or fifteen minutes, or a maximum of thirty minutes, being required to put through a call. Customarily, however, the embassy reported by telegraph. (Berezhkov, personal communication, March, 1968; I. F. Filippov, *Zapiski o Tretiyem Reikhe*, Moscow, 1966, p. 24.)

larly of what Molotov described as indications that the German Government was dissatisfied with the conduct of the Soviet Government.

Molotov mentioned rumors that war was impending between the two countries and added that he could not understand what grounds there might be for German complaint. He asked Schulenburg to enlighten him as to the trouble. .

"I replied that I could not answer his question, as I lacked the pertinent information," Schulenburg reported in an urgent telegram to Berlin which he sent off at 1:17 A.M., Sunday morning. It was the last message the German Embassy in Moscow was to file for many years.

Molotov continued to press the matter, saying he wondered if there might not be something to the rumors of impending war. He had been informed, he said, that all German business people had left the country and that wives and children of embassy personnel had also departed.

Von der Schulenburg, an honest, principled man, was embarrassed. He knew from his own private sources (but not yet officially) that war was imminent. Deeply alarmed at what was going on in the Reich, he had sent a trusted agent to Berlin who had returned only the previous Sunday, bringing word that the likely date of attack was June 22.

The Ambassador had no ready answer for Molotov. He said rather lamely that the German women and children had gone home for vacation, that the climate in Moscow was very severe. Not all the women had left, he added, an allusion to the wife of Gustav Hilger, second secretary of the embassy, who accompanied Schulenberg to the interview.

At this point, Hilger recalled, Molotov gave up the effort, shrugged his shoulders and the interview was at an end. The Germans drove back to their embassy in the late evening twilight. An excursion boat was moving down the Moskva River, blazing with light, a jazz band blaring out an American song.

Admiral Kuznetsov became convinced in later years that some time after noon on Saturday Stalin finally realized that conflict with Germany, if not inescapable, was more and more likely. Kuznetsov's theory is supported to some extent by the evidence of Army General I. V. Tyulenev, who in June, 1941, was in command of the Moscow Military District.

General Tyulenev was a Red Army veteran. He had commanded the Soviet troops which took over the Polish areas adjacent to the Ukraine in 1939. He had won his spurs in the Civil War. He had served in the Czar's Army and had been with the Red Army's 1st Cavalry.

As Moscow commandant he was in close touch with Stalin and the Kremlin. He was well briefed on the threatening situation on the Western frontiers. He knew there had been hundreds of Nazi overflights. He knew that Soviet forces had been forbidden to respond to such incidents, and he was uneasy about the situation. However, like many other officers, his con-

The Fateful Saturday . 27

cern was eased by a Tass communiqué published June 14 denying there was any basis for rumors of impending war. As he said, "It was impossible not to believe our official organs."

Some time on Saturday[8] General Tyulenev was told that the Kremlin was calling. When he picked up the receiver, he heard the harsh voice of Stalin, who asked: "Comrade Tyulenev, how are we fixed so far as antiaircraft defense of Moscow is concerned?"

Tyulenev gave him a brief outline of the status of air precautions as of that Saturday.

Stalin then said: "Considering the disturbing situation, you should bring the Moscow antiaircraft forces to 75 percent readiness for action."

That was the end of the conversation. Tyulenev asked no questions, but he called his chief of air defense, Major General M. S. Gromadin, and told him not to send the AA batteries to summer camp, but to order them on full alert.

Another decision was made June 21—although possibly by coincidence. A unified fighter command for Moscow air defense was set up and orders for its operation were signed and given to Colonel I. D. Klimov. It was designated as the 6th Fighter Corps but did not actually become operative until after war had begun. It ultimately comprised 11 fighter squadrons with 602 planes. On June 22 its strength was zero.

Before leaving for the day General Tyulenev checked with Defense Commissar Timoshenko, who advised him there had been more evidence of German war preparations: there were suspicious activities at the German Embassy; many of the embassy personnel had left, either departing the country or driving out of Moscow. Tyulenev telephoned General Staff headquarters as well. He was told that Soviet border commanders reported a quiet day but that intelligence sources continued to indicate an imminent German attack. The information had been relayed to Stalin, who said there was no point in stirring up panic.

Stalin's question about the Moscow air defenses did not arouse alarm in General Tyulenev's mind. He had his chauffeur drive him to the quiet little side street, Rzhevsky Pereulok, where he lived with his wife and two children. He glanced at the newspaper, *Vechernaya Moskva*, as he drove through the main streets. No special news. He noticed that posters had been put up for Leonid Utyosov's first summer jazz concert at the Hermitage Park. On Monday a movie was opening—*The Treasure of the Gorge*. The General heard some youngsters singing from an open window, one of the new popular songs: "*Lyubimy gorod* . . . beloved city."

He wondered what to do on Sunday. Should he spend the day at his summer villa at Serebrany Bor, just outside Moscow, or should he take the youngsters to the opening of the water stadium at Khimki?

[8] Kuznetsov gives the time as 2 P.M. Tyulenev's memoirs merely indicate Saturday afternoon.

He decided to postpone a decision until morning and, picking up his wife and children in Rzhevsky Pereulok, drove on out to his dacha.

Tyulenev's account leaves no doubt that if Stalin reached the conviction on Saturday afternoon that war with Germany was imminent, he did not communicate a feeling of urgency to his military associates. No evidence has come to light that he took other precautionary action on Saturday afternoon until after 5 P.M., when Marshal Timoshenko and General Zhukov were summoned to the Kremlin.

There a meeting of the Politburo was discussing the possibility that the Germans might attack either Saturday night or on Sunday. Marshal Semyon Budyonny is the only source for what happened, but his account conveys a sense of the unreality of the occasion.[9] Those present were called upon to offer their views of what should be done. Budyonny suggested that all armies east of the Dnieper be ordered to start moving in the direction of the frontier. Once they were in motion, he said, "it doesn't matter what happens. Whether the Germans attack or not, they will be in position."

It seems not to have occurred to Budyonny or any one else at the meeting that such a plan would put thousands of troops in motion on highways and railroads, an easy target for the German dive bombers.

Budyonny's second proposal was to "take all the ropes off the planes" and put them on a No. 1 Alert. In normal Soviet practice the planes were secured to the ground by ropes and wires. Budyonny's proposal meant that they would be freed and that the Soviet pilots would sit in readiness for take-off in their cockpits.

Budyonny's third proposal was that a line of deep defense be set up on the Dnieper and Dvina from Kiev to Riga. He proposed that the population be mobilized with spades and shovels to transform the banks of the rivers into an impassable tank barrier. He thought that such a defense line would probably be needed because the Germans were in a stage of full military readiness whereas the Soviet forces were in the opposite condition.

There was some discussion, and then Stalin intervened: "Budyonny seems to know what to do, so let him be in charge."

Budyonny forthwith was named to command the Soviet Reserve Army with the construction of the Dnieper defense line as his immediate assignment. Georgi M. Malenkov was made his political commissar. The appointment came nine hours before the Nazis attacked. Budyonny had nothing with which to carry out his task—no staff, no troops, no equipment, nothing. He hurried off to army headquarters on Frunze Street and told Malenkov he would telephone him as soon as he had a staff put together.[10]

[9] There is no reference to this meeting in the memoirs of such high military figures as Tyulenev, Kuznetsov, Voronov and Zhukov. Nor is it mentioned in official Soviet histories. Budyonny did not indicate precisely who was present. (Budyonny, personal communication, July, 1967.)

[10] Many Soviet sources confirm that Budyonny was named Reserve Forces Commander and instructed to move reserve forces to the Dnieper River line. The Politburo decision of June 21 is reported by V. Khvostov and A. Grylev (*Kommunist*, No. 12, August, 1968).

At that time, or so Admiral Kuznetsov believes, Stalin must have decided to put Soviet armed forces on a state of combat alert and to order them, in case of need, to oppose a German attack by force.

Such a decision by Stalin, Kuznetsov concluded, would explain the pile of telegraph blanks which he saw in front of Timoshenko and Zhukov when he was summoned to the Defense Commissariat at 11 P.M. Saturday evening. They had been working for hours at Stalin's instructions, Kuznetsov believed, drafting orders to put the commands on the alert. These orders were not actually dispatched until about 12:30 A.M. on the twenty-second. So the possibility exists that whatever instructions Stalin may have given at the Politburo meeting were contingent on developments in the course of the evening, such as a possible talk with Ribbentrop.[11]

One more action was taken. Special representatives of the High Command were dispatched to border military districts and to the fleets to warn them of the dangers and instruct them to put their units on combat alert.

It was this mission which put General Meretskov on the Red Arrow to Leningrad Saturday night. But since the High Command's emissaries were sent by railroad trains which would not arrive at the command points before some hour on Sunday (and in some cases not before Monday)[12] it would hardly seem that the Kremlin was convinced that German attack was only hours away.

Indeed, the texts of the warnings which Timoshenko and Zhukov sent out (many of which arrived hours after the German attack) were only cautionary. They instructed the units to be alert, but they prohibited forward reconnaissance into enemy territory. And they warned sternly against provocations.

A serious question arose in Admiral Kuznetsov's mind that Saturday night. "I could not throw off some grievous thoughts," he recalled. "When had the Defense Commissar [Timoshenko] learned of the possible attack of the Hitlerites? What time had he been ordered to put the forces on combat alert? Why had not the government [Stalin] instead of the Defense Commissar given me the order putting the fleet on combat alert? And why was it all semiofficial and so very, very late?"

Twenty-five years later the Admiral's questions still awaited a full answer.

11 This view is supported by the fact that at 4 A.M., June 22, an urgent message was sent by Molotov to Dekanozov, reporting the contents of the Molotov-Schulenburg talk and specifically asking Dekanozov to raise with Ribbentrop or his deputy the three questions to which Schulenburg did not respond: what reasons Germany had for being dissatisfied with her relations with the Soviet Union, what the basis was for the rumors of impending Soviet-German war, and why Germany had not responded to the Tass statement of June 14. (V. L. Izraelyan, L. N. Kutakov, *Diplomatiya Agressorov*, Moscow, 1967, p. 184.) Dekanozov was never to have an opportunity to raise the questions.

12 Marshal G. I. Kulik, another Deputy Defense Commissar, was sent to the Special Western Military District. He did not arrive at Bialystok, headquarters of the Tenth Army, until late Monday, June 23. By that hour he seemed to General I. V. Boldin to be dazed and at sea. Marshal Kulik reached Bialystok only a few hours before Major General M. G. Khazelevich of the Tenth Army was killed and his army virtually destroyed. (I. V. Boldin, *Stranitsii Zhizn*, Moscow, 1961.)

4 . *The Night Wears On*

WHEN THE BALTIC FLEET COMMAND GOT WORD FROM Admiral Kuznetsov that the Germans might attack in the early hours of Sunday morning, it came as no surprise. In fact, as Admiral Panteleyev, Chief of Staff, recalled, they had been expecting "minute by minute that the next telegram or telephone call would bring the dark word—war!"

It was almost midnight Saturday when Panteleyev was summoned to join his superior, Fleet Commander Admiral Tributs. "It's happened," he thought as he hurried out of the big war room to the Admiral's private office. There he found Tributs with his Military Council member, Commissar M. G. Yakovlenko. Tributs was leaning back in his black-leather chair, nervously tapping his knee with a long pencil. He displayed no other sign of emotion.

"I've just talked with Kuznetsov," he said without preliminaries. "Tonight we must expect an attack by Germany."

Panteleyev dashed back to his desk and started sending alerts to all fleet units, to the Fleet Air Staff and the Administration of Rear Services and Supplies.

Actually, the fleet was not in bad shape to meet the emergency. Some progress had been made in preparing the Leningrad sea approaches to repel German attack. As early as May 7 Admiral Tributs decided to post patrol ships at the entrance of the Gulf of Finland and at all naval bases in order to intercept Nazi submarines or surface vessels. However, the cold weather, the late break-up of the ice and the persistent fog delayed Admiral Tributs in making his dispositions. It was not till the second half of May that one submarine, the *S-7*, took station in the Irben Strait, which gives access to the Gulf of Riga. On May 27 the patrol submarine *S-309* assumed a position at the mouth of the Gulf of Finland. At the same time picket ships were posted at Hangö on the Finnish shore across the Gulf of Finland from Tallinn, at Libau (Liepaja), the westernmost Soviet harbor, only seventy miles east of the Soviet-German frontier, and at Tallinn and Kronstadt.

Before June 1 all Soviet cruisers and most of the mine layers and submarines, as well as the floating submarine base, had been pulled back from

Libau to Ust-Dvinsk, the fortress and naval base near Riga, where antiair-craft protection was superior to that in exposed Libau. The *Oka*, a special mine layer equipped to put down antisubmarine nets, was sent from Libau to Tallinn, and the battleship *Marat* was returned from Tallinn to its old base at Kronstadt.

Neither the Baltic commander, Admiral Tributs, nor his superior, Admiral Kuznetsov, had much taste for Libau. It was an open harbor only a few minutes' flight from the German air bases in East Prussia, and the naval commanders did not regard it as suitable for wartime use. The Russian Imperial Navy had taken the same view. Under the imperial war plans all warships were evacuated from Libau on the opening day of World War I.

When Libau fell into Soviet hands with the incorporation of the Baltic states into the Soviet Union in July, 1940, Stalin raised the question of what to do with it. He wanted to put a battleship there. Admiral Kuznetsov argued vigorously against this. Stalin listened silently and in the end agreed to station only light naval vessels, principally a submarine brigade, at Libau.

At the same time, as a sop to Stalin, two old battleships, the *Marat* and the *October Revolution*,[1] were transferred from their secure, well-equipped base at Kronstadt to the new Tallinn base. There they stood in the open roadstead, awaiting the construction of a protective mole. This work, in the hands of the NKVD (police) labor force, was proceeding with utmost dilatoriness (as was most base and fortification work in the Baltic areas).

In April Admiral Panteleyev and several other fleet commanders went to Riga to confer with the recently formed staff of the Special Baltic Military District, which was commanded by Colonel General F. I. Kuznetsov. The army and naval commanders sat long over their maps. In the eight months since the Baltic states had been absorbed by the Soviets much had been done, but much remained to be done. Fortifications along the new frontier were far from complete. The Baltic District was short of troops, short of tanks, short of antiaircraft guns, short of planes. Work on airfields for the new fast fighters and long-range bombers (which they hoped to receive) was going very slowly. Worst of all, the army men said that since the construction was in the hands of the police there was no way to speed it up.

The naval men had equally serious complaints. The new coastal artillery batteries, including those designed to defend Libau from sea attack, were far behind schedule. The new naval bases on the Baltic coast were just being organized. Even the facilities at Riga were not ready and would not be until May 25. Eighty percent of the naval aircraft had to be stationed at rear bases, far from the potential war theater, because the airstrips had not been finished. One officer who inspected the advance fortifications was shocked to find that concrete gun pits were sited so close to the frontier that they had no

---

[1] Originally called the *Petropavlovsk* and the *Gangut,* these 23,000-ton ships somewhat resembling World War I Italian battleships were part of the Czarist Navy's 1909 building program, the first large-scale imperial construction after the 1905 defeat by Japan. They carried twelve 12-inch guns.

protective mine fields or barriers in front of them. Others lacked any means of swinging guns in directions other than to the west—they would be useless once an attacker got behind them. Some embrasures were too narrow to contain the weapons they were supposed to receive.

By May the shore batteries at Libau had been installed, but there was no protection from the land side. The naval commander was responsible for defense against sea attacks, but land action was in the hands of the army's Special Baltic Military District. Coordination between the two services had not been worked out. Army GHQ was at Riga, that of the navy at Tallinn, 180 miles away. The question of supreme command in case of war was not settled. The situation was similar at all Baltic bases in the Leningrad Defense area with the exception of Hangö, where the navy had been given supreme command.

The army's attitude was epitomized by the Baltic Military Commander, Colonel General F. I. Kuznetsov. When Admiral Kuznetsov sought to discuss with his army namesake a project for constructing a defensive ring on the land approaches to Libau and Riga, General Kuznetsov exclaimed in indignation: "Do you really think we would permit the enemy to get to Riga?"

Only after repeated urging by Tributs, a lively, energetic, impetuous and highly qualified naval officer who could not conceal his feeling of alarm, was the 67th Infantry Division sent to man the land defenses of Libau. But this was on the eve of war, and formal liaison between army and navy was still unresolved as late as midnight, June 21.[2]

In view of these conditions Admiral Tributs' proposal that he move his ships out of the dangerously exposed port of Libau made elementary common sense. But there was a major obstacle. Stalin held a different opinion. Stalin had wanted to station a battleship in Libau in the summer of 1940, and he might not welcome the further weakening of the base.

"We were aware that this force was too much for Libau, and when the war threat grew, it was proposed to transfer some of the ships to Riga," Kuznetsov observed. "Because Stalin's viewpoint was known I was not willing to issue an order for this without higher sanction."

Kuznetsov procrastinated but finally agreed to bring the matter up in the Supreme Naval Council in the presence of Andrei A. Zhdanov. Zhdanov, a pasty-faced Party functionary of forty-five, was one of the most powerful of Stalin's associates. In 1941 his prestige was so high that many spoke of him as a possible successor in the event of Stalin's death. He was the Party chief of Leningrad and, as such, in general charge of the Baltic region and the Politburo member most concerned with naval affairs. In the curious confusion of Kremlin responsibilities Foreign Minister Molotov in his dual role

---

[2] Libau had neither the organization nor the forces to meet a German attack in the opinion of Vice Admiral N. K. Smirnov, Political Commissar of the Baltic Fleet. (N. K. Smirnov, *Matrosy Zashchishchayut Rodinu*, Moscow, 1968, p. 20.)

as Deputy Chairman of the Council of People's Commissars was charged with ministerial responsibility for the Soviet Navy, but it was Zhdanov, the Leningrad leader and active aspirant for Stalin's mantle, who as secretary of the Central Committee was in political (and actual) charge of most naval matters.

Half an hour before the Supreme Naval Council met in late April or early May Zhdanov appeared in Kuznetsov's office.

"Why and what do you want to transfer from Libau?" he asked.

Kuznetsov was ready with his facts and figures. He told Zhdanov the Soviet warships were "like herrings in a barrel" at Libau and that there was a fine base near Riga from which the ships could operate easily in any direction.

Zhdanov was noncommittal. "Let's see what the others say," he grunted. No dissent was voiced in the Council, but Zhdanov insisted that the decision be referred to Stalin.

Kuznetsov sent his report to Stalin but got no reply. He had kept a carbon and decided to take the matter up personally with the dictator the next time he had a chance. In mid-May he managed to get Stalin's approval. He immediately telephoned Tributs: "Go ahead. We have received approval."

Admiral Tributs continued to worry about the two battleships at Tallinn. The port was open to attack from the north. Neither booms nor nets had yet been placed to protect the battleships from torpedoes. He requested permission to transfer the ships to Kronstadt. It came through on the eve of war. By the evening of June 21 the *Marat* had safely made its way back to Kronstadt, but the *October Revolution* still stood in the Tallinn Roads and was not pulled out until early July.

The night of June 21–22 was cool on the Tallinn shore. When Admiral Panteleyev stepped outside the fleet command post after sending off his messages putting the command on the alert, he found a raw wind blowing off the sea. From the nearby fields came the scent of uncut hay. Here, as in Leningrad, it was barely dusk, although the hour was past midnight.

Already the trawler *Krambol* had put out to strengthen the patrol off Tallinn. The Chief of Rear Services, Major General Mitrofan I. Moskalenko, had asked Moscow for permission to divert the tanker *Zhelesnodorozhnik*, en route to Libau with a load of fuel oil, to Ust-Dvinsk and Tanker No. 11 from Kronstadt to Tallinn. Fuel supplies were short in both places, and if war came each would badly need it. Two hours later permission came in.

At 1:40 A.M. Panteleyev received confirmation that the entire fleet and its bases had gone on No. 1 Combat Alert. The Libau commander had been given orders to send his remaining type-M submarines (except three on patrol duty) to Ust-Dvinsk and his other craft to Ventspils, further north on the Latvian coast. The commander of the Hangö base was ordered to send his submarines and torpedo boats across the Gulf of Finland to the base of Paldiski, west of Tallinn. There were in the Tallinn Harbor some new ships, not quite finished. Tributs ordered those fit for immediate service incorporated into the fleet in the morning. Those not ready for duty were to go back to the Leningrad shipyards immediately.

After telephoning Tributs just before midnight Kuznetsov placed calls to Golovko at Northern Fleet headquarters at Polyarny and to the Black Sea Fleet at Sevastopol.

The Black Sea Fleet had just concluded spring training exercises. Kuznetsov had been in doubt whether to permit the maneuvers, but decided that if war came the fleet might as well be at sea as at its bases.

The exercises concluded June 18, and on June 20 the fleet was back in port in Sevastopol, where a seminar on the maneuvers was scheduled for Monday, June 23.

The fleet had gone on a No. 2 Alert as soon as it reached harbor. However, on Saturday evening many officers and men were ashore, strolling along the Grafsky embankment. Cutters and barges busily plied back and forth between ships and shore. A big concert was in progress at Navy House, with Fleet Commander F. S. Oktyabrsky in attendance. At the movie house on Red Fleet Boulevard a Soviet version of the Fred Astaire–Ginger Rogers picture called by the Russians *Musical History* was playing.

Some Moscow officers who had come down for the maneuvers had already left, but Rear Admiral I. I. Azarov, chief of the navy's Political Department, a salty sea dog who had spent his life in the navy, was still in Sevastopol. He spent the evening in the summer garden restaurant at Navy House with an old friend from the Baltic Fleet, Aleksandr V. Solodunov, now in charge of hydrographic studies for the Black Sea Fleet. The two men drank beer, told stories and had no thought of going to bed. The next day was Sunday. They would sleep late.

Suddenly Azarov noticed the director of Navy House and another officer speaking to a group of commanders at a neighboring table. The men grabbed their uniform caps and hurried out. As they passed Azarov's table one leaned over and said: "No. 1 Alert has been announced."

Azarov went straight to headquarters. He found that Chief of Staff I. D. Eliseyev had been on the point of going home when Kuznetsov's warning call came through. The officer of the day, Captain N. G. Rybalko, had spent a quiet evening. At 10:32 P.M. he telephoned the Inkerman and Kherson lighthouses and ordered the lights turned on so that a tug could tow the nightly garbage scow from the harbor.

Now, a little after 1 A.M., as Azarov stood in the office he could see from the windows the lights of the city begin to dim in accordance with the No. 1 Alert. A siren sounded and there were signal shots from batteries. The radio loudspeakers began to call sailors back to their posts: "*Vnimaniye . . . Vnimaniye . . .*"

City authorities, thinking another practice alert was under way, telephoned staff headquarters, protesting the blackout: "Why is it necessary to black out the city so quickly? The fleet has just come back from maneuvers. Let the people have a chance to rest."

They were told to obey orders and not to ask questions. Meanwhile, navy headquarters called the power station and the main switch was thrown. The city sank into darkness.

The city and fleet were fully blacked out, but from the sea still shone the beams of the two lighthouses. Telephone connections to the lights, it developed, were out of order, possibly sabotaged. Finally, a motorcyclist was dispatched and the lights were shut off.

Here and there antiaircraft batteries fired a round of tracer bullets to test their weapons. Fighter planes revved up their motors. Sailors and commanders streamed back aboard their ships to the signal "General Quarters" issued at 1:55 A.M. By 2 A.M. Officer of the Day Rybalko noted that the fleet was in readiness to meet attack.

At about 3 A.M. or a little later the acoustic listening posts on the coast at Yevpatoriya and Sarych Cape reported the sound of airplane motors. Officer of the Day Rybalko checked with the Fleet Air Command and the Air Force. No Soviet planes were in the air. Lieutenant I. S. Zhilin of the Antiaircraft Command telephoned, asking permission to open fire at "unknown planes."

Rybalko called the fleet commander, Admiral Oktyabrsky.

"Are any of our planes in the air?" Oktyabrsky asked.

Rybalko replied: "No, none of our planes."

"Bear in mind that if there is a single plane of ours in the air you will be shot tomorrow," Oktyabrsky rejoined.

"Comrade Commander," Rybalko persisted, "may we have permission to open fire?"

"Act according to your orders," snapped Oktyabrsky.

Rybalko turned to Vice Admiral Eliseyev. The answer was so equivocal the young officer did not know what to do.

"What answer shall I give Zhilin?" Rybalko asked.

"Give him orders to open fire," Eliseyev said decisively.

"Open fire," Rybalko told Zhilin.

Zhilin understood the personal risks of such action.

"Bear in mind," he said, "that you are taking full responsibility for this order. I am putting this note into my operations journal."

"Write what you want," shouted Rybalko, "but open fire on those planes."

Almost without interval the roar of planes approaching Sevastopol at low altitude was heard, followed by the chatter of antiaircraft guns, the whine of bombs, the searing stab of powerful searchlights. Planes began to fall in flames. Battery No. 59 brought down the first. The crash of bombs rumbled over the harbor.

It was now some time after 3 A.M., Sunday, June 22.

By 3 A.M. in Moscow Admiral Kuznetsov had stretched out on a leather divan in the corner of his office. He could not sleep. He kept thinking of the fleets, of what might be in progress. He had great difficulty in keeping from picking up the telephone and again calling Admiral Tributs for it was the Baltic Fleet that gave him the gravest concern.

However, he managed to restrain himself by repeating Moltke's aphorism that once you have given the order for mobilization there is nothing to do but go to sleep for now the machine is working on its own. But he could get no sleep.

A strident ring from the telephone brought him to his feet. It was now fully light.

He lifted the receiver.

"The Commander of the Black Sea Fleet is reporting."

Kuznetsov knew from Oktyabrsky's excited voice that something unusual had happened.

"An air attack is being carried out on Sevastopol," Oktyabrsky gasped. "Our antiaircraft guns are beating off enemy planes. Some bombs have fallen in the city. . . ."

Kuznetsov looked at his watch. The time was 3:15. It had started. He had no doubt. The war had begun.[3]

He took up the phone again and asked for Stalin's office. A duty officer answered: "Comrade Stalin is not here, and I don't know where he is."

"I have a report of exceptional importance which I must give immediately to Comrade Stalin personally," Kuznetsov said.

"I cannot help you," the officer replied, hanging up quietly.

Without replacing the receiver Kuznetsov called Defense Commissar Timoshenko. He repeated precisely what Oktyabrsky had told him.

"Do you hear me?" Kuznetsov asked.

"Yes, I hear you," Timoshenko replied calmly.

Kuznetsov hung up. A few minutes later he tried another number in an effort to get to Stalin. No answer. He called back the duty officer at the Kremlin and told him: "Please advise Comrade Stalin that German planes are bombing Sevastopol. It's war."

"I'll do what I can," the officer replied.

A few minutes later Kuznetsov's telephone rang.

"Do you understand what you have reported?" The voice was that of Georgi M. Malenkov, member of the Politburo and one of Stalin's closest associates. Kuznetsov thought Malenkov sounded displeased and irritated.

"I understand," Kuznetsov said, "and I report on my own responsibility. War has started."

---

[3] Kuznetsov's timing of events on the night of June 21–22 leaves much to be desired. He gives different times in different versions of his memoirs. For example, Vice Admiral Azarov says he heard the first burst of antiaircraft fire at Sevastopol at 3:30 A.M. Officer of the Day Rybalko timed the first burst at 3:13 A.M. Admiral Kuznetsov, apparently basing himself on Rybalko's notes, gives the time of the approach of German planes as 3:07 A.M. It probably would have taken Oktyabrsky's call at least ten minutes to get through to Moscow. Thus it probably was closer to 3:30 A.M. that Kuznetsov got the call from Sevastopol.

Malenkov did not believe Kuznetsov. He rang up Sevastopol himself and got through to Admiral Oktyabrsky just as Azarov entered the commander's office. Azarov heard Oktyabrsky's end of the conversation.

"Yes, yes," Oktyabrsky was saying. "We are being bombed. . . ."

As he spoke, there was a resounding explosion. The windows rattled.

"Just now," Oktyabrsky shouted excitedly, "a bomb exploded quite close to staff headquarters."

Azarov and a friend exchanged glances.

"In Moscow they don't believe that Sevastopol is being bombed," the friend said. He was right.[4]

Within an hour Timoshenko telephoned General Boldin, Deputy Commander of the Special Western Military District, four times. Each time he warned against acting against German provocations, even when Boldin told him his troops were being attacked, towns were burning and people dying.

Marshal Nikolai Voronov, Chief of Antiaircraft Defense, had stayed at his desk, on orders, all evening long. About 4 A.M. he received the first word of the bombing of Sevastopol and of attacks on Ventspils and Libau. He hurried to Timoshenko and found L. Z. Mekhlis, Chief of the Army Political Administration and a close colleague of Police Chief Lavrenti P. Beria, with him. Voronov reported on the bombings. Timoshenko then gave him a big notebook and told him to write down what he had just said. Mekhlis stood behind Voronov, checking the statement word by word, and ordered him to sign it. Voronov was excused without any instructions, any orders, at a moment when, as he observed, every second, every minute counted.

"I left the office with a stone in my heart," Voronov recalled. "I realized that they did not believe that war actually had started. My brain worked feverishly. It was clear that the war had begun whether the Defense Commissariat admitted it or not."

He got back to his own office to find his desk heaped with telegrams reporting Nazi air attacks from the Gulf of Finland to the Black Sea. A young woman duty officer, wearing a beret, a revolver at her belt, dashed in from the next-door headquarters of the Armored Forces Administration. In the "secret safe" of the administration, she said excitedly, there was a big packet with many seals on which was written: "Open in Case of Mobilization." Mobilization hadn't been announced, but the war had begun—what should they do? Voronov said, "Open the packet and get to work." He turned to his own officers and began to issue orders.

War had indeed begun, but when General Zhukov, Chief of Staff, reported

---

[4] Marshal Budyonny disputes this. "There wasn't a single small child who didn't believe the Germans were getting ready to attack," he insists. "If Stalin didn't believe this, then why was I appointed nine hours before to command the Reserve Army?" He insists there was no question of disbelieving the bombing reports. He heard them about 4 A.M. and called Admiral Kuznetsov to obtain confirmation. As for difficulties in getting through to Stalin, everyone was trying to telephone him and naturally some of the calls were taken by duty officers. (Budyonny, personal conversation, July, 1967.)

to Stalin that the Germans were bombing Kovno, Rovno, Odessa and Sevastopol, Stalin still insisted it must be a provocation by the "German generals." He clung to this conviction for hours.

As the sky brightened outside the windows of Kuznetsov's office, he waited for orders from someone announcing a formal state of war—or at least for instructions to advise the navy that the attack had started. Nothing happened. His telephone did not ring. It was evident, as he later was to note, that hope for avoiding war still lingered. He could put no other interpretation on the curious response to news of the attack on Sevastopol.

Kuznetsov could contain himself no longer. He dispatched to Admiral Tributs and his other commanders a curt order. It said: "Germany has begun an attack on our bases and ports. Resist with force of arms any attempted attack by the enemy."

In fleet headquarters at Tallinn Admiral Panteleyev was at his desk in the long, vaulted, coastal artillery gallery which served Tributs as the war room of his combat command post. The gallery dated back to World War I times. It was completely underground. There were no windows. The only illumination was provided by naked strings of electric light bulbs.

Along one wall stood small desks for the telegraph and radio operators. In the center of the chamber was a big situation board with maps of the Baltic area.

Panteleyev's desk was at the entrance of the noisy room. Officers were coming and going. The telephones rang constantly. His task was to filter the reports, passing on the most urgent to Admiral Tributs. Captain F. V. Zozulya called from Kronstadt. "They've dropped sixteen mines at the entrance to the Kronstadt Roads," he said. "But the channel remains clear." A report came in from Libau. Captain Mikhail S. Klevensky reported that shortly after 4 A.M. bombs had been dropped on the military quarter of the city and around the airfield.

The Baltic Merchant Fleet relayed a message from V. M. Mironov, captain of the steamer *Luga*. He was returning to Leningrad from Hangö. About 3:30 A.M. his ship was attacked by a German plane. A score of bullets were fired, and Sergei I. Klimenov, a sailor, was slightly wounded. About the same time the Latvian steamer *Gaisma*, en route to Germany with a cargo of wood, was torpedoed in an attack by four German cutters off the Swedish island of Gotland. The action occurred about 3:20 A.M. The Germans turned their machine guns on the Soviet sailors in the water, killing several, including Captain Nikolai Duve. These probably were the first casualties of the Soviet-German war.

Panteleyev looked about. Officers were barking orders. The clock on the wall pointed to 4:50 A.M. He received a call to report to Admiral Tributs. Panteleyev found him striding briskly to his desk, long pencil in hand. The Admiral raised his tired eyes to Panteleyev, who silently handed him a telegraph blank. The Admiral slowly filled in the blank, reading aloud to Panteleyev as he wrote:

"Germany has begun to attack our bases and ports. Resist the enemy with force of arms. . . ."

He sighed, then affixed his signature with a bold stroke. Officer Kashin grabbed the telegram. In an instant it was humming through the air and by the wires to every base and ship in the Baltic.

By 5:17 A.M. word had reached every Baltic unit: "Resist German attack." Thus, in at least one sector, the vital sea approaches to Leningrad, Soviet forces knew that war had started; that the Germans had attacked; that they must resist with all strength.

Panteleyev went back to his desk. He felt relieved. The die was cast. War had begun. He listened to the hurried chatter of the telegraph keys as the operators tapped out the orders to the fleet. Then he went up the stone staircase and out into the open air.

The sun was rising. The sea was quiet. In the Surop Strait a tug was hauling a string of barges toward Tallinn Harbor. Aboard the tug the sailors were impatient. Harbor and home were in sight. Of war they as yet had no knowledge.

5 . Dawn, June 22

ON THE MORNING OF JUNE 22 THE LENINGRAD MILITARY
Command was housed, as it had been for more than a century, in the grandiose ensemble of the Russian General Staff building, ten years in construction
—from 1819 to 1829—probably the finest of Rossi's architectural achievements. Placed at the head of Nevsky Prospekt, opposite the Winter Palace,
the General Staff building was formed of two wings, joined by an arch
dedicated to the Russian victory over Napoleon in 1812. The central entrance
was 40 feet wide and towered 75 feet high. Some 768 windows sparkled
from three tierlike stories.

A week ago, on June 15, Colonel (now Lieutenant General) B. V.
Bychevsky, chief of the Leningrad District Engineers, had returned to this
monument to Russian military glory from a trip to inspect the fortified zone
being built to protect Russia's newly leased Hangö military base from attack
from the Finnish mainland. He found the work progressing fairly well and,
as he drove back to Leningrad, was happy to see that the Pioneer camps and
children's homes in Karelia were beginning to fill up with summer guests.
The forest seemed particularly green and fresh after the cold, wet spring.

Bychevsky, young, vigorous, blue-eyed and slightly balding, knew that
Leningrad had received disturbing intelligence, particularly from naval units
and points along the Finnish border, of the arrival of German troops in
Finland. However, the tempo of activity in the General Staff building did
not seem to have quickened. Lieutenant General Markian M. Popov had
gone off on a field trip, as scheduled. His departure left the building half-
empty since most of the senior aides and lieutenants had accompanied him.
When Bychevsky arrived at headquarters on Monday morning, June 16, he
had never seen it more peaceful. His own deputy had gone off with General
Popov. The weekend war news from Western Europe could not have been
more dull. About the only item of passing note was an announcement by the
U. S. State Department of the sinking of the freighter *Robin Moore* by a
German submarine off the Brazilian coast.

What had eased the atmosphere in Leningrad (and throughout the Soviet Union) had been the publication in Saturday's papers of an official statement by Tass, dated Friday, June 13.

The statement (given in advance to the German Embassy for transmission to Berlin) denied rumors of impending war between Russia and Germany. It said such rumors had been current before the recent departure from Moscow of the British Ambassador, Sir Stafford Cripps, and had become especially widespread since his arrival in London. The implication was that the rumors had been inspired by Cripps or the British.

The reports, Tass continued, alleged that Germany had made various territorial and economic demands on Russia; that Russia had rejected the demands; that as a result Germany had begun to concentrate troops on the Soviet frontier and that now Soviet troops were being gathered on the German frontier.

"Despite the obvious absurdity of these rumors," Tass declared, "responsible circles in Moscow have thought it necessary, in view of the persistent spread of these rumors, to authorize Tass to state that they are a clumsy propaganda maneuver of the forces arrayed against the Soviet Union and Germany which are interested in the spread and intensification of the war."

The statement added that

in the opinion of Soviet circles the rumors of the intention of Germany to break the [Nonaggression] Pact and to launch an attack against the Soviet Union are completely without foundation, while the recent movements of German troops which have completed their operations in the Balkans to the eastern and northern parts of Germany must be explained by other motives which have no connection with Soviet-German relations . . . as a result all the rumors according to which the Soviet Union is preparing for a war with Germany are false and provocative.

In the face of this declaration the worries of many commanders had been allayed. "Moscow knows what it's doing," some said. Others insisted that Stalin must be right because Stalin always had all the facts in his possession. Especially comforting was the circumstance that not even in the secret meetings of the Party elite had there been any mention, any warning, any suggestion that war might be near.

The atmosphere in Leningrad eased even more when word spread that Party Secretary Andrei A. Zhdanov, chief of both the Leningrad City and the Leningrad Regional Party organizations, member of the Military Council of the Leningrad District, secretary of the Central Committee of the Communist Party and right-hand man of Stalin himself, was leaving for his summer vacation.

On Thursday, June 19, Zhdanov left by train for his favorite holiday spot, Sochi on the Caucasian Black Sea coast. Sochi, a resort of white villas, semitropical shrubbery and a rather stony beach, was also Stalin's retreat.

Zhdanov often joined him there for two or three weeks at a time. The fact that Zhdanov had gone to Sochi seemed to many a guarantee that nothing of consequence would happen. This view was supported by the press. The only news from Berlin in Thursday's *Leningradskaya Pravda* was an announcement of the signing of a German-Turkish friendship pact.

Bychevsky drove out to Karelia every day to check on fortifications work. He was there on Friday when he got a call from Major General Dmitri N. Nikishev, Leningrad Chief of Staff.

"Come back immediately," Nikishev said. "Hurry."

"I'm glad I found you," Nikishev said, when Bychevsky arrived at the General Staff building three hours later. "The situation, my friend, is getting a little complicated. The Finns along the Karelian isthmus are beginning to get ready for action. We have got to begin military protection of the frontier. Is that clear?"

"Not exactly."

"Prepare your engineers to lay mine fields along the frontier."

Bychevsky protested that his personnel were occupied in work on fortifications.

"Take them off that!"

"And do you have orders from Moscow to that effect?" Bychevsky rejoined. "I don't see how I can halt work on the fortifications."

"I don't care what you think," Nikishev snapped. "There's no time to wait for orders. Just plain work is what's needed. Collect all the mines there are in the stores and issue them to the troops. Meanwhile, we'll write the orders to the army."

Nikishev stalked off and locked himself in his office with his intelligence staff and operational chiefs. Bychevsky pulled out of his files the contingency plans for mining the frontier and began to draft orders for the Fourteenth, Seventh and Twenty-third armies. These were the forces of the Leningrad Military District which were deployed along the eight-hundred-mile Finnish frontier from the Barents Sea to the Gulf of Finland. It was no small task to mine this long border.

Meantime, Nikishev ordered Lieutenant General P. S. Pshennikov, commanding the Twenty-third Army, which covered the Karelian isthmus just north of Leningrad, to move one division from the rear to a forward position at Vyborg on the Finnish frontier.

The southern and western approaches to Leningrad Province were not the defensive responsibility of the Leningrad Military District. When the Baltic states were incorporated into the Soviet Union in 1940, these areas had been split off from the Leningrad Command and put under the new Special Baltic Military District with headquarters at Riga. The Leningrad Command had no troops south or west of the city except for some artillery units that had gone to summer training camps.

In recent weeks, however, on orders from the General Staff, Bychevsky had been concentrating his attention on building a fortified zone in the region of Pskov-Ostrov for the Special Baltic District. These fortifications lay about 180 miles southwest of Leningrad along the Velikaya River. The zone was designed as a defense in depth against attack on Leningrad from the southwest.

All day Friday Bychevsky worked on plans for the new mine fields on the Finnish frontier. Although he ordinarily kept in touch with Major General V. F. Zotov, chief of engineers of the Baltic District, he was too busy on Saturday to telephone him. Later Zotov told him that on Saturday he, too, was working on mine fields. He started to lay mines along part of the East Prussian border and mobilized some of the local populace to dig trenches and dugouts. However, he was compelled to halt when cows from a collective farm got into the fields and started touching off mines. He was told to quit for fear of spreading panic.

Bychevsky did not leave the General Staff building until late on Saturday. He had been home hardly an hour when the duty officer telephoned and said an alert had been announced. Back at General Staff, Bychevsky found officers milling around, trying to find the reason for the call. No one seemed to know. Nikishev made no announcement. Bychevsky did manage to learn that it was connected with an alarming situation on the frontier. He told his engineering aides to hold themselves ready to leave at a moment's notice to join the units along the frontier.

What was going on behind the scenes?

With the Leningrad Military Commander, Lieutenant General Popov, in the field (along with most of his top commanders) and Party Secretary Zhdanov on vacation, the situation was difficult. No second- or third-echelon Soviet official was accustomed to acting without precise instructions from above. These had not been forthcoming.

The man in charge of Leningrad on June 22 was Zhdanov's deputy, Party Secretary Aleksei A. Kuznetsov, a thin intense man with dark, deep-set blue eyes. Intelligent and alert, Secretary Kuznetsov had become aware in the course of Saturday that a possibly dangerous situation was building up on the frontiers. He knew that for weeks the Germans had been continuously violating the air frontiers. He knew that the Soviet base at Hangö had reported landings of German troops in Finland. He knew that all German freighters to the last ship had cleared out of Leningrad, many of them not even waiting to load cargo. He had been consulted by the Baltic Merchant Shipping Administration about the apparent detention of Soviet ships in German waters, and it was he who had quietly approached the chief officials of the Leningrad Party as they left the meeting at Smolny on Saturday evening and warned them to stay close to their telephones in case of an emergency. He also went to Colonel Ye. S. Lagutkin, Chief of Antiaircraft Defense, and asked him where he was planning to be on Sunday.

"What's the matter?" Lagutkin asked.

"We've got to be alert," Secretary Kuznetsov replied. "The situation on the frontier is alarming."

Further than that Kuznetsov did not feel he could go without exposing himself to charges of panic, but he did ask several top officials to join him at Smolny about midnight. It was, he thought, a pity that Zhdanov should be on vacation.

Precisely what time the Leningrad Military District received the circular telegram from Defense Commissar Timoshenko and General Zhukov ordering a combat alert is not known. The standard Soviet sources assert the telegrams were not sent out by the Defense Commissariat in Moscow until 12:30 A.M. They were dispatched to the Leningrad, Special Baltic, Western, Kiev and Odessa Military Districts. It seems likely that the alert reached the Leningrad military staff a little before 2 A.M.[1]

It was about 2 A.M. when Leningrad staff officers began to be recalled to the General Staff building and General Nikishev and several of his aides went to Smolny, where Party Secretary Kuznetsov had summoned a meeting of the top officials of the city.

One after another the Party chiefs arrived. They quickly mounted the stairs to Kuznetsov's third-floor office. It was brilliantly lit, but the shutters had been carefully drawn. Here were the oblast or regional Party secretaries, the City Party leaders, the Chairman of the Leningrad City Soviet, Mayor P. S. Popkov, General Nikishev and his associates.

As each man arrived, he was motioned to a place at the long table with its cover of crimson baize. Secretary Kuznetsov sat at the head of the table smoking quietly. He said nothing until all had arrived. Then, glancing at his watch, which showed almost 3 A.M., he said, "Let's begin, comrades."

Nikishev read to the assembled group the telegram transmitted from Moscow. It warned of the possibility of sudden attack on the twenty-second or twenty-third in a number of border areas, including the Leningrad region. The attack, the telegram stressed, might begin with a provocative action. Soviet military forces were strictly warned against giving any provocation, but must be in full preparedness to meet the blow of the Germans.

In contrast to the brief warning given to the navy, the land and air forces received detailed orders—all to be carried out before dawn. In the case of Leningrad, of course, dawn had arrived before the orders.

The orders provided:

A. In the course of the night of 22.6.41 secretly occupy firing points in fortified regions on the state frontier.

B. Before dawn 22.6.41 disperse to field airdromes all aircraft, including military, under careful camouflage.

[1] The navy alert telegram took one to two hours for delivery. The army telegrams probably took longer. The warning did not arrive at Fourth Army headquarters at Kobrin until nearly 5:30 A.M. One source claims the telegrams were sent at 11:45 P.M. but in cipher, which caused further delay. (V. Khvostov, A. Grylev, op. cit.)

C. All units to be put on combat alert; troops to be dispersed and camouflaged.

D. Antiaircraft defenses to be placed on combat alert without supplemental increase in staff. Prepare all measures for blacking out cities and objectives.

Take no other measures without special authorization.

At the conclusion of the reading there was silence. Finally, someone asked, "How shall we understand the telegram? Does it mean war?"

"War—possibly," was Secretary Kuznetsov's cautious reply.

Obviously the Leningrad Military Command could not have carried out the orders during the 100 to 130 minutes that intervened between their receipt and the onset of German attack. The caution concerning secrecy and camouflage was made ludicrous by Leningrad's "white nights."

As a matter of fact, the meeting in Secretary Kuznetsov's office was still in progress when he was called to the telephone by Moscow. The hour was close to 5 A.M.

Moscow advised him that German planes had bombed Kiev, Minsk, Sevastopol, Murmansk. Kuznetsov made the announcement with his customary complete lack of emotion.

While Smolny deliberated, the officers at General Staff remained in a state of nervous anticipation. They consulted one another and waited for orders. The same scene was enacted at other Soviet military commands, where officers, suddenly tumbled out of their beds by the word "Alert," found themselves assembled without clear ideas of what was going on or what to do.

On Leningrad's approaches the Special Baltic Military District, commanded by Colonel General F. I. Kuznetsov, was charged with guarding against attack from East Prussia. General Kuznetsov's units were scattered over an area of hundreds of miles. Many were in summer training camps, others were moving to new assignments.

General Kuznetsov was a very senior officer with great theoretical knowledge but little practical experience in command. He had been an instructor for some years at the Frunze Military Academy. Later, he was to command the Central Front briefly and then the special Fifty-first Army participating in the defense of the Crimea. His record on all these assignments was mediocre. He was characterized by his colleagues as a man of indecision, a poor organizer who was gifted with such aplomb that he was almost impervious to suggestion and incapable of swift reaction in an emergency. It would have been difficult to find a man less competent to deal with the fluid and chaotic situation which began to unfold on the morning of June 22.

The situation in the Baltic Military District reflected Kuznetsov's weaknesses. One of his officers, Major General M. M. Ivanov, commander of the 16th Rifle Corps, had quietly instructed his corps to occupy defenses along the frontier and had brought shells up to the front lines. Kuznetsov ordered the ammunition returned to the supply depot. Ivanov disregarded the order, and when the Germans attacked his corps they were beaten off.

Kuznetsov was so dilatory that not until June 15 did he request Moscow to hurry up with the delivery of 100,000 antitank mines, 40,000 tons of explosives and 45,000 tons of barbed wire that had been ordered long ago.

He called for a blackout of Baltic cities and military objectives on June 18, but when General Zhukov in Moscow ordered him to cancel the blackout, Kuznetsov meekly obeyed and the lights stayed on in Riga, Kaunas, Libau, Siauliai, Vilnius, Dvinsk (Daugavpils) and Evgav.[2]

Ordinary summer maneuvers began early in June. Kuznetsov and his staff set up a special field headquarters near Panevezys on the eve of the war.

On the evening of June 21 a large group of political workers from the Central Political Administration of the Red Army visited almost every unit of the Eleventh Army, one of the three commanded by Kuznetsov. The political workers assured officers and troops that there would be no war and that the rumors were simple provocations. Influenced by these views, emanating from Moscow, some commanders canceled precautionary instructions which they had given earlier. Work on laying down a mine field near Taurage was suspended.

At about 2:30 A.M., June 22, Kuznetsov, having received the alert sent out by Timoshenko, ordered his armies to occupy their forward positions, to issue live ammunition, to lay down mine fields and tank traps and prepare to repel any major action by the Germans—but not to fire on German planes or respond to provocations. Not many front units got the order before they found themselves engaged in what seemed to them completely mysterious combat.[3]

Lieutenant General P. P. Sobennikov commanded the Eighth Army of the Special Baltic Military District. He was charged with defense of the East Prussian littoral, the coastal areas. To the greater part of his forces, Sobennikov was to recall, the attack came completely without warning. During the predawn hours he managed to issue orders to some units to begin moving up to the frontier. But the troops from the rear had no notion of

[2] The authors of the official fiftieth anniversary volume on the Soviet armed forces make the assertion that commanders of border districts were ordered between June 14 and 19 to put their frontier troops into field dispositions and instructed on June 19 to camouflage airports and military installations. No source for this order is cited nor is a text given. The recollections of field commanders and the operational journals of border units indicate that when efforts were made to move to a higher degree of preparedness on the eve of the war, very sharp, very serious reprimands were forthcoming from Moscow. (V. D. Ivanov, editor, *50 Let Sovetskikh Vooruzhennykh Sil SSSR*, Moscow, 1967, p. 250.) V. Khvostov and A. Grylev (*op. cit.*) claim border commands were ordered to field headquarters June 19.

[3] One German Army unit intercepted Soviet field messages saying, "We are being fired on. What shall we do?" Headquarters replied: "You must be crazy. Why is your signal not in code?" (John Erickson, *The Soviet High Command*, London, 1962, p. 587.)

what was going on to their west, where the German attack had already started.

In the General Staff building in Leningrad the situation was not quite so catastrophic. General Nikishev rushed back to headquarters from Smolny and at about 5 A.M. called in his waiting commanders and staff.

"It's war, comrades," he said. "Fascist Germany has attacked us. Proceed to carry out the mobilization plans."

The commanders dashed to their offices. With trembling hands they fitted keys into the locks of the big war safes and drew out the sealed red packets containing the mobilization orders and ripped them open.

"Suddenly," Bychevsky recalled, "there loomed before us heaps of unfinished business. Two engineer regiments and one pontoon regiment had to be reorganized into individual battalions and prepared for dispatch to reinforce army units. We had to break off work on laying the concrete in the fortified regions."

Even then not all the officers were prepared to act.

Major Nikolai Ivanov said doubtfully, "Maybe we should not hurry with this? After all we haven't any orders from Moscow."

Bychevsky sternly instructed Ivanov to carry out his orders. All available steel and cement must be thrown into second-line fortifications.

Ivanov thought a minute. He cleaned his glasses with a white handkerchief. "That means it's war!" he said decisively. "All right. We'll fight."

Another officer who had been summoned hurriedly to the General Staff building was General Mikhail Dukhanov, soon to become known as the heroic commander of the Sixty-seventh Army, one of the toughest fighting units on the Leningrad front. Dukhanov was an old cavalry man. His career dated back to czarist times. In recent years he had been an inspector of Soviet military academies.

He was roused from sleep by a phone call and found a staff car waiting on the street outside his building before he was dressed. The streets were empty of traffic as he whirled down Profsoyuz Boulevard and past the Admiralty, sputtering about "fools who call training alerts in peacetime."

In his office he had hardly stopped sputtering when word was passed along of the German attack. Automatically he looked at his calendar and was surprised to see staring at him in red letters the new date: "June 22 Sunday." The year, 1941, was in black letters. His adjutant had torn off Saturday's leaf before leaving the previous afternoon.

Within the hour Dukhanov had his orders. He was to go to Kingisepp, sixty-five miles to the southwest, with instructions for the 191st Infantry Division to deploy along the Finnish Gulf coast and protect the sandy shore from Kunda to Ust-Narva against possible troop landings.

Dukhanov's chauffeur awaited him outside the General Staff building.

Dukhanov looked across the broad Palace Square, freshly washed. The rosy tints of sunrise were reflected from the windows of the Winter Palace and shafts of sunlight threw the gray statues into sharp relief. The tip of the Alexander I column was caught in the sun's rays. Not a person was in sight.

Dukhanov took his place in the front seat of his car, the driver beside him. From under the great arch of the General Staff building a boy and girl appeared. The boy put his arm around the girl and tenderly kissed her. The girl's happy laughter sounded gaily in the quiet morning air.

Soon, thought Dukhanov, that charming laugh will be stifled by the grim word "War!" He turned to his chauffeur. "Let's go! It's a long way."

It was still early morning when Dukhanov arrived at 191st Division head-quarters. The duty officer mechanically saluted: "Nothing of importance has happened."

All through his discussion with the 191st Division commander Dukhanov could not get those words out of his mind. "Nothing of importance has happened."

It was a troubled night in the solid stone house on Leontiyevsky Pereulok, a narrow lane which leads from Gorky Boulevard through the old Moscow merchant quarter to emerge at the Nikitsky Gates. The house, at No. 10, with its sturdy columns guarding a massive door, was heavily curtained. From the street there was no sign of unusual activity, but there had been no sleep in the German Embassy that night. After returning from his mid-evening Kremlin conference with Molotov the Ambassador, Count von der Schulenburg, sat down with his trusted friend and confidant, Gustav Hilger, to draft what was to be his last dispatch from Russia.

The task was a painful one. For days the embassy had been destroying its secret files and documents. Schulenburg knew that only a sudden and un-expected turn of events could keep Germany from going to war against Russia—in all likelihood before dawn. The prospect filled him with gloom. Hilger shared his despondency, indeed felt it even more keenly. Hilger had been born in Moscow, son of a prosperous German merchant family, and had devoted his life to Russia. He was almost as Russian as he was German. He and the Ambassador had done everything in their power to halt the onrush of war. They had even taken their lives in their hands and attempted to warn the Russian Ambassador to Berlin, Dekanozov, when he chanced to be in Moscow in mid-May. They told him as plainly as they dared that Hitler was preparing to attack. This was treason, they knew, and they would be shot if Hitler ever learned what they had done, but the danger to Germany of the prospective war was so great, in their belief, as to justify the risk. Dekanozov, with that stubbornness of which only Stalin's best-trained lackeys were capable, shut his ears to von der Schulenburg. He insisted he could not talk of such matters; only Molotov was competent to listen.

Finally, von der Schulenburg and Hilger, utterly balked, gave up their perilous effort.[4]

Now on this evening of June 21-22 von der Schulenburg drafted a telegram to the Foreign Office in Berlin, reporting the curious conversation he had had an hour before in the Kremlin with Molotov, patiently explaining to his chiefs Molotov's almost pitiful effort to open up at this hour (when Hitler's armies already were moving to the frontier for their dawn assault) new conversations aimed at appeasing whatever appetites Hitler might have.

Neither Schulenburg nor Hilger had hope that this cablegram would affect Berlin's action. Both knew the die had been cast. Yet they were determined to play out the game.

The cable was drafted, encoded and sent to the message center. It was timed at 1:17 A.M., and the Ambassador went to his residence to await events. One of his aides, Gebhardt von Walther, went with him. Hilger remained at the embassy. There were few persons left there. Not only the women and children and German businessmen, but the German experts in Russia on various missions (many of them in connection with the supplies Russia was providing to the Nazis) had gone back home. The German technicians who had been working in Leningrad to supervise the completion of the new cruiser *Lützow* had vanished. The naval attaché, Captain von Baumbach, in charge of the *Lützow* work had left that very evening—the last to go. The consulates had packed up. Everyone had been rounded up except a small group of Germans aboard the Trans-Siberian express, bound from Tokyo to Moscow.

Now it was the morning of June 22. The Ambassador had known for a week that this was the date set for the attack. He knew that the hour was supposed to be 4 A.M. Walther had brought this information from Berlin only the day before. Suddenly, the duty officer telephoned. A long telegram was starting in from Berlin. There was hardly any doubt what it might be. The Ambassador arose with a sigh and returned to his chancellery. The time was 3 A.M. The message was prefixed: "Very Urgent. State Secret." It was for delivery to the Ambassador personally.

As soon as von der Schulenburg read the opening words he knew what the remainder would say. It began:

(1) Upon receipt of this telegram, all of the cipher material still there is to be destroyed. The radio set is to be put out of commission.

---

[4] V. I. Pavlov, who served as Stalin's principal translator at the Big Three conferences in World War II, accompanied Dekanozov as interpreter. In personal conversation with Dr. Gebhardt von Walther, then a secretary of the German Embassy in Moscow (in 1967 West German Ambassador to Moscow), he still insisted twenty-five years later that the Russians thought the warning by von der Schulenburg was a "blackmail" attempt. Walther, who was present at the Dekanozov–von der Schulenburg talk, recalled that Pavlov telephoned him the day after the fateful interview, asking him "how the conversation should be understood." Walther assured him the Ambassador's words should be taken just as they had been spoken. (Walther, personal conversation, June 16, 1967.)

(2) Please inform Herr Molotov at once that you have an urgent communication to make to him and would therefore like to call on him immediately. . . .[5]

The weary Ambassador turned to Hilger and Walther. The men shook their heads. The message was long. It took nearly two hours to transmit and decode. A clerk was ordered to telephone the Kremlin. The Ambassador's limousine was brought around front again.

A little after 5 A.M. von der Schulenburg and Hilger were moving swiftly down Herzen Street toward the Kremlin. Their car swung right on the Mokhovaya and then made the left turn up the raised approaches beside the Alexandrinsky Gardens to the Borovitsky Gate of the Kremlin. The city slept, but it was already almost full daylight. Beyond the rose-brick Kremlin walls the Moskva River flowed softly and smoothly, its waters mirror-calm. The air was heavy with the scent of acacia and early roses from the Alexandrinsky Gardens.

The Kremlin guards brought their hands up to their blue-and-red caps in a smart salute, glanced at the diplomats and waved them inside.

Von der Schulenburg and Hilger entered Molotov's offices in the cream-and-yellow Government Palace just about 5:30 A.M. Molotov, tired, worn and dour, showed them to seats at a long table covered by green baize. Von der Schulenburg drew out his message and began to read: "The Soviet Ambassador in Berlin is receiving at this hour from the Reich Minister for Foreign Affairs a memorandum—"

Unable to contain himself Molotov blurted out: "Heavy bombing has been going on for three hours!"

Von der Schulenburg looked up from his papers but said nothing. He droned on for ten minutes and concluded: "Thereby the Soviet Government has broken its treaties and is about to attack Germany from the rear, in its struggle for life. The Führer has therefore ordered the German armed forces to oppose this threat with all the means at their disposal."

Several moments of complete silence followed. Molotov seemed to be struggling to maintain his stony demeanor. Finally he said, "Is this supposed to be a declaration of war?"

Schulenburg lifted his shoulders helplessly.

Molotov then spoke with indignation. He said the message could be nothing but a declaration of war since German troops had already crossed the border and Soviet citizens had already been bombed. He called the Nazi action a "breach of confidence without precedent." He said Germany had attacked Russia without reason, that the excuses given were nothing but pretexts, that the allegations of Soviet troop concentrations were sheer nonsense, that if the German Government had felt offense, it merely needed to send a note to the Soviet Government instead of unleashing war.

[5] The text is from the German Foreign Ministry files. Hilger is quoted as saying it was not received in precisely this form in Moscow. But no other text has been discovered. (*Documents on German Foreign Policy*, Series D, Vol. XII, p. 1063.)

"Surely we have not deserved that," said Molotov.

The Ambassador replied with a request that the embassy staff be permitted to leave the Soviet Union in conformity with international law. Molotov icily rejoined that the Germans would be treated with strict reciprocity.

The Ambassador and Hilger shook hands with Molotov and re-entered their car. As it purred down the gentle slopes and out of the Kremlin compound, they saw, Hilger later recalled, a number of cars arriving. He thought he recognized several high-ranking generals in the machines.

The Germans drove in silence back to the embassy, which lay less than five minutes from the Kremlin. It was a region of Moscow with which Hilger had been familiar since boyhood. As he passed through the streets, he thought with sinking heart that he would never see them again.[6]

The telephone in the Soviet Embassy in Berlin rang at 3 A.M., awakening Counselor Valentin Berezhkov from a restless sleep. A voice that was unfamiliar said that Foreign Minister Joachim von Ribbentrop was in his office and wished to see Ambassador Dekanozov immediately. The unknown voice and the official tone of the language struck a sudden chill into Berezhkov, but he shook off his apprehension and said he was pleased that the Foreign Minister was prepared to receive Dekanozov in response to his repeated requests.

"We know nothing of any requests," the voice said coldly. "I have been instructed to advise you that Reich Minister Ribbentrop wishes to see the Soviet representative immediately."

Berezhkov said it would take a little time to rouse Dekanozov and get the car sent around. He was told that Ribbentrop had sent a car which was already outside the Soviet Embassy.

When Berezhkov and Dekanozov emerged on the Unter den Linden, they found a black Mercedes waiting. A uniformed officer of the SS Totenkopf Division, death's head gleaming on his cap, escorted them, together with a Foreign Office protocol officer, also in uniform. Over the Brandenburg Gates the first rays of the sun were already visible. It was going to be a fine, clear, warm day.

Entering the Wilhelmstrasse they saw a crowd. Floodlights illuminated the entrance to the Foreign Office. There were cameramen, movie crews, journalists, officials. Berezhkov's sense of alarm deepened. The two Russians walked up the long staircase and down a corridor to Ribbentrop's suite. The corridor was lined with uniformed men who snapped to a smart salute and clicked their heels. They turned to the right into Ribbentrop's office,

[6] While von der Schulenburg and Hilger were at the Kremlin, Walther gathered up some of the embassy personnel from their homes and brought them to the embassy. He then went to the railroad station to await the arrival of the Trans-Siberian in order to escort the German party from the train to the embassy. While he waited there, an NKVD officer appeared and politely told him that he must return to the German Embassy. Walther did so. The Russians did not even bother to accompany him. The German diplomats in Moscow were treated throughout with complete courtesy. In contrast, the Soviet personnel in Berlin and elsewhere in Germany were subjected to rude and even brutal treatment. (Walther, personal communication, July, 1967.)

a vast room with a desk at the far end where Ribbentrop sat in his gray-green minister's uniform. To the right of the door was a group of Nazi officials. They did not move when the Russians entered. Dekanozov walked silently across the long room, and Ribbentrop finally rose, silently bent his head, offered his hand and invited the two Russians to sit at a round table nearby. Berezhkov noticed that Ribbentrop's face was bloated. It was muddy in color and his eyes were bloodshot. He swayed a bit as he walked, and the thought entered Berezhkov's mind: "The man is drunk." As they sat at the table and Ribbentrop began to speak, slurring his words, it was obvious that he was, in fact, intoxicated.

Dekanozov had brought the text of his latest instructions from Moscow with him. But Ribbentrop brushed the subject aside. It was another matter that he wished to discuss. The German Government had become aware of concentrations of Soviet troops along the German frontier. It was apprised of the hostile attitude of the Soviet Government and the serious threat this presented to the German state. The Soviet forces had repeatedly violated the German state frontiers. He presented Dekanozov with a memorandum detailing the Nazi allegations. The Soviet Government was preparing to strike a deadly blow at the Nazi rear at a moment when it was engaged in a life-and-death struggle with the Anglo-Saxons. The Führer could not endure such a threat and had ordered appropriate military countermeasures.

Dekanozov interrupted. He said that he had been seeking an interview with Ribbentrop, that his government had instructed him to raise certain questions concerning Soviet-German relations which required clarification.

Ribbentrop cut Dekanozov off sharply. He had nothing to add to what he had said except to say that the German action was not to be regarded as aggression. He rose a bit unsteadily and said: "The Führer ordered me to announce to you officially these defensive measures."

The Russians rose. Ribbentrop said that he was sorry that matters had arrived at this pass for he had earnestly sought to put relations between the two countries on a sound and sensible basis. Dekanozov said he, too, was very sorry. The German Government had a completely erroneous conception of the position of the Soviet Union.

As the Russians neared the door, Ribbentrop hurried after them. Speaking very rapidly, the words tumbling one after the other in a hoarse whisper, he said, "Tell Moscow that I was against the attack."

The Russians walked out into the street. It was fully light. The cameras clicked. The movie cameras whirred. Back at the embassy they tried to call Moscow. The time was 4 A.M. (6 A.M. in Moscow). The telephone connections had been broken. They tried to send a messenger to the telegraph office. He was turned back. Berezhkov slipped out the rear door in a small Opel Olympia. He managed to make his way to the main post office and handed in his telegram to a clerk.

"Moscow!" the clerk said. "Haven't you heard what has happened?"

"Go ahead," Berezhkov said. "Send it anyway."

The telegram never arrived in Moscow.

What took place in the Kremlin once the formal declaration of war—despite its Hitlerian perversity—had been delivered is still not easy to determine.

Directive No. 1 of the Defense Commissariat signed by Marshal Timoshenko and General Zhukov was not issued until 7:15 A.M., after the German attack had been under way for nearly four hours. It was received in Leningrad at General Staff headquarters at 8 A.M. The order was a curious one. It did not define Russia and Germany as actually being in a state of war. It read like the document of men who were by no means certain that they were dealing with actual war. Little wonder that the Soviet armed forces were confused.

The Soviet commanders were instructed to attack and exterminate enemy troops which had entered Soviet territory, but they were barred from crossing into German territory. They were permitted air reconnaissance and attacks but only to a depth of sixty-six to a hundred miles. Permission was given to bomb Königsberg and Memel. Flights over Rumania or Finland were forbidden without special permission.

If this was war, then surely it was limited war. When the Leningrad commanders read the prohibition on flights over Finland, they were dumfounded. They had already shot down at least one German plane based in Finland.

Colonel Bychevsky met one of his old Leningrad colleagues, P. P. Yevstigneyev, chief of intelligence, in the General Staff corridor.

"Have you read the order?" Yevstigneyev asked.

"I read it," Bychevsky said. "What do you think, Pyotr Petrovich, will the Finns fight?"

Yevstigneyev snorted. "Of course they will. The Germans are heading for Murmansk and Kandalaksha. And Mannerheim is dreaming of revenge. Their aviation is already in action."

In Moscow Admiral Kuznetsov grew more and more nervous as the hours rolled by. He had two major concerns—possible landing attempts in the Baltic behind the Soviet lines and German air attacks on his Baltic naval bases. And what was most alarming was the silence of the Kremlin. The last communication he had had was Malenkov's surly call displaying anger and distrust of Kuznetsov's report of the German attack on Sevastopol. No orders came to Kuznetsov from the Kremlin, none from the Defense Commissar. Although on his own responsibility he had ordered his fleets to oppose the German attack, it was not enough simply to "oppose the enemy." It was time to direct the Soviet forces to strike counterblows as swiftly and effectively as possible.

Yet he, the most independent of the Soviet commanders, was not willing to order this on his own responsibility.

"The fleet could not do this alone," he noted. "There had to be agreed plans and unity of action by all the armed forces."

He knew his fleets were ready; he was confident they would meet the challenge. But what really was going on in Libau, in Tallinn, in Hangö and throughout the Baltic approaches to Leningrad?

The morning flowered—beautiful, sunny, fresh. Finally about ten o'clock Kuznetsov could no longer contain himself. He decided to go in person to the Kremlin and report on the situation. He found the traffic light as he drove down Komintern Street. Not too many people in the center of town. Everyone, he thought, was already on his way to the country. A normal peacetime scene. Here and there a fast-moving car, sending pedestrians scurrying with the horn.

At the Kremlin it was quiet. The flowers, newly set out in the Alexandrinsky Gardens, blazed with purple and red. The walks had been freshly raked with reddish sand for the benefit of Sunday strollers. Elderly babushkas with their grandchildren were already sunning themselves on the park benches. The guards at the Borovitsky Gate, in their parade white jackets and blue trousers with the wide red stripes, snapped to a salute, glanced into the car and waved it on. The Admiral's machine speeded up the incline and whirled into the courtyard outside the Government Palace.

Kuznetsov peered in all directions. No cars. No strollers. No signs of activity. Nothing. One car was coming out. It halted to let the Admiral have the right of way in the narrow drive.

"Apparently the leadership has met somewhere else," Kuznetsov decided. "But why hasn't there yet been any official announcement about the war?"

Where could the leaders be? What was going on?

He was still pondering this question when he got back to the Naval Commissariat.

"Did anyone call?" Kuznetsov asked his duty officer.

"No," the officer replied. "No one called."

Kuznetsov waited all day. No one called from the government. He did not hear from Stalin. Not until evening did Molotov telephone to ask how the fleet was making out.

6 . *What Stalin Heard*

THE GREAT WHITE MARBLE-AND-GILT HALL OF ST. GEORGE in the Kremlin Palace was thronged with Soviet military men. It was December 31, 1940, and several hundred top army commanders had been meeting in Moscow for the past fortnight, discussing urgent matters. The big question in the minds of all, as General M. I. Kalinin, commander of the West Siberian Military District, recalled, was: Will Germany attack and when can we expect it?

"It was obvious that the Fascists were in a hurry," he recalled. "They were doing everything they could to test our strength."

Up to New Year's Eve nothing had been said officially about Germany, but tonight the officers had been told that Stalin would speak. Most of them anticipated he would use the occasion to warn that war with Germany was possible within a few months. This was the gossip as the officers strolled about the parquet floor, looking up at the white marble tablets on which were engraved the golden lists of holders of the St. George's cross, the highest czarist military decoration, Russian equivalent of the Victoria Cross. Although the czarist regime had long since fallen, the names of the great Russian military heroes had remained on the walls without change.

Suddenly came a stir. Stalin appeared. He walked to the upper end of the hall from the interior reception rooms of the palace and stood there mechanically clapping his hands in the customary Russian way during the prolonged applause. Finally, it died down and the officers waited expectantly. Stalin smiled cryptically. "*S novym godom!*" he said. "*S novym schastyem!—*Happy New Year! The best to you all!"

He spoke a few more words of formal welcome, then turned the reception over to Marshal Kliment Voroshilov and walked out. Voroshilov offered a slightly warmer New Year's greeting, and that was all. The reception was over.

The officers straggled out of the Kremlin into the snowy night puzzled. They returned to the Central House of the Red Army for a rousing celebration, punctuated by more vodka toasts than some of them could remember.

"Evidently, this isn't the time to talk about the matter," Kalinin and his comrades concluded. They asked no more questions. They had long since learned that Stalin was an enigma and that questions were not only futile but often dangerous.

The military meeting went on until January 7. Lesser commanders then returned to their posts, and a war game was run off between January 8 and 11 for top-ranking officers. This was followed by a conference at the Kremlin on January 13 in which Stalin and the Politburo participated. To this restricted audience Stalin did mention the gathering signs of war but offered no indication of when he thought it might break out. He talked in general terms. He spoke of the possibility of two-front war—with Germany on the west and Japan on the east—for which Russia must be prepared. He thought that the future war would be one of maneuver, and he proposed to increase the mobility of infantry units and decrease their size. Such a war, he warned, would be a mass war and it was essential to maintain an over-all superiority in men and material of two to one or three to one over a possible enemy. The employment of fast-moving motorized units, equipped with automatic weapons, demanded exceptional organization of supply sources and great reserves of material. Some of his listeners were astonished to hear him expound at length on the wisdom of the czarist government in laying in reserves of hardtack against possible war. He praised hardtack highly, called it a very good product, very nourishing, especially when taken with tea.

Other listeners were deeply disturbed at Stalin's pronouncement (faithfully approved by the meeting) that a superiority of at least two to one was required for a successful offensive not only in the area of the principal breakthrough but on the whole operational front. The application of such a doctrine would require numbers, equipment and rear support far beyond anything heretofore contemplated. The Soviet commanders agreed that overwhelming superiority was needed in the breakthrough area, but they did not see why such great numerical concentrations were required on the nonactive parts of the front as well.

They were even more disturbed that the plans and estimates for bringing the Red Army up to strength to meet the German threat were not intended to be completed before early 1942. War might not wait that long.

The corridors of the Kremlin and of the Defense Commissariat on Frunze Street sputtered with rumors, but the actions flowing from the meeting carried no feeling of crisis or urgency. There was another big shake-up of commands. Marshal Meretskov was replaced as Chief of Staff by General Zhukov, principally because Meretskov made a poor impression at the Kremlin when he gave his report on the war games on January 13.[1]

---

[1] Meretskov was scheduled to deliver an evaluation of the military exercises at the Defense Commissariat January 14. Stalin suddenly telephoned and ordered the discus-

General M. P. Kirponos was shifted from Leningrad to Kiev, and General Markian M. Popov was brought back from the Far East to take Kirponos' post in Leningrad.

The great mistake of January, 1941, in the opinion of Soviet marshals who survived the war, was that Stalin simply refused to believe that a German attack was near and therefore did not order the drafting of urgent plans.

Not that Stalin was lacking concrete evidence of German intentions. It had already begun to pile up impressively. The earliest hint of what the future held may have been a report of the Soviet intelligence agency, the NKGB, to the Kremlin in July, 1940, revealing that the Nazi General Staff had asked the German Transport Ministry to provide data on rail capabilities for movement of troops from west to east. It was at this time that Hitler and the General Staff first began seriously to examine the question of an attack on Russia, and by July 31, 1940, the German planning was in full swing.[2]

There is no indication that Stalin or any other high Soviet official paid heed to the early intelligence warnings. Indeed, it was not until after Molotov's frosty conversations with Hitler in Berlin in November, 1940, at which Nazi-Soviet differences over spheres of influence and plans for dividing up the world became obvious, that talk began to be heard among some Soviet military men of a change in relations with Germany which might bring war. Marshal A. M. Vasilevsky, who accompanied Molotov to Berlin, returned convinced that Germany would attack the Soviet Union. His opinion was shared by many of his colleagues. Vasilevsky believed Molotov reported to Stalin the general conviction that Hitler sooner or later would attack and that Stalin did not believe him. Draft plans for the strategic deployment of the Soviet armed forces in case of German attack were twice laid before the Soviet Government by the High Command in the fall of 1940 but were not acted upon. As early as September, 1940, Soviet commanders along the Western Front were talking about Hitler's *"Drang nach Osten"* and his habit of carrying around in his pocket a picture of Frederick Barbarossa. War games predicated on a German attack were discussed, but the generals were reprimanded by their political superiors for "Germanophobia."

It was not healthy for military men to speak their minds openly about Germany so long as Stalin clung to his conviction that Hitler would respect

sions held at the Kremlin a day earlier. Meretskov's data were incomplete, his notes skimpy and his presentation unavoidably halting. Whether the change of plans was a political trick on the part of Stalin or an intrigue by someone in the Kremlin is not clear. Zhukov was named immediately (January 14) to replace Meretskov, although public announcement was deferred to February 12. (A. I. Yeremenko, *V Nachale Voiny*, Moscow, 1964, p. 45; Kuznetsov, *Oktyabr*, No. 11, November, 1965, p. 149; M. I. Kazakov, *Nad Kartoi Bylikh Srazhenii*, Moscow, 1965, pp. 61–66.) Marshal Bagramyan is mistaken in claiming that the Zhukov appointment was announced in the papers of January 15. His memory seems to have played him a trick. (Bagramyan, *Voyenno-Istoricheskii Zhurnal*, No. 1, January, 1967, p. 55.)

[2] The earliest published reference to Nazi planning for the war in the East is Halder's diary entry for July 22, 1940.

the Soviet-German pact. Occasionally, after the Hitler-Molotov talks Stalin or Molotov remarked that Germany was no longer so punctual or careful about fulfilling her obligations under the pact. But no serious significance seemed to be attached to this.

Hitler gave approval to Operation Barbarossa, the military plan for attacking Russia, on December 18. At noon the next day he received the new Soviet Ambassador, V. G. Dekanozov, who had been cooling his heels in Berlin, waiting to present his credentials for nearly a month. Hitler received Dekanozov with great courtesy, apologizing that he had been "so busy with military affairs" that he had not had time to meet with him earlier. A week later, on Christmas Day, the Soviet military attaché in Berlin received an anonymous letter, saying the Germans were preparing for an attack on Russia in the spring of 1941. By December 29 Soviet intelligence agencies had in their hands the basic facts about Barbarossa, its scope and intended time of execution.

Toward the end of January the Japanese military attaché, Yamaguchi, returned to Moscow from Berlin. He gave a member of the Soviet naval diplomatic service his impressions of Germany. The Germans, he said, were extremely dissatisfied with Italy and were seeking another field of action.

"I do not exclude the possibility of conflict between Berlin and Moscow," Yamaguchi said.

This information was reported to Marshal Voroshilov January 30, 1941.

Before the end of January the Defense Commissariat had become sufficiently concerned to begin drafting a general directive to the border commands and the fleets which would for the first time name Germany as the likely opponent in a future war.

At about this time the Chief Political Administration of the Army proposed to Zhdanov—who was in charge of Party ideological work—that they shift the basis of army propaganda to a stronger line. They warned that a mood of overconfidence was being fostered by excessive emphasis on the theme of the "all-victorious strength" of Soviet forces and the constant implication that Russia was too powerful for anyone to attack her. The Political Administration wanted a line emphasizing vigilance, the need for preparedness and the danger of attack. But Stalin categorically forbade this approach for fear it would be regarded by the Germans as Soviet preparation for an attack.

In the first days of February the Naval Commissariat began to receive almost daily reports concerning the arrival of German military specialists in the Bulgarian ports of Varna and Burgas and of preparations for the installation of shore batteries and antiaircraft units. This information was reported to Stalin February 7. At the same time the Leningrad Command reported German movements in Finland and German conversations with the Swedes concerning transit of their troops.

About February 15 a German typographical worker appeared at the

Soviet Consulate in Berlin. He brought with him a German-Russian phrase book which was being run off in his printing shop in a very large edition. Included were such phrases as: "Where is the chairman of the Collective Farm?"; "Are you a Communist?"; "What is the name of the secretary of the Party committee?"; "Hands up or I'll shoot"; "Surrender."

The implications were obvious.

The embassy in Berlin noted that more and more little items were appearing in the German press about "military preparations" on the Soviet side of the German border. Such ominous news releases had preceded the German attacks on Poland and Czechoslovakia.

There was no sign that any of this intelligence disturbed Stalin's Olympian composure.

On Red Army Day, February 23, the Defense Commissariat issued the directive ordered by Meretskov naming Germany as the probable enemy and instructing the frontier regions to make appropriate preparations. However, by this time Meretskov had been replaced as Chief of Staff by Zhukov, and little was done by the new chief to follow the order up. It was decided to organize twenty new mechanized corps and many new air units, but little progress was made because the needed tanks, planes and other material were not available.

The daily bulletins of the General Staff and of the Naval Staff now began to carry items about German preparations for war against Russia. At the end of February and in early March German reconnaissance flights over the Baltic became an almost daily occurrence. The State Security organs obtained information that the German attack on the British Isles had been indefinitely postponed—until the end of the war against Russia.

The German flights were so frequent over Libau, Tallinn, the island of Ösel and the Moonzund Archipelago that the Baltic Fleet was given permission by Admiral Kuznetsov to open interdictory fire without warning. Kuznetsov's directive was approved March 3. On March 17 and 18 German planes appeared over Libau and were fired on. Nazi planes also appeared over the approaches to Odessa. After one such incident Admiral Kuznetsov was summoned to the Kremlin. He found Police Chief Beria alone with Stalin. Kuznetsov was asked why he had issued the order to fire on the German planes. When he attempted an explanation, Stalin cut him off with a stiff reprimand and instructions to revoke his order. He did so on April 1, and the German reconnaissance flights resumed in force. Kuznetsov's actions had violated orders issued by Beria forbidding border generals or any military units to fire on German planes.[3]

The intelligence data piled up. The State Security forces obtained a report

---

[3] Not long thereafter a German reconnaissance pilot made a forced landing just outside Libau Harbor. His plane was towed in, he was given a dinner, his plane was refueled and he was sent off with a hearty greeting—on special orders from Moscow. (Orlov, *op. cit.*, p. 36.)

in March concerning a meeting of Marshal Antonescu, the Rumanian dictator, with Bering, a German official, at which the question of war against Russia was discussed. On March 22 the NKGB received what it regarded as reliable information that "Hitler has given secret instructions to suspend the fulfillment of orders for the Soviet Union." On March 25 the NKGB compiled a special report of its data on the concentration of German forces in the East. This disclosed that 120 German divisions had now been moved to the vicinity of the Soviet Union.

The NKGB had one truly remarkable source. This was the master spy, Richard Sorge, a German Communist and intelligence agent, who had for some years been in Tokyo, ostensibly as a correspondent for German newspapers but actually a Soviet spy of unmatched capability and insight. Sorge had made himself a close confidant of the German Ambassador in Tokyo, Hermann Ott. Thus he was privy to the most intimate German military and diplomatic information.

Utilizing a secret wireless station—and an elaborate courier system—Sorge sent back to Moscow a stream of incredibly accurate information about both Japan and Germany. In 1939 he transmitted 60 reports totaling 23,139 words, and in 1940 his volume was about 30,000.

His first message to Moscow reporting German preparations for an eastern offensive was dispatched November 18, 1940. Month by month his reports accumulated more data: that in Leipzig a new German reserve army of forty divisions was being formed (on December 28, 1940); that eighty German divisions had been concentrated on Soviet frontiers; that twenty divisions which had participated in the assault on France had been shifted to Poland. On March 5 Sorge was able to transmit to Moscow a sensational item. He sent off a microfilm of a telegram from Ribbentrop to Ambassador Ott which gave the date of the German attack as mid-June.

Did this mass of data obtained by Soviet intelligence agencies, particularly those agencies controlled by Police Chief Beria, actually reach Stalin, Zhdanov and other members of the Politburo? Some Soviet military figures, in the virulence of their hatred for Beria, have hinted that he suppressed or distorted these materials.

This is possible. It is also true that Dekanozov, the Soviet Ambassador in Berlin, was a close associate of Beria's and thus in a position to color, slant or suppress information on Beria's instructions. Another Beria henchman, Bogdan Kobulov (one of the six police officials executed with Beria December 23, 1953), was Counselor of Embassy in Berlin and in charge of intelligence operations. There is evidence that Dekanozov did, in fact, minimize reports indicating German preparations for attack. Andrei Y. Vishinsky, a Beria lieutenant, had been installed in the Foreign Commissariat as Molotov's chief aide. Vishinsky's influence may have been weighted against finding cause for alarm. However, these men could not have kept the military intelligence reports from reaching Stalin.

Marshal F. I. Golikov was chief of intelligence for the General Staff from mid-July, 1940, until the beginning of the war. He insists that all reports bearing on German plans were forwarded to Stalin and that they clearly indicated that an attack was being prepared.

Some of Golikov's critics contend that while he forwarded the reports he labeled them of "dubious authenticity" or suggested that they came from *agents provocateurs*. However, it is probable that it was precisely the "dubious" reports which would particularly appeal to Stalin's suspicious mind.

The evidence indicates that Stalin, Zhdanov and the others received the intelligence but consistently misinterpreted it, regarding it as provocative or indicative of a situation less immediately pressing and thus fitting Stalin's concept of an attack by Germany not earlier than autumn 1941 or spring 1942.

"It was clear that the General Staff did not anticipate that war would begin in 1941," Marshal Voronov, wartime head of Soviet artillery, concluded. "This viewpoint emanated from Stalin, who beyond reason believed in the nonaggression pact with Germany, who had full confidence in it and refused to see the obvious danger which threatened."

It took a strong will to ignore all evidence. For months there had been a stream of worrisome reports from the Soviet military attaché, in France, Major General I. A. Susloparov. The Germans had systematically restricted Soviet Embassy activities, and in February, 1941, the embassy was shifted from Paris to Vichy, leaving only a consulate in Paris.

In April Susloparov sent word to Moscow that the Germans planned to attack Russia in the last days of May. A bit later he advised that the attack had been delayed a month because of the difficult spring weather. By the end of April Susloparov had obtained information about the impending attack from his Yugoslav, American, Chinese, Turkish and Bulgarian colleagues. All these data were forwarded to Moscow by the middle of May.

In April a Czech agent named Skvor reported that the Germans were moving troops to the border and that the Czech Skoda plant had been given instructions to halt deliveries to the Soviet Union. Stalin red-inked the report: "This informant is an English provocator. Find out who is making this provocation and punish him."

An account quickly reached Moscow of an incident in Berlin at a reception at the Bulgarian Embassy. The chief of the German Western press department, a man named Karl Bemer, got drunk and shouted out: "Inside of two months our dear Rosenberg will be boss of all Russia and Stalin will be dead. We will demolish the Russians quicker than we did the French." I. F. Filippov, the Berlin Tass correspondent, heard of the incident almost immediately and also that Bemer had been arrested as a result of his loose talking.

The reports came not only from Soviet sources. As early as January Under Secretary of State Sumner Welles warned the Soviet Ambassador in

Washington, Konstantin Umansky, that the United States had information indicating the Germans were preparing war against Russia in the spring.

On April 3 Winston Churchill, through Sir Stafford Cripps, the British Ambassador in Moscow, sought to warn Stalin that British intelligence data indicated the Germans were regrouping to attack Russia. Sir Stafford had difficulty in relaying the message, in part because of touchy Soviet-British relations. He had instructions to hand the message to either Molotov or Stalin. In the end he gave it to Vishinsky, who may or may not have passed it higher.[4]

Toward the end of April Jefferson Patterson, then the First Secretary of the American Embassy in Berlin, invited Valentin Berezhkov, First Secretary of the Soviet Embassy, to cocktails at his pleasant Charlottenburg house. Among the guests was a German Air Force Major who was introduced as having just come home on leave from North Africa. Toward the end of the evening the Major sought out Berezhkov.

"There's something Patterson wants me to tell you," he said. "The fact is I'm not here on leave. My squadron was recalled from North Africa, and yesterday we got orders to transfer to the east, to the region of Łódź. There may be nothing special in that, but I know many other units have also been transferred to your frontiers recently. I don't know what it may mean, but I personally would not like to have something happen between my country and yours. Naturally, I am telling you this completely confidentially."

Berezhkov was taken aback. Never before had one of Hitler's officers passed on this kind of top-secret information. The embassy had been repeatedly warned by Moscow to avoid provocations, so, fearful of a trap, Berezhkov did not attempt to draw out the officer. He did, however, relay the data to Moscow.

Berezhkov's report went forward with a stream of similar information from the Berlin Embassy. Beginning in March the embassy heard a series of possible dates for the invasion—April 6, April 20, May 18 and June 22. All of them were Sundays. The embassy became convinced a multiplicity of dates was being deliberately circulated as a smoke screen.

---

[4] Churchill drafted a brief, cryptic warning which he wished conveyed personally to Stalin by Cripps. This was dispatched with covering instructions to Moscow by Eden, a few days after April 3. Cripps did not respond to the instruction until April 12, when he advised London that he had just sent Vishinsky a long personal letter along similar lines. He objected that if he forwarded the message from Churchill it would only confuse matters. After some back-and-forth between Churchill, Eden and Cripps, the message was finally delivered to Vishinsky for Stalin on April 19. On April 23 Vishinsky confirmed that it had been given to Stalin, but nothing further was ever heard of the matter. Whether or not the information got to Stalin, it seems to have gotten to Hitler. A top-secret communication from the German Foreign Office to the German Embassy in Moscow on April 22 reported the contents of Cripps's communication and said it had been delivered April 11. The Germans must have had a spy in the Soviet Foreign Office or, possibly, in the Soviet Embassy in Berlin, which may have been informed of Cripps's letter. (Churchill, *The Grand Alliance*, Boston, 1950, pp. 356–361; *Documents on German Foreign Policy 1918–45*, Series D, Vol. XII, p. 604.)

It did not escape embassy notice that the German press, after several years, was again serializing excerpts from *Mein Kampf*. The passages republished were devoted to Hitler's "*Lebensraum*" theories, the need for expansion to the east. Was the German public being prepared for events to come? This conclusion fitted other data coming into the hands of Soviet diplomats.

March and early April, 1941, were a tense period in relations between Germany and Russia. This was the moment in which Yugoslavia with tacit (or more than tacit) encouragement from Moscow defied the Germans and in which the Germans moved rapidly and decisively to end the war in Greece and occupy the whole of the Balkans. When Moscow signed a treaty with Yugoslavia April 6—the day Hitler attacked Belgrade—the German reaction was so savage that Stalin became alarmed.[5] He ostentatiously closed down the diplomatic missions of countries occupied by the Germans (Belgium, Greece, Yugoslavia, Norway, Denmark) and even gave diplomatic recognition to the fleeting pro-Nazi government of Rashid Ali in Iraq. He seized on the departure of Japan's Foreign Minister Matsuoka (who had just concluded a friendship pact with Molotov) for a demonstrative gesture toward the Germans. At the Kazan railroad station ceremonies for Matsuoka's departure April 13 he threw his arms around Count von der Schulenburg's shoulders and declared: "We must remain friends and you must do everything to that end." He then sought out the German military attaché, Colonel Hans Krebs, and blurted: "We will remain friends with you—in any event!" It was on this same ebullient occasion that Stalin embraced Matsuoka and proclaimed: "We, too, are Asiatics!"

The diplomatic significance of Stalin's conduct was not lost on Schulenburg, who promptly telegraphed a report to Berlin. Stalin's conduct may have been influenced by a report submitted to him and to Molotov by the NKGB on April 10 summarizing a conversation between Hitler and Prince Paul of Yugoslavia. Hitler was described as telling Prince Paul he would open military action against Russia at the end of June.

It may have been Stalin's fear of growing German hostility that led him to speed deliveries of Soviet supplies to the Germans. These deliveries rose to new highs in April—208,000 tons of grain, 90,000 tons of oil, 8,300 tons of cotton, 6,340 tons of copper, tin, nickel and other metals, and 4,000 tons of rubber. For the first time the Russians began to transport rubber and other materials ordered by the Germans via the Trans-Siberian line by special express train. Much of this matériel, including the rubber, was purchased abroad and was destined, of course, to be used by the Nazi forces in their attack on Russia.

The stream of messages, microfilms and dispatches coming to the NKGB

---

[5] The treaty was signed in Moscow at 1:30 A.M., April 6. The Germans attacked Yugoslavia at 7 A.M., April 6. Possibly in the knowledge that German attack was imminent, the treaty was backdated to April 5. (Henry C. Cassidy, *Moscow Dateline*, Cambridge, Mass., 1943, p. 10.)

from Sorge by this time was reaching imposing dimensions. During the absence of Ambassador Ott (who had accompanied Foreign Minister Matsuoka to Berlin and Moscow) Colonel Kretschmer, the German military attaché in Tokyo, received word of Germany's intention of attacking Russia. Sorge dispatched a message dated April 11 which said: "Representative of General Staff in Tokyo reports that immediately after the end of war in Europe war will begin against the Soviet Union."

Throughout April the daily bulletins of the Soviet General Staff and the Naval Staff reported German troop movements to the Soviet frontier. The May 1 information bulletin of the General Staff to the frontier military districts summarized the situation in these words:

"In the course of all March and April along the Western Front from the central regions of Germany the German Command has carried out an accelerated transfer of troops to the borders of the Soviet Union."

Such concentrations were particularly visible in the Memel area across the Soviet-German frontier from the advanced Baltic base of Libau.

The movements were so obvious along the central Bug River frontier near Lvov that the chief of frontier guards asked Moscow for permission to evacuate the families of his troops. Permission was categorically refused, and the commander was rebuked for his "panic."

German overflights of Soviet territory continued to increase, and the German chargé in Moscow, Tippelskirch, was summoned to the Foreign Commissariat April 22 and presented with a stiff protest. The Russians claimed there had been eighty overflights from March 28 to April 18, including one in which a German plane had been forced down near Rovno April 15 and found to be carrying a camera, exposed film and a topographical map of the U.S.S.R. The Germans were warned of "serious incidents" if the flights continued, and they were reminded that Soviet instructions to border forces not to fire on German planes might be withdrawn.

Rumors of Soviet-German war were so persistent in Moscow (being fed by every traveler and diplomat arriving in Russia who had passed through Germany) that German diplomatic and military personnel begged Berlin for some excuse, however lame, with which to combat them. The efficient network of Soviet secret police informers reported all the rumors to the NKGB.

Now there came from Richard Sorge what could only be described as final confirmation of German plans. In a telegram sent by secret wireless from Tokyo May 2 Sorge reported:

> Hitler has resolved to begin war and destroy the U.S.S.R. in order to utilize the European part of the Union as a raw materials and grain base. The critical term for the possible beginning of war:
> A. The completion of the defeat of Yugoslavia.
> B. Completion of the spring sowing.
> C. Completion of conversations between Germany and Turkey.

The decision regarding the start of the war will be taken by Hitler in May. . . .

Stalin received from his intelligence forces on May 5 a report which said: "Military preparations are going forward openly in Poland. German officers and soldiers speak openly of the coming war between Germany and the Soviet Union as a matter already decided. The war is expected to start after the completion of spring planting."

Sorge's messages tumbled one after the other. In a day or two he was reporting: "A group of German representatives returning from Berlin report that war against the U.S.S.R. will begin at the end of May." On May 15 he gave the date specifically as June 20–22. On May 19 he reported: "Against the Soviet Union will be concentrated 9 armies, 150 divisions."

By this time Admiral Kuznetsov had ordered his Northern Fleet to carry out reconnaissance as far west as Cape Nordkyn in Norway, to strengthen its naval patrols and reinforce its fighter and AA (antiaircraft) crews. He sent similar orders to other fleet units.

He issued the order a day after the Soviet naval attaché in Berlin, Admiral M. A. Vorontsov, advised Moscow that he had obtained a statement by an officer attached to Hitler's headquarters to the effect that Germany was preparing to attack Russia through Finland and the Baltic states. Moscow and Leningrad were to be attacked by air and paratroops landed. Madame Kollontai, the Soviet Minister in Stockholm, reported in mid-May that German troop concentrations on the Russian frontier were the largest in history.

A deputy military attaché in Berlin named Khlopov reported on May 22 that the attack of the Germans was scheduled for June 15 but might begin in early June. The military attaché, General Tupikov, was sending almost daily reports of German preparations.

The top personnel of the Soviet Embassy in Berlin met in early May and analyzed all the information available concerning German preparations for war. They drafted a report which concluded that the Germans were almost ready and on a scale that, considering the concentration of troops and matériel, left no doubt that an attack on Russia was to be expected at any moment. This report was sent to Moscow but not until late in the month. Possibly it was deliberately delayed by Dekanozov.

There was no diminution of the information from Sorge. He obtained from the German military attaché in Tokyo a German map of Soviet military dispositions, indicating the German plans for assault, and advised that the general German objective was to occupy the Ukraine and impress one to two million Russian prisoners of war into their labor force. He sent information that 170 to 190 divisions were being concentrated, that the assault would begin without an ultimatum or declaration of war and that the Germans expected total collapse of the Red Army and the Soviet regime within two months.

About June 1 Admiral Vorontsov, the naval attaché in Berlin, advised Admiral Kuznetsov in Moscow that the Germans would attack about June 20–22. Kuznetsov checked to be certain Stalin received a copy of the telegram. He did.

On June 1 Sorge sent another message from Tokyo explaining the German offensive tactics which were to be employed: strong reliance on cutting off, surrounding and destroying isolated Russian units.

Stalin could not have had more specific, more detailed, more comprehensive information. Probably no nation ever had been so well informed of an impending enemy attack. The encyclopedic mass of Soviet intelligence makes even the imposing data which the United States possessed concerning Japan's intention to attack Pearl Harbor look quite skimpy.

But the Soviet experience reveals that neither the quantity nor the quality of intelligence reporting and analysis determines whether a national leadership acts in timely and resolute fashion. It is the ability of the leadership to comprehend what is reported, to assimilate the findings of the spies and the warnings of the diplomats. Unless there is a clear channel from lower to top levels, unless the leadership insists upon honest and objective reporting and is prepared to act upon such reports, regardless of preconceptions, prejudices, past commitments and personal politics, the best intelligence in the world goes to waste—or, even worse, is turned into an instrument of self-deceit. This was clearly the case with Stalin. Nothing in the Bolshevik experience so plainly exposed the fatal defects of the Soviet power monopoly when the man who held that power was ruled by his own internal obsessions.

7 . *What Stalin Believed*

WHAT WAS STALIN THINKING DURING THE LONG, COLD
Russian spring of 1941, as the intelligence data piled up, as the evidence that
his erstwhile partner, Adolf Hitler, was—in contradiction to his sworn
pledges—preparing to attack the Soviet Union?

Certainly, Stalin knew that times were changing, that the heyday of the
Nazi-Soviet *entente* had passed.

The novelist Ilya Ehrenburg had returned to Moscow from Paris after
the fall of France. He was a violent Francophile, and the Nazi rape of France
had deeply moved him. He was writing a novel about the French events,
called *The Fall of Paris*. Because of the Nazi-Soviet pact no Moscow publisher would touch it. The censorship would not even clear his chapters for
serial publication.

At his wit's end Ehrenburg sent a copy of the book to Stalin, hoping that
he might get some support. One morning in April his telephone rang. It was
Stalin. Ehrenburg was flustered. His daughter's dog was yapping. He had
never spoken to Stalin before. Stalin said, "We've never met, but I know
your work." Ehrenburg mumbled, "Yes, I know yours, too."

Stalin told him he had read the manuscript and that he would try to help
get it through the censorship. "We'll work together on this," Stalin said.

The politically sophisticated Ehrenburg knew that this meant only one
thing: war. Stalin was preparing for war with Germany.

Ten days later Stalin gave a reception in the Kremlin to young officers
graduating from the Soviet military and naval academies. It was May 5. He
spoke for forty minutes and mentioned the threat of war in serious terms.
He indicated he did not believe the Red Army was yet ready to fight the
Wehrmacht. "Keep your powder dry," he said, warning the officers to be
prepared for anything.

One account of the speech quotes Stalin as observing that the next few
months would be critical in relations between Germany and Russia and that
he hoped to stave off war until 1942. But in 1942, he indicated, war was

certain to come. Another account suggested Stalin sought to prepare a "new compromise" with Germany.[1]

The next day, May 6, Stalin for the first time in his career assumed governmental office. He became Premier in place of Molotov, who was made Deputy Premier and continued as Foreign Commissar. Stalin ordered certain precautionary steps in this period. Instructions were issued in May for the transfer of a number of reserve forces from the Urals and the Volga region to the vicinity of the Dnieper, the western Dvina and border areas.

Some Soviet students find in Stalin's conduct in May contradictory signs: on the one hand he clung to his old dogma that there would be no attack; on the other he began to display concern lest the Germans actually would move against Russia.

How the situation looked to others may be judged by the tart comment of Aleksandr Zonin, a Soviet naval writer, speaking of the atmosphere of that time:

"Everything clearly shouted that Hitler soon would break his treaty. It demanded the supercilious blindness of Nicholas I or the pompous naïveté of an actor to insist with confidence that there would be no war, to declare: 'Be quiet. We will decide, we will announce when the time has come to mow down the weeds.' "

The epidemic of rumors about German attack, the visible evidence along the frontiers of concentrations and overflights, began to affect the morale of the armed forces. The Chief Naval Political Commissar, I. V. Rogov, reported "unhealthy moods" among fleet personnel. Rogov was a strict, demanding man. His nickname was "Ivan the Terrible" (his name and patronymic were "Ivan Vasilyevich," the same as those of the terrible Czar). He was in the habit of shifting his staff without explanation from one fleet to another, from the Arctic Command to the Black Sea, from the Danube to the Pacific. He arbitrarily promoted men "by two"—two ranks—and demoted them "by two" with equal arbitrariness. His eyes were slightly hooded, and he had heavy black eyebrows. He was suffering from a heart

---

[1] This reconstruction of Stalin's speech was obtained by Alexander Werth from Soviet sources. It coincides closely with several other evaluations of Stalin's attitude. For example, Stalin told Lord Beaverbrook in October, 1941, that he never doubted that war would come but hoped to hold it off for six months or so. Margaret Bourke-White, who was in Moscow in May, 1941, heard that the theme of Stalin's talk was: "Germany is our real enemy." She found gossip about the speech general in Moscow. The Soviet censorship killed dispatches on the topic, and one correspondent, she said, was expelled within a week for smuggling out the story. The suggestion of a "new compromise" was contained in a version of the remarks obtained by the German DNB correspondent and forwarded to Berlin by the German Embassy June 4. Some Soviet commentators suggest that the flight of Rudolf Hess from Germany to England on May 8, 1941, tended to disorient Stalin, reinforcing in some manner his Anglophobia. (Alexander Werth, *Russia at War, 1941–1945*, New York, 1965, pp. 122–123; Gustav Hilger and Alfred G. Meyer, *The Incompatible Allies*, New York, 1953, p. 330; *Nazi-Soviet Relations, 1939–1941*, Washington, 1948, p. 337; Henry C. Cassidy, *Moscow Dateline*, Cambridge, 1943, p. 2; Margaret Bourke-White, *Shooting the Russian War*, New York, 1942, p. 31; *Documents on German Foreign Policy*, Series D, Vol. XII, p. 964.)

complaint, but none of his associates were aware of this. Now this stern, self-contained, imperious man lacked confidence in what line to take.

"What are we going to do about all the talk that the Germans are preparing to attack the Soviet Union?" he asked Admiral Kuznetsov. The difficulty lay, of course, in the dichotomy between the rumors and the bland tone of the press. Persons who talked of war were branded "*provocateurs*." Rogov and Kuznetsov decided to order their political workers to hew to the line that vigilance must be heightened and that Germany was the probable enemy.

This was done in the navy. But it was not done generally in the military and for an excellent reason. On June 3 a meeting of the Supreme Military Council was convened in Moscow to approve a draft of instructions for the army's political workers which would emphasize the need of vigilance and the danger of war. Stalin's close associate, Georgi M. Malenkov, attacked the draft in the sharpest terms, contending that it sought to prepare the troops for the possibility of war in the nearest future. Such a presentation, he said, was entirely unacceptable.

"The document is formulated in primitive terms," Malenkov sneered, "as though we were going to war tomorrow."[2]

Stalin supported Malenkov's opinion, and the instructions were not issued. The official attitude was unchanging: all rumors and reports of war were but a British trick to sow trouble between Russia and Germany.

The strongest support for the conclusion that Stalin remained confident even on the eve of war in his ability to prevent its outbreak is provided by the fact that on June 6 he approved a comprehensive plan for the shift-over of Soviet industry to war production. This timetable called for completion of the plan *by the end of 1942*! It was an excellent, detailed schedule, calling for the conversion of large numbers of civilian plants to military purposes and the construction of much-needed defense facilities.

"Stalin underevaluated the real threat of war against the Soviet Union from the side of Fascist Germany and did not believe in the possibility of attack on the U.S.S.R. in the summer of 1941," the Soviet economist Kravchenko commented after a careful examination of the Soviet economic military plans of the period. As of June 22, 1941, the Soviet Air Force had on hand only 593 new-model fighters and bombers. Only 594 of the powerful new 60-ton KV tanks and 1,225 of the serviceable new medium T-34 tanks had been put in the hands of the army.[3]

---

[2] *Velikaya Otechestvennaya Voina Sovetskogo Soyuza, 1941–1945,* Moscow, 1965, p. 58. *Survey,* June, 1967, mistakenly dates this discussion June 17, 1941, and makes the argument take place between Malenkov and Kuznetsov.

[3] Kravchenko concluded that the "cult of personality" adversely affected Soviet military preparations throughout the prewar period. There were great delays in putting new military items into production. For example, in 1940 Germany produced 10,250 planes of advanced design; England 15,000. The Soviet turned out only 64 YAK-1's, 20 MIG-3's and 2 PE-2's. In 1940 only 2,794 tanks were produced, mostly

"Stalin never believed in the possibility that Germany would attack the U.S.S.R. in June, 1941," concluded Marshal Andrei Grechko, onetime Chief of Staff.

On the very day (June 6) that Stalin approved the plan for converting Soviet industry to a wartime basis by the end of 1942, the NKGB put before him an intelligence evaluation that German concentrations on the Soviet frontiers had reached the four-million mark.

Warnings came from all directions. There were more from London. Lord Cadogan, permanent Under Secretary of the Foreign Office, on June 10 called in Ambassador Maisky.

"Take a piece of paper," Cadogan said, "and write down what I'm going to dictate." He proceeded to list for Maisky (with dates and military designations) the identity and location of units the Germans had concentrated on the Soviet frontier. Maisky sent the data by urgent cipher to Moscow. The only response Maisky ever got—if it was a response—was the June 13 Tass statement brushing aside rumors of Soviet-German war as a British provocation.

The Soviet Embassy in Berlin noted a curious and alarming circumstance. Near the embassy on Unter den Linden stood the studio of Hoffmann, Hitler's court photographer, the man who took the pictures of Eva Braun. Hoffmann had a display window in which he put up maps of European theaters in which operations were contemplated. In the spring of 1940 he put up maps of Holland and Scandinavia. In April, 1941, it was Yugoslavia and Greece. Toward the end of May a huge map of Eastern Europe, the Baltic states, Byelorussia and the Ukraine appeared. The hint was obvious.

Yet Moscow showed no signs of alarm. Large numbers of Soviet personnel, their wives—even pregnant wives—and children continued to arrive in Germany after June 1.

The consequences of Malenkov's intervention against realistic political instructions for the army quickly assumed a sinister aspect. Officers who continued to warn about German attack or speak out on the danger of war were branded as *provocateurs*. Some were arrested. Others were threatened with arrest.[4] Political commissars were sent out from Moscow. They de-

---

old model T-26's and BT's. Only 243 60-ton KV's and 115 T-34's were built. The production of the 45-mm antitank gun was phased out, but the 57-mm gun had not yet been put into production. Only 2,760 antiaircraft guns were manufactured. (G. Kravchenko, *Voyenno-Istoricheskii Zhurnal*, No. 4, April, 1965, p. 37.) In the first half of 1941 production of T-34's rose to 1,110, according to I. Krapchenko. (*Voyenno-Istoricheskii Zhurnal*, No. 10, November, 1966, p. 48.) In the first half of 1941, 1,946 MIG-3's, YAK-1's and LAGG-3's were produced, as well as 458 PE-2's and 249 IL-2 Stormoviks. (A. Yakovlev, *Tsel Zhizni*, Moscow, 1966, p. 239.)

[4] Aleksandr Rozen's novel, *Posledniye Dve Nedely*, Moscow, 1963, treats this subject extensively. The Soviet critic A. Plotkin finds Rozen's account fully justified by the historical data. (A. Plotkin, *Literatura i Voina*, Moscow–Leningrad, 1967.)

scribed Stalin as carrying out the most delicate balancing act in order to avoid war. "Stalin," one said, "can walk so quietly he doesn't even shake the china." They referred to Bismarck's dictum that Germany could not fight a war on two fronts.

This atmosphere produced disaster. For instance, on the vital Bug River frontier, defended by the Fourth Army, more than 40 German divisions had been identified by June 5. It was known that at least 15 infantry, 5 tank, 2 motorized and 2 cavalry divisions were massing in the direction of Brest-Litovsk. Yet, on June 10, after getting the latest evaluations from Army General D. G. Pavlov at district military headquarters in Minsk, General A. A. Korobkov assured his associates that Moscow did not fear German attack.

Marshal Ivan K. Bagramyan was then a colonel attached to the Kiev Military District and Deputy Chief of Staff. By late May he had intelligence reports that the Germans were moving all civilians out of border areas. On June 6 the Germans replaced their border guards with field troops and put military directors in charge of all hospitals. An estimated two hundred troop trains a day were arriving at the Ukraine frontier, and the rumble of truck traffic all along the border was sufficient to keep residents from sleeping at night.

Colonel General M. P. Kirponos, the Kiev commander, ordered some of his troops to occupy sections of the frontier fortifications which had not yet been completed. The move had hardly started when the Chief of Staff, General Zhukov, telegraphed peremptory orders from Moscow: "The chief of NKVD border troops reports the chief of the fortified region has received orders to occupy the forward works. Such action may quickly provoke the Germans to armed clash with serious consequences. You are ordered to revoke it immediately and report specifically who ordered such an arbitrary disposition." According to one version, this intervention was directly inspired by Police Chief Beria.

Actually, a good deal was being done in Kirponos' command to prepare for possible war. Bagramyan had been working since winter on plans for meeting any threat to the Western border. A variant had been approved in early February and sent to the General Staff in Moscow, but delay followed delay and revision followed revision. Not until May 10 was the plan approved by the Kremlin.

At the same time, on May 5 the frontier districts got new directives about disposition of their forces for defense, providing for concentration of heavy reserves, especially tanks in a deep interior defense region. The Kiev Command was instructed to prepare to receive large reinforcements from the Caucasus, including the 34th Infantry Corps of five divisions, headed by Lieutenant General M. A. Reiter, and three divisions of the 25th Corps. This group was transformed into the Nineteenth Army, and Lieutenant General I. S. Konev was placed at its head. A bit later the district was advised that it would receive the Sixteenth Army headed by Lieutenant General M. F.

Lukin from the Trans-Baikal district. It was due to arrive between June 15 and July 10.[5]

Did Stalin still believe that Germany was not planning to attack or that, if she did harbor such plans, he could outmaneuver Hitler?

Admiral Kuznetsov visited the Kremlin June 13 or 14. He saw Stalin for the last time before the outbreak of war. He gave him the latest intelligence evaluations from each fleet, advised him that the Black Sea Fleet was about to begin maneuvers and that the Germans had for all practical purposes abandoned work on the unfinished cruiser *Lützow* in Leningrad. He submitted a report on the number of German ships in Soviet ports and a chart drawn up by his Chief of Staff showing how quickly these numbers had fallen. Kuznetsov felt that the chart provided dramatic evidence of German preparations for war and of the little time that remained. Should not orders be given to Soviet ships to avoid German waters? Kuznetsov wanted to put the matter to Stalin, but, as he recalled, "it appeared to me that my further presence was clearly not desired." He left Stalin's office without a question having been raised about preparing the fleets for action. There was no evidence that his presentation was ever followed up.

This was the day that Stalin approved publication of the Tass statement implying that rumors of war were a British trick. Kuznetsov believed that Stalin's intense suspicion of the British (and to a lesser extent of the Americans) blinded him to the validity of the intelligence evaluations he received. Anything that came from Churchill or the British was, Stalin was certain, part of a scheme to draw him into war. Thus, when Ambassador Maisky in London passed on British information about the divisions Germany had concentrated on the Soviet border, Stalin rejected the data. He took the same attitude when Maisky reported on June 13 that the British were ready to send a military mission immediately to Moscow in event of German attack and when Maisky advised on June 18 that Cripps had told him the German attack was imminent and that the Germans now had 147 divisions on the Soviet frontier.

By curious irony Richard Sorge in Tokyo turned over to his wireless operator the last message he was to send before the outbreak of war on the very day he read in the Japanese press the Tass statement of June 13. Sorge had received a message from Moscow on June 12 strongly doubting the validity of his earlier reports of German preparations for attack. Sorge expressed to a colleague his concern. He wondered whether Stalin could be doubting his information. He dictated a new telegram, saying: "I repeat:

---

[5] On June 13 General M. I. Kazakov, flying from Tashkent to Moscow, saw below him on the Trans-Siberian railroad, train after train, headed west. He recognized the trains as troop convoys. He knew they did not come from Central Asia (his own command) and deduced that a large-scale movement from Eastern Siberia or Trans-Baikalia was in progress. The next day his guess was confirmed when he met General Lukin, the Trans-Baikal commander, in the Defense Commissariat. (M. I. Kazakov, *op. cit.*, p. 68.)

nine armies of 150 divisions will attack on a wide front at dawn June 22, 1941." The message was signed with his customary code name, "Ramsey."[6]

In the opinion of Soviet historians none of the intelligence data altered the fixed opinion of Stalin and his closest associates, Zhdanov, Beria and Malenkov, that there would be no immediate Nazi attack. Order after order in the last ten days before the war forbade moves along the frontier lest they be interpreted by the Germans as provocations.[7]

Not even when German reconnaissance planes accidentally landed at Soviet airports June 19 was Moscow's evaluation shaken. True, that same day General Kirponos was instructed to advance his command post to Ternopol, closer to the border. The shift was to be made June 22. But no orders came through to move up troops or put planes on the ready.[8]

Political workers in the army were briefed to carry out a new line which was said to reflect the intentions of the Tass communiqué. There were three main points: first, talk of war is provocational; second, the communiqué proves that there is no disagreement with Germany; third, thanks to Stalin's policy peace has been secured for a long time.

These views certainly were shared by both Stalin and Zhdanov. Zhdanov was Chief of the Party's Propaganda and Agitation Department. The Party line of "No War" was being laid down under his strict guidance.

Only in the navy did it prove possible to maintain some vigilance. There, due to Kuznetsov and his chief political officer, I. V. Rogov, the line of imminent danger and possible attack by Germany continued to be presented in lectures to the troops.[9] But not without repercussions. When the Deputy Political Chief Kalachev lectured along these lines to the Military Medical Academy in Leningrad, a letter quickly turned up in Moscow complaining that the press spoke of peace and Kalachev of war.

[6] The date of transmission is given as June 17 by M. Kolesnikov. (*Takim Byl Rikhard Sorge*, Moscow, 1965, p. 171.) Sorge's information was transmitted to Stalin. (P. N. Pospelov, *Velikaya Otechestvennaya Voina Sovetskogo Soyuza, 1941–1945*, Moscow, 1965, p. 58.)

[7] The Soviet Defense Ministry's study of the Communist Party's role in World War II flatly says that Stalin had ample and excellent intelligence data on the date when he could expect war. He ignored it, and so, asserts the ministry, did Marshal Zhukov and the responsible Defense Chiefs. (I. M. Shlyapin, M. A. Shvarev, I. Ya. Fomichenko, *Kommunisticheskaya Partiya v Period Velikoi Otechestvennoi Voiny*, Moscow, 1958, p. 42.)

[8] General Bagramyan was in command of the headquarters detachment which left Kiev for Ternopol on the morning of June 21. He had been too busy to read the papers, and en route he looked at *Red Star*, the army paper. Nothing alarming struck his eye, but he was seriously disturbed by the intelligence reports from the frontier. About 5 A.M. the morning of the twenty-second his column passed through Brody, just as the fighter field was bombed by Nazi planes. The headquarters detachment arrived at Ternopol between 6 and 7 A.M. after going through two Nazi air attacks. (Bagramyan *Voyenno-Istoricheskii Zhurnal*, No. 3, March, 1967, p. 61.)

[9] Vice Admiral V. N. Yeroshenko recalls that the Black Sea Commander, Admiral F. S. Oktyabrsky, visited the refitting yards at Nikolayev in mid-June to warn his commanders of the imminence and possibility of a Nazi attack. (V. N. Yeroshenko, *Lider Tashkent*, Moscow, 1966, p. 22.)

Rogov sent a strong group of propagandists to lecture to the Black Sea Fleet during their maneuvers. The group was headed by Vice Admiral I. I. Azarov. The Party line was to warn the sailors of the threatening situation with Germany. On the very day Azarov spoke before the personnel of the cruiser *Krasny Kavkaz*, Tass denounced war rumors as a provocation.

Captain A. V. Bushchin came to Azarov and said: "Comrade Commissar, you will have to speak again before the command and tell them whom to believe. Are those who talk of the nearness of war *provocateurs* or not?"

It was a difficult moment for Azarov, but he held to his position, telling the men the Tass communiqué was solely for foreign consumption.

Throughout the Black Sea maneuvers alarming naval reports came in. The Danube flotilla commander advised that Nazi military engineering work was being pressed night and day on the west bank of the river. Deserters said that military action was expected by month's end. Marine units were seen at Rumanian ports and German officers along the Danube. Daily calls from the Baltic commanders told of German ship and plane movements.

The NKGB reported to Stalin personally June 11 that the German Embassy in Moscow had on June 9 received instructions to prepare to evacuate its quarters in the course of seven days. There was evidence that the embassy was burning documents in the basement. Five days later the NKGB reported that German troops concentrated in East Prussia had been ordered to occupy take-off positions for attacking Russia by June 13. Then the date was changed to June 18.

By this time rumors had begun to circulate among high staff officers of warnings which Stalin had received from Churchill and Roosevelt. Tension in the Defense Commissariat was high.[10] Marshal A. M. Vasilevsky told a questioner June 18: "Things will be all right if Germany doesn't attack in the next fifteen or twenty days."

On what did Vasilevsky base this remark? In part, certainly, on the move-

---

[10] However, General Kazakov was astonished to find Defense Commissar Timoshenko and General Zhukov spending Wednesday night, June 18, watching a long—and poor—German documentary film rather than coping with urgent defense problems. Two days later, June 20, General P. I. Batov was received by Timoshenko and given a new command—the land defenses of the Crimea. Batov had heard much talk and rumor of German preparations for attack, but Timoshenko assured him there was nothing dangerous in the frontier situation and that Batov's apprehensions were groundless. Batov received no special instructions, no contingency orders in the event of war, no plans for cooperation with the Black Sea Fleet nor for preparing the Crimea for military operations. "This was the twentieth of June, 1941," Batov wryly recalls. (P. I. Batov, *V Pokhodakh i Boyakh*, Moscow, 1966, p. 7.) On the other hand, on June 19 General S. I. Kabanov, in charge of the Soviet base at Hangö on leased Finnish territory, learned that the Soviet military attaché in Helsinki and the Soviet political representative had suddenly removed their families from a country villa near Hangö. He guessed correctly that they acted in the belief that war was imminent. (Vice Admiral N. K. Smirnov, *Matrosy Zashchishchayut Rodinu*, Moscow, 1968, p. 16.) Admiral N. G. Kuznetsov claims S. I. Zotov, the Soviet emissary in Finland, warned Kabanov June 19 of the impending Nazi attack. (*Oktyabr*, No. 8, August, 1968, p. 164.)

ment of reinforcements to the west, which was now, belatedly, under way on a fairly large scale. There had been a steady build-up of Soviet forces, roughly parallel to that of the Germans.

The German troop movement had been carried out in three stages. About thirty divisions were sent to East Prussia and Poland in the fall of 1940. This force was built up to seventy divisions by mid-May. In the same period Soviet forces in the west were increased to about seventy divisions, but with the difference that the Soviet divisions generally were not at war strength nor disposed in frontier positions.

The Germans began heavy troop movements May 25, sending in about one hundred military formations each twenty-four hours. The Soviet reinforcements, ordered in mid-May, soon began to arrive in the west. These movements were carried out on an urgent basis, troops being moved without equipment and arms. They were concentrated on the line of the western Dvina and the Dnieper from Kraslava to Kremenchug. This was the destination of Konev's troops from the north Caucasus and Lukin's Trans-Baikal army. They were assembling at Shepetovka, southeast of Rovno. But only slowly were the frontier troops advanced to border positions.

The movement of troops from the interior was to be completed only in the second half of July—the critical period to which Vasilevsky referred.[11]

By June 21, 1941, the Soviet had deployed about 2.9 million troops in the Western defense districts against an estimated 4.2 million Germans. The total strength of the Soviet military establishment had been strongly expanded from the 1939 level—up to 4.2 million in January, 1941, against 2.5 million in January, 1939. The total stood just below 5 million June 1. The air force had been tripled and land forces increased 2.7 times. The army had 125 new rifle divisions.

But the numbers were deceptive. The army had only 30 percent of the automatic weapons provided by the table of organization; only 20 percent of the planes were of new modern types and only 9 percent of the tanks. When General S. M. Shtemenko took over the 34th Cavalry Division in July, 1941, he found it had no arms whatever. He finally got some 1927 vintage cannons but was unable to obtain enough rifles or ammunition to

---

[11] The strategic deployment of troops to cover the Soviet frontiers was carried out according to plans which had been worked out by the General Staff in autumn 1940. However, the very extensive movements up to the western Dvina and Dnieper river lines were not designed to be completed before the latter part of July. By that time the Red Army was fighting for its life around Smolensk. (General V. Ivanov, *Voyenno-Istoricheskii Zhurnal*, No. 6, June, 1965, p. 80; P. Korodinov, *Voyenno-Istoricheskii Zhurnal*, No. 10, October, 1965, p. 30.) General S. M. Shtemenko reports that five armies had been ordered to move from the interior to western areas: the Twenty-second under General F. A. Yermakov, the Twentieth under General F. N. Remizov, the Twenty-first under General G. F. Gerasimenko, the Nineteenth under Konev and the Sixteenth under Lukin. (S. M. Shtemenko, *Generalnyi Shtab v Gody Voiny*, Moscow, 1968, p. 26.) V. Kvostov and A. Grylev (*op. cit.*) contend the Trans-Baikal and Far East commands were ordered April 26 to prepare to send a mechanized corps and two infantry corps west.

equip his troops. There were no antitank guns—nothing but Molotov cocktails (gasoline bottles with wicks). He got twelve antitank guns, but not until October, 1941.

The chiefs of the Soviet Air Force and the air construction industry were hastily summoned to the Kremlin in early June and denounced for failure to develop a system of camouflaging Soviet planes. Stalin had learned, through a letter from an aviator, that air force planes along the Western border were parked in parade formation at the airdromes, gleaming in aluminum, beautiful targets for attack. No one had ever given the question of camouflage the slightest thought. The Air Construction Commissariat was ordered to come forward with a comprehensive plan for camouflage within three days. The plan was submitted in early June but had not been carried out, except in part, by the time the attack started.

Thus some precautions, even though sluggish, were being taken.

Is it credible in the face of all the evidence that Stalin genuinely believed Germany would not attack—or that he could stave off the attack by a diplomatic maneuver?

It seems not only possible but certain. In mid-June Major General A. A. Korobkov of the Soviet Fourth Army on the Bug River told his commanders that the higher-ups in Moscow were inclined to interpret the German concentrations as a blackmailing maneuver, designed "to strengthen the argument of Germany in the decision of some political discussions" with the Soviet Union.

The Soviet historian A. M. Nekrich observed that if this represented Stalin's view, he had no real idea of what was going on in the world.

This seems to have been the case. Marshal Voronov is certain that Stalin persisted to the end in believing that war between Russia and Germany could only arise as a result of provocations, not by Hitler, but by "military revanchists." In other words, Stalin trusted Hitler but not his generals!

There were some final efforts by field commanders to take the necessary steps before it was too late. General M. P. Kirponos, the commander in Kiev, became convinced a week or so before June 22 that war was coming. He sent Stalin a personal letter asking permission to evacuate from frontier regions along the Bug River 300,000 civilians, to prepare defense works and set up antitank barriers. To this the reply was the same as all the others: This would be a provocative act. Do not move.

There is a possibility that Stalin thought he had an ace in the hole. Beginning about mid-May there circulated in both Moscow and Berlin rumors that Russia and Germany were exploring the possibility of reaching a new economic and political accord. Grigore Gafencu, the Rumanian Minister in Moscow, thought there might be substance to the reports. He heard that the Germans had made very stiff demands—the right to exploit the Ukraine, the turning over of all Russia's airplane production and other proposals which sounded outrageous. But some felt Stalin was ready to pay an extremely high price to avoid war.

Ulrich von Hassell, the famous German diplomat and diarist, in Berlin heard much the same thing. There were, he noted in his diary, "whispers everywhere that Stalin will make a kind of peaceful capitulation." Von Hassell was skeptical of this, and so, he noted, was Weizsäcker. Von Hassell was certain Hitler was going to carry out his campaign against Russia.

But as time passed, as German preparations for war mounted at an ever-faster tempo, the rumors did not die. They grew. Von Hassell again took note of them, just after the fateful Tass communiqué of June 13. His entry for June 15 reported: "With astonishing unanimity come rumors—in the opinion of 'knowing men' spread for propaganda (why?)—that an understanding with Russia is imminent, Stalin is coming here, etc."[12]

Was this Stalin's ace in the hole? Did he plan, if worse came to worst, if Hitler was really preparing to attack, to make the pilgrimage himself? To emulate Ivan Kalita (Moneybags), the medieval Czar, who solidified his power by making the submission to the great Tatar Khans, by accepting the yarlik? Did he harbor the intention of going to Berlin at the last moment and buying his way out of the cul-de-sac into which his policy had led his country and himself?

Some curious evidence points in this direction.

On June 18 Ambassador Dekanozov in Berlin asked to see Weizsäcker. The Soviet Ambassador was received, but, according to one account, "nothing important resulted" because Weizsäcker had no instructions.

Weizsäcker's own report stated that Dekanozov brought up only "a few current matters." He described Dekanozov as chatting "with complete unconstraint and in a cheerful mood" about such trivialities as Weizsäcker's recent trip to Budapest and the situation in Iraq. He got into no detailed discussion of Soviet-German relations.

On June 20 Halder placed a cryptic note in his diary: "Molotov wanted to see the Führer on June 18."

Was this subject raised in the Dekanozov meeting on the eighteenth? Was there an eleventh-hour effort to arrange a Hitler-Stalin meeting? The Italian Ambassador in Berlin, L. Simoni, heard rumors of a Stalin trip for the purpose of making last-minute concessions.

This hypothesis is given support by the fruitless efforts of Molotov and Dekanozov to get into meaningful discussions with the Germans on the evening of June 21, when the preparations for attack could hardly have been overlooked by a ten-year-old child.

As good a portrait of Stalin in these days as is available is that drawn by Admiral Kuznetsov. In the Admiral's view, Stalin unquestionably expected war with Hitler. Stalin regarded the Nazi-Soviet pact as a time-gaining stop-gap, but the time span proved much shorter than he anticipated. His chief mistake was in underestimating the period he had available for preparation.

"The suspiciousness of Stalin relative to England and America made

---

[12] I. F. Filippov, Tass correspondent, heard these rumors from Schneider, editor of the *National Zeitung*, in the latter part of May. (Filippov, *op. cit.*, p. 194.)

matters worse," Kuznetsov concluded. "He doubted all evidence about Hitler's activity which he received from the English and Americans and simply threw it to one side."[13]

The suspiciousness of Stalin complicated matters in other ways. It was not ordinary suspiciousness, but what Kuznetsov called the "sick suspiciousness peculiar to [Stalin] at that time." And under its influence Stalin not only rejected the plain evidence before him but refused to share with anyone whatever plans he had for the conduct of war should it break out.

"I did not know in that time [the eve of the war] whether we had any kind of operative-strategic plan in case of war," observed Marshal Voronov, one of the highest officers in the Soviet Army. "I only knew that the plan for artillery and combat artillery tactics had not yet been approved, although the first draft had been worked out in 1938."

It was not possible for responsible commanders in the General Staff or the High Command to take even ordinary precautions. They had no war plans —except offensive plans for carrying war beyond the frontiers of the Soviet Union. They had no contingency plans for liaison between staffs. They had no prepared schemes on which to fall back in event of sudden Nazi attack because *Stalin had decreed that there would be no Nazi attack*. If a dictator decrees that there will be no attack, an officer who prepares for one is liable to execution as a traitor.

The men around Stalin were so dominated by him that when the crisis came, in Admiral Kuznetsov's words, "they could not take in their hands the levers of direction."

"They were," he noted, "not accustomed to independent action and were able only to fulfill the will of Stalin standing over them. This was the tragedy of those hours."

General Tyulenev, commandant of the Moscow area, and Marshal Voroshilov met in the Kremlin on the morning of June 22 a few hours after the German attack.

"Where has the combat command post been prepared for the Supreme Command?" Voroshilov asked.

Tyulenev noted that the question "considerably embarrassed me."

And with good reason. No underground bomb shelter for the Supreme Command existed. None had ever been provided. No orders had been given to Tyulenev. Neither Stalin nor his associates of the Politburo nor his top generals had lifted a finger to prepare for this simple eventuality. Admiral Kuznetsov had provided a concrete shelter for the Navy Commissariat. But he did so without orders and at his "own risk and fear."

In the end Tyulenev gave to the Supreme Command his own Moscow District Command underground headquarters.

[13] Marshal A. M. Vasilevsky noted that the more the evidence of German preparations for war mounted, the more firmly Stalin denied its authenticity. (M. Bragin, *Novy Mir*, No. 9, September, 1961, p. 268.)

An even stranger circumstance: On Tuesday, June 24, a group of naval political workers arrived at Kronstadt from Moscow. These men had been studying in the Military Political Academy in Moscow. They heard about the war on June 22 while eating their Sunday midday meal. Two hours later they were assembled by the director of their courses, a battalion commissar, in a building on the Bolshaya Sadovaya. They were told to collect their things and meet at 6 P.M. at the Leningrad railroad station. They were being sent to the front.

Each man was told to pack a white uniform, starched shirt and collar, and complete parade paraphernalia. They were told that victory would be forthcoming very soon and they must be prepared for the celebration.

The men, following instructions, arrived with their parade uniforms. It was a long time before they had a chance to use them.

What possible motivation could there have been for these orders? Whence did they come?

Stalin's authority was so great that it went unchallenged until a fortnight or so before the attack. Only then did some officers begin to speak cautiously, questioning what was happening. But it was too late. And there were still too many commanders who took the attitude: since there are no orders from Moscow to prepare for war, there will be no war.

Thus it went to the end, Stalin trying in the final hours to stave off attack by ordering his armed forces not to fire at German planes, not to approach the frontiers, not to make any move which might provoke German action.

He held this conviction so stubbornly that (as Khrushchev was to point out) when the firing started on the morning of June 22, Moscow still ordered the Soviet forces not to return it. Even then Stalin sought to convince himself that he was only contending with a provocation on the part of "several undisciplined portions of the German Army."

Between 7:15 A.M. of June 22, when the Defense Commissariat first officially advised the armed forces to resist the German attack, and the speech to the Russian people at noon by Molotov informing them that war had started, Stalin was still trying to stave off war.[14]

Russian historians make several allusions to the fact that even after the attack Stalin was casting about for diplomatic means of averting the fatal collision. "Only when it became clear that it was impossible to halt the enemy offensive by *diplomatic action*," says Karasev, one of the most precise

[14] A. Yakovlev, one of the Soviets' leading military aircraft builders and Deputy Commissar of Aviation Construction at the moment of the outbreak of war, writes: "It is perfectly incomprehensible why our troops were forbidden (in Timoshenko's 7:15 A.M. directive) to cross the frontier without special permission." He called the directive "more than cautious, even confusing." "Why was the air force forbidden to attack at a depth of greater than 100-150 kilometers into German territory? War had already started, but the command didn't know what it was: An isolated incident? A German mistake? A provocation? Not to mention that the Commissar's directive was extremely tardy and didn't reflect knowledge of what was happening at the front." (A. Yakovlev, *Tsel Zhizni*, Moscow, 1966, pp. 240-240.)

of Soviet historians, "was the government announcement about the attack of Germany and the start of war for the Soviet Union made at noon."

What was this "diplomatic" action? There is a clue in the Halder diary, which notes under date of June 22:

"Noon. Russians have asked Japan to act as intermediaries in the political and economic relations between Russia and Germany and are in constant radio contact with the German Foreign Office."[15]

The evidence is overwhelming that the Nazi attack came as a total surprise and shock to Stalin. Describing Stalin's reaction to the events of June 22, Nikita Khrushchev pictured him in collapse, thinking "this was the end."

"All that Lenin created we have lost forever," Stalin exclaimed. In Khrushchev's words, Stalin "ceased to do anything whatever," did not for a long time direct military operations and finally returned to activity only when the Politburo persuaded him he must because of the national crisis.

Ivan Maisky paints a similar picture. From the moment of the Nazi attack, he says, Stalin locked himself in his office, refused to see anyone and took no part in the affairs of government. For the first four or five days of the war Ambassador Maisky in London was without instructions from Moscow, and "neither Molotov nor Stalin showed any signs of life."[16]

[15] Dr. Gebhardt von Walther, now German Ambassador to Moscow and then a secretary in the German Embassy, regards it as inconceivable that Stalin could have supposed the attack to have been made by Nazi generals, acting without Hitler's orders. He regards it as equally impossible that the Russians should have made an effort to contact Berlin through the Japanese. At the same time he feels certain Stalin believed until the last that Hitler was trying to blackmail him and that war could be averted. (Walther, personal conversation, June 16, 1967.)

[16] The question of Stalin's leadership and the precise assessment of responsibility for the terrible failures of policy and intelligence in the months before the Nazi attack is one of the most sensitive topics in Soviet historiography—so sensitive as to reveal clearly the role Stalin and his conduct still play in Kremlin politics. For example, Maisky spoke freely of his doubts about Stalin and his alienation from Stalin's policies in the version of his memoirs published in *Novy Mir* (No. 12, December, 1964). But when the book version of the memoirs appeared six months later, Maisky's expressions of doubt regarding Stalin's leadership had vanished. And Maisky's description of Stalin's difficult, labored broadcast of July 3, 1941, was sharply censored. (I. M. Maisky, *Vospominaniya Sovetskogo Posla*, Moscow, 1965, pp. 140-147.) Also compare Admiral N. G. Kuznetsov's account of 1965 and that of 1968, in which Stalin's collapse vanishes! (*Oktyabr*, No. 11, November, 1965, and *Oktyabr*, No. 8, August, 1968.)

Even more striking is the controversy over the work of one of the ablest Soviet historians, A. M. Nekrich. Nekrich published in 1966 an intensive study of the pre-June 22, 1941, events, called *1941, 22 Iyunya*. Nekrich presents an account of the warnings, intelligence reports and growing concerns of the front commanders over the mounting evidence that Hitler was preparing to attack. He concludes that Stalin consistently discounted this evidence and continued to assume that no attack was likely before autumn 1941 or spring 1942. Nekrich's work was reviewed favorably in *Novy Mir* (No. 1, January, 1966, p. 260), which called it "clear, intelligent and interesting" and highly recommended the book to the general public. Nekrich's work was published under the auspices of the Marxism-Leninism Institute, the highest Marxist scholarly institution in the country. It was translated in other Eastern European countries, where it was reviewed in glowing terms. Then, after an acrimonious discussion under the auspices of the Institute of History in Moscow, Nekrich was expelled from the Communist Party in June, 1967, and his work was severely censured. It was plain that twenty-five years after the events the moves and countermoves of the period 1940-41 still possessed major significance in Soviet contemporary politics.

Why was Hitler's assault such a stunning surprise to Stalin?

The real question, as Marshal Andrei Grechko puts it, was "not so much one of suddenness as of evaluation."

"Probably," Marshal Bagramyan remarks dryly, "certain figures among Stalin's entourage shared this evaluation."

The record strongly suggests that Stalin, Zhdanov and his associates were living in a world turned inside out, in which black was assumed to be white, in which danger was seen as security, in which vigilance was assessed as treason and friendly warning as cunning provocation. Indeed, had anyone in the inner circle suggested to Stalin that his estimate of the situation was mistaken, he would, in all probability, have been ordered to the firing squad.

8 . *Cloudless Skies*

EARLY SUNDAY MORNING, JUNE 22, FYODOR TROFIMOV, A veteran Leningrad Harbor pilot, rose to carry out a routine assignment. He was to pilot the Estonian passenger-freight steamer *Ruhno* out of Leningrad Harbor. The *Ruhno* was sailing that morning for Tallinn. Trofimov emerged from the bunkhouse of the pilot station to find the sun not yet as high as the tall banks of the nearby Leningrad grain elevators. There was only a breath of wind off the gulf, but the air was clean and smelled of the morning. In the quiet harbor oil slicks lay on the water without a ripple.

A launch was waiting for Trofimov. He shook hands with the boatman and directed him to Pier 21, where the *Ruhno* waited. There were few ships in the Barochny anchorage. They passed the northern breakwater and then slowed to permit a big excursion boat to enter the Sea Canal. Early though it was, a band was playing on the boat's deck and pretty girls waved and shouted. Trofimov lifted his cap and waved back. The launch passed under the bow of a high Danish refrigerator ship, and ahead loomed the *Ruhno*, its name neatly painted in white letters; below that, in gold, was lettered its home port, Tallinn. The *Ruhno* was a beautiful small ship, more like a yacht than a commercial vessel. It was rich with mahogany and bright with gleaming white work. It was on the regular Tallinn-Leningrad passenger run.

Trofimov boarded the *Ruhno*, introduced himself to the young captain and soon headed the ship into the Gutuyevsky basin. The sun was rising over the city now, burnishing the cupolas with gold. High above gleamed the great dome of St. Isaac's and the needle spire of the Admiralty.

Hundreds of times Trofimov had taken the familiar route from the port to the lee of Kronstadt, where he would be dropped and the *Ruhno* would head into the open gulf. His task was to guide the ship into the Sea Canal which traversed the shallow Neva estuary, a distance of fifteen miles, taking the ship out the invisible sea gates of Leningrad and setting it on course. As the *Ruhno* entered the Neva inlet, an overladen barge with sand from

82

the London banks in the Gulf of Finland appeared. Trofimov had to slow the *Rukhno* to keep from swamping the barge. He shouted a curse at the barge captain, then picked up speed.

The harbor was unusually beautiful on this Sunday morning. Dozens of white sailboats dotted the horizon. As the sun rose higher, it grew warmer. The green forests of Strelna came into view and the *Ruhno* passed the first Sergyevsky buoy. No ships appeared. Trofimov loosened his collar. He was beginning to feel drowsy and he cushioned his chin in his hand. As he did so, he smelled the meerschaum and resin imbedded in his palm. He was about to tell the *Ruhno*'s captain how he loved the smells of the sea when the world exploded before his eyes. He lost consciousness. Gradually, he regained his senses to find himself covered with blood. His head hurt. What had happened he could not guess.[1] The sun still shone brightly and the green woods of Strelna lay off to the north. From somewhere in the distance he heard the shout: "All hands abandon ship!" There was a roar of escaping steam. The ship was beginning to sink. Suddenly Trofimov noted the position. The center of the channel! Should the *Ruhno* sink there, Leningrad's port would be completely blocked. He pulled himself up to the bridge. If only the steering chain still worked. He yanked it. At first no result. Then, as he watched, the nose of the ship swung slowly and the *Ruhno* headed for the channel side. Slowly, slowly the ship inched forward. Slowly, it lost speed. Slowly, it sank lower. A moment before it went under, Trofimov leaped. He was pulled into a lifeboat as the *Ruhno* nosed down on the very edge of the canal.

The hour was still well before noon, and the sun stood high in a blue and cloudless sky.

Summer had hardly begun when Ilya Glazunov went with his mother, as they did each year, from the big apartment in the gloomy Petrograd Quarter to their country cottage, a few miles beyond Detskoye Selo, in the forest south of Leningrad. The little boy loved the Russian countryside. Here he had drawn his first conscious breath. Here he had heard his first rooster crow, seen his first pine trees, first watched white clouds lazily float across blue skies.

Sunday, June 22, brought the kind of morning country boys like best—warm, sunny, lazy. It was sheer joy to get up, to stretch, to run down the dirt road and feel the soft dust under tender bare feet.

Ilya and some friends had found a quiet corner—an old courtyard, strewn with lumber and broken bricks. Clotheslines stretched across it, and bulky chemises and purple undershirts fluttered in the breeze. Along the blind wall at the back of the court a tethered goat was nibbling the new grass.

---

[1] The Germans had sown mines in the Leningrad waters during the night of June 21–22. The *Ruhno* was one of the first victims. The Merchant Fleet at this hour had still issued no warning to pilots or captains of possible German action.

The youngsters were playing soldier—White Russians against Red Russians. Finally they paused to catch a breath. One boy looked out through a chink in the wall to the street. A crowd was gathering at the corner—the biggest crowd he had ever seen. The boys raced through the courtyard and into the street just as a voice began to speak from the radio loudspeaker, set up on the telephone pole.

Vladimir Gankevich was up early on Sunday morning. This was an important day for Vladimir—the day of the track and field meet between teams representing Leningrad and the Baltic republics. Vladimir was a star of the Leningrad team, second only to the champion, Dmitri Ionov. The two were a dual entry in the running broad jump, and Vladimir was determined to make a fine showing.

He ate a light breakfast of bread and cheese, washed down with tea, and, putting his sweatshirt and shorts in a canvas bag, left the house about eleven o'clock. There were only a few people at the stop where he got on the bus, but Vladimir paid little attention. He was thinking about the meet. It was going to be a warm day. Already the sun felt hot. He hoped there might be a breeze off the gulf before the competition started.

He got off near the stadium and hurried toward the dressing rooms. Gradually, he became aware of something strange. There was no one in sight! Certainly he hadn't got the date wrong. He was looking around in some confusion when he heard the sound of running steps. It was his younger brother, Kostya.

"Vladimir!" the boy shouted. "Vladimir! There's news."

Yelena Skryabina planned to visit nearby Pushkin that Sunday with her neighbor, Irina Klyuyeva, to see a sick child. Her older boy, Dima, and his inseparable friend, Sergei, were going to Peterhof, the palace which Peter and Catherine built to rival Versailles. This was the day that the Peterhof fountains, the famous golden Samson, and the long cascade down to the Baltic seashore was to open. Madame Skryabina was hurrying to finish her work on the typewriter when the telephone rang. It was her husband calling from his office. He had only a moment—no time to explain. He told her not to go out and to keep Dima at home. Then he hung up. But Dima had already left. What had happened? Madame Skryabina turned on the radio to see if there was any news.

The youngsters in Gryady, a little railroad town eighty miles southeast of Leningrad, stayed up most of Saturday night, singing and dancing at their high school graduation party, and most of them decided to gather on Sunday for a picnic at the lake. Ivan Kanashin said he'd meet his chum Andrei Piven at noon. The friends soon would separate, for Andrei planned to spend the summer working with a geological expedition surveying peat deposits around Gryady. Ivan was entering the engineering institute. It was almost breakfast time before Ivan went to bed, and when he felt his mother shaking his shoulder, he closed his eyes firmly and turned his head to the wall. His mother shook him again and said, "Wake up, Ivan. Wake up." There was a strange note, something like terror, in her voice. Suddenly Ivan found himself wide-awake. The sun was streaming into the room and his mother was speaking to him.

Ivan Krutikov, a lathe operator, loved Leningrad's white nights—the scent of the cherry blossoms, the heavy fragrance of the lilacs, the strolling all through the night. He and his friend Vasya Tyulyagin worked on the Saturday night shift, and Sunday morning they didn't feel like going home. They went to the park at Pushkin and, toward noon, rented a boat and rowed about the idyllic little lake in the warm sun. They felt relaxed, tired and drowsy. Suddenly they noticed people running toward the great Cameron Gallery, the loveliest wing of the Catherine Palace.

The two young men pulled at the oars. Something had happened! As they drew near the shore, they could hear a voice talking over the radio loudspeaker.

It was quiet in Dmitri Konstantinov's apartment. His relatives had gone to the country. In two weeks he would finish his studies at the institute and take a vacation. This morning he occupied himself with household chores. He and a neighbor had tickets for the performance at the Maly Opera Theater where *The Gypsy Baron* was playing—one of the season's successes.

Konstantinov was about to leave to meet his friend when the telephone rang.

"Did you hear?" his friend said. "Shall we go to the theater or not? I'm almost out of my mind."

"What are you talking about?" Konstantinov asked.

"What's the matter with you?" his friend responded. "Haven't you heard?"

"No."

"Well, it's like this. . . ."

The expanse of Palace Square still glistened from its morning washing as the guards and guides of the Hermitage Museum began to arrive at the employees' entrance, across the square from the General Staff building.

The barometer beside the door stood at "clear." The weather bureau predicted a fair, bright day. Already the sun was high over the blue Neva, and the wet paving stones reflected in aquarelle tints both the sun and the sky.

The museum workers straggled in through the service doors. One set of steps led up to the galleries. Another, small and curving, led to a room below where, once or twice a year, members of the staff assigned to air-raid protection gathered for a Civil Defense drill.

Today the staff, as it arrived, went down the narrow, curved staircase. A drill had been called. They were issued helmets, gas masks, first-aid kits, and told to wait.

Time passed slowly. The room was close. It was tiring. No one knew why the drill had been called. Then someone said the radio would announce an important government communiqué. About what? Nothing but music was to be heard on the radio.[2]

The museum workers looked at the Sunday issue of *Leningradskaya Pravda*. Just the same old war news from Europe, Africa and Asia. A new dispatch from Samarkand: "Today work is continuing in the Gur Emir mausoleum."

Eleven o'clock struck. The doors of the Hermitage swung open. Within minutes thousands of visitors scattered through the great halls. The guides began to take their groups around. They moved from room to room . . . the ceremonial apartments of the Winter Palace, the military gallery dedicated to the War of 1812, the Renoir collection, the Degas', the great Rembrandt galleries, the collections of Leonardo da Vinci and Raphael. Finally, one guide, somewhat weary, brought some visitors to the Tamerlane rooms.

It was past twelve now, and below in the crowded room where museum guards, scientific workers, researchers and museum staff had gathered the radio was bringing the news.

All the Leningrad railroad stations were crowded that morning, most of all the Finland Station. It was here that Lenin was greeted on his return from Switzerland via Germany in the famous sealed train to Russia on April 16, 1917. Here he spoke from an armored car to the throngs of his revolutionary supporters. On this lovely June morning few of those who streamed to the Finland Station had thoughts of revolution in mind, although there were as always fresh flowers in a vase below the bust of Lenin which marked the historic spot. Crowds were buying tickets and cramming aboard trains for the resorts just north of the city along the Finnish Gulf and in Karelia—Sestroretsk and Terijoki. They bought ice-cream sandwiches from white-aproned *morozhenoye* girls as they waited for the trains to pull out and dropped twenty-kopek coins into the cap of the blind beggar who slowly made his way through the crowd, mournfully singing to the accompaniment of his accordion. Trains were leaving every half-hour, and there wasn't a seat to spare. There were families with picnic baskets and young people with guitars and light haversacks over their shoulders.

Others were coming into Leningrad. The suburban train from Oranienbaum was filled with seamen from the training ships. Among them was

[2] A "practice" Civil Defense exercise was called by the Leningrad Antiaircraft Defense Command for 10 A.M., Sunday morning. The drill was ordered by Colonel Ye. S. Lagutkin of the Leningrad Antiaircraft Command because he could get no orders from the Chief Antiaircraft Command in Moscow, a branch of the Ministry of Internal Affairs, one of the police ministries directed by Lavrenti P. Beria. Lagutkin was told to act on his own discretion. In order to get the AA units to their posts in the event of German attack he ordered the "practice" alert. (*Na Zashchite Nevskoi Tverdyni*, p. 11.)

Ivan Larin, captain of the thirty-five-ton trawler, *KTS-706*, one of a squadron whose command was based on the famous old cruiser *Aurora*, now tied up at Oranienbaum. The *Aurora* was the naval hero of the Revolution—the ship whose guns opened fire with blanks on the Winter Palace on the evening of November 7, bringing about the surrender of the Kerensky supporters still holding out within the palace.

Larin, a veteran of service in the Pacific and the Black Sea, was planning to spend Sunday with his wife and three children in the little house where they lived in Okhta. The suburban train glided to a smooth stop at the Baltic Station. Larin stepped off with a firm quick stride and was nearing the entrance when he saw a crowd gathered around a radio loudspeaker. He made his way in that direction.

The naval fortress of Kronstadt was a special place, more like a great floating battleship than a city. It had its own life, its own customs, its own traditions. On the morning of Sunday, June 22, it was holding a holiday fete. On the Field of Bulls, an ancient pasture on the western side of Kronstadt, the traditional spring carnival was opening. From early morning buses had plied back and forth between the "city" of the fortress island and the field, bringing the sailors and their families to the *gulyaniye*.

There on the open meadows had been set up pavilions, bazaars, sideshows and entertainments. There were orchestras for dancing and buffets well supplied with beer and vodka.

During the night, of course, most of the garrison at Kronstadt had heard some shooting. There were rumors about. But it was always like that with a garrison: training, exercises, threats and rumors of war.

The bands were playing, the Field of Bulls was bright with girls in their holiday dresses and sailors in their Sunday whites. Suddenly over the crowd came a hush. A voice on the radio loudspeaker was saying: "*Vnimaniye . . . Vnimaniye . . .* Attention . . ."

Mariya Petrova was an actress. She had pondered before giving up the stage for the new and untried field of radio. Now, after ten years in radio, she was happy in her decision. She felt that her audience was far greater than it would have been on the stage. Her specialty was reading aloud fairy tales, verses and stories, both for children and grownups. She had read the stories of the Brothers Grimm, Hans Christian Andersen, Samuil Marshak, Kornei Chukovsky, Lev Kvitko and Gaidar. She also read childhood tales by Leo Tolstoy, Anton Chekhov and Gorky.

She had looked forward to this Sunday. Early in the morning she was to read a chapter from a new story by Lev Kassil called "The Great Adversaries." Then she and some friends from Radio Leningrad were going to the country. Soon her vacation would start and she would join her little daughter, Larisa, at the dacha in Rozhdestveno.

She gave her broadcast, met her friends, and they started out to the country. As they drove through the bright June day, they sang and joked about where to spread their picnic lunch in the birch forest.

They noticed that there seemed to be many more cars than usual on the highway, and all headed back toward Leningrad. There was something alarming, something strange, about it. No other cars were leaving the city. Finally, a truck driver leaned from his cab and shouted: "Haven't you heard the radio?"

Vissarion Sayanov answered the doorbell on Sunday morning in time to take his mail from the hands of the red-cheeked postgirl. He was pleased at what he found, the kind of mail an author enjoys—a letter from a man who had been an aviator in the Russian Air Force in World War I.

The retired aviator lived now in a little town in northern Russia. He enclosed a photograph album of pictures from World War I. One showed a Russian village on which a German plane had dropped four bombs in 1915, one of the earliest air attacks of the war. The writer suggested that Sayanov might use the pictures if he were to republish his novel about the war in the air during 1914–17.

There was something even more interesting in Sayanov's mail—proof sheets from the magazine *Zvezda* of his poem about General Kulnev, who died leading the Russian rear guard against Napoleon.

Sayanov glanced down the sheets. His eye caught a passage:

> The year 1812 . . . the month June . . . Uneasy
> Were those days . . . a time of change and of alarm. . . .
> And what up to now had been a small
> War now became a great war.
> The enemy attacked Russia. . . .

Sayanov spread out the sheets and patiently began to read line by line, checking the proof against his manuscript. Engaged in this pleasant work he lost all sense of time. The telephone rang and he picked it up, his eyes still on the manuscript.

"You haven't heard anything yet?" a friend asked breathlessly.

"About what?" he said.

"About the war . . ."

Sayanov turned on the radio. A military march was playing. He threw open the window. The sky was cloudless. Along the wide Leningrad boulevards strolled men in their pressed Sunday suits, girls in summer dresses, youngsters in blue sport shirts, swinging tennis rackets as they hurried to the courts. On the Neva he could see launches cutting through the water, white sailboats bending to the wind and seagulls swirling around the bridges.

Sayanov thought of St. Petersburg as it had been in imperial days, of Petrograd as it became during the war against the Kaiser, and of the Leningrad it now was.

Like all Leningraders, he loved his city. Each time a Leningrader returned from an absence it was with the excitement of a young lover again meeting his love. How difficult to be separated from it for long!

Generation after generation the city had been celebrated by its poets. Never had they lacked passion. Innokenti Annensky called the city "Peter's cursed error." Pushkin wrote in awe and terror of the giant Peter, of his will, of his iron purpose in building the great capital in the marshy wastes of the Neva estuary, heedless of life, heedless of cost, heedless of flood, of storm, of cold, of sickness, of suffering and of death. To Dostoyevsky it was a double-imaged city, a city of fog and of abyss . . . the bronze horseman in the marsh . . . the edge of Russia. It was Russia and it was not Russia. It was the place at which Russia faded into infinity, the boundless sea, the invisible barrier between the end of Russia and the beginning of Europe.

All this and more passed through Sayanov's mind as he looked out the window and across the golden spires, the needle point of the Admiralty, the upward-thrusting blade of the Peter and Paul Fortress, the dome of St. Isaac's, the terrible gold and tatterdemalion enamel of the Church of the Blood, the cathedral erected at the spot along the Catherine Canal where Alexander II lay shattered, his body broken and bleeding from the assassin's bombs.

And now, as so often in the past, as in 1919 when workers battalions marched out to stem the German tide, as in earlier times the Russians marched and countermarched in endless military minuet against the Poles, against the Lithuanians, against the Baltic knights, the Swedes and all the rest, the terrible sound of war was clamoring down the broad avenues.

Sayanov heard a band strike up a military march, and from the distance came the shout of a command and the sound of cheering. Somewhere closer a woman sobbed, low and continuously. Russia was at war.

There was a warm breeze blowing off the Gulf of Finland when Aleksei Lebedev, a young poet (he was also a junior officer in the navy), and his wife, Vera, finished their late breakfast at a friend's cottage. The water was cold, but Aleksei went for a dip nonetheless. It was bracing after the drinking, dancing, toasts and laughter of the evening. Aleksei had recited poetry. He was a solidly built young man with a face some found sullen or even gloomy, but he had been gay and relaxed at the party. Later he and Vera had strolled in the luminous Leningrad night. They talked of the future, of their plans, of their love. He read to her some verses:

> In June, in the northern June,
> When no lantern is needed:
> When from the sharp-edged dunes
> The sunset rays never fade:
> And the resin heather bares
> Its lilac colors to the

Warm closeness of twilight
And the moon's brilliance again beckons
Us to sea aboard a black schooner—
Then I love you. I love you
In June. In the northern June.

As he spoke, the air seemed unearthly still. The birches, their trunks pale and ghostly, their leaves spring-green, did not quiver. A light fog crept over the mirrored waters of the Gulf of Finland.

Now in the morning sunlight the couple walked into the forest and found a quiet glade. They stretched on the new grass. Aleksei had a volume of Jack London in his pocket. He drew it out and asked Vera to read, resting his head against her knee. Presently, she saw that he had drowsed off. She put down the book and, careful not to disturb him, moved so that she could watch him. She rested there, gazing at the sleeping poet for a long time. She had almost drowsed off herself when a young girl she had never seen before ran into the glade.

"Haven't you heard the radio?" the girl asked. "It's war!"

War. Vera's heart trembled. She softly touched Aleksei with her hand and said very quietly, "War, Alex, war."

He was wide-awake instantly.

"Well, it's begun," he said, clenching his teeth. "And we'll fight them."

Not far distant—at the resort villa owned by *Leningradskaya Pravda* at Fox's Bridge—Vsevolod Kochetov, a brash cub reporter, and some of his seniors were playing volleyball on the court to the rear of the house, surrounded by pines. It was noon—almost time for lunch—when someone brought the word: War!

These were newspapermen. They didn't stop to ponder implications or complications. They had only one thought: to get back to Leningrad, to get to the paper as fast as possible, to cover the story.

Within minutes a dozen or more of them were running toward the highway, the Leningrad-Vyborg road. They halted a passing ton-and-a-half truck and ordered the nonprotesting chauffeur to take them to Leningrad, to No. 57 Fontanka Street.

The men stood in the back of the truck. There was no conversation. Each was lost in his own thoughts. Near Novaya Derevnya where the road turns off to the Serafimov Cemetery the truck met a funeral procession—a white hearse, a coffin covered with red cotton, white horses with black funeral draperies. Behind the coffin walked the weeping relatives, and behind them a group of fifty friends. A band played Chopin, rather raggedly. The procession brought a somber hush over the newspapermen—except for one cynic who, motioning toward the coffin, said from the side of his mouth, "Reinsurer!"

It was the kind of a remark which sounded vaguely funny, vaguely gauche in Russia, where the perpetual preoccupation of bureaucrats was to "reinsure" themselves against any possible eventuality.

The truck rumbled on, and by late afternoon the newsmen were in their office. The editor and his chief assistant were waiting. None of them knew any more than the radio had reported. But all were ready to get to their task—the publication of a special edition of the *Leningradskaya Pravda*, the first "extra" that had ever been issued.

9 . *A Matter of Detail*

THERE WERE PRACTICALLY NO QUESTIONS LEFT FOR decision when Adolf Hitler summoned his High Command to meet on June 14 in the Reich Chancellery in Berlin for a final preview of Operation Barbarossa. Field Marshal Walther von Brauchitsch had returned the day before from another inspection of the forces in East Prussia, his second within a month. He was accompanied by General Adolf Heusinger. Von Brauchitsch reported that the troops gave a "pleasing impression." Staff work generally was very good. Chief of Staff Colonel General Franz Halder had also been in the East and found the armies in excellent spirits. Their preparations, he noted, would be completed by June 22.

Hitler shared the general optimism. He addressed the commanders for an hour and a half with his customary fervor, dwelling at length on the reasons why it was necessary that Russia be destroyed.

The text of Hitler's remarks has not been preserved, but several listeners recorded their impressions. Halder noted in his diary:

"After luncheon the Führer delivers a lengthy political address in which he explains the reasons for his intention to attack Russia and evolves his calculation that Russia's collapse would induce England to give in."

General Heinz Guderian, the Panzer general and one of the forty-five general officers present, recalling Hitler's address, said: "He could not defeat England. In order to bring the war to a close he must win complete victory on the continent. Germany's position on the mainland would be unassailable when Russia had been defeated.

"The detailed presentation of the reasons that led him to fight a preventive war against the Russians was unconvincing."

Field Marshal Erich von Manstein described Hitler's strategic aims as based primarily on political and economic considerations.

"These were," he noted, "(a) the capture of Leningrad (a city he regarded as the cradle of Bolshevism), by which he proposed to join up with the Finns and dominate the Baltic; and (b) the possession of the raw-material

92

regions of the Ukraine, the industrial centers of the Donets and later the Caucasus oil fields."

After the meeting General Erich Höppner, commander of the 4th Panzer Group which was to lead the armored assault on Leningrad, told a friend, "Now I am really convinced that the war against Russia is necessary."

No one at the staff conference seems to have found irony in the fact that the final confirmation of plans for the war was given on the precise day that the Soviet (but not the German) press published the Kremlin's agonizingly detailed Tass denial that there was any basis for rumors of a Soviet-German war.

Not everything went entirely smoothly, however. One argument arose. At what hour should the German offensive begin? Von Brauchitsch, having just returned from talks with his field commanders, argued that the attack should coincide with sunrise, which on June 22 in East Prussia would be at 3:05 A.M. In accordance with von Brauchitsch's view the decision was taken to start operations at 3 A.M. instead of 3:30 or possibly 4 A.M.

The matter did not end there, however. Three A.M. on the Baltic shores of East Prussia would be virtually full daylight. Not so, farther south— there at 3 A.M. it would still be dark.

The German attack forces had been divided into three groups: Army Group Nord, Army Group Center and Army Group Süd. The commanders of the Center and South wanted a later H-hour, 4 A.M. at the earliest. On June 20 the argument was still going on. Like so many military questions it was finally resolved by compromise. The jump-off was fixed for 3:30 A.M.

The general objective of Operation Barbarossa, as outlined in Hitler's draft of December 18, 1940, was to occupy Russia up to a line drawn from Archangel to the Volga, to crush it as a military power, and to turn Soviet territorial, agricultural and raw-materials resources to the use of the German war machine.

The ultimate target was Moscow, but the plan did not call for direct frontal assault on the Soviet capital. Barbarossa provided that Moscow would be attacked only after the fall of Leningrad.

Leningrad had a peculiar fascination for Hitler. In part this arose out of his view that the city was the mainspring and incubator of the ideology against which he was leading the holy Nazi crusade. Another source of his feeling was the ancient Teutonic mystique concerning the Baltic. For centuries the Germans had regarded the Baltic as *their* sea. Once they had controlled it through the militancy of the Teutonic knights and the cunning of the Hanseatic League. Hitler saw Leningrad not only as the birthplace of revolutionary Communism but as St. Petersburg, the fortress capital which Peter I built as the foundation for Russian power in the Baltic.

Thus, in the original draft of Barbarossa, and in the variants of German military plans which would develop during the fateful summer of 1941,

Leningrad and the Baltic became for Hitler an *idée fixe*, a preoccupation which never left him.

Leningrad *must* be captured; the Baltic littoral *must* be secured; Soviet naval power *must* be destroyed; Kronstadt *must* be leveled. Then—and only then—would Hitler permit the assault on Moscow.

Thus Hitler stipulated on the eve of the war that the first German objective was to drive straight across from East Prussia, liquidating the Soviet positions along the Baltic, eliminating the bases of the Baltic Fleet, annihilating the remnants of Soviet naval power and capturing Kronstadt and Leningrad.

Then, having linked arms with the Finns, the Nazi armies would sweep down from the north while the main German forces closed in from the west. Moscow would fall in a gigantic pincers movement.

The army group assigned to capture Leningrad, Army Group Nord, was commanded by Field Marshal Ritter von Leeb, the senior German commander who had led the successful assault on the Maginot Line. Von Leeb, then sixty-five represented the Prussian old guard. He was no favorite of Hitler's and, indeed, was cool to the Nazis. But he had proved an able commander in the takeover of the Sudetenland, and he won promotion to Field Marshal and the Knight's Cross for his Maginot achievement.

Von Leeb was given two armies, the Sixteenth commanded by Colonel General Ernst Busch, and the Eighteenth, commanded by Colonel General Georg von Küchler. In addition, he had the 4th Armored Group led by General Höppner and the First Air Fleet, commanded by Colonel General Keller. Von Leeb had at his disposal probably 29 divisions, including 3 armored and 3 motorized divisions, numbering more than 500,000 men.[1] These forces mustered more than 12,000 heavy weapons, 1,500 tanks and about 1,070 planes. Von Leeb commanded roughly 30 percent of the forces which Hitler committed to Operation Barbarossa.

According to the plan of operations, von Leeb was expected to capture Leningrad within four weeks, that is, by July 21.

Von Leeb's attack was designed as a double-pronged offensive. The Eighteenth Army had been concentrated close to the Baltic coast, with its main strength packed into a sixty-mile front from Memel, on the Baltic, to Tilsit on the south. It was to strike along the Tilsit-Riga highway, forcing the western Dvina at Plavinas, southeast of Riga, and then head dagger-straight northeast to Pskov and Ostrov on the distant southwest approaches to Leningrad. This thrust would cut communications between the Baltic states and the main Russian fronts.

---

[1] Some Soviet estimates make it 42 or 43 divisions, 725,000 men, 500 tanks, 12,000 weapons and 1,200 planes. Dmitri V. Pavlov, *Leningrad v Blokade* (Moscow, 1958), uses the figures 500,000 men and 29 divisions; the authoritative *Na Zashchite Nevskoi Tverdyni* (p. 37), says 29 divisions, including 3 tank, 3 motorized. A. V. Karasev, *Leningradtsy v Gody Blokady* (Moscow, 1959, p. 30), makes it 43 divisions, including 7 tank and 6 motorized, and 700,000 men. German sources give the figure of 28 divisions. (Orlov, *op. cit.*, p. 40.)

At the same time the Sixteenth Army, just to the south, was positioned east of Insterburg where von Leeb set up his headquarters. Its lines spread south almost to the Neman River. Its task was to smash east on a broad front to Kaunas, then drive northeast to the western Dvina and secure a crossing at Dvinsk (Daugavpils).

Once these maneuvers were carried out, von Leeb would have flanked the whole center of the Russian defense system. He would be within striking distance of enveloping Leningrad from the south, the southwest and the west.

The hammer of von Leeb's drive was provided by the 4th Panzer Group, one of the finest armored forces in the Wehrmacht, commanded by Höppner. The 4th Panzer was a powerful striking group. It was composed of two corps. One was the 56th, commanded by Field Marshal Erich von Manstein, and including the 8th Panzer Division, the 3rd Motorized Division and the 290th Infantry. The second was the 41st Panzer Corps, commanded by General Georg-Hans Reinhardt, comprising the 1st and 6th Panzer divisions, the 36th Motorized Division and the 209th Infantry. The SS Death's Head Division was to follow the Panzers in a mopping-up operation.

The 4th Panzer Group was directly attached to Field Marshal von Leeb. It constituted an independent striking force, although its actions were carefully coordinated with the two field armies, the Sixteenth and Eighteenth.

The task of von Manstein's 56th Panzer Corps was to slash out of the flat pine forests north of Memel and east of Tilsit and head break-neck for Dvinsk, 175 miles to the northeast. His first objective was the Dubisa River bridges at Argala, fifty miles to the east. Von Manstein remembered the country well from fighting over it during World War I.

At a few minutes after 3 A.M., June 22, his Panzers broke across the frontier with a rush which overwhelmed the weak resistance on the border. Soon the tanks encountered a pillbox system which slowed them a bit.

Nevertheless, by 8 P.M. Sunday evening General Brandenberger, commanding the 8th Panzer Division, secured the two Dubisa River crossings at Argala, according to plan. The shattered Soviet forces had no time to destroy the bridges. Behind Brandenberger's tanks the 3rd Nazi Motorized Division and the 290th Infantry had crossed the frontier by noon and were moving rapidly in the path cleared by the armor.

The 41st Panzer Corps under General Reinhardt was to drive to the Dvina at Jekabpils (Jakobstadt), an old fortress town which was the midpoint between Riga and Dvinsk. The corps was held up temporarily by stiff resistance around Siauliai, but the Soviet units were quickly crushed.

The armored forces moved with a rapidity which astonished even veteran commanders like von Manstein. By the twenty-fourth, his 56th Corps had seized the river crossings near Ukmerge (Wilkomierz), 105 miles inside Soviet territory and less than 80 miles away from Dvinsk on the main highway. By early morning of the twenty-sixth the Panzers were outside Dvinsk, and by 8 A.M. they had captured the two big Dvinsk bridges intact.

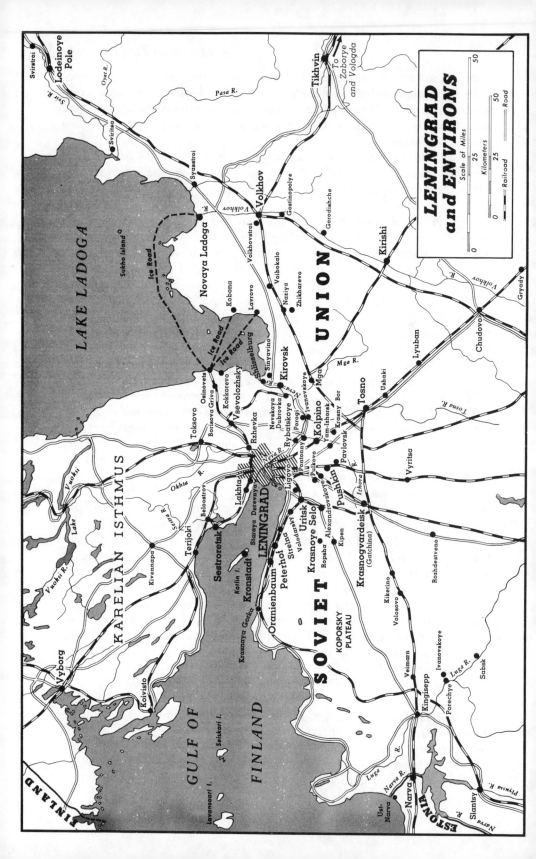

LENINGRAD and ENVIRONS

Scale of Miles

Kilometers

━━━ Railroad
━━━ Road

LAKE LADOGA

Svirstroi
Lodeinoye Pole
Svir R.
Oyat R.
Sviritsa
Pasa R.
Syasstroi
Novaya Ladoga
Volkhov R.
Volkhov
Volkhovstroi
Sukho Island
Ice Road
Kobona
Lavrovo
Voibokalo
Naziya
Zhikharevo
Gostinopolye
Gorodiahche
Kirishi
To Zaborye and Vologda
Tikhvin
UNION
Volkhov R.
Gryady
Chudovo
Osinovets
Ice Road
Ice Road
Kokkorevo
Shlisselburg
Sinyavino
Kirovsk
Mga R.
Mga
Ushaki
Lyuban
Borisova Griva
Vsevolozhsky
Neva R.
Ivanovskoye
Krasny Bor
Tosno
Toksovo
Rzhevka
Nevskaya Dubrovka
Porogi
Rybatskoye
Yam-Izhorsk
Tosna R.
Vyritsa
KARELIAN ISTHMUS
Okhta R.
Lakhta
Neva R.
Ligovo
Pontonny
Kolpino
Pavlovsk
Izhora R.
Vuoksi R.
Sestra R.
Beloostrov
Staraya Derevnya
LENINGRAD
Volodarsky
Pulkovo
Pushkin
Ropsha
Alexandrovskoye
Vuoksi
Lake
Terijoki
Uritsk
Strelna
Krasnoye Selo
Kipen
Kivennapa
Sestroretsk
Oranienbaum
Peterhof
Rozhdestveno
Koivisto
Kotlin I.
Kronstadt
Krasnaya Gorka
SOVIET
Krasnogvardeisk
(Gatchina)
Kikerino
Volosovo
Vyborg
Seiskari I.
lavansaari I.
KOPORSKY PLATEAU
Veimarn
Ivanovskoye
Luga R.
Sabsk
GULF OF FINLAND
Kingisepp
Potechye
Luga R.
Plyussa R.
FINLAND
Narva R.
Ust-Narva
Narva
Slantsy
ESTONIA

The 3rd German Armored Corps under General Hoth, part of the Nazi Army Group Center, just to the south, drove to the Neman River so rapidly that it was able to capture the bridges at Alytus and Myarkin, forty miles south of Kaunas, before the Soviets could demolish them.

This feat turned the Soviet Neman River line which protected Kaunas and made the fall of the city inevitable.

Small wonder that Hitler's Chief of Staff, Colonel General Halder, summing up the first hours of the Nazi attack, wrote in his operational diary:

> The offensive of our forces caught the enemy with full tactical surprise. Evidence of the complete unexpectedness for the enemy of our attack is the fact that units were captured quite unawares in their barracks, aircraft stood on the airdromes secured by tarpaulins, and forward units, attacked by our troops, asked their command what they should do.
>
> We may anticipate even more influence from the element of suddenness on the further course of events as a result of the rapid movement of our advancing troops.

In view of what had happened in the opening hours of the war Halder's statement must be regarded as a marvel of understatement. The Nazi performance in the initial phase of the attack gave Hitler every reason for self-congratulation. He had taken his enemy once again completely by surprise. The pattern of the blitzkrieg, the lightning war, which first had been demonstrated in Poland, then refined in Scandinavia, the Low Countries and France, was being spectacularly repeated. The optimistic forecasts that Russia would simply fall apart under a few weeks' pounding by the Panzers and the Luftwaffe seemed on the verge of fulfillment. There was no one in the Führer's headquarters in those exciting days who was likely to recall the ominous precedent of Napoleon's Russian venture. Once again the genius of the Führer was being proclaimed by the triumph of his strategy and arms.

10 . On the Distant Approaches

THE GERMANS HAD SELECTED THE TILSIT-RIGA HIGHWAY as one of the main avenues of their thrust toward Leningrad. The highway crossed the Soviet-German border at a town called Taurage on the Ura River.

Taurage held a central position in the shield which was being created by Colonel General F. I. Kuznetsov's Special Baltic Military Command as a protection against any thrust toward Leningrad across the Baltic states. This command, set up after the absorption of the Baltic states into the Soviet Union in the summer of 1940, was supposed to hold back an attack hundreds of miles to the west of Leningrad.

Despite its obvious importance, Taurage was garrisoned on the evening of June 21 only by special police border troops rather than by regular Red Army units. Some time during the evening a border patrol intercepted a letter which said the Germans planned to attack either Saturday night or Sunday morning. At about 2 A.M. June 22 Lieutenant Colonel Golovkin of the border force ordered his men to battle stations. They could plainly hear the noise of heavy machines, obviously tanks, across the river. It was a cool night and quiet except for the clank of heavy equipment on the German side where no lights were showing.

At 4 A.M. came a roar like thunder. A shell smashed into the command post at Taurage, and a second knocked out the switchboard. Over a field telephone came a cry from a border sentry: "Osoka calling. Osoka calling. Germans have crossed the frontier. This is Osoka. It's war. I see tanks. Many tanks."

The border guards blew up the bridge across the Ura but did not have the strength to offer much opposition. In the commandant's office they were busy burning secret papers and getting the money out of the office safe. At about 2 P.M. the frontier guards managed to make their way to Skaudvile, about seven miles east of Taurage. Low-flying Nazi planes strafed them, and they fired back with pistols and machine guns. They had no antiaircraft weapons.

Not until 4 P.M. did they get their first communication from the regular Red Army Command. It was a message from 125th Division headquarters, ordering them to set up roadblocks, to liquidate the Nazi "intruders," to hold up disorganized units and soldiers and halt the spread of panic. The description of the Germans as "intruders" suggested that even twelve hours after the war had started the 125th Division commander was not sure Russia really was at war.

The border guards did their best with the "intruders," but "it wasn't easy," one survivor recalled.

The weight of the Nazi attack was so heavy that it simply crushed many Soviet units in its path. This was the fate of the 125th Division. It was attacked by three German armored divisions of the 4th Nazi Panzers and three infantry divisions. It fell apart. Within hours it had no tanks, hardly any antiaircraft guns, little transport and was running out of hand grenades. Helplessly, it staggered back to the rear.

The 125th Division was part of the Soviet Eleventh Army, which was commanded by Lieutenant General Vasily I. Morozov, a handsome, quiet, self-controlled, mustached officer of great experience. He had an able staff, headed by Major General Ivan T. Shlemin and Ivan V. Zuyev, a political commissar who had served in Spain.

The Soviet Eleventh Army was one of three which made up the Baltic Military Command of Colonel General F. I. Kuznetsov. Kuznetsov was a very senior Red Army officer, but he had never seen active combat. His Chief of Staff was Lieutenant General P. S. Klenov and his Military Commissar was P. A. Dibrov.

The Germans possessed a superiority over Kuznetsov of about three to one in infantry and two to one in artillery. In armor the two forces were roughly equal.[2] However, the figures were deceptive. Kuznetsov had dispersed his troops widely through the whole Baltic area. Many units were 100 to 300 miles to the rear. Only seven divisions were in the frontier region, and most of them had only one regiment in line, the rest being in barracks and camps, 25 or 30 miles away. This reflected the general situation on the Western Front, where of a total of 170 Soviet divisions facing the Germans only 56 were in the first echelon on June 22.

Not only were troops badly positioned (Stalin specifically had refused requests by Kuznetsov to concentrate his forces on the frontiers), but the fortified regions on the new state borders were far from complete—only 50 percent by one estimate. Many heavy forts were not due to be ready until 1942 or even 1943. A visitor on the eve of June 22 was shocked to find Baltic frontier works which supposedly had been finished but had no weap-

[2] The authoritative Soviet study of the Baltic campaign gives the German superiority as 1.66 to 1 in divisions, 1.3 to 1 in armor, 1.8 to 1 in weapons, 1.37 to 1 in planes. (Orlov, *op. cit.*, p. 40.)

ons in place except for a few gun positions fitted out for "show" to inspectors sent out from Moscow.

Kuznetsov's frontier commanders were excellently informed as to German forces concentrated across the border from their lines. Often they knew not only the numbers but the designations of the units and names of German commanders. But they could not obtain orders to position their troops properly to meet an attack.

Nor did Colonel General Kuznetsov have any detailed plan of action in event of German attack. It was no accident that the very suggestion to set up plans to defend his Riga General Headquarters struck him as unthinkable. Like most commanders in the field, as well as the Supreme Command in Moscow, he was dominated by Stalin's official doctrine that "war will be fought on alien territory with a minimum of bloodshed." This thesis had been preached for years both in the military academies and in the Communist Party. The Soviet Army, the Soviet Government and the Soviet people had become accustomed to thinking that if war came their armies would strike quickly to the west and carry the attack to the enemy. Comparatively little attention had been given to defense tactics or to problems which might be encountered as a result of Nazi blitzkrieg tactics.

Thus Colonel General Kuznetsov was by no means ready militarily or psychologically for the crisis which arose. Many—possibly half—of his officers were on leave. More than half the border units were understrength and had only a fraction of the arms and equipment called for by the table of organization.

Almost all Kuznetsov's tanks were old models—1,045 out of a total of 1,150. And 75 percent of these needed repairs. Three-quarters of his planes were five or more years old and almost unserviceable. Many guns had no mechanized transport, and most of them were not powerful enough to match the German artillery or German tanks. In the 12th Mechanized Corps 16 percent of the tanks were out of service, being repaired. In the 3rd Corps the percentage was 45. An authoritative estimate placed only five of the thirty divisions which saw service on the Northwest Front as fully equipped. The remainder were 15 to 30 percent below level in personnel and equipment.

The new fortified system was not complete; the old installations in the Pskov-Ostrov area had been dismantled; the new airfields had not yet been finished and many old ones were being reconstructed. There was a shortage of shells, ammunition and spare parts. This situation prevailed throughout the Soviet Army.

When Marshal A. I. Yeremenko took command of the 3rd Mechanized Corps, he found it had only 50 percent of its authorized tanks, mostly old T-26's. He had hardly any new T-34's, which became the work horses of World War II, and only two new KV 60-ton tanks, which were superior to anything the Germans possessed. The 7th Mechanized Corps, constituted on July 1, had 40 of its rated 120 KV tanks and none of the rated 420 T-34's. The Western Front entered the war with 60 percent of its allotted rifles, 75 percent of its mortars, 80 percent of its AA guns, 75 percent of its artillery, 56.5 percent of its tanks and 55 percent of its trucks. The ratios in Kuznetsov's Special Baltic District were about the same.

General Kuznetsov had available for the protection of Leningrad's approaches two principal armies—the Eighth, commanded by Major General P. P. Sobennikov, and the Eleventh, commanded by Lieutenant General V. I. Morozov, and the understrength Twenty-seventh Army, commanded by Major General A. Ye. Berzarin. The Twenty-seventh Army was located east and north of the Dvina. The Eighth Army defended the coastal sector which was attacked by the Eighteenth German Army. The Eleventh Soviet Army was just to the south, where it met the brunt of assault by the German Sixteenth Army. The heaviest blow of the 4th German Panzers struck at the hinge of the Eighth and Eleventh Soviet armies.

The German intelligence estimated Kuznetsov's forces at 28 divisions, including 2 armored, 2 cavalry and 6 mechanized.[3]

Because of the indecisiveness of Colonel General Kuznetsov and his reluctance to give precise instructions there was a vast variation in the state of preparedness of his subordinate commands on the eve of the war.

Lieutenant General Morozov of the Eleventh Army had been convinced that war was coming and coming very soon. Acting on his own initiative, Morozov ordered a number of precautionary steps for his Eleventh Army, only to bring down Moscow's wrath. A special investigating commission appeared at his headquarters at Kaunas to inquire into charges that he and his political aide, Commissar Zuyev, were exaggerating the war threat and creating dangerous tensions.

Morozov was compelled to soft-pedal his preparations, but after the Tass communiqué of June 13 he took the risk of resuming them because activity by the Germans was so open and so obvious—daily overflights by Nazi reconnaissance planes, the arrival of more German units on the frontier, the drone of Nazi motor transport, day and night, audible at his forward positions.

Finally, on June 18 Colonel General Kuznetsov issued Order No. 1, which instructed his forces to move to a higher degree of preparedness. Morozov summoned his Military Council and directed the 16th Rifle Corps, comprising the 188th, 5th and 33rd Rifle Divisions, to occupy their forward positions. He gave similar orders to the 128th Infantry Division. The four divisions were instructed to leave only a single regiment each in the Kasly-Rudy area, about thirty miles east of the frontier, where most of them had

---

[3] John Erickson, *The Soviet High Command*, estimates them at 28 rifle divisions, 3 mechanized corps, 4 cavalry divisions, 7 mechanized brigades, 1,000 tanks. Pavlov (*op. cit.*, 3rd edition, p. 10) gives the figures as 12 rifle, 2 motorized, 4 armored divisions. Orlov (*op. cit.*, p. 40) makes it 22 divisions, including a separate rifle brigade.

been engaged in summer training exercises since early June.

However, the orders came so tardily that at the moment of the Nazi attack the bulk of Morozov's troops were still in the training areas. For instance, his 188th Division met the attack with only four rifle battalions and one artillery unit on the line—all the rest were still in the Kasly-Rudy camps.

Simultaneously, Morozov moved his command post from his headquarters in the heart of Kaunas, an ancient Baltic city of round stone towers and crenelated walls, to Fort No. 6. This fort had been built before World War I at the bend in the Neman River between Zhalyakalnis and Pyatrashunai, just east of the old city. It was of sturdy construction, designed to withstand heavy bombardment by the World War I Big Berthas. There were reinforced-concrete bunkers, underground shelters and walls protected by thirty to forty feet of brick-and-earthen barriers. Morozov felt it should be secure against any dive-bombing attack by the Nazis.

Fort No. 6 was one of two built by the czarist regime before 1914 to protect Kaunas. The other, Fort No. 9, was located about five miles out of Kaunas in the Zhamaitsk highway leading to the Baltic coast. Fort No. 9 was even more powerfully built than Fort No. 6, possessing very deep bastions, concrete pillboxes and heavy gun positions.

Despite the excellence of their construction both forts had fallen almost immediately in World War I. In fact, Fort No. 9 surrendered without ever firing a shot.

In the intervening years Fort No. 9 had been turned into a high-security prison by the Lithuanian Government, and it was used for the same purpose by the Soviets when they took over Lithuania in the summer of 1940.

Both forts were soon to acquire sinister names. Fort No. 9 became, under the Nazis, the chief death camp in the Baltic region, a rival of Auschwitz and Dachau. Here an estimated 80,000 Lithuanians, Jews, Russians, Poles, French and Belgians were to die in the gas ovens. Fort No. 6 was utilized by the Nazis as Prisoner of War Camp No. 336. Some 35,000 Soviet military passed through its heavy steel gates. Only a handful emerged. A prison "hospital" was set up at Fort No. 6. In eleven months, from September, 1941, to July, 1942, 36,473 Soviet prisoners were admitted. Of that number 13,936 died. At the end of the war 67 mass graves were found in the vicinity of Fort No. 6, in one of which, according to German records, some 7,708 individuals had been buried.

These horrors lay in the future. For the moment, it seemed on June 18 a wise precaution to General Morozov to move his headquarters to this more secure place—secure not only from Nazi air attack but from sudden assault from the population. Neither Morozov nor his staff were under illusions as to the reliability of Kaunas in event of German attack. Manifestations by the Lithuanian nationalists occurred almost daily. Sometimes it was just an old woman, caught sewing on a Lithuanian flag. Other times it was a shot in the dark that took the life of a Soviet officer.

Major V. P. Agafonov, a communications officer, was occupied all day June 19 installing his equipment in Fort No. 6.

Late that evening Lieutenant Colonel Aleksei A. Soshalsky, chief of intelligence, told Agafonov he was concerned about German preparations for attack. Word was circulating that the date had been fixed for Sunday, June 22. Agafonov reminded him that there had been earlier rumors of June 15, but Soshalsky was not reassured. He pointed out that only that day had they found the communications lines of the 188th Division cut.

Agafonov was worried about the safety of his two children. But he was fearful that if he tried to send them to the rear he would be branded a "panicmonger." He knew, too, that General Morozov had just sent his own daughter to a summer camp almost on the frontier.

On June 21 Colonel General Kuznetsov came down from his Baltic field headquarters near Panevezys, about three hours' drive due north of Kaunas. He was disturbed about the orders Morozov had given for moving troops into border positions. Moscow was insisting again that nothing be done which might be interpreted by the Germans as a provocation. It was this fear, not worry over the concentration of Nazi divisions, which preoccupied the Kremlin.

"Aren't you carrying out your concentrations along the frontier too openly?" Kuznetsov asked. "Don't you think they are going to smell this out on the other side of the line? If they do, there will be unpleasant consequences."

"We've done everything possible," said General Shlemin, Morozov's Chief of Staff, "to assure that our movements will not be noticed."

"I hear," Kuznetsov said, "that ammunition is being provided to the troops."

"That's correct."

"Well," said Kuznetsov, "be careful with it. One accidental shot from our side may be used by the Germans as an excuse for a provocation."

"We understand," General Shlemin replied. "Our people have been strictly cautioned."

The tall, dignified Kuznetsov and the small, shaven-headed Shlemin stared at each other a moment. Then Kuznetsov nervously pulled on his gloves, muttering, "What a muddled situation . . . fantastically muddled . . ."

He strode off to his car, sat there a moment as though about to say something more, then slapped his hand on his knee and drove off.

Major Agafonov hurried ahead with his work at Fort No. 6. He labored all day and into the evening Saturday, June 21. He was too busy to attend one of the many meetings held that night in almost every Eleventh Army unit by a special team of political commissars, sent out by the Central Political Administration of the Red Army in Moscow. This team was instructed to carry out seminars throughout the Eleventh Army, assuring the troops that war with Germany was not imminent. The exercise had been ordered to dampen down the vigilance and "militancy" of the Eleventh Army.

Major Agafonov worked well past midnight. There was nothing new from the frontier, all quiet as far as he knew. He finally got his telegraph, radio and telephone positions manned and connected.

It was nearly 3 A.M. when he and General Shlemin started for their barracks to get a little rest. They ran into Colonel S. M. Firsov, chief of engineers for the Eleventh Army. Firsov was angry. He had obtained from the Baltic Military District a shipment of about ten thousand mines, which he proposed to emplace along the frontier, protecting areas of possible German tank assault. He had started on Saturday laying out the mine fields. But the chief of engineers of the district, Major General V. F. Zotov, had ordered him to halt.

"Apparently," he said with a grim smile, "I'm in too much of a hurry."

Firsov put the blame on Zotov. Actually, the orders came from higher up and were part of the effort by Moscow to "cool" the Eleventh Army and the Baltic Military District in hopes of averting a German attack.

Few hopes could have been more vain. Within two hours Agafonov was routed from his sleep. He raced to the command post, deep in the interior of Fort No. 6. Every telegraph, telephone and wireless receiver was jangling: "The enemy has opened strong artillery fire. . . . The enemy is attacking our forward positions. . . . Artillery fire on our positions. . . . German tanks are attacking. . . . We are beating off a German infantry assault. . . ."

One telephone operator threw up his hands. "Comrade Major! I quit! Everyone is swearing at me, threatening me with arrest. . . . I don't know what to do."

The training camp at Kasly-Rudy was under air attack. General Shlemin made his first report to Colonel General Kuznetsov at Baltic headquarters: "All units are occupying defenses along the frontier line. All along the line the enemy has opened fire. . . ."

A radio operator reported: "No contact with the 128th Division." This was serious business. Major Agafonov set to work to restore communications. Finally a brief flash came in from the 128th Division: "German tanks have surrounded headquarters." Nothing more. General Shlemin attempted to get through to the 5th Tank Division near Alytus, a key crossing of the Neman River just north of the 128th Division position. The radio operator tried again and again: "Neman! Dunai calling. Alytus! Alytus! Alytus! Dunai calling!" But Alytus did not answer. Nor did it answer for the rest of the night. A courier was sent by car to Alytus, forty miles away. He did not return.

General Morozov grew more and more concerned.

"German tanks are advancing on Alytus," he said. "If they seize the bridge there, they will turn the flank of our army."

He was pondering the situation when Lieutenant Colonel Soshalsky entered the room. He walked up to Morozov and whispered hoarsely, "Vasily Ivanovich, the Germans have broken into the children's camp. The children—"

"What about the children?" Morozov asked, his tone still hopeful.

"I can't tell you," Soshalsky cried. "The children . . . the tanks."

Major Agafonov's children were in that camp. So was Morozov's daughter, Lida.[4]

Still no word from Alytus.

At 6 P.M. the evening of June 22 Major Agafonov himself set out to try to reach Alytus. A few miles out of Kaunas he met a blue tourist bus bringing back twenty commanders from a vacation in the countryside. No point in going any farther, they told him. Alytus was occupied by the Germans.

It was, indeed. Four armored and four infantry divisions, including nearly five hundred German tanks, forming the 3rd Nazi Tank Group of Army Group Center, had smashed across the Neman, splintering the 128th Rifle Division and badly bruising the 126th. The 5th Soviet Tank Division, moving up to protect Alytus, was caught in motion and found itself cut off and surrounded. The blow crushed the hinge between the Eleventh Army and the Central Front and threatened to isolate the Eleventh Army from its neighbor to the north, the Eighth Army. Before nightfall on Sunday, June 22, the Germans had secured excellent crossings of the Neman River at Alytus and a few miles farther south at Myarkin.

The fate of Kaunas was sealed. By the time Major Agafonov got back to Fort No. 6 he found that headquarters was being shifted to Kaisiadorys, about twenty miles to the east. He had two hours to tear out his installations. Before morning a new system must be operating from Kaisiadorys. He proposed shifting over to wireless, but this was forbidden. The Germans had captured the staff of the 128th Division, including the commander, General Aleksandr Zotov. Presumably they had captured the Soviet ciphers. Wireless was to be used only in the direst necessity. The 5th Tank Division had still not been heard from, and the whole of the 16th Corps was retiring to Jonava, twenty miles northeast of Kaunas. The city was being abandoned without a battle. Left behind were the families of the army men, Major Agafonov's among them.

The German attack caught the Soviet Air Force in the Special Baltic Military District on the ground. It was, in the words of Lieutenant General P. P. Sobennikov, Commander of the Eighth Army, virtually destroyed in the first two or three hours of war. Lieutenant General P. V. Rychagov, Air Commander of the Baltic District, was ordered to Moscow and shot. Lieutenant General of Aviation Kopets, Chief of the Soviet Bomber Command, committed suicide June 23. He had lost 800 bombers to a handful by

[4] In 1944 General Morozov by great good fortune found his daughter. She had made her way into Latvia and there had survived the Nazi occupation. (Boris Gusev, Dmitri Mamleyev, *Smert Komissara*, Moscow, 1967, p. 84.)

the Germans. In the first day of war the Western and Special Kiev Military Districts lost half their air strength. Soviet losses to 1:30 P.M. on June 22 were put at 800 by Halder. At that hour the Nazis had lost 10 planes. The total Soviet loss on the first day was 1,200 planes—900 on the ground and 300 in combat.

The speed and impact of the German assault had a catastrophic effect on communications within the Baltic Command. Before noon on June 22 General Kuznetsov had lost contact with almost all his forward units. Reinforcements were headed for fronts which no longer existed and were wiped out by German armor scores of miles from where the enemy was supposed to be found. The closer to the frontier, the worse the situation.[5]

The Germans had little difficulty in overpowering individual Soviet units which they encountered near the frontier. Most of the troops had neither instructions nor battle plans. All they could do was fight back with any weapon that was at hand.

At many points in the first hours of war the only opposition was put up by the paramilitary frontier police, the NKVD Border Guards, whose nominal commander was Lavrenti P. Beria, Stalin's sinister chief of secret police.

This was the case in the region just north of Memel, where the Germans crossed the frontier, advancing toward Palanga, key to the Nazi push up the Baltic coast to the port of Libau.

By 6 A.M. Palanga, defended only by the 12th Border Guards, was in flames and battle was raging in the streets. By 8:45 A.M. the 12th Border Guards reported Palanga had fallen and they were retreating.

At noon the 24th and 35th companies of the 12th Guards had been driven back along the road toward Libau. Up to this time—after eight hours of heavy combat—no regular Red Army units had come to the aid of the border forces. The reason is quite clear. They had simply been wiped out. Soviet historians trying to reconstruct the battle have little to work with. Destruction of the units was so complete that not even their operational journals have survived.

Libau was the second largest port in Latvia. This was the port which the Baltic Fleet Commander, Admiral Tributs, considered indefensible because of its closeness to East Prussia and from which all major fleet units had been withdrawn shortly before the German attack. Colonel General Kuznetsov had reluctantly assigned the 67th Division to defend the city only a few

---

[5] Typically, Colonel General I. Lyudnikov, commanding the 200th Rifle Division, was moving his troops on forced march to a concentration point six to ten miles northwest of Kovel. About midnight June 22 he heard heavy aircraft overhead. At 3:40 A.M. a flight of nineteen German JU-88's, their black swastikas plainly marked, appeared just north of his column. At about 4 A.M. he heard heavy firing to the west, and five minutes later nine JU-88's attacked Lyudnikov's 661st Regiment. Lyudnikov had no orders. He put his troops under cover and told them not to fire on any planes without special instructions. He got through to 31st Corps about 6 A.M., but his commander, Major General A. I. Lopatin, had no instructions. All day Lyudnikov waited for orders. None came. (I. Lyudnikov, *Voyenno-Istoricheskii Zhurnal*, No. 9, September, 1966, pp. 67–69.)

days earlier. Major General N. A. Dedayev of the 67th had two regiments—the 56th and 281st—and a scattering of sailors and coastal artillery at his command.

Not until June 21, less than twenty-four hours before the attack, had Major General Dedayev's artillery commander, Colonel Korneyev, sat down with his naval counterpart, Captain Kashin, and worked out the coordinates for the artillery defense of Libau.[6]

Acting on his own and largely because of nervousness engendered by reports from naval intelligence, Major General Dedayev on the evening of the twenty-first ordered those units of his 67th Infantry which were not engaged on construction work (most of his troops were so employed) out of their barracks on military exercises. Three battalions moved from town to the banks of the Barta River and set up a camp. General Dedayev spent most of the evening driving about Libau and its military installations, trying to convince himself that all was in order. Returning to headquarters in late evening he heard that Captain Mikhail S. Klevensky, the Naval Commander, had received a warning from the Baltic Fleet Headquarters of possible action that night.

Dedayev listened to the 11:30 P.M. news from Moscow. There was nothing special. The Spassky chimes played the Internationale. Not until 3 A.M. did a message come through from Colonel General Kuznetsov at Baltic Military Headquarters, alerting all units to occupy forward positions with full field ammunition, prepared for action, but to avoid provocations and not to open fire on overflights of Nazi planes.

General Dedayev went straight to the naval base and spent an hour with Captain Klevensky, working out a triple system of defense lines around Libau. It was the first time they had sat down to work out a joint defense plan. On his way back to headquarters Dedayev heard the drone of planes. It was three waves of JU-88's coming in from the sea.

No one fired on them. They swung over the city, suddenly dove, dropped their bombs and zoomed away. Only then did the ack-ack guns protecting Libau open fire.

General Dedayev checked the reports from all his units. It was obvious that the Nazis were driving hard toward Libau. He telephoned General Berzarin of the Twenty-seventh Army, his commander in chief. Berzarin's answer was curt. Dedayev was on his own. The Germans were attacking on the whole frontier. Hold on with what you have. Fight to the last man.

The General sighed. He would do what he could. But the odds were very long.

The situation of the Eighth Army was even worse. Lieutenant General P. P. Sobennikov had received the alert from Colonel General Kuznetsov so

---

[6] R. Velevitnev, A. Los, *Krepost bez Fortov*, Moscow, 1966, p. 27. Another account gives the date of the meeting as June 20. (*Na Strazhe Morskikh Gorizontov*, Moscow, 1967, p. 146.)

tardily that many Eighth Army units found themselves being attacked by German armored units even before they knew that war had started.

Sobennikov's 48th Infantry Division, commanded by Major General P. V. Bogdanov, moving toward the frontier from Riga, early Sunday morning was marching in parade order behind its band in the region of Raseinyai. Martial music filled the air. Suddenly, "not knowing that war had started," the 48th Infantry was hit by German attack bombers. A little after noon the division was attacked near Erzhvilkas by German armor which had broken through at Taurage. The 48th Infantry had nothing but rifles and hand grenades with which to fight. At 10 P.M. Bogdanov advised headquarters that he had lost 60 to 70 percent of his forces and had run out of ammunition.

One of Sobennikov's heavy artillery units, advancing to the front by rail, at dawn on Sunday morning witnessed an attack on the Soviet airdrome at Siauliai. The artillerymen saw the German planes, watched the bombs fall and fires break out, but thought it was all a training exercise.

'Actually," Sobennikov observed, "at this time almost all the air force of the Special Baltic Military District was being destroyed on the ground."

Within twenty-four hours of the outbreak of war Sobennikov reported to Colonel General Kuznetsov:

"The Army [the Eighth] is in a helpless situation. We have no communications with you, nor with the rifle and mechanized corps. I beg you to do all that you can to provide me with fuel. As for what depends on me —I am doing it."

The problem of the Soviet command in the first hours of the war was compounded by the fact that at higher echelons there persisted the strange feeling that *this might not be war*. The commander of the 125th Division was not alone in this. General Fedyuninsky, who commanded the 15th Soviet Infantry Corps along the Bug River, had the definite impression that many hours after the German attack his chief, General M. I. Potapov of the Fifth Army, was "still not quite sure that the Nazis had started a war."

The same atmosphere prevailed at the headquarters of the Special Western Military District at Minsk, where Army General D. G. Pavlov was attending the theater June 21 when the first reports of an attack came in. "It can't be," he said. "It's just nonsense."

Colonel General Leonid M. Sandalov was chief of staff of one of the armies of Pavlov's command—the Fourth Army with headquarters at Kobrin near the Bug River. Sandalov reported to Pavlov repeatedly during the night of June 21–22 signs of German preparations for attack. The same information had come in from all the frontier points, including the Brest garrison. This information was sent both to Pavlov and to the General Staff in Moscow.

At 2 A.M. Kobrin and many other points reported interruptions of communications. A Fifth Column was at work. This information, also, went to Pavlov and to Moscow.

Nonetheless, at 3:30 A.M. Pavlov telephoned the Fourth Army commander,

Major General A. A. Korobkov,[7] that a "raid by Fascist bands" might be expected on the Bug River frontier during the night. Korobkov was ordered to give no provocation, to seize the "bands" if possible, but not to pursue them across the frontier.

Pavlov did order the 42nd Division moved up to fortified positions and told Korobkov to issue a general alert.

Within the hour Lieutenant General V. I. Kuznetsov, Commander of the Third Army, communicated with Pavlov, using the radio since telephone lines had been severed. He reported that the Germans were attacking on a wide front and bombing Grodno. Similar information came from Major General K. D. Golubev commanding the Tenth Army at Bialystok.

Pavlov told his deputy front commander, Lieutenant General I. V. Boldin, that he "couldn't quite make out" what was happening.

With the telephone at Pavlov's headquarters constantly ringing with reports of German attacks, Defense Commissar Timoshenko called from Moscow and ordered Pavlov to take no action against the Germans without prior notification to Moscow.

"Comrade Stalin has forbidden opening artillery fire against the Germans," Timoshenko said.

The confusion grew worse and worse as the day wore on. Unable to get a picture of what was going on at the front, General Boldin proposed to fly to Tenth Army headquarters at Bialystok. But the airports had been bombed. No planes were available. He decided to drive despite reports of Nazi paratroop landings. He managed to get to Tenth Army headquarters Sunday evening. By this time the Tenth Army had been moved out of Bialystok to escape savage German dive-bombing. General Golubev reported that his Tenth Army had almost ceased to exist. He was unable to get through to forward units and had only occasional communication with General Pavlov at Minsk.

"It's hard, very hard, Ivan Vasilyevich," General Golubev told Boldin. "Where there is a chance of clinging to something we hold on. The frontier guards are fighting well, but few of them are left and we have no way of supporting them. And this is the first day of the war! What will happen next?"

---

[7] General Korobkov was removed from his command July 8 and shot a few days later as a penalty for permitting the destruction of his army by the Germans.

11 • The Red Arrow Pulls In

WITH A HISS OF STEAM AND A SLOW FINAL TURN OF THE
driving wheels the Red Arrow express came to a halt in the train shed of
Leningrad's October Station. A small delegation of officers had arrived a
few minutes before, and now they stood on the platform, waiting for
General Meretskov to emerge from the International sleeping car, the last
car on the train. The hour was 11:45 A.M., June 22. The usual Sunday morning bustle filled the station.

There had been little sleep for Meretskov during his night-long journey
to the north. His mind was filled with deep worries. All day Saturday he had
worked in the Defense Commissariat, sharing the rising concern of his colleagues over the threatening reports. At midevening he had been instructed
to go immediately to Leningrad to act as the High Command liaison in
carrying out urgent preparations for meeting a German attack which might
come at any time, possibly within a few days.

Few Soviet commanders were more familiar than Meretskov with modern
warfare. He had been a military adviser in Spain during the Civil War, along
with men like Marshal Rodion Ya. Malinovsky (Comrade Malino), the
artillery specialist; Marshal N. N. Voronov; Tank General A. I. Rodimtsev
(Captain Pavlito); the Navy Commissar, Admiral Kuznetsov; and Generals
P. I. Batov, Georgi M. Shtern and Dmitri G. Pavlov. Indeed, Meretskov, as
"Comrade Petrovich," had been an architect of the great Loyalist victory at
Guadalajara.

Meretskov, an imposing, bulky man (his blond complexion, his wide
Slavic face and his bearlike figure had looked almost comic in the beret and
wide cape which he affected in Spain), had acquired a healthy respect for
Nazi military power and the striking force of Nazi Panzers on the battlefield
of Spain.

None knew better than he the strengths and weaknesses of the Soviet
Army. He knew, of course, as did every Red Army officer, the terrible
toll taken by the purges of 1937–38. The roll of the victims was endless—

three of the five Soviet marshals who at that time held this rank: M. N. Tukhachevsky, V. K. Blücher and A. I. Yegorov; every officer who then commanded a military district, including such men as I. P. Uborevich and I. E. Yakir; two of the four fleet commanders, Admirals V. M. Orlov and M. V. Viktorov. Every commander of an army corps had been shot. Almost every division commander had been shot or sent to Siberia. Half the regimental commanders, members of military councils and chiefs of political work in the military districts had vanished. The majority of military commissars of corps, divisions and brigades had been removed. One-third of the regimental commissars had been lost. How many individuals did this total? Not Meretskov nor any surviving high officer could estimate the number. Certainly one-third to one-half of the 75,000 officers in the Red Army in 1938 had been arrested. The percentages were far higher in upper ranks.

Among Meretskov's companions in Spain the casualties were striking.[1] The results could everywhere be seen. By the beginning of 1940 more than 70 percent of the divisional commanders, almost 70 percent of the regimental commanders and 60 percent of the political commissars were newly promoted. In the autumn of 1940 a tally of 225 regimental commanders disclosed not a single officer who had completed a course in a higher military institution. Only twenty-five had even been to military academies (high-school grade). The remainder of the two hundred had only finished courses for junior lieutenants. The results were appalling. In the army as a whole only 7 percent of the officers had had higher military education; 37 percent had never even had a course in a military institution.

When Lieutenant General S. A. Kalinin arrived at Novosibirsk in 1938 to take up his duties as commander of the Siberian Military District, he was astounded to be met by a captain, serving as acting commander. The captain was the highest-ranking man left in the command. The Chief of Political Administration, Captain V. V. Bogatkin, had arrived in Novosibirsk a few months earlier. On the very night of Bogatkin's arrival two NKVD men called with orders for the arrest of the Siberian District Commander. Bogatkin put the NKVD men off, flew to Moscow the next day and at great personal risk got the orders for arrest withdrawn.

To be sure, some commanders had been returned from exile.[2] Marshal Konstantin Rokossovsky, soon to become the hero of the defense of Moscow, had come back from Siberian exile, having successfully overturned false evidence, supposedly given by a Red Army Commander, Adolf Yushkevich,

---

[1] Meretskov himself was named by Khrushchev among officers who had suffered from the purge, but whether this occurred on his return from Spain in 1937 or later is not certain. By 1938 Meretskov was in good standing and was made commander of the Leningrad Military District. Robert Conquest is mistaken in saying Meretskov was released from prison in 1939. (Robert Conquest, *The Great Terror*, New York, Macmillan, 1968, p. 486.)

[2] But in October, 1941, and again in the summer of 1942 some of the Red Army officers still held in the camps were shot at Stalin's order, perhaps in panic because of the disasters at the fronts. After his "interrogation" in 1938 Marshal Rokossovsky had no fingernails left on one of his hands.

who had been dead for more than ten years at the time he allegedly gave his testimony. General A. V. Gorbatov, a magnificent commander, survived two years of physical torture by the NKVD and exile to one of the worst camps in the Far East. On March 5, 1941, at 2 A.M. he was released from prison. That very day he was named by Marshal Timoshenko to command the 25th Rifle Corps in the Ukraine. Timoshenko himself, now Defense Commissar, had been denounced as an "enemy of the people" in 1938 at the spring Communist Party conference in Kiev. It took intervention by Khrushchev to keep the Commissar from the black wagons of the secret police. As late as May, 1941, when General Leonid A. Govorov (who had been Meretskov's chief of staff with the Seventh Army during the Finnish war and whose name soon would be inextricably linked with that of Leningrad) was appointed chief of the principal artillery school, the Academy named for Dzerzhinsky, the secret police put him on the list for arrest. The charge was that he fought in the White Russian forces under Admiral Kolchak. In a sense, this was true. Govorov, a poor peasant lad in the Vyatka Gubernia, was impressed into the Kolchak army when his village was captured by the Whites in 1918, but at the first opportunity he led his comrades over to the Communist side. Personal action by Mikhail I. Kalinin, the Soviet President, spared Govorov from possible execution.

Marshal Ivan Bagramyan had a similar experience. In December, 1940, he was named deputy chief of staff to Marshal Georgi K. Zhukov, then commander of the Kiev Military District. In January, 1941, he was summoned before the new District Commissar, Nikolai N. Vashugin, who coldly informed him that he had an "uncertain" past. Bagramyan was outraged. "What's bad about my biography?" he demanded. "My father was a worker, my brothers, too, and I have always honestly served my country."

Vashugin charged that Bagramyan had fought for the Dashnaks, the Armenian nationalist movement. Bagramyan managed to show that he led a local Communist uprising against the Dashnaks rather than the reverse.

On the very eve of war, in the first days of June, B. L. Vannikov,[3] Commissar for Arms Production, was arrested, after an ugly dispute over weapons production that involved Stalin, Andrei Zhdanov and G. I. Kulik, then head of the Chief Artillery Administration. B. I. Sharurin, another Soviet arms specialist, narrowly escaped arrest. Kulik was an associate of Police Chief Beria. He was responsible for Vannikov's arrest and was blamed by Red Army commanders for a variety of errors. Vannikov described him as "incompetent and light-minded." Marshal Voronov, who worked with him on artillery matters, called him "disorganized." Kulik's style was called "Prison or a Medal." If a subordinate pleased him, he got an award; if not, he went to jail. The constructors of the best Soviet tank, the 60-ton KV, blamed Kulik for endless delay in acting on their proposal to fit the machine with a diesel motor. Finally, at personal risk, they went ahead with a diesel-motored machine after General D. G. Pavlov (soon to be shot for the

---

[3] Vannikov's memoirs, first suppressed, now are being published in a highly tendentious version (*Voprosy Istorii,* No. 10, October, 1968, p. 116).

disaster which befell Soviet arms on the Western Front), who had seen tank warfare in Spain, warned that a gasoline-powered tank was nothing but a "flaming torch."

It was not only officers who were caught up in these tragic events. Colonel D. A. Morozov, serving in the east in 1938, recalled going into a big grocery store. The wife of General Georgi Ye. Degtyarev[4] was coming out, tears streaming from her eyes. "What's happened?" he asked. "They won't sell anything to me," she replied. Her husband had been arrested as an "enemy of the people" a few days before. Morozov went into the store with her and bought the food she needed. He heard the clerks whispering, "There goes another. They'll get him next."

Now, as Meretskov well knew, the Soviet Army faced its most critical test. To say that it had not been affected and would not be affected by the tragic events of the past two or three years was ridiculous. The cream of the military cadres, the best and most experienced commanders, had been eliminated, and the morale of the remainder had suffered wounds which would require years in the healing—if, indeed, this generation was ever to recover.

Speaking long after these tragic events, Konstantin Simonov, the Russian novelist, who came to know the Red Army as did few other individuals, concluded that the performance of the Soviet Army against the Germans in World War II had to be examined through the "prism of the tragic events of 1937–38."

"The matter is not only that in these years we lost a pleiad of major military leaders," he said, "but that hundreds and thousands of honest people among the higher and middle echelons of commanders were subject to repression.

"The matter lies in the spirit of the people who remained to serve in the army, in the force of the blow that had been dealt against them. At the beginning of the war this process had not yet been finished, it was still going on. The army found itself not only in the most difficult of times incompletely rearmed but in a no less difficult period with its moral values, confidence and discipline incompletely restored after the destructive events of 1937–38."

If thoughts of his martyred comrades and of the strength which they might have brought to the Soviet Army this moment passed through the mind of Meretskov, it would hardly be surprising.

And he had other food for thought. Leningrad was inextricably connected with his personal fortunes. He had commanded the Leningrad Military District in 1938, and he held this post at the outbreak of war with Finland November 30, 1939. It was upon his shoulders and the striking force of his Seventh Army that the task of bringing the Finns to terms had initially fallen.

The early period of the Finnish war had not gone well for the Russians—

---

[4] Degtyarev was released from camp in time to take his place in the Fifty-fourth Army, which defended the Leningrad supply route.

or for Meretskov. This was not exactly his fault. Plans for the Finnish campaign had originally been drafted in detail by the Chief of the General Staff, Marshal Boris M. Shaposhnikov. They were based on careful estimates of Soviet capabilities and took into full account the strength of the Mannerheim Line and the fighting potential of the Finnish Army. Shaposhnikov calculated (correctly) that the Red Army would meet strong and stubborn opposition from the Finns and that a major offensive would be required.

Stalin was furious when Shaposhnikov submitted his plan to the Supreme War Council. He said Shaposhnikov underestimated the Red Army and overvalued the Finns.

The Shaposhnikov plan was junked and the task was turned over to the Leningrad Military District, headed by General Meretskov. Acting quite possibly on Zhdanov's advice, Stalin decided to set up a Finnish government in exile under the veteran Russian-Finnish Communist, Otto Kuusinen. Stalin was certain that a demonstration by Russian border troops and the propaganda of the Finnish "liberation" movement would bring the Finns to their knees. What Meretskov thought is not known. He was given two or three days to draw up a plan and then was sent into action.

Less than a month's fighting demonstrated the unreality of Stalin's conception. On January 7, 1940, Marshal Timoshenko took command of the Finnish front. Meretskov remained in charge of the Seventh Army. He enlisted the cooperation of Zhdanov in developing a new and effective mine detector, capable of locating Finnish mines under the ice and snow. He also developed a better means of reducing Finnish concrete defenses, principally by point-blank fire of heavy-caliber 203-mm and 280-mm cannons. As an outgrowth of these activities he established a firm and—as it was to prove—an enduring friendship with Zhdanov.

With Timoshenko's takeover new troops were brought in, Shaposhnikov's original plans were put into motion, and on March 12, 1940, the war came to an end with the signing of a treaty which pushed the Soviet frontier about a hundred miles north of Leningrad and gave Russia what she had originally wanted, a thirty-year lease on the Hangö Peninsula (to guard the Gulf of Finland approaches to Leningrad) and a few minor territorial concessions.

Meretskov could consider himself fortunate. He came out of the bitter March, 1940, post-mortem by the Central Committee on the Finnish operations in fairly good order. Many had been sharply criticized, especially the Defense Commissar, Marshal Kliment Voroshilov. L. Z. Mekhlis, Beria's secret police crony, who was sent by Stalin to advise the Ninth Soviet Army, arrested many commanders and sought to shift the blame from himself but underwent some criticism as well.

A series of decisions flowed from the spring post-mortem, many of them useful and sound. Young commanders with battle experience in Spain, the Manchurian border war with the Japanese at Khalkin-Gol and the Finnish campaign were promoted to new responsibilities.[5]

The fact that Meretskov was given only three days to work out a plan for his offensive against Finland probably saved him from serious consequences. In any event, he was promoted to the rank of full general in June and became Chief of Staff in August, 1940.

Now, in the last minutes before his arrival in Leningrad, Meretskov could look back on the past two years and, speaking as a military man, find much for which to be thankful.

The defensive position of Leningrad, for example, was infinitely better, at least on paper, than it had been in 1939. Before 1939 the frontier had lain only twenty miles to the north. Leningrad had been within long-range artillery fire from the Finnish frontier. The sea approaches had been equally vulnerable. Finnish forts commanded the entrance to the Gulf of Finland from Hangö and the nearby shore. Soviet warships came in and out of the Kronstadt base at their peril.

The situation along the Baltic littoral in 1939 was equally dangerous. Now, with the incorporation into the Soviet Union of the Baltic states, the frontiers had been pushed four hundred miles to the west. There was depth for maneuver, breathing space. Leningrad no longer lay open to attack by enemy planes based only a few minutes' flight to the west or north.

The Baltic Fleet had new bases two and three hundred miles closer to the enemy.

Leningrad again might be regarded as a secure military bastion, the bastion Peter intended it to be.

Today—or so it might well seem to a military man like Meretskov—thanks to the foresight of Stalin and Zhdanov, Leningrad once more stood strong and powerful, a defensible position even under conditions of modern warfare.

But, to be sure, a thousand things must be done. Work on the fortifications must be speeded. Troops must be moved to the frontiers. Airports must be put in working order. Guns must be installed in forward positions. All of this must go ahead at fever pace because at any moment the German attack might start. Yet, at the same time, *every effort*—and these were the last words from Timoshenko and Zhukov before Meretskov took leave of them in the Defense Commissariat Saturday night—*every effort* must be made to avoid action which might provoke a German attack. In no case must fire be opened upon a German plane. And no unusual move—of any kind—was to be taken without prior consultation with Moscow.

How would Russia emerge from the crisis? How ought he to begin in

---

[5] Following the April post-mortem into the Finnish campaign Marshal Timoshenko replaced Marshal Voroshilov as Defense Commissar. A special commission headed by Zhdanov and N. A. Voznesensky, Soviet Planning Chief and a close associate of Zhdanov's, was set up by the Party Central Committee to seek to strengthen the army, improve its vigilance and fighting ability and heighten its political awareness. (*50 Let Sovetskikh Vooruzhennykh Sil SSSR*, p. 244.)

order in the shortest possible time to bring the Leningrad Military District to the peak of fighting effectiveness? What steps had to be taken to strengthen the city's defenses? And what had been happening along the troubled frontier as he traveled north through the long white night?

The questions chased around and around in Meretskov's head as he watched the approaches of the October Station glide past the open window of his compartment. He rose and went to the corridor. An aide carried his briefcase and bag. The train came to a gentle stop, and Meretskov stepped onto the platform.

The Leningrad officers saluted. Meretskov was surprised to see that General Popov, the district commander, was not on hand—contrary to protocol. From the solemn faces of the welcoming delegates he could see that something had happened.

"Well?" Meretskov asked.

"It's started," one of them replied.

The group walked swiftly through the side entrance of the station to the military limousine which waited, its motor running. Meretskov took the customary seat of honor, next to the chauffeur. The others piled in back, two on jump seats. The car moved swiftly forward, circling the square and down the Nevsky Prospekt. The Prospekt was alive with pedestrians, going in and out of the great stores, sauntering down the street, basking in the warm sun. At the kiosks yellow daffodils and pink cherry blossoms were on sale. No one gave heed to the black Packard as it whirled past Eliseyev's grocery store, past the bright-windowed shops of the Gostiny Dvor, past the clock tower of the City Hall, the circular façade of the Kazan Cathedral, past the Admiralty, through Palace Square and on to Smolny Institute, the Party headquarters.

Here Meretskov and his colleagues listened to the government broadcast at noon which brought to the still peaceful city the news that Russia had been at war since 4 A.M.

The eloquent words of Molotov—"Our cause is just. The enemy will be beaten. We shall triumph"—still echoed from the loudspeakers when Meretskov sat down with the Leningrad Military Council. Absent was Andrei Zhdanov, the city's boss, the master of every detail of Leningrad's fate. Absent, too, was Lieutenant General Markian M. Popov and most of the top Leningrad commanders.[6]

Those who met in the council room to determine what first steps must be taken to secure Leningrad's defense were: General Meretskov; A. A. Kuznetsov, Party Secretary and Zhdanov's first deputy; Deputy Commander

---

[6] Colonel B. V. Bychevsky, chief of Leningrad engineering troops, in one context reports that Popov returned to his command post from a field trip about 10 A.M. Sunday. In another he speaks of getting orders from Popov on the General's return June 23. Had Popov been in Leningrad, he certainly would have attended the Council, which did not meet before 1 P.M. The Leningrad Party history says he was not present and that General Pyadyshev presided in his place. (*Na Zashchite Nevskoi Tverdyni*, p. 16.)

of the District, General K. P. Pyadyshev; Terenti F. Shtykov, a Leningrad Party secretary closely identified with military and security questions; N. N. Klementyev, political officer for the Leningrad Military District (who had been in the field with Popov but returned ahead of him); and General D. N. Nikishev, Chief of Staff and the man who had taken such action as had been accomplished for the city's defense.

Four major decisions were made that afternoon by the Military Council, and each was to play a vital role in Leningrad's defense.

First, the Pskov-Ostrov fortifications 150 miles southwest of the city were to be completed immediately. Second, a new fortified line was to be built along the Luga River, about 120 miles southwest of the city from Lake Ilmen to the vicinity of Kingisepp. Third, the fortifications north of Leningrad, along the old (not the new) frontier with Finland, were to be put into full defensive order. Fourth, a new defense line was to be built in the Volkhov region, southeast of the city.

There was one notable feature about the decisions. Each was predicated upon the necessity of defending Leningrad in depth, of protecting the city against an encircling attack which might overrun the half-finished fortifications along the new frontiers to the west and to the north.

Thus on the very first day of war the acting commanders of the Leningrad front sought to correct what had suddenly smashed into their consciousness as the weakness inherent in the whole new concept of Leningrad's defense. Because for so many years Leningrad had lived with a frontier only twenty miles to the north, because it had been obvious for so long that an enemy to the north might almost instantly overwhelm the city, almost all of the Leningrad defense precautions had been concentrated to the north.

The splitting off from the Leningrad Command of direct responsibility for defense of the Baltic littoral and the creation of the Special Baltic Military District were evidence of Leningrad's preoccupation with the threat to the north. The Baltic Command was to provide a shield for the state frontiers, four hundred miles to the west. It was to protect the new states of Lithuania, Latvia and Estonia from attack. It was to keep an aggressor from plunging through the littoral and jabbing deep into the Russian heartland.

Now on this afternoon of June 22 the Finnish frontier, however dangerous, was still quiet. It had not gone into action. But from the southwest the din and clatter of the German Panzers had already begun.

Leningrad had not one division, not one regiment, not one active military unit deployed to the south or southwest of the capital.

What if the Germans broke through those new frontiers so far west? What then?

All the decisions taken by the makeshift Leningrad Military Council were designed to cope with this new and unforeseen danger. From now on all powers connected with defense, with social order, with state security, were concentrated in the hands of the Military Council. It formed a junta with powers of life and death over Leningrad.

These first-hour decisions would go far to spell the difference between success and failure of the German drive to capture Leningrad.

12 . *Even the Dead*

THE PEOPLE—IN THE STREETS, IN THE PARKS, IN THE SHOPS, in the working factories—listened to Molotov's broadcast at noon, announcing the outbreak of war with rapt attention. He spoke flatly in his usual unemotional way. Only an occasional tremor revealed his tension. He began:

"Men and women, citizens of the Soviet Union, the Soviet Government and its head, Comrade Stalin, have instructed me to make the following announcement: At 4 A.M., without declaration of war and without any claims being made on the Soviet Union, German troops attacked our country, attacked our frontier in many places and bombed from the air Zhitomir, Kiev, Sevastopol, Kaunas and other cities. . . . This attack has been made despite the fact that there was a nonaggression pact between the Soviet Union and Germany, a pact the terms of which were scrupulously observed by the Soviet Union. We have been attacked although during the period of the pact the German Government had not made the slightest complaint about the U.S.S.R.'s not carrying out its obligations. . . .

"The government calls upon you, men and women citizens of the Soviet Union, to rally even more closely around the glorious Bolshevik Party, around the Soviet Government and our great leader, Comrade Stalin. Our cause is just. The enemy will be crushed. Victory will be ours."

Only a few wondered why it was Molotov, not Stalin, who spoke to the country. And certainly none, outside the tightest, inmost circle of the Kremlin, suspected the truth—that Stalin had been thrust into traumatic depression from which he would not emerge for many days and weeks.

What people did realize was that war had started. By 1 P.M., a few minutes after Molotov's speech, queues, especially in the food stores, began to grow. At the State Savings Banks lines formed. Depositors wanted their money. The women shoppers in the *gastronoms* or grocery stores started to buy indiscriminately—canned goods (which Russians do not like very much), butter, sugar, lard, flour, groats, sausage, matches, salt. In twenty years of Soviet power Leningraders had learned by bitter experience what to expect in time of crisis. They rushed to the stores to buy what they could. They gave preference to foods which would keep. But they were not particular. One shopper bought five kilos of caviar, another ten.

At the savings banks the people clutched worn and greasy passbooks in their hands. They were drawing out every ruble that stood to their accounts. Many headed straight for the commission shops. There they turned over fat packets of paper money for diamond rings, gold watches, emerald earrings, oriental rugs, brass samovars.

The crowds outside the savings banks quickly became disorderly. No one wanted to wait. They demanded their money *seichas*—immediately. Police detachments appeared. By 3 P.M. the banks had closed, having exhausted their supply of currency. They did not reopen again until Tuesday (Monday was their closed day). When they opened again, the government had imposed a limit on withdrawals of two hundred rubles per person per month.

The food and department stores stayed open. So did the commission shops. Many persons had hoards of paper rubles hidden at home. They took the money and bought anything which had a hard value.

Leningrad housewives cleaned out many smaller grocery stores on Sunday afternoon. It was their second recent experience in food hoarding. They had descended like locusts on the stores at the time of the winter war with Finland. Hoarding was an old Russian custom. No one who had lived in Leningrad since World War I had much confidence in the government's ability to maintain normal supplies of food. The story of every past war— and not a few peacetime years—had been one of short supplies and hardship.

There was a run on vodka stocks. By midevening bottle supplies were exhausted. Not a few cafés and restaurants sold out, too. The vodka was not for immediate drinking. It was also being hoarded.

In the factories and offices mass meetings were called. Many big factories were operating that Sunday, among them the Elektrosila, the Krasny Viborzhets, the Skorokhod, because the city was experiencing a power shortage and Sunday operations had been instituted to spread the load. Party secretaries at these plants got a warning call from Smolny about 9 A.M., and in many of them there were secret meetings of key Party workers before 11 A.M. Then, after Molotov's radio speech, public meetings for all the plants were held.

That Sunday afternoon, Olga Berggolts was sitting in her flat in Leningrad. She lived in a curious apartment built as a cooperative early in the 1930's by a group of young (very young, it now seemed) engineers and artists. The official name of the building at No. 9 Ulitsa Rubinshtein was "The Communal House of Artists and Engineers." But to all Leningrad it had long been known as the "Tears of Socialism." It was an unusual house— a monument to the burning passion of the writers and engineers in the early days of the Revolution to have done with the hideous trappings of bourgeois existence. There was nothing in the "Tears of Socialism" to remind one of old, outmoded ways. No kitchens. No mops. No place in the whole building for cooking or individual meals. No entryways with coat racks. No coat racks—except for communal ones.

The house had been built for collective living of the most collective kind. Its architecture was pseudo Le Corbusier. Leningraders liked to joke that in the "Phalanstery on Rubinshtein" no families were permitted.

The jokes long since had gone as stale as the experimental theories of communal existence. But Olga Berggolts and most of the inhabitants of the building had a desperate fondness for it, despite its crankiness. It was, in a sense, a link to their youth and to a time of enthusiasm which now seemed to belong to a different age and even to a different generation and different people.

It was not merely that communal living had turned out to be a more depressing fad than anyone could have imagined. It was all the rest that had happened during the 1930's. Olga Berggolts was a poet, a child of the Revolution, a woman of talent and of courage, a woman whose clear blue eyes saw the world with a sad honesty taught by the harsh Russian life, a woman whose wide Russian brow bore the imprint of suffering, a woman whose gentle tenderness had been forged in sorrow and injustice. As a schoolgirl on the day of Lenin's funeral, at 4 P.M., Sunday, January 27, 1924, Olga Berggolts stood with a friend outside the old house near the Narva Gates where she lived. She listened to the din of the factory whistles, the blast of the steam locomotives, the bells and the sirens which at that moment sounded all over Russia in tribute to Lenin. When quiet returned and the air still seemed to vibrate with the departing echo of the sound, she turned to her friend and announced: "I'm going to join the Young Communists and be a professional revolutionary. Like Lenin."

By the 1930's that brave resolution was being sorely tested. The thirties took from her two daughters, one dying after the other. And then came what she still called the "heavy experience" of 1937–39, the years in which she was in prison and labor camps, one of the countless victims of Stalin's endless purges.

Before the years in prison she had been a lyric poet, a writer of verses and stories for children. But prison brought her to maturity, as a woman and as an artist. Now on this lovely June 22 Olga Berggolts put down on paper her thoughts—a poem which was not (and could not be) published for many years. She tried to express what she felt for her country, for her Motherland, for herself:

> I did not on this day forget
> The bitter years of oppression and of evil.
> But in a blinding flash I understood:
> It was not I but you who suffered and waited.
> No, I have forgotten nothing,
> But even the dead and the victims

Will rise from the grave at your call;
We will all rise, and not I alone.
I love you with a new love
Bitter, all-forgiving, bright—
My Motherland with the wreath of thorns
And the dark rainbow over your head. . . .
I love you—I cannot otherwise—
And you and I are one again, as before.

In those hours after the German attack became known many citizens of
Leningrad were subjecting themselves to a new examination of conscience,
a difficult and searching inquiry into the precise nature of their feelings.

Not all were like Olga Berggolts; not all were able to put behind them
the cruelty, the suffering, the savagery, the smashed dreams and the broken
illusions of the past decade; not all were able to feel in this fateful hour that
patriotism and the Motherland came first. There were those who privately,
or perhaps not so privately, saw in the German attack a cause for rejoicing.
The Germans, they thought, would liberate Leningrad and Russia from the
rule of the hated Bolsheviks.

It is not likely that anyone will ever know how many of these dissidents
there were, but certainly some thousands of people in that first moment did
not view the German attack as sheer tragedy. Dmitri Konstantinov, who
went on to become a Red Army commander and who fought through the
most savage Leningrad battles, was one whose thoughts were a mixture on
that Sunday afternoon.

The idea of war was terrible, but he could not turn his mind away from
the past decade—the executions, the exiles, the arrests, the terror, the in-
former, the fear, the midnight knock on the door. How many now languished in Stalin's prisons and camps? Possibly twenty million, he thought.
Might not the war bring freedom to them? Might not this new horror bring
in its train some good? Might it not lift from Russia's back the savage
burden of the Bolsheviks and give the nation a chance for a new, normal,
humane life?

The answer was beyond discovery. He well knew the agony of modern
war. He knew, too, the bestiality of Hitler, his racist theories, the insane
pretenses of *Mein Kampf*. Which would bring the worse tragedy to Russia
—Stalin or Hitler? Who could say?

That evening Konstantinov and a friend went to the Maly Opera Theater
and sat through the performance of *Gypsy Baron*. The theater was two-
thirds full. During the entr'acte the audience promenaded in the foyer. But
there was not the usual animation. People were silent or spoke in hushed
whispers.

After the performance Konstantinov and his friend walked as far as the
Troitsky Bridge. It was full daylight, of course, but automobiles had begun
to show dim blue headlights. Blue lights had been installed on the streetcars
and in the entrance halls of buildings.

The Neva flowed quietly and grandly past the great buildings of the city, washing the granite embankments with its restless current.

The talk of Konstantinov and his friend was gloomy. They would, of course, go into the army and fight for their country. But what would the future bring?

In the communal apartment where Yelena Skryabina lived there lived as well a microcosm of Leningrad. Across the hall resided Lyubov Nikolayevna Kurakina. For the past two years Lyubov's husband, a dedicated Communist and Party worker, had languished in prison, convicted as an "enemy of the people." He was still there. His wife, a staunch Communist, had wavered in her convictions during the imprisonment of her husband, but on Sunday evening her Communist feelings flowed back in full vigor. She forgot the injuries she had suffered and treated her neighbors to a windy oration about the invincibility of Soviet Russia.

Listening from a perch on a tall chest was another neighbor, Anastasiya Vladimirovna. She smiled sarcastically at the oratory of Lyubov. She had never bothered to conceal her hatred for the Soviet regime. With the onset of war she saw for the first time hope of rescue from the Bolsheviks.

Yelena Skryabina shared not a few of Vladimirovna's sentiments. But she was wise and experienced enough to know that the future held no simple or easy choice. She, like most of her countrywomen, was a Russian patriot. She could not wish for Russia's defeat at the hands of an hereditary enemy. Yet she knew that such a defeat might well be the only way of ending a regime which was cruel, eccentric and vicious.

The question was different for Dmitri A. Shcheglov, a writer and a firm Party member. He had come back Saturday night from Petrozavodsk in Karelo-Finland, where he had gone for the premiere of a new play, *The Treasure of Sampo*. In the train compartment a Red Army colonel and a major were talking about the large numbers of German troops in Finland. The talk left him worried. He was not too surprised when his wife, who had gone to the theater where she worked, telephoned on Sunday and told him about the war. His wife was going on to a Party meeting.

Shcheglov sat for a time, trying to decide what to do. It was quiet. The clock ticked monotonously. Probably this is the last quiet moment in a long time, he thought. His daughter came into the room.

"What shall we do?" she asked.

By this time his mind was clear. "Go on the same as every day," he said firmly, little knowing that within ten days he would be signing up for the front in the People's Volunteers.

It was different, too, for youngsters like Ivan Kanashin and Andrei Piven in the town of Gryady in the Leningrad region. The two boys found most of their high school graduating class gathered in the central park a little after noon. The whole town was there as well. Grigori Vasilyevich Volkhonsky, the Soviet deputy, was making a patriotic speech.

When the talk was over, the youngsters conferred excitedly. What should they do? Where should they go? They were seventeen, too young for the Red Army. But there must be some place. They headed for Malaya Vishera, the nearest larger town. There they were sure they would be able to volunteer. They went to the Communist Youth office. Dozens of youngsters were ahead of them. Only seventeen-year-olds were accepted. Exactly what their duties would be none knew. But Andrei Piven, Kolya Grishin, the best football player in school, Misha Vasilyev and Ivan Kanashin signed up. They were told to go home, collect some clothes, say good-bye and report for duty on Tuesday. Their parents cried, but there were no clouds in the minds of the youngsters. They were off to serve their country.

The reasons for the doubts, the torment, the hesitations, the mixed mood of so many Leningraders were deeply rooted and profoundly tragic.

From the moment of its founding by Peter on May 16, 1703, Leningrad, or Petrograd, or St. Petersburg—whatever name it had borne—had been a special city and its people a special people. The character of the northern capital was fully formed long before the 1917 Revolution, and it was this character which gave to that Revolution its essential spirit.

In St. Petersburg for a hundred years before 1917 the Revolution had been in gestation. The tragic failure of the noble young officers who in 1825 sought to bring the government enlightenment within the framework of czarism by converting it to European parliamentarianism—the ill-fated Decembrist movement—had been the initial effort by the northern capital to propel the Romanovs out of medieval tyranny.

When the Decembrists failed (and were executed or exiled with their young wives to the most remote and harsh lands of the Empire, east of Irkutsk to the dismal mines of Petrovsky Zavod), their example lived on as an inspiration for generation after generation of Petersburg youth.

To this was joined the legend of Pushkin, the poet whose Byronesque image became the ideal of Russian youth. Pushkin was a martyr in the same cause. There was hardly a youngster in "Piter" (as they called their northern capital) who did not believe that Czar Nicholas I had a hand in provoking the quarrel which led to Pushkin's fatal duel and death.

Decade succeeded decade through the nineteenth century. Each brought to St. Petersburg new martyrs, new revolutionaries, new idols. The roll grew too long to recite—Alexander Herzen, Belinsky, Dobrolyubov, Chernyshevsky, the young men and women of the Narodnya Volya—the People's Will. The anarchists, Bakunin, the assassins, young Aleksandr Ulyanov, Lenin's older brother, the writers, the Dostoyevskys, the Turgenevs, the Chekhovs, the Tolstoys. Not all lived or worked in "Piter." But they contributed to its spirit.

The city grew great. It was Russia's window on the West—the center of the most advanced, the richest, the most cultured, the most revolutionary society of the land and a burgeoning industrial center. Here the new Russian industrial aristocracy had its birth. Here rose the smoky chimneys of the

Putilov steel works. Here became established the big foreign entrepreneurs, Siemens and Hals, Thornton, Langesippen, Laferme, Grapp, James Beck, Stieglitz, Maxwell, Frank, Singer Sewing Machine, International Harvester, McCormick.

On the Nevsky Prospekt, great billboards proclaimed the virtues of the Singer Sewing Machine. The Equitable Life Insurance Company occupied handsome quarters, and nearby were the stores of the Bessels and the brothers Mory.

It was here that the Academy of Sciences had been founded by Peter and developed by Catherine. Here the flower of Russian science and scholarship —Lomonosov, Mendeleyev, Sechenov and the great Pavlov—had lived and worked.

St. Petersburg was an imperial city, *the* Imperial City. It had been created in imperial scope. Its architecture, its buildings echoed this theme. Peter and Catherine and their successors consciously and devotedly sought to erect on the Neva a capital grander than any in the world. In this they in large measure succeeded. The great ensembles, the long promenade of palaces along the Neva embankments, the network of canals and small streams—the Fontanka, the Moika, the Catherine Canal, Nevsky Prospekt and the palaces of the Stroganovs, the Anichkovs, the Engineers Castle, the Tauride Palace, the Champs de Mars, the Summer Gardens, the more distant grandeurs of Peterhof, the Catherine Palace at Tsarskoye Selo—all this made "Piter" a magical and remarkable metropolis.

Yet the capital not only was built on a dismal marsh which had claimed the lives of thousands of the laborers whom Peter assigned to it; it was erected upon the ramshackle, shoddy, cruel foundations of czarist despotism combined with the worst oppressions of the early industrial era. Poverty, starvation, beggary, prostitution, all the diseases of malnutrition and the afflictions of illiteracy marked the slums and the workers' quarters of the Petrograd side and the Vyborg quarter.

Out of this breeding ground and the incredible decadence of the court of Nicholas II in its last phases of Rasputin and World War I the Russian Revolution had been born.

It was born as every Leningrader knew (and took pride in) in Petrograd. It was born of Petrograd suffering, Petrograd spirit, the Petrograd milieu. And it was born, as it were, spontaneously. No one organized it. No one plotted it (although generations of young Russians had plotted revolution for years, they had no hand in this). It took its origin from the despair and rebellion of women, standing in queues at the bread shops, day after day, only to receive no bread. Finally, in March of 1917 (February 26 by the old Russian calendar) these feelings boiled over.

Within three days the structure of the Russian imperial rule collapsed like a punctured puffball. All that remained was a little dirty powder in the palm of the hand.

Petrograd was the site and scene of the second revolution—the Bolshevik Revolution. It was to Petrograd that Lenin returned, to the Finland Station, on that April day of 1917 to proclaim his Maximalist demands—revolution, no quarter to the provisional government, all power to the Soviets—the demands which so disturbed, frightened and surprised his home-grown followers like Stalin and Molotov, the young men of the Bolshevik movement who really did not know what Bolshevism was until Lenin had defined it with his quick, dark brush strokes.

Here Lenin brewed his *coup d'état* and rode to power over the backs of Kerensky and his provisional moderates, who fell almost as easily as had imperial czardom.

It was a Petrograd tragedy, still deeply felt by its citizens, that in the hour of desperate German threat in March of 1918 Lenin "temporarily" removed the seat of Soviet Government to Moscow.

More than twenty years had now passed on this June 22, 1941, and the Soviet capital was still in Moscow. The years had not been easy for Leningrad. Even before Lenin's death in 1924 the change had begun. With Moscow as the center, the Revolution took on a different tone, a different content. Perhaps this was inevitable. Perhaps it would have happened even if the capital had not been moved to Moscow. But no one in "Piter" felt quite sure of this.

For the fact was that for two hundred years a struggle for the soul of Russia, for the leadership of the great Slav land, had been in progress.

On the one side were the Muscovites, dowdy, greedy, rude, vigorous, led by the conservative Orthodox clergy and the grasping Moscow merchant class, the *"meshchanstvo,"* the tough, heavy-handed, vodka-drinking families which had risen from the peasantry over the backs of their own kind, conservative, set against change, isolationist, fearing and hating Europe, fearing and hating St. Petersburg, which symbolized for them all that was new, progressive, stylish—and dangerous.

And on the other side was St. Petersburg, its eyes on the brilliance of Paris and Rome (although its heart might still be on the Volga), its style set by the West, ecumenical, industrial, heavily foreign (French, not Russian, was the language of society), looking down on backward, muddy, dusty Moscow as the back country from which it had sprung, regarding Moscow as the symbol of red tape, backwardness, crudeness, vulgarity, provinciality.

With the transfer of the capital back to Moscow, Leningrad began to feel the change—and to fear it a little. For two hundred years "Piter" had lorded it over Moscow. Now it was Moscow's turn.

And so it proved to be—with a vengeance, the vengeance of a paranoid and dictatorial ruler whose like Russia had not seen since Ivan the Terrible.

The first signs became evident within a year or two of Lenin's death—in the sharpening struggle between Stalin and the Old Guard Bolsheviks, among whom was numbered Grigori Zinovyev, the Party boss of Leningrad, one of Lenin's closest associates, the second or third most influential man in Russia.

Zinovyev fell in 1927, and Leningrad saw that its fears of Moscow were not without foundation. Still, at first the change was not too great. Stalin was involved in launching the first Five-Year Plan and embarking on the tragic and bloody collectivization of the peasants. Leningrad stood aside from these massive conflicts. Moreover, she had developed a new and brilliant leader, Sergei Kirov, an adherent of Stalin's but an attractive, able man who was winning the heart of Leningrad and the support of members of the Central Committee who had been frightened and appalled by Stalin's heavy-handed ruthlessness. Indeed, it was rumored that at the great "Congress of Victors," the Party Congress in January, 1934, at which the worst troubles of both industrialization and collectivization seemed over, Kirov had gotten more votes than Stalin in the elections to the Central Committee.

Then on December 1, 1934, occurred an event which was to mutilate life in Leningrad for years to come. On that day a young man named Leonid V. Nikolayev walked into Kirov's office in Smolny and shot him dead.

That act unleashed upon Leningrad such terror as the world had not seen since the Paris Commune, and not even then. Thousands were arrested. They were shot or sent to concentration camps, labor camps and so-called "isolator prisons." They were so numerous that they came in later years to be nicknamed "Kirov's assassins." Swept into the net with these Leningraders (the arrests heavily concentrated among young people, intellectuals, anyone who might by remote classification have indicated in the past any lack of sympathy for the regime), of course, was Zinovyev and with him most of the Old Bolshevik opposition to Stalin.

In fact, the Kirov assassination was the keystone to the terror of the 1930's. It was on the day of Kirov's assassination that the secret police were given special powers, never before granted, under which they could sentence and execute by administrative process anyone in the Soviet Union.

From this assassination flowed the whole regime of terror which bloodied Russia from one end to the other in the ensuing years, continuing up to the start of World War II (although beginning in 1939 a damper was placed on word of arrests—the formality of trial long since had been dispensed with —and many persons, even in Russia, were not quite aware that the purges were continuing).

Nowhere did the terror strike more harshly than in Leningrad.

In Leningrad occurred the worst repressions of 1937–38. Hundreds of leading Party members and important officials were wiped out—among them four secretaries of the city and regional Party committees, four chairmen of the city executive, the head of the young Komsomols and dozens of other top Party figures.

The story of the purge in just one Leningrad factory—the great Red Putilov steel works—has been painstakingly pieced together. The first blows fell on all who had in any manner been connected with the old Zinovyev group. The plant had hardly been rechristened in Kirov's name before the deputy director, the chief of the Party committee and the foremen of a dozen shops were summarily thrown out of the Party and out of their jobs. In January, 1935, more than 140 persons were discharged—and then arrested—on grounds they had some past connection with the czarist regime, with former industrialists, businessmen, shopkeepers or well-to-do farmers. In short order another 700 persons were rounded up under the category of "class enemies."

Production declined. Every failure to meet a quota and every mistake was blamed on "enemies of the state," either already unmasked or about to be unmasked.

The plant director, Karl Martovich Ots, an honorable man, one of the outstanding industrial executives in the Soviet Union, attempted to maintain some order, to protect his personnel from the waves of arrest and vilification. But it was hopeless. One day a T-28 tank was being checked out for delivery to the army when a bolt was found missing. Demands were made to bring the "enemy saboteurs" to light. Ots knew that the fault lay with a mechanic who had simply forgotten to screw in the bolt. At personal risk, Ots refused to permit a witch hunt. But it was like attempting to hold back the tide with a sand pail. A purge of Party members in the factory was carried out, in which more hundreds vanished.

The pace of arrests slackened a bit in 1936, then resumed with a rush in 1937. Into the maw vanished Ots, who had just been named to head the great Izhorsk factory and for whom a gleaming tablet of honor had been erected in the reception room of the Kirov plant. Along with him went his successor at the Kirov works, M. Ye. Ter-Asaturov, the heads of the bookkeeping department, the tank production units, the personnel department, the machine-tool shop and dozens of others. Not to mention former Kirov plant workers who had risen to high government and Party posts—the Mayor of Leningrad, Aleksei Petrovsky; the secretary of the Neva Party region and the Novosibirsk Party secretary, Ivan Alekseyev.

Most of the chiefs of big industrial organizations were shot, among them Ots, Ter-Asaturov, and I. F. Antyukhin, head of the Power Trust. Almost every Leningrad industry lost its director and most of its top personnel. The Leningrad military command was wiped out with the execution of the District Commander, General P. Ye. Dybenko, and the commander of the Baltic Fleet, Admiral A. K. Sivkov.

A new Party leadership was installed and Zhdanov was brought in from Nizhni-Novgorod (now Gorky) for that purpose. Zhdanov, a powerful, ambitious man, never won the love of Leningrad, but by the outbreak of World War II he had stamped his mark on the city and was to impress it even more indelibly as the war went on.

Not only did the purges start in Leningrad. It was in Leningrad that they were given their characteristic leitmotiv of macabre paranoia. For, as was obvious even at the time, long suspected by Leningraders, and confirmed after Stalin's death, the assassination of Kirov was not the act of a single disgruntled, deranged individual. There was something very, very peculiar about the murder. It was, in fact, inspired or contrived by Stalin himself. The murder was arranged by Stalin's own police, and among the first victims of the post-assassination purge were the police officers who had a hand in setting up the situation which made Kirov's killing possible.

It was this circumstance—the impelling evidence that Moscow now had ascendancy over Leningrad; the tangible clues of a persisting fear, if not hatred, of Leningrad on the part of Stalin; the general atmosphere of terror, banality and vulgarity which had been brought to the Soviet scene by Stalin —which created in Leningrad at the outbreak of war an atmosphere of unusual inwardness and self-examination.

There were few Leningraders of intellectual capacity who would not have viewed the overthrow of Stalin with emotions ranging from grim satisfaction to unrestrained delight. But few were so unsophisticated as to suppose they would be confronted with a simple choice. The alternative of Hitler— even though they had not yet experienced directly the horrors of Nazism— was not really a viable alternative to the horror of Stalin.

With occasional exceptions, therefore, it could be predicted on June 22 that Leningrad and the Leningraders would close ranks and defend their great city with the patriotism and love which had always been their strongest characteristic.

It was, after all, *their* city and *their* Russia, and for those of revolutionary spirit it was *their* Revolution—not Stalin's. Leningrad was steadfast. As their greatest poetess, Anna Akhmatova, had written in a time of incredible tragedy only a year or so before:

> No, I lived not under foreign skies,
> Sheltering under foreign wings:
> I then stayed with my people,
> There where my people, unhappily, were.

Leningrad would, when all was said and done, fight—fight to the best of its capacity and hope that victory might bring a better day.

This, quite naturally, was the mood of Iosif Orbeli, director of the Hermitage, that Sunday afternoon. He slammed the door of his office and charged up the staircase to the long corridor that flanked the galleries. He strode forward, looking to neither one side nor the other. But he was on no urgent mission; he was simply working off anger. He had telephoned the Committee on Arts in Moscow half a dozen times in the past two hours, trying to get instructions, or clearance to go ahead with the evacuation of the Hermitage. That it must be evacuated he had no doubt. Already German bombers had attacked a dozen cities. At any moment they might appear over

Leningrad. He stopped a moment and looked out across the Neva. He saw beyond the spire of the Peter and Paul Fortress a fat gray sausage—one of the first antiaircraft balloons rising into the air. Orbeli made up his mind. He told the guards to close the museum halls and admit no more visitors. Then he went to his office and summoned his colleagues. Moscow hadn't called yet. All right. He would go ahead without Moscow. Forty of the most precious treasures—the Leonardo da Vincis, Raphaels, Rembrandts and Rubenses—would be taken from the walls and carried down to stone vaults in the cellars. Plans would be made for evacuation. If it wasn't possible to begin packing this afternoon, then the work must start first thing Monday morning.

Suddenly he looked at the calendar. It still showed Saturday's date. Mechanically, he tore off the Saturday sheet. The new date, Sunday, June 22, appeared.

Orbeli looked up. A thought had come to him: "Napoleon, if I'm not mistaken, attacked Russia also in June—was it the twenty-fourth of June?"

The thought of Napoleon changed Orbeli's mood. He smiled, looking a bit like Mephistopheles when he did so. Napoleon and now Hitler. Not a bad precedent to bear in mind.

PART II

The Summer War

Beat, heart!
Hammer away—no matter how tired.
Listen!
The city has sworn that the enemy will not
*   enter.*

13 . The Dark Days

THE FIRST DAYS OF WAR SET IN TRAIN A DEADLY SEQUENCE
of events within the Kremlin. Two men shared primary responsibility for
the catastrophe which struck Russia—Iosif Stalin and his Leningrad lieutenant, the man whom most believed he had chosen as his successor, Andrei
Zhdanov.

It was Stalin who had held his country on the path of collaboration with
Nazi Germany, who had refused to believe on the war's eve that Hitler
would betray him and who was confident down to the last hours that, if
Germany was bent on attack, some way out could be found, even if a huge
price had to be paid.

It was Zhdanov who had been the architect of Stalin's policy vis-à-vis
Germany, the man who had conceived the idea of opening a diplomatic
initiative with Germany, the man who had said again and again, after the
outbreak of war in 1939, that Germany "cannot and will not fight on two
fronts."

Now the Nazi attack sent Stalin into a state of psychic collapse which
verged on a nervous breakdown. He was confined to his room, unable or
unwilling to participate in affairs of state. And Zhdanov was neither in Leningrad nor in Moscow; he was on vacation in the Crimea. For days the great
Soviet state was virtually leaderless, drifting like a rudderless dreadnought
without a pilot, in the face of mortal danger.

Zhdanov's responsibility for the crisis was deep. It was he who had first
publicly sounded a note of skepticism over the possibility of Russia's reaching agreement with England and France on the eve of war in 1939. It was
he who wrote and published in *Pravda* on June 29, 1939, an article in which
he expressed what he described as his "personal views" that England and
France were not serious about an alliance with Russia, that they were engaged in a maneuver to entrap Russia into war with Hitler. He conceded
that "some of my friends" disagreed with this assessment but added that he
would attempt to prove its validity.

The fact that Zhdanov had been named by Stalin to be chairman of the Party Central Committee Department of Propaganda and Agitation and was, of course, generally known to be Stalin's heir apparent left no doubt as to the significance of the article. It was a warning to the West that Russia might look elsewhere for arrangements to guarantee her security and was so interpreted by the Germans, already deep in preliminary conversations with the Russians. With the signing of the Nazi-Soviet pact on August 23, 1939, Zhdanov emerged as the author of the new Soviet policy of alignment with Germany. Diplomats in Moscow called him the "architect" and Molotov the "builder" of the German-Soviet treaty.

The exact nature of the divisions within Stalin's Politburo over the German pact has never been revealed. That there were differences was never doubted and, indeed, was explicit in the wording of Zhdanov's article of June 29, 1939.

The Politburo under Stalin (and after him) was the scene of acute rivalries, tensions and ambitions. Zhdanov was the rising star, but there were other men of great power and skill in intrigue. There was Beria, the police chief, who was busy completing the "purge of the purgers"—the liquidation of the old police apparatus which had carried out the final phase of Stalin's mad repression of the 1930's, the so-called "*Yezhovshchina.*" Beria had come up to Moscow from Stalin's native Georgia in December, 1938, after a decade as chief of politics and police in his native Caucasus. Now he was bidding for broader powers and already had deeply involved himself with foreign affairs. One of his closest lieutenants, Dekanozov, had been installed as First Vice Commissar of Foreign Affairs under Molotov, and in November, 1940, Dekanozov was sent to Berlin as Soviet Ambassador, there to remain during the last fatal months. Another Beria lieutenant, Andrei Y. Vishinsky, the infamous prosecutor of the purge trials, had also been placed in the Foreign Commissariat as deputy to Molotov.

There was another powerful contender for influence within the Politburo. He was Georgi M. Malenkov, then the newest of Stalin's secretaries, a daring young man who was being set into very rapid orbit by Stalin. Malenkov, too, was deeply involved in the new German policy.

In political prestige Zhdanov held many advantages over Beria and Malenkov. He had occupied a high Party post since December, 1934, when he was summoned from the comparative obscurity of provincial Nizhni-Novgorod on the Volga to take over leadership of Leningrad after Kirov's assassination. Zhdanov was Stalin's choice to bring stability and order to the city of the Revolution's birth, a city and a milieu which Stalin found difficult, unfamiliar and dangerous.

Stalin's relationship to Leningrad was anomalous. While he had lived in Petrograd and St. Petersburg, as an underground Bolshevik and briefly as a very junior editor of *Pravda* before World War I, he never visited it between the time of Lenin's death in 1924 and that of Kirov in 1934. Actually, Stalin rarely left Moscow for any reason except for vacations to the Crimea or Sochi. He made one trip to Siberia during the 1920's. He visited his native Georgia two or three times, principally to see his mother. Aside from these excursions he usually kept to a narrow path that led from the Kremlin to his dacha on the Mozhaisk Chaussée and back again.

There were many who thought that Stalin felt that the northern city might challenge, and perhaps had already challenged, his power. Possibly a lurking feeling of inferiority toward Leningrad's superior culture and vivid revolutionary tradition may have played a role in Stalin's attitude toward that city.

Zhdanov had built himself into Stalin's confidence in his six or seven years in Leningrad. He not only was unchallenged in Leningrad; he was extraordinarily close to Stalin. He often spent weeks at a time in Moscow or accompanying Stalin on extended stays in the Crimea or in Sochi. Stalin seemed to like Zhdanov and the Zhdanov family and even entertained hopes for a closer association—ultimately fulfilled when his daughter, Svetlana, married Zhdanov's son, Yuri.

Zhdanov played a special role with Stalin in the launching of the most savage of the purges of the 1930's. Khrushchev made public in his secret speech of 1956 a telegram dispatched over the names of Stalin and Zhdanov from Sochi September 25, 1936, to the other members of the Politburo in Moscow.

The telegram said:

We deem it absolutely necessary and urgent that Comrade Yezhov be nominated to the post of People's Commissar for Internal Affairs. Yagoda [the police chief who carried out the earlier phase of the purge] has definitely proved himself to be incapable of unmasking the Trotskyite-Zinovyev bloc. The OGPU is four years behind in this matter. This is noted by all Party workers and by the majority of the representatives of the NKVD.

Khrushchev's implication was explicit. Zhdanov shared with Stalin full responsibility for launching the worst of the purges—the *Yezhovshchina*.

Zhdanov was a dark-haired man with brown eyes and, in his early years, considerable physical attraction. But as with many Soviet functionaries the ceaseless hours of work (often at night because of Stalin's habit of keeping late evening hours), the lack of physical exercise, the multitude of ceremonial banquets took their toll. By the eve of the war Zhdanov was overweight, pasty-faced and prey to severe asthmatic attacks. He was a chain smoker, lighting one Belomor after the other until the *pepelnitsa* on his desk was cluttered with stubs. He was forty-five years old and had come a long, long way from his boyhood in Mariupol on the Black Sea shores. Like many prewar Bolsheviks his background was bourgeois. His father was an inspector of schools and possibly a member of the "white" or secular Orthodox clergy.

Zhdanov's preoccupation with foreign affairs dated from 1938, when he became head of the parliamentary Foreign Affairs Commission. He had watched the events of the 1930's with concern. He was acutely aware of the threat which Hitler posed. But he was also confident that a policy could be devised which would avert that threat—at least for a time.

Speaking with Admiral Kuznetsov during a long trip which the two made to the Soviet Far East between March 28, 1939, and April 26, 1939—at a time when the air was filled with repercussions of Hitler's takeover of Czechoslovakia and his occupation of Memel—Zhdanov expressed conviction that Europe was headed for war. He said that he doubted that "such a fatal turn of events" could be avoided.

Admiral Kuznetsov, who shared this opinion, was alarmed. The Soviet Union was just embarking on a very ambitious long-term program of naval construction. Would there be time to complete it if events were hurrying toward so fateful a conclusion?

"The program will be completed," Zhdanov said firmly.

Kuznetsov (unknown to himself, he was being sized up by Zhdanov, who was soon to recommend to Stalin that the Admiral be named Navy Commissar) formed a favorable opinion of Zhdanov during the long train journey. The two spent hours, sitting in their compartment, gazing out as the Siberian taiga flowed past, discussing politics and personalities. Kuznetsov had headed the Soviet naval mission to the Spanish Republicans during the Civil War. There was talk about Spain and of men whom Kuznetsov had known well there—Marshal Kirill Meretskov, Marshal N. N. Voronov, General D. G. Pavlov and others. Zhdanov was a font of questions concerning naval commanders. Kuznetsov spoke his mind freely and frankly. The two men were delighted to find that in most instances their views coincided. Occasionally, however, a chill came into the conversation—or so it seemed to Kuznetsov as he looked back twenty-five years later. Once Zhdanov casually remarked that he had never dreamed that Admiral M. V. Viktorov, former fleet commander in the Baltic and the Pacific, could be "an enemy of the people." The names of other naval "enemies of the people" swam in and out of the conversation. Judging by his tone of voice, Kuznetsov recalled, Zhdanov's feeling in these matters was one of surprise. Certainly there was no hint of skepticism or disbelief.

Zhdanov spoke little of himself. As the train crossed the long bridge over the Kama River at Perm, he remarked that he had fought over this territory in the Civil War days and had started his Party work in this region.

"In general," he remarked, "I am more of a river man than a seaman. But I love ships and enjoy naval affairs."

At the end of July, 1939, almost on the eve of war and of the Nazi-Soviet pact, Zhdanov accepted Admiral Kuznetsov's invitation to join him on a brief cruise in the Baltic. They boarded a cruiser at Kronstadt and headed out to sea. Kuznetsov drew to Zhdanov's attention the fact that they could not go a hundred miles without threading their way through Baltic islands—Seiskari,

Lavansaari, Gogland—all belonging to Finland, all potential enemy bases in event of war, all in a position to observe the slightest move by the Leningrad fleet. The next day they sailed past Tallinn and Helsinki, two great ports long linked to the glory of Russian naval power, now both in other hands, Estonian and Finnish. Two senior commanders who had served in the Imperial Navy in World War I, L. M. Galler and N. N. Nesvitsky, pointed out to Zhdanov the area in which mine fields had been laid down in 1914, from the island of Naissaar off Estonia to the Porkkala peninsula in Finland, to bar German access to the Russian bases at Kronstadt.

The talk with Zhdanov centered not on ancient history, however, but on the problems which would confront the Baltic Fleet in event of war. The Baltic Fleet was Russia's strongest. But how could it get to sea? Even when the ships were at anchor at Kronstadt, they lay under direct observation from the Finnish shore near Sestroretsk. A man with a pair of binoculars could see exactly which ships were at harbor, when they were preparing to go to sea and when and if they returned. What would happen if war should come?

The admirals and Zhdanov may well have talked about the possibility of coercing Finland, by military threat or diplomatic maneuver, into making concessions which would increase the security of the chief Russian naval base, Kronstadt, and the chief Russian fleet, the Baltic.

There is no record of such conversations. But the topic must have come to mind. The admirals were showing Zhdanov the kind of protective barriers the czarist Imperial Navy possessed. They would hardly have been human had they not suggested that the time was at hand when the Soviet Union must have similar protection for the Soviet fleet.

It seems logical to suppose that the genesis of the winter war with Finland, which lay only a few months distant, can be found in this pleasant summer cruise in the wooded islands and blue waters of the Gulf of Finland. For Zhdanov was destined to play the leading role in that war. If he was not the inspirer of the policy which led to hostilities with Finland, he was the man who was charged with the ill-fated effort to carry it out, using the local forces of his Leningrad Military District.

To many of his associates Zhdanov was a difficult, domineering individual. They found little in his character to attract them and seldom had occasion for personal or confidential chats with him. In the memoirs of men who worked with him through the long, difficult years of World War II in Leningrad there is a paucity of anecdote and an absence of warmth, but much respect for his ability to carry enormous burdens of work and responsibility. It is likely that many of those in the higher echelons of government and Party were reluctant to come too close to Zhdanov, fearing his power and his role in the terrible and self-destructive purges. Admiral Kuznetsov was in a somewhat different situation. He had not infrequent opportunities for probing Zhdanov's views. In a way he was Zhdanov's protégé, and he was thrown constantly with Zhdanov in his work on naval questions.

During most of 1940 Zhdanov held firmly to the belief that both sides in the West were fully enmeshed in war. There was nothing to fear from them. The Soviet Union could quietly go ahead with its own business.

During the December, 1940, military seminars held in the Defense Commissariat every member of the Politburo attended some sessions, but Zhdanov was in constant attendance. Later on, staff members recollected that he was present at almost every meeting.

By February, 1941, Admiral Kuznetsov was filled with concern over Soviet policy, over the reliability of the Nazi-Soviet pact, over the growing possibility of a Nazi attack. He sought a private talk with Zhdanov and specifically asked him why he thought the Germans were moving troops to the east and whether they were not preparing for war.

Zhdanov held to his previous position. He insisted that Germany was in no condition to fight on two fronts. He cited the German experience of World War I and contended that this demonstrated clearly that Germany did not have the strength to conduct war in the east and the west at the same time. He cited the well-known views of Bismarck to back up his evaluation. As for German reconnaissance flights and troop movements, he suggested they were either precautionary measures by the Germans or a kind of psychological warfare, nothing more.

Kuznetsov pressed his points. He noted that the Germans were moving troops to Rumania and Finland and flying over Hangö and Polyarny. Zhdanov did not budge. Kuznetsov could not understand the Leningrad chief. Perhaps Zhdanov based his confidence on private knowledge of the enormous defense works which were being undertaken on the Western frontiers.[1] Perhaps he knew something from Stalin which was top secret. Many Soviet general officers believed that Stalin had convinced himself Hitler would not attack Russia until he had finished with England. Whatever may have been his reasons, Zhdanov did not explain them. Kuznetsov never understood the basis for Zhdanov's evaluation. That it remained unchanged up to the eve of war was, however, demonstrated by Zhdanov's action in leaving Leningrad on June 19. It was not conceivable that he would have departed the northern capital at that moment had he believed German attack was imminent.

Zhdanov's authority in Leningrad was very nearly as absolute as that of Stalin in Moscow—subject always, of course, to the *diktat* of Stalin.

This meant, in effect, that not the smallest detail of Leningrad business was transacted without Zhdanov's approval. He had several capable assistants,

[1] These works were, indeed, conceived on a vast scale. By spring of 1941 a force of 135,714 workers was engaged on the task, including 84 special construction battalions, 25 construction regiments, 201 engineer and sapper battalions, etc. However, by the outbreak of war fewer than 1,000 of 2,300 major artillery emplacements had been completed or equipped. (Review of N. A. Anfilov, *Nachalo Velikoi Otechestvennoi Voiny*, Moscow, 1963, *Voyenno-Istoricheskii Zhurnal*, No. 8, August, 1963, p. 84.)

headed by his principal deputy, Party Secretary A. A. Kuznetsov. Kuznetsov, young, vigorous, energetic, kept the city at his fingertips. He was a competent deputy. But he was trained never to act without authority from above.

The totality of this prohibition on independent action became evident only in the emergency on the eve of the war. Because of the absence of Zhdanov from Leningrad, Secretary Kuznetsov found himself literally incapable of taking the normal steps which a deputy would be expected to carry out.

In his total subordination to Zhdanov he reproduced, in miniature, the total subordination of the members of the Politburo to Stalin's dictatorship. In Leningrad no one challenged Zhdanov. In Moscow no one challenged Stalin. Out of this absolutism, medieval in concept, was to flow the principal source of the tragedy in Russia's military ordeal, now beginning.

Without Stalin who was to lead? The Defense Commissariat was so much Stalin's creature that Timoshenko and Zhukov could hardly be expected to give genuine shape and movement to an extraordinarily complex military effort. A new Stavka, or Supreme Command, was set up June 23, but it was nothing but a paper reorganization of the existing High Command. Of course, mobilization of the country's manpower was fairly simple since, in general, it must follow predetermined lines. But strategy, tactics and diplomacy were another matter. New arrangements, new treaties were pressing. Yet Russia's diplomats got no instructions for at least a week—clear evidence of the total paralysis of the decision-making apparatus.[2]

Admiral Kuznetsov was a member of the Stavka and has given a picture of its "work" in the early days of the war. Stalin was not present at any meetings in June and probably not until nearly the middle of July.[3] Marshal Timoshenko, Defense Commissar, acted as chairman of the Stavka, but the role was only nominal. "It was not difficult to observe," Kuznetsov recalled, "that the Defense Commissar was not prepared for the role that he had to play. Nor the members of the Stavka either."

The function of the Stavka was not clear. It had little connection with reality. The members of the Stavka were not subordinate to Timoshenko. Instead of Timoshenko calling upon them for reports, they demanded that he report to them what he was doing. The Stavka's deliberations concerned only land armies. Only once did Kuznetsov report on naval matters. That was when he advised the Stavka that the cruiser *Maxim Gorky* had been

[2] Maisky in London was dumfounded at his inability to get any response from the Foreign Commissariat.

[3] Marshal Andrei Grechko spent the first twelve days of war in the General Staff. It was his task to keep the operations map up to date—no easy matter. He reports that General Georgi K. Zhukov, then Chief of Staff, frequently came to the operations room, studied the map, then took it off to Stavka "to report to I. V. Stalin." It does not seem likely, in fact, that Stalin participated in Stavka decisions during this period. (Grechko, *Voyenno-Istoricheskii Zhurnal*, No. 6, June, 1966, p. 12.) Incredible as it may seem, Admiral Kuznetsov in a new version of his memoirs published in 1968 insists that Stalin worked "energetically" on June 22 and 23 and that he saw him at a Kremlin meeting June 24, (*Oktyabr*, No. 8, August, 1968, p. 138.)

damaged by a mine and that Soviet forces had abandoned Libau. Zhdanov was a permanent member of the Stavka, but his post seems to have been more ceremonial than real.

The first clear-cut action to emerge from the Kremlin was a series of decrees dated June 27, 29 and 30. Those of June 27 and June 29 were general, designed to mobilize the resources of the country. But the wording was suggestive of the difficulty in which the uncertain leadership found itself. The decrees emphasized that despite the "serious threat" to the nation a number of Party, government and social organizations had not yet realized its gravity.

The next day, June 30, a decree was promulgated naming a Committee for State Defense, headed by Stalin. The members of this committee were Molotov, Marshal Voroshilov, Georgi Malenkov and Lavrenti Beria. There is no evidence that Stalin participated actively in their decisions. On June 27 the British Ambassador, Sir Stafford Cripps, returned to Moscow from London with Lieutenant General F. N. Mason-Macfarlane and other military specialists for high-level discussions. To his surprise, he and his group were received by Molotov rather than Stalin.[4]

The Committee for State Defense, in essence, was a junta. It was given all powers of state, and from what is apparent about Stalin's condition it appears to have been a junta to run the state with or *without* Stalin. Its membership is a prime clue as to what was happening within the Kremlin, who was in a position of power, who was not.

Voroshilov's membership on the committee may be disregarded. At no time in his long career did Voroshilov display political initiative. He was Stalin's crony and creature, and by July he had been sent off to take command in Leningrad. The active members of the junta were Molotov, Malenkov and Beria. Molotov's role may have been equivocal. Those of Beria and Malenkov were not. These two men were not even full members of the Politburo, the highest political organ of the Communist Party. They were very junior. Indeed, they were among the newest *candidate* members of the Politburo—a very junior status. Beria had attained that stature only two years earlier when Stalin brought him up from Georgia to head the secret police. And Malenkov had been made a candidate member only in February, 1941, a scant four months previously. The core of the junta, thus, was Molotov, Beria and Malenkov, but the two junior members were in a position to outvote the senior one, Molotov.

How these two junior men were able to insinuate themselves into a position of such great influence is not precisely clear. But despite his junior status Beria controlled the police and was an extremely powerful man. The police had infiltrated the Red Army and held a major role in the Foreign

---

[4] Stalin's first quasi-public appearance was a radio broadcast July 3 at the unlikely hour of 6:30 A.M. He received the British group July 12, his first meeting with nonintimates after the outbreak of war. (Cassidy, *op. cit.*, pp. 57–66.)

Service, in the espionage service and in the Party itself. It is likely that the alliance of Beria and Malenkov, which came fully to light only after Stalin's death in 1953, had already been forged. In a time of crisis the security forces in any country come to the fore. With Russia at war and in deathly peril, with Stalin incapable of conducting affairs, Beria and Malenkov turned matters to their personal advantage.

If the precise mechanism which they employed is not clear, one thing is plain. While Nazi Panzers ripped apart the country and Stalin was locked in his room in a state of nervous collapse, intrigue, plots and maneuvers held the day within the Kremlin. When the Florentine byplay was over, Zhdanov had lost his role as Stalin's heir. He was dispatched back to Leningrad to link his personal fate with that of the northern capital, sink or swim.[5]

It is more than possible that his colleagues saddled Zhdanov with responsibility for the incredible disaster of Soviet foreign policy, of which he had been a leading architect—for the gargantuan error in miscalculating Hitler's appetites and psychology. The question may even be posed whether Malenkov and Beria—both of whom opposed putting Soviet forces on combat alert and both of whom (with Molotov) had full access to the intelligence warnings of the German attack—did not deliberately permit their country to drift into war with Germany out of some motive of intrigue or ambition. Kremlin politics bars nothing—nothing in the realm of possible goals, nothing in the realm of possible means. Malenkov and Beria may have seen a chance to seize the government and, possibly, negotiating behind Stalin's back, to extricate Russia from the war by suing for peace with Germany. The cost would be enormous, but their hands would inherit the power.

Whatever the game, whatever the motive, with the creation of the junta the senior members of the Politburo were deliberately excluded from the inner circle. L. M. Kaganovich, A. A. Andreyev (long since forgotten, but in those days often spoken of as a possible successor to Stalin), Anastas Mikoyan, Kalinin, Khrushchev, and the candidate members, N. M. Shvernik, Nikolai Voznesensky and Aleksandr Shcherbakov—all were excluded.

But most notable was the exclusion of Zhdanov. Later on, all this would change. Stalin would resume his primacy. Mikoyan, Kaganovich, Bulganin and Voznesensky would be added to the State Defense Committee. It would cease to be a junta. But Zhdanov would never be named to the charmed circle.

[5] Undoubtedly Zhdanov was severely handicapped by his absence from Moscow and Leningrad. By the time he got back from the Crimea the basic decisions probably had been made.

14 . *Zhdanov in Action*

ON THE STREETS OF LENINGRAD THERE WAS EVERY SIGN
that the people were rising in patriotic anger to meet the German threat.
Troops paraded down Nevsky Prospekt, singing as only Russian soldiers
can sing:

> Rise up, mighty land,
> Rise up for the deadly battle. . . .
> Let noble anger
> Boil like a wave.
> We march to the People's War,
> The Holy War. . . .

Mobilization points swarmed with volunteers—100,000 the first day,
212,000 within a week.[1] *Leningradskaya Pravda* patrioteered in every column. The leading Party workers were summoned to Smolny on Monday,
June 23. Party Secretary Aleksei Kuznetsov ordered them within one hour
to submit estimates of the number of workers needed for war production.
Another Party Secretary, Ya. F. Kapustin, ordered all essential industry to
go onto an eleven-hour day.

But behind the façade of convention and cliché there were gaps in the
accomplishment.

Not everyone put patriotism first. Some local Party organizations in the
Leningrad area were very slow to turn over tractors and trucks, which were
being mobilized for military use. Often they turned over machines which
were decrepit or out of repair and held on to the best ones for themselves.

The first days were filled with rumor and alarm. The vagueness of the
communiqués concealed the enormity of the disaster at the front. Yet that
very vagueness gave rise to the most disquieting rumors.

---

[1] It had originally not been planned to start mobilization until midnight, June 22–23.
But so many men appeared at the mobilization points that enrollment was begun at many
of them on the evening of June 22. The Party sent 14,000 Komsomols to help handle the
crowds. (*Na Zashchite Nevskoi Tverdyni*, pp. 17–18.)

Two days after the start of the war Ilya Brazhin, a correspondent, went to the October Station to catch a train for Murmansk. He had to wait in line five hours to buy a ticket. The station was calm but jammed with patient, resigned people, mostly women and children. When the train finally pulled up, it was filled within minutes. No one had any real idea of how the war was going. Some had heard rumors that Brest had fallen (Brest already lay a hundred miles behind the German lines, although a small fortress was still holding out). Others had heard that Helsinki had fallen (actually, war between Finland and Russia did not start until the next day, following savage bombing attacks, largely by Soviet naval planes, on bases from which German aircraft were operating).

Thousands of parents sent their children out of Leningrad in the first few days of war, most of them to summer camps west and southwest of the city —to Luga, Tolmachevo, Gatchina—points which were to be directly in the path of German advance. But, of course, no one supposed the enemy might get this close. The danger they feared was the kind of bombing London had suffered. Most of the children were sent off in large groups without their parents—a circumstance which complicated the task of re-evacuation when that became necessary. Within a few weeks thousands of these children (and many of their parents) would be lost in the advance of the German tanks. Many were killed during evacuation. One trainload of more than two thousand youngsters was bombed at Yedrovo with very heavy casualties. A similar incident occurred at Lychkovo. As parents heard rumors of the attacks, they pressed authorities for word of their children, many of whom they were never again to see.

The Leningrad authorities had decided at the end of June to remove 392,000 children from the city. They managed to send out 212,209 in one week, June 29–July 5, of whom 162,439 went into the nearby country and the remainder largely to Yaroslavl. At best estimates, about 115,000 children were re-evacuated from the path of German advance. But thousands fell into German hands.[2]

No one in the early weeks could visualize what the war would bring. In many villages of the Leningrad region Party officials took no defense or evacuation precautions at all.

The great Nazi blitz of London was the horror which filled the minds of most Leningraders, official and unofficial. At any moment, they feared, the Luftwaffe might launch its attack. True, the first nights of the war were comparatively peaceful. No major Nazi attempt on the city was made. But the threat was omnipresent. German planes had been seen frequently in the vicinity of Leningrad, and the first alert had been sounded at 1:45 A.M., June 23. A group of twelve German JU-88's flew over the Leningrad area,

---

[2] The figures on evacuation vary. One estimate puts the total of children sent out of the city at 235,000, of whom 164,000 went into nearby areas. (*Na Zashchite Nevskoi Tverdyni*, pp. 25, 49.)

of which five were claimed to have been shot down.

By nightfall of the first day of war 14,000 air-raid workers had been assigned to posts. The Leningrad City Council quickly ordered the creation of 10,000 special fire-fighting units in factories, offices, stores and apartment houses. A twenty-four-hour, round-the-clock watch was established on the roofs of most buildings. Anything burnable was removed from 18,000 attics. The fire department built new concrete water-storage basins with a capacity of 220,000 cubic yards and installed 500 new water hydrants. It set up 156 fire-fighting platforms and 142 stationary fire reservoirs.

These were the facilities which played a major role in preventing destruction of the city by fire when the Luftwaffe offensive was launched in September.

Leningrad was not only the target of the German offensive. It was a great industrial city, making a major contribution to the Soviet war effort. It had 520 factories and 780,000 workers. It produced 91 percent of Soviet hydroturbines, 82 percent of turbine generators, 58 percent of steam turbines, 100 percent of direct-current boilers, one-fifth of the country's machine tools and 10 percent of the total Soviet industrial production. It made much high-quality paper, cloth, yarn, shoes and textiles. It was particularly important in specialized engineering and metalworking—the kinds of industry which had No. 1 priority in the war effort. The Kirov works, founded by the Putilov family, was the greatest machinery plant in the country. It turned out the new heavy KV tanks—60-ton monsters of whose existence the Germans did not dream. The same tanks were produced in the famous Izhorsk metallurgical combine. Other factories made armor plate, heavy artillery, signal equipment, radio transmitters, aircraft. The Baltic shipyards built and supplied the Soviet Fleet.

Typically, Moscow seemed more concerned about the security of these establishments than the defense of Leningrad. On Monday the twenty-third I. M. Zaltsman, director of the Kirov plant, was instructed by Moscow to proceed as quickly as possible to Chelyabinsk in the Urals and investigate whether production of the KV tank could be shifted to the Chelyabinsk tractor works. On Tuesday morning Zaltsman and his chief engineer, Z. Y. Kotin, landed in a special plane on the grounds of the Chelyabinsk factory. They inspected the tractor works, consulted the engineers and sent back their opinion within two days.[3]

If, the Kirov men reported, their cadres of workers and special equipment were shipped to Chelyabinsk, the plant could within two or three months

[3] One account (S. Kostyuchenko, Yu. Fedorov, I. Khrenov, "*Sozdateli Groznykh Tankov*," *Zvezda*, No. 5, May, 1964, p. 168) gives the impression that Zaltsman and Kotin went to the Urals at the order of Stalin, returned in two days to Moscow and that Stalin proposed that the factory be evacuated. Stalin is quoted as saying: "You'll not be able to work [in Leningrad] anyway once the air raids and shelling begin." Actually, the conversation with Stalin must have occurred much later than June, probably not before late July or August. Zaltsman and Kotin are represented as opposing any evacuation as premature. Stalin is said to have agreed to defer the idea. There is no evidence that Stalin participated in any decisions whatever from June 22 until some time in early July.

produce fifteen KV tanks a day. They opposed an immediate move, and Moscow acquiesced to their view—one in a lengthening train of miscalculations which within weeks was to bring Leningrad, and the whole nation with it, to the brink of disaster.

Instead, on June 25 Moscow ordered the Kirov plant to get the KV tanks into serial production immediately. Parts and sections were subcontracted to fourteen other Leningrad factories, and by July the plant, on a twenty-four-hour shift, had doubled production. It had cut assembly time for the KV to ten hours.

It was not until June 27 that Zhdanov got back into action in Leningrad.[4] He had been absent since June 19, and the war had been in progress for five days before he returned to take over the direction of the affairs of the city of which he was the leader. Meetings began immediately at Smolny and went on far into the night. Four thousand Party members were sent on that day to join military units to stiffen morale.

The great Smolny ensemble on the Neva embankment began to take on a shape and form which made it almost unrecognizable to visitors. Camouflage nets were strung over it and spattered with brown, green and gray paint. Many nets were sewn in the Leningrad theaters, and among the seamstresses was Galina Ulanova, the famed ballerina. From the air, it was hoped, the Germans would mistake the site for the Summer Gardens. When Lieutenant General A. V. Sukhomlin was driven there for the first time, he asked the sentry, "Am I at Smolny?" "Yes, this is Smolny," the guard said impassively. Sukhomlin saw nothing familiar about the buildings. The needle spire of the Peter and Paul Fortress gave the camouflage command great difficulties. They had no time to erect a wooden scaffolding. Finally, an engineer clambered up the interior stonework to a height of three hundred feet and found a narrow window which gave onto an outside ladder leading to the top. A workman managed to scale the ladder and put up a rigging from which the spire could be covered.

The Admiralty tower presented even greater problems. An effort was made to drop a rigging onto it from one of the AA balloons. But after two weeks of failures amateur Alpinists, including a music teacher, Olga Fersova, were rounded up. They scaled the tower and splashed the gilded surfaces with dirty gray paint. (It took several years' effort and enormous expense to remove the camouflage at the war's end. Scientists experimented with various solvents, and fire towers tried to wash the paint off without success. Finally, Alpinists were called upon again and, protected by great nets, managed to remove the camouflage with chemical solvents.)

Whether the German planes were fooled by these efforts is hard to say,

[4] Bychevsky, who reports Zhdanov's departure on vacation June 19, does not give the precise date of his return but mentions it in a context that suggests June 27. There is no mention in the standard Soviet references of Zhdanov participating in Leningrad decisions before June 27. *Na Zashchite Nevskoi Tverdyni* (hereafter referred to as *N.Z.*), which is most detailed, first mentions Zhdanov's presence in Leningrad as on June 27 (p. 35).

but Soviet airmen insisted loyally they could no longer recognize Smolny, the Winter Palace or the General Staff building.

On the last Friday in June Zhdanov called in one group after another. Workers from the City and District Party organizations were directed to organize a vast cooperative effort with the military. Factories were ordered to carry out four hours of military drill daily in addition to their eleven-hour working shift.

Zhdanov must have been aware by this time of the enormous losses in manpower being suffered on the Leningrad fronts—the virtual destruction of the Eleventh Army, the cruel damage to the Eighth and the melting away of the understrength Twenty-seventh Army. He ordered that a People's Volunteer Corps be formed—a civilian army that would be given summary training and sent to the front or used as a security force in the rear. Later, other Russian cities adopted the device, but it originated in Leningrad.

The task was placed in the hands of L. M. Antyufeyev, a Party propaganda officer, and N. N. Nikitin, chairman of the Volunteer Air Society. It was decided to enroll 200,000 Volunteers aged eighteen to fifty. In its first days it was called the "Volunteers' Army," the "People's Army" or the "Army for Destroying Fascism." Later it got the formal name "The Popular Draft." Major General A. I. Subbotin, one of the Leningrad Party secretaries, was named commander. Arms and officers were to be supplied by the regular army. No thought was given to uniforms.

Once Zhdanov got moving, he moved fast. On July 1—the day after the State Defense Committee, nominally headed by Stalin, was announced—Zhdanov set up his own Leningrad Defense Committee, headed by himself and including Party Secretaries Kuznetsov, Shtykov, Chairman N. V. Solovyev of the Regional Soviet and Mayor P. S. Popkov of the City Soviet. This became known as the "Big Five." It was empowered to handle almost any operational question in the Leningrad area. Zhdanov set up "quartets"—four-man committees to handle regional and city industrial matters. Troikas were formed in each region of the city. Another troika was set up to handle questions relating to the Young Communists. Many other extraordinary dictatorial groups were also used by Zhdanov to speed the war effort.

The conversion of the city to military production went forward rapidly. By the beginning of July 5 factories had begun to produce artillery and 11 were turning out mortars, 12 were making tanks and armored cars, and 14 were producing flame-throwers. Mass production of grenades had begun in 13 plants, including a toy factory and a stove works. Antitank mines were being made by musical-instrument shops and perfume factories. By August one million Molotov cocktails had been turned out by Leningrad distilleries, filling their bottles with alcohol or gasoline.

But the production of materials for the front encountered ever-increasing difficulties as raw materials and semifinished products failed to be delivered to Leningrad, as factory workers were mobilized into the army, the People's

Volunteers and fortifications work, and as some factories began to be evacuated to the east.

Mobilization of the regular army went well in Leningrad. Two hours
after mobilization was announced 91 percent of the men in the Moscow
region had reported for duty, and within six hours 98.2 percent had shown
up. In the first week of war 212,000 Leningraders signed up to volunteer
for military duty, subject to acceptance and physical examination. The
numbers ultimately enrolled in the People's Volunteers are stated differently
by different authorities, but it was between 160,000 and 200,000. By the
end of enrollment the first day, June 30, 10,890 had signed up. By July 4
the number reached 77,413. In addition, about 90,000 (mostly underage
youngsters) were enrolled in auxiliary police detachments.

The first topic which Zhdanov had raised on his return to Leningrad was
fortifications. He told an assemblage at Smolny headquarters that "three-
quarters of our effort" must be put into the rapid creation of a network of
defense works around Leningrad.

This had also been on the mind of General Popov, the Leningrad commander, the moment he got back to Leningrad from the inspection tour
he was making when war broke out. He ordered a secondary defense line
built along the Luga River, about a hundred miles southwest of the city.
He placed Colonel Bychevsky in charge of this work and named General
Konstantin P. Pyadyshev, deputy Leningrad commander, to head what
would soon become the Luga Operating Group, a special army to defend
the to-be-created line. The Military Council gave approval to the project
June 25 at a meeting attended by General Popov, Military Council Member
N. N. Klementyev, and Party Secretaries Kuznetsov and Shtykov.

Bychevsky now had far more fortifications work than he could carry out.
He and his deputy, Colonel N. M. Pilipets, checked the supply depot. There
were 57,000 mines on hand, of which 21,000 were antitank mines. The three
armies needed at least 100,000. That meant production of 300 to 350 tons
of explosives a day. They called the Leningrad Explosives Trust. It could
provide only 25 tons, and this was ammonal, not TNT. There were, it transpired, only 284 tons of TNT in the Leningrad supply depots—a shortage
which was soon to call into play the ingenuity of Professor A. N. Kuznetsov,
who invented a substitute using sinal, a mixture of saltpeter and sawdust. It
was christened "AK." This was the first shortage to be discovered in
Leningrad. It was not to be the last.

Bychevsky and Pilipets telegraphed Moscow. They got back the answer
they might have expected: "To cover your needs from the Center is impossible. There are more important fronts than yours. Use your local
resources." They explained the situation to Mikhail V. Basov, chief of the
industrial department of the Leningrad City Party. Basov was a businesslike
man of few words. At this point he had been working for forty-eight hours
without sleep.

"The picture is clear," he said. "Will 100,000 mines the first five days be enough?"

It would be fine. Basov ordered 40,000 from the Aurora factory and 60,000 from the Woodworking Trust. If he couldn't find enough explosives at the Explosives Trust, he would get some from local construction outfits.

The Leningrad population was drafted into the fortifications work. Everyone without a job was ordered to put in eight hours a day, digging trenches and constructing shelters. Factory workers were supposed to work three hours a day—after an eleven-hour shift on the production line. Actually, the whole idea of a "working day" had vanished. Everyone in the city was devoting fourteen, sixteen or eighteen hours a day to production and military tasks.

The Leningrad Soviet Executive approved a decision under which ordinary citizens of Leningrad, Pushkin, Kolpino and Kronstadt would be mobilized for obligatory labor on field fortifications, trenches and tank barriers.

The Military Council of the front ordered all large civilian construction work in the Leningrad area halted. The labor forces and equipment were sent to work on fortifications. The biggest crew was that engaged in building the Leningrad subway system. Led by Chief Engineer I. G. Zubkov, this organization was placed at the service of Bychevsky to build the proposed iron ring around the city. Work on the Upper Svir hydroelectric station, the ENSO power plant and the ENSO power line was halted also.

One more decision was made by Zhdanov that fateful Friday, June 27. Henceforth no factory whistle, no locomotive bell, no church chime was to sound in Leningrad except to signal air-raid alarms. Little did Zhdanov realize that the day lay not far ahead when no whistle *could* sound—because there would be neither steam nor electricity in the city.

Thus, when on the ninth day after the outbreak of war a thirty-one-car train pulled by two engines moved out of the freight station of the October line at dawn, carrying more than half a million precious objects from the Hermitage Museum, no whistles blew, no bells rang.

First, a pilot locomotive went ahead to clear the tracks. Then came the long train: two powerful locomotives, an armored car in which the most valued objects were carried, four linked Pullmans for other special treasures, a flatcar with an antiaircraft battery, twenty-two freight cars filled with canvases, statues, objects of art, two passenger cars—one for museum workers, headed by Art Scholar Vladimir T. Levinson-Lessing, another for the military guard—and finally, at the rear, another flatcar bearing another antiaircraft battery.

The train originally had been ordered to move out units of the great Kirov defense plant. Then plans changed. Evacuation of the Kirov plant was delayed, and the formidable aggregate was turned over to Professor Orbeli. Since Tuesday morning, clad in blue overalls speckled with cotton wisps from packing stuffs, Orbeli had been overseeing the loading of his treasures — Rembrandt's *Holy Family*, delicately removed from its frame by Nikolai Mikheyev, and packed in a box strengthened with planks and protected by layer upon layer of paper; all the Titians, the Giorgiones, the Rubenses, the Murillos, the Van Dycks, the Velázquezes, the El Grecos, Da Vinci's Madonnas — the *Madonna Litta*, the *Madonna Benois*; those of Raphael — the *Madonna Alba*, the petite *Madonna Conestabile* — all in their golden frames; and Rembrandt's *Return of the Prodigal*, a massive 12-foot 6-inch by 9-foot 10-inch canvas in its own heavy case. Three ministers had observed the packing from Orbeli's office — the Minister of Interior (the NKVD): the Minister of State Security (the NKGB), and the Chairman of the State Committee for Cultural Affairs — each concerned not so much with evaluation but to make certain no one stole anything.

On the train traveled the museum's great *Pallas Athena* and the magnificent museum collection of diamonds, precious stones, crown jewels and ancient artifacts of gold. Along with them went the marble Venus acquired by Peter I, the Venus the old boyars called the "white devil." And here, too, were Rastrelli's sculpture of Peter and his collection of wax figures, packed in great crates marked in black letters: "Wax Figures — Do Not Drop."

The tons of boxes had been stacked in the great Hermitage Hall of Twenty Columns, sometimes called the Hall of Money. Soldiers and sailors loaded them on the trucks which drew up in an endless column beside the Winter Palace and the Hermitage all through the night of July 1. The trucks rumbled down the Nevsky Prospekt in the semidusk, for the white nights had not yet ended in Leningrad.

Never had so valuable a train been loaded. As it moved slowly out of the October freight station, Orbeli stood beside the lamp post at the end of the platform. His hat rested on his breast and tears ran down his cheeks. Not until the last car, the flatcar with the AA guns on it, had disappeared, did he turn and walk down the platform. Half a million treasures had been dispatched. A million more still awaited exit.

The prompt, efficient evacuation of the Hermitage was due almost entirely to the foresight and courage of Orbeli. Although almost all the Armenians in Leningrad had been purged by Stalin in 1938 Orbeli stood and fought for the Hermitage. He managed by a personal letter to Stalin to block the sale of many priceless Hermitage paintings abroad and he insisted on making detailed plans for evacuation of the Hermitage treasure as early as 1939 long before the German attack.

15 . The White Swans

THE MEN WORE ICE-CREAM SUITS AND THE *DÉCOLLETAGE*
of the ladies sparkled with diamonds. They sat under the striped awnings
at the Gloria and the Golden Swan, chatting lazily, eating parfaits and sip-
ping colored drinks through straws. Nothing in the world seemed to bother
them. There was no need to hurry. They sat, shaded from the sun, and
watched behind their dark glasses. They sat waiting. . . .

They were waiting, thought Nikolai Mikhailovsky, a correspondent who
had just arrived in Tallinn, for the Germans and they cared very little
whether anyone noticed or not. Across the street someone was putting up
fresh posters. They read: "Comrades! Stand as one in the defense of our
freedom and our life."

Down the street hurried military cars daubed with mustard paint. Trucks
rumbled by. Crowds walked along the boulevard, staring at the bulletins
posted in the windows.

Did the men in the ice-cream suits notice what was going on? Mikhailovsky did not think so. He strolled through Kadriorg Park. The swans sailed
proudly across the pond, their necks a curve of snowy white. A little stream
splashed over the rocks and pigeons pouted on the newly swept walks.
Chattering squirrels leaped in the trees.

It seemed so quiet, so peaceful.

But no one knew better than Mikhailovsky how false was the illusion of
peace and security. He had spent a good deal of time in the prewar months
in the Baltic states. He knew the danger that lay below this glittering surface. By day the shops were filled and people strolled lazily in the parks.
By night shots rang out—the Fifth Column at work. The Russians took no
chances. The naval writer Vsevolod Vishnevsky went around armed, as
he said, like a cowboy with an automatic in a holster and a carbine on his
back. Anatoly Tarasenkov, another writer, carried grenades in his gas mask,
a rifle under his arm and, Vishnevsky joked, wanted a small cannon, too.

Soviet rule was far from secure. The strictest security precautions prevailed. You had to have a special visa to enter the Baltic states from Russia,

and they were hard to get. There were checks on the frontiers between each Baltic state to control movements from Latvia to Estonia, from Lithuania to Latvia.

Many Russians hesitated to enter the Baltic area, fearing the general state of insecurity. Some wives of naval officers refused to accompany their husbands to Riga. They had heard too much about the Latvian nationalists, about terrorists, snipers and bombings.

Beginning on June 13, at the very moment when the Tass communiqué was denying rumors of war, special detachments of the Soviet secret police had been concentrated in the principal Baltic cities. That day and each day thereafter they carried out mass arrests. In Lithuania possibly 35,000 persons were taken into custody. The number arrested in Estonia and Latvia was on the same order. The total was close to 100,000.

The police rounded up members of non-Communist parties, former military and police officers, priests, ministers, businessmen and well-to-do farmers. Persons who had been arrested in the early months of Soviet rule were taken from their prison cells and loaded on trains for the long journey east to Siberian prison camps.

The purge was far from complete when war broke out. Many remained in prisons in Vilnius, Kaunas, Riga and Tallinn, awaiting transport to the east. Nor was care taken by the police as to who was arrested. Soviet publications later delicately noted that "in conditions of the Stalin cult of personality not a few mistakes were perpetrated."

Vladimir Rudny, a young Moscow newspaperman, witnessed the action in Riga. On June 17 the entire Riga Party organization was mobilized to assist in the arrests. Among those mobilized, as later became evident, were secret members of the Latvian underground, who protected their cohorts and managed to send to prison persons either neutral or inclined to the Soviet cause.

Late in the evening, walking through the Riga streets, Rudny heard firing. A colonel of the Latvian nationalist army was shooting it out with an NKVD detachment, trying to save a cache of arms and radio transmitters.

As Rudny watched the battle, a young Latvian woman came up and they fell to talking. She warned Rudny to get out of Riga, saying she knew that war was about to start and that the Germans would quickly be in Riga. Rudny replied in anger. That kind of rumor spread panic. That was why the arrests were being made, to round up the Fifth Column so there would be no repetition of events in Spain.

"Do leave, I beg you. Do leave," the woman insisted and melted into the darkness.

Later Rudny met two colleagues—Vyacheslav Susoyev and the playwright Sergei Mikhalkov, a man of extraordinary thinness and height—six feet five inches tall and weighing, then, only 150 pounds.

To Rudny's amazement, Mikhalkov also said war was only a few days distant.

"Nonsense," snapped Rudny. "That's a fairy story for beginners in Civil Defense."

"Wait and see," said Mikhalkov calmly. "Time will tell."

The trio were drinking wine in the ancient cellar of the Fokstrotdil. Nothing more was said. But Rudny was never to forget the conversation.

Soviet authorities did not explain to the population what was going on. Panic and rumors spread. The NKVD sent off to Siberia a considerable number of Soviet supporters and left untouched many bitter opponents. The result fanned the hatred already felt by many Balts for their Soviet masters. The round-up underlined the dichotomy with which the Soviet leadership viewed the possibility of conflict—on the one hand acting with hysterical haste to prepare for war and on the other banning talk of war as virtual treason.[1]

The Latvians, Estonians and Lithuanians had welcomed the Soviet takeover in 1940 with little enthusiasm. They enjoyed independence. Their feeling of nationalism was strong. It was reinforced by passionate anti-Communism and, quite often, chauvinistic hatred for Russians.

For a thousand years the Baltic states had boasted a strong German minority. The Germans played a leading role in cultural, economic, political and military life. Even in St. Petersburg the Germans had been an important factor. Many settled there in the time of Peter and Catherine. The German influence in the Romanov court had been profound and was blamed by many for the final collapse of the czarist dynasty.

At the time of the Soviet takeover the German minority in Latvia numbered 60,000, passionately pro-Hitler and banded together in 268 Nazi organizations. Some 52,000 of these Germans were repatriated in October-December, 1939, but official German missions had been established in both Riga and Tallinn, and as late as March 7, 1941, Berlin was still trying to get consular status for them.

In all the Baltic states fiercely nationalistic anti-Soviet organizations remained in the underground along with a network of German spies. Soviet intelligence agents had been at war with them for months. They uncovered one spy in the code room of the Latvian Ministry of Foreign Affairs. From July, 1940, to May, 1941, the NKGB rounded up 75 underground nationalist groups in Lithuania. Throughout 1940 and the first quarter of 1941 the NKGB took into custody 66 resident German intelligence agents and 1,596 individual operatives. Of this number 1,338 were in the western areas, the Baltic states and the Ukraine.[2]

---

[1] When Operational Alert No. 1 was received in Kingisepp after midnight on June 22, Major Pavlovsky asked his commander, General Eliseyev, whether something might have miscarried with the Germans. Eliseyev sharply replied: "Do you understand what you are saying? Get hold of yourself. Words are not sparrows."

[2] The figure of 5,000 in the 1939–41 period is given in *Istoriya VOVSS*, Vol. I. *Red Star* used the same figure for the eleven months before the war (May 14, 1965). (V. V. Platonov, *Eto Bylo Na Buge*, Moscow, 1966, p. 24.)

In preparation for the attack on Russia the Germans established in 1940 a special organization known as Brandenburg-800 to carry out diversionary operations behind the Russian lines—the destruction of bridges, blocking of tunnels, capture of rear fortifications and similar objectives. It was to operate in liaison with agents already inside the Soviet Union—nationalist and other anti-Soviet groups.

"At the disposal of the staff of the German Army," reported Admiral Canaris, chief of German intelligence, on July 4, 1941,

> there has been made available a large number of groups of agents of the native population, that is, Russians, Poles, Ukrainians, Finns, Estonians, etc. Each group numbers 25 or more men. At the head of each group is a German officer. The groups use captured Soviet arms, military trucks and motorcycles. They are capable of penetrating the Soviet rear to a depth of 35 to 200 miles ahead of the advancing German armies to which they report by radio the results of observations, devoting special attention to the collection of information on Russian reserves, the condition of railroads and highways and also all measures being carried out by the enemy.

Among the nationalist groups in Lithuania were the Union of Lithuanians, the Front of Lithuanian Activists and the Committee for Rescuing Lithuania. In Latvia they included the Perkinkrusts, and in Estonia the underground Legion of the East and the Committee of Rescue, otherwise known as the Izmailites and the Kaitzelites. The Estonians before the outbreak of war had organized so-called Erna battalions to carry out diversions behind the lines of the Red Army.

In prewar weeks tension was high in Latvia. Several mysterious forest fires were attributed by Soviet police to Latvian nationalists. In many villages the kulaks or richer peasants were in open rebellion against the Soviet Union. Agitation against the regime was widespread. There had been interference with spring sowing and growing reluctance on the part of poor peasants to join in Soviet agricultural projects. Sabotage was reported in sawmills. From the pulpits priests and ministers were giving frank voice to their antagonism to Soviet power.

Nowhere was the situation sharper than in Lithuania. The Lithuanian Activist Front had been established in Berlin November 17, 1939, by Colonel Kazys Shkirpa, former Lithuanian military attaché in Germany. He formulated a program for liberation of Lithuania and on March 24, 1941, smuggled into Lithuania directives for carrying out an uprising to be timed with the German attack on the Soviet Union.

LAF cells of three or five persons were assigned individual tasks—the taking over of police stations, seizure of telephone exchanges, etc.

By the eve of the war the LAF estimated its membership at 36,000. It was damaged by the Soviet round-up of June 14, but not seriously. Two command centers were established, one in Vilnius and the other in Kaunas.

There were other nationalist organizations active in Lithuania: the Lithuanian Defense League, the Iron Wolf at Sakiai, the Lithuanian Freedom Army in Siauliai and the Union of Lithuanian Freedom Fighters.

The dissident Balts were encouraged by the overt Nazi preparations for attack. By mid-June the Nazis hardly bothered to conceal their work along the Baltic frontier. Engineers labored openly, setting up fire points and observation posts, strengthening bridges on roads leading to the Soviet frontier and putting down pontoons along the streams. In some places new mine fields were laid, in others old ones were taken up. Beginning about June 17 groups of German officers in cars began to cruise along the border, studying the terrain and the deployment of Soviet troops. On the night of the twentieth a skirmish was fought near Buraki, where a group of German scouts tried to force their way into Soviet territory. Three were killed and two captured.

With the outbreak of war the Baltic states were quickly in turmoil. Soviet authorities were so uncertain of the population that they made no effort to order mobilization, fearing that they could not rely on such forces. As a result even elements loyal to the Soviet Union had no weapons and no means of defending themselves against the Germans or anti-Soviet Latvian, Lithuanian and Estonian nationalist bands.

The former Lithuanian, Latvian and Estonian armies had been incorporated into the Red Army, where they formed three territorial corps, the 29th (Lithuanian), the 24th (Latvian) and the 22nd (Estonian). Each consisted of two rifle divisions with corps artillery, communications and engineering units. Most of these were at summer camps when war broke out, and none played a role of consequence in the defense of the Baltic littoral— probably because the Soviet command had grave doubts of their loyalty.

Neither the Baltic armies, commanded by Colonel General F. I. Kuznetsov, nor the Baltic Fleet, under Admiral Tributs, had plans for evacuation of their forces or of the civilian population. There were no plans for carrying out any operations whatever on Baltic soil. All the Soviet war plans called for carrying the war to the enemy's territory. There was nothing in the directives about fighting on the home ground.

Within twenty-four hours the radio station at Kaunas had been seized by the Lithuanian underground organization. At 11:30 A.M. Radio Kaunas proclaimed Lithuanian independence. It announced the formation of a new government headed by Shkirpa, with General Rastikis (who was also in Berlin) as Minister of National Defense.[3] Lithuanian underground groups seized the police stations, captured the prison, freed political prisoners and

[3] Shkirpa got a cool reception at the Wilhelmstrasse when he reported these developments later in the day of June 23. He was dressed down for not consulting the Foreign Office, and German anger was not ameliorated when he plaintively noted that he sent a memorandum June 19 outlining the whole plan. In the end the Germans did not permit independent or puppet governments to be set up in any of the Baltic states. (*Documents on German Foreign Policy, 1918–45*, Series D, Vol. XIII.)

took control of the automatic telephone station. Fighting between the Lithuanians and Soviet troops was severe. Some two hundred Lithuanians were killed in the Kaunas battle and possibly two thousand in other cities and villages.

By the time Colonel General Georg von Küchler marched into Kaunas June 25 in parade formation at the head of the Eighteenth Nazi Army, the Lithuanian rebels controlled the city. The Lithuanians estimated that nearly 100,000 persons joined the uprising.

Only too swiftly did it become apparent that the glacis which the Soviets had hoped to create in the Baltic states as a reliable defensive zone and protection to Leningrad was a deadly trap.

Nothing was secure within it. The Russians found themselves overwhelmed at the front by the swift German Panzer thrusts. They were cut off from communication from their headquarters and isolated in hostile country where every village might contain an ambush and every street corner might conceal deadly peril. German paratroops dropped into the countryside. German agents, native patriots, bands of dissident elements seemed to spring out of the very ground.

Major M. P. Pavlovsky served in the coastal command at Kingisepp in the Moonzund Archipelago of Estonia. For weeks before the war he had been alarmed by the attitude of the local population. A German agent named Rosenberg had been arrested among the workers building emplacements for the 315th, 317th and 318th batteries of 180-mm coastal guns. German officers had appeared in the midst of the new fortified areas—a grave-location team, it was said, come to make arrangements about transfer to the homeland of the bodies of German soldiers killed in World War I. There was difficulty in getting reliable local labor to work on the batteries. At night around Tallinn there were bursts of gunfire.

With the outbreak of war Pavlovsky's worst apprehensions about the local populace were confirmed. That Sunday evening a young Soviet commander was shot and killed as he emerged from a restaurant in Kingisepp. The next morning anti-Soviet leaflets showered through the streets of Kuressaare. They called on the population to assist the advancing Nazi armies. Armed bands appeared near Virtsu and Lihula. Radio messages in cipher to Nazi agents were intercepted. The Germans dropped a battalion of troops by parachute near Pärnu.

At any moment a Soviet unit might be struck from the back.

The situation at Riga was even worse. The Germans bombed the city in the first hours of the war and anti-Soviet skirmishers quickly took positions in the streets. There were practically no troops to maintain order—only infantry cadets and an NKVD regiment. The other military elements in the city were not combat forces—the staff of the Special Military District, rear-echelon forces and a staff regiment.

When the Germans dropped parachutists in Riga, there weren't enough

Soviet patrols to cope with them. Bands of workers were mobilized to help out, and a dozen battles were fought in the city in an effort to restore order.

A squadron of mine layers under Vice Admiral V. P. Drozd came into Riga Monday night, June 24. They found fires raging and random shooting near the harbor.

Drozd ordered his sailors to bend all efforts to loading the ships with mines and ammunition. Even engineers and machinists were pressed into duty.

The firing came closer and closer.

"Who was shooting and why they were shooting no one knew," Drozd told companions later. "We did not know how the fires had been set. Our troops had already left the city. There were no Soviet police. Persons brought in rumors that the Germans were entering the city. My sailors captured two *provocateurs* at the very gates to the depot. But to whom should they turn them over?"

The moment Drozd had reloaded his squadron he went back to sea.

"It's much more peaceful at sea," he observed.

To Admiral Tributs, the Baltic Fleet Commander, it was apparent that the new advanced positions in the Baltic states were so insecure as to endanger the whole fleet. All the reservations he had offered to Stalin's insistence upon the forward Baltic bases had proved well founded.

Admiral Tributs concluded that Riga would prove no more secure than Libau and Ventspils, which fell in a matter of two or three days. The Riga authorities, panicky at the hostile attitude of the Latvians, had almost ceased to function. The Aisargi, the Latvian nationalists, began sporadic firing from rooftops. German paratroops and saboteurs threatened the naval base at Ust-Dvinsk. Tributs gave orders to evacuate Riga.

But this presented difficulties. The Germans had heavily mined the Irben Strait, and Admiral Drozd did not have enough mine sweepers to clear a path for his retreating squadron. The only mine-free route to the east and Tallinn lay through the narrow, shallow Muhu-Väin Strait, separating the coast from the Moonzund Islands.

Drozd's small craft could navigate this channel easily. But there were heavily laden transports and the 7,000-ton cruiser *Kirov*, put on duty in 1936, Soviet-built, Drozd's flagship, the pride of the Baltic.

Heavy ships had not used the passage since World War I when the Russian battleship *Slava* traversed the shallow waters, fleeing German attack. Later, blockships, filled with cement, had been sunk in the channel.

The choice was difficult. But rather than risk the German mine fields, Drozd determined to squeeze the *Kirov* through the shore channel. Draggers and trawlers were put to work deepening its shallowest portions. Cargo was shifted to smaller ships. Finally, the *Vtoraya Pyatiletka* (which had been bound for Germany on the night of June 21–22) managed to scrape through.

Only the *Kirov* and the powerful icebreaker, the *K. Voldemars*, remained in Riga. Drozd could wait no longer. The Germans had reached Riga's outskirts by June 27. On the night of June 29, with work on the northern part of the channel unfinished, Drozd led his remaining ships, escorted by the destroyers, *Stoiki, Smetlivy* and *Grozyashchi,* into the shallow path.

Later, Drozd called the trip worse than any battle he had ever fought.

All started well. But as they reached the point where the World War I blockships had been sunk, the cruiser scraped bottom, first on sand, then on the cement. It came to a full stop.

"We on the bridge shuddered. But we had to hurry," Drozd recalled, "while it was still dark. Again I ordered slow speed ahead. The cruiser moved a little."

Buoys with tiny lights had marked the course of the dredged channel. The cruiser steered a painful path along this route. At midnight it ran completely aground. Tugs finally freed it. But almost immediately the cruiser headed into a shoal, nose on. It took three hours to get off.

The next day with Drozd[4] still on the bridge the *Kirov* sailed into Tallinn.

The fleet got out of Riga just in time. On June 29 a Nazi tank group broke into Riga on the Bausky Chaussée and raced for the bridge across the Daugava (or Dvina) River. Two bridges had been destroyed, and the Germans made for the railroad bridge, which was intact. A ton of high explosive had been placed under it, but when the plunger was pushed, the charge did not ignite.

The Russians threw together some units from the 10th and 125th rifle divisions and the NKVD regiment. With the support of an armored train they managed to smash three German tanks which got over the bridge. Then a second and successful effort was made by Lieutenant S. G. Baikov and a detachment of seven sappers to blow it up. Baikov was killed in the explosion.

Foiled in their attempt at direct entry, the Nazis circled around to the east. The broken Soviet forces hastily pulled out of Riga and hurried down the Pskov highway to Sigulda. On July 1 the German 26th Army Corps victoriously marched into Riga.

Ten days of war, Admiral Panteleyev noted. The fleet had lost the whole Baltic littoral up to Tallinn, and now it must prepare to fight for its life for its principal base.

For all the work that filled almost every hour of day and night, the minds of Panteleyev and his fellow officers could not shake off the remorseless question: What had happened at the front and why had the retreat been so sudden and so deep?

---

[4] Drozd died in an unusual accident in the winter of 1941–42. Driving on the ice from Kronstadt to Leningrad, his car fell into a bomb hole and he drowned. (Kuznetsov, *Oktyabr*, No. 8, August, 1968, p. 170.)

16 . The Red Army Retreats

TO MANY—IF NOT MOST—LENINGRADERS, LULLED BY YEARS of propaganda about Soviet military might, it seemed certain that within a few days the Red Army would turn the tables on the Nazi invaders and begin to drive them back toward the frontiers of the Third Reich. This seemed a plausible conclusion from the stories which were published by *Leningradskaya Pravda,* quoting shot-down pilots as saying the German soldiers did not want to fight, that the German workers had set fire to Nazi naval stores at Kiel and that Finnish troops were deserting to the Red Army lines rather than carry out orders given them by their commanders.

Even the Leningrad military had no sense of the colossal disaster which was beginning to unfold. General Dukhanov discovered this a couple of days after the outbreak of war when talking with Colonel G. V. Mukhin, chief of the Leningrad Infantry Academy, a fine officer and a man soon to add his name to the honor roll of Leningrad's defenders.

Dukhanov was shocked to find that Mukhin imagined that the tide would soon turn along the frontier. Mukhin had not been able to grasp from reading the official communiqués that the German armies were already one hundred miles within the Soviet borders. The truth was that by the evening of June 23 the redoubtable 4th Nazi Panzers had blasted an eighty-five-mile wedge between the Soviet Eighth and the Soviet Eleventh armies. By June 25 Nazi units were ninety miles inside the Baltic Military District (the name had now been changed to the Northwest Front) in the direction of Dvinsk and 150 miles inside Russia in the direction of Vilnius and Minsk. No one in Leningrad knew this. Not even the command in the General Staff building. The press continued to stress that German proletarians in the Nazi Army would rise against Hitler and aid a Soviet victory and that the spirit of the German Army had been crushed. Some factory papers even treated the war as a joke, and as late as July the magazine *Leningrad* printed a poor limerick treating the whole thing as a kind of gigantic prank.

If confusion was profound in Leningrad, it was almost total at the High

Command in Moscow. It had prevailed since the start of the war. On the evening of June 22 orders were issued at 9:15 P.M. to all front commands to launch an immediate counteroffensive to drive the Germans back inside Germany. The Baltic Command, acting in coordination with the Western Front, within twenty-four hours was to drive the Germans across the border to the region of Suwalki. Only a headquarters completely at sea could have issued such an optimistic order.[1]

Unreal as were these instructions, General Kuznetsov attempted to carry them out—with one change. He shifted the direction of the operation from Suwalki to Tilsit. A war game based on an offensive toward Tilsit had been carried out recently, and his commanders were familiar with the terrain. Moreover, he had issued orders for an attack toward Tilsit ten hours earlier and could not countermand them. The shift toward Tilsit meant there would be no cooperation with the Central Front offensive, but he did not seem to have thought of that.

The operation was doomed to failure. There wasn't time to prepare, there was little air strength, artillery was out of ammunition and had no motive power, and tanks were short on fuel. Kuznetsov had only tenuous communication with his armies, and his armies had little connection with their divisions.

An heroic attempt by Sobennikov's Eighth Army was made to carry out the counteroffensive. But the hastily collected tank force of the Eighth Army collided head on with the 4th Nazi Panzers. Most of the precious Soviet armor was destroyed.

One unit involved in the desperate action was the 28th Soviet Tank Division, commanded by Colonel (later Army General) Ivan D. Chernyakhovsky, a talented armored specialist. He got his orders while his forces were moving headlong toward the front. He had time for neither reconnaissance nor preparation. With his 55th Tank Regiment already involved in a fire fight with the German 1st Tank Division, Chernyakhovsky decided to try to advance toward Siauliai with the aid of the remnants of the 125th Rifle Division.

He attacked at 10 P.M., June 23, and drove the Nazis back three miles. A company of Nazi motorcyclists was wiped out on the Kaltinenai-Raseinyai road. Just to the north the Soviet 2nd Tank Division attacked a Nazi tank column advancing along the Tilsit-Siauliai highway.

The battle developed rapidly into the first large armored encounter on

[1] "Now, it is not difficult to note that the decision of the Supreme Command of the Soviet Army taken on the evening of the first day of war did not correspond to the actual existing situation. Moreover, it simply did not provide for concentrating forces and organizing a very complicated operation," comments Major General P. Korkodinov, a conservative and thoughtful Soviet military critic. (*Voyenno-Istoricheskii Zhurnal*, No. 10, October, 1965, p. 33.) Because of broken communications the High Command had only a most imperfect picture of the front-line situation. (Shtemenko, *op cit.*, pp. 28-29.)

the Northwest Front, ranging over an area of about forty miles from Kaltinenai to Raseinyai. Nearly 1,000 tanks took part. The 2nd Soviet Tank Division wiped out more than 40 Nazi tanks and 18 guns near Skaudvile. But before the day was over the 2nd Division had been surrounded by the 41st German Motorized Corps. With the support of the 12th Soviet Mechanized Corps, it fought its way out with terrible losses.

Chernyakhovsky's 28th Division started June 25 with 84 tanks, mostly old ones. By nightfall it had lost all its armor. It was no longer an armored division, merely a shell of shattered combat units. Moscow hastily yanked the crack 21st Armored Group out of the Stavka pool and ordered it to try to hold the north bank of the western Dvina (supposedly about seventy-five miles to the rear of the fighting line).

The 21st Armored was commanded by Army General D. D. Lelyushenko, a tough and experienced tank officer. Lelyushenko had organized this corps in the spring of 1941 and had chosen very good officers. Nikolai I. Voikov, a man with great theoretical background as well as combat experience, commanded his 42nd Tank Division. The 46th Tank Division was commanded by Vasily A. Koptsov, who had won his spurs in tank actions against the Japanese at Khalkin-Gol. He was one of the best young commanders in the Red Army. The commander of the 185th Motorized Division was Pyotr L. Rudchuk, whom Lelyushenko had known as far back as the Civil War days when both served in Budyonny's famous First Cavalry Army.

Lelyushenko's force was well trained and comparatively well armed, although he had only 97 old tanks instead of the 400 new KV's and T-34's which were due to be issued.[2] When war broke out, Lelyushenko recalled with bitterness a conversation he had had a month earlier with Lieutenant General Yakov N. Fedorenko, chief of the Armored Forces Administration of the Red Army. Fedorenko assured him that his corps would get its full quota of tanks by 1942.

"And if war comes?" Lelyushenko asked.

"The Red Army has enough strength without your corps," Fedorenko replied.

Lelyushenko had been in Moscow for staff consultations on June 22. He was immediately ordered back to his corps, which was stationed to the southeast of Dvinsk (Daugavpils). He rejoined his troops June 23. That day he received 96 antitank guns, but when his units were twice attacked by German bombers, he could not reply as he had no antiaircraft guns, and suffered serious losses in munitions, fuel and personnel. On June 24 he got two battalions from the Armored Academy, equipped with old BT-7 tanks, and reorganized his forces so that each tank division had 45 tanks and included motorized units and artillery as well. On June 25 the corps was again heavily bombed, but late in the day obtained some antiaircraft guns.

[2] D. D. Lelyushenko, *Zarya Pobedy*, Moscow, 1966, pp. 4–28. According to another source, 98 tanks and 129 guns. (Orlov, *op. cit.*, p. 90.)

Two JU-87's were shot down. One of the German aviators said he had seen a Nazi tank column only ten to fifteen miles southwest of Dvinsk.

Timoshenko ordered Lelyushenko to advance his corps into the Dvinsk region in an effort to keep the Germans from occupying Dvinsk and crossing the Dvina River. At 4 P.M. on the twenty-fifth Lelyushenko was moving toward Dvinsk under heavy Nazi air attack.

As the tanks rumbled into the little town of Dagda, fifty miles east of Dvinsk, Lelyushenko saw a sight he long remembered—a little girl lying beside the road, her leg broken by a bomb blast, covered with blood. The child was conscious and cried again and again for her mother. The General ordered his adjutant to rush the youngster to a medical unit.

It was June 27 before Lelyushenko managed to get within striking distance of Dvinsk. His forces were dispersed in broken forest thickets about twenty miles northeast of Dvinsk when Lieutenant General Sergei D. Akimov, second in command to Colonel General F. I. Kuznetsov of the Northwest (Baltic) Front, appeared. Akimov was tired, dusty and sunburned. He looked as though he had not slept for many days. He brought desolate news. He had been given a pick-up force, made up of local volunteers and the 5th Paratroop Corps, and told to hold Dvinsk until Lelyushenko's 21st Corps arrived. The German 8th Tank Division had thrown him out. As he had just reported to Kuznetsov: "Our attack was smothered. Individual units penetrated the city from the north and northwest, but when the enemy's reserves appeared, they were thrown out. The reason for our failure lay in our absence of tanks, insufficient artillery (we had only six guns) and weak air cover."

General Akimov advised Lelyushenko that his 21st Corps was being subordinated to the Twenty-seventh Army under Major General Berzarin, who was now in charge of a fifty-mile front covering the western Dvina from Livani to Kraslava.

With Akimov's weary assent, Lelyushenko proposed that he try to drive the Germans from Dvinsk and establish a protective line on the north side of the Dvina along a ten-to-twelve-mile front.

Early on the morning of the twenty-eighth Lelyushenko launched his attack. By 7 A.M. his advance guard had broken into the village of Malinovka, seven miles north of Dvinsk, and an hour and a half later the 46th Division, with some air support, entered Dvinsk. Hand-to-hand and house-to-house fighting broke out. The Soviet tanks closed in on Manstein's 56th Corps and even rammed the enemy machines.

The Nazis fought desperately. Hundreds of bodies strewed the streets around the burning tanks and blasted guns. The commander of the German 8th Tank Division, General Brandenberger, took cover with his staff in a fort on the southern outskirts of Dvinsk.

Soviet losses were heavy. The commander of the Soviet 46th Tank Division, the brilliant young Vasily Koptsov, was wounded fighting in the center of the town but continued to direct his forces.

Soon the Soviet machines began to run out of fuel and ammunition. The 42nd and 185th divisions were badly needed to bolster the 46th, but they were held up by Nazi bombing. Lelyushenko turned direction of the Dvinsk fighting over to Akimov and raced off to the 42nd and 185th. He found the 42nd had run into the leading units of the 121st Division of the Sixteenth German Army near Kraslava on the western Dvina about twenty-five miles due east of Dvinsk.

Lelyushenko radioed the 42nd in an improvised five-word code, "Grach [nickname for commander] Hurry Hit Dag [for Dvinsk]," and signed it "Lom" (for Lelyushenko).

Lelyushenko managed to get both the 42nd and 185th into action along the western Dvina, cutting off and encircling several German units. About 400 soldiers of the 3rd German Motorized Division were wiped out and 285 prisoners were taken. A detachment under A. M. Goryaunov was sent across the western Dvina and knocked out a company of infantry and 35 vehicles of the 56th Panzer staff.

But the Germans brought in heavy reinforcements and by evening, after air preparation, methodically began to cut the Soviet forces to bits. Lelyushenko decided to pull back to a chain of lakes running from Rushoni to Dridza about thirty miles northeast of Dvinsk.

The experiences of the Eighth Army under General Sobennikov were being duplicated by the Eleventh Army commanded by the very able Lieutenant General V. I. Morozov. If anything, Morozov's difficulties were even worse.

Having lost Kaunas in the first hours of war, General Morozov had pulled his headquarters back to Kaisiadorys, twenty miles to the east. With the German armored force across the Neman River, the question was what steps Morozov might take to halt them. He called his military council into session on the night of June 24–25 to consider the situation. There were, he said, two possibilities. He might move northwest to attack the German 4th Panzers, driving northeastward on the highway toward Dvinsk. Or he could attack to the southwest and try to re-establish connections with the Western Front command.

After outlining the two possibilities he paused.

"Comrade Commander," one of his subordinates intervened, "why did we give up Kaunas without a battle?"

Morozov explained patiently that if the Eighth Army had been able to hold the east bank of the Neman River, they would have fought to the end to save Kaunas. But once the Germans had secured bridgeheads across the river, to hold on to Kaunas would simply have meant they would fall into Nazi encirclement.

At that point Morozov was summoned to the VC high-security wire to take a call from General Kuznetsov at Northwest Front headquarters. He returned a few minutes later, hardly recognizable. His face was stone. His eyes glowed in their deep sockets. He looked at no one but went to the map and picked up the pointer. He hunted about a moment, then pointed to Kaunas.

"There," he said, carefully avoiding all eyes. "From the area of Jonava we will attack Kaunas and then East Prussia. That is the order of the Defense Commissariat."

"And what about our plan?" asked General Shlemin.

"We have no answer on our plan," Morozov muttered. Then, seeming to gather all his strength, he said, "Comrades, the order from headquarters permits no discussion. All members of the Military Council must return immediately to their troops."

The orders for the counterattack had been issued by Colonel General Kuznetsov at a meeting of the Military Council of the Northwest Front at 3 A.M., June 25.

The counterattack was carried out by Major General M. M. Ivanov of the 16th Rifle Corps. It was extremely difficult for him to get in touch with his units, inform them of the orders and get elementary information about the German dispositions. Nonetheless, he made the attempt. The remnants of his 23rd and 33rd rifle divisions advanced along the Jonava highway toward Kaunas, and the 5th Rifle Division drove in from the east. Some units got to the outskirts of Kaunas, but not in strength. They were hurled back in disorder, and for all practical purposes the 12th Corps ceased to exist. Major General V. F. Pavlov of the 23rd Division was killed. So was the deputy commander of the 33rd Rifles, Commissar Silantyev.

Worse was to follow. Almost immediately the Eleventh Army lost contact with Colonel General Kuznetsov. It was not to be restored for days.

With the capture of Soviet ciphers by the Germans and the interference of Nazi transmitters on Soviet frequencies, Major Agafonov became extraordinarily nervous about the security of communications. His fears were intensified when he got a call on the radiotelephone for General Morozov and Commissar Zuyev just as a Nazi plane began to circle over their Jonava headquarters. Suspecting a Nazi trick, Agafonov refused the call, saying that Morozov and Zuyev had moved to another spot. The plane then disappeared.

Soon another message came in on the radiotelephone. It was from Kuznetsov's chief of staff. Agafonov wasn't to be fooled a second time. "Who are you calling?" he snapped back. "You know very well we don't have any Zuyev here."[3]

The connection was broken. Fatally—for this call was genuine. It was being made by Kuznetsov's orders. The Commanding General was also

[3] V. P. Agafonov, *Neman! Neman! Ya—Dunai!*, Moscow, 1967, pp. 36–37. According to another account, twenty Nazi planes were circling overhead at the time of this call. They vanished when the call was refused. (Boris Gusev, *Smert Komissara*, Moscow, 1967, p. 88.)

nervous about the security of communications. He had received a telegram from Morozov demanding reinforcements and sharply criticizing Kuznetsov for "passivity." He didn't think this sounded like Morozov's style. It might be a Nazi fake. Even when his aides insisted that under the conditions in which the Eleventh Army was fighting a commander might lose his temper, Kuznetsov insisted on verification. It was his effort which was rebuffed by Agafonov.

That was the end of communications between the Eleventh Army and headquarters. Thereafter the remnants of Morozov's command straggled back through the Baltic marshes in small, disorderly units, only vaguely in touch with their commanders.

The destruction of the Eleventh Army exposed the flanks of the Eighth Soviet Army to the north and the Third Soviet Army to the south, leaving them easy prey to the German Panzers. No Soviet force remained in the Kaunas-Vilnius area capable of handling the German threat.

Contact between Sobennikov's Eighth Army and Morozov's Eleventh Army had vanished, and General Kuznetsov of the Northwest Front had little idea of what was going on at the front. Fearful of using wireless for communications, not knowing where his units were located, General Kuznetsov had no notion of where to send munitions and fuel supplies. Most of the armored and mechanized units were out of fuel. By the morning of the fourth day of war, Soviet military historians concede, the situation on the Northwest Front was critical.

General Kuznetsov himself had lost all command of events. An officer who had known him at the Frunze Military Academy hardly recognized him. Another old friend said he was "woefully changed." At the academy he had been neat, clean-shaven, impeccably groomed. He was weary now, dirty, rumpled, his face pale, his eyes red-rimmed. He gave orders testily and threatened his subordinates with court-martial if they were not fulfilled.

To add to his plight, he had been wounded—not a serious wound, but a painful laceration of the leg which hampered his movements and made it even more difficult for him to concentrate on the confusing swirl of military events.

In this situation he received one of the contradictory orders which so often came from Moscow. It was from the Supreme Command and it ordered him *simultaneously* to hold the Dvina River line and to establish secure defenses on the Velikaya River, based on the old fortified regions of Pskov and Ostrov. He ordered the Eighth Army to fall back to the Pskov and Ostrov regions. The Twenty-seventh Army was to stay on the defensive until the new Velikaya River line was established, then retire into the fortified zone.

The commanders began to carry out the orders. At about 2 A.M., July 2, General Lelyushenko of the 21st Armored was told by his chief, Major General A. Ye. Berzarin of the Twenty-seventh Army: Hold your front firm and retire only under heavy pressure, taking care that the Germans don't break through at any point and sever contact between units of the Twenty-seventh Army.

Lelyushenko wholeheartedly approved. Then at 8 A.M. a new order came through. General Berzarin ordered the 21st Corps to launch an offensive "to liquidate the German position on the northern bank of the western Dvina and reconquer Dvinsk."

To Lelyushenko it seemed that once again Colonel General Kuznetsov had "mistakenly evaluated the actual situation." The Twenty-seventh Army had neither the troops, the arms nor the fuel for such an undertaking. It was vastly outnumbered in armor and planes. The Germans had nine divisions poised for offensive action.

What happened was that Kuznetsov reread the exact wording of his instructions from Moscow: "to hold a firm defense line along the river Dvina." Kuznetsov's troops no longer held the Dvina line. Long since, they had been forced back. In a pedantic attempt to carry out precisely the Moscow edict, he issued what the official Soviet history called orders "that did not reflect either the actual situation and condition of the troops and which did not take into account the real possibilities of the element of time."

Lelyushenko did what any good commander would. He did not hurry to go over to the offensive. It was just as well. About noon the Germans began to attack, throwing at him the 8th Panzers, the 2nd Motorized, the SS Death's Head Division and the 290th and 121st infantry divisions.

In heavy fighting, Lelyushenko fell back steadily. Had he taken his troops to the offensive, he would have been wiped out. Even so, he lost half his personnel and equipment and was left with only four thousand men. Still, he continued to exact a heavy toll on the Nazis. He positioned his shattered 42nd Division in the little town of Dagda, carefully masking its location. When the advance guard of the Death's Head Division entered the town, he sprang his trap, wiping out several hundred Germans. The 42nd Division held its lines near Dagda until July 3. But the crack 41st Nazi Motorized Corps broke through on the right flank of the Soviet Twenty-seventh Army near Rezekne, sixty-five miles northeast of Dvinsk. Lieutenant General Akimov tried to drive the Germans back but did not succeed and had to fall back in the direction of Karsava and Ostrov.

On the evening of July 3 Lelyushenko ordered his 185th and 46th divisions to retreat toward Ludza-Laudrei. The 42nd had trouble disengaging, but a counterattack by the redoubtable Goryainov broke into the command point of the German 121st Division of the Sixteenth Nazi Army. The German commander, Major General Lancelle, was killed.

The 21st Corps held along the Ludza-Laudrei line on the fourth, then fell back toward Sebezh and Opochka. The retreat was carrying them into a land of endless marshes, peat bogs and dismal thickets. On the evening of July 5 the 21st at the order of General Berzarin, commander of the Twenty-seventh Army, began to retire to the old Soviet frontier, to a line along the rivers Lezh and Sinaya. The evening of July 6 found them defending Opochka against a fierce offensive, which the 185th Division once again met with a counterattack. That same day, the 21st Corps, a remnant of the outfit which had gone into action eleven days previously, was ordered out of combat and into reserve for re-equipment. Actually, the remnants were so closely engaged with the Germans that they could not be pulled out. Lelyushenko continued to fight on for nearly a month before returning to Moscow for reassignment.

The Germans were now in a position to turn the Pskov-Ostrov-Opochka line, almost the last natural barrier to their direct advance on Leningrad. They were a little behind Hitler's timetable—but not too much.

With the situation developing in this catastrophic fashion, Moscow decided to move three corps up from interior reserves and try to establish a new line on the Velikaya River, roughly from Pskov to Ostrov to Opochka, about 125–150 miles southwest of Leningrad. But before the troops could reach their positions the broken elements of the Twenty-seventh Army had fallen back to the southeast. The Germans seized Ostrov on July 5 and Pskov on July 9.

Within three weeks, of the thirty-one divisions which had been allotted to the Northwest Front twenty-two had lost 50 percent or more of their strength, many of them in the first few days of fighting. This was comparable to losses on the other fronts. By this date twenty-eight Soviet front-line divisions had been obliterated—they no longer existed—and more than seventy divisions had lost 50 percent of their strength. By June 28 the commander of the 2nd Infantry Corps of the Thirteenth Army of the Western Front reported he had no ammunition, no fuel, no food, no transport for supply or evacuation, no means of communication, no hospitals and no instructions where to evacuate his wounded. His situation was typical. By June 29 the Western Front had lost 60 important supply depots, including 10 artillery, 25 fuel, 14 provisions, 3 armored-mechanized.[4] It had lost more than 2,000 wagons of munitions (30 percent of its total), 50,000 tons of fuel (50 percent of reserves), 500 wagons of mechanized materials, 40,000 tons of forage (half the supply) and 85–90 percent of hospital and engineering supplies.

By this time General Kuznetsov had been relieved of command. He had headed the Baltic front for a total of only nine days when, after being wounded, he was ordered to relinquish his post to Major General Sobennikov of the Eighth Army. So chaotic was the situation that it was four days before the two generals could meet and the command be turned over.

---

[4] The General Staff had proposed in 1940 to remove all the principal supply depots from Byelorussia and other forward areas and locate them behind the Volga River. Stalin vetoed the idea and ordered depots concentrated in the frontier commands. (Nekrich, *op. cit.,* p. 84.)

Why did the distant Leningrad, or Northwest Front, collapse with such rapidity? Why did General Kuznetsov's troops fall back again and again?

"The Commander of the troops of the Northwest Front, Colonel General F. I. Kuznetsov, for all his positive qualities, did not possess the necessary operative-strategic preparation and experience in leading large operating units in conditions of war," reads the verdict of the official Soviet military historians. "Placed in a very critical position by the sudden enemy attack, he was unable correctly to evaluate the evolving situation and display the necessary initiative and wisdom in utilizing the large forces which he had at his disposal."

The verdict is mild. Many of Kuznetsov's peers, suffering far less critical reverses, were shot. Among them was his chief of staff, Lieutenant General P. S. Klenov.

The Soviet military histories cite the overwhelming German numerical superiority as the prime factor in the disaster. But they also cite bad direction, faulty command, poor management, poor leadership, poor coordination— almost all the faults imaginable. There was nearly total incomprehension on the part of Soviet commanders as to how to halt the Nazi Panzers. The Soviet infantry did not know how to coordinate action with Soviet tank units, and no one understood how to use shock tactics to smash back at the onrushing Germans.

The mass attacks of Nazi tanks and planes terrified the Soviet troops. A soldier named Nikitin of the 163rd Infantry Division tried to tell a Northwest Front brigade commissar what it was like: "We start our attack, shouting 'Hurrah!' The Germans start to run. And then out of nowhere their tanks and planes hit us. . . . It's terrible. And on our side we have no planes, no tanks, just infantry. How can we stand up against that kind of force?"

Thus the direct military threat to Leningrad developed with startling rapidity—far more speedily than anyone in Leningrad could conceive. More and more evident became the wisdom of the Leningrad leaders in the war's first days in putting so much emphasis on the erection of new lines of field defenses. Now the task was under way. The whole city was throwing its shoulder into the effort. But the hour was late.

17 . *The First Days*

THE FIRST WEEKS OF WAR DID NOT SEEM SO DIFFERENT IN Leningrad. The air-raid sirens sounded occasionally, but no bombs fell. When the Hermitage ARP workers heard the first alarm on the radio, they quickly mounted to the roof and took their posts at the entrances and in the court-yards. The cool early-morning light of June filtered down on them and reflected from the gray Neva. Before the museum spread the broad expanse of Palace Square, a desert of granite, empty, lifeless. In truth, the museum was still an open target for German destruction. But fortunately no planes appeared, and in the morning Academician Orbeli issued Order No. 170, congratulating the museum staff for its excellent ARP work.

The danger of air attack on Leningrad had been a great worry to the government long before the outbreak of war. From the second day, June 23, volunteers were put to work, digging air-raid shelters in the Champs de Mars, the Summer Gardens and other parks. The city was defended by a Special Army Corps of Antiaircraft Artillery and a network of fighter fields on which 25,000 men were at work. More than one million Leningraders had participated in ARP training as early as 1940. Now in these first days the occasional German planes which appeared over the city flew at very great height, and no bombs were dropped. But each night fire fighters sat on the roofs with sand pails, water buckets, shovels and axes. A blond girl named Natasha was one of them. She was seventeen, serious and gray-eyed.

"What did you do this past year?" someone asked her later.

"I sat on the roof," the girl said.

"Like a cat," a friend added.

"I'm not a cat," Natasha replied. "There are no cats left in the city. The roof was my post. I stayed at my post."

At first she and her friends sat on the moonlit rooftops and read poetry—Byron, Pushkin.

"It was so quiet," she said. "Hardly any cars on the street. Strange. I felt as though I were flying over the city—a silvery city, each roof and each spire engraved against the sky. And the blimps! On the ground they looked like sausages, fat and green. But at night, in the air, they swam like white whales under the clouds."

It was only later that the horror, the fear, the tragedy came.

Along the streets windows blossomed with paper strips, pasted on to prevent the glass from shattering under the impact of bombs. Some householders cut out elaborate designs. In one house on the Fontanka the windows were decorated with paper palm trees. Below the trees sat gay groups of monkeys. Others carefully pasted crosses on their windows, possibly hoping for divine protection.

Ordinarily the theater season in Leningrad ended by July 1. The great Mariinsky Opera House shut for the summer. So did the Conservatory. The Philharmonic closed even earlier. The Theater of Comedy and the principal drama theaters toured the provinces; only visiting companies and the Operetta Theater performed in Leningrad. Now all this changed. The Mariinsky resumed its season after a two-day interval. *Ivan Susanin* and *Swan Lake* returned to the Leningrad stage. All the theaters stayed open. Actors were mobilized in defense tasks. Olga Iordan and a friend, N. A. Zubkovsky, rehearsing in the new ballet, *Gayane* or *Happiness*, found their ARP duties more pleasant than difficult. They relaxed in comfortable chairs in the lobby of the theater through the long summer twilight, gas masks dangling from their necks, looking out on the Kryukov Canal and listening for the sound of German planes. War still seemed far, far away. Day after day the weather stayed sunny, warm and bright.

But there were other worries. Yelena Skryabina's friend, Lyubov Nikolayevna, boarded a plane to try to find her children, who had been visiting in a Byelorussian village. Most of Byelorussia had already been overrun by the Germans. But she did not know this. By amazing good fortune she found the children, unharmed, and managed to make her way with them back to Leningrad unscathed.

The police began to clamp down. On June 28 was published Order No. 1 of the Leningrad Garrison "to secure social order and state security." It fixed hours for the operation of all industrial enterprises, offices, theaters, parks, cinemas and stores. Entry into the city was forbidden except for bona fide residents and persons on official business, and 25 control points manned by a force of 232 police checked movements in and out. Those living in the suburbs and working in Leningrad got special passes. Picture taking was forbidden. Workers' "troikas" were formed to guard railroad stations. Violations were subject to punishment under military law, that is, by shooting. Detachments of trusted Party workers were enrolled in every factory and office to maintain order. They were armed with submachine guns, revolvers and grenades. Evacuation centers—forty-two in all—were set up to receive and process refugees from the Baltic states.

Ordinary crime fell off spectacularly with the excitement of war. The police were amazed to record a 60 percent drop in the first weeks. Robberies were down 95.6 and drunkenness 78 percent.

But the secret police did not relax. Yelena Skryabina heard on July 1 of the arrest of her good friend and fellow worker, Madame Belskaya. The police had come at night, conducted a search and taken the woman off without explanation. Why? Possibly because the father of her daughter (born out of wedlock) was a French engineer who had lived for a time in Leningrad.

Madame Skryabina went to see her friend's family, a sister ill of tuberculosis, an aged mother, a three-year-old daughter and a brother already mobilized in the Red Army. When she was late getting home, Madame Skryabina's family feared that she, too, had been arrested.

Spy mania seized the city. A well-known academician was riding in a streetcar. Suddenly, a group of teen-agers surrounded him. One yanked at his full, flowing beard. Another shouted: "He's a spy!" With difficulty the scholar managed to disengage first his beard and then himself.

Security patrols roved the streets. Alexei Brusnichkin, a Leningrad newspaperman, was walking down the Nevsky, wearing a brown shirt. He had a slight limp. A patrol seized him, certain he was a Nazi paratrooper who had injured his foot in jumping. Photographer Georgi Shulyatin dashed off to Pskov, on assignment for "Northern Newsreel." He was wearing an English tweed jacket, a foreign-looking cap and carrying a movie camera. He stopped someone to ask the whereabouts of staff headquarters and was instantly arrested. Fortunately, the police escorted him to headquarters, where he managed to get himself released. He also got a war correspondent's uniform.

There were ugly rumors. It was said that a well-known poet, mobilized for front-line duty, had wounded himself in the hand, hoping to escape active combat. Instead, he was put before the firing squad as an ordinary shirker.

Daniel Harms, an eccentric poet, lived at No. 11 Mayakovsky Street, just beyond the Anichkov Bridge. Tall and thin, Harms wore a cavalier's hat, like those of the Three Musketeers. Around his neck dangled a chain of amulets, carved of tortoise shell and ivory. It was said that he existed mostly on milk, and it was known that he had so little money he was always near starvation. He supported himself—poorly—by publishing occasional verses for children. During his life only two of his poems for adults were published. But, to his "desk drawer," as the Russian phrase has it, he was a voluminous contributor—a brilliant satirist, a philosopher of Gothic tendencies, a true poet of the absurd, long before the school of the absurd became chic. Such a man, an original in dress, manner, thought, habits and philosophy, did not find life easy in the Leningrad of the 1930's. But, unlike many others, he had survived.

Not long after the war started the writer Leonid Panteleyev spent an evening with Harms, whom he had known for many years as a talented man whose eccentricity was a mere mask, a man whose true personality had little in common with that of the clown he pretended to be.

The two friends drank cheap red wine, ate white bread—white bread was still available in every Leningrad bakery—and spoke of the war. Harms talked with optimism. He was a patriot who knew the danger of the Germans but was confident that Leningrad—and precisely Leningrad—would decide the course of the war. The bravery and firmness of the Leningraders would prove the rock on which the Nazi war machine would be smashed.

A few days later the hall porter knocked at Harms's door. Someone wanted to see him in the courtyard below. Immediately. Half-dressed, one foot bare and the other in a sandal, Harms went to the courtyard. The "black crow" —the secret police van—was waiting. Off he went to prison, there to rot and die in the arctic winter of 1941–42. No one in Leningrad knew why. No one knows today. Perhaps because he wore a funny hat.

The prison traffic was not all one way. Colonel N. B. Ivushkin was a minor party official in Demyansk. He was arrested in 1938 and imprisoned. On the eve of war he was released—in time to join the 55th Infantry and march two hundred miles in the last days of June from Demyansk to Velikiye Luki. Kurakin, the husband of Madame Skryabina's neighbor, Lyubov Nikolayevna, suddenly came home after two years in a labor camp. At first Lyubov was in seventh heaven. But her husband was so old, so tired, so despondent, so ill—he had a broken rib and had been deafened in one ear— that the joy of his return faded. And there was the husband of Aleksandr Shtein's sister, a soldier solid as a rock, a colonel, a man who would end the war commanding an antitank brigade in Berlin, his chest glittering with medals, who began the war with handcuffs still on his wrists (after four years in prison camp as "an enemy of the people") and went from the prison office to the military commissariat, and from there to the battlefield.

Indeed, there were those who saw detachments of prisoners transported directly from labor camps to the front lines and sent into battle with NKVD guards holding machine guns at their backs. Other prisoners were mobilized for work on the fortifications. As the Red Army staggered back from the Baltic, some NKVD prisoners were released. Some escaped. Some were shot.

The question that haunted Leningrad in these days was the same that had been raised by Zhdanov the day of his return to the city from Moscow— fortifications: the Luga line.

Since almost the first day of the war Colonel Bychevsky had been working night and day on the Luga line, the new system of fortifications running along the Luga River, roughly forty to seventy-five miles southwest of Leningrad. Each day that passed made it more apparent that if the Nazis were to be halted short of Leningrad's gates it would only be on the Luga line.

The other lines were crumbling, one by one. The fleeting hope that the

Germans might be stopped on the Velikaya River line running from Ostrov to Pskov and on to Lakes Pskov and Peipus, roughly 150 miles southwest of Leningrad, had dissolved. Colonel Bychevsky had spent the summer of 1939 creating a system of reinforced-concrete gun positions throughout the Ostrov area—at Kolotilovsky, Olkhovsky, Gilevsky and Zorinsky. The bunkers covered every possible approach to Ostrov, and the same kind of fortifications protected Pskov. Bychevsky could hardly believe his ears when he was told the system had fallen to the Germans. But he knew then, if he had not known before, that the Luga line was almost the city's last hope.

Bychevsky had reason to suppose that Zhdanov felt the same way. Indeed, it was possible that Zhdanov did not think that any line would halt the Germans before they got to Leningrad. As early as June 28 Zhdanov had ordered Bychevsky to set up munitions depots in the forests and marshes northeast of Pskov and between Pskov and Gdov for the use of partisans, should the Germans reach these areas. Zhdanov personally selected the points for the caches, working over a map with Bychevsky. At Zhdanov's orders Bychevsky planted radio-controlled mines at many key points which might be overrun by the Germans. These could be detonated by radio signals from mobile field transmitters—one of the Leningrad Command's most secret weapons.

More than thirty thousand Leningraders had been mobilized on the Luga line to dig trenches, mine fields and dig gun emplacements, dugouts and tank traps. A small group of army sappers directed the work, but the brunt was borne by women. With the fall of Ostrov another fifteen thousand workers were sent to the Luga line. Concrete antitank barriers were loaded up from the Karelian isthmus and trucked to Luga positions. Three factories, the Nevgvozd, Barricade and No. 189 Construction Trust, turned out rails for tank barricades.

This work, in large measure, was directed by Party secretaries or Party representatives. Not all Party chiefs, in the smaller towns and villages, however, acquitted themselves with honor. In the Volosovo region the Party chiefs panicked and fled to the rear. They were charged with desertion and excluded from the Party. In the Batetsk region the Party chiefs, frightened of air attacks, took shelter in a dugout so well camouflaged no one could find it. They were expelled from the Party.

There were other problems, some of which only became apparent later when the Germans stormed up to the defense zones. Much construction was left in the hands of local Party organizations or low-ranking military men who often had no idea what kind of defenses to build. The local barriers and tank traps were not connected. Firing positions were badly sited. Then, as the swift approach of the Panzers threw the situation into crisis, changes would be ordered, often too late. This kind of error proved almost fatal in September when the Germans reached the Pulkovo Heights. New firing positions and new gun sightings had been ordered, but little of the work had been completed.

Youngsters from the universities and institutes were corraled into the fortifications tasks. Unlike the ordinary Leningraders, who were drafted without pay, the youngsters got nine rubles a day—more than their scholarship allowances.

One morning Bychevsky got a telephone call from his oldest daughter, a first-year student at Leningrad University.

"Good-bye, Papa," the youngster said, "I'm off to work."

"Where?"

"You know where, I think. We're going in a car. I have to hurry."

"What are you taking with you?"

"What do I need?" the girl replied. "A towel. Some soap. I don't need anything else."

"Wait a minute," her father said. "Wait a minute, young lady. Have you got a coat, a kettle, a spoon or a knapsack? And you must take some bread, some sugar, some linen."

"You're joking, Papa," the girl replied gaily. "None of the girls is taking anything. We won't be gone long. We'll sleep in a haystack. Tell Mama not to worry. See you soon."

But, as Bychevsky noted, the girls did not return so quickly. Nor did all return. They came back, not by car, but on foot, weary to exhaustion, their clothes in rags, their bodies aching, their hands raw, their feet bruised, black with dirt and heavy with sweat. Many bore bloody bandages over their wounds. Some were buried (and some were not) in the open fields and beside the roads, where they were caught by flights of low-flying JU-88's and Heinkel attack bombers. The planes flew over, day after day, bombing and strafing. How many thousands were killed? No one knows. There was no accurate count of those engaged on the job and no way of identifying who returned and who did not.

Day and night the work went ahead, regardless of air attack, regardless of losses, regardless of the exhaustion of the women, old men and young people who made up most of the force. On the approaches to Kingisepp the Leningrad subway construction crew was sent in with mechanical excavators, steam shovels and powerful cranes. But the principal instruments were picks and shovels, and the principal motive power the backs and muscles of inexperienced women and men.

Thus the Luga line took shape, almost two hundred miles long, running from Narva and Kingisepp near the coast, then southeast along the Luga River through Luga city to Medved and Shimsk at Lake Ilmen. Its distance from Leningrad was about sixty miles south of Kingisepp, about a hundred miles at Lake Ilmen. Though the position was strong, it could be flanked if the Germans managed to penetrate east of Lake Ilmen to Novgorod.

The Luga River was 120 to 180 feet wide, with a shore that was marshy in some places but in others suitable for mechanized forces. To protect the line, Bychevsky erected mine fields and antitank barricades, covered by fortified and semifortified gun positions to a depth of about two and a half to three miles. Soon, to Bychevsky's horror, he discovered that some mine fields had no effect on the heavy new German armor. The light Soviet mines exploded, but the tanks rolled ahead unharmed.

Zhdanov and the Leningrad Command knew that the broken armies rapidly falling back could hardly stand on the Luga. They were retreating too rapidly and in too great disorder. Even retreat was becoming difficult. The highways from the Baltic were clogged with refugees. Some eighty thousand workers who had been engaged in constructing fortifications in the Baltic states were trying to flee east. Mixed with the refugees were shattered army units, individual soldiers, peasants trying to herd their cattle to safer fields, German agents, anti-Soviet farmers, deserters and ordinary people, filled with fear and panic.

If the Luga line was to be held, it would be held not with such material but in spite of it.

The commander of the Luga line—the Luga Operating Group, as it was called—was Major General K. P. Pyadyshev, a brilliant, rather sardonic man of great military experience and few illusions. It was obvious to him, as to all, that Leningrad did not have trained troops to throw into the breach.

The retreating armies of the Leningrad (Northwest) Front were incredibly battered. By July 10 they had fallen back 300 to 325 miles in eighteen days of constant fighting. They now possessed only 1,442 guns, cannon and mortars. They had lost all their air support, most of it in the first four hours of the war. The armored and mechanized divisions had lost so much equipment that they were, in fact, mere rifle divisions. The three armies, the Eighth, the Eleventh and the Twenty-seventh, had a paper strength of 31 divisions and 2 brigades. It was just paper. In 22 of the divisions the losses were above 50 percent. In 6 divisions—the 33rd, the 126th, the 181st, the 183rd, the 188th Rifle and the 220th Motorized—the strength had fallen to an average of 2,000 men. Several divisions had fewer than 30 percent effectives. The three armies may have mustered 150,000 men. The Eighth Army was running out of arms. It had an average of 1.7 mines per mortar and 0.5 shells per weapon. The 10th Rifle Division had 2,577 men, 89 machine guns, 1 antiaircraft gun and 27 cannon and mortars. The 125th Rifles had 3,145 men, 53 machine guns, 7 antiaircraft guns and 22 other cannon.

Any hope for holding the Luga line lay with the People's Volunteers. The call for volunteers went out June 30. That day 10,890 signed up. By July 6, 100,000 had volunteered. By July 7, the total reached 160,000, including 32,000 women, 20,000 Communists and 18,000 Young Communists.[1] Dmitri Shostakovich, the composer, was among them. In his application he

---

[1] There are minor differences in figures on the Volunteers, as given in various Soviet sources. For instance, Karasev puts the figure of women volunteers at 27,000 after one month. Another source gives the total for July 7 as 200,000, possibly meaning applications rather than acceptances (B. Malkin and M. Likhomarov, *Voyenno-Istoricheskii Zhurnal*, No. 1, January, 1964, p. 17), and *Leningrad v Velikoi Otechestvennoi Voine* (p. 51) gives the July 7 total as 110,000.

wrote: "Up to now I have known only peaceful work. Now I am ready to take up arms. Only by fighting can we save humanity from destruction." Shostakovich was not accepted. He was assigned to air-raid duty. The actor Nikolai Cherkasov signed up. So did the forty-six-year-old poet, Vsevolod Rozhdestvensky. He served for four years on the Leningrad, Volkhov and Karelia fronts, mostly as a correspondent for army papers. He also wrote poems and, in intervals, managed to finish a book of memoirs.

Not all the writers had an easy time getting into the armed forces. Lev Uspensky tried to join the navy but ran into a problem. He wore Russian size 47 (English equivalent, size 14) boots. The navy quartermaster didn't stock boots that large. His application was held up until they found boots big enough to put him into proper uniform.

Yevgeny Shvarts, a nervous, gentle, half-ill satirist and writer of children's fairy tales, tried to join the Volunteers, although his hands shook so badly (he had Parkinson's disease) he could hardly sign the application.

"How can you hold a rifle?" someone asked.

"Never mind," Shvarts replied. "There are other things to do."

When Shvarts was not accepted, he and the humorist Mikhail Zoshchenko worked night and day for a week and completed a satire, *Under the Lindens of Berlin*. It was put on at the Comedy Theater. When the Comedy Theater was evacuated in August, Shvarts and his wife refused to leave. They stayed on as members of the defense unit for their house at No. 9 Griboyedov Canal.

Boris M. Levin, a jolly man whom the writer Samuil Marshak nicknamed the "Himalayan bear," signed up. He lost his good nature with the start of the war and was deep in gloom. "All over the world," he said, "the lights are going out." Levin attended an officers' short course. On his first night in the front lines he was killed in a Nazi attack on his dugout. He hadn't even been issued a gun. Only eight days after the war started, the first Leningrad writer fell in action. He was Lev Kantorovich, member of a border detachment, killed June 30 near Enso.

Enlistment points were set up in every quarter of the city. Leonid Panteleyev noticed one in a lane near the Narva Gates in a new school. A crowd surrounded a curious little man, narrow-chested, middle-aged, wearing the People's Volunteers arm band. He was shouting in a teary voice, and beating his narrow chest: "Citizens, I beg you always to remember. I have three sons: Vladimir. Pyotr. Vasily. All three are at the front. I beg you to remember. And tomorrow I myself will go to the front and fight for all citizens of the Soviet Union—without exception." Panteleyev could never decide whether the man was drunk or simply excited.

The life of the writer Dmitri Shcheglov had changed very little since the start of the war. Each day he got up at the same time. He worked at his desk. He listened to the war bulletins. The Red Army was being thrown back. But people said this was not too significant. "It's a war of maneuver,"

176 . PART II: The Summer War

they insisted. The mood of the city seemed good, but he knew the situation was getting worse. He sent off his thirteen-year-old son Alexei to the East. The father and son both held back their tears, but Shcheglov had to turn away at the last moment, he did not want his youngster to see him crying.

The Kirov Theater asked Shcheglov to act as consultant on the libretto of a new ballet, *White Nights*, to be put on after the defeat of Germany. At the Alexandrinsky Theater *Flandria* was playing; at the Radlov Theater, *The Good Soldier Schweik*. At the Gostiny Dvor the ads still proclaimed: "Buy Eskimo Pies," "Hot Cocoa" and "Meat Pasties 25 Kopeks Apiece." But the monuments were disappearing—Catherine's famous bronze horseman of Peter I was hidden in a great sandbox (the first proposal was to sink it to the bottom of the Neva River, as had been planned at the time of Napoleon's invasion of Russia). The statues of General Kutuzov and General Suvorov, the conquerors of Napoleon, remained in place—as a matter of military pride—on the Nevsky and at the Kirov Bridge but were protected with sandbags. The gigantic bulls by the sculptor V. I. Demut-Malinovsky at the Leningrad Packing Plant were placed on runners and hauled to the necropolis of the Alexander Nevsky Lavra. The idea was to put them underground, but it was never carried out. They stayed among the monuments and headstones all through the war, a frightening spectacle for rare visitors, especially when camouflaged in white for the winter.

On July 8 Shcheglov and his friends, Vladimir Belyayev, Boris Chetvernikov and Mikhail Rosenberg, went to the enlistment point and signed up for the Volunteers—a month's training and they would go to the front. Meanwhile, Shcheglov's wife came by the barracks each evening with a thermos of coffee and homemade sandwiches.

Everyone was signing up for something. Fifteen thousand registered for the People's Volunteers from the Kirov works—enough for a whole division. More than 2,500 Leningrad University students joined the army and the Volunteers, including 200 Party members and 500 Young Communists. The university provided seven battalions of Volunteers. The Railroad Engineering Institute mobilized 900, the Mining Institute 960, the Shipbuilding Institute 450, the Electrotechnical 1,200. Almost every student in the Lesgaft Institute signed up, led by their professors. One hundred and fifty of the 400 members of the Artists Union volunteered the first day. Pavel Armand, director of the film, *Man with a Gun*, was named commander of a machine-gun unit. By July 5 Public Order battalions numbering 17,167, mostly youngsters and oldsters, had been organized to maintain internal order. An additional six regiments of about 6,000, including 2,500 Communists and Young Communists, were formed by July 15. About 200 partisan units, including perhaps 15,000 men and women, were organized for fighting behind the Nazi lines.

At first it was planned to form 15 divisions of Volunteers. But it was quickly found that this would exhaust Leningrad's manpower. The figure was cut to 7 divisions at a Military Council meeting July 4.

The first three divisions went into barracks at 6 P.M., July 4, and by July 7 (!) were supposed to be en route to their positions in the Luga line. Volunteers were accepted in the age bracket eighteen to fifty. Generally their average age was much higher than in the regular army. There were few officers with command experience, particularly in infantry. Many reserve officers were engineers and scientists, and others had little or no military background. It was not possible to fill more than 5 or 10 percent of line-officer posts with men of experience. Half the Volunteers had no military background of any kind. Squads and companies were made up of men from the same office or shop. All knew each other. Instead of using military language, they politely said: "Please do so and so," "I beg of you," etc. *Leningradskaya Pravda* published a picture showing a Volunteer standing at full height, throwing a Molotov cocktail at an oncoming tank. Marshal Voroshilov was furious. He made the paper publish new pictures and articles, pointing out that if the Volunteers tried to hurl gasoline bottles or grenades like that, they would be mowed down before they could lift an arm.

The haste and carelessness with which the People's Volunteers were organized took a deadly toll once the units went into action. Many men never reached the firing line. One commander reported that 200 of his 1,000 men dropped out on the march into action because of illness, fatigue, age and physical exhaustion.

Most of the officers had little more training than the men. In the 1st Division of 1,824 commanders only 10 were regular army men. Only 50 percent of the officers of the 2nd Division had had any previous practice with weapons. Almost none had experience in digging trenches, camouflage, military tactics or command. In the artillery regiment of the 2nd Division, commanders were changed five times between July and October, in an attempt to find a qualified man. The longest a commander lasted was nineteen days. The commanders of the 1st Division and the 2nd Guards Division had to be removed almost the moment the units went into action.

The first three divisions had a very high ratio of Party members (20 to 46 percent) and ordinary workers (up to 61 percent). The 1st Division was organized by the Kirov region Party secretary, V. S. Yefremov. It went into training the night of July 3–4, using the playing grounds of the 5th School on Stachek Prospekt as its drill field. It comprised between 10,000 and 11,000 men, of whom nearly one-third were Party members or Young Communists.[2] In the 1st Regiment of this division were 2,496 Kirov workers

[2] The figures are given differently by different sources. N.Z. (p. 69) gives the total as 12,102 as does *900 Geroicheskii Dnei* (p. 51). *900* (p. 51) gives the Party total as 1,258 and the Komsomol as 1,015. However, S. Kostyuchenko and his fellow authors of the official history of the Kirov factory give the figure as 11,584, including 1,285 Party members and 1,196 Young Communists. They first published these figures in *Neva* (No. 11, November, 1964, p. 170) and repeated them without change in *Istoriya Kirovskogo Zavod* (Moscow, 1966, p. 97). The differences are insignificant but throw light on the difficulty of establishing exact statistics in connnection with the Leningrad blockade. For instance, *Vtoraya Mirovaya Voina* (p. 150), citing Defense Commissariat statistics, gives the total as 10,431, with 3,493 Party and Komsomol members. So does *Leningrad v VOV* (p. 54).

and 439 men from other regional organizations, including about 1,250 Party members and 1,015 Young Communists. The 2nd Division, from the Moscow and Leningrad regions, had members from the Elektrosila, Karburator, Skorokhod and Proletarian Victory factories. Of its approximately 9,000 members, 1,197 were Party members and 1,750 Young Communists. The 3rd Division had 950 Party and 1,475 Young Communists in a total of 10,094.

The heavy participation of Party members in the Volunteers was matched by their enrollment in the regular army. For instance, of 10,403 Communists in the Neva region of Leningrad 4,215 went into the regular army. In the summer of 1941 nearly 90,000 Leningrad Party members and Young Communists went to the front.

The Leningrad City Party as of May 1, 1941, had 121,415 members and 32,173 candidates, a total of 153,588. Membership July 1 was 122,849 and 30,682 candidates, a total of 153,531. There were on July 1, 1941, 28,346 members and 19,844 candidates in the Leningrad region or oblast. This made a total membership in the city and region of 201,721 as of July 1. About 70 percent of the Party membership and 90 percent of the Young Communists went into military duty. In the first three months of war 57 percent of the membership went into service, including 1,142 primary Party secretaries. By October 1, 431,000 persons had been mobilized in Leningrad for combat duty, including 54,000 Party members and 93,000 Young Communists.

On the morning of July 10 the 1st (Kirov) Division of Volunteers under command of Major General F. P. Rodin was mustered for the front. Hand grenades and Molotov cocktails were issued to each man. There were not enough rifles to go around. The unit was starting into battle with 35 percent of its allotted machine guns, 13 percent of its artillery and 8 percent of its authorized mortars. Many men carried only picks, shovels, axes or hunting knives. Some had guns last used by the Bolsheviks against General Yudenich's attack on Petrograd in 1918. Many had nothing but empty hands and brave hearts.

There were some who watched the Leningraders form up who could not help recalling the July days just twenty-seven years earlier. That was the month when the Czar's armies assembled by the million and moved west against the forces of Wilhelm II and Franz Josef. Then, too, rank after rank had no rifles. Not until their comrades fell in combat would they be able to arm themselves. History was repeating itself on the Russian battlefield.

But those who thought such gloomy thoughts did not speak them. At the

---

Karasev (p. 44) gives the total for the 2nd Division as 9,210. So does *Leningrad v VOV* (p. 705). N.Z. makes it 8,751. There are parallel discrepancies in the figures on the "Public Order" battalions. Karasev (p. 48) gives the figure of 17,167 enrolled in 79 battalions by July 5. N.Z. (p. 25) gives a figure of 168 battalions, numbering 36,000 persons, including 10,000 Party members and 1,500 Young Communists. *Vtoraya Mirovaya Voina* (p. 155) gives a figure of 90 battalions, including 19,000 "by the beginning of July."

head of the column of Volunteers waved a red and gold banner, presented by the Kirov factory workers. Next came a band. An hour later the men boarded boxcars at the Vitebsk freight station. As they unloaded at their destination, Batetsk, just east of Luga, German attack bombers struck. The division's first casualty, a military engineer named Nikolai Safronov, was buried in the green fields nearby. The Volunteers quickly moved out and took over an eighteen-mile front from Unomer through Lubinets, Shchepino and Ozhogin Volochek to Kositskoye.

The 2nd Volunteers set up headquarters in the Institute of Aviation Mechanics. On the night of July 13, headed by Lieutenant N. I. Ugryumov, it embarked on freight cars, and went to Veimarn Station, just east of Kingisepp. The troops detrained under air attack and headed for their positions at Ivanovskoye, past burning *izbas*, or peasant huts, madly galloping horses, bellowing cattle, barking dogs and wildly fluttering chickens. The roads were clogged with refugees, many of them women with babies at the breast or old men hobbling with canes.

In the fortifications system still toiled nearly sixty thousand workers, although the battle had almost reached them.

It was a scene of chaos that might have been painted by Vereshchagin, the Russian battle portraitist.

The People's Volunteers, tumbling out of the freight cars, shielding their mouths from the acrid smoke of the burning villages, groping their way toward the unfamiliar trenches, did not know that more than two weeks ago when Army Group Nord was still in the Siauliai region the methodical Germans had completed plans for their victory parade in Leningrad. SS General Knut was to be Leningrad commandant. The Nazi troops would march in triumph through Palace Square, column after column, past the General Staff building and the Winter Palace. There, it was anticipated, the happy Führer would review his victorious armies.[3]

[3]Guidebooks to the sights of Leningrad had been printed and distributed, to both soldiers and officers. Soviet writers contend that invitations had been printed for a great banquet of honor to be held in the Hotel Astoria, across from St. Isaac's. Even the date had been fixed—July 21, just a week away. The story of the banquet and the invitations was first reported in accounts written in the spring of 1942. But none of the sources reproduce either invitations, tickets or menus. The suspicion persists that the story is apocryphal. However, special permits for automobiles in Leningrad were printed by the Germans, and examples can be seen in the Central Museum of the Red Army. (Karasev, *op. cit.*, p. 102.)

18 . *The Luga Line*

VSEVOLOD KOCHETOV AND HIS FELLOW WAR CORRE-
spondent of *Leningradskaya Pravda*, Mikhail Mikhalev, drove out of
Leningrad just after midnight on July 14 in the office Ford, which, because
of the war, was painted a kind of dirty brown.

Kochetov felt quite proud. He had managed to wangle from his paper
not only a car and a Ukrainian chauffeur, Serafim Boiko, but from the Military Commissariat on Angleterre Street he had gotten a new TT pistol, still
in factory grease, and two dozen bullets. He had a permit to keep the gun
until September 1, when (happy thought!) the war might be over. He also
had a big birthday cake in a cardboard box, some candy and a letter. These
were for Comrade Molvo, director of the new military newspaper, *To Victory*, which had been set up for the 2nd Division of People's Volunteers.

Kochetov was especially proud because he had barely managed to become a war correspondent. He was exempt from military service because
of a heart illness and, not having military status, had not been picked to go
to the front by *Leningradskaya Pravda*. He wangled his assignment after
meeting Mikhalev and three other correspondents one day on the street.
They were all in brand-new uniforms. Kochetov was wearing a dark-blue
jacket and bright-colored shoes. Very thin, very gloomy, he begged his
colleagues: "Take me along, fellows." They interceded with the editor,
P. V. Zolotukhin, and now he and Mikhalev were on their way to the front
for the first time to visit the 2nd Division, located near Opolye, or, perhaps,
Veimarn or Ivanovskoye. No one quite knew. The night was lovely and
warm. There was hardly any traffic. They passed through Krasnoye Selo, a
dark quiet village, and the turn-off road to Ropsha, a place Kochetov knew
well. Ropsha had once been a hunting grounds of the czars. In the palace
where Peter III, husband of Catherine, was murdered in a drunken brawl
by the lover of his wife, Count Orlov, Kochetov and his fellow students at
the Agricultural School had had their dormitory.

It was hard to believe that war was at hand, but, at a crossroads, they saw a bullet-riddled truck. In the next village a church had been bombed. About sixty-five miles from Leningrad they came to Opolye, a big village of well-built houses, well-painted, tin-roofed. An archway led into what had been in the old days a horse market. They found that Comrade Molvo was fast asleep. Kochetov decided to leave the birthday cake until the morrow. He located an empty room above the village store and tumbled in for a little rest before setting out for the front. In the morning Kochetov was disappointed to see no signs of action. He went off to a hay barn, and there in its quiet coolness, with the comfortable feel of the new pistol in its shiny brown holster against his hip, drafted his first dispatch, which he optimistically datelined: "From the Fighting Front."

The bucolic scene at Opolye could hardly have been more deceptive. The truth was that Leningrad's defenses were in crisis. Once again the speed of von Leeb's Panzers had outpaced the desperate Soviet effort to erect a firm line. Racing on from Pskov the 41st Panzer Corps had driven straight along the highway toward Luga. They brushed aside the remnants of the 118th Soviet Rifles and crushed the 90th Infantry, which was just coming up, unaware that the Germans were at hand. The Panzers smashed across the river Plyussa, only eighteen miles from Luga, where they had finally been halted in desperate fighting.

While Kochetov blithely was driving through the night to the "front," the 41st Panzers had switched the axis of their attack and were moving northeast to ram a shattering blow at the very segment of the line which Kochetov had selected to visit.

By this time the Leningrad Command was in frenzy. Marshal Voroshilov had been named Supreme Commander on July 10. Three days later—why the delay?—Zhdanov was named his co-commander, or Military Council member.

Draconian measures were taken.

The whole Soviet command setup was being wildly shaken up in a desperate effort at survival. Aside from the replacement of General Kuznetsov as Northwest Front commander by General Sobennikov of the Eighth Army, Lieutenant General P. S. Klenov, Chief of Staff of the Northwest Front, was dismissed for incompetence and "weak leadership."

The situation on the Western Front was the same as that on the Northwest Front. Marshal (then General) A. I. Yeremenko, Soviet commander in the Far East, was called into Moscow. He left the Far East on June 22 and arrived (going most of the way by train!) on June 29. He was told by Marshal Timoshenko that the Western Front was in chaos and that the government had decided to remove General Dmitri Pavlov and his chief of staff, Major General V. Ye. Klimovsky, putting Yeremenko and Lieutenant G. K. Malandin in their places.

Yeremenko located Pavlov early the next morning, breakfasting in a small tent outside Mogilev, where he had set up his headquarters. Pavlov, one of

Russia's most experienced soldiers, veteran of the Spanish Civil War, greeted Yeremenko in his usual joking manner.

"How many years it's been!" he said with a smile. "What fate has brought you here? Will you stay long?"

For an answer Yeremenko handed over the order removing Pavlov from command. The General read it dumfounded and asked, "And where do I go?"

"The Commissar has ordered you to Moscow," Yeremenko said.

Pavlov blinked. Then, recovering his manners, he invited Yeremenko to join him at breakfast. Yeremenko declined, saying he had no time and needed an immediate briefing.

Pavlov sat silent for a moment or two, then began: "What can I tell you about the situation? The stunning blows of the enemy caught our troops by surprise. We were not ready for battle. We were in peacetime conditions, carrying out exercises in our camps and firing ranges. And, for this reason, we suffered heavy losses, in air power, artillery and tanks and in manpower, too. The enemy deeply penetrated our territory, occupying Bobruisk, Minsk."

Pavlov mentioned to Yeremenko the late hour at which he had received orders to go on Combat Alert.

While Pavlov and Yeremenko talked, Marshals Voroshilov and B. M. Shaposhnikov arrived at Pavlov's headquarters, driving up in a long black Packard limousine. They confirmed Pavlov's gloomy picture.

"It's a bad business," Voroshilov said. "There is no firm front. We have separate strongpoints in which our units are holding off the attacks of superior enemy forces. Communications with them are weak."

That afternoon Generals Pavlov and Klimovsky flew off to Moscow. Yeremenko never saw them again. They were shot immediately. Their guilt, in the view of Marshal S. S. Biryuzov, who knew them well, lay in the fact that to the very last moment they meticulously carried out the orders issued by Marshal Timoshenko and the General Staff at Stalin's personal direction.[1]

Creation of a new command in Leningrad did not provide troops for the Luga fortifications.

Against the crippled Soviet armies von Leeb was estimated to have 21 to 23 crack divisions of Group Nord, led by the redoubtable 4th Armored, possibly 340,000 men in all. He had 326 tanks and 6,000 guns. Soviet sources estimated German superiority July 10 at 2.4 times in infantry, 4 in artillery, 5.8 in mortars, 1.2 in tanks. The Northwest Front that day had 102 planes

---

[1] The removal from command of Generals Pavlov, Klimovsky and V. Ya. Semenov, Pavlov's Chief of Operations, had a grave effect on morale. General Shtemenko, an officer in Stavka, reports the action was not explained, that no one dared mention the names of the generals aloud. Stavka officers were badly affected. Suspicions and suspicious allegations began to be made within the Stavka but, he contends, were quelled by the Party Secretary at headquarters. (Shtemenko, *op. cit.*, p. 31.)

in service. Group Nord had about 1,000.

With the fall of Pskov the 4th Nazi Armored Group, now heading up the highway toward Luga, was breaking the way for an estimated dozen Nazi divisions. Six German divisions drove toward the Narva-Kingisepp sector.

Desperate, the Leningrad Command decided to shift forces from the north (where the Karelian front with the Finns was relatively inactive) to the Luga line.

The 10th Mechanized Corps and the 70th and 237th rifle divisions were ordered south. But before these crack units could get into position they were diverted by Voroshilov to the southeast to halt a threat of the Germans to overrun the Luga line by flanking it east of Lake Ilmen in the vicinity of Novgorod.

What was to be done now? Not many troops remained at Leningrad's disposal. Finally, General Pyadyshev was given the 191st Rifle Division to protect his right flank at Kingisepp and the 2nd Division of People's Volunteers just to the south. The key position in the middle of the Luga line was held by Colonel G. V. Mukhin and his cadets of the Leningrad Infantry School. To Mukhin's left was another People's Volunteer division, the 3rd. The 177th Rifle Division protected the approaches to Luga city and on the south; covering the span from Luga city to Lake Ilmen, were the 70th Rifle Division, the 1st People's Volunteers and the 1st Mountain Brigade. The units were strung like beads on a chain. The 191st had a fifty-mile front to defend, the 2nd Volunteers a thirty-mile front. The approaches to Kingisepp were covered only by the retreating 118th Division. There were gaps of as much as fifteen miles, not defended by any forces.

To back up this makeshift force Pyadyshev had a strong artillery unit, led by a brilliant young colonel, G. F. Odintsov, who was destined to play an outstanding role in the defense of Leningrad.

The artillery group was made up of a regiment of officers from the Red Army Higher Artillery School, a division of the 28th Corps Regiment, artillery regiments of the 1st, 2nd and 3rd Leningrad artillery schools and an antiaircraft unit from the Leningrad artillery technical schools. Later, the group acquired the 51st Corps Regiment, retreating from the Baltic.

Half of the manpower to defend the Luga line, thus, was People's Volunteers. The fate of Leningrad might well depend on how these hastily mobilized, totally untrained, poorly armed workers' battalions stood up under the hammer blows of Hitler's finest, fastest-moving, best-equipped Panzer spearheads.

Colonel Bychevsky spent July 11 on the Luga line. He installed heavy, electronically activated mines under some large buildings at Strugi Krasnye, Gorodishche and Nikolayevo, where German tanks could be expected at any moment. He placed a radio transmitter in a secluded corner of the big park at Gatchina, ready to transmit the signal touching off the electronic mines as soon as the Germans reached the three points.

All day Bychevsky encountered throngs of refugees, low-flying Messerschmitts, blown-up bridges, corpses beside the roads, fleeing soldiers and officers trying to rally them to a stand.

The night of the eleventh he was summoned with other top commanders to Smolny for a meeting with Voroshilov and Zhdanov. Voroshilov seemed nervous and ill at ease.

General Popov, the Leningrad field commander, a tall, rather handsome man who was always restless indoors, described the situation. Reports from the front were not clear and often contradicted each other. An argument quickly developed over the direction of the main German thrust. Deputy Commander Pyadyshev, leader of the Luga group, believed the Germans had reached the line of the 483rd Regiment of the 177th Division and were fighting on the river Plyussa. However, Major General A. A. Novikov, air commander of the front, contended that his reconnaissance showed the main German strength, two hundred tanks or so, was at Strugi Krasnye.

"What's the value of that kind of intelligence?" Voroshilov asked. "You haven't got a single prisoner, not one document. How many tanks are there at Strugi Krasnye? Who is moving on Gdov?"

General Pyotr P. Yevstigneyev, chief of intelligence, couldn't say.

"What units are approaching the Luga?" Voroshilov asked.

Yevstigneyev couldn't answer that either.

The weight of evidence seemed to indicate that the chief German attack was to be expected at Luga city on the direct road to Leningrad.

But what if the Germans struck south of Kingisepp? In that case the first units of the 2nd People's Volunteers should be arriving the next day at Veimarn, only a few miles from the Luga line. The crack infantry cadet school unit under Colonel Mukhin was already in position at nearby Sabsk. After examining the plans for the Luga fortified zone, Voroshilov and Zhdanov went to Novgorod, where the headquarters of the Northwest Front was then located. They spent the day of July 12 there and approved plans for a counterattack by the Eleventh Army against the fast-moving 56th Nazi Motorized Corps. They strengthened the Eleventh Army with a tank division and two infantry divisions and ordered the attack to be launched early in the morning of the fourteenth.[2]

On the twelfth and thirteenth Bychevsky was busy with fortifications and mining. Soon after dawn on the thirteenth he transmitted the radio signal that touched off the three great bombs he had put under the buildings at Strugi Krasnye. German motorized units were quartered there and the casualties were large. That evening, back at Smolny, Voroshilov and Zhdanov called in the commanders and political commissars of four newly formed guerrilla battalions, each composed of 10 units numbering 80 to 100 men. They were ordered immediately to cut behind the German lines and

---

[2] *N.Z.*, p. 63. The date of the Voroshilov-Zhdanov visit is mistakenly given as July 14 by A. N. Tsamumali (*Na Beregakh Volkhova*, Leningrad, 1967, p. 7).

attempt by any possible means to halt or hamper the pace of Nazi advance. They had orders to attack units of Nazi motorized infantry, blow up bridges, destroy communications, burn supply dumps and warehouses left in the wake of the hectic Russian retreat and carry out other "special tasks." Before dawn the "destroyer" battalions, as the Russians called them, had been transported to the Gdov-Slantsy area and left to make their way behind the lines.

There was an atmosphere of desperation about every act of the High Command. A few hours after the "destroyer" groups had been dispatched, early on the fourteenth, Bychevsky got a frantic call from Leningrad. The 41st Panzers had smashed into Porechye, crossed the Luga River and the fortified line, seizing a foothold at Ivanovskoye within the Soviet defense system. A similar attempt at Sabsk had been narrowly beaten off by the infantry school men.

Porechye was the heart of the 2nd People's Volunteers sector. Once again the Germans had reached the line before the Soviet troops. Twenty German tanks roared through Porechye and into Ivanovskoye, just beyond it, as the first units of the 2nd Volunteers clambered out of the boxcars which had brought them up from Leningrad.[3] When they formed up hastily to march to Ivanovskoye, they were hit by the Germans. Firing seemed to come from every direction. Peasant *telegi* or carts creaked down the road. Goats bleated. Horses neighed. The Volunteers began to drop, wounded or dead. Those who had guns fired wildly, often standing at full height with weapons on their shoulders as though on the rifle range. The Germans replied with cannon over open sights. Soon the dry turf and the forest debris caught fire, sending clouds of smoke billowing over the scene.

If the Germans broke through here, they had a smooth highway sixty miles to the Winter Palace. There was not a single organized unit, not one manned defense position, to halt them all the way to Leningrad.

The telephone call which Bychevsky received from Leningrad ordered him to report immediately to the Commander in Chief and bring with him a company of field engineers. Leningrad told him they were dispatching a thousand mines by truck. Bychevsky gathered up the 106th Sappers Battalion and, traveling a roundabout way to avoid Nazi dive-bomber attacks, managed to get to command headquarters in five hours. He found the whole Leningrad Front Command there, including both General Popov and Marshal Voroshilov.

The two generals were standing on an open hillside about five hundred yards from Ivanovskoye, watching the 2nd Volunteers straggle back from an unsuccessful counterattack.

[3] Actually, the Volunteers assumed they were going to a quiet sector of the lines where they would be able to complete their scanty training before going into action. Many had never fired a gun or thrown a grenade. (Vissarion Sayanov, *Leningradskii Dnevnik*, Leningrad, 1958, p. 25.)

Soviet artillery was laying shells into the center of Ivanovskoye. The *izbas* were going up in clouds of smoke. Through his binoculars Bychevsky saw German tanks moving through the smoke to the edge of the village, their ugly guns flashing with fire. Three or four bawling goats stood still tethered to wooden slat fences in front of the *izbas*.

Voroshilov greeted Bychevsky rudely. He snapped, "Sappers are always late!" Then he turned and, paying no heed to shells bursting nearby or to the splinters whistling through the air, continued to examine the battlefield.

Bychevsky heard some machine gunners talking:

"That's him—Voroshilov! Klim!"

"Look how he stands, as though he grew out of the earth."

"My mother says there are people who have a charm against bullets."

"Bullets maybe. But those are shells!"

Voroshilov was not amused at what he saw. He wanted to know why the artillery was firing on an empty village with the German armor already on the outskirts. Popov started to explain that the artillery hadn't had time to reconnoiter the village, then broke off. Before Voroshilov could interfere Popov climbed into a tank and headed for the village himself.

"What the hell!" Voroshilov shouted, clapping his hands.

Soon, however, the tank was hit by a shell and lumbered back. Popov climbed out, shaken.

"What's the idea?" Voroshilov yelled. "Have you lost your mind? If you are going to reconnoiter the positions, who's going to command the front?"

Voroshilov encountered a pretty Red Cross girl named Klavdia and told her she should not be in such a dangerous position. Klavdia pertly replied: "And what about you, Comrade Marshal? You go right to the center of the fire. Why? Because you are needed. I go where I'm needed—to where the wounded lie."

A few moments later Popov and Voroshilov whirled off. Not, however, without leaving orders that the *place d'armes* at Porechye-Ivanovskoye be promptly liquidated—orders that cost the 2nd People's Volunteers dearly in a vain attempt at fulfillment. Years later the picture of the corpse-strewn battlefield was still in the mind of a participant.

For all his warnings to Popov about reckless conduct, Voroshilov found it hard to restrain himself. On the same part of the front at the village of Sredneye, a few miles from Ivanovskoye, troops of the 2nd Volunteers had broken under a German attack just as Voroshilov came up. They were falling back in ones and twos and small groups. Voroshilov got out of his command car and personally halted the retreating men. At this moment a Soviet tank unit and some infantry reinforcements appeared. Drawing his pistol, the sixty-year-old hero of the Bolshevik Civil War led the troops across the field toward the Germans. The shout of "Hurrah!" rang out. The German attack petered out, and the 2nd Volunteers stiffened their lines, their morale restored by the old cavalryman's personal example of bravery.

The fourteenth was a day of dark alarms. The Germans crossed the Luga on the Sabsk front held by the infantry cadets but made little progress in sharp fighting. The Russians could not dislodge them from Porechye no matter how hard they tried.

In an effort to stiffen the crumbling People's Volunteers, the Supreme Defense Command in Moscow agreed to release to each infantry division three to five tanks, either the monster KV's or the work-horse T-34's.

Before the day was over Zhdanov issued in his name and that of Voroshilov a decree or *Prikaz* which was the first of what was to be a series of dramatic exhortations.

"Comrade Red Army men! Commanders and political workers!" it began. "Over the city of Lenin, the cradle of the Proletarian Revolution, there looms the immediate danger of the invading enemy."

The decree took note of what was a fact—the disorder and panic that were engulfing the front. "Individual panicmongers and cowards," said the *Prikaz*, "not only voluntarily leave the front, but they sow disorder among the ranks of honest and brave soldiers. Commanders and political workers not only do not suppress panic but do not organize and lead their units in battle. By their shameful conduct they even increase disorganization and fear along the front lines."

The proclamation decreed that anyone leaving the front regardless of rank or responsibility would go before a field tribunal and be shot on the spot.

Confusion and tension had been heightened by the alarming reports from the Supreme Command in Moscow. On July 10 the Supreme Command warned the Leningrad Command that the Germans planned a mass paratroop attack on the Leningrad area. Leningrad was ordered to strengthen its air reconnaissance and create reserves (from what?) of fighter and bomber aircraft to wipe out the Nazis when they landed.

New air observation points were set up throughout Leningrad, hasty efforts were made to mobilize the population for defense (youngsters eight to sixteen were to be trained to fight in hand-to-hand combat). An effort was made to turn the whole area into a hornet's nest of fire points from which the Germans would not emerge alive.

The landing of the Germans never occurred. It was one of many such rumors which swept Leningrad. Because of the Nazi tactics in the West the Russians feared, above almost any other possibility, German air and sea landings behind their lines.

The speed with which the Germans penetrated the Luga line stimulated Zhdanov to redoubled efforts to fortify the near approaches to Leningrad. He placed his first deputy, Party Secretary Aleksei A. Kuznetsov, in charge of this work, with Bychevsky as his chief lieutenant.

One of Kuznetsov's first acts was to call in the NKVD and mobilize all the prisoners in the NKVD labor camps. The prisoners were sent first to the Kingisepp region, where there was every reason to anticipate an early breakthrough. Because of constant German air attack the women who had been working there were transferred to locations closer to Leningrad.

Colonel Bychevsky, the tireless engineer, was fond of Kuznetsov, whom he called the "human spring" because his energy and even temper seemed inexhaustible. Kuznetsov was under forty, very thin, very pale. His sharp face and nose gave him an appearance of strictness, but Kuznetsov was soft, attentive and almost always tactful. He seldom raised his voice, and he did not rebuke people without reason. In this he was in sharp contrast to many Party executives, including his chief, Andrei Zhdanov.

One night Bychevsky was working at his desk. It was 4 A.M. The telephone rang. It was Kuznetsov, asking him to come immediately to the Mariinsky Theater. Bychevsky could not imagine what emergency had arisen. He hurried to the theater, where he found Kuznetsov bubbling with excitement. He showed Bychevsky an array of papier-mâché guns and tanks which the theater's scenic artists had built. He proposed to issue immediate orders to get the decoys up to suitable positions behind the front.

Now there came a momentary respite in the Nazi pressure. The battered Soviet Eleventh Army, protecting the approaches to Shimsk, the Lake Ilmen anchor of the Luga line, had been reinforced with troops from the Karelia front—the 21st Tank Division, the 70th Guards and the 237th Rifle Division. Finding Manstein's 56th Motorized Corps badly exposed, the Soviet force struck in a pincers attack. Between July 14 and 18 they drove the Germans back nearly thirty miles.

As Manstein dryly noted: "It's impossible to say that the position of the corps at this moment is very enviable. The last few days have been critical, and the enemy with all his strength is attempting to close the ring of encirclement." The 8th Nazi Panzer Division had to retire for refitting. The 56th lost about four hundred vehicles. The immediate threat to Novgorod was liquidated. For the moment Leningrad could breathe a bit easier.

Hitler showed some concern over the situation. In a directive of July 19 he warned that further advance toward Leningrad could be achieved only when the eastern flank of Group Nord had been secured by the Sixteenth Army. The 3rd Panzer Group of Army Group Center was switched to a northeast axis in order to cut connections between the Leningrad front and Moscow and shore up the right flank of von Leeb's forces.

Hitler followed his admonitions with a personal visit to von Leeb's headquarters July 21 at which he demanded that Leningrad be "finished off speedily."

Nikolai Tikhonov and Vissarion Sayanov visited Major General Andrei E. Fedyunin, commander of the 70th Guards, after his successful rollback of von Manstein's 56th Motorized Corps. Fedyunin's headquarters were in Sheloni, in a clearing amid a defense forest, near a big village called Medved (Bear). Tikhonov had known Fedyunin in the days of the winter war with

Finland. It was a hot summer day, a good day for picking berries, for sauntering in the woods and finding a cool stream to lie beside.

For nearly ten days his front had been quiet. But General Fedyunin was neither relaxed nor cheerful.

"This quiet is deceptive," he said. "It will happen—and soon. We helped our Luga force, but now the enemy has regrouped. He will hit us here. Not this division, perhaps. He knows us. We have licked him. But he will hit the 1st Volunteers and move on Novgorod. . . . It is going to be hard for us, but we have no alternative: fight to the last!"

Tikhonov and Sayanov watched the shadows grow longer. Toward evening a woman came by with a shovel. A guard stopped her and told her the Germans were laying mortar fire into her potato field. She shrugged her shoulders and went on. "It will be dark; maybe they won't see me," she said.

Someone asked General Fedyunin why he was wearing his dress uniform. He laughed. He had been wearing it when the war started and hadn't gotten around to getting his field clothes sent to him.

"I'll do it tomorrow," he said.

The correspondents went their way. A day later, August 13, Tikhonov was in Novgorod, the most ancient of Russian cities. Its old walls rattled to the sound of artillery fire. People streamed through the square. The Novgorod lands were once again aflame with war.

Tikhonov asked an officer about the 70th Guards. They were falling back northwest of the city, the officer said, under attack by fresh German divisions.

"When did you leave the 70th?" the officer asked.

Tikhonov told him. "You're lucky," the officer replied. "The Germans hit an hour later. General Fedyunin has been killed."[4]

The Germans were not the only enemy.

Bychevsky worked almost daily in close liaison with Lieutenant General K. P. Pyadyshev, commander of the Luga Operating Group defending the Luga line. On July 23 Bychevsky received a copy of a new order dividing the Luga front into three sectors, each with an individual commander and staff. This might make some sense, Bychevsky thought. After all, Supreme Headquarters as early as July 15 had recommended reducing the size of units since so many Soviet commanders had proved incapable of handling large bodies of troops. But each division of the front increased the chance of openings on the flanks, of bad liaison, of gaps through which German armor could penetrate. This had been the story of the German success to now. Why suddenly split the Luga line? And what about Pyadyshev? There was nothing in the communiqué to indicate his assignment. "Pyadyshev,"

---

[4] General Fedyunin committed suicide. He shot himself rather than fall captive to the Nazis. However, some of his troops escaped and brought his body out with them. (Sayanov, *op. cit.*, p. 36.)

Bychevsky noted, "simply vanished from the horizon."

Rumors began to circulate that Pyadyshev had been arrested. Bychevsky did not want to believe this. He asked the Chief of Staff, General Nikishev. Nikishev replied: "I don't know"—and made plain he wanted no more talk about the matter.

Pyadyshev was no military novice. For ten years he had served in the Leningrad Military District. In the 1930's he headed military schools and conducted exercises and maneuvers. He had been chief of various commissions entrusted with work on Leningrad's fortifications. He wore two Orders of the Red Banner, won in victories in the Civil War. He was a military scholar, a man of tact and even temper, straightforward in personal relations and solicitous of the opinion of others.

It had been thanks to his initiative, in the absence of Zhdanov and of Popov, that work had got under way so rapidly on the Luga line. He it was who organized the special Luga artillery group and the units from the military schools. Bychevsky's high opinion of Pyadyshev was not unique. General Mikhail Dukhanov, another Leningrad veteran, called him one of the best officers in the command, a man of wisdom, experience and vigor, exceptionally able at preparing troops for battle and directing them, even in a situation in which blunder and confusion were inescapable.

Neither the reason nor the circumstances of Pyadyshev's arrest were ever made known. Even today no public explanation has been given.[5]

However, Pyadyshev's removal was only one of a series of moves taken on July 23. A unified antiaircraft command was created, covering not only the fighting fronts but also Leningrad itself. The direction of defense construction in the Luga zone was lodged in a troika headed by Party Secretary Kuznetsov, and the fortifications work was divided into five sectors.

One other event may have been connected with this shake-up. On July 23, Vyacheslav A. Malyshev, Commissar of Heavy Machine Building, telephoned the great Kirov factory and gave the plant director personal instructions for the organization of antiaircraft defense and fire-protection activities.

The impression left by these moves is one of frenetic activity, bordering on hysteria if not panic.

Perhaps Pyadyshev was shot to show his fellow officers that the warning in the Voroshilov-Zhdanov decree of July 14 meant business. Or perhaps he fell victim to a secret police plot, too confused, too complex, ever to be sorted out.

Later on, after the war, when Soviet military historians began to examine the Leningrad battle, they tended to give more and more credit to the Luga line for saving the city from total disaster. The Germans were held up on the Luga front from July 9 or 10 to August 8—close to a month. The blitzkrieg was thrown off pace, the Nazi timetable out of balance. The date for Hitler's

[5] After the Twentieth Congress of the Communist Party in 1956 Pyadyshev was publicly "rehabilitated."

victory parade on Palace Square had to be postponed and then postponed again. During the month, despite fierce fighting, despite unconscionable Soviet losses, only minor German penetrations were made from Kingisepp to Lake Ilmen and old Novgorod. The line held. It held in spite of casualties that almost wiped out the units of the People's Volunteers—losses which an experienced officer like Dmitri Konstantinov regarded as sheer scandal. Even F. I. Sirota, a patriotic historian of the Leningrad epic, conceded the "very low military capability of the People's Volunteers." The officers were no more experienced than the men. Brigadier Commander Malinnikov of the 1st Volunteers, the highly regarded Kirov division, had to be removed for what was euphemistically called "losing direction of his troops." The fact was that many Volunteers broke and fled, and no one could have halted them. The men had no training and few arms. Often they did not even remember to fire their guns at the enemy. So many lost their weapons in their first engagements that army propagandists launched a special campaign of slogans: "The weapon is the power of the soldier." "To lose your gun is a crime against the Motherland."

After disastrous experiences with the 2nd People's Volunteers, steps were ordered to try to give these units a more experienced officer cadre. When the 2nd Guards Division of People's Volunteers was formed, its officers and commissars were called to Smolny and then sent out to towns near Leningrad to try to enlist volunteers with some military experience. Some were found in Novgorod, and one hundred were brought in from the Urals. Despite all this Voroshilov and Zhdanov found the division poorly organized, trained and led.

Nor was it only the wanton sacrifice of the Volunteers. General Dukhanov never was able to reconcile himself to the use of the infantry school cadets as a line regiment. These were fifteen hundred infantry officers, veterans of the Finnish war, who had been taking advanced training courses when war broke out. Almost all had battle experience and command experience. There was nothing—nothing—the Leningrad forces needed more than battletrained, command-experienced officers. To use these men as cannon fodder to halt the Nazi battering ram with the naked bayonet—this was military insanity. General Pyadyshev agreed with Dukhanov. At the first opportunity he planned to take them out of the line. Before the chance came, Pyadyshev had been dismissed and shot; most of the infantry school men had died in battle.

In the end, of course, the lines could not be held. Under the conditions which Dukhanov found when he himself was directed on July 19 to take over command of the Sabsk-Ivanovskoye sector of the Luga line, it was a miracle they had held so long. This was the section of the line manned by the cadet officers and the 2nd Volunteers. When Dukhanov arrived at Volosovo, the point where he was to meet his troops, he found only Commandant (now Colonel General) A. D. Tsirlin of the Engineers Academy, an adjutant, a driver, and an engineers detachment. The other units were in the lines. There was no means of communicating with them.

"This is like a fairy tale," Tsirlin said. "There isn't enough of anything. There is a staff of three men and a command post on wheels. For means of communication, you have yourself. And the units are scattered like seeds in a field."

While hunting the command post of the infantry school unit Dukhanov met a communications unit. He asked the commander whose it was. "We're assigned to General Dukhanov," the officer replied.

"Where is he to be found?" Dukhanov asked.

"Who knows?" the commander said. "I was told to come to Sabsk and I'd find him there. We're looking right now."

Dukhanov told him his search had ended. But he still had to find the Kirov infantry command post. Hearing the rumble of artillery fire, he ordered his driver to put on speed. They met a truck driver, who motioned them to halt.

"What's the matter?" the General asked.

"Tanks. German tanks have broken through the infantry school front." The soldier spoke quickly and in panic. Dukhanov hurried forward and found that, true enough, two tanks had broken through, but both had been destroyed. They lay afire in an antitank ditch.

In these days the writer Dmitri Shcheglov was still training in the officers' short course of the People's Volunteers. His unit was quartered in the Pavlovsky Barracks where the Czar's Life Guards once made their headquarters. The Pavlovsky corridors were filled with iron cots for the Volunteers. They drilled on the Champs de Mars amid rows of AA guns manned by solemn-faced girls, installed in dugouts and earthen huts, dug into the ancient czarist parade grounds. Every evening Shcheglov went for a walk in the old gardens next to the Russian Museum. It was a secluded spot, an historic one.

Shcheglov's spirits were buoyant. He had heard of the success of the counteroffensive near Shimsk in which the 56th German Panzers were bloodied. At last the Nazis were being held up. Soon, it might be, the Russians would have their day. But quickly the news was bad again. The Germans had broken through to the river Plyussa.

The Volunteers had a concert on the evening of July 26. Yelena Rubina, a poetess, gave an imitation of Hitler: "Everything's fine, I swear, *mein Führer*." It was a great success. Then Nikolai Cherkasov recited the monologue of old Professor Polezhayev in the great patriotic film, *Deputy of the Baltic*, winding up with the line: "Happy journey to you, you Red fighters."

On July 30 the Volunteers were called together. The next day they were to leave for the front.

Shcheglov spoke.

"Comrades," he said, "many of us here are fathers. Each of us must face the future—our children to whom we must give an answer. Our sons and daughters someday will ask, 'What did you do to beat the enemy?' And not only our children will ask—their mothers and our wives will ask, 'What did you do to destroy the invaders?' How and what our answers shall be soon will be clear."

The men cheered. The next day most of them were assigned to units, but Shcheglov was held up in Leningrad. He was still in Leningrad four days later when his daughter returned from digging trenches at Kingisepp. She had walked nearly thirty-five miles and caught the last train from Izhorsk, fighting her way onto the car and clinging to the hand grasp and the lower step.

"The enemy is near," Shcheglov noted in his diary.

He was, indeed. And soon he would be much nearer.

19 . *The Luga Line Crumbles*

ON HIS CEASELESS, NEVER COMPLETED EFFORT TO BUILD some kind of barrier that would slow the German advance Colonel Bychevsky found himself spending the night of August 7–8 with Colonel G. V. Mukhin and the remnants of the infantry cadet school. At eight in the morning the dugout where he sat with Mukhin shook as though an earthquake had struck. Every timber quivered and earth trickled down between the planks like rivulets of water. The German offensive to crush the Luga line had started.

Von Leeb had been reshuffling his forces. Operating under a new directive from the Supreme Command, Directive No. 34, issued July 30, his two armies and the redoubtable 4th Panzers had been strengthened by the assignment of the 8th Air Corps of attack bombers. Von Leeb's task was to break through the Soviet defenses on the Luga, encircle Leningrad and make contact with the Finnish armies on the Karelian peninsula.

Von Leeb now had at his disposal twenty-nine divisions of 80 to 90 percent muster strength. Against him were fifteen weak Soviet divisions. Halder noted in his diary for August 3 that in view of the disparity "Army Group Nord obviously should not meet with irresistible difficulties."

Von Leeb had divided his armies into three groups. The 41st Motorized and 38th Army Corps of the 4th Panzer Group were assigned to strike at Ivanovskoye and Sabsk, aiming for Leningrad via the Koporsky Plateau. To the north and west von Leeb had placed the 58th Nazi Infantry which covered the territory from the source of the river Plyussa to Peipus Lake.

Just to the south was what von Leeb called his Luga group—three divisions and the 56th Motorized Corps of the 4th Panzers. This was to strike for Leningrad via Luga city and the direct Luga-Leningrad highway. The 8th Panzer Division was held in reserve here.

The southernmost group comprised the 28th and 1st Army Corps, aimed at the Novgorod-Chudovo front held by the Forty-eighth Soviet Army.

Von Leeb hoped soon to have the five divisions of his Eighteenth Army, now occupied in the investment of Tallinn, available to add punch to his offensive. Further south his Sixteenth Army was pushing around Lake Ilmen against the Soviet Eleventh and Twenty-seventh armies.

The thunderous cannonading which shook the timbers of the dugout in which Bychevsky sat with Mukhin marked the launching of von Leeb's attack.

An adjutant shouted to Bychevsky: "Last night one of our scouts went to Redkino. He counted about sixty Nazi tanks there. And we haven't much artillery."

Mukhin and Bychevsky slithered along a lateral trench to an observation point in the forward line. They saw a flight of thirty Junkers-88's roaring in low over the lines. Nine peeled off and dropped their bombs as the officers slid for cover into a sandbagged dugout.

After a half-hour preparation the German artillery halted. Mukhin was on the field telephone to Captain Volkhov of his 2nd Battalion. Twenty-five tanks were bearing down on Volkhov's position. Five minutes later Volkhov reported three tanks afire and German infantry attacking. Mukhin called a bit later. The attack had been beaten off.

Vsevolod Kochetov, the fledgling war correspondent, and his companion Mikhalev spent the night of August 7–8 camping among the gravestones in a churchyard at Opolye. It was a dry, warm night. Kochetov had managed to acquire a carbine to add to his TT revolver. His pockets were filled with grenades, and he was using a field knapsack for a pillow. It was stuffed with his battered notebooks, towels, soap and a razor.

The reason Kochetov was spending the night in such a high degree of military preparedness, as he later explained, was that there were so many signs of an imminent German offensive.

He was awakened by what sounded to him like a volcanic eruption. A blinding light flashed over the horizon. The earth shook. Kochetov guessed that railroad artillery must be in action.

He started out for the 2nd People's Volunteers but found the roads jammed with ambulances, communications cars, motorcyclists, refugees driving cows, goats and pigs, and peasants pulling cartloads of household goods. Alongside the mob ran dozens of mongrel dogs, howling and barking. Kochetov decided to make for the infantry cadet school sector instead. Reaching the village of Yablonitsy, he and Mikhalev encountered a full-scale retreat—Red Army trucks, heavy guns, mobile radio transmitters, crowds of soldiers, tired, dirty-faced, bandaged, some with glazed eyes, many without weapons. Behind them could be heard the sound of heavy guns.

Kochetov had never seen a retreat before. It was a terrifying sight—soldiers, soldiers, soldiers, hopelessly slogging along the road. No one in charge, no one to direct the men, no way to halt the hopeless tide of humanity. Finally he saw a lieutenant and asked where the infantry school men were.

"They are still there," the lieutenant said, waving back toward the battle-field.

Kochetov talked to some of the retreating men. They told of the over-whelming German fire, of the terrible tanks, of the paratroops, of the en-circling movements. The Germans, it appeared, were all-powerful, merciless, unconquerable. Their army was an irresistible machine. They were raining down leaflets conveying the (false) claim that Leningrad and Kiev had already fallen.

The situation was not quite so terrifying as it seemed to the inexperienced Kochetov. But it was difficult. He decided to abandon his search for the infantry school outfit.

In reality, bad as things looked from the Russian side, they looked none too good from the German. Halder noted in his diary for August 10 that von Leeb's gains had been "very insignificant."

"What we are doing now," he wrote, "is the last desperate attempt to prevent our front line becoming frozen in positional warfare. . . . The critical situation makes it increasingly plain that we underestimated the Russian colossus."

The front was devouring Soviet manpower voraciously. On July 23 Zhdanov ordered 105,000 persons mobilized for work on the Luga fortified line and 87,000 for work in the Gatchina fortified area. Local Party secretaries got the order shortly before noon and were instructed to have the cadres ready with equipment, shovels, picks and field rations by 5 P.M.

Party workers were sent out on mission after mission to spur the work, for in some places morale was bad and crews were influenced by German leaflets emphasizing the futility of resistance. Three secretaries, V. S. Yef-remov, A. M. Grigoryev and P. A. Ivanov, were sent to the Kingisepp region. They arrived about 8 A.M., July 28.

"The residents had already fled," Ivanov recalled. "The city was burning. The only force remaining was a unit of railroad troops defending the station and getting ready to blow up the bridge across the river.

"The next morning we went to Veimarn, where there were still some echelons at work on fortifications. We had only begun to assign the people to their tasks when a flight of Junkers came over the station. Some of the people took cover in the woods. But there were many casualties. Hundreds of them went on to their tasks, working first under air attack and then under mortar fire. They performed no worse than experienced army sappers."

Although between 500,000 and 1,000,000 Leningraders[1] had been mobilized for work on trenches and fortifications—even children of fourteen and fifteen were laboring in the field—there were never enough hands. Thirty thousand were put to work on the Koporsky Plateau, between Kingisepp and Leningrad. Nearly 100,000 worked in the Gatchina area.

Notice after notice appeared on factory and office bulletin boards. The

[1] The figure was "up to 500,000" by the end of July or early August. (N.Z., p. 80.)

board at the Hermitage Museum was covered with calls: "To the trenches!"
"At Luga—to the trenches!" "At Kingisepp—to the trenches!" Ada Vilm,
the scientific secretary of the Hermitage, went with a group of workers near
Tolmachevo. It was a place she had known since childhood. Here she had
picked berries and gathered mushrooms. Here she had strolled through the
long summer nights. Now she and her comrades dug trenches.

"When we arrived with spades, picks and shovels," she recalled, "the constant sound of the artillery cannonade was still distant. Then we became
accustomed to the whine of shells, to nearby explosions.

"We went on digging until the Fascist tanks approached our sector. That
evening we were prepared to return to Leningrad."

By that time Tolmachevo had fallen and the flames of burning Luga
reached toward the sky. The Hermitage workers struggled all night through
the forest and at dawn came to a station where they caught the last train
back to Leningrad.

Dirty, dusty, exhausted, their clothes torn and grimy, packsacks on their
backs, shovels in hand, they arrived back at the Hermitage and were called
immediately to a meeting addressed by Militsa Mate, deputy director, in
charge of packing the third trainload of Hermitage treasures. No time must
be lost. To work! To work!

General Popov and Party Secretary A. A. Kuznetsov were constantly on
the move to try to stiffen the front. Now they were with Mukhin and the
infantry cadets; now with the 2nd People's Volunteers; now with Major
General V. V. Semashko, commander of this whole sector, including Kingisepp.

They threw into the lines another People's Volunteer Division, the 4th,
and attempted to carry out a counterattack together with the Kirov men.
The 4th Division numbered 10,815 men, including 2,850 Communists and
Young Communists. But it had only 270 machine guns, 32 cannon and 78
mortars. Only one out of 10 officers had had army experience.[2]

The task was hopeless. The Soviets ran up against five German divisions,
including two Panzers. The attack fell apart, its direction confused, its communications shot to bits.

Bychevsky walked into Semashko's headquarters toward the end of an
ugly post-mortem on the night of August 11.

Kuznetsov was upbraiding Semashko for faulty direction of the 4th Volunteers. "Remember," Kuznetsov said sharply, "these are the workers of
Leningrad."

[2] On July 25 the Military Council had ordered the formation of four more divisions of
People's Volunteers from the 34,000 enrollees still in the city. They were to be called
Guards Volunteers. The 1st went into the lines at Volosovo August 11, the 2nd at
Gatchina on the seventeenth, the 3rd at Ropsha. The 4th was reorganized as the 5th
before ever going into service. It went into the Pulkovo line September 12–13. The 6th
went into action at the Rybatskoye meat plant September 16 and the 7th at Avtovo
September 30.

"Aleksei Aleksandrovich," protested Semashko. "I don't want to throw the tiniest shadow of doubt on the working people. But this division was formed three days ago. It hasn't had a drop of fighting experience. The men have never even fired a gun. They marched twenty-five miles to take up their position, and I had already been ordered to carry out the counterattack. And they immediately ran into tanks. . . ."

"Untrained, never under fire," Kuznetsov snapped. "And who held up the enemy for a whole month on the Luga line but the People's Volunteers? Who on this very day set fire to half a hundred tanks? The brothers Ivanov and other workers from the Meat Combine! They hadn't been under fire either, but they fought back with Molotov cocktails. . . . Comrade Semashko, we haven't any other division to send you. You are going to have to do with what you have.

"And the road from Kingisepp to Volosovo is not to be cut by the enemy. That is the categorical order of the Military Council."

"Yes, sir," said Semashko, looking at his watch. "It will soon be dawn." He left the dugout to do what he could.

General Popov remained in the shelter, pacing like a tiger from corner to corner. He nervously snapped his finger joints.

"The whole 4th Panzers is hitting here, the bastards," he said. "There'll be two times two hundred tanks here before long."

Semashko had less than fifty tanks left.

His lines did not hold despite the categorical orders of the Military Council, despite the fighting qualities of the Leningrad workers, despite the threats of Kuznetsov. The line from Kingisepp to Volosovo was cut—and within twenty-four hours. No orders, no heroism, no blood could halt the Nazi Panzers. Thousands of men and women worked on antitank ditches and trenches. They dug and dug and dug. But the lines could not hold. Von Leeb threw in his reserve Panzer division—the 8th. It cut the Kingisepp-Gatchina railroad August 12 and captured Veimarn. Kingisepp was doomed. But the Red Army fought on. It was almost driven out of the city August 13 but fought back in. On August 16 the defenders, exhausted, dirty, wounded, slipped out and fell back toward the Gatchina fortified zone. But the battle was still not over. On the twentieth the 11th Soviet Rifles stormed Kingisepp from the west and briefly liberated it. They were thrown out in less than twenty-four hours.

Once the line started to crumble, it crumbled almost everywhere. It fell apart along the Luga. The Novgorod position disintegrated almost at the same moment. Novgorod fell August 13 despite valiant counterattacks by the Forty-eighth and Eleventh Soviet armies. Faulty staff work by the Thirty-fourth Soviet Army, which was supposed to join the operation, bungled the desperate Soviet effort. The Germans won control of the whole Lake Ilmen–Staraya Russa position and drove the Russians back of the river Lovat by August 25.

The cost to the Russians of this kind of fighting may be judged from the roster of the Forty-eighth Soviet Army, commanded by Major General S. D. Akimov, after it had retired north where it tried to hold a thirty-mile front around Lake Peipus. As of August 24 this army—so called—had a total strength of 6,235 men. It had 5,043 rifles, or a ratio of five rifles to every six men. It had 31 heavy weapons—three 45-mm's, ten 76-mm's, twelve antiaircraft 76-mm field guns, four 122-mm mortars and two 152-mm mortars. It had 104 machine guns and 75 submachine guns.

In fact, the Forty-eighth Army was the equal in numbers (but not in arms) to a half-strength peacetime Soviet division.

The Forty-eighth Army was more badly mauled than some units defending Leningrad. But not much. Nor were the German losses light. One Nazi officer called the Luga offensive "the road of death." General Höppner, commanding the German 4th Panzers, noted that his men had to fight their way through 1,236 field fortified points and 26,588 mines.

There was some truth in the call which von Leeb broadcast to his troops as they crashed forward across the Luga line:

"Soldiers! You see before you not only the remains of the Bolshevik Army but the last inhabitants of Leningrad. The city is empty. One last push and the Army Group Nord will celebrate victory!

"Soon the battle with Russia will be ended!"

But as von Leeb rallied his troops with these ringing words, he was using quite different ones in his desperate appeals for reinforcement and aid to the German Supreme Command. Halder reported grimly on August 15 that because of the punishment von Leeb was taking "there will be no way of getting around issuing the order for transfer to Army Group Nord of the motorized corps. To my mind it is a grave mistake." He noted further that "wild requests by Army Group Nord for engineering troops, artillery, antiaircraft, antitank units (on top of three armored divisions) are turned down."

Day by day, hour by hour, the options open to the Leningrad Command diminished.

Tallinn, the Baltic Fleet base, had been left to the rear, fighting in close encirclement. How long it might hold on was questionable. The Karelian front was coming apart as Voroshilov and Zhdanov bled it of troops to reinforce the line just outside Leningrad. At any moment the Finns and Germans might break through north of the city.

There were no reserves left. As Leningrad's Chief of Staff, General Nikishev, reported to Marshal B. M. Shaposhnikov, Chief of Staff of the High Command, August 13: "The difficulty in the present situation is that neither the commanders of divisions, the commanders of armies, nor the commanders of fronts have any reserves whatever. Even the smallest breakthrough can be halted only by hurried improvisations of one unit or another."

Nikishev told Shaposhnikov that the Leningrad front had little left with which to oppose von Leeb beyond the untrained People's Volunteers and the battered units which had fallen back all the way from Lithuania and Latvia.

These forces, Nikishev declared, simply could not be expected to stop the Germans, who continued to throw into battle relatively intact motorized and armored units.

His request to the General Staff was staggering: "a minimum" of 12 divisions, 400 planes and 250 tanks.

Nikishev told Bychevsky about his letter to the General Staff sometime between 5 and 6 A.M. on the morning of August 14 when Bychevsky called to get the latest information. This was the only quiet hour of twenty-four at Nikishev's headquarters. The General had the habit of snatching an hour or two of sleep, his head buried in the papers on his desk and his hand still grasping his pen.

Tired and bitter, Nikishev asked Bychevsky whether he thought the General Staff would provide the troops to save Leningrad. Nikishev glanced at the wall where the map of the front showed the blue arrows of Nazi columns penetrating deeply into the front. He did not wait for an answer.

"Well, of course," Nikishev said. "They won't give us the troops. But we had to send the request just the same."

Nikishev was bitter at Voroshilov, Chief of the Leningrad High Command, whom he blamed for siphoning off troops from the northern sector to the Northwest Front of the Leningrad region.

Three days later orders came from Moscow, responding to Nikishev's plea. Three divisions were transferred from the Northwest Front to the Northern Front (the main Leningrad front) and on the nineteenth the Forty-eighth Army was shifted from the Northwest to the Northern Front.

The military value of the move was dubious. In fact, it may have opened the path to German encirclement of Leningrad.

The Northwest Front had launched a fairly successful counterattack in the region of Staraya Russa and had driven the Nazis back thirty or thirty-five miles. To counter the blow, von Leeb had been compelled to put his 56th Motorized Corps and his SS Death's Head Division into action in the Staraya Russa area. He also committed the 39th Motorized Corps, which had been shifted up from Smolensk. The Germans described their plight as a "temporary crisis."

The Soviet Eleventh and Thirty-fourth armies were holding off this Nazi counterattack, although they were no real match for such a powerful striking force. Moreover, the Thirty-fourth Soviet Army, in particular, was badly directed.

Just at this moment these armies were weakened by the command shifts, requested by Nikishev. As Nikishev himself commented bitterly: "Now we can get them with a whole German corps on their tail!"

The shift of the Forty-eighth Army was a fatal move. This bedraggled outfit, nothing but a hulk, chanced to be the only unit in the path of four fast-moving German divisions, heading for the Moscow-Leningrad railroad.

The Nazi divisions struck at the hinge between the two Leningrad fronts, the Northern and the Northwest. They shouldered aside the wreck of the Forty-eighth Army, pushing it east. General Dukhanov was on the scene. When he learned that the Forty-eighth was retreating to the east along with units of the Northwest Front, it was, he said, "like a terrible, stupid dream." The movement of the Soviet forces east (rather than falling back to the north) uncovered the whole approach to Leningrad.

This error, Dukhanov believed, enabled the Germans to encircle the city. True, the over-all strength of Leningrad might still have been unable to prevent the Germans from closing the ring. But by withdrawing to the east the Soviet troops left a gap of a dozen miles open, unprotected. The Nazis paraded right into it.

"The army in that period was on wheels," Lieutenant General A. V. Sukhomlin, Chief of Staff of the Fifty-fourth Army, recalled. Moscow was trying valiantly to shuffle units north to Leningrad from the reserve echelons which had been created to the east of Moscow. Troops were constantly being moved from the Karelian peninsula to the south and west of Leningrad. They were shuffled around between west, southwest and east day and night.

It was a never-ending task, like trying to keep a sieve full of water. As fast as units were pulled from the north to strengthen the south or southwest, there was new deterioration to the southeast.

Nothing which Leningrad tried to do in those fateful August days could halt the hemorrhage of manpower or the irresistible tide which swept the Nazi Panzers closer and closer to the city's gates.

20 . *The Enemy at the Gates*

THE HUB OF THE DEFENSE OF LENINGRAD WAS SMOLNY, the great compound along the Neva, only a mile or two from the Winter Palace, Party headquarters since Lenin's day. Long since, Smolny had displaced the General Staff building as the directing center of the battle. Here Zhdanov worked and lived around the clock, his figure growing more slack as sleepless night and endless day succeeded each other. He smoked more and more, the boxes of Belomors and Pamirs piling up on his desk in disorderly litter until they were removed by his aides.

There was a large underground command center at Smolny. There at a long table was the communications center, men and women in military uniform, sitting behind the Baudot telegraph transmitters, rattling out orders and messages to all corners of the front. Here was the VC high-security line connecting Leningrad with Moscow. And here, when air alerts sounded, worked Zhdanov, together with the top echelon of the Party, the government and the Leningrad front.

Smolny was heavily defended. Antiaircraft guns had been mounted on neighboring buildings and in the surrounding park. The building was protected by a maze of trenches and machine-gun nests. Four tanks stood guard near the entrance, and a gunboat was stationed on the Neva embankment nearby.

There were no direct hits on Smolny during the heavy air attacks, but beginning with the great raid of September 8, many 500- and 1,000-pound bombs dropped in its vicinity. There were direct hits on the water pumping station and the Peasant House, only a hundred yards from the main Smolny buildings.

Most of the time Zhdanov worked in his office on the third floor of the right wing of the Smolny complex. This was convenient for him since his Party colleagues, the other Leningrad secretaries, A. A. Kuznetsov, Ya. F. Kapustin, M. N. Nikitin and T. F. Shtykov, had their offices in the same wing. On the floor below were the headquarters of the Leningrad front and staff, and next to the central staircase was the front commander's suite. Here the Military Council met.

Behind Zhdanov's desk a portrait of Stalin hung. To the left were pictures of Marx and Engels. There was no other decoration in the room. The long table that extended down from his desk was covered with red baize and heaped with maps and *papki*, paper folders of ocher and liver hue, tied with heavy mauve ribbon, which are the daily work load of the Russian bureaucrat.

Zhdanov's desk had only a few permanent fixtures—a desk set of soap-colored Urals stone, decorated with steel, the gift to him of the workers of the Kirov factory. There was a bookshelf with glass doors, neatly covered with green baize, at one side of his desk. It was filled with stacks of *papki*.

Here he worked hour after hour and day after day, wheezing and coughing as his asthma grew more and more difficult with the endless consumption of cigarettes. He did not wear a military uniform, although he held the military rank (as did all the top Party officers) of lieutenant general, but the old olive-drab Party blouse, of the early revolutionary tradition. It tucked into his broad belt, billowing a bit, for Zhdanov was a chunky man running to fat around his middle.

His dark eyes burned like coals in their deep sockets, and the stress lines across his face sharpened as the hours of night work went on. He seldom left the confines of Smolny, even to walk around the dilapidated grounds, now filled with military debris—antiaircraft batteries, field radio stations, trucks for troops, small encampments, searchlight crews, parks of courier and command cars.

His brown hair shot with auburn tints showed no sign of gray. His fat fingers were deeply stained by nicotine, although he preferred the traditional Russian *papirosy* with their long cardboard draw to the conventional cigarettes.

There were kitchens and dining rooms in Smolny, but Zhdanov did not often eat anywhere but in his office. A tray of food was brought to him, and he would wolf it as he conducted business or, infrequently, would share a dinner, often at 3 A.M., with one or two of his principal aides. Day and night he consumed tea, drinking it in the Russian style from a glass in an embossed German silver holder, a lump of sugar in his mouth and, if possible, a slice of lemon in the tea.

Smolny was as busy after midnight as it was at high noon. Bychevsky often reached Smolny in the early hours of morning. At 5 A.M. he found every office occupied, doors opening and closing, messengers and clerks busily carrying papers from one room to another, officers going in and out, telephones ringing, telegraph keys chattering in the communications rooms.

It was at Smolny that Zhdanov and Voroshilov planned their strategy in the defense of the city. Here it was that Zhdanov met with the top commanders, with the officials of the city upon whom he relied to carry out so many defense measures. Here he harangued the Young Communists upon whose slender shoulders more and more burdens were destined to fall, and the active members of the Party, who, in the last resort, would be called upon to fight to the end to save Leningrad from falling to the Germans.

The prospect that the Party members would, in fact, be summoned to fight street by street, house by house, room by room, in savage city guerrilla warfare such as the world had only seen previously in the university city of Madrid was becoming more and more real.

All night long Zhdanov and Voroshilov labored over military problems. All day and into the evening there were meetings, conferences, rallies, pep talks. The procedures were often informal; front commanders, Party workers, engineers and specialists wandered in and out of Military Council sessions, taking part or not according to circumstance or whim.

Zhdanov and Voroshilov met with the editors of *Leningradskaya Pravda* in an effort to stiffen its propaganda line. They managed to shake loose from the army some of the paper's experienced correspondents and set them to covering the fighting in a more realistic way than was possible for cub reporters like Vsevolod Kochetov and his chum, Mikhalev. Efforts were made to make available more information, particularly regarding the fighting on the Leningrad front. Rumor and confusion as to the reality of the situation were still general among the public.

The top military and political officers were brought into Smolny on July 21. Both Zhdanov and Voroshilov warned them that there was not the slightest reason for self-confidence. Speaker after speaker stressed the need for the rapid building of fortifications. Flaws in construction work and disputes among fortifications experts were aired. It was decided to lodge responsibility in a single unified defense construction administration with Secretary Kuznetsov in charge.

Another rally was called at Smolny July 24, a meeting of the Communist Party *aktiv*. Secretary Kuznetsov was chairman.

Voroshilov spoke first. "The task of tasks is not to let the enemy into this city," he said. Then Zhdanov spoke. "The enemy wants to destroy our homes, seize our factories, exterminate our achievements, wash our streets and squares with the blood of countless victims and enslave the free sons of the Motherland. It shall not be!"

The entire Leningrad Party *aktiv* rose at Zhdanov's call and, standing in the chamber where Lenin had decreed that the Bolshevik Revolution should begin, swore a solemn oath to "die before yielding the city of Lenin." Then they sang the Internationale. Every member of the Party and every Party candidate was mustered to twenty-four-hour round-the-clock duty at Party headquarters. Plans were drafted for Party workers, Young Communists and workers' detachments to defend the city, block by block and house by house.

In all the alarm and crisis no special measures were taken to conserve food. The run on food stores began June 22, but there had been no organized attempt to control reserves. All the big Soviet cities went on a ration-card system July 18. Leningrad's ration was the same as that of the rest of the country—800 grams[1] of bread a day for workers, 600 for employees, 400 for dependents and children. The meat ration was 2,200 grams a month for workers, dropping to 600 for dependents and children. There were ample rations of cereals, fats and sugar.

As Yelena Skryabina noted in her diary: "Nothing terrible so far. We can live."

Commercial stores—seventy-one in all—opened the day rationing started. In these stores without ration cards you could buy anything you wanted—and any amounts: sugar, butter, meat, caviar. But prices were high. A kilo (2 1/5 pounds) of sugar sold for seventeen rubles. People crowded into the stores, looked at the prices and went away muttering. Restaurant meals were not rationed and tasted as good—or bad—as ever.

The Hermitage work went on night and day. Professor Orbeli would not cease worrying until all of his treasures had been shipped away. More and more the packing was impeded by the drafting of Hermitage workers for digging trenches and military service. By extraordinary efforts a second shipment was dispatched July 20. It filled 23 cars. There were 422 boxes, 700,000 separate articles. Fourteen members of the staff accompanied the train to its mysterious destination—now known to be Sverdlovsk. A third train, Orbeli thought, would complete the job.

On the Hermitage bulletin board, where once had been posted notices of art lectures and archaeological finds, now appeared a different kind of announcement: the death of Sergei N. Anosov, an archaeologist, the first Hermitage casualty, killed on duty with the Red Army.

And on Orbeli's desk the telephonograms piled up from the Party Secretariat, from the Military Council, from the City Soviet:

> We ask you to mobilize from those physically able to engage in defense work 75 men. All those mobilized must be provided with shovels, picks, crowbars, saws and axes. Each must carry five days' food supplies, and a cup, spoon and pot, a change of underwear, warm clothing and money. Advise all those mobilized that they will be on the assignment not less than two weeks.

Aleksandr Shtein, the playwright whose wife was an artist at Lenfilm, was working now with the Baltic Fleet at Kronstadt. One late July day he got a four-hour leave to visit Leningrad. The evacuation of children was in full sway—those who had been brought back from the Luga area, those who had never been sent away. He found Nevsky Prospekt filled with buses and streetcars, packed with crying children, worried parents. Military

[1] Ration figures can be converted from the metric system by using the rough equivalent of 450 grams to the pound.

music blared from radio loudspeakers. The youngsters carried huge bundles and boxes. At the Anichkov Bridge—naked without the famous Klodt horses, long since buried against bombing attack—there was a traffic jam.

The windows of the big Nevsky shops were surrounded with sandbags and crisscrossed with paper strips, cut from old newspapers. War placards were everywhere: "Have you signed up yet in the People's Volunteers?" Another showed an ultramarine sea with a battleship, its cannons spouting red flame.

The stream of buses flowed to the stations, where huge crowds had gathered. Women kept counting their charges . . . 110 . . . 112 . . . 114. Many children carried small khaki knapsacks on their backs. Shtein's wife was there with their six-year-old daughter Tanya—off to the deep rear, somewhere in the Urals . . . just for two weeks, the mothers reassured their children—and themselves.

Evacuation from Leningrad had been on-again off-again. For the most part it involved children, first sent to the nearby countryside and then re-evacuated to the Urals and other distant areas. To organize the exodus, a special department had been created by the Leningrad Soviet. Up to the eleventh of August it sent out of Leningrad 467,648 persons.[2] But that figure had been largely nullified by the inward flow of refugees from the Baltic states. On August 10 it was decided to send another 400,000 women and children out of the city. The figure was upped to 700,000 only four days later. In reality, nothing like these numbers were evacuated. When the circle closed, 216,000 persons had been processed but not evacuated. The railroads were not able to handle the volume. They were being heavily bombed. For instance, on August 15 105 German bombers attacked the Chudovo railroad station, and on August 18 they damaged the Volkhov River bridge on the Leningrad-Moscow line, tying up traffic.

"With catastrophic lateness," one witness noted, "we attempted to send out of the city women and children. We collected them, put them on cars and moved them six or seven miles from Sortirovochnaya Station to Rybatskoye or somewhere else where they stayed on the tracks, eight- or ten-train echelons. They waited three days, five days, a week, expecting to be sent on any minute, unable to communicate with their families, who thought they had long since gone. Most of them had no money, and the food for their trip was eaten on the spot."

Until the last moment most Leningraders considered it bad form, almost cowardice, to leave. For this the city was soon to pay dearly. The responsibility here, as in so many areas, lay directly with the Party organization. For it was the Party bosses, from Zhdanov on down to the shop stewards, who encouraged people not to leave and excoriated those (except for women and children) who sought to get out.

Along with the children evacuated from Leningrad went large quantities

[2] Karasev, *op. cit.*, p. 91. The figure is given as 477,648 in *N.Z.* (p. 144). Probably a misprint.

of food to sustain them in the remote areas of the Urals, Central Asia and the Volga. Exactly how much food was shipped from Leningrad is not known, but on one day, August 7, Leningrad shipped 30 tons of sugar, 11 tons of butter and quantities of flour and cereals to the Kirov Oblast.

The problem of maintaining production, especially of war necessities, grew difficult. Factories were being removed from the city—if slowly—in line with orders issued by the State Defense Committee as early as July 11. By August 1 the Nevsky machine-building plant had been loaded onto 180 freight cars and sent to Sverdlovsk, the Kirov machine plant[3] had sent out 81 cars of equipment to Barnaul, and the Russian diesel plant had been moved on 70 cars to Gorky. There was considerable hesitation about evacuating big plants like the Kirov steel and the Izhorsk works. But in August about 3,000 Kirov workers and some equipment were sent to Chelyabinsk. Some Izhorsk equipment was also moved out. There was enormous confusion. As late as 1943 the director of the big Zhdanov plant was still trying to get his equipment assembled. Part of the machinery had been shipped to Tashkent and the rest to the Urals. By August 27 some 59,280 cars of machinery had been shipped, including 56,000 electric motors, 22 boiler assemblies and 23 hydroturbines. By September 1 nearly 100 plants had been evacuated in whole or in part.

Some plants took raw materials and supplies along with them. On July 29 this was categorically forbidden for iron, steel and metals. About a week later all Leningrad plants were put on fuel quotas and work was begun to equip large boilers, such as those at Power Station No. 5, the Kirov factory and others, to burn peat and wood.

The task of fulfilling high-priority orders of the State Defense Committee, such as a directive to the Kirov plant to begin serial production of field guns, became harder and harder. The order was subcontracted to thirty-eight separate factories but, even so, in July only 133 guns were turned out.

Another high-priority order was for rocket shells for the famous Russian secret weapon, the Katyusha, an eight- and twelve-barreled rocket gun. This work had to be subcontracted to seventeen factories, and not until August 27 were the first shells produced.

The Germans plunged ahead with deadly vigor. Their forward units had begun to break into the areas of Leningrad's exurbia—if a later concept may be applied to Leningrad—the regions where many people had summer villas or commuting homes.

Zhdanov summoned to Smolny August 16 what was called in Party circles a "narrow *aktiv*"—that is, a meeting not of the full active membership of the higher Party ranks but of key people: secretaries of the Party districts, the *raions* or counties and wards of the city and its environs, the chairmen of the governmental units, directors of big factories, the backbone of the Leningrad Party. The time had come for frank talk. Already there were grumbling and concern in the factories. Workers could not understand

[3] Not to be confused with the great Kirov metallurgical (former Putilov) works.

why the Red Army retreated, retreated, retreated. Nor were they re-assured by the fact that rumor after rumor of bad news, the fall of cities and further withdrawals was confirmed days later by the official communiqués. Zhdanov talked bluntly. He said all must be prepared for a serious worsening of the situation.

"We must expect at any moment," he said, "mass air attacks upon areas of the city. We must immediately inspect and bring to full strength all ranks of the ARP, the fire-fighting and the first-aid commands."

Peter S. Popkov, Mayor of Leningrad, reported that about 400,000 persons had been evacuated from Leningrad, leaving some three million in the city. Popkov was an extremely able, energetic man. He spent little time at Smolny and usually was to be found at factories, power stations or other industrial sites, lending a hand with production problems. He was hot-tempered and nervous and not always able to maintain a calm exterior. He reported there were only five thousand air-raid shelters and that they would not accommodate more than one-third of the populace. New air-raid shelters must be built immediately.

A. K. Kozlovsky, a Party worker at the great Northern Cable plant, attended the meeting. He jotted his impressions in his diary:

> Today I was at the narrow *aktiv*. Report by Marshal Voroshilov. Then Comrade Zhdanov spoke. In the most open and direct manner he laid out the situation of the Leningrad front. The situation is far from jolly. . . .
> But the Red Army will not permit the enemy to break into the city. Today we begin to form new workers units on the factory principle. The city will be surrounded by a belt of forts.

Bychevsky came away from the meeting grim and determined. "We left this meeting filled with thought about the urgent matters which must be done immediately, this very night, tomorrow," he recalled. "The streets seemed more tense than ever. The whistle of a militiaman invisible in the blackout seemed particularly sharp. From somewhere sounded a single shot."

Well the streets might seem more tense. The Germans were broadcasting by radio and leaflet to the Leningrad area that only Vasilevsky Island was still holding out and that Kronstadt "is burning." SS and police units for "maintaining order" in Leningrad had been designated. Special passes in the name of the "Commandant of Leningrad" had been printed for cars entering Leningrad. Leaflets were dropped over Leningrad saying: "If you think that Leningrad can be defended, you are mistaken. If you oppose the German troops, you will perish in the wreckage of Leningrad under the hurricane of German bombs and shells. We will level Leningrad to the earth and destroy Kronstadt to the water line."

"Only hours remain before the fall of Leningrad, the stronghold of the Soviets on the Baltic Sea," the Berlin radio announced.

The deadly seriousness of it all was apparent to everyone. On August 20 Zhdanov and Voroshilov set up a special Leningrad City Council of Defense, headed by General A. I. Subbotin, head of the People's Volunteers. It included Party Secretary Kuznetsov, Party Secretary Ya. F. Kapustin, Mayor Popkov, and L. M. Antyufeyev, member of the Military Council of the People's Volunteers. The Defense Staff was to comprise Subbotin, Colonel Antonov as Chief of Staff, and Antyufeyev as Military Commissar. Its task was to direct block-by-block defense of the city. Under the Council were created all-powerful troikas—three-member directorates—in each region of the city. The troika consisted of the Party secretary, the local city executive chairman, the local NKVD commandant. The area Volunteer Military Command was attached to the troika. In each factory a small troika was named, charged with defense of the plant. Each district was divided into sectors, each sector into subsectors. One hundred fifty workers battalions of 600 men, women and teen-agers were to defend the sectors; 77 of the battalions were to be mobilized before nightfall. They were to be armed with rifles, shotguns, pistols, submachine guns, Molotov cocktails, sabers, daggers, pikes. In the neighborhoods street barricades, fire points, machine-gun nests and antitank traps began to be set up. In parks and open fields machine-gun posts were erected to protect against German parachutists. Heavy posts were fixed into the ground to wreck planes or gliders attempting to land. The fortified system was to be completed within four or five days.

Zhdanov called to Smolny a full party *aktiv* on August 20. It was the second of the war. No invitation tickets were issued. Word of the meeting was spread from Party cell to Party cell. Only the participants knew the place and time. The meeting was held in Lepny Hall. There were no formalities, no election of a presidium, no reports. The participants were red-eyed, gaunt-faced, exhausted and openly alarmed. They carried their side arms into the meeting. Both Zhdanov and Voroshilov, pistols in holsters, spoke—Voroshilov first, with a map and pointer. He showed mile by mile the line defending the city, the new breakthrough points (Gatchina was closest). He warned that the Germans were preparing a savage attack but promised that "Leningrad will become its grave."

Zhdanov spoke slowly, solemnly.

"We have to teach people in the shortest possible time the main and most important methods of combat: shooting, throwing grenades, street fighting, digging trenches, crawling. . . .

"The enemy is at the gates. It is a question of life or death. Either the working class of Leningrad will be enslaved and its finest flower destroyed, or we must gather all the strength we have, hit back twice as hard and dig Fascism a grave in front of Leningrad."

It was a short meeting. There was no time for talk. An order was issued to the troops: "No backward step!"

The next day a proclamation, signed by Voroshilov, Zhdanov and Popkov, carried the same message to the people. All over the city gigantic posters appeared on the walls: "The enemy is at the gates!"

At this precise moment—unknown to Leningrad and its leaders—Hitler had squarely joined the issue: Leningrad must first be fought and won. Only after that would the battle of Moscow begin.

Hitler issued a new directive August 21 decreeing that the principal Nazi objective was not the capture of Moscow but (in the north) the encirclement of Leningrad and junction with the Finns.

"Not until we have tightly encircled Leningrad, linking up with the Finns and destroyed the Russian Fifth Army [the Leningrad force] shall we have set the stage and can we free the forces for attacking and destroying the Center Army Group Timoshenko [defending Moscow]," Hitler said.

In Leningrad, security clamped down. When Kochetov and his ever-present friend Mikhalev arrived in their Ford at the Leningrad outskirts on August 22, they were halted by a patrol of the newly created Komendatura. The officer explained that the patrol was designed to prevent the Germans from infiltrating the city in the guise of refugees. "We will not permit any Fifth Column," the officer said. He also mentioned the problem of deserters.

While it was true that the Komendatura patrols would halt any organized German units, their chief target was spies, saboteurs, deserters from the Soviet armed forces and "other hostile elements." No one was permitted into the city without proper papers. Anyone without them was taken into immediate custody. The disorderly flow of refugees into the city was summarily halted. Refugees were to be collected in central gathering points and then, it was hoped, directed to the rear.

Ilya Glazunov, the little boy of the Red-Russian-versus-White-Russian game, was among those refugees. His parents had delayed until the last moment leaving their place in the country. Now thousands of people swarmed the roads. The children were serious and silent. Each had his own burden. In Ilya's knapsack was a little porcelain Napoleon. He never could remember why he had saved it except that he'd just got it on his eleventh birthday. German planes roared over the torrent of humanity, again and again. The only shelters were the bomb pits made by earlier strafing runs. The Glazunovs managed to board one of the last trains for Leningrad. It passed through a "dead zone," the suburban area cleansed of population where, hour by hour, the German advance guard was expected. Everywhere there were field works and trenches. The passengers talked of nothing but saboteurs and spies, about shooting, about murdered children. Someone said that the train just ahead had been attacked by German planes, almost all the passengers killed. Ilya's mother, thinking him asleep, quietly asked a neighbor: if she covered him with her body, would that protect against the German bullets? The neighbor thought it wouldn't. His father smoked his pipe, looked out the window and stared up at the cloudy sky.

A curfew was imposed within the city. No one was permitted on the street between 10 P.M. and 5 A.M. without a special pass.

The police were strengthened. The city possessed 36 police divisions, broken into 352 units of 2,341 men. In addition, there were 1,250 police posts in institutions and 80 special observation posts on building roofs.

New enrollment of workers battalions was undertaken, and by August 28 another 36,658 individuals had been enlisted. In September these formed the cadres for the 5th and 6th People's Volunteers.

The new Council for the Defense of the city of Leningrad met August 20, the very day of its formation. Colonel Antonov was ordered to submit by 4 P.M., August 21, a plan for the internal defense of the city.

Guns, grenades, Molotov cocktails were stocked on streetcar platforms. Guns were mounted on trucks—twenty heavy weapons per sector—for mobile movement from one part of the city to another.

The city was surveyed for areas where the Germans might drop paratroops. Haymarket, Theater Place, Vorovsky, Champs de Mars, Palace Square, the Tauride Palace Gardens, the Volkov Cemetery, the Botanical Gardens and the Smolensk Cemetery were singled out as special danger points.

Round-the-clock observation posts were established in the rotunda of St. Isaac's Cathedral (at 330 feet, the tallest building in Leningrad), the roof of the Lenin flour mill, the Troitsky Cathedral and the Red Banner factory.

The city was sown with dragon's teeth—great cement blocks to bar the passage of German tanks. Railroad iron was crisscrossed into jungles along the outskirts of the city where the Nazis might break through.

Some measure of the task thrown upon the backs of Leningrad men—and women, mostly women—is afforded by the statistics: 450 miles of antitank ditches, 18,000 miles of open trenches, 15,000 reinforced-concrete firing points, 22 miles of barricades, 4,600 bomb shelters.

When Pavel Luknitsky returned to Leningrad from the Karelian front August 14, the city at first glance seemed not to have changed too much. There were crowds at the stations, trying to get aboard trains leaving the city. Few buses were running, and he noticed how empty the shelves were in the grocery stores.

But within ten days he noted in his diary: "How quickly has the Leningrad situation changed in the last 10 days!"

"Will we drive the enemy from Leningrad?" he asked himself. "Will they fall back in panic, pursued and attacked by our troops? Or . . . I don't want to think about the alternative. . . ."

Rumors ran through the city: Kingisepp had been recaptured. . . . Narva had been retaken. . . . Also Smolensk and Staraya Russa . . .

"Even if one of these rumors is correct, the situation is better," Luknitsky wrote. Unfortunately, none was true.

The Germans were said to be using gas. . . . This, also, was not true.

A powerful relief force was coming to the aid of Leningrad. . . . Nor was this true.

The city began to take on the appearance of a fortress. The big stores and office buildings on the Nevsky, the Liteiny, the factories on the Petrograd side, the industrial establishments beyond the Narva Gates—all were turning into sandbagged fire points. Luknitsky thought the Gostiny Dvor, an ancient merchant arcade, now looked like a miniature Kremlin under its sandbags. Every park in the city had been dug up for air-raid trenches. They crisscrossed the Summer Gardens and the Champs de Mars.

Some eighty Leningrad writers had joined the People's Volunteers. But there were others, too. There were people who were trying to escape Leningrad, Luknitsky noted, "like rats leaving a ship in danger."

One such coward, he regretted, had been found within the Writers Union and had been expelled for "desertion."

"How could he look us in the eyes after the war?" Luknitsky asked himself.

Luknitsky's father was a sixty-five-year-old professor in a naval institute. Together with Academician B. G. Galerkin, he had joined a special commission to provide Party Secretary Kuznetsov with scientific advice on constructing fortifications and air defenses, for turning the city into a "contemporary fortress," as Bychevsky put it. On the twenty-second of August Luknitsky helped his father pack a small bag of essentials. Henceforth he would live and work in a naval barracks.

Just at this time Kochetov got back to Leningrad from the Luga front and the area of the Kingisepp breakthrough. The evening he arrived, August 22, he and his friend Mikhalev had a fine lamb cutlet at the old Kvissisana Café on Nevsky Prospekt. Kochetov enjoyed his meal, but he had been upset by the Komendatura officer's remarks about desertions at the front. Kochetov kept telling himself there were no such cases.

His mood did not improve when he met the editor of his newspaper. He got into a row about a story concerning a Red Army man whom Kochetov had brought into a field hospital, suffering from thirty-two shrapnel wounds. The editor felt the story was too bloody, too terrible, would sow demoralization. He also suggested that Kochetov try not to make so much noise as he clumped around the corridors in his military boots.

In a huff Kochetov decided to get out of the city and go back to the front. He visited the offices of the newspaper *For the Defense of Leningrad*. There he got a better reception. He had his picture taken with the staff, "just in case," as he put it. Then he sat down to a meal with the newspaper staff. What a meal! Not even the government members ate so well. This was more to Kochetov's taste. Maybe he could get a transfer from the *Leningradskaya Pravda*.

It must have been that same day, August 25, that Pavel Luknitsky paid a call on Anna Akhmatova, the great Leningrad poet. He found her in the same cluttered apartment in Karelsky Pereulok beside the Fontanka where she had lived for so many years.

Anna Akhmatova was sick in bed, but she greeted Luknitsky with her usual politeness. She was in good spirits, despite her illness, despite the danger to her beloved Leningrad. She had been invited, she told Luknitsky, to speak on the radio.

"She is a patriot," Luknitsky wrote in his diary, "and the consciousness that her spirit is shared by all fills her with courage." The invitation was remarkable. Since 1925 Akhmatova had been forbidden under a secret police decree to speak in public.

Thus Leningrad, a city of three million people, a city of cowards and of patriots, of sleazy sharpers and men and women of endless dedication, of blundering military men and feuding Party leaders, moved toward the time of trial.

21 . *Stalin on the Phone*

IT WAS DAILY ROUTINE FOR STALIN TO TELEPHONE FROM the Kremlin in Moscow to Party Secretary Andrei Zhdanov and Marshal Voroshilov at their Smolny headquarters on the Neva. The calls came through at almost any hour but were more frequent after midnight. The war might be on, Russia might be in deadly danger, but Stalin had not changed his habits of a lifetime. He continued to do most of his work late at night.

The normal Stalin working day started shortly before noon. He rose, ate a light breakfast, ran quickly over the most urgent situation reports and telegrams and then began his conferences with the Supreme Command, fellow Politburo members, generals about to receive or being considered for posts of great responsibility, the industrial chiefs charged with producing tanks, airplanes and artillery, and diplomats representing his new allies of the West.

He spent much time in the communications room of the Kremlin, adjacent to his office, where direct teletype wires connected him with most of the chief cities, and VC or high-priority high-security telephone linked him with the military fronts and commands.

Stalin had now in late August apparently recovered from the breakdown he suffered at the onset of war. He had assumed supreme command of the Soviet armed forces as head of what was called the Stavka or the Supreme Command on July 10, a week after the delivery of a radio speech to the nation on July 3—a performance so halting, so filled with pauses, hesitations, sighs audible to the radio audience, interludes of noisy water-drinking, that it impressed many as the effort of a man barely in control of himself. On July 19 Stalin took over the post of Defense Commissar, and on August 8 he was named Supreme Commander of the Soviet Union or, as the title later came to be used, Generalissimo.

Some time after July 10—he does not seem to recall the precise date— Admiral Kuznetsov saw Stalin for the first time since the outbreak of war. He found him in the office of Defense Commissar Timoshenko, standing before a long table strewn with maps of the fighting fronts. Kuznetsov was quick to note that there were no naval maps among them.

Stalin questioned Kuznetsov about the situation in the Baltic, particularly the defense of Tallinn and the islands of Ösel and Dagö.[1] He wanted to shift the heavy guns from the islands, but when Kuznetsov said it was almost impossible to move coastal artillery, Stalin dropped the question.

By the end of July the Stavka had begun meeting in Stalin's Kremlin offices, being summoned at Stalin's personal whim, its composition varying according to Stalin's desires. In other words, by the end of July the Soviet Government was running again in the familiar Stalin style.

Stalin's working habits put a murderous burden on his chief associates and upon the General Staff in particular. In order to cover the long hours during which they were subject to call—from 10 A.M. to possibly 4 or 5 A.M.—they were compelled to divide their working shifts. For example, Marshal Aleksei I. Antonov, Deputy Chief of Staff, was permitted to sleep from 5 or 6 A.M. to noon. The rest of the twenty-four hours he was subject to call at any moment. General Semyon Shtemenko, his deputy, was given free time between 2 and 6 or 7 P.M.

Stalin received three reports daily from the General Staff. The first was between 10 and 11 A.M. by telephone, usually by Shtemenko. At 4 or 5 P.M. Antonov reported. But the main report came at night, often close to midnight. If Stalin was at his villa on the Mozhaisk Chaussée, the officers drove there. If he was in the Kremlin, the General Staff officers entered through the Borovitsky Gate, circling around the Great Palace in which the Supreme Soviet met, and crossed ancient Ivanovsky Square to the little corner where Stalin's apartment and office were to be found. They went in through the offices of his *chef de cabinet*, the loathsome General Poskrebyshev,[2] passed through the anteroom in which the chief of Stalin's personal guard was stationed, and then into Stalin's familiar office.

On the left side of the room was a long table where the officers spread their maps and a large globe on which, Khrushchev said, Stalin plotted operations.[3]

[1] The questions about the defense of Tallinn, Ösel and Dagö suggest a meeting toward the end of July. It was not until July 14 that the Supreme Leningrad Command ordered the Eighth Army to prepare to defend Tallinn and the two islands, and not until the end of the month did their situation become really serious. In a 1968 rewrite of his memoirs Kuznetsov puts this meeting in "the last days of June." (*Oktyabr*, No. 8, August, 1968, p. 160.) In 1963 he fixed the date as "in July when the enemy was attacking toward Tallinn" (V. M. Kovalchuk, editor, *Oborona Leningrada*, Leningrad, 1968, p. 237).

[2] Poskrebyshev vanished from public view the day after Stalin's death March 5, 1953. Outside of one sarcastic reference to him by Khrushchev as Stalin's "shield-bearer," his name did not appear in print for several years, and it was generally thought that he had been executed for his role in Stalin's purges. However, he survived until autumn 1966, according to the evidence of Galina Serebryakova, the Soviet writer, who met him in the Kremlin hospital in 1964. She found him completely callous about Stalin's crimes, even taking a grim humor in the plight of the victims. She quoted him as saying that "we"—meaning Stalin, Beria and himself—began to use poison to kill purge victims in 1939 or 1940.

[3] General Shtemenko and other writers of memoirs universally ridicule Khrushchev's contention. In fact, however, Stalin may well, occasionally, have pointed out locations on his globe if a military map was not immediately available. (Shtemenko, p. 117.)

Stalin went over the reports from the fronts. They were made orally and usually without notes. The military sat on one side of the room and the Politburo on the other. Stalin paced the room fitfully, occasionally returning to his desk in the far corner, picking up two *papirosy* (he preferred a brand called "Herzegovina Flor"), breaking them open, filtering the tobacco into the bowl of his pipe, tamping it down, and lighting it in a blue cloud of smoke.

Although he was now in better command of himself, he was still nervous and jittery. Indeed, it was not until more than two years later that Marshal Voronov, on returning from an extended trip to the front, noted that Stalin had become "significantly more quiet and self-confident." He was, Voronov said, much less "nervous and hot-tempered" than in the early months of the war.[4]

The General Staff, with the assistance of the chiefs of the various branches of service, reported to Stalin the action of the past twenty-four hours, referring to the fronts, the mechanized and armored corps by the names of commanders. The divisions were referred to by number. This was Stalin's way of conducting business.

After the briefings Stalin dictated orders, usually written out on the spot by Shtemenko and corrected by Stalin in his own hand. These were often put directly on the teletype to the front commanders without being typed up.

It was 3 or 4 A.M. before this procedure was finished. Then the commanders had to return to their headquarters and issue the necessary supporting orders.

The Stalin system was one of enormous centralization. Stalin refused to permit a single important decision or document relating to artillery to issue from the General Staff without Voronov's signature. Nor would he consider or even read a report until Voronov had personally cleared it. Stalin would not permit even the smallest question to be decided without his concurrence. Since many individuals were fearful of reporting to him, the net result was incalculable delay and confusion in the conduct of the war.[5]

Despite the improvement of his physical condition, Stalin had not yet begun to attach his name to major communiqués and decrees. That would

---

[4] General P. A. Belov had an interview with Stalin November 14, 1941. He had not seen him since 1933. He found him enormously changed. "In eight years," Belov said, "he seemed to have aged twenty." Stalin had lost his previous confidence, and his eyes were not steady. Marshal Zhukov spoke sharply to him, as though he, Zhukov, were his superior. Stalin accepted it all as though this were normal. Sometimes, Belov thought, Stalin seemed confused. (P. A. Belov, *Za Nami Moskva*, Moscow, 1963, p. 43.)

[5] The strain of this system was so intense that many officers broke down and many, their health wrecked, retired prematurely at the end of the war. Often Stalin invited the staff to stay on after reporting and watch a movie, sometimes with a foreign statesman or other guest. This would prolong the evening two or three hours more while urgent orders remained unexecuted in their briefcases. (Shtemenko, *op. cit.*, p. 137.)

wait a bit—until the Soviet Union began to achieve successes rather than appalling disasters.[6]

However, Stalin was sufficiently in command of himself so that Harry Hopkins at the end of July found him in what seemed to be perfectly normal spirits. Indeed, Hopkins was impressed with Stalin's conviction that the Russian armies would be able to halt the German attack not more than 60 or 70 miles east of the lines then held. Stalin told Hopkins on July 31 that the Russians would go into the winter still holding Moscow, Kiev and Leningrad.

Hopkins left Moscow without a hint of the traumatic period from which Stalin had so recently emerged. Hopkins had every confidence that the Soviet leader was correctly evaluating the military situation.

Stalin was now following the details of the Leningrad crisis with his usual minuteness. He was especially interested in the internal defenses of Leningrad, the system of fortifications and street barricades, the mobilization of the population into Volunteer battalions, the formation of block-by-block fighting units.

Not infrequently he telephoned directly to Party Secretary Kuznetsov, who was in charge of fortifications, giving him specific instructions as to how barricades should be built, where they were to be placed and how the population should be prepared to fight the Germans.

It was not easy for Kuznetsov to carry out the peremptory and often arbitrary instructions which Stalin gave him. But he was a man of unusual capacity for work, great zeal and great optimism. His humor was usually good. He knew his technical staff, knew the industrial capabilities of the city and for the most part was able to meet Stalin's demands.

As the Germans closed in on Leningrad, the issue of internal defense grew more and more pressing. The Leningrad Command, headed by Zhdanov and Voroshilov, did not have the time or energy to cope with the task efficiently. For this reason, acting on their own initiative, they had created the Council for the Defense of Leningrad on August 20, staffing it with the men who were concerned with these local matters.

The moment was one of the greatest tension. The twenty-first was the day proclamations went up on the city walls—on the Nevsky, on Kirov Prospekt, on Lieutenant Schmidt Embankment: "The enemy is at the gates!"

This was the day—or evening—that Stalin called Zhdanov and Voroshilov to an urgent consultation on the VC telephone. Stalin was in a rage. Why had they set up the Council for the Defense of Leningrad without consulting

---

[6] Marshal S. S. Biryuzov reported that in this period almost all documents and orders were signed "at the order of the Supreme Command" by Marshal B. M. Shaposhnikov, Chief of Staff. (S. S. Biryuzov, *Kogda Gremeli Pushki*, Moscow, 1963, p. 247.) After the war began to go in Russia's favor the orders were signed by the Supreme Commander (Stalin) and the Chief of Staff or his deputy. Lesser orders were signed "by the authority of the Supreme Headquarters." (Shtemenko, *Voyenno-Istoricheskii Zhurnal*, No. 9, September, 1965.)

him? And why were they not personally members of the Council?

It was in vain that Zhdanov attempted to explain that the Council was designed to handle matters to which the Leningrad Front Command had no time to attend—the block-by-block plans, the location of the tank traps, the sandbagging of machine-gun posts, the issuance of Molotov cocktails, the thousand and one details of getting the great city ready for street battle and Nazi storming.

Stalin refused to be appeased. Perhaps he thought that Zhdanov and Voroshilov were seeking to evade responsibility for the city's fall. Or he (or one of his Kremlin associates) may have seen a dark plot to yield up Leningrad. It may have been anger at a manifestation of independence which might forebode greater independence later on. There well may have been others in the Kremlin (or Stalin himself) who sought to find grounds for criticism of Zhdanov and Voroshilov for their failure to halt the German drive on the city. Stalin may have seen in the creation of the special Council visible evidence of panic.

The precise motives of the strange and disturbed dictator are not clear. What is clear is that Stalin would not accept the action of his Leningrad proconsuls.

The truth is that Stalin had become increasingly critical of the conduct of Leningrad's defense as the situation worsened. He and his deputy, Chief of Staff Marshal B. M. Shaposhnikov, examined every decision affecting Leningrad. Repeatedly Stalin or Shaposhnikov (at Stalin's insistence) ordered changes in dispositions, in the use of troops or weapons.

As the Leningrad forces fell back toward the northern capital, Stalin began to hector Voroshilov and Zhdanov. He called them "specialists in retreat." Zhdanov, he insisted, "concerns himself with only one thing—how to retreat."

Not infrequently, Stalin rejected proposals out of hand. He did not seem to understand the relative strength of the German attacking forces and those available for Leningrad's defense.

His dissatisfaction with Leningrad's leaders reached culmination August 21. Not only did he peremptorily order that the Council for the Defense of Leningrad be "reviewed" and its membership "revised" to include Voroshilov and Zhdanov, but he administered a formal rebuke to both men. He assailed what he called their "enthusiasm" for forming workers battalions with insufficient weapons. He ordered that the commanders who had been picked to head the battalions be changed for others, nominated by Moscow. Here again his concern for the minutiae of the city's internal defense suggested a fear that Leningrad might be delivered to the Germans from within. These fears may have been inflamed by reports from the NKVD that the Leningrad populace was not to be trusted; or the secret police may have circulated rumors of some kind of plot by Zhdanov and Voroshilov. Or Stalin may simply have had a pathological fear of putting weapons into the hands of ordinary Soviet citizens.

This same day Stalin rejected a proposal by Admiral Tributs for a naval offensive to be launched from Tallinn toward Narva in hope of undermining the German troops advancing on Leningrad.

Although the Baltic Fleet was fighting for its life at Tallinn, Admiral Tributs and his Military Council, N. K. Smirnov and A. D. Verbitsky, suggested that the fleet mobilize all its resources, the men defending Tallinn (a group 20,000 to 25,000 strong called the 10th Corps), the garrisons remaining on the Baltic islands and on Ösel, Dagö and Hangö, plus all of the fleet marines. This force would number about 60,000 men plus three artillery regiments. It would be hurled at the rear of the German Group Nord in a sudden offensive from Tallinn toward Narva.

Tributs said that his air intelligence and reports of scouts indicated the Germans had no reserves in the rear and that there was every prospect of catching them by surprise and delivering a stunning defeat. It was a Churchillian concept, brave, imaginative and bold, one of the few creative military schemes to emerge in Soviet councils during the war.

Stalin turned it down out of hand. The official reason was that it would uncover the Gulfs of Riga and Finland to German entry and that it was too difficult to assemble the forces in the time available. Actually, the rejection may have been grounded in politics, not in military concerns.

The interventions by Stalin desperately handicapped Leningrad's defenses. They handicapped the task of the men whose responsibility it was to save the city from the Germans. They were compelled to name themselves to the Council for the Defense of Leningrad, and, as a result, by August 30 it had been discarded as a useless appendage since it merely duplicated the Leningrad Front Council.

Whatever the motivation for Stalin's conduct, its significance has been underlined by a multitude of circumstances. The very existence of the Council for Defense had not been revealed until Dmitri V. Pavlov did so in his slender volume, *Leningrad v Blokade*, which appeared in 1958. Not one word of elaboration of his account was added until 1965, when a few details were set forth in a civilian history of Leningrad in the war.[7] Finally, in 1966 the full text of the order establishing the Council was published in a collection of official Leningrad documents. Even so, every Soviet historical and public reference continues to be couched in virtually the words of Pavlov's original reference—a sign that the wording was cleared at the highest level of Soviet Government and that nothing else was cleared or has been cleared. In other words, the question of the Council for Defense was still a sensitive issue in Soviet politics more than twenty-five years after the event.

[7] As late as 1964 the official military history of the Leningrad siege glossed over this critical point. It made no mention of the dispute with Stalin nor the naming of the original Council for the Defense of Leningrad on August 20. Instead, it reported the formation of the Council as occurring August 24 and gave its membership as that dictated by Stalin. There was no reference to the August 20 action nor to the dissolution of the Council on August 30. (I. P. Barbashin *et al.*, *Bitva Za Leningrad, 1941-1944*, Moscow, 1964. p. 60.)

There can be no doubt that the savage row between Stalin and the Leningrad defenders, Zhdanov and Voroshilov, was of import not only in the defense of the city but in the higher game of Kremlin politics which went on throughout the war between Stalin and those of his associates who sought, by one means or another, to advance their personal fortunes, regardless of its effect on the war.

Stalin's suspicions concerning the internal defense plans for Leningrad almost certainly were stimulated by Beria, who seems to have done everything possible to prevent the organization in Leningrad and elsewhere of civilian militia, paramilitary or partisan outfits, insisting that all such functions be kept in the hands of the police.[8]

The care with which one author after another uses almost the same language to describe these matters supports the view that the whole complex of Leningrad decisions—the formation of Volunteer units, the organization of local paramilitary forces, the attempt to vest in local Leningrad officials responsibility for internal defense of the city—became in later days part of the pseudo-legal foundation on which the bizarre charges of the so-called "Leningrad Affair" were, at least in part, based. The men who devoted the last ounce of energy and ability to protecting their city from German conquest were, within a few years, to be executed for fulfilling these very acts.

At just this time—middle or late August—Stalin widened extraordinarily the powers of the Commissariat of Internal Affairs to maintain "social order." These powers, as well as other special military weapons placed in the hands of the police for dealing with rumormongering, sowing alarm and panic among the population, were used by Beria and his lieutenants as a basis for accusations of anti-Soviet activity and counterrevolutionary thoughts among the military as well as the civilian population.

Beria's interference was so effective that he managed to prevent the setting up of any centrally directed guerrilla movement until late spring 1942. Under the direction of Zhdanov, Leningrad had taken a lead in forming People's Volunteers and in sending partisans behind the lines. It had gone further than any other Soviet city in creating informal workers battalions.

Stalin's dissatisfaction with Leningrad thus was reinforced by Beria, possibly working together with or parallel to Malenkov.

[8] Panteleimon K. Ponomarenko, who eventually organized the Soviet partisan movement, reported that a commission to set up this movement was approved in July, 1941, with himself, L. Z. Mekhlis and others as members. But the existence of the order was not revealed until near the end of the war. In November, 1941, a central partisan staff was set up under Ponomarenko but was killed by Beria's interference. On May 30, 1942, the State Defense Committee again ordered the Commission activated, but its activity was sharply limited at Beria's initiative. Terenti Shtykov, the only Leningrad Party Secretary to survive the murderous "Leningrad Affair" (possibly because he was in eastern Siberia when it occurred in late 1948 and early 1949), flatly blames Beria and hints that the whole question of paramilitary and partisan activity was in some manner related by Beria to the Leningrad Affair. Beria apparently had full responsibility for all underground activities, for he is blamed for destroying the foundations of such units in the purges of 1938-41. (Ponomarenko, *Voyenno-Istoricheskii Zhurnal*, No. 4, April, 1965, p. 33; Shtykov in *Khrabreishiye iz Khrabrykh*, Leningrad, 1964, p. 5; *VOVSS*, p. 108.)

22 . The Tallinn Disaster

WEEK BY WEEK THE NAVAL CORRESPONDENT NIKOLAI Mikhailovsky had watched them—the golden people on the bright sands of Pirita where the blue waves of the Baltic gently caressed the clean sweep of beach. They lay there in the blazing sun, growing more and more brown, their eyes invisible behind the dark glasses, white towels about their shoulders, lazily idling on the sand, seldom going near the water. He watched them as they sauntered to the white-and-green-striped bathing machines. He watched as they emerged in light linens and, toward the end of day, took their places at the tables in the boulevard cafés. They had been waiting since June. It was mid-August now, and it did not seem likely that they had much longer to wait, the well-to-do of Tallinn, the bourgeoisie, the secret and not-so-secret sympathizers with the Germans. Day by day they grew more bold, more insolent, more self-confident—or so it seemed to Mikhailovsky. Hardly a day went by without a sumptuous wedding at one of the great churches and a festive procession with flowers and holiday costumes through the central streets of the city. It was as if they deliberately wanted the city to see—"Yes, we are here, we are waiting. Soon that rabble will be gone and once again we will be in charge."

Old Johannes Lauristin, the chairman of Soviet Estonia, a man who had spent half his life in the prisons of pre-Soviet Estonia, better known as Yuhan Madarik, author of two or three novels, mused in his offices in the Old City over the "golden people."

"They exist, you know," he said sadly, then went on to talk of the "patriots," the workers of the docks and the ports and the factories who were supporting the Soviet forces.

Tallinn had changed since Mikhailovsky arrived on the first day of the war. Week by week the tension had grown. "Their" forces, the sympathizers with the Germans, had grown more and more active. From the ninth of July onward the countryside had become so dangerous for Soviet citizens that few ventured out alone. The Germans captured Ainazi July 6 and quickly seized Pärnu. There was no real force between Pärnu and

Tallinn. Had the Germans driven straight up the highway, a distance of less than a hundred miles, they would have captured Tallinn out of hand. The city was seized with panic. The wildest rumors circulated. Enormous stores of oil and munitions were set afire to keep them from "falling into German hands." The Baltic Fleet Staff boarded the packet *Pikker* and the *Virona* and kept steam up. Even the director of the Baltic Fleet newspaper fled along with many other Russians. They were terrified that Estonian nationalists would attack them en route.[1]

Hearing the news of the German breakthrough, Admiral Tributs called Moscow: "Who is going to defend Tallinn from the land side? We have no forces." The Eighth Army, he was told, would protect Tallinn. He got the same answer from Leningrad. The truth was that no plan existed for the land defense of Tallinn. No one ever imagined it would be attacked.

The Eighth Army had been the answer when the Germans crossed the frontier; when they took Libau; when they took Ventspils; when they crossed the western Dvina; when they captured Riga. Admiral Tributs no longer believed in the Eighth Army. He turned to the Estonian Soviet Government, and they provided 25,000 men and women with spades and picks to throw up three lines of trenches.

The move saved Tallinn for the moment. But it came almost too late. Admiral Panteleyev went out to meet the makeshift Estonian defense staff —only twelve or fourteen miles outside the city. He got caught in a skirmish between a detachment of Estonian nationalists and a fire truck on which were riding Soviet firemen, armed with rifles. He had a narrow escape.

On July 9 the Germans landed by plane and parachute two trained units of Estonian guerrillas called Erna-I and Erna-II. The situation grew more tense.

"We had to be on guard," Mikhailovsky recalled. "We had to be careful. The *Kaitseliitovtsi*, the Estonian nationalists, began to raise their heads. In cellars, in storehouses or in holes in the ground they had hidden their guns and just waited for a favorable moment to put them to use.

"There were places where the local Fascists shot our retreating soldiers in the back and met the Hitlerites with flowers, like liberators."

The struggle against traitors, Nazi sympathizers, cowards and panicmongers was nip and tuck. Vsevolod Vishnevsky didn't even want to write about it. Only the stiffest measures—firing squads, military tribunals, summary executions, on the spot—maintained a semblance of order.

Mikhailovsky shared a room in the Golden Swan Hotel with a prominent Dostoyevsky scholar, Orest V. Tsekhnovitser, one of the most revered men on the faculty of Leningrad University. He had volunteered his services to the Baltic Fleet.

---

[1] The staff went back ashore July 22 in order to boost morale in Tallinn. (Smirnov, *op. cit.*, p. 31.) Tributs proposed moving his flag headquarters to the Luga gulf, 120 miles to the east but permission was refused. (Kuznetsov, *Oktyabr*, No. 8, August, 1968, pp. 154-155.)

They walked through the Old City and the spreading expanse of Kadriorg Park, the rambling ensemble of forests, lakes, formal gardens, streams and recreation areas which spread along the Baltic shore in the heart of Tallinn. The park stretched beside the sea for a mile and a half and was three-quarters of a mile wide. Here, facing the embankment, was the monument to the old Russian cruiser, the *Rusalka*, sunk in the terrible storm of 1893. They visited the little house of Peter the Great, the house in which he lived while he watched his labor crews build the great port of Revel, the port now called Tallinn. They admired the round mirrors, the wide oak bed under a rotting canopy, the mahogany bureau, the high chair with the artistic carving on its back in Peter's house. They walked silently into the cool, gloomy precincts of the ancient cathedral, Toomkirka, as it was called, six centuries old, the burying place of the great Russian admirals, Krusentern and Greig. An old caretaker told them that Krusentern and his wife occupied the newest graves in the church, only two hundred years old. Some mummies in the vaults were three and four hundred years old.

The professor occasionally wrote letters back to his wife in Leningrad. Mikhailovsky copied a few lines from one:

> I see how history is being made, and I am happy that I am not on the sidelines in these decisive days. I want to tell you all something more significant. Don't be worried about me and, in general, not only "me" but "us." I see around me such heroic dedication, such love for our native land that all this makes me quite another person.
>
> It is incredibly difficult for us now. But we clearly see the perspective of the struggle. We know that we will win in Europe, that we will get to Berlin and for all time destroy this hated Fascist regime. Victory unquestionably will be ours.

The spirit, the enthusiasm and the energy of Professor Tsekhnovitser filled Mikhailovsky with confidence.

Not all the Soviet colony in Tallinn was so solemn. Anatoly Tarasenkov, who had inherited the editorship of the Baltic Fleet paper when its director fled to the rear, lived in a barracks at No. 20 Vaitenberg with a communications company. All they did, Tarasenkov recalled, was dream about girls— and chase them. A very moral political commissar was wild about Selma, an Estonian street girl, whom he picked up on a Kadriorg Park bench. The girl was small, young and very dull. But, observed Tarasenkov, "she was a very erotic girl for the age of seventeen or eighteen." Another member of the company had a romance with an Estonian nurse named Elsa. Sometimes, Tarasenkov went to the Rom Restaurant with or without feminine company. In the winter to come in starving Leningrad his mind would go back again and again to the cauliflower, the oily borsht, the fat *kolbasa* and the meat pies at the Rom. In the market there were beautiful flowers—and beautiful flower girls.

But, as Tarasenkov was to note, "the vacation was soon to end."

The aid which the Eighth Army could give to Tallinn was minimal. The fleet organized a scratch force of marines which halted the Germans on the Pärnu-Tallinn road in actions around July 30. More troops, including a construction battalion, were sent to cover the Paldiski region, just west of Tallinn, and NKVD detachments were pressed into service. Retreat had carried the Eighth Army considerably east of Tallinn. It was falling back on Narva, where it called for help. The fleet answered by sending in warships from Tallinn and Kronstadt.

By August 8 the Germans had cut off Tallinn, both east and west, telephone communication with Leningrad was lost, and Admiral Tributs and his associates had begun to consider possible means of getting out of the trap.

Various proposals were taken up. One called for massing all available forces and attempting to break through the German lines in the direction of Narva. This was the plan ultimately rejected by Stalin August 21. Another variant advanced by N. K. Smirnov, a member of the Military Council of the Baltic Fleet, called for transferring the Tallinn forces to the Finnish shore and fighting through the Finnish-German lines to Leningrad. Both of these proposals required intricate movement of men and ships through heavily mined waters under German gunfire, German observation and German bombing. Both in the end were rejected by the Soviet Supreme Command.

With the capture of Kunda on the Gulf of Finland, east of Tallinn, on August 8 the port was surrounded. Its narrow streets settled into a gloomy quiet, broken only by the shout of patrols and the quick step of marines. Barricades covered the main approaches.

A rain of artillery shells plunged down on the city, on the varicolored beach houses at Pirita, on the fishing villages with their unpainted huts and drying nets.

In the harbor the 6-inch guns of the cruiser *Kirov* and the 4.5-inch weapons of the destroyer leader *Leningrad* began to drop shells on the German positions. From the old harbor watchers saw the orange flash of flame as the great guns trained in on the Nazi targets. First the flash, then . . . one second . . . two seconds . . . the thunder of the gun and a moment later the dull roar as the shell exploded to the rear.

The Germans brought up long-range artillery and zeroed in on the warships. On one day, August 23, the Germans dropped more than six hundred shells into the harbor. German planes, high above the range of Soviet antiaircraft, bombed the fleet.

Business life in Tallinn dwindled to nothing. No one walked the streets. The Tallinn cabbies vanished. Streetcars halted. The radio loudspeakers fell silent. No newspapers appeared at the kiosks.

Mikhailovsky took a quick stroll in Kadriorg Park. The red squirrels swore angrily at him. They were hungry. No one came to feed them. The narrow lanes were quiet and empty. Debris piled up in the streets. For days no street cleaners had appeared. Porters with their white aprons, their brooms and dustpans, vanished. In a barbershop window he saw a sign: "*Suletud* (Closed)." The owners of the shops on Hara Street put down their heavy steel shutters. At the end of the street Mikhailovsky heard a carpenter hammering. He was putting the last nails into a wooden coffin.

In the comfortable restaurant of the Golden Swan a fat headwaiter with two chins met Mikhailovsky each evening. Now his face grew as stony as that of an Egyptian mummy.

"What do you want?" the waiter asked.

"Is it possible to dine?"

The man in the morning coat smiled sarcastically. "It's finished, all finished, respected comrade. . . ."

The whistles of the factories were silent, and without them Mikhailovsky felt a great emptiness. It seemed, indeed, that all was finished.

The defense of the city was placed in the hands of Admiral Tributs August 17.[2] The defense force comprised what was optimistically called the 10th Corps. Actually, it represented about 4,000 weary, dispirited men holding a line fifteen or sixteen miles outside the city. From the beginning Major General Nikolayev, Tributs' deputy, flatly declared that "the forces are completely insufficient." Many in the fleet harshly criticized Nikolayev, but there was little anyone could have done. A few Tallinn workers were drafted, all the sailors that could be spared from the ships were sent ashore, together with such police and political workers as could be scraped together. Marshal Voroshilov sent in 425 Communists and Young Communists from Leningrad. There were 73 Party workers from the fleet and 100 from the army to stiffen the defense units.

The backbone of the defense was provided by the guns of the cruiser *Kirov*, the destroyer leaders *Leningrad* and *Minsk*, and the nine destroyers and three gunboats which stayed in the roadstead. The final defense force comprised about 20,000 men, including nearly 14,000 sailors and 1,000 or more police. They had 13 T-26 tanks.

As rapidly as possible Tributs had sought to evacuate from Tallinn the wounded and those not needed for the city's defense. The turboelectric ship, the *BT-509*, now called the *Baltika*, got away with 3,500 wounded in earlier fighting. It was hit by a mine but managed to transfer its passengers safely and arrived at Kronstadt in tow August 13. The *Siberia*, which brought Tributs and his staff to Tallinn in July, 1940, was lost in a bombing attack. It carried 3,000 wounded, but many were saved.

The final German attack on Tallinn opened about midevening August 19 at a moment when Admiral Tributs and Admiral Panteleyev were taking a stroll in the empty lanes of Kadriorg Park. They knew from captured Nazi

[2] The decision to unify the defense under Admiral Tributs came much too late, in the opinion of Smirnov (*op. cit.*, p. 36).

soldiers that the German command had been ordered to take Tallinn by August 24.

That day Orest Tsekhnovitser wrote another letter to his family:

> Very worried not to get any news. I must know:
> How is your health?
> Did you get the money voucher, Zhenia?
> Where are you living?
> What are you thinking about?
> Have you gotten my letters?
> I am healthy. Life is very, very tense. We are doing something very important. More than that I can't write about myself. I haven't heard from Grandma for two weeks. Very worried about you. My best to those who know me and love me a little.
>
> I embrace you and kiss you
> OREST

> Yuka [his son]: Oh! If I live (as Leo Tolstoy used to say), what talks we will have when the Fascists are licked! The enemy is so strong that we have to work fiercely to beat him. And we will. But we have to keep up the fight.

It was the last word the family had from him.

August 23 was a sunny day. The weather throughout August had been exceptionally good. It reminded Vsevolod Vishnevsky, the playwright and senior correspondent with the Baltic Fleet, of Spain. Vishnevsky went to staff headquarters that morning and got a briefing from Major General Zashikhin. The Germans were attacking in strength. A Soviet mixed regiment had been forced back, but General Zashikhin thought the lines would hold.

At about 4 P.M. it began to rain. Vishnevsky was pleased to learn that telegraph connections with Moscow had been restored. He went to the offices of the newspaper, *Soviet Estonia*, and found a good deal of nervousness there. This bothered him. He was a big, bold, self-confident man. Even in the worst moments he insisted that all would be well. He had spent part of the morning reading over the front communiqués of the first two months of the war. This put him in an optimistic mood—God knows why.

Nikolai Chukovsky, then a young correspondent attached to the 10th Bomber Group of the Baltic Fleet air arm, recalled meeting Vishnevsky about this time. He saw Vishnevsky standing on the boulevard in front of staff headquarters, talking with a well-known writer who was in naval uniform.

Vishnevsky glared at the writer, his round puffy face white with anger. Chukovsky decided it was no moment to intervene and tried to go past without speaking, but Vishnevsky grasped him by the arm and detained him.

"You also want to get out!" Vishnevsky accused Chukovsky in fierce tones. "But we will hold out! We will stop them!"

It was with difficulty that Chukovsky convinced Vishnevsky that unlike the writer in naval uniform he had no intention of quitting Tallinn.

Now, amid obvious signs that the Germans were closing in for their final attack, Vishnevsky busied himself with his notes, jotting down every impression. He went to the Political Administration of the Baltic Fleet and sat there at a window in late afternoon, looking out to sea, filling notebook after notebook with nervous, almost cryptic comments.

Suddenly the alarm rang: General Quarters. "Be ready to board the *Virona*. Leave no papers behind."

He gathered his possessions, swept them into a haversack, and was ready to go. He jotted down one more note: "Evidently the situation is getting worse. The marines have suffered losses. The German fire is very heavy. The commissar is wounded. . . ."

That night he slept aboard the *Virona*. Cabins No. 111 and 112 were assigned to correspondents. He lay on the bed without undressing. It was cold. It was cold when he awoke the next morning to hear the cruiser *Kirov* lobbing shells over the city. A tug, the *C-103*, kept swinging the *Kirov* around so the Germans could not get the range. Gray clouds obscured the sun. It was getting colder. Vishnevsky spent the day on the *Virona*, writing a leaflet to be distributed to the Baltic Fleet. He saw fires burning in the city and watched two heavy German shells explode in Kadriorg Park. The fighting grew more intense in the city outskirts. The weather changed again and again. Two rainbows appeared over the harbor.

All day on the twenty-fourth Vishnevsky made hurried jottings in his notebook:

Black smoke . . . Two fighters overhead . . . the *Tsiklon* [*Cyclone*, a Soviet gunboat] moves away from the wall. . . . The fire on the point has gone out. . . . 10:12 A.M. Two trawlers . . . Sunny . . . Tugboats . . . Two torpedo boats come into the harbor. . . . Comrade Karyakin says the sailors are holding up the Germans on the Narva highway . . . sailors from the *Kirov* and a mine layer—off to the front, singing . . . The *Virona* prepares to depart. . . . Many fires . . .

The Nazis missed their date, although in the confusion of August 24 they almost wiped out the Tallinn field command. General Nikolayev, his Military Council Member and General Moskalenko had decided to visit the command post of Colonel T. M. Parafilo. They did not know the Germans had overrun the position until they came under mortar fire. They had a close call. By nightfall the Nazis pushed into the lovely beach community of Pirita, and along the walls of the Minna Harbor the last reserves of the command had been assembled—the cadets of the Frunze Naval Academy.

In the gloom of the gray evening Admiral Panteleyev's eyes were caught by the glitter of the gold emblems and blue collars of the cadets. They were tall, staunch lads, well uniformed.

Panteleyev looked at the fresh, red-cheeked, blond young men, and his heart turned over. They represented the future of the fleet. And they were being sent into action from which few would emerge.

Admiral Tributs stepped before them and made a speech. They could hardly distinguish his words in the roar of cannonading. Then they marched through the gates of the harborage with a quick close step. That night the Germans overran the thin line of sailors defending Paldiski. Almost all perished in the hand-to-hand battle. Admiral Tributs ordered fleet personnel to board their ships, leaving only guards on shore.

"It was a tense alarming night," Panteleyev recalled. "The Germans were within six miles of Tallinn. Everyone was at the front, even the policemen. The city was empty. It held out only because of the naval guns and shore batteries. Once the Kirov stopped firing and General Nikolayev telephoned: 'What's the matter? Why are the ships silent? The Fascists are mounting an attack. Give us support immediately!' "[3]

On the twenty-fifth smoke screens were laid down over the harbor to protect the warships from Nazi air attack. One bit of good news brightened the day. Another convoy of nine transports with wounded made it back to Kronstadt. The transport Daugava was sunk, but all hands were saved. That day Admiral Tributs gave orders for a massive mine-sweeping operation to clear the path for the expected evacuation. But hardly had the orders been issued to Vice Admiral Rall than the wind began to rise from the northeast to gale force. The trawlers could do nothing in the high seas.

The night of the 25th–26th was even more alarming than the previous one. General Nikolayev called from his command post. He asked that the Military Council come to him. Tributs and the divisional commissar left and returned almost immediately, ordering all commanders to be summoned. The worst had happened. The Nazis had broken through both from the east and from the south. The warships were ordered to double their rate of fire.

All night the firing went on. At dawn Panteleyev noted in his operational journal:

26 August 6 A.M. During the night beat off strong attack on city. Enemy changed tactics, infiltrating small groups into the objectives. . . . All airfields captured by enemy. Our planes flew off to east. Fleet and city under bombing and shelling. Beautiful Pirita is burning. . . . Other suburbs also burning. Big fires in the city. Barricades and obstacles being built at approaches to harbor. Smoke everywhere . . . Fire of ships and shore batteries has not slackened. Our command post on Minna Harbor constantly under fire.

It was the last notation Panteleyev was to make in Tallinn.

Early in the day the Stavka in Moscow ordered Tallinn evacuated.

[3] It was heavy guns that enabled the Russians to hold Tallinn as long as they did. In all, 11,488 shells were expended in the defense, 7,505 by shore and railroad batteries. (Yu. Perechnev, Yu. Vinogradov, Na Strazhe Morskikh Gorizontov, p. 152.)

Vishnevsky went ashore that morning. He found barricades in all the principal streets. Smoke billowed over the city and a battle was in progress around the airport. Strong machine-gun fire echoed around the Rusalka monument. Ambulances clanged through the streets with the wounded. The Russians were slowly falling back toward the harbor. Shrapnel burst over Kadriorg Park.

The typesetters at the fleet newspaper were ordered to dig trenches in the park, and Editor Tarasenkov stationed himself near the Rusalka monument to halt the fleeing soldiers and sailors and try to form a new defense line. He saw Vishnevsky, gloomy, his glasses pushed down on his nose, going back toward the port. Until nightfall Tarasenkov held his post. At one moment a wild-eyed sailor rushed at him, automatic in hand, shouting, "Halt!" Tarasenkov, mustering all his will power, ordered the sailor to join the defense lines. The sailor hesitated, then hurled his weapon away and threw himself, writhing, to the ground.

By this time Paldiski had been cut off from Tallinn. The staff of the newspaper *Soviet Estonia* was taken aboard an icebreaker. Vishnevsky went back aboard the *Virona* at 6 P.M. Two planes were attacking the *Kirov*, and the harbor was quickly enveloped in smoke from the smoke ships. He watched two fires rise up over the city, dense clouds of pitch-black smoke high in the sky, as the sun set. He guessed that the oil tanks were burning. The first evacuation convoy, he heard, was to leave that night. He had a copy of Tarle's *Napoleon*. He opened it and began to read.

The next morning the city was still holding out, but the Germans had set up automatic weapons in Kadriorg Park. The Germans showered leaflets over the city: "The great Baltic Fleet is encircled."

Waves of smoke rose higher and higher. The sound of explosions was continuous. The Russians were setting fire to supply and ammunition dumps as they moved back to the harbor. By 12:15 P.M. the power station, the grain elevators and the arsenal were in flames. Sailors with gasoline cans were touching off warehouses. The smoke was so thick Vishnevsky had difficulty breathing. The NKVD units and the prosecutor's staff left their stations and hurried to the evacuation ships.

Mikhailovsky was still ashore. As he came toward the harbor, he passed a grassy patch right at the edge of the sea and saw a small group of Red Army men. Before them was a newly dug grave, red earth heaped up beside it. Lying on a stretcher beside the grave was a young girl in uniform, her face white as marble, her lips still smiling, her fair hair tossed back. A soldier was speaking:

"We say farewell to Zina, our good friend. She was as young as us. She saved our lives and she herself wanted to live. And now she is gone and we must leave her here in the raw earth. . . ."

Mikhailovsky went on. On Narva Street wounded were being carried out of a school and placed in ambulances. Soldiers trailed down the street, some carrying two or three rifles, their own and those of wounded or fallen comrades. The air was filled with the smell of fire and explosives. The barricades left narrow passages at one side through which the last retreating men could pass.

These were the men who would hold the lines while the ships loaded and got away from the Minna and the freight harbors. Overhead roared salvo after salvo of shells from the *Kirov*. Close to the piers from which Soviet troops were boarding transports, stores of ammunition burned, rattling and crackling like the battlefield itself.

A crane operator cursed as he loaded huge crates onto one of the ships: "What the hell is the point of loading these boxes? There isn't enough room for people and we are overloading the boats with crates."

"It's munitions, stupid," a soldier replied.

"Munitions, munitions," the operator snapped. "Who needs them at sea?"

The packet *Pikker*, which had been the command point for the Military Council, now stood empty. Only the cook, wearing his white cap, sat on the deck, watching the scene with curiosity.

An infantry captain arrived at the pier, worn and bedraggled. He approached a vice admiral. "Can I bring my men aboard?" he asked. "I've no equipment left. I destroyed my last cannon."

"I can't do it," the admiral said sharply. "The transport is overloaded. You'll have to get on the tanker."

Mikhailovsky watched a small gray car come up to the pier. Out of it stepped Vishnevsky, who motioned to the chauffeur. "You can destroy the car here."

The chauffeur was hesitant. "Maybe I can just remove the carburetor."

"You heard the order," Vishnevsky said sternly. "Nothing is to be left for the enemy. Carry out the order."

The chauffeur finally moved the car into a narrow driveway, took out a grenade, threw it in and flung himself to the ground. The machine blew up with a bang.   .

An idea suddenly came to Vishnevsky. The papers! No one had brought the last edition of the *Soviet Estonia* from the print shop. Together with Mikhailovsky, Anatoly Tarasenkov of *Komsomolskaya Pravda* and Yuri Inge, a poet, they went back into town, past the barricades, past the burning buildings to the gray structure that housed the newspaper. A four-story building was afire across the street.

They tramped into the newspaper office. It was gloomy and still. A stack of fresh newspapers lay at the mail window. The Estonian printers were still there. They looked at the four Russians with surprise. Each grabbed a bundle of papers and walked out. A woman with a blue kerchief on her head cried. They made their way back to the Minna Harbor through streets in which firing echoed again and again.

At 2:40 P.M. Vishnevsky boarded a cutter with Commissar Karyakin and went to the destroyer leader, *Leningrad*, command ship of the evacuation squadron. The noise of explosions in the city and bombs dropping in the harbor was deafening.

Tarasenkov, Mikhailovsky and most of the other journalists went aboard the *Virona*. So did Tsekhnovitser, the professor, a rucksack on his back. His face was thin, covered with several days' beard, his uniform torn and his boots muddy. But he was as brisk and bright as ever.

"Well," he said gaily, "we fell into the devil's meat grinder! What kind of miracle got us out I just don't know. We had been fighting for three days, and I thought the only way we'd get out would be in a coffin with a band playing. Suddenly, we got orders to get out and come to the harbor."

"You were born under a lucky star," someone said.

"Exactly," said Tsekhnovitser.

Johannes Lauristin, the chairman of Soviet Estonia, appeared. He was looking for the icebreaker *Surtyl*, on which he was supposed to be evacuated. It had already left, most of its passengers members of the fleet theatrical troupe.

"Never mind," he shouted, "I'll go on the mine layer *Volodarsky*. I'll see you in Leningrad."

Night fell. From the ships in the harbor could be seen ancient Vyshgorod, its balustrades outlined against the rosy sky. The great tower of Long Herman loomed over the scene, and on its heights waved a red flag. From the city came the rumble of explosions. The last guard still held its lines.

The loading of the transports began at 4 P.M., August 27. An evacuation plan had been prepared in twenty-four hours for upwards of 190 ships to be moved out of Tallinn Harbor, including 70 transports of more than 6,000 tons each. For safe passage through the narrow mine-filled waters (one witness compared the waters to "soup with dumplings," so filled were they with mines) a minimum of 100 mine sweepers was needed. There were available 10 fleet mine sweepers and 17 light trawlers. The best guess at the number of German mines in the waters through which the convoys would pass was 3,000 to 4,000.[4] Admiral Tributs asked for the emergency loan of 16 light cutters to protect his convoys and for a pre-emptive air strike against German coastal air bases to reduce the dangers to his convoy. Orders for these precautions came through from Leningrad, but only after the fleet had left Tallinn.

As evening drew on, the fleet guns redoubled their fire to cover the loading of the transports. The commercial wharfs fell under German fire, and ships had to be shifted to the Bekerovsky port. At 9 P.M. the rear guard fell back to their last positions. The destruction of the last stores began.

Admiral Panteleyev watched for a while from the bridge of the *Virona*.

[4] The figure is given as "more than 3,000" by one writer (Achkasov, *Voyenno-Istoricheskii Zhurnal*, No. 10, October, 1966, p. 19) and as 4,000 by another (Orlov, *op. cit.*, p. 134).

He saw the destroyer leader *Minsk* break off fire and turn sharply. The mine layer *Skory* did the same. They were dodging bombs. At midnight the *Virona* moved off to take its place in the convoy, between the islands of Naissaar and Aegna. The weather had not improved.

A gale rocked the ships from stem to stern. The big transports strained at the lines of the tugs. Rain swept the harbor in sharp gusts. At the entrance to the channel stood the old mine layer *Amur*. It was destined to be sunk to block access by the Germans. Now the harbor was dark. The piers were empty. There remained only two cutters and the last ship, the *Pikker*, to bring the Military Council of the fleet to the cruiser *Kirov*.

Aboard the *Virona* there was lively talk. Most of the journalists were on this ship. So was a nurse named Budalova who had been in Spain with the Russian group during the Civil War. All night long they talked with her about the war, about art, about artists, about Ilya Ehrenburg, who had been in Spain and whom they all knew. Tarasenkov thought the girl was a lot like Vera Milman, Ehrenburg's secretary—well educated, with good taste, cynical, a keen observer and sharp-witted. The night wore on, and aboard the *Virona* the war seemed as distant as the rose-velvet horizon where Tallinn lay burning.

Suddenly a profound roar shook the harbor and the sky glistened with stars of every color. It was the fleet stock of signal rockets, going up in one heavenly shower.

Panteleyev now was aboard the *Pikker* at the wharf. It was decided to move the Military Council to the *Minsk* in stages, beginning at 4 A.M. Panteleyev was in the second echelon, due to go at 7 A.M. The last would leave at 8 A.M., headed by General Moskalenko.

Time dragged on. The night grew more raw and cold. The Germans were almost at the entrance to the Minna piers. The crossfire died down. Panteleyev checked his reports. Nearly 23,000 persons had been loaded aboard the evacuation ships, as well as 66,000 tons of freight, mostly military materials.[5]

At 4 A.M. the Military Council was sent to the *Kirov*. Two cutters stayed behind, a little gunboat for Panteleyev and a torpedo boat for Moskalenko. The harbor was empty and quiet. The docks stood deserted. Slowly it began to get light. At 7 A.M. Panteleyev bade good-bye to Moskalenko and took off with his deputy, Captain N. A. Pitersky, and Commissar L. V. Serebrennikov. The wind was fresh, and the cutter threw up a splashing wave. Soon Panteleyev was aboard the *Minsk*, relaxing in a warm cabin and drinking coffee.

---

[5] This is Panteleyev's figure and probably is correct. The figures are given as more than 20,000 persons and 15,000 tons of materials by Orlov (*op. cit.*, p. 135).

23 ♦ The Russian Dunkirk

THE 190 SHIPS OF THE TALLINN EVACUATION HAD BEEN divided into four convoys. They formed up off Tallinn, waiting for orders to proceed. Desultory German fire splashed toward the ships. At 11:30 the signal to be prepared to proceed at noon was run up. Ahead of the convoy stretched an odyssey of 220 miles, of which 150 miles lay between two coasts occupied by the Germans and 75 miles were heavily mined. German airports were in easy range of almost the whole course. No Soviet air cover could be expected before the ships got to the immediate vicinity of Kronstadt.

Shortly after noon the first ships got under way—nine troop transports, including the *Virona*, and an escort of three submarines, five trawlers, five mine sweepers and five coastal cutters. The torpedo boat *Surovy* (*Grim*) commanded the escort. From the *Minsk*, Panteleyev could see how jammed were the transports, not a free spot on deck. They waddled along behind the tiny trawlers like turtles after frogs. Next came Convoy No. 2, headed by the *Kazakhstan*, guarded by the gunboat *Moskva*.

The signal officer reported: "The *Virona* has raised anchor. . . . The *Kazakhstan* has raised anchor. . . ."

The first and second convoys had just begun to move out of the harbor when the first of the German contact mines were touched off.

"It's begun!" someone on the bridge of the *Minsk* exclaimed.

Admiral Panteleyev kept his binoculars fixed on the shore. At about 1:35 P.M. the red flag on the ancient tower of Long Herman fluttered down and the tricolor of bourgeois Estonia was run up in its place.

At 2 P.M. Convoy No. 4 began to move. It was composed of nine ships, including self-propelled barges and tugs. It was protected by two cutters and nine trawlers.

Convoy No. 2 started moving again at 2:50 P.M.—ten large transports, four mine sweepers, nine trawlers and four gunboats.

Twenty minutes later came Convoy No. 3, the last and largest—nine big transports, including the *Luga*, the *Tobol*, the *Lucerne*, the *Balkhash*, the

Asumaa, the *Kumari* and the *Vtoraya Pyatiletka*.

It was protected by five gunboats and cutters and eight trawlers. The two transports which rescued the garrison from Paldiski joined this convoy.

The channel was clear. The ships drew off to the north and further on, at the very horizon, moved to the east. Now that the transports had gotten away General Moskalenko touched off the last depots at the water's edge. The *Amur* was sunk at one channel entrance, the transport *Gasma* at another and the tug *Mardus* at the eastern approach to Minna Harbor.

Under the direction of Vice Admiral Yu. F. Rall, the mine layers *Burya* (*Storm*), *Sneg* (*Snow*) and *Tsiklon* (*Cyclone*) planted mine barrages around the harbor and in the channel. Finally, at 4 P.M. the Baltic Fleet itself raised anchor. Five fleet trawlers led the procession. Then came the *Kirov*, bearing the fleet commander's flag, followed by the *Leningrad*, a squadron of mine layers, submarines and other warships. In all there were 28 fighting ships in the contingent, including rescue boats and icebreakers.

Not until 5:15 P.M. did the *Minsk* leave the harbor under German shrapnel fire. It headed a detachment of some 21 naval vessels. The *Minsk* steamed out, allowing an interval of twelve cable lengths behind her escorting trawlers. Finally, the rear guard of 13 ships under Admiral Rall departed at 9:15 P.M.

The hegira to Kronstadt was under way—a line of ships that stretched out over fifteen miles.

At 6 P.M. the dinner bell sounded on the *Minsk*. The steward laid the officers' mess with the usual white linen and gleaming crystal. But Panteleyev remained on the bridge. Already over the long line of transports stretching into the horizon the German air attack had begun, and the first ship had gone down, the transport *Ella*.

Aboard the *Virona* it was also the mess hour. Mikhailovsky, his notebook in hand, sat down at the long table. Among those waiting on table was a young girl with black braids, sensitive face, blue eyes. She looked to Mikhailovsky like a girl graduate. After dinner everyone went on deck to watch the German planes. The girl, her hair neatly braided, stood next to Mikhailovsky.

"How strange war begins," she said. "So unexpected. I just don't understand anything."

"Are you from Leningrad?" he asked.

"Yes," she said, "and I happened to be in Tallinn quite by accident."

They talked a while, then the ship moved on to the east. The islands of Naissaar and Aegna lay far behind. Again the German planes attacked. Nine struck at a tanker and a steamer. A smoke screen concealed the results. Suddenly the cruiser *Kirov* steamed ahead with its protective cover of trawlers. Fog began to spread over the sea.

They were coming into heavily mined waters now. The ships put out paravanes to touch them off. About suppertime a fierce new air attack was launched. The *Virona*'s antiaircraft guns chattered ceaselessly. The ship swung wide and zigzagged madly. Wave after wave of German JU-88's plunged down, attacking singly and then in trios.

Passengers began to run from side to side, but the stern base voice of Professor Tsekhnovitser halted them: "Comrades! Be calm! Nothing is going to happen to us. Panic is the most dangerous thing!"

The whistle of falling bombs filled the air. Suddenly Mikhailovsky felt the ship shudder. The deck under his feet seemed to rise up. The next moment he was under water, sinking to the bottom. The end. So it seemed. Then he rose. Blood was flowing from his forehead and into his left eye. Bullets flew through the water. He turned on his back and saw planes in the sky. They seemed to zero in on him. He ducked his head under water. When he came up again, the sky was clear. The sound of motors was fading into the distance. He felt something in the water—something firm and cold. He turned about and saw a body floating, the skull crushed and the face a mass of pulp. Only by the black braids did he recognize the schoolgirl from Leningrad who had found herself in Tallinn by sheer chance.

Mikhailovsky swam away. He swam for a while, then turned on his back and rested. He was miles from shore. All around him he heard cries for help. He saw a box float by. It had on it the letters: "Theater: Baltic Fleet." He grabbed for it, but had not the strength. The sun was setting and its red rays ran like tongues across the sky. He saw no people. Darkness—that is the worst, he thought. He grew cold. Suddenly, almost on top of him, a cutter appeared. Strong hands reached out and pulled him from the sea.

Admiral Panteleyev witnessed the *Virona* tragedy. He saw the ship, standing without movement, listing to the right. Over it rose a heavy cloud of oily smoke. The rescue ship *Saturn* made its way to the *Virona* to bring it under tow. The gunboat *Surovy* stood by, and the transport *Alev* hove to. But disaster followed on disaster. First, the *Saturn* was mined and sunk, then the *Virona* and finally the *Alev* and two more transports.

A sailor on the gunboat *Sneg* saw the *Virona* sink. The passengers were mostly staff of the Baltic Fleet, officers' wives, propaganda workers, newspapermen, Party officials. The quarterdeck was crowded, but in the sea the sailor could perceive the dark figures of people swimming. Across the watery expanse he heard the faint sound of the Internationale. The crowd on the deck was singing, and the stirring strains rolled over the waves. Then the sailor heard the thin crack of shots and the yellow flash of flame as officers took their own lives in the last moment before the ship disappeared below the waves.

The *Sneg* picked up dozens of survivors. Some of the women had lost all their clothes. Some of the men were hysterical. Later another gunboat picked up a woman who had clung to a German mine for hours before she was taken off. She was a commander's wife. She had sung the Internationale with the others. But she put no bullet in her head. She simply leaped into the water and eighteen hours later was rescued. Anatoly Tarasenkov jumped from the ship in full uniform, wearing his greatcoat, his pockets filled with manuscripts and notes, his pistol in his belt. He joined a circle of passengers who were holding hands and attempting to support each other with the help of life belts. Soon his limbs grew stiff, and he slowly swam off. How long he had been swimming he did not know when a tug appeared and he was hauled aboard.

As the tug plowed through the murky waters, he heard the cry again and again: "Save us! Help! Help!"

The tragedy of the *Virona* shook those who saw it. A commissar on the *Sneg* said bitterly: "Did you ever think we would drown like blind cats in a puddle? Where were our planes?" He was bitter at the commander of the *Kirov* for steaming proudly ahead, as though trailing his cape to the Germans. Why, he demanded, did not the commander go ahead with torpedo boats and organize aid?

The poet Yuri Inge watched the *Virona* sink from the foredeck of the icebreaker *K. Voldemars*. Inge was thirty-five years old, a tall, straight man with serious gray eyes and blond hair which was only beginning to darken a little. Vissarion Sayanov, his fellow poet, thought he looked like a Scandinavian.

"What bastards!" a friend heard Inge exclaim as, notebook in hand, he tried to jot down impressions for the poem already taking shape in his mind. Every life preserver on board the *Voldemars* was thrown to the struggling victims of the *Virona*. A moment later the *Voldemars* itself was hit and sank immediately.

Inge's wife, Yelena Vechtomova, knew of the tragedy as soon as the survivors got back to Kronstadt. A young boatswain named Virchik said, "I saw him almost at the end." But no one wanted to believe in Inge's death, and the letters he had written Yelena kept coming by slow military post week after week: "Good morning, Alenushka. It's a perfectly beautiful morning . . ."; "Broushtein has come and he brought two letters from you . . ."; "I've been to the post office and there are no letters . . ."; "How is Serezhenka? . . ."; "I've bought you some blue wool gloves." It was almost too much for Yelena Vechtomova.

The losses of the *Virona* were great: the writers F. Knyazev and Ye. Sobolevsky, Professor Tsekhnovitser, the poet Vasya Skrulev, the *Pravda* photographer Misha Prekhner. The elderly novelist and revolutionary president of Estonia, Johannes Lauristin, was lost on the *Volodarsky*.

No witness of the tragedies ever erased the scene from his memory. On the distant horizon the lagging ships of the rear guard loomed as dark shadows silhouetted against the rose-and-black sky where Tallinn lay burning. Enormous plumes of dense smoke poured upward and curved inward over the heavens, reaching toward the enactments of horror in the nearer sea. In the total blackout the burning carcasses of sinking ships glowed like campfires in a watery desert. Occasionally the sea would be blindingly lightened as the thunder of a torpedo or mine sent another ship to its end. The antiaircraft guns of the warships chattered ceaselessly at German dive bombers which swarmed in for the kill, their bomb paths illuminated by the flames of vessels already afire. The sea boiled with wreckage amid which swam survivors, some clinging to planks, others staying afloat with the aid of life preservers. The few lifeboats were loaded to the gunwale. Patrol boats and submarines picked their way through the waters, saving as many of the swimming men and women as they could. All around was the shuddering roar of mines, being exploded by the paravanes of the surviving ships. Within one hour the *Minsk* had touched off a dozen. The *Kirov* exploded five in half an hour.

As the ships neared Cape Uminda-Nina, they came under shellfire from German shore batteries. Coveys of German attack boats launched torpedoes amid the stricken convoys.

Just after 8 P.M. the submarine *S-5*, which was escorting the cruiser *Kirov*, struck a mine and disappeared under the water. A few moments later the right paravane of the *Kirov* caught a mine and, to the horror of the crew, began to draw it aboard the cruiser. Sailors managed to cut loose the paravane at the last moment, preventing an explosion aboard the cruiser. While the *Kirov* struggled with the faulty paravane, another escort, the mine layer *Gordy*, blew up at 8:36 P.M., followed in a few moments by the *Yakov Sverdlov*, which took a torpedo aimed at the *Kirov*. Many sailors were drowned. The flagman on the *Kirov*'s lookout kept up a continuous call of mine sweepers and minor ships sinking in the purée of mines. Another mine caught in the *Kirov*'s paravane just as a German torpedo boat dashed in for the kill. The torpedo boat was beaten off by the *Kirov*'s main guns. Simultaneously shore batteries opened up, but the cruiser silenced them and finally won a moment's respite when the mine layer *Smetly* covered it with a smoke screen.

It was much the same on the destroyer leader, *Minsk*. At 9:40 P.M. a mine exploded in one of the *Minsk*'s paravanes. Vice Admiral Panteleyev estimated that the ship took on 650 tons of water. The mine layer *Skory* came to the aid of the *Minsk* as it lay in the water without movement. The *Skory* and a tugboat took the *Minsk* in tow, but were sunk by a mine. The five base trawlers at the head of the *Minsk* detachment did not notice what had happened and steamed ahead, leaving only one trawler with the *Minsk*. Without escort amid waters filled with mines, Vice Admiral Panteleyev ordered his protective detachment and convoy to cast anchor. He did not resume course until after daylight the next day.

The rear guard was almost obliterated. About 10 P.M. the guard ships, *Sneg* and *Tsiklon*, were sunk and twenty minutes later the squadron leader, *Kalinin*, was lost off Cape Uminda-Nina. The *Kalinin* stayed afloat for an hour, and most of its wounded and personnel were removed. But at the same

time the mine layers *Artem* and *Volodarsky* went down. Vice Admiral Yu. F.
Rall, commander of the detachment, suffered severe wounds. The transports
Luga, Everitis and *Yarvamaa* were sunk.

In view of the density of the mines, the terrible losses already suffered
and the inability to cope with the hazards in the night, the fleet commander
ordered all ships to anchor until daylight. Patrols were set up to ward off
torpedo attacks.

What were the Tallinn evacuation losses? Of the 29 large transports which
left Tallinn, 25 were lost, 3 were beached on Hogland Island and only 1
reached Leningrad. One of the three ships beached on Hogland, the *Saule*,
later was towed to Leningrad. In all, the Baltic Merchant (noncombat) Fleet
lost 38 ships in the Gulf of Riga and the Irben Strait. More than 10,000 lives
were lost. In addition, 16 warships, mostly gunboats, mine sweepers and
cutters, were sunk and 6 small transports were sunk. Among the great ships
which went down were the *Ivan Papanin*, carrying 3,000 troops; the *Vtoraya
Pyatiletka* with about 3,000; the *Luga* with 300 wounded; the *Balkhash* and
the *Tobol*, each carrying several hundred. Of a total of 67 non-Navy ships,
34 were lost; of something over 100 naval craft, 87.5 percent were saved
along with about 18,000 personnel.[1]

The *Kazakhstan*, carrying 3,600 troops, including 500 wounded, was the
largest transport in the convoy. It was captained by Vyacheslav Kaliteyev,
one of the most experienced Baltic skippers. He had been captain of the
steamer *Cooperation*, which brought to Russia children of the Spanish Republicans. He had taken the *Kazakhstan* on several dangerous trips through
the Arctic, and he had captained his boat through the Baltic from the
beginning of the war.

The *Kazakhstan* took its place in the first convoy to leave Tallinn. Kaliteyev,
was on the bridge. The ship quickly drew German attention. First there
were submarine attacks and then wave after wave of JU-88's struck. A
stick of bombs fell harmlessly in the water. Then one struck. It hit a glancing
blow at the bridge, killing the commander of the antiaircraft battery, the
signalman and all those on the upper bridge.

The *Kazakhstan* was left without command. It lost speed and dropped out
of the convoy. More than a hundred bombs fell around the ship. Flames
broke out. The decks swarmed with hundreds of persons, most of whom had

[1] By comparison with Dunkirk the Tallinn evacuation was sheer catastrophe. Dunkirk
was a far larger operation, involving the safe evacuation of 338,226 men. The casualty figures are not entirely precise but are given as 9,291 (8,061 British and 1,230 Allied). In the
retreat to Dunkirk and in the action on the beaches and in transit to England, a total of
68,111 British troops were lost. The British employed 1,084 ships in the evacuation, many
of them very small. Only 108 of these were lost. The distance from Dunkirk to Dover
and the channel ports was only forty to fifty miles, and there was complete command of
the sea route by the British Navy and no problem of mines; even the Luftwaffe was not
terribly active. (David Divine, *The Nine Days of Dunkirk*.) Incidentally, there is some
confusion in the Soviet sources as to the number of men brought safely out of Tallinn.
One source contends that 18,233 men were saved out of a total of 23,000 who started
from Tallinn. This seems to be an obvious underestimate of casualties. (*Vtoraya Mirovaya Voina*, Vol. II, p. 100, citing archives of the Baltic Fleet Command.)

never before been at sea. Soldiers and passengers were pressed into service to fight the fire. For nine hours the battle raged before the flames were brought under control. Only seven members of the thirty-five-man crew survived. Headed by Second Boatswain L. N. Zagurko, they managed to get steam up and steered the *Kazakhstan* to a lonely spit of land called Vaindlo or Stenskjiner, about 500 yards long and 150 yards wide. There stood a lighthouse, a round cast-iron tower, painted white, manned by a small detachment of sailors. It was located about sixteen miles off the coast, between Naissaar and Gogland. The passengers were landed and picked up by sloops and small boats, which brought them to Kronstadt. Then, lightened of its load, the *Kazakhstan*, still under the command of its seven-man crew, was navigated, without charts, with field telephones connecting the bridge and the engine room, to Kronstadt. It got there September 1. All seven members of the crew won Orders of the Red Banner for their achievement.

But what of Captain Kaliteyev? There was no word of him in the Supreme Command's communiqué No. 303 of September 12, 1941, hailing the achievement of the *Kazakhstan*, sole troop ship to survive the nightmare of Tallinn.

Nor was this an accident. For Captain Kaliteyev was trapped in another nightmare. He was not dead, as most of those aboard the *Kazakhstan* had supposed.

The bomb which killed the men on the bridge did not kill Kalitayev. It merely knocked him unconscious.

"I heard the crash," he said later, "and felt the crack of the ceiling breaking and I don't remember anything more."

When he came to himself, he was lying on the right side of the bridge with his head toward the ladder leading to the upper bridge. He felt that his head was wet and putting his hand to it found it covered with blood. But he saw no wounds on his body.

He then lost consciousness again and apparently slipped from the bridge for when he came to he was in the water with the ship sliding past him. There were many others in the water around him, and about 60 or 80 yards away was a small sloop, afire, with ten or fifteen persons clinging to it. He slipped out of his coat and boots. He wore no life jacket as he had felt that to don one would have aroused fear among the passengers.

He kept afloat for half an hour and then with a sailor named Yermakov was picked up by the submarine *S-322*. The submarine was unable to return him to his ship. Instead, it took him to Kronstadt, where he arrived ahead of the *Kazakhstan*.

An investigation was immediately launched into the captain's conduct. Why had he left his ship? Why had he returned ahead of it? At first all went well. His associates in the merchant shipping service vouched for his character. The seven who saved the ship spoke up for him. Two medical experts said his story rang true.

But then came derogatory stories from passengers on the boat. The captain had abandoned his post. He had leaped into the water in fear. Gossip went to work. The suspicious investigators of the NKVD grew more suspicious. Kronstadt at that moment was gripped by panic. Some measure of the atmosphere in which the case was judged can be grasped from the fact that Vladimir Rudny, a Moscow correspondent, and Yuli Zenkorsky, a Tass correspondent, were picked up as "spies" a few days before the Tallinn ships came in. A few days later the writer Mikhail Godenko saw a young sailor, drunk on a couple of bottles of eau de cologne, shouting, "Down with the Soviets." A commander drew his *nagan*, his holster pistol, and shouted, "Stop!"

"What do you mean stop?" said the sailor. "You rats of the rear. Where were you when we were fighting at Gatchina, at Detskoye Selo?"

"I'll shoot," the commander warned.

"Shoot. Shoot ahead," the sailor yelled. "Shoot me. But tomorrow the Germans will be fighting in Piter."

A single shot brought the sailor to the pavement.

Admiral Kuznetsov, the Naval Commissar, visited Kronstadt August 31 —the day the evacuation of Tallinn was completed. Even before he arrived at Kronstadt he fell under the influence of the disorganized, panicky events. He found at Oranienbaum, where he embarked in his cutter for Kronstadt, undisciplined gangs of sailors, not in uniform, separated from their units, wandering aimlessly, seemingly oblivious to what was going on around them. Kronstadt was gloomy. The officers and the sailors were filled with depression.

That was the atmosphere in Kronstadt in which the case of Captain Kalitayev was judged by the secret police. Their verdict: death before the firing squad. The charge: desertion under fire, cowardice.

Seventeen days after Order No. 303 was issued, honoring the seven men of Kalitayev's crew for saving the *Kazakhstan*, the captain went before the firing squad and was executed.

Not until January 27, 1962, did the Leningrad Military District Court get around to "rehabilitating" the reputation of Kalitayev and informing his widow, the actress, Vera Nikolayevna Tutcheva, that the charges against her husband were quite without foundation. So closed one of the last and most tragic episodes of the Tallinn disaster.[2]

[2] The "rehabilitation" of Captain Kaliteyev is in itself an epic and throws a penetrating light on the atmosphere which prevailed in Stalin's Russia, during the war and after. The naval correspondent and playwright, Aleksandr Ilych Zonin, was a passenger on the *Kazakhstan* and a witness to what happened. Zonin did his utmost to establish the true facts and again and again implored his colleagues not to write the story as though it was the tale of "Seven Who Saved the Transport." He placed his own version of the *Kazakhstan* affair in the naval archives, although he could not get it published. Orders had been issued coincident with the Order No. 303 honoring the "Seven" that Kaliteyev's name was to be "blacked out." The chief credit for establishing the truth is assigned by Vladimir Rudny, who long interested himself in the case, to Georgi Aleksandrovich Bregman, a correspondent of the newspaper *Water Transport*. Bregman had known Kaliteyev

Admiral Kuznetsov, Admiral Tributs, Admiral Panteleyev, Admiral Drozd and the other top naval men conducted a lengthy post-mortem in the ensuing weeks into the Tallinn affair. Admiral Kuznetsov tended to blame the Leningrad Command, which had operational control of the Baltic Fleet, for delay in ordering that evacuation plans be drafted for Tallinn—if necessary.

Panteleyev felt that, while the decision to defend Tallinn to the last regardless of cost was right and necessary in order to draw as much German strength off Leningrad as possible, a major error had been made in not evacuating from Estonia long before the end thousands of civilians and all nonmilitary organizations, as well as the rear echelons of the fleet. Some officers felt the basic concept of the Baltic defense had been wrong—that the fleet should have evacuated Hangö and the islands, thrown up a strong defense line at Tallinn and then pulled back to the secure base at Kronstadt.

As for the effort to plow through the German mine field, all admitted this had been a disastrous mistake. A later study by the fleet's mine experts reached the conclusion that the mine field had the extraordinary density of not less than 155 mines and 104 mine protectors per mile. To traverse such a field with any safety would have required not less than a hundred seagoing mine sweepers.[3]

The worst handicap, Panteleyev concluded, was the fact that the fleet had no secure bases. From the beginning of the war it had been in movement, falling back from Libau, to Riga, to Tallinn and finally back to Kronstadt. It would have been far better off never to have moved.

The magnitude of the losses stimulated the search for scapegoats. The

---

before the war and was completely confident of his bravery and honesty. He was in a military hospital recovering from wounds when he heard of the catastrophe which had befallen his friend. He began to collect evidence and after *sixteen years of work* managed to get the verdict against Kalitayev reversed. (Vladimir Rudny, *Deistvuyushchii Flot*, Moscow, 1965, pp. 57–72.) Zonin narrowly escaped the fate of Kalitayev. He was expelled from the Communist Party as a result of one of the literary political quarrels of the late 1920's but, unlike most of his colleagues, was not arrested at that time. He served with great distinction in wartime as a Baltic Fleet correspondent and was recommended for readmission to the Party. But the Party control officials rejected him. In 1949 he was arrested and sent to a concentration camp. He survived to be released after Stalin's death but died soon of a heart attack, his health crippled by his sufferings. His son, Sergei, is now an officer in the Soviet Navy. (A. Shtein, *Znamya*, No. 4, April, 1964, pp. 78–84; *Literaturnaya Gazeta*, December 8, 1964.)

[3] After World War II when Soviet naval specialists subjected the Tallinn disaster to careful analysis, they concluded that the Baltic Fleet seriously overestimated the dangers of Nazi submarine attack. Had the fleet steamed straight out to sea, it would have been able to avoid most of the German mine fields and shore batteries. It would have risked attack by Nazi submarines, but the Germans were not present in strength in that area and, moreover, the Baltic Fleet was much better equipped to cope with submarine attack than with mines. There was also a channel close to the shore which Soviet ships had been using and which was known to be comparatively free of mines. However, it had been closed August 12 by order of the Northwest Front Command after the Nazis reached the Finnish Gulf at Kunda. (V. Achkasov, *Voyenno-Istoricheskii Zhurnal*, No. 10, October, 1966, p. 30.)

whole affair came under high-level security review. Vsevolod Vishnevsky, a fervent naval partisan and keen observer, wrote a sixteen-page report in the first days of his return to Kronstadt and submitted it to the Fleet Military Council and the Political Administration. He also wrote a fourteen-page report for publication in the fleet newspaper, *Red Fleet*. The public report was never published. The formidable Ivan Rogov, Political Commissar of the Fleet, had Vishnevsky in his black books. Moreover, the Tallinn disaster was a matter for very high-level politics. It was, in fact, a case for Lavrenti P. Beria and the secret police.

Panteleyev and his fellow command officers were the subject of sweeping inquiry by police and prosecutors. They attempted honestly and realistically to explain what had happened. The explanations were not accepted.

"A live criminal was what they wanted," Panteleyev concluded, after going through a long night of questioning.

The memory of one confrontation burned long in his consciousness. It was with an individual whom Panteleyev described as "a highly placed officer." Could this have been Malenkov or Beria—or one of their chief aides? He does not specify.

"Comrade Chief of Staff," said this official, "why didn't our fleet fight? Why have the Fascists been able to fight and we have not?"

Panteleyev attempted to explain the complicated situation. The official would not listen.

"No, no," he said, "I do not agree with you. The staff is not supposed to concern itself with that kind of business. It must work out active operations and fight, and attack, and . . ."

As Panteleyev dryly notes: "In the eyes of this important official the staff of the fleet came very close to being guilty for all the tragedies that had occurred."

Looking back at the Tallinn tragedy from a perspective of twenty-five years, the Soviet naval historian, Captain V. Achkasov, was convinced that its cause lay in the reluctance of any of the commanders—of either the Baltic Fleet, the Leningrad Command or the High Command in Moscow— to order preparations for evacuating the fleet.

The reason for this reluctance, he felt, was a well-founded knowledge on the part of all that commanders of encircled units had repeatedly been subjected to the gravest charges of cowardice and panic, often with fatal consequences. Rather than risk a firing squad, the commanders withheld any recommendations for withdrawal until a tragic outcome became inescapable.

24 . *The Northern Crisis*

THE COMMANDERS OF LENINGRAD'S DEFENSES TREATED
the Northern Front—that with Finland—like a savings bank. From almost
the beginning of the war they systematically transferred troops and matériel
from the north to feed into the bleeding fronts on Leningrad's south, southwest and southeast.

But the Northern Front was not an inexhaustible reservoir of manpower.
Marshal Voroshilov and Zhdanov could rob Peter to pay Paul, but sooner
or later there was going to be a serious overdraft.

For weeks the Twenty-third Army, first under General P. S. Pshennikov
and now under Major General Mikhail N. Gerasimov, had held off Finnish
forces north of Leningrad which were estimated at nearly twice its size. The
Finns had a margin in guns of 1.2 and a 2.2 ratio of air superiority.

But now the Twenty-third Army was falling into serious trouble. The
Finns launched an offensive July 31, driving in the Keksholm direction,
hoping to reach the northern shores of Lake Ladoga and split the Twenty-
third Army in two.

General Gerasimov had taken command of the army on August 4. A man
of great self-confidence, his presence exuded calm. Once Colonel B. V.
Bychevsky, the fortifications specialist, heard him report on a serious Finnish
breakthrough. He showed no signs of nervousness. When he finished his
report, he began to whistle a pleasant melody from an operetta.

General Gerasimov's task was complicated by the fact that he had no
reserves. None whatever. All had been drained off into the defense of
Leningrad's southern approaches. Nor was that all. The High Command
kept drawing on both the Twenty-third Army and its northern neighbor, the
Seventh, to reinforce the shattered Leningrad front. It was a policy that was
bound to lead to disaster. Now that disaster seemed near.

The Finns drove through to the shores of Lake Ladoga near Khitola,
northwest of Keksgolm, on August 6. Gerasimov's eastern units—the 168th

Rifle Regiment, the 367th Rifle Regiment and the 708th Rifle Regiment—
were cut off from the west, fighting a defensive battle north of Sortavala.
Another group, the 142nd Rifle Regiment and the 198th Motorized Division,
continued to fight north and northeast of Kiitola. A third group was fighting
south and west of Keksgolm.

Only one division could be spared to reinforce Gerasimov. This was the
265th Rifle Division. The Finns had opened a gap of nearly twenty miles
between Gerasimov's divisions and were heading for the Lake Vuoksa, with
the aim of getting behind him and encircling the forces defending Vyborg at
the new Soviet-Finnish border.

By August 15 the Finns had smashed across the Lake Vuoksa, east of
Vyborg. The threat of encirclement to Gerasimov's main forces was grave,
and there were no troops available to help him. The Finnish front was
crumbling at the precise moment when the Nazi offensive south and southwest of Leningrad was gaining in momentum.

Because Leningrad had lived for so long under the danger of the nearby
frontier with Finland, the Leningrad Military Command before World War
II had always considered the north as the most critical area. Here the Soviets
had invested tens of millions of rubles in concrete underground fortifications.
Here were located the heaviest gun emplacements, the most powerful siege
guns. The 1940 war with Finland had been fought to secure Leningrad's
northern approaches.

Now the command was confronted with the tragic decision of abandoning
the northern shield which had been wrested from Finland in the winter war.
There was no alternative. The demands of the Southern Front were in-
satiable. On August 20—the very day that Zhdanov and Voroshilov prepared
their "enemy at the gates" proclamation—the Supreme Command ordered the
Twenty-third Army to retire to a shorter, more easily defensible line that
ran from Lake Pukya to Lake Vuoksi and the right bank of the Vuoksi River,
just north of Vyborg.

The Vyborg defense group began to demolish the heavy fortifications
along the new Finnish-Soviet frontier and fall back to the Vyborg area.
But the Finns were too fast for them. The 2nd Finnish Corps cut behind
the Russians and reached the Vuoksi, driving to within seven miles of Vyborg
by the twenty-sixth of August.

The options available to the Soviet commanders suddenly began to
vanish. On August 28 Gerasimov was ordered to withdraw his three divisions
to the old Mannerheim Line, along Lake Muolan and Rokkala. He was
instructed to blow up all fortifications in Vyborg, to dig in on the new line
and hold there.

This was the news which greeted Colonel Bychevsky when he arrived at
General Staff headquarters the night of August 28. He knew that Gerasimov
had proposed withdrawal to General Popov, the Leningrad commander,
several days earlier, fearing that the Twenty-third Army might be cut off.

But Popov summarily forbade such a move and reprimanded Gerasimov for what he called his "passivity."

The retreat in Karelia came as a personal blow to Bychevsky. He had directed the construction of much of the heavily fortified system which was now being destroyed. It was probably the best defensive line which the Soviets had ever built. He had overseen the mounting of the great guns just before the war started. He had laid the enormous and powerful mine fields which protected the forts. Now all this was lost. In fact, in the considered opinion of the Leningrad commander, General M. M. Popov, the new fortifications "played no special role" in the city's defense. Bychevsky could not help feeling that by some means the Finns should have been halted on the fortified lines rather than on new ones which would have to be hastily improvised.

"What is to be done now?" Bychevsky asked his assistant, Colonel Nikolai Pilipets.

Pilipets spread his hands.

"Nobody knows," he replied. "Army staff already has changed its location twice today, and now communications with Gerasimov have been interrupted. One thing is clear: the three Vyborg divisions are in a trap."

The Vyborg divisions, the 42nd, the 115th and the 123rd, had no chance to reach the Mannerheim Line on the Finnish side of the old frontier. They had virtually no ammunition and were cut off from headquarters. On their own initiative they retreated southwest to the little fishing port of Koivisto on the northern shore of the Finnish Gulf. The Finns drove steadily forward, occupying Vyborg August 29; Kivennapa, thirty miles south, on the same night; Raivola on the thirtieth; and Terijoki, on the old Soviet-Finnish frontier, August 31. The 168th Division, which had been isolated, defending Sortavala on the northern coast of Lake Ladoga, suffered extraordinary losses and finally had to be removed across Lake Ladoga to Leningrad.

The remnants of the Twenty-third Army attempted to move back to the old Karelian fortified area and occupy the system which had defended Leningrad's northern approaches prior to the 1939–40 winter war with Finland. This line was only twenty miles from the Leningrad city limits.

Even this was not accomplished without great difficulty and risk. The retreating troops, destroying their equipment, attempted to slip out in small groups through the dense forest and boggy marshes. Many units lost their way and became disoriented in the gloomy wilderness. Some became demoralized. Others managed to make their way to the Sestra River and the Sestroretsk fortified line.

For two or three critical days at the end of August there was almost no organized defense. The Finns could have pushed ahead and stormed the Beloostrov fortifications, marching into the northern suburbs of Leningrad. The only units holding on were some detachments hurriedly taken from the Baltic Fleet and thrown into battle as land marines. This handful of Soviet units staved off the storming of the northern capital by the Finnish troops.

One of these units was a small reconnaissance outfit headed by Anatoly Osovsky. He had twenty-six men. On September 1 he found himself in Sestroretsk, where he reported to the local Party secretary and the head of the NKVD, who sent him to the highway just north of Sestroretsk where a Nazi tank column had been reported. There he discovered a handful of soldiers, who joined his group. A mile north of the city near the local customshouse he spotted a German T-3 medium tank firing down the highway. His men took cover in a sand pit. The tank slowly advanced, but Osovsky disabled it with two accurately hurled grenades which tore off its treads.

Soon two more tanks and forty or fifty infantrymen appeared. Osovsky had fifteen men left. They opened fire with small arms and brought the advance to a halt. Osovsky's men stayed in their positions for six days, winning personal congratulations from Party Secretary Andrei Zhdanov.

Leonid Zakharkov, member of a naval air unit, volunteered for a naval detachment which was hurriedly thrown into the same Beloostrov front.

"We sloshed all night through the marsh," he recalled, "up to our waists in water. We carried our equipment over our heads—guns, mortars, ammunition. Suddenly we found ourselves almost to our necks in water. We moved ahead under machine-gun fire from the railroad tracks."

Fighting beside him were two girls, Valya Potapova, wife of a scout, and black-eyed, black-haired Anna Dunayeva. They lived in Terijoki and had joined a patrol battalion which on August 31 found itself fighting a Finnish parachute detachment in the Pukhtolovo Hills. There were 10 girls in the unit of 140. They had three machine guns and several dozen rifles.

Forced to retreat to Terijoki, they found the city burning and empty. The bakery was on fire, the city hall ablaze. By nightfall they reached the road to Sestroretsk. There they got a ride part of the way and joined the little band of defenders. On that first night the lines ran through a swamp beside the Sestra River. After two days they fell back into the fortified lines, where the naval brigade joined them.

The battle for Beloostrov went on and on into September. Twice the Russians were thrown out of the city and fought their way back in hand-to-hand combat in which an outstanding Soviet tank commander, Major General Lavrionovich, was killed. But his tanks moved forward in heavy rain and mud and managed to secure the city. Finnish attacks went on for the next three months, but the Soviet lines held.

The collapse of the Twenty-third Army was marked by savage fighting. Ivan Kanashin, one of the youngsters who had volunteered at Komsomol headquarters at Gryady on Sunday, June 22, now was serving with a detachment of twenty-eight Young Communists, defending an airfield outside Vyborg. They had beaten off a heavy paratroop attack and on the windy, dark morning of August 29 lay in field positions and watched the thin red sunrise streak the sky. Soon an enemy tank column appeared on the Vyborg highway. The tanks halted to inspect some ditches beside the road where lay the bodies of several hundred paratroopers, killed in an attack of the previous day.

The young troopers held their fire until the last possible moment, then opened up with hand grenades. The Finns tossed back grenades, and Kanashin dropped with a splinter wound in his neck. When he regained consciousness, he saw an officer standing over him and a group of eight Russian wounded.

"The valiant German troops already are marching down the boulevards of Leningrad," the officer said, in Russian. "And you stupid kids think you are going to save Russia. What's the idea of this suicide, I ask you? Soviet Russia is *kaput*."

A youngster named Misha Anisimov raised himself, blood streaming from his mouth and down his face. "Hitlerite baboons!" he shouted. "I spit on you. Go ahead. Shoot."

The officer kicked Anisimov, drew his pistol and shot him. Then he shot a youngster named Ilyusha Osipov.

"What's the matter, you Russian bastards?" he said. "Are you dying of terror? Maybe you'll come to your senses before it's too late. One word for mercy and I'll give you your lives."

Kanashin lifted himself and spat in the officer's face.

A minute later he was yanked to his feet. Two troopers put a chain around his neck, attached it to their car and started to drive off. Kanashin with his last strength grabbed the collar as he felt his body swaying behind the careening machine.

A cold rain brought him to consciousness. He lay beside the road, half in, half out of a small stream. He had been left for dead by the troopers. Staggering to his feet, he entered the forest. Somehow he managed to make his way across the countryside, through marshes and underbrush. He stumbled into the Russian lines beyond Terijoki at the Sestra River on September 8.

On the morning of September 1 Admiral Panteleyev had gone out into the staff garden at Kronstadt to get a little fresh air. He had been working since the night before on plans for new mine barriers to guard the approaches to Leningrad and on means of supporting the garrisons at Hangö and on the Moonzund Islands, which still held out at the entrance to the Gulf of Finland.

As he strolled in the open, listening to the roar of the Kronstadt guns, backing up the heavy fighting on the Leningrad approaches ashore, an aide called him to Admiral Tributs.

"There's a call from Smolny," Tributs said. "The 115th and 123rd divisions, falling back from Vyborg, have suffered heavy losses and they are surrounded almost without supplies and weapons along the shore at Koivisto. We don't know the exact situation. Communications are cut. They should be somewhere near here."

The Admiral stepped to a chart and made a black circle with his long pencil between Koivisto and Makslakhti.

"Is everything clear?" Tributs asked.

Nothing at all was clear, but Panteleyev waited for Tributs to continue.

"Voroshilov has ordered us to collect the divisions from Koivisto and bring them to Leningrad. You are in charge. Is it clear now?"

Tributs gave Panteleyev permission to telephone his family in Leningrad —he had not had time to see them since the Tallinn evacuation. Panteleyev talked to his family, then made his plans. He would need six or seven transports for the new evacuation. While they were being collected, he decided to go to Koivisto and see for himself what the situation was.

Protection for the rescue convoys would be provided by armored cutters and gunboats. The fleet batteries on Krasnaya Gorka and the Bjerkoe Peninsula could lay down protective fire.

Panteleyev set off in a wooden patrol boat—the best defense he could think of against the magnetic mines which were plaguing Soviet ships in the Gulf of Finland. The weather was fine—a lazy southwest wind and gentle waves. The patrol boat skirted the Finnish coast. Panteleyev saw an occasional summer villa, no people, no horses, no cows. He had known the Koivisto cove since he was a youngster and had sailed there. It was a picturesque coast and this was where the yachts began their cruise to the Gulf of Bothnia.

In the Koivisto Harbor Panteleyev found two Soviet gunboats, an ironclad and a landing barge. The Soviet forces had set up a defensive ring, and it seemed probable that they would be able to hold out against attack until the evacuation was completed. Word came from Kronstadt that two transports were on the way.

Some army men appeared on the pier, gloomy, with drawn faces and hoarse voices. They were commanders of various broken units. There were many wounded. Finally a division commander came up with the remnants of his staff. He was as tired as the others but still carried himself with vigor.

"I've neither guns nor tanks left," he said.

"Never mind," Panteleyev assured him. "We have 130-mm guns on the ship. They will support us."

In the darkness the first transport appeared. It was decided to load the two thousand wounded first. Next unwounded soldiers would be boarded, but only those who still had their guns. This was a purposeful order. The officers had noticed many men throwing away their weapons. Now the troops started to scurry about. Miraculously unit after unit appeared, each man with a gun or submachine gun.

"Our tickets for the steamboat," one man said.

Three ships had been assembled for the operation—the *Barta*, under Captain A. Farmakovsky, the *Otto Schmidt*, captained by N. Fafurin, and the *Meero*, commanded by Captain V. A. Tsybulkin.

The *Barta* arrived first. It loaded 2,350 men and took off.

Thousands still waited on the shore when word came that one of the transports—it was the *Meero*—had been sunk near the Bjerkesund, by either a mine or a torpedo.

Then the *Otto Schmidt* ran aground, but managed to get off and picked up its load. All night long the evacuation went on. The last transport vanished to sea, and still men and women kept appearing from the forest. A gunboat was sent off, loaded to the water line with evacuees.

Panteleyev stood by with several cutters in case more people appeared. Finally, he gave the order to cast off. His boat had gone only a short distance when the sailors spotted a dog, panting with exhaustion, running down the pier.

"It's our dog from the gunboat!" a sailor shouted. The boat drew back to the pier and the dog jumped aboard, wild with happiness.

Panteleyev's boat moved out to sea. As they approached the Stirsudden lighthouse, they hailed it. No answer. "Maybe they're asleep," someone said. Then the answer came: a shot from a field gun. Then another. Clear enough! The enemy had occupied the lighthouse.

Before noon the convoy had reached Kronstadt—14,000 men had been evacuated safely, 12,000 "fit for combat" and 2,000 wounded.

Pavel Luknitsky, the correspondent, had spent much time on the Karelian front. He had seen the tenseness, the near-panic in Petrozavodsk when women and children were evacuated with the heightening of the Finnish August offensive. Now he met the survivors of the Twenty-third Army when they arrived in Leningrad. He thought them far from fit for battle. Many were emaciated, exhausted. Many were wounded. Many had fought to the last of their strength. Others had become demoralized when they found them-selves trapped in encirclement. It would take time to form these bedraggled troops into new first-class fighting units. But time was one asset Leningrad did not possess. The men were assigned to new units and sent up to the front almost as rapidly as they landed in the cutters from Kronstadt.

In Karelia the Soviet troops dug in on the old lines, there to sit it out until 1944. To the east, on the Seventh Army front, there was another month of action. The Seventh Army positions east of Lake Ladoga had been unhinged by the disintegration of the Twenty-third Army. The Finns massed nine infantry divisions and three brigades against the Seventh Army—a manpower superiority of almost three to one. Beginning September 4 they went on the offensive. In harsh fighting the Finns captured Olonets the next day and drove to the Svir River by September 10, cutting the Kirov railroad which connected the Karelian front with the rest of the country. After a bitter battle the Finns finally occupied Petrozavodsk October 2.

By this time—as of September 24—General Meretskov, one of the best of the Soviet generals, had taken command of the Seventh Army. He stabilized the front along the whole Finnish littoral, and for practical purposes there was no more movement until the opening of the Soviet counterdrives in 1944.

On the line of the river Svir and on the old Finnish-Soviet frontier positional warfare became the rule of the day. The objective which Hitler had advanced before launching his attack on Russia—that the Germans and the Finns join hands across the Karelian peninsula in preparation for the final great sweeping drive south on Moscow—was not now achieved—nor would it be. But critical days lay ahead before this was to become clear.

25 . *The Last Days of Summer*

THE TRAIN ON WHICH VERA INBER WAS RIDING SLOWED to a halt just after daybreak. No station was in sight, no plane in the sky, no sound of gunfire. All was stillness. Even the men in the compartment where an endless game of preference was in progress played with stealthy quietness. The Lieutenant General, whistling under his breath, named his suit. A military engineer next to him tapped his pipe so gently on the edge of the table it sounded like a distant woodpecker. A single wisp of tobacco smoke floated out the door and into the corridor, where it was caught in the rays of the rising sun.

So still was it that to Vera Inber the train seemed to be moving on velvet rails.

She had seen few signs of war. At Volkhov two fighter planes flew over the train for a while, and a small detachment of marines, the golden anchors on their uniforms glittering in the sun's first rays, marched down the platform.

To the right and the left of the track the holes, filled with water, seemed to be more frequent. Along the telegraph line there were also holes, but smaller ones. The Germans, she thought, are very economical, very German in their bombing. They wasted nothing: big bombs for the railroad tracks, small bombs for the telegraph poles. Now the forest was scorched by explosions and there were uprooted trees. She saw a birch, its bark crisscrossed with names and messages. The history of a lifetime had been scratched out on the white surface. Now it sagged, half-burnt, blackened, torn.

When the train pulled through the next station, Vera Inber read the name, neatly outlined on white-painted stones that stood among a bed of red and white petunias. The name was Mga. Vera Inber had never heard it before. These stations, she thought, all had drowsy, ancient Russian names . . . names that smelled of the pitch and the honey of the pine and birch forests: Mga . . . Budogoshch . . . Khvoinaya . . .

In those days the novelist Vera Ketlinskaya spent most of her time in an old stone mansion at No. 18 Ulitsa Voinova, just off Liteiny Prospekt, a stone's throw from the Neva. Here was the headquarters of the Leningrad Writers Union, and here she sought to organize her colleagues in Leningrad's war effort. An aeon had passed since that Sunday in the country at Sviritsa, where she had been teaching her ten-month-old son, Serezhka, to take his first halting steps and someone interrupted with the news: War!

In the last days of August her task was not easy. She was besieged with requests for permission to leave the city. People wanted a pass to get out before the Germans came.

There was panic and nervousness. Not that Vera Ketlinskaya was inclined to blame anyone. The situation was frightening. The city was preparing for battle in the streets. The examples of Madrid and of London were vivid in the minds of all. Block-by-block defense units were being set up. Because there were so few guns, Finnish knives—long-bladed hunting weapons—were being passed out.

She tried to persuade some of the writers who obviously could make little contribution to Leningrad's defense to leave. But many refused to go. One was Yevgeny Shvarts, the playwright whose *The Naked King* reminded more than one Leningrader of life under Stalin (which may be the reason it remained in Shvarts's literary archives after his death and was only performed ten years after Stalin's death and eight years after Shvarts's).

The Leningrad Theater of Comedy was being evacuated. But Shvarts would not join his associates. He said he would stay on in his granite building at No. 9 Griboyedov Canal, where he was a member of the fire brigade and his wife belonged to the first-aid team.

Shvarts was no Communist, but he was a patriot.[1] A few months before the war started he wrote a play in which a foreign spy plane landed somewhere on the steppes of southwest Russia. The censors banned the play. "Really," they told Nikolai Akimov, director of the Theater of Comedy, "do you think our air frontiers are not secure? The basic theme of this play is unjustified and impossible."

Shvarts volunteered to help Vera Ketlinskaya. He was with her when a Party secretary telephoned from Smolny about a uniformed war correspondent. The secretary wanted the man released so he could be sent to the rear. "This is a military question," said the Party man, "not a literary one."

"Indeed," Shvarts commented wryly, "it is a military matter—a matter of getting out of the military."

Two days after the correspondent escaped to the safety of Moscow an article he had written earlier was published by *Leningradskaya Pravda*, proclaiming: "We will defend Leningrad with our naked breasts!"

One day—it was August 27—the office door opened, and Vera Ketlinskaya

---

[1] For many years Shvarts and Nikolai M. Oleinikov had edited a children's magazine called *Chizh i Yezh*. Oleinikov had been a Party member since the first days of the Revolution. He was arrested and executed in 1937 as an "enemy of the people." Shvarts was so shaken he was unable to write for several years.

saw a small, graceful woman wearing a light coat and a coquettish hat under which struggled a mop of curly grayish hair.

"How do you do!" the woman said. "I'm Vera Inber."

She walked across the room, her high heels ringing on the parquet.

To Vera Ketlinskaya it was like an appearance from Mars. Vera Inber was fifty-three years old and a well-known Moscow poet. Her husband was the distinguished physician, Professor Ilya Davidovich Strashun. What was she doing in Leningrad?

"My husband and I have come to live in Leningrad," she said simply. "I don't know for how long, but at least until spring."

Was it possible that this chic, self-possessed woman did not know what she had walked into, did not know that at any moment the Germans might break into the streets of Leningrad, that the city might soon be encircled, indeed might already be within a German ring?

Vera Ketlinskaya hurriedly cleared the room and began to speak confidentially with Vera Inber.

"I know all that," Vera Inber replied. "You see, my husband had a choice —to be chief of a hospital in Archangel or in Leningrad. We decided that since my daughter and granddaughter have been evacuated and since, as a poet, I should in time of war be in the center of events, naturally Leningrad would be much more interesting."

"But—" Vera Ketlinskaya interrupted.

"I know what you're going to say," Vera Inber continued. "But, first of all, I believe that Leningrad will not give up. And second, well, we are not young. And for the middle-aged to sit in the rear is somehow very shameful."

That night Leningrad was put under curfew. Movement in the streets between 10 in the evening and 5 A.M. was forbidden without special pass. And that evening Vera Inber spoke for the first time on the Leningrad radio. She recalled that Alexander Herzen, the nineteenth-century Russian critic, democrat and patriot, once said that "tales of the burning of Moscow, of the Battle of Borodino, of the Berezina Battle, of the fall of Paris, were the fairy stories of my childhood—my *Iliad* and my *Odyssey*." So in these present days, she told her listeners, Russia was creating for future generations new Odysseys, new Iliads.

In the fortnight during which August imperceptibly blended into September the city never had seemed more beautiful. It stood brooding and grim, Peter's military city, on guard, under heavy attack, firm, belligerent. Never had there been such an August—hot, dry, summery, a clear sky of distant blue curved like a saucer high over the city, the trees and shrubs flowering magnificently. The great lindens glowed with gold and purple and russet along the wide avenues, under the trees carpets of mushrooms. An ill omen, the babushkas said. Many mushrooms, many deaths. The green lawns and flowerbeds of the parks were crisscrossed with trenches and packed with gun sites.

Leningrad was preparing to meet the enemy. Catherine's equestrian Peter

no longer reared his mighty charger on the banks of the Neva. Around the
heroic figure were piled layer after layer of sandbags, covered with gray
wooden planking. Gone were the Klodt stallions from the Anichkov Bridge,
buried in the Summer Gardens and protected by mounds of earth. Only the
stone sphinxes with their great paws still guarded the Neva embankment,
and the bowed caryatids still shouldered their terrible burdens at the
portals of the Hermitage. And the ugly monument to Catherine II stood in
all its ugliness in Ostrovsky Square.

The weather continued hot. Kirov Prospekt, always so clean and sparkling,
always washed down each morning just after dawn, always swept each night,
now was dusty and dirty. Rubbish was collecting in the gutters. The Prospekt
was the grand boulevard that cut across Kamenny Ostrov—stone island.
Once it had been Kamenny Ostrov Prospekt, but like so many of Leningrad's
boulevards its name had changed. Thus, Sadovaya (Garden) Boulevard had
become Third of July Street. Morsky (Sea), Teatralny (Theater), Ofitsersky
(Officer), Millionnaya (Million)—all had been changed. You could almost
write a history of Leningrad by chronicling the names of the streets. There
was the time early in the 1920's when Nevsky Prospekt was known as
NEPsky—after the NEP men or private traders whom Lenin had brought
back under NEP or the New Economic Policy. In those days NEPsky was
graced by the fine fish monger, Zolotsev, and the sausage king, Marshan.
There was a gambling club on Grafsky (Count) Street, across from the
trotters on Troitsky (Trinity). Later Grafsky was changed to Proletarian
Street. But always, whatever the changes, the streets seemed to come back
to their original names. No one ever got used to calling the Nevsky Twenty-
fifth of October Street, and soon it would be officially the Nevsky once
again.[2]

Day by day long military columns moved through the city, slowly pushing
down the boulevards, many made up of broken units, men who had survived
one battle and were en route to another which they might not survive.
Beside the Karpovka embankment stood a number of dusty carts and horses.
Red Army men clambered down to the river with buckets and pans. A
crowd of forty or fifty silently watched them.

The sight of the Red Army men drinking water from the river when there
was a tap in every apartment in the city somehow seemed unbelievably
grievous.

Finally someone shouted, "Fellows! What are you drinking that dirty water
for? Come around to the courtyard."

Aleksandr Shtein had a room at the Astoria Hotel. That was the hostelry
where the Germans planned to hold a joint victory dinner with the Finns.
Residence in the hotel was controlled by the Leningrad City commandant.
Shtein gave the hotel director Shanikhin his order and got the key to a

---

[2] The change was made January 15, 1944.

corner room on the mezzanine floor, looking out on the square across from the handsome monument to Nicholas I.

The Astoria had become headquarters for Soviet war correspondents, for the pilots of the Soviet-produced Douglas DC—3's who flew back and forth, low over the fighting lines, usually without fighter cover. Here were the chiefs and technical assistants of big Leningrad factories, awaiting evacuation, representatives of the central ministries, important and not-so-important refugees from the Baltic states. Here were a few ordinary Leningraders and singers like Lydiya Sukharevskaya and Boris Tenin. Here the newspaper *Red Star* parked its Emka, the battered light car used by the poet, Mikhail Svetlov, and the prose writer, Lev Slavin.

Shtein looked out on the cast-iron figure of Nicholas I, astride his cast-iron horse, and beyond that to the dark-red granite of the old German consulate. It had flown up to June 21st an enormous Nazi banner which flapped from the roof. It had been broken by angry demonstrators on the second day of the war and not repaired.

At dusk a maid made the rounds of every room to be certain that the heavy blackout curtains were drawn. If any light showed, Shanikhin was on the spot instantly with his chief assistant, Nina.

Down the corridor from Shtein came the sound of a husky, bold, coarse voice singing:

> My Marusichka
> Oh, my darling,
> My Marusichka,
> Oh, my sweetheart.

Shtein had heard the voice and the song before—in the Golden Lion in Tallinn. It was a record by the White Russian café singer Leshchenko singing his favorite Paris song, "Marusichka." Who was playing it? Shtein found the room occupied by a big, bluff submarine commissar, a man who had fought through the Finnish war, the wearer of an Order of Lenin, a man who reminded him of the correspondent Vsevolod Vishnevsky. The commissar was suffering from a light case of tuberculosis and had been sent back from Kronstadt for treatment. He had gotten as far as the Astoria. Where he would go next no one could say. He sat in his room playing "Marusichka." Then he played "Tatyana"; then "Vanya"; finally, "Masha." He was indefatigable. So was Leshchenko.

The commissar had a stock of Leshchenko records and a case of beer. As long as the beer lasted, as long as the records lasted, the commissar sat in his room. Finally, the beer ran out, the phonograph broke. He packed up his things and went back to Kronstadt.

In the restaurant the band still played. No one had thought of evacuating the musicians. No one had thought of mobilizing them to military duties.

They were incorporated in the ARP squad "without release from production duties." They played on.

The restaurant was directed by a lady with a grand manner whom the correspondents called "Lady Astor." One night when all the rumors were bad S. Abramovich-Black, director of one of the fleet newspapers and the descendant of a long line of Russian and non-Russian naval officers, approached her with all his gallantry and announced: "My cutter is at your service at the pier on Lake Ladoga. I give you my word of honor as an officer, madam, that without you we will not leave. You may go on working in peace."

The fact that Abramovich-Black had no cutter and that there was no cutter waiting on Lake Ladoga made no difference.

The band struck up the "Barcarole." Everyone felt better.

German leaflets began to appear in town, scattered from planes by parachute: "Beat the Jews. Beat the Commissars. Their mugs beg to be bashed in. Wait for the full moon. Bayonets in the earth! Surrender!"

A well-known writer visited Shtein's next-door neighbor. The writer's lips were white, his hands shook and somehow he looked obnoxious. He knew that the Germans had launched a new assault on the city and he had read the leaflets. He began to reason with himself aloud: "I have never said anything publicly against Fascism. I never signed any petitions. I'm not a Party man. My mother, it is true, was a Jew, but, on the other hand, my father was from the nobility. I've found some papers which verify that."

In a three-room de luxe suite lived some young Estonians. One was playing a ukulele. Each had a wine glass, and a bottle of champagne stood on the table. A young girl in a tight sweater was doing a tango with a blond young man. They didn't seem to have a care in the world. But at dawn they would be parachuted behind the German lines to organize resistance in Estonia.

Vladimir Gankevich, the Leningrad athlete who was now a Red Army lieutenant, had been given a responsible task by his commander, Colonel Pavlov. The order came from Marshal Voroshilov himself. Gankevich was to go to Murmansk and inspect the Fourteenth Army preparations for ski operations, which would commence once the snow had fallen. On the morning of August 29 Gankevich kissed his sweetheart, Galya, good-bye at the Moscow station. The hubbub was overwhelming. He heard a woman crying, "Senushka, what will happen to you? And to me? God help us! You are abandoning your home and going God knows where!"

Gankevich looked from the window as the train pulled out and saw mostly men in uniform. Some had handkerchiefs at their eyes. Most of the passengers were women and children, part of the hasty new effort to evacuate from Leningrad those not necessary for the city's defense.

Across the compartment sat a youngster, eight or nine years old. His mother was crying. The youngster said, "Don't cry! We'll beat the Germans and soon be back with Papa. Did you see the gun he was carrying?"

Gankevich turned to a woman beside him and asked where she was going. "I don't know," she said. "The evacuation has begun. All those with children are supposed to leave Leningrad—for somewhere in the Urals."

Suddenly a youngster named Volodya shouted, "Look at the balloons. Look, Mama! So many!"

Gankevich looked, too. To his amazement he saw German paratroops descending in a broad meadow near the railroad tracks. He heard the heavy thump of antiaircraft guns and saw the Germans begin to form up at the far edge of the field.

The train picked up speed and roared down the tracks past a small station without stopping. Gankevich got just a glimpse of the name: Mga.

An army captain quieted the passengers. "Don't be alarmed," he said. "Nothing dangerous about that. The Germans will all be wiped out before we get to Volkhov."

He walked from compartment to compartment, joking with the children. Finally he slid into the seat beside Gankevich.

"Do you have some tobacco?" he asked pleasantly, then whispered, "You understand what's happened? The Germans have captured Mga. Connections with Leningrad have been broken."

Aleksandr Rozen, the war correspondent, made his weary way into Leningrad. He had been with the 70th Division at Medved during the exciting days in July when they roughed up Manstein's 56th Panzers at Soltsy. He was wounded in the savage Nazi assault which broke the division and sent it reeling back toward Leningrad. Sent to Novgorod, the day the city was falling to the Germans, he wandered through the city's ancient Kremlin, older than Moscow's, through echoing corridors, empty rooms, the abandoned headquarters of the Soviet command, which had already evacuated the city.

Painfully, he had made his way north, stage by stage, seeking the remnants of the division, remnants which constantly eluded him. Valdai, Kuzhenkino, Bologoye, Uglovka, Borovichi, Khvoinaya. At each ancient Russian village he was a little late. Finally, at Khvoinaya a commandant—against strictest orders—put him on a hospital train for Leningrad. The old engine pulled the train through one station after another, all in ruins. He saw smashed trains lying on sidings, stations burning, towns leveled.

The train passed through a little station—Mga. Rozen had never heard the name before. Soon he was at Obukhovo on Leningrad's outskirts. One more stop, then the Leningrad freight station.

At headquarters he inquired about the 70th Division. It was in bits—one unit fighting at Lisino-Korpus, another near Tosno, a third at Ushaki. He hunted out the commanders. Fedyunin was dead. Krasnov was in the hospital. Not a man remained of Krasnov's regiment. Colonel Podlutsky of the artillery unit was heavily wounded—in the hospital. He had led his detachment out of encirclement 125 miles behind the German lines.

Rozen walked out of the hospital down Engineers Street and turned into the Sadovaya. He went slowly, not hurrying. Strangely, his spirits had begun to lift as he walked down Leningrad's boulevards. It seemed to him that he had already survived the worst, that Leningrad would stand, that Leningrad would survive, that Leningrad would conquer death.

He walked on down the street to the offices of the newspaper, *On Guard of the Fatherland*, for which he had written during the winter war with Finland. He met Editorial Chief Litvinov and asked what he could do to be useful. Litvinov thought for a moment.

"I think I'd like to have you go over to Lake Ladoga and interview the chief of the Ladoga flotilla."

Rozen couldn't understand. Why should he go to Lake Ladoga? The battle was being fought at Pushkin, at Kolpino.

"Well," said Litvinov, "you see, railroad connections between Leningrad and the rest of the country have been cut."

Mga . . . Rozen's hospital train had been the last to go through the little station.

The Leningrad Public Library had shipped off 360,000 of its most priceless items (out of a collection of 9,000,000). Voltaire's Library, the Pushkin archives and the incunabula had gone off in July. Now the attic had been filled with sand and the most precious remaining books were removed to the cellars. The main reading room was closed, and a smaller room on the first floor was opened for 150 readers. The card catalogue, the information bureau, the print collections, had been put in the subbasement, and many treasures had been transferred to the gloomy subterranean galleries of the Peter and Paul Fortress and the Alexander Nevsky catacombs.

Some fifty-two boxes of treasures from the great Pushkin palaces of Catherine and Alexander had been shipped out before the Germans swept in. The valuables of the Russian Museum were sent to Gorky and then, to the horror of Director P. K. Baltun, on to Perm by river barge.

During the second half of July most of the animals in the Zoological Gardens had been evacuated. So had the Lenfilm studios, the scientific institutes of the Academy of Science and other institutes, totaling ninety-two in all.

Most of the great artistic ensembles had now left Leningrad. The Philharmonic and the Pushkin Drama Theater went to Novosibirsk, the Conservatory to Tashkent, the Mariinsky Opera and Ballet to Perm, the Maly Opera to Orenburg. Two great trains, on July 1 and July 20, had carried off the treasures of the Hermitage and a third was being prepared.

Director Orbeli had fifty tons of shavings and three tons of cotton wadding in which to pack the first two trainloads. But for the third he had nothing but wood for boxes. By August 30 he had packed 350 boxes. Work was starting on the 351st when the order came through to halt. The Germans it seemed, had captured Mga, a little station on the last railroad linking

Leningrad with mainland Russia. Perhaps it would soon be recovered. Meanwhile, hold up on the packing. The boxes stayed for a time in the main vestibule of the Hermitage. Just outside, the lindens had begun to turn yellow, but their leaves did not fall. The days were so sunny. It was still as warm as midsummer with nights that were calm, clear, moonlit.

26 . Will the City Be Abandoned?

ADMIRAL KUZNETSOV ARRIVED IN LENINGRAD SHORTLY before the fall of Mga. He does not give the exact date of his departure from Moscow in his memoirs, but it must have been August 27, and he arrived in Leningrad on August 28. Kuznetsov says he originally planned to go to Leningrad somewhat earlier but that "I was summoned by Stalin on some question or another at the end of August" and was then dispatched to Leningrad with what he calls "responsible representatives of the Stavka," as part of a special commission representing the Central Committee of the Party and the State Defense Committee. At no point in his wordy memoirs does Kuznetsov name those "responsible representatives." The only name he mentions is that of Marshal Voronov, who left nearly a week earlier.

This is not accidental. The fact is that the "responsible representatives" were none other than two members of the State Defense Committee, Vyacheslav M. Molotov and Georgi M. Malenkov.

The other members of the mission were A. N. Kosygin (later to become Premier of the Soviet Union), who was deputy chairman of the State Committee on Evacuation; Air Marshal P. F. Zhigarev, Soviet Air Commander in Chief; Voronov and Kuznetsov. Technically, Voroshilov and Zhdanov were members of the Commission as well.[1]

The Commission was assigned the task of "evaluating the complicated situation" and rendering on-the-spot aid to the military command, the city and the regional Party organizations. It was endowed with the widest discretionary authority. Obviously, it held in its hands the fate of Leningrad, specifically the question of whether it could or should be held.

Kuznetsov did not fly directly to Leningrad; instead, he flew with the party to Cherepovets, where a special train was made available. The route itself is a clue to the desperation which must have been felt in Moscow

---

[1] Kuznetsov's memoirs are a political document, and the Admiral is a master of half-truth. He often deliberately confuses the picture. In a 1968 version he mentions Molotov and Kosygin but not Malenkov. Kosygin had been in Leningrad since mid-July.

concerning the Leningrad situation. Cherepovets is nearly two hundred miles due east of Leningrad and is a point on the east-west Leningrad-Vologda railroad, rather than the direct north-south Leningrad-Moscow railroad.

The distinguished party boarded the special train at the provincial station of Cherepovets and moved westward, through Tikhvin and Volkhov until they got to the little station of Mga, about twenty-five miles southeast of Leningrad. There, for reasons not immediately clear to Kuznetsov, the semaphore was set red against further progress. An air attack was just coming to an end; German bombers, their motors clearly audible, were flying away; antiaircraft guns were banging; explosions could be heard and fires were springing up not far from the railroad.

"To wait for dawn was not desirable," Kuznetsov thought. But what to do? A number of bombs had fallen on the trackage, and it was not possible for the train to move forward. The party disembarked and picked its way down the tracks, boarded an interurban streetcar and presently met an armored train which Voroshilov had thoughtfully sent to Mga to pick up the bedraggled members of the State Defense Committee.

It is not likely that Malenkov and Molotov arrived in Leningrad with any great confidence in the military position.

As Kuznetsov remarked: "In a military situation one sometimes encounters unexpected situations. However, the position in which the Stavka representatives found themselves speaks of the insufficiencies of information and of control over situations even in those cases where it was essential."

What Malenkov and Molotov did not realize until after their arrival in Leningrad was that the bombing of Mga which they witnessed was the prelude to a Nazi attack on the station which would on August 30 cut the last rail connection—that of the Northern Railroad—between Leningrad and the mainland of Russia.

The Commission members spent about ten days in Leningrad. The exact nature of their decisions is not clear from any of the Soviet accounts. There is no published record of the conversations between Malenkov, Molotov and Zhdanov. There is not to be found in any front-line reminiscences, officers' tales or specialized histories a reference to the presence of Malenkov or Molotov on any fighting front during the time of their visit. Kuznetsov gives the impression that he concerned himself wholly with fleet matters and was not privy to the discussions.

Marshal Zhigarev is said to have aided in overcoming deficiencies in air defenses (the city was on the eve of savage German air attacks but thus far had not been bombed). Voronov helped on antitank defenses. Admiral Kuznetsov, the naval member, worked on the collaboration of Baltic Fleet units in artillery support of the Leningrad front. Assistance in plans for the internal defense of the city was rendered. Once again minute details were spelled out. The line of defense was to run from the Finnish Gulf and the Predportovaya Station along the October Railroad tracks through the village of Rybatskoye to the Utkin factory, the Kudrovo State Farm, to Rzhevka and along the line Udelnoye–Kolomyagi–Staraya Derevnya. If the Germans broke into the city, they would be met by 26 rifle divisions and 6 tank battalions, armed with 1,205 guns, or 30 per mile of front.

Much attention was given to the problem of evacuating population, factories and scientific institutions and improving Leningrad's food position, although by this time all rail routes had been severed.

During this period Admiral Panteleyev went to Smolny at Voroshilov's summons. A big meeting was in progress. The room was filled with people, most of them military but many civilians as well. Some were women. Voroshilov sat against the wall at a long table covered with a dark cloth. He looked tired, gloomy and discouraged. He talked in a quiet, soft voice, not at all like himself. The windows were blacked out, and the room was dark and dismal.

Panteleyev did not recognize anyone in the room besides Marshal Voroshilov, although there were many high officials present. He does not name them. Were the members of the State Defense Committee present?

The meeting was one long catalogue of disaster—of people who had refused to be evacuated, of people (especially children) evacuated into the path of the Germans, of special trains which stood on dangerous sidings for days without moving, subject to Nazi air attack, of children sent off thousands of miles to the east with no word to their families as to their destination.

Again and again someone would say: "But who would have thought the enemy would get so close to Leningrad?"

Voroshilov sternly demanded an answer as to why the government orders to evacuate the population had not been fulfilled.

The meeting didn't take long. It left Panteleyev filled with despondency. The next day orders were issued to continue to evacuate civilians—not less than a million through Shlisselburg. Shlisselburg fell three days later.

The visit of Malenkov and Molotov to Leningrad has dropped out of Soviet historiography. But it once was firmly fixed as a stellar event. Malenkov proudly noted in his biography in the *Bolshaya Sovetskaya Entsyklopedia*, published in 1952, that he "in August, 1941, was to be found on the Leningrad front." Standard histories written as late as 1953 mentioned the visit. In fact, the official version then was that "under their [Malenkov's and Molotov's] firm leadership plans were worked out and measures carried out directed at organizing the defeat of the enemy." Or, as another historian put it: "In September at the sharpest moment of the struggle for Leningrad the Central Committee sent V. M. Molotov and G. M. Malenkov into the besieged city to organize its defense."

The mission may have been designed to assist the hard-pressed defenders of Leningrad. But it may—and this possibility is hinted at by Kuznetsov—have been entrusted with the task of deciding whether Leningrad should be abandoned.

Voronov, a tall, thoughtful man whose quiet manner inspired confidence, was first on the ground. He was there by August 22. His impressions were troubled.

"To my surprise," he recalled, "the city continued to live very peacefully. You might have thought that the battle was being fought on the nearest approaches to Berlin and not under the walls of Leningrad."

He was appalled to find practically nothing had been done about evacuating the population. He saw in this clear evidence of an underevaluation of the threat which now hung over the city. He was right.

The State Defense Commission, Voronov recalled, demanded the immediate evacuation from Leningrad of children, women and old persons and also all scientific institutions and factories which could not be used for the essential needs of the front or city. The Commission called for the immediate reconstruction of the life of the city on military terms.

Just though Voronov's criticisms were, the time was far too late to undo the fatal results of weeks of false optimism.

On August 26 Zhdanov and Voroshilov, presumably joined by Voronov, talked via the VC phone with Stalin in Moscow. Reporting the desperate situation which had been created by the German capture of Lyuban Station, about fifty miles southeast of the city, and the cutting of the October Railroad between Moscow and Leningrad—the principal communications route to the city—they said they must have additional forces if the city was to be held.

Stalin responded to the plea of desperation. He agreed that Leningrad should receive the next four days' supply of tanks from the Leningrad tank factories (principally, the KV 60-ton monsters turned out by the Kirov and the Izhorsk factories). These were two of the main producers of armored weapons in the Soviet Union, and, desperate though the Leningrad situation was, their production had continued to go almost entirely into the central strategic reserves of the Red Army in the Moscow area.[2] Stalin's order meant twenty-five to thirty tanks for the Leningrad front. Many of them moved straight into battle, their steel bodies unpainted and glistening.

Moreover, Stalin promised to send to Leningrad four aviation regiments and ten infantry battalions. This would bring the number of reserves sent to the Leningrad front since the outbreak of war to seventy battalions. At the same time Stalin grimly ordered the Leningrad Command to "put in order" the Forty-eighth Army (actually, little more than a figure on a piece of military paper after its latest disasters) and to mine heavily the Moscow-Leningrad highway and the approaches to Leningrad. In fact, of course, the Germans had already cut the Moscow-Leningrad highway.

Each of the ten battalions which Stalin agreed to send to Leningrad com-

---

[2] The State Defense Committee August 4 had approved a plan by the Leningrad defenders that the Kirov factory produce as many KV tanks above the planned quota as possible and that these extra tanks go to the Leningrad front. In August the plant had a quota of 180 tanks. It produced 207. The 27 extra tanks went to the Leningrad defenses. (*N.Z.*, p. 126.)

prised a thousand or more men. But not all were experienced and not all had weapons.

"Don't hurry about throwing them into battle," Zhdanov warned G. Kh. Bumagin, Military Council member of the Forty-eighth Army. "The new recruits need a little preparation for the battle front."

But the caution was in vain. The Nazi 39th Panzer Corps of the 3rd Panzer Group was driving forward from Lyuban to Tosno and Mga on the outskirts of Leningrad. The commander of the luckless Forty-eighth Army threw everything he could lay his hands on into the battle in an attempt to halt the German advance. Nothing helped. The Germans drove remorselessly on.

Stalin had defined the basic task of the Leningrad Command in these terms: to protect the city from attack from the west, southwest and southeast; to prevent the Germans from cutting the October, Pechora and Northern railroads; to hold firmly the Koporsky Plateau to insure the defense of Leningrad from the sea; to halt the Finnish offensive at the Vuoksi River and keep the Finns from cutting the Kirov railroad.

It was a task beyond the capability of the forces defending Leningrad— or of any reinforcements which the city could hope to obtain.

This was the grim moment at which Malenkov and Molotov appeared on the scene.

Malenkov was Zhdanov's keenest rival as a possible successor to Stalin and court favorite. Molotov's role was anomalous, but the indications are that he was playing at Malenkov's side, not Zhdanov's. These were two members of the three-man junta which had taken power during the days of Stalin's incapacity in June; two of the three men who had sent Zhdanov back to Leningrad to defend his fief, who had cut him off from decision-making or ambition-satisfying exercises in Moscow. Zhdanov had been in Leningrad now for two months, directing its defense. His record was hardly brilliant. Now the gravest decisions had to be made. Could the city be held? Was there any way of thwarting the Nazi offensive?

Only echoes of the icy conversations of the high Soviet leaders with their brutal underlay of anxiety and emotion come through the reports of the survivors. All mention of Malenkov and Molotov in this connection has been banished from the Soviet press since their ignoble defeat in the 1957 attempt to oust Nikita Khrushchev. Zhdanov left no record before his untimely death August 31, 1948. Most of Zhdanov's closest associates were shot in the following years.[3]

---

[3] There is a remarkable absence of direct source materials on Zhdanov and by Zhdanov. There are only the rarest citations of him in the Soviet historical works on the Leningrad siege. For example, the official collection of Leningrad documents (*900 Geroicheskii Dnei* —hereafter referred to as *900*) publishes only one Zhdanov document from the fund of his personal materials in the Central Party Archives at the Institute of Marxism-Leninism in Moscow: a report to the State Defense Committee submitted in October, 1943, on the evacuation of industry from Leningrad. There are no references to this or any other

However, without question the fateful issue of abandoning Leningrad arose. If there were opposing positions in these discussions, they must have been: Zhdanov for holding on, Malenkov and Molotov for giving up.

The usual command upheavals and reshuffles, a certain sign of crisis on a Soviet front, occurred. On the twenty-third of August Karelia had been split off from the Leningrad Command. On the twenty-ninth the State Defense Committee (was the idea that of Malenkov and Molotov?) named Voroshilov as the Leningrad front commander, with Zhdanov and Party Secretary Kuznetsov as Military Council members, and General Popov as Chief of Staff. The move made considerable sense, yet it marked a down-grading of the roles of Voroshilov and Zhdanov. They formerly had been in charge of the whole complex of fronts and armies in the Leningrad area. Now they had only the single front—essentially that of the city itself. The next day the Council for the Defense of Leningrad was dissolved and all its functions taken over by the Leningrad Front Command of Zhdanov and Voroshilov.

On September 1 Stalin delivered a formal reprimand to Zhdanov and Voroshilov. In a message from the Stavka to the Leningrad Command he laid down the line that errors of organization and lack of firmness had marked the defense of the approaches to Leningrad. He demanded that more active measures be taken for the defense of the city.[4]

It is likely that this reprimand was the first fruit of the intervention of Malenkov and Molotov. It may have been stimulated by an act of hopeless deception which was attempted by the Leningrad Command. Leningrad did not promptly report the loss of Mga to Moscow. Presumably, it did not report this fact because it hoped to recapture Mga and restore the situation. The hope, like so many others, was vain.

The battered Forty-eighth Army was ordered by the Leningrad Command to retake Mga Station at any price. The 1st Division of NKVD troops, with-

---

collection of Zhdanov materials in the official history of the Leningrad siege (*Leningrad v VOV*). Indeed, the only available texts (usually partial) of many Zhdanov speeches in this period come from the personal notes of persons present, notably D. V. Pavlov in his classic *Leningrad v Blokade*. Pavlov's notes are quoted and requoted endlessly in other source materials. There is a comparable lacuna in direct quotations of speeches by Zhdanov's Leningrad lieutenants. In view of the Soviet habit of taking stenographic notes of all meetings and the care with which archival materials are preserved, this seems very strange. Moreover, there has been no published collection of Zhdanov speeches or papers, contrary to the practice followed with many of his less prominent contemporaries. The suspicion persists that the Zhdanov archive either was destroyed by his enemies (presumably Malenkov and Beria) or more likely is still retained under the highest security classification as an outgrowth of the Leningrad Affair.

[4] At the end of August the State Defense Committee gave orders which Achkasov calls "of exceptionally important influence on the further course of the Leningrad battle." He described these as formation of new units, reorganization of troops, defending the southeast and southern approaches to Leningrad, creation of new defense lines, preparation for evacuation of part of the Leningrad institutions and for organization of institutions remaining in the city for production of military needs of the front. (*Krasnoznamennyi Baltiiskii Flot v VOV*, p. 99.)

drawn from the Karelian front, was thrown in. No luck. The Germans had Mga and they would retain it.

The record was beginning to be built up against Zhdanov and Voroshilov. First, they had been "masters of the art of retreat." Next, they had set up an internal defense committee which Stalin seemed to regard as a possible device for the surrender of the city. They made arrangements for street fighting in the city which aroused his suspicions.

Now they were caught red-handed concealing a terrible defeat.

If Leningrad were to fall, Malenkov and Molotov would have little difficulty in presenting a record which would put full blame on Zhdanov and Voroshilov.

The fall of Leningrad from the standpoint of the junta of Malenkov and Molotov would have one favorable consequence. It would eliminate for all time a dangerous and able rival for political power within the Kremlin. Not that Zhdanov was entirely without allies in Moscow. On September 2 *Izvestiya* published an eloquent declaration, expressing confidence that Leningrad and the Leningraders would fulfill their great honor and duty by defeating the Germans and driving them back from the city. It was signed, "N. Petrov." But its author was the venerable Mikhail I. Kalinin, President of the U.S.S.R. and himself a native of Leningrad. He at least gave a vote of confidence to the Leningrad defenders. But Kalinin was by no means the equal in power and intrigue of Zhdanov's opponents. The war on the front with the Nazis might be deadly. That behind the scenes was even more so.

Kuznetsov did not return to Moscow with the other members of the State Defense Committee. Naval matters held him up, and he did not fly back to Moscow until September 12, to the accompaniment of a thunderstorm which tossed his plane about as it flew low over the stormy waters of Lake Ladoga.

The next day he was summoned to the Kremlin at the unusual hour of noon. Ordinarily he was never called until evening. During the day Stalin worked in his Kremlin office, but at night, when air raids were likely, he often transferred his work to a suite near the Kremlin air-raid shelter. Kuznetsov felt that only an urgent matter would have brought the call at the unusual midday hour. He was right.

Stalin opened the meeting abruptly by advising Kuznetsov that the Leningrad Command had been put in the hands of General Georgi Zhukov. The decision had been made the night before,[5] and Zhukov was already in Leningrad or on his way.

What Stalin did not say—or Kuznetsov did not report—was that Voroshilov had been removed after another tremendous row between Leningrad and Moscow.

[5] The Stavka decision was made September 11. Zhukov took over the command September 13. (A. V. Karasev, *Istoriya SSSR*, No. 2, 1957, p. 5.)

Once again Leningrad had been caught out.

The Germans had smashed their way into Shlisselburg, the fortress on the Neva, and closed the circle around Leningrad on September 8. But the Leningrad Command did not report this fact—no more than it had reported the loss of Mga. It did not report the loss of Shlisselburg on September 8. It did not report it September 9. On September 9 Moscow learned about the loss from another source—the official German communiqué.

Stalin demanded an explanation.

The explanation was hardly satisfactory. On September 11 Voroshilov and Zhdanov advised the Kremlin that for two months they had been trying to create a shock group to seize the initiative from the Germans but that as fast as troops were provided they had had to be thrown into the breach. Thus their efforts to organize a powerful counteroffensive and throw the Germans back from the breakthrough to Mga and Shlisselburg had failed.

This merely confirmed Stalin in his conviction that it was the "passiveness" of Voroshilov that had caused the Leningrad disasters. He ordered Voroshilov removed and Zhukov sent in to replace him.[6]

Apparently, Stalin did not go into this detail with Admiral Kuznetsov. Nor, apparently, did Kuznetsov tell Stalin of a curious experience which occurred while he was sitting in Admiral I. S. Isakov's office in Smolny on August 30 waiting for the Admiral to return from a meeting of the Military Council. The telephone rang—not the military telephone but the ordinary city line. Kuznetsov answered it. It was a young girl, who said despairingly: "The Germans have gotten to the Neva River in the region of Ivanovskoye."

The news was completely unexpected. Admiral Kuznetsov reported it to General Popov, the Leningrad Commander, who was inclined to think it was the fruit of panic or fantasy. But, unfortunately, it was neither. The Germans had broken through to the Neva, and they stayed there until 1943.

None of this came up in the conversation between Stalin and Kuznetsov.

Stalin strolled about his office nervously and finally sat down on a black-leather couch, peppering Kuznetsov with questions. How many ships remained in the Baltic? Where were they? Were they playing any role in the battle for Leningrad? He referred to the city by its old familiar nickname of "Piter" rather than Leningrad.

Kuznetsov sought to steer the conversation to broader naval matters. But Stalin would have none of it. He had a map on the wall, a small one, showing the German lines running right up to Leningrad, and now he got to the question for which he had summoned Kuznetsov. The situation of Leningrad was extraordinarily serious, he said.

---

[6] Failure to admit the loss of a town in the hope of quickly retaking it was regarded by Stalin as the gravest of crimes. He removed from command and harshly punished every commander caught in such an attempt at deception. (Shtemenko, *op. cit.*, p. 116.) One source claims Secretary Kuznetsov told a Smolny meeting the morning of September 9 that Leningrad had been cut off. (A. Kostin, *Zvezda*, No. 6, June, 1968.)

"It is possible that it may be abandoned," he added. Then, asking Kuznetsov to run over again the number and classes of warships in the Baltic Fleet, he snapped: "Not one warship must fall into the hands of the enemy. Not one," he repeated. Moreover, he made plain that if his order was not carried out, the guilty parties would be "strictly judged." This term, in Stalin's vocabulary, meant one thing: the firing squad.

"I understood that this was not the time to discuss this question," said Kuznetsov later. He awaited further orders.

The orders were simple: to prepare and send to the commanders of all ships instructions to prepare for scuttling.

To his own surprise—and obviously to Stalin's—Kuznetsov blurted out: "I cannot sign such a telegram."

Stalin wanted to know why. Kuznetsov suddenly recalled that the fleet was under the operational control of the Leningrad front. Such orders, he said, required Stalin's signature as chief of the Stavka.

Kuznetsov was not entirely certain why Stalin wanted the order signed by the Naval Commissar, but the implication was he wanted to shift the blame.

Stalin then suggested that Kuznetsov go to the Chief of Staff, Marshal Shaposhnikov, and have the telegrams prepared with two signatures, Shaposhnikov's and Kuznetsov's.

But Shaposhnikov was not interested in putting his hand to such an order either. "This matter is entirely for the fleet," he told Kuznetsov. "I will not put my signature to it."

Kuznetsov told him the idea was Stalin's. Shaposhnikov still objected. Finally, the men decided to draft the telegram and send it to Stalin for his signature. Stalin agreed but didn't send the orders off immediately. Eventually, however, they went out.

A year later Kuznetsov had reason to congratulate himself on his foresight. Police Chief Beria sent to Stalin a report charging the Baltic Fleet Commander, Admiral V. F. Tributs, with yielding to panic in issuing "premature orders" to prepare the fleet for scuttling. A copy went to Kuznetsov.

"I quickly reminded them what the situation was and removed the blame from the leaders of the fleet," Kuznetsov recalled.

The curious reluctance of Stalin to sign the order, the accusation by the police and the apparent conviction on Stalin's part that the fall of Leningrad was likely hint at the desperate politics being played around the city.[7]

Stalin clearly was under pressure to abandon Leningrad. It is possible that this counsel came to him from Malenkov and Molotov, backed by complaints of the failure of Zhdanov and Voroshilov properly to defend Leningrad, of the cost of defending the city, of the impossibility of making a firm stand, of the need to use every resource for the defense of Moscow, which itself was approaching the most perilous of days.

[7] Kuznetsov also claims preparation of a plan to scuttle the Baltic Fleet began in late August.

Zhdanov was fighting for his political life, his actual life, as well as that of the city to which his fate had been linked.

Stalin also must have felt that he was fighting for his political life. On September 4 he sent a message to Prime Minister Winston Churchill couched in most gloomy terms: "We have lost more than half the Ukraine, and in addition the enemy is at the gates of Leningrad."

He asked that Britain immediately create a second front to draw off 30 to 40 German divisions and that she send "by October 1 30,000 tons of aluminum, 400 planes and 500 tanks."

The alternative was that "the Soviet Union will either suffer defeat or be weakened to such an extent that it will lose for a long period any capacity to render assistance to its allies by its actual operations."

Churchill thought he recognized in the message and in the manner of Ambassador Maisky's presentation hints of a possible bid by Moscow to Germany for a separate peace.[8]

Eleven days later Stalin asked that the British land twenty-five to thirty divisions at Archangel or via Iran. On September 12 Churchill proposed that if Russia was forced to yield Leningrad and destroy the Baltic Fleet, the British would partially recompense the Russians for the destruction of warships. To which Stalin replied that he would submit his bill to the Germans after the war if such an event should occur.

Under all these circumstances was Stalin prepared to abandon Leningrad? "Unquestionably" was Kuznetsov's response. Not that Stalin wanted to surrender the city, but he felt that the fall of Leningrad was only too likely. Otherwise, Kuznetsov concluded, Stalin never would have given orders so serious as those calling for the preparation of the fleet for scuttling.

The actions flowing from the September crisis—the reprimand to Zhdanov and Voroshilov, the removal of Voroshilov from command, the dispatch of Zhukov to Leningrad, the orders by Stalin to prepare the city for its fall— suggest a political compromise. Blame for the plight of the city was placed on both Voroshilov and Zhdanov, but Voroshilov had to take the major portion. He was sacked and saddled with military responsibility for the situation. Zhdanov was given one last chance: with Marshal Zhukov's aid he might save the city if he could. But the terms were harsh. The city must be saved very quickly because a total effort to halt the Germans before Moscow was already getting under way. Perhaps it was because Leningrad's continued defense would divert German troops from Moscow that Zhdanov and Zhukov were instructed to try to hold the line. But it was also plain that unless Zhdanov and Zhukov turned the situation around very, very quickly, Stalin was prepared to sacrifice Leningrad, if need be, in order to save

---

[8] Maisky insists there was no hint of separate peace in his presentation and suggests this interpretation arose from Churchill's "guilty conscience" about not opening a second front. But Maisky admits he made a deliberately passionate presentation. He suggests he himself instigated Stalin's message and adds that the fear of a separate peace helped him get more for Russia. (Maisky, *op. cit.*, pp. 172–173.)

Moscow. If Leningrad did fall, the full blame would fall on Zhdanov, the Party leader, not on Marshal Zhukov, the military technician, sent in at the last moment. Indeed, the expectation in the Kremlin, or even the order, may well have been that Zhdanov was to go down fighting street by street and block by block in a Russian Götterdämmerung. But the scene of Zhdanov's final act would be Smolny, the cradle of the Bolshevik Revolution.

Not the least difficult aspect of Leningrad's suicidal struggle behind the scenes was the burden on energy and morale to which it subjected the fighting naval and military commanders within Leningrad.

At a moment when they were bending every effort to save the city from the Germans came sudden orders to put highest priority on mining the great ships, the naval depots, the military installations throughout the city. It was a cruel burden and a cruel blow. The bitterness which the Leningrad commanders felt has been reflected down through the years. In many it implanted a permanent, undeviating hatred for Moscow and Stalin. They became convinced that at the most critical of all moments Stalin was prepared to sell them out.

From this time onward popular feeling toward Zhdanov began to change in Leningrad, even though few in the city knew these details of high politics. Until these critical days the city and its populace had held aloof from this dynamic, humorless man, so immersed in his own aims and ambitions. Now he began more and more to symbolize to Leningrad its isolated, desperate battle. Week by week and month by month the portrait of Zhdanov spread from one area to another, one office to another, one street corner to another.

It spread so widely and so universally that two years later visitors to Leningrad could hardly believe their eyes. Almost nowhere was a portrait of Stalin to be seen except, perhaps, in some official office—and not always there. Everywhere the figure of Zhdanov glowed down from the walls. Stalin, so the people had decided, was no friend of Leningrad. Zhdanov was no friend, perhaps, but he had shared the city's trials and desperations. He had by this become one with them.

PART III

Leningrad in Blockade

With each step the feet grow heavier
But better not to pause for rest.
Perhaps, Death sits beside the road,
Just resting, too. . . .

PART III

27 . *The Circle Closed*

NO ONE HAD PLANNED TO FIGHT A BATTLE AT MGA. THE little railroad station figured on no strategic charts, either German or Russian. In fact, the engagement at Mga was accidental, small-scale, haphazard. It was the consequences of Mga that were so far-reaching.

What gave Mga importance was that once the Nazis firmly grasped the town they severed all of the rail connections between Leningrad and the remainder of Russia—the "mainland" as it came to be called—and they cut all the highways.

The first sign of danger in this direction came when the battered Soviet Forty-eighth Army, which was defending the main Moscow-Leningrad railroad line in the vicinity of Ushaki and Tosno, about thirty-five miles southeast of Leningrad, began to crumble under the Nazi Panzer attacks. Instead of falling back northward toward Leningrad, the broken regiments of the Forty-eighth Army drifted *eastward*, opening up a gap which the Nazis quickly managed to exploit.

The Leningrad Command, back to the wall, striving to stem the Nazi tide at a dozen critical points, did not immediately realize what had happened.

Colonel Bychevsky, chief of Leningrad's sappers, for example, occupied around the clock placing mines, blowing up bridges, ceaselessly seeking to build barriers against the Germans, had no inkling of the new danger. For him August 28 began very much as did each of the days of late August which later came to form in his mind a blurred calendar of disaster.

Bychevsky was disturbed that morning for a different reason. In the midst of battle the Chief of Staff, the sardonic General D. N. Nikishev, whose skepticism of Moscow's desire or ability to provide sufficient resources for Leningrad's defenses had never been concealed, had vanished.[1] Along with Nikishev went his deputy, N. G. Tikhomirov. Why? Bychevsky had

---

[1] More fortunate than most, General Nikishev was not shot. He survived to participate in the Stalingrad battle. (*N.Z.*, p. 444.)

no better idea than he had of the other strange, never-explained command changes which so often caused his colleagues to disappear. He guessed that possibly Nikishev had offended Voroshilov. But this was only a guess. In Nikishev's place appeared Colonel N. V. Gorodetsky from the Twenty-third Army, a good, vigorous officer. But it was not easy to pick up the threads of the complex battles then raging. Gorodetsky made mistakes, some of which cost Leningrad dearly.

On this bright August morning with the scent of buckwheat and golden-rod heavy in the hedgerows outside Leningrad, the new Chief of Staff advised Bychevsky that the Forty-eighth Army was heavily engaged in defending the Moscow-Leningrad railroad and that it needed help. He told Bychevsky to send a detachment of sappers to Tosno to lay down a series of mine fields and to destroy any bridges which might be seized by the Germans. Tosno was located about fifteen miles south and west of Mga.

Bychevsky sent off a small unit from his 2nd Reserve Pontoon Battalion and decided to go to Tosno with Commissar Nikolai Mukha and look at the situation himself.

They drove out the Moscow highway, which runs almost arrow-straight, paralleling the railroad. When they got as far as Krasny Bor, a large village fifteen miles outside the city, they heard firing in the forest. Leaving the car, they started on foot in the direction of the sound, moving very care-fully. At this point they were less than five miles south of the Kolpino fortified region, established along a little stream, the Izhora River. The fortifications had just been occupied by the Izhorsk workers artillery and machine-gun battalion, a volunteer unit, which had had no training in firing from stationary batteries. Behind this small unit there was nothing—just the broad, empty Moscow highway leading straight to the southeast gates of Leningrad.

What, thought Bychevsky, is going to happen if the Germans break through here? The two officers came up to a wooden barricade thrown across the highway. Beside it was an armored car where they found two generals, A. I. Cherepanov and P. A. Zaitsev. The generals were directing a field regiment and the small engineering detachment which Bychevsky had ordered to Tosno in a fire fight against German units. The field regiment had only about fifteen cartridges per rifle and three submachine guns.

The Germans, it seemed, had broken through the remnants of the Forty-eighth Army and swept beyond Tosno. It was their armored reconnaissance that was being held up in the fire fight.

General Zaitsev went back to the Izhora River line to try to organize a defense there. The other officers stayed on the highway to hold up the German advance as long as they could.

The German fire grew hot. The Russians fell back a couple of hundred yards as the sappers hastily put up heavy wooden barriers along the highway and dug in some antitank mines. But the field regiment was running out of ammunition. The Russians would certainly have been overwhelmed had not five heavy Soviet tanks come up and laid down covering fire. Two German light tanks appeared on the highway, but one hit a mine and caught fire and the other was hit by its own artillery. The Germans began to lay in heavy mortar fire and two Messerschmitts roared down the highway, machine guns blazing.

The Russians had no alternative. They fell back into the fortified positions at Yam-Izhorsk and Bychevsky's men mined the bridge across the little Izhora River. As the Germans approached the bridge, the mines were touched off, halting them temporarily. The Germans were advance reconnaissance units of the 39th Army Corps of the Sixteenth Army, comprising the 12th Panzer Division and the 121st and 96th Infantry divisions (with the 122nd Infantry in the second echelon).

Dusk was beginning to fall. Bychevsky and Mukha had to report to Smolny. Artillery exchanges already had begun between the Izhorsk battalion and the Germans. The officers stopped a moment to wish good luck to one of the workers units, headed by I. F. Chernenko, an engineer in the great Izhorsk works.

Chernenko had gotten back to Kolpino that afternoon from Leningrad. At the station he found he could only buy a ticket as far as Pontonny. The girl at the ticket window said the rail line was under fire and a train had been hit. He rode to Pontonny and walked into Kolpino. Within an hour or so he was sent up to the lines. He decided to wear his leather jacket even though the afternoon was hot. It probably would be cold that night in the trenches. He was right.

The Izhorsk factory where Chernenko worked was one of the greatest in Russian industry. Founded by order of Peter the Great in 1722 to produce timbers for ship construction, in the mid-eighteenth century it began to make anchors and copper sheeting and in the nineteenth century pioneered in machine building, boiler construction, engines, turbines, armor plate and heavy military equipment. It produced the armor for Russia's early dreadnaughts—the *Petropavlovsk*, the *Sevastopol*, the *Gangut* and the *Poltava*.

Under Soviet aegis it vastly expanded. Now it boasted blooming mills, steel rolling mills and a whole series of specialized plants, including artillery works, a shell factory and—extremely important at this moment—a heavy tank plant. It was turning out both the reliable Soviet T-34 and the massive KV 60-ton monster of whose existence the Germans were beginning to become aware.

Not only had the Germans driven to the entrance to Leningrad; they had gotten within close artillery range of a military factory whose production was vital to Leningrad's defenses and to the whole Soviet war effort.

At this moment there were about a thousand men, members of Izhorsk factory volunteer units, in the fortified lines along the little Izhora River. Most of them were armed with rifles from drill halls, carbines, hand grenades and pistols. Few had more than a day or two of training. They were supported by a homemade armored unit—ton-and-a-half and three-ton trucks which had been fitted out in the shops with light armor plate. How long they might hold out in the face of serious attack by the 39th German Corps was questionable.

By early evening word spread through the sprawling red-brick Izhorsk shops that the Germans were nearing the city. Cannonading could be heard in the distance, rumbling like summer thunder. It was a dark night without stars, and on the distant horizon there appeared to be the dull reflection of fires.

G. L. Zimin, chairman of the factory Party committee, called his Party workers to a meeting.

"We don't need anyone who's drooling in terror," he said roughly. "Let the real Izhorites take up their guns and—forward march! There's no time to waste. If we do not halt them, the Germans will advance to the Neva Gates and the Obukhovo factory."

He told the men that German reconnaissance had penetrated as far as the stadium—just outside the city. The Moscow road was cut. Yam-Izhorsk was in the hands of the Germans.

He looked at the crowd, among them elderly workers, some trembling with fatigue.

"Who is not feeling well?" he asked.

A few raised their hands.

"Go back to the shops. . . . Who hasn't served in the army?"

Several more raised their hands.

"You are released, comrades," he said. There were protests, but he waved them away.

"And are there any cowards here?"

The room was deathly still.

"All right," he said. "Tonight we'll form a factory battalion and before dawn we'll be on the firing line."

Only six or seven of the workers present failed to join the battalion.

By 11 P.M. about sixty Communists and Young Communists headed by Chairman Aleksandr V. Anisimov of the region executive committee had formed up in the darkened streets. They wore their factory overalls. There had been no time for farewells to wives and sweethearts.

The battalion marched up the road past the stadium and on down toward the Kolpino settlements where many of the workers lived. Behind them rose the tall column in the center of town on which was mounted the figure of a factory worker, gun in hand, dedicated to the Petrograd workers of the 1917 Revolution.

It was dawn before the unit neared the positions which they were to occupy.

"We were coming along with our rifles when suddenly we met a youngster with a blue bundle," Anisimov recalled. "He was a good lad, worked at the Martin oven. His name was Sasha. He saw us and asked where we were going. We answered and then asked, 'You—where are you going with the blue bundle?' "

Sasha had been to the bakery to pick up a loaf of bread and now he was on his way to the factory. What was going on there?

Anisimov said it wasn't a question of defending the factory but of defending the city.

"How can I?" Sasha asked. "I haven't a gun."

"Come along," Anisimov answered. "We've got some spare guns and we'll find you a uniform."

Sasha shrugged his shoulders, put his blue packet into the pocket of a uniform jacket and marched along in the cold misty morning with his companions. Two days later they buried Sasha, killed by a shell fragment. They put the blue bundle under his head for a pillow.

Anisimov posted his little unit in the lines beside the other Izhorsk workers at about 6 A.M. An hour later he went forward to the northern outskirts of Yam-Izhorsk. He and Commander Georgi V. Vodopyanov got as far as the cemetery when bullets began to fly. One whined off a cross just beside Anisimov. They decided to get back to their lines quickly.

The Germans did not break the Izhorsk line, but they were now close enough to bring the great defense plant under point-blank artillery fire. The shelling began at 7:30 A.M., August 30, and went on for weeks with hardly any interruption. Some units of the plant had been evacuated in August, but most had not and the systematic German bombardment virtually halted production. Forty-five workers were killed and 235 wounded. In October, when fighting came to a lull, the Izhorsk battalions began to divide their time between the front lines and the plant. The government on October 4 decided to evacuate as much of the plant as possible to the Urals (production in September had dropped to a third of the August level), and over the ensuing weeks several of the principal shops were disassembled with enormous difficulty and flown out of Leningrad.

The fierce resistance of the Izhorsk workers stopped the Germans in their headlong thrust straight toward Leningrad. But it had startling and unforeseen consequences. Halted along the Izhorsk line, the Germans were deflected to the east in the same direction as the retreat of the shattered units of the Forty-eighth Army. The Nazi Panzers, finding no opposition, pushed swiftly northward along the Tosna River. The 20th Panzer Division was in the lead, and it found the going very easy. Not many Germans realized that they had broken into one of the most famous battlegrounds in Russian history. Just 701 years earlier on the ancient soil at the mouth of the Izhora, Alexander Yaroslavovich, one of Russia's legendary heroes, won the title of Alexander Nevsky. Here in the low ground along the Neva he led his knights from Novgorod the Great against the Swedes, headed by Prince Birger.

278 . PART III: Leningrad in Blockade

Birger planned to advance across the Neva, across Lake Ladoga and descend via the Volkhov River to attack Novgorod, the great northern capital of ancient Russia. Strategically, his plan bore great resemblance to that of Hitler. Nevsky unexpectedly attacked the Swedes and routed them July 15, 1240, in a battle which for centuries was Russia's most famous.

Now again the Izhorsk earth trembled to the roar of fighting men, again the fate of Russia stood in the balance. But where was the twentieth-century Nevsky?

None appeared. The Forty-eighth Army was in shreds. It stumbled back north and east, permitting the Nazi armor to drive up the excellent suburban road network with hardly any opposition. Before evening of August 28 the outriders of the Nazi 20th Panzers were approaching Mga. Mga was located on the Northern Railroad. This was not the main Leningrad-Moscow railroad, which had already been cut. The Northern Railroad was the line which connected Leningrad with Vologda, and through that junction point with Moscow.

As the Nazi attack developed, only a handful of Soviet troops found themselves, largely by accident, in Mga. The principal unit was a group under the command of a Major Leshchev. Major Leshchev and his soldiers had retreated all the way from Novgorod. They constantly found themselves just ahead of the Nazi armor, which nagged at their heels and inflicted heavy punishment. By the time they arrived at Mga they had no artillery and almost no cartridges.

The only other Soviet unit in Mga was a small group of Bychevsky's sappers under the command of Lieutenant Colonel S. I. Lisovsky. A week after the fall of Mga, Lisovsky, his hair bleached by exposure to the sun, his face worn and wrinkled, made his way into Leningrad and told Bychevsky what had happened. He had tried to mine the highway along which the Nazis were advancing, but they came on too fast. There was no real battle of Mga—just a series of small skirmishes in which the ill-armed, exhausted Soviet units managed to slow down the Nazis until the main German strength of tanks and motorized artillery came up. By August 30 the Nazis held Mga and had cut the Northern Railroad. They quickly fanned out, and their first units reached the Neva River the same day in the region of Ivanovskoye, just southwest of Otradnoye—the breakthrough which the excited young Komsomol girl had so accidentally reported to Admiral Kuznetsov as he sat by chance in the office of Admiral Isakov at Smolny.

Belatedly, the Leningrad Command realized what had been happening and the implications of the loss of Mga. They had few troops to throw into the breach. The first division of NKVD troops was hurried to the scene under the command of a tough police general, Colonel S. I. Donskov. It was the first to reach the Mga area. It was followed by a Border Guard division under an able general, G. A. Stepanov, and the 168th Division under Colonel Andrei L. Bondarev. But these troops had been heavily engaged against the

Finns in Karelia and had just been withdrawn from that front. They were too exhausted to be effective. Other pick-up units were rushed in—part of the 237th Rifle Division, the 1st Division of the People's Volunteers, units from the Border Guards school, two tank regiments, one of T-26's and one of KV 60-ton monsters, a division of 155-mm howitzers.

They went into action as early as August 31, against the 20th Nazi Panzers within Mga and against the German 122nd Infantry Division which had now occupied Ivanovskoye and Pavlovo at the estuary of the Mga River. The first attack of Donskov's NKVD troops was successful. The Nazis were hurled out of Mga on September 1. But on September 2 the Germans brought in powerful units of the 39th Motorized Corps and the 1st and 28th Army Corps of the Sixteenth Nazi Army. By this time it was evident to both Nazis and Russians that Mga had become the key to the encirclement of Leningrad.

The German strength was far too great for the Russians. The Soviet problem quickly became not one of trying to hold or win back Mga but to keep the Nazis from striking across the Neva River itself.

This problem preoccupied Bychevsky. The key to holding the Neva line and to preventing the Germans from getting across was a railroad bridge at Ostrovki, halfway between the Tosna and the Mga rivers. If the Nazis seized this bridge, they would be across the Neva in an instant, knifing behind the Soviet lines, in a position to strike only forty-five miles northward to make a junction with the Finns and lock a vise around Leningrad.

If the Germans got across the bridge—or the river—in any strength, there was hardly a chance that the Leningrad defenders could prevent close-in encirclement of the northern capital, its inevitable fall and an opportunity for Hitler to carry out his strategic design of a massive sweep from the north to encircle Moscow from the rear.

This bridge was on the mind of Colonel Bychevsky on the morning of August 30. He had spent the whole night trying to get the exact details on the situation at the front. It was not easy. The situation was too fluid. The NKVD units were moving up to the Mga region, and the 168th Division had been ordered into position on the Izhorsk line just east of Kolpino.

Bychevsky had been unable to see the Leningrad commander, General Popov, all night long. Popov was in continuous conference with the High Command and the special commission of the State Defense Committee.

It was morning before Bychevsky got into Popov's office. On the General's desk was a glass of ink-black coffee. And in the air Bychevsky caught a whiff of valerian drops, a favorite Russian restorative.

When Bychevsky walked in, Popov grumbled, "What do you want, Bychevsky? I was just going to shave."

Popov ran his hand over the stubble on his beard and grimaced as though he had a sore tooth. "You know what the situation is," he snapped. "You know the orders. Let's get to work."

Bychevsky said he wanted to go to the Neva and see about the railroad bridge at Ostrovki-Kuzminki.

"Do we have any troops there?" he asked.

Popov said that General Stepanov had been put in charge of the area. Some People's Volunteers were supposed to man the northern bank of the Neva, and on the southern side the 168th Division and NKVD units under Colonel Donskov were supposed to be moving into place.

"What about the bridge?" Bychevsky persisted.

"Of course, get it ready to be blown up," Popov snapped.

A moment's silence followed. Then Popov said, "Have you heard about the changes? The State Defense Committee has named Marshal Voroshilov commander of the front and I am Chief of Staff."

Bychevsky left almost immediately for the threatened railroad bridge. He brought with him his deputy, Pilipets, and a detachment of sappers under Lieutenant Rubin. From the region of Porogi, on the north side of the Neva opposite the mouth of the Tosna, on toward Shlisselburg there were hardly any troops. Bychevsky found only one antiaircraft battery, manned by Baltic sailors who were preparing to use their weapon as field artillery.

So far as he could see there were no troops whatever on the southern side of the Neva, although he heard the distant sound of battle.

The railroad bridge was completely undefended.

The moment the sappers arrived Bychevsky ordered them to cut the metal girders and mine all the approaches. As Bychevsky laconically noted: "These measures were very timely. The next day the Hitlerites arrived at the Neva right in the region of the destroyed bridge."

The blowing up of the bridge by Bychevsky's men may well have saved Leningrad. The Nazi 39th Corps under General Rudolf Schmidt had been entrusted with the task of securing the bridge. Schmidt had a special diversionary unit of the so-called Brandenburg Corps, which was supposed to cut behind the Russians and seize the bridge before it could be knocked out.

Bychevsky's timely action thwarted this plan. The 39th Corps had no pontoon bridges in its supply column. Instead of attempting to force the Neva, the 39th drove north along the near bank of the stream toward Shlisselburg.

But the circle around Leningrad had been effectively closed.

V. M. Gankevich, the officer and former athlete who had been sent to Murmansk to make certain that the Fourteenth Army's ski equipment was in order, had finished his assignment and was returning to Leningrad. His train brought him as far as Volkhov. No further. Anyone who wanted to get to Leningrad would have to walk. The distance was seventy-five miles by a roundabout and dubious route—north to Staraya Ladoga, then west across the Old and New Ladoga canals which paralleled the lake shore, through Shlisselburg and on into Leningrad.

Gankevich decided to try it on foot. He set off and at dusk overtook another man, a naval lieutenant named Aleksandr Radchenko. Radchenko was slow to become friends with Gankevich until he discovered the sportsman-officer was also trying to get to Leningrad. Then they joined forces and pushed on through the night. They could hear the sound of distant cannon fire almost constantly. There was little traffic, but occasionally they met a truck. When they got to the river station at Staraya Ladoga, they heard a woman crying and in the corner of the waiting room found a man's body, covered with a rug. The woman was sobbing beside him. The body was that of Aleksandr Ilyin-Zhenkovsky, a leader in the 1917 Bolshevik Revolution, a Party propagandist, a onetime Soviet diplomat and a leading chess player. The woman was his wife. They had been on a barge being towed across the Volkhov River. A German flier dropped a bomb on the craft. Ilin-Zhenevsky was killed, but the other passengers miraculously escaped.

The two men arranged for the burial of Ilyin-Zhenkovsky, and in the morning he was entombed in the Staraya Ladoga cemetery beside the Volkhov River.

The officers then continued their hike. About ten miles beyond Staraya Ladoga they began to encounter Soviet infantry and tanks. The two men were intermittently under fire. By the time they got to the New Ladoga Canal they were exhausted. Gankevich was barely able to swim. There was no boat, not even a plank, in sight. However, Radchenko managed to help him across both the New and the Old Ladoga canals. The two men stumbled into Shlisselburg. The Nazis were battering at its approaches. German tanks rumbled forward over the bodies of German soldiers who had fallen in earlier waves. The Russians were suffering heavy losses from Nazi dive-bombing. Under German fire a Soviet engineering detachment was putting a pontoon across the Neva. Tugboats on the river helped to hold it in place. The two men made their way along the outskirts of the city. In an abandoned barn beside the river they found a boat without oars. With a couple of loose boards they cast off onto the Neva just as some unknown man shouted to them to halt. Their boat swirled out into the current and they paddled furiously for the opposite shore. The danger was not over. They were apt to be fired on at any moment, especially from the north bank. And they might well be taken by their own comrades as fleeing deserters.

As they bumped onto the shore, a tall, thin Soviet lieutenant with an automatic in his hand halted them.

"Who are you and from where do you come?" he demanded.

The pair handed over their documents. They found themselves in the midst of a well-constructed trench system equipped with fire points, dugouts and fully manned.

A few hours later the two men made their way into Leningrad. It had taken Gankevich ten days to make the trip from Murmansk. He got back September 8. This was the day the Germans took Shlisselburg.

The NKVD division commanded by Colonel Donskov was forced back from Mga, back from Power Station No. 8, the Mustolovo and the Kelkolovo workers settlements toward Shlisselburg.

It was Lieutenant Colonel S. I. Sisovsky's opinion (expressed to Bychevsky) that the Germans could have gotten across the Neva at some point north of the Tosna estuary, but that they had elected to drive for Shlisselburg instead.

The German strength was far superior to that of the Russians. Von Leeb sent in the 12th Panzer Division on September 7 and more than three hundred supporting planes. The NKVD troops melted away, and the road along the south bank of the Neva was left free for the Germans to move to Shlisselburg.

The broken Forty-eighth Army had been taken out of the hands of General Akimov August 31 and put under the command of Lieutenant General M. A. Antonyuk. It had less than ten thousand men left. The command change was in line with Stalin's directive to put the Forty-eighth Army "in order." Antonyuk proved unable to get any grasp whatever of his troops, and on September 12 the remnants were thrown into the newly created Fifty-fourth Army. This army, based on Volkhov, was designed to relieve the pressure on Leningrad and, hopefully, deblockade the city. But it was headed by as great an incompetent as the Red Army boasted, the political and police officer, Marshal G. I. Kulik, who was once described by a Soviet observer as "operatively illiterate and impermissibly procrastinating." Kulik held the command until September 25, when he was replaced by the reliable Lieutenant General M. S. Khozin.

The incompetence of Kulik, the ineptness of Antonyuk and the mismanagement of the Forty-eighth Army and the Northwest Front, then commanded by Voroshilov, were blamed by General Dukhanov for the disastrous breakthrough along the whole line from Lyuban to Tosno to Kolpino. To what extent these factors were responsible for the success of the Nazis in reaching the Neva it is difficult to assess. Soviet military commanders, who to a man hated and perhaps feared Kulik, place a major share of the blame on him for the success of the Germans in encircling Leningrad and closing the vise about the city.

There was certainly Soviet incompetence, confusion, cowardice, failure of coordination and poor direction. But the greatest handicaps were lack of manpower, inferior and inadequately trained troops and, on a higher level, consistent underestimation of the Nazi danger.

Here and there were bright exceptions. One was the Izhorsk battalions. The lines at Kolpino did not break. Indeed, within a fortnight the Izhorsk workers units went on the offensive and pushed back the Germans a bit.

But even this action has been obscured in some measure by political factors. The wartime hero of these actions was A. V. Anisimov, the man who led out the battalion of sixty workers at dawn. It was he who in February, 1942, was singled out for special honors in a ceremony conducted at Smolny by Party Secretary A. A. Kuznetsov. It was he who was credited for organizing the defense and honored with the award of the Order of Lenin. It was he who took the salute: "Honor and glory to the Izhorsk workers!" But with the passage of years Anisimov's image faded. Other names replaced it. Why? The answer is not clear. The question of the glory of Izhorsk seems to have shifted away from reality into the savage world of Kremlin politics—a world more deadly than that of the Soviet-German lines in September, 1941. There are two official reports of the work of the Izhorsk factory, one dated September 6 and one about January 1, 1942, included in the documentary collection of the Leningrad blockade. The factory director's name is not signed to either report. All other factory reports in the collection are signed. The official Leningrad war history "rehabilitates" the name of the wartime Izhorsk hero, A. V. Anisimov. But it, too, omits the Izhorsk director's name —a certain sign that high-level politics is involved.

At least three literary works touching on the Izhorsk defense and the workers' battle to save Kolpino were written after the war. Yevgeny Ryss started to publish a novel in 1945 which he called *At the City Gates*. It dealt with the Izhorsk factory which he called "Starozavod." Only two parts of the novel ever came out. He ran into endless "critical" difficulties and finally abandoned the idea. Nikolai Chukovsky touched on the subject in his novel *Baltic Skies*, and Leonid Rakhmanov, who had been a war correspondent with the Izhorsk workers, wrote a play about them. Neither work ever saw the light of day in its original form. Only in 1959 did Rakhmanov finish his play.

Vera Ketlinskaya is blunt in placing responsibility for these difficulties. It was, she said, the "Leningrad Affair" which caused them. That is a euphemism for the savage political war between Zhdanov, on the one hand, and Georgi Malenkov and Lavrenti Beria, on the other, which, in the end, took countless lives in Leningrad.

The shadow of Mga was quick to lengthen, but on September 1 there were still signs of peacetime normalcy in Leningrad. The university had sent 2,500 students, 8 professors, 60 docents, 47 senior lecturers and 109 assistants into the armed forces. Yet 2,000 students registered for classes on September 1. One girl complained that a lecture had lasted five hours—her class was trapped with its professor in a bomb shelter and he never stopped talking. Forty higher educational institutions opened their doors September 1 and in the two weeks following. It was not business as usual. Schoolchildren collected a million bottles for Molotov cocktails in a fortnight.

September 1 was the day Dmitri Shostakovich spoke on the Leningrad radio.

"Just an hour ago," he said, "I completed the score of the second part of my new large symphonic work."

If he completed the third and fourth parts, he said, he would entitle it his

Seventh Symphony. He had been working on the composition since July.

"Notwithstanding war conditions, notwithstanding the dangers threatening Leningrad," he said, "I have been able to work quickly and to finish the first two parts of my symphony.

"Why do I tell you about this? I tell you this so that those Leningraders who are now listening to me shall know that the life of our city is going on normally. All of us now carry our military burdens."

Leningrad, he said, was his native city. Here was his home and here his heart.

"Soviet musicians, my many and dear colleagues, my friends," he said. "Remember that our art is threatened with great danger. We will defend our music. We will work with honesty and self-sacrifice that no one may destroy it."

Then Shostakovich returned to his apartment on Skorokhod Ulitsa on the Petrograd side, there to continue his work and to serve his duty with the fire service, protecting the apartment house against bombs. The day was an exceptionally clear one and the air had a special quality. Those who heard Shostakovich talk said each word rang like the note of a great piano.

He had, he told his friends, never composed with greater ease. He spent hours at his desk in his flat on the top floor of the five-story building where he lived, sometimes working around the clock. And he still went to the conservatory, where he had a few students left. Most had gone to the front, including the most talented of all, a young man named Fleishman who joined the People's Volunteers and was killed at the front in July.

Repeatedly Shostakovich was asked to leave Leningrad. He refused. Not until early October, after finishing the third movement of his symphony, did he reluctantly obey a command by the government. He and his family were evacuated to Moscow and within a few days to Kuibyshev. There he finished his symphony. There in March it was performed for the first time and on March 29 was given its formal premiere in the Hall of Columns in Moscow—Shostakovich's Seventh, the Leningrad Symphony, with its broad sweep of anger, agony and military panoply.

The sheets on which Shostakovich wrote his September 1 radio address have been preserved. On the reverse side are the hasty notes of the studio director:

Plans for next broadcasts to the city
1. Organize detachments.
2. Communications in the streets.
3. Construction of barricades.
4. Fighting with Molotov cocktails.
5. Defense of houses.
6. Especially emphasize on all instructional transmissions that the battle is nearing the closest approaches to the city, that over us hangs deadly danger.

Olga Berggolts preserved that souvenir of Shostakovich's broadcast. She preserved another souvenir—a sheet of lined paper torn from a book-keeper's ledger on which she wrote down at the dictation of Anna Akhmatova the speech which the poetess gave over Leningrad radio, the dictation carefully corrected by Anna Akhmatova in her own hand. It was dictated not at Anna Akhmatova's own house but in the so-called writers' "skyscraper," in the apartment of Mikhail Zoshchenko, the satirist. They had gone there because a heavy bombardment was in progress and the skyscraper was supposed to be a safer place.

Anna Akhmatova was Leningrad's "muse of tears," intensely feminine, personal and emotional. But it was with another voice that she spoke that evening over the radio to "my dear fellow citizens, mothers, wives and sisters of Leningrad."

For months, she said, the Germans had sought to take prisoner "the city of Peter, the city of Lenin, the city of Pushkin, of Dostoyevsky and Blok, the city of great culture and great achievement."

"All my life is connected with Leningrad," she said. "In Leningrad I became a poet. Leningrad gave my poetry its spirit. I, like all of you now, live with one unconquerable belief—that Leningrad never will be Fascist."

After the broadcast they went back to the building on the Fontanka, the former Sheremetyev Palace where Akhmatova lived. Olga Berggolts long remembered her beside the wrought-iron gates, her face stony with anger, a gas mask over her shoulder, standing duty as a member of the ARP team. Anna Akhmatova sewed bags for sand, which protected the shelter trenches in the gardens of the palace under the great maple of which she wrote in "Poem Without a Hero." All through September Anna Akhmatova stood by her post, guarding the roofs, placing the sandbags, writing her verses, fighting for her country. Only with October would she, too, reluctantly accept evacuation to Tashkent in distant Central Asia.

It was in these days that Olga Berggolts wrote of her beloved city:

> Leningrad in September, Leningrad in September,
> Golden twilight, the regal fall of the leaves,
> The crunch of the first bombs, the sob of the sirens,
> The dark and rusty contour of the barricades . . .

Valerian Bogdanov-Berezovsky had lived with his wife in Pushkin for nearly ten years. Then, in late August, he collected his writings, his most essential reference books, a few other personal possessions and came to Leningrad. It was no longer possible to work in Pushkin. The beautiful city on Leningrad's outskirts with its great parks, its palaces, its villas, its deep associations with Russian history and Russian culture overflowed with refugees from the Baltic, from Pskov, from Velikiye Luki, from Gatchina. At the Conservatory, where Bogdanov-Berezovsky taught a course in the history of Soviet music, they tried to persuade him to join the group of composers and musicologists which was being evacuated to Tashkent. He declined to go. His mother was ill and could not be moved from Leningrad, and he had been asked to head the organization directing the work of those remaining in Leningrad. The Conservatory group was evacuated without him on the night of August 22. The train was held up at Mga because the Germans had bombed out the bridge at Volkhovstroi, en route to Vologda. Finally, the train was diverted to the Pestovo line, the only one remaining open. Shortly after the train pulled out of Mga, German bombers savagely attacked Mga railroad station.

On August 30 Bogdanov-Berezovsky went to Smolny to talk with Party officials about setting up a small mobile orchestra and singing group which would present operatic scenes to troops at the front and in the hospitals. After the conference he and other composers assembled for rifle drill under the direction of a "very nice but very demanding young lieutenant." The musicians loaded their guns, fired at targets, cleaned them. They were preparing for the block-by-block defense of Leningrad. On September 1 Bogdanov-Berezovsky rose at 6:30 A.M. He worked at his desk until nearly 10. Then he went to the Union of Composers. He and his colleagues held an audition of military songs for a military song book which they were putting out for the Leningrad troops. This was his new life—a life which differed only in minor detail from that of most of his fellow citizens.

September 4 was a foggy, cloudy day. All night there had been the sound of cannon. The shelling seemed nearer. By noon reports began to come to Smolny: German long-range artillery was firing into the city. A shell plunged into the Vitebsk freight station. Another hit the Dalolin factory. Then the Krasny Neftyanik plant was hit, followed by the Bolshevik factory and Hydroelectric Station No. 5. There were heavy casualties. The shells, it was quickly determined, were being fired by long-range 240-mm siege artillery from the region of Tosno.

Word of the shelling spread from one end of Leningrad to another, and with it word of the fall of Mga which had cut the last railroad to Moscow. It was the fall of Mga which had enabled the Germans to begin shelling the city. Vissarion Sayanov walked through the Leningrad streets that day. The posters were up for the premiere of *Maritza* at the Musical Comedy Theater September 6. He found a long line at the railroad station. He asked the people why they went there. The window was shut. No tickets were being sold. Didn't they know Mga had fallen? A woman with three little children beside her answered, "Maybe they will take Mga back and then the road will be open and then the people in line here will get the first tickets. That's why."

A white-aproned girl was selling soda pop in the station, and people walked past eating Eskimo pies. A little girl had chalked squares on the sidewalk and was solemnly playing hopscotch. That was the day Sayanov met a girl walking on Nevsky Prospekt with two gas masks over her shoulder and a cat in her arms.

"You're well prepared for a gas attack," he observed.

"Yes," she said. "I'm practicing."

"But why two masks?"

"What about my cat?" she said. "Do you think I'd let her die in a gas attack?"

Sayanov was often to think of the girl and her cat in the weeks to come as Leningrad belts drew tighter.

People talked of Mga and little else. Sayanov heard a man say on the street, "The German soldiers say they hold Mga so strongly that if we take it they'll have to fall all the way back to Berlin. They say it's impossible to take Mga."

It was strange, Sayanov thought, that people's attention fastened so on Mga—not only that of civilians but of the military as well.

28 . *The Blood-Red Clouds*

VERA INBER HAD NEVER SEEN SUCH AN AUTUMN: NO RAIN; the air warm and dry; the leaves purple, amber and lemon-yellow, still rustling on the trees. Her husband, Dr. I. D. Strashun, was busy all day at the great hospital on Aptekarsky Island. Occasionally there was an air-raid alert, and Vera Inber would stand on the balcony of their apartment on Pesochnaya Ulitsa and look out beyond the pleasant trees and walks of the Botanical Gardens to the vista of the great city.

On September 8 she went with some friends to the Musical Comedy Theater to see *The Bat*. When the sirens sounded between the first and second acts, the theater director asked the audience to take seats close to the walls because there was no air-raid shelter. The performance went on to the counterpoint of AA guns.

When Vera Inber and her friends came out of the theater, they noticed a strange reddish light reflected across the square in the dusk. Suddenly their chauffeur appeared and said, "I thought I'd come for you. It's better to get home quickly."

As their car turned out of the square, they saw mountains of smoke pouring up toward the sky, the smoke shot through with long tongues of reddish flame, the flames and the smoke reaching thousands of feet over the city.

"The Germans have set fire to the food warehouses," the chauffeur said.

They drove rapidly through St. Isaac's Square, past the Admiralty and its slender spire, across Palace Square and over the Neva by the Kirov Bridge. As they looked back, they could see the waves of smoke, oily-black and ember-red, curling ever higher and higher.

Alarm followed alarm. For the first time Vera Inber went down to the shelter. The sound of German planes was still overhead and the AA guns had not been silent.

Pavel Luknitsky had a front-row seat for the raid—the window of a friend's sixth-floor apartment at the corner of Borovaya Ulitsa and Rasstannaya. It overlooked the Vitebsk locomotive depot, the great Badayev warehouses, the freight station and beyond toward Avtovo and the Kirov metallurgical works.

The Badayev warehouses had been built by an old St. Petersburg merchant named Rasterayev just before World War I. They were wooden buildings, put up one next to the other with gaps of not more than 25 or 30 feet between them. The compound covered several acres in the southwest quarter of the city. Luknitsky and his friend, Lyudmila Fedorovna, walked to her apartment on Borovaya in early evening. They stopped with many other Leningraders to peer at a building at the corner of Glazovskaya and Voronezh streets which had been hit by a German shell. The German shelling had started only September 4, and the building, No. 13 Glazovskaya, was one of the first to be hit. There had been many casualties, mostly women and children. The evening was pleasant and clear. There were a few white clouds in the blue sky. Suddenly a factory whistle sounded an air alert. Almost immediately they saw hundreds of incendiary bombs showering into the Vitebsk freight yards. Dozens of fires of blinding brilliance burst out.

Clouds of black and red smoke began to rise. Bombs continued to fall and the AA guns to bark. Some women gathered in the courtyard of the building, chattering in curiosity about what was going on. Luknitsky climbed to the roof. From there he could see that the whole city was gradually being covered with smoke from huge fires burning in the vicinity of Ligovo and the freight station. At first he thought it must be an oil depot. Later he learned it was the Badayev warehouses.

About 8 P.M. the all-clear sounded and Luknitsky started back to the Petrograd side. But he found the trams were halted by crowds moving toward the fires. He had to go on foot to Five Corners where the streetcars were running. Along a wall on Chernyshevsky Street he saw a group of youngsters with guitars and mandolins playing for their girl friends. The blood-red smoke spread farther and farther across the sky, and after 10 P.M. when he got back home a new air alert sounded.

To Olga Berggolts the greasy clouds brought a premonition of alarm. They reminded her of an eclipse of the sun—a red eclipse. She thought of the leaflets which the Germans had dropped: "Wait for the full moon!" And below in smaller letters: "Bayonets in the earth." Superstitious people might take panic. But as yet she had no idea that the red clouds were casting the fateful shadow of famine over her beloved Leningrad.

Vsevolod Kochetov had returned from the front to the *Leningradskaya Pravda* on September 8 and was talking with his colleagues when the alert sounded. They saw planes, high in the sky, heard the AA guns and the sound of fire trucks and ambulances. Then they went up to the roof and someone said, "It's the Badayev warehouses."

The tower of flame and smoke rising more than three miles provided an easy marker for the German planes when they returned to bomb the city again about 11 P.M. Yet it seemed to Kochetov that the Germans were being aided by rockets fired inside Leningrad, by signals sent up to guide the Nazi bombers. Who were these traitors? Former imperial bureaucrats? Elderly members of the old Russian intelligentsia? Kulaks? Old White Guard officers? Traders? Businessmen ready to greet Hitler with the traditional Russian offering of bread and salt? Kochetov, ever ready to suspect the worst, felt there was treachery all about him.

Kochetov was not the only one to see Nazi agents and traitors signaling from windows and rooftops. That night and for weeks to come rumors of Nazi activity flooded the city. The Nazis did send agents into the city. There was hardly a Leningrader who did not believe that Nazi "rocketmen" were active. The reports found their way into official accounts, police documents, military reports, personal reminiscences and official histories.

In reality, the "rocketmen" did not exist. They were a product of the hysteria and suspicion of the times.[1]

Colonel B. V. Bychevsky was returning on the evening of September 8 from one of his endless trips to the front, this time to the Neva region, where he was working on a pontoon bridge. He was deep in thought when his chauffeur, Pavel Yakovlev, suddenly stopped the car, saying, "Comrade Chief, look at what's happening in the city!"

Bychevsky looked. The whole horizon over Leningrad was colored deep blood-red. The sky was crisscrossed by searchlights, and the flames of the fires, reflected back from the smoke clouds, filled the streets and squares with a strange light. People were running toward the conflagration with loads of sand and carts of water. AA guns rattled and bombs kept falling.

It was midnight when Bychevsky got back to Smolny Institute. The news was all bad. The German air attack had been going on for hours. At the front the offensive was gathering strength. Secretary Kuznetsov had been at the great Peterhof Palace, the pride of Russia, the rival of Versailles. He ordered

[1] Reports of rocketmen can be found, for example, in the official account of Pavlov, head of the Leningrad City Military Department, to Party Secretary A. A. Kuznetsov, October 23, 1943, telling of the success of the Young Communists in combating them (*900 Geroicheskikh Dnei*, p. 122). There are similar reports by Lieutenant General G. Stepanov, former chief of the Leningrad garrison (S. Bubenshchikov, *V Ognennom Koltse*, Moscow, 1963, p. 51); I. Ya. Lorkish, writing of the struggle against Abwehr agents in Leningrad (*Nevidimye Boi*, Leningrad, 1967, p. 11); the history of the Leningrad militia (A. Skilyagin, V. Lesov, U. Pimenov, I. Savchenko, *Dela i Lyudi*, Leningrad, 1967, p. 261); the October 31 report of the Petrograd regional council to the Leningrad City Council (*900*, p. 75); the official history of the Leningrad blockade (*Leningrad v VOV*, p. 98); and in many, many other works. To all these reports the men in charge of Leningrad's defenses offer a negative response. The authorities who investigated the rumors became convinced that in the vast majority of cases what Leningraders took for "rocket" signals were, in fact, tracer bullets of antiaircraft guns firing from rooftop positions at German planes or in some instances flares dropped by Nazi aircraft. As Ye. S. Lagutkin, chief of Leningrad's wartime AA defense, put it: "If some authors of books and articles write that in Leningrad there were many rocketmen, then these statements do not conform to reality." (*N.Z.*, p. 168.) D. V. Pavlov, the Leningrad food chief, supports Lagutkin's view. (Pavlov, personal communication, April 30, 1968.)

.ts treasures evacuated but forbade the sappers to mine the noble buildings. By now the Germans probably were there. Bychevsky was still talking with M. V. Basov[2] of the Leningrad Party organization when N. M. Shekhovtsev, deputy of the City Soviet, came in from the fire, his wide face lined with deep creases and smeared with soot. He sank into a chair, letting his heavy hands fall to his lap. It was now 6 A.M., and the fight with the fire was still going on.

"Has it all burned?" asked Basov, referring to the tons of flour, sugar, meat and other provisions in the warehouse.

"It's burned," Shekhovtsev sighed. "We kept all these riches in wooden buildings, practically cheek by jowl. Now we will pay for our heedlessness. It's a sea of flames. The sugar has flowed into the cellars—two and a half thousand tons."

Shekhovtsev launched into a bitter denunciation of himself, of the city authorities for their carelessness, for not dispersing the supplies, for not putting them in secure buildings, for the shortage of fire-fighting apparatus.

"Well," snapped Basov, "the leaders are to blame—ourselves among them. The people have good grounds for hurling some nasty words at us. What are the people saying?"

"They're saying nothing," Shekhovtsev replied. "They are fighting the fire, trying to save what they can. . . ."

The German air attack on Leningrad had begun September 6, but the first intensive raid was that of September 8. The Germans came that night in two main waves. The first, at 6:55 P.M., was carried out by 27 Junkers, dropping 6,327[3] incendiary bombs, of which 5,000 fell on the Moscow region, 1,311 in the Smolny region and 16 in the Red Guard region. These incendiary bombs set 178 fires.[4] At 10:35 P.M. a second wave of bombers dropped 48 high-explosive bombs of 500 to 1,000 pounds, mostly near Smolny Institute and the Finland Station. A pumping plant at the city waterworks was hit, and 24 people were killed and 122 wounded.

Almost all the city's fire-fighting apparatus, 168 units, was brought out to fight the Badayev fire, which blazed over an area of more than four acres. It took all night to bring it under control.

Not a person in Leningrad on the morning after the Badayev fire had reason any longer to doubt that the city faced the grimmest trial of its history. The smell of burning meat, the acrid stench of carbonized sugar, the heavy scent of burning oil and flour filled the air. Everyone knew Badayev was the city's greatest warehouse. Everyone knew that here the grain, the sugar, the meat, the lard and the butter for the city were stored. Now it was

[2] Basov was executed in 1950, one of the many victims of the so-called "Leningrad Affair." (G. Odintsev, *Voyenno-Istoricheskii Zhurnal*, No. 12, December, 1964, p. 61.)

[3] Pavlov, *op cit.*, 2nd edition, p. 32. The figure is given as 12,000 by the official history. (*Leningrad v VOV*, p. 172.)

[4] Pavlov, *op. cit.*, p. 32. The figure is given as 183 in the official ARP report. (*900*, p. 139.)

lost. "Badayev has burned," the babushkas said. "It's the end—famine!"

The iron ring of Hitler had closed. Indeed, Nazi troops were pounding into Shlisselburg and sealing the circle during the very hours in which Badayev went up in a pillar of flame. And even before Badayev went the city's position had been desperate.

For weeks Leningrad had glided along. To be sure, food was rationed, but no more strictly than in any other big city in Russia.

Even now Kochetov could buy at the lunch counter at *Leningradskaya Pravda* luxury products without ration coupons—first-quality crabmeat, gray full-grained caviar. At a special "closed store" for generals the salesgirl pressed Kochetov to buy champagne. "It's very nourishing," she said, "full of vitamins." At first he was going to take a bottle, but she insisted that he take more. He wound up coming away with a case. Thousands of Leningraders hoarded as much food as they could buy. Luknitsky visited a photographer with whom he had once traveled in Asia. The photographer showed him a special shelter which he had built in his apartment, filled with shelf after shelf of canned goods, food of every conceivable kind. He was certain there would soon be famine in the city. Luknitsky left the apartment with a feeling of revulsion. He recalled another friend, Major Boris Likharev, chairman of the Leningrad Writers Union. Likharev's wife had found a ten-pound can of caviar in the store and bought it "just in case." Likharev made her give it to a children's home because he thought it was showing a bad example.[5] Olga Iordan could still buy fresh caviar, real coffee, blackberry juice and sea cabbage. But shopping was getting more difficult.

Yelena Skryabina had to spend long hours in queues. She was able to buy butter in the commercial stores (of which there were seventy-one in Leningrad) and sometimes sugar. But she had to scurry from one end of town to another, sometimes to Vasilevsky Island, sometimes to the Petrograd side. She had about a month's supply of food on hand September 1.

No one in Leningrad—up to September 8—had actually suffered for food. White bread was sold as late as September 10. The rationing imposed July 1 was close to the average normal food consumption. The bread ration was nearly two pounds (800 grams) a day for workers and about a pound for dependents and children. The 1940 average consumption had been 531 grams of bread a day. The cereal ration of 2,000 grams a month compared with 1940 consumption of 1,740; meat was 2,200 grams compared with 3,330 average; butter and fats 800 compared with 1,020 average, and sugar and sweets 1,500 compared with 3,630 average.

No alarm about Leningrad's food situation had been expressed until the special mission of the State Defense Committee discovered that on August 27, the date when for all practical purposes rail communications with Leningrad

[5] Two years later Likharev admitted to Alexander Werth that he and his wife had many times regretted their action. "We were haunted by the memory of that tin of caviar. It was like paradise lost." (Alexander Werth, *Leningrad*, New York, 1944, p. 77.)

were severed, the city had on hand the following supplies: flour, exclusive of grain, 17 days' supply; cereals, 29 days'; fish, 16 days'; meat, 25 days'; dried fish, 22 days'; butter, 28 days'.

An urgent telegram was sent to the State Defense Committee in Moscow August 29 asking that emergency food shipments be sent to Leningrad. The committee decided to provide Leningrad with a 45-day reserve of food. It proposed to ship in 135,000 tons of flour, 7,800 tons of cereals, 24,000 tons of meat and fish, 3,500 tons of dried fish, 3,000 tons of butter.

It recommended that Leningrad reduce its free commercial sale of food (at high government prices) and put tea, eggs and matches on a ration basis. The government approved these recommendations and ordered the Transport Ministry to begin on August 31 sending eight food trains daily to Volkhovstroi and Lodeinoye Pole with food for the city. From those points the food was to be sent by barge, tugboat and tanker via Lake Ladoga and the Neva River to Leningrad.

In line with these decisions, on September 2 the Leningrad rations were reduced. The bread ration was cut to 600 grams—a little more than a pound —a day for workers, 400 grams for office workers and 300 grams—about half a pound—for dependents and children under twelve. The meat ration was cut to three pounds a month, cereals to the same level, fats to a pound and a half, and sugar and candy to five pounds. This meant belt-tightening. But it was not insupportable—especially since it was still possible to eat in restaurants or dining rooms attached to factories, institutions and offices without giving up ration coupons.

But behind the façade of these still generous controls a deadly picture assumed shape.

On September 6—two days before Badayev's pillar of flame—Peter S. Popkov, Mayor of Leningrad, sent a cipher telegram to the State Defense Committee reporting that Leningrad was on the verge of exhausting her food reserves. Food trains must be expedited or the city would starve.

Popkov's telegram was based on an inventory which disclosed that the city then had on hand only these supplies: flour, 14.1 days; cereals, 23 days; meat and meat products, 18.7 days; fats, 20.8 days; sugar and confectionery, 47.9 days.

In eight days—between the State Committee telegram of August 29 and Popkov's—the city's reserves of flour had dropped by three days, of cereals by six days, of meat by nearly seven.

Should Leningrad's consumption continue at these levels and delivery of supplies show no improvement, the city would be down to bare shelves within two or three weeks—possibly less. The time had come for extraordinary measures. Two days later Dmitri V. Pavlov arrived in Leningrad from Moscow, clothed with powers to handle all food questions in Leningrad, both for the civilian population and the army.

Pavlov was one of the ablest and most energetic supply officials in the

Soviet Union. He was thirty-six years old, a graduate of the All-Union Academy of Foreign Trade, and had devoted his whole career to food distribution and production. He was Commissar of Trade for the Russian Federated Republic and an important executive of the Main Administration of Food Supplies of the Defense Commissariat. He was a direct, honest, vigorous man who saw from the moment of his arrival in Leningrad that only spartan measures, applied with an iron hand, offered a chance for the city's survival. The first thing he had to know was the facts, the tough, naked facts—not anyone's political or propaganda-tinged facts. What was the actual position of Leningrad so far as food was concerned? Was the city down to two or three weeks' reserves? What supplies had the army? The navy? What was the population load? What kind of supplies could be got into the city?

Pavlov was at work almost before he clambered out of the Douglas DC-3 which brought him in low over Lake Ladoga to the Leningrad airport. He spent September 10 and 11 inventorying the city's reserves. The figures were grim—he had known they would be—but not quite as bad as Popkov's alarming telegram of September 6. Based on the actual rate of expenditure of food for the armed forces and the civilian population, the city's reserves totaled: grain, flour, hardtack, 35 days; cereals and macaroni, 30; meat and meat products including live cattle, 33; fats, 45; sugar and confectionery, 60. The only food not included in Pavlov's inventory was a small amount of "iron rations" (hardtack and canned goods) in the army and fleet reserves and a small amount of flour in the hands of the navy.

The chief differences between Pavlov's estimates and those of Popkov were that Pavlov included all the food in the city—that in military hands as well as civilian and unprocessed materials (unmilled grain and unslaughtered cattle), as well as flour and meat in cold storage. Moreover, by the time Pavlov cast his estimates the ration had been again cut (as of September 12) to 500 grams of bread per day for workers, 300 for office employees, 250 for dependents and 300 for children under twelve.

Pavlov calculated—correctly—that there was no hope for any supplies whatever from the outside for a considerable time. The only route open was across Lake Ladoga, and there were no boats, piers, highway and rail facilities or warehouses which could handle substantial shipments. To create them would require time.

Leningrad, he was certain, must live on what it had on hand—for how long no one knew.

How many people did he have to feed? This was not easy to establish. Pavlov estimated, on the basis of the distribution of ration cards, figures on evacuation, refugees and prewar population, that he had a civilian population of about 2,544,000, including about 400,000 children, in the city, and another 343,000 in the suburban areas within the blockade ring. The total was roughly 2,887,000. In addition, there were the military forces defending the city. No exact figure has ever been given for them, but they must have been in the neighborhood of 500,000. The number of mouths which he had to feed for an indefinite period of time, thus, was close to 3,400,000.[6] It was no small task, and he was filled with the gravest foreboding. Like all Leningrad's leadership, he inevitably lived for news that the city had been deblockaded. But, unlike the others, Pavlov had to face each day the reality of the city's dwindling food reserves.

Almost Pavlov's first act was to evaluate the consequences of the Badayev fire. They were serious, but perhaps not quite so serious as most Leningraders thought. The destruction of Badayev did not doom the city to famine.

Pavlov estimated the Badayev losses at 3,000 tons of flour and about 2,500 tons of sugar, of which, in the grimmest months of the winter that lay ahead, about 700 tons, blackened, dirty and scorched, would be reclaimed and converted into "candy."[7]

Nevertheless, he took no chances on a new Badayev. Almost all Leningrad's flour was stored at the city's two big milling combines—the Lenin and the Kirov. He ordered it dispersed throughout the city. He did the same with the grain in harbor elevators and storehouses.

Despite Pavlov's insistence that Badayev was not the key to Leningrad's future suffering, many Leningraders—Pavel Luknitsky among them—remained convinced that the great fire had more to do with the city's suffering than the authorities have ever been willing to acknowledge.[8]

Pavlov blamed other causes. Ten different economic agencies had a hand in administration of food supplies. Each operated on orders from its Moscow headquarters. So long as Moscow did not forbid the sale or distribution of food, they continued. The commercial restaurants fell in this category. And they were dispersing 7 percent of Leningrad's total food consumption, 12 percent of all fats, 10 percent of the meat and 8 percent of the sugar and candy. Cattle slaughter was being carried out without care or plan. Vegetable fat was stored in commercial warehouses, animal fats in military supply dumps. Because of consumer prejudice against crabmeat it was sold without ration coupons. Invalids in hospitals and children in nurseries were fed off-ration, but got ration cards besides. In mid-September the Moscow Sugar Administration ordered its Leningrad subsidiary to send several freight cars of sugar to Vologda—although Leningrad, of course, had lost all rail connections with the rest of the country.

Pavlov moved in. He halted the sale of food without ration coupons. He

[6] In July, 2,562,000 ration cards were issued in Leningrad; in August, 2,669,000; in September, 2,480,400; in October, 2,443,400. About 636,283 persons were evacuated through Leningrad from June 29 through August 27, of whom Pavlov estimates 400,000 were Leningraders, the remainder refugees from the Baltic states. (Pavlov, *op. cit.*, 1st edition, pp. 59, 60.) Karasev estimates the September 6 population at "over 2.5 million." Leningrad's population by the census of 1939 was 3,191,300. (Karasev 120, p. 17.) An unpublished document has been found in the Leningrad archives which reports "in all 227,335 persons" were evacuated up to December 4, 1941. This casts doubt on the authenticity of the 636,283 figure (which supposedly included 488,703 Leningraders) (*Voprosy Istorii*, No. 11, November, 1968, p. 167). Thus, the number trapped in Leningrad may have been 260,000 more than earlier estimated.

[7] N.Z. claims 900 tons of sugar and 1,000 tons of flour were reclaimed. (*N.Z.*, p. 195.)

[8] Dmitri V. Pavlov insists his report is exact and that all other versions are "fantasies." (Personal communication, April 30, 1968.)

closed down the public commercial restaurants. He stopped the making of beer, ice cream, pirogi (meat pies) and pastry. He canceled all orders to food agencies from Moscow and took control of these supplies, insisting on immediate and accurate inventories. He eliminated ration cards for persons being fed in hospitals or children's homes, cutting the total by 80,000.

But he made mistakes—as he was later publicly to admit. Even after his first harsh cuts in rations the city was still consuming more than 2,000 tons of flour a day. He permitted an increase in the sugar and fat rations in September to make up for the cuts in meat and cereals. That took 2,500 tons of sugar and 600 tons of fats—quantities which could have been saved in September and October and used to help tide over the terrible December which lay ahead.

Leningrad had entered the war with a normal reserve of food. On June 21 she had 52 days' supply of flour and grain, including stores in the port elevators which were intended for export, 89 days' supply of cereals, 38 days' supply of meat, 47 days' of butter and fats, 29 days' supply of vegetable oils.

In July and August Leningrad received far less than normal food shipments from the nearby Yaroslavl and Kalinin regions—only 45,000 tons of wheat, 14,000 tons of flour and 3,000 tons of cereal. About 23,300 tons of grain and flour came in from Latvia and Estonia before the Germans occupied those areas. About 8,146 tons of meat were obtained from the Leningrad suburbs up to the end of the year. The Leningrad area had 25,407 pigs, 4,357 cattle and 568 goats on September 1. Total meat reserves, slaughtered and on the hoof, were 12,112 tons. Daily consumption after the September 12 ration cut was 246 tons.

The city got only a handful of the market produce she normally consumed. In 1941 Leningrad received only 6,960 tons of potatoes against a supply of 245,032 in 1940—and potatoes were the basic diet of tens of thousands. The city received 30,376 tons of vegetables against 154,682 the previous year and 508 tons of fruit against 15,234.

Leningrad used more food than usual in the weeks after the outbreak of war. The output of flour in July, for example, was 40,000 tons. In August consumption of bread went up 12.4 percent from an average of 2,112 tons to 2,305 tons daily, largely because of the influx of refugees.

Pavlov found the city was using 2,100 tons of flour per day at the start of September. This rate of consumption continued to September 11, when he brought it down to 1,300 tons. From September 16 to October 1 he cut it to 1,100 tons. In September—exclusive of the Leningrad front and the Baltic Fleet—Leningrad used a daily average of 146 tons of meat, 220 tons of cereals and 202 tons of sugar.

When the calendar turned to November and then to December, Pavlov looked back again and again at those consumption figures for early September. What he would not have given for the 8,000 tons of flour that he could have saved had the cuts gone into effect September 1 instead of September

10—not to mention the hundreds of tons of meat and other foodstuffs.

The air raids did not halt with the September 8 attack on Badayev. The next night bombs fell on the Zoo. The elephant, Betty, was killed. So were some apes. Betty's death throes went on for hours and her howling terrified those who heard her. Several sables, frantic with fear, were released into the streets. Dogs in the Pavlov Institute, windows in their stomachs, howled like dirges during the attacks. The raids went on the next day and the next and the next.

Leningrad's air defenses could not hold off the Nazi bombers. Because of errors and mistakes the city ARP had been reorganized and put in the hands of a troika in August. The Leningrad fighter command started the war with 401 planes, but by September the figure was sharply reduced. The main protection came from 160 AA batteries mustering 600 guns. About 300 barrage balloons hovered over Leningrad, day and night, and there were 3,500 ARP units manned by 124,000 workers.

But the Nazi attacks continued.

"Now begins our life on the roofs," Pavel Gubchevsky, scientific colleague at the Hermitage, told his fellow ARP workers. Two posts were set up— one above the Hall of Arms of the Winter Palace and the other on the roof of the New Hermitage next to the huge skylight which gave onto the main picture gallery. For many nights no bombs fell on the Winter Palace or the Hermitage, but the rain of shrapnel from AA guns crackled and sparkled like heat lightning on the vast pavement of Palace Square. From his observation post Gubchevsky saw just across the Neva German bombers shower down incendiary bombs around the ancient Peter and Paul Fortress, where generation after generation of Russian rebels, state criminals and revolutionaries had been imprisoned. The incendiaries rolled down the thick walls of the fortress like rivers of fire and burned out on the sandy banks of the Neva. Then came a thunderous explosion and a thousand tongues of flame lashed around the *"Amerikanskye Gory"*—the roller coaster which was the main attraction of the amusement park in the adjacent gardens. Night turned to day as the wooden structure blazed toward the sky. The wind blew toward the Winter Palace, and soon sparks and soot rained down on the Hermitage roof along with heavy particles of blackened paint from the gay decorations of the amusement park. The fretwork of the roller coaster, a hodgepodge of twisted girders, stood charred and twisted throughout the war, a reminder of the fire-filled night.

The air raid on September 10 was almost as big as that of the eighth. Three more Badayev warehouses burned—fortunately they were empty. But the big Red Star creamery was hit and tons of butter were lost. The Zhdanov Shipworks were badly damaged. More than 700 Leningraders were killed and wounded and more than 80 big fires were set. On that day over the Kirov metallurgical works suddenly was heard a low-flying plane. A moment later Leonid Sanin, ARP officer, reported that paratroops were attacking the plant and hurried toward the descending chute. The next instant a tremendous shock wave knocked him unconscious. It was not parachutists the Nazis had dropped but a one-ton delayed-action bomb suspended in a parachute.

There were 23 big raids in Leningrad in September and 200 shellings. More than 675 German planes took part in the raids. They dropped 987 explosive and 15,100 incendiary bombs, and they killed or wounded 4,409 Leningraders. The worst attacks were those of September 19 and 27. There were six raids on the nineteenth, four by day and two by night, with 280 planes participating. On September 27, 200 planes attacked the city.

That of the nineteenth was the worst of the war. One bomb fell on a hospital in Suvorov Prospekt. There were heavy casualties among the 600 wounded who were sheltered there. Another hit the Gostiny Dvor, the big shopping center in the heart of the city, killing 98 and wounding 148.[9]

The offices of the Soviet Pisatel Publishing house were located in the Gostiny Dvor. Eight editors, among them Taisiya Aleksandrova and Tatanya Gurevich, were killed and Director A. M. Semenov was severely wounded. Most of the victims in the Gostiny Dvor were women, many of them workers in a clothing factory. A week later Pavel Luknitsky visited the site and learned that several were still alive, trapped in the wreckage, being fed with food lowered to them through a narrow hole.

On the night the Gostiny Dvor was hit Dmitri Shostakovich invited some of his friends—Valerian Bogdanov-Berezovsky, the musicologist, and the composers, Gavrül Popov and Yuri Kochurov—to his fifth-floor flat. They found him surrounded by orchestration sheets on which he was scoring his Seventh Symphony. He sat at the piano and began to play with enormous enthusiasm. He was in such a state of emotional tension that it seemed to his listeners he was striving to extract from the piano every last atom of sound.

Suddenly the air-raid siren sounded, and overhead the musicians could hear Leningrad's fighter planes. Shostakovich played on. When he finished the First Movement of the symphony, he asked his wife and children to go to the bomb shelter but proposed to his friends that he continue to play. He went through the Second Movement to the crashing accompaniment of anti-aircraft guns. The Third Movement was incomplete.

Shostakovich's friends made their way back home after the all-clear had sounded. They saw from their streetcar clouds of smoke rising over the city. It was the Gostiny Dvor. It burned for days.

Shostakovich's music, the roar of the guns, the fires springing up, the bombs, the sirens, the planes—all seemed to Bogdanov-Berezovsky to blend into a cacophony in which reality and art were inextricably intermingled.

On the day of the Gostiny Dvor disaster Ivan Bondarenko, a Tass man, noted in his diary: "Explosions, explosions, more explosions. Yellow dust and black smoke over Socialist Street."

And that same day a Moscow woman living on Stremyannaya Ulitsa

[9] N.Z., p. 166. The date of this disaster is mistakenly given as September 24 in *Leningrad v VOV*, p. 176.

rushed into the Leningrad radio studios. Her house had just been smashed by a bomb, and under the wreckage lay her two children, dead.

"Let me talk on the radio," she begged. "I want to speak."

She was permitted to go to the microphone, and there, her voice breaking with emotion, her words heavy with sorrow, she told of the death of her son and daughter.

"I can remember not only her words but even the sound of her breathing," Olga Berggolts wrote twenty years later.

The air of the city grew thicker and thicker with the smashing of buildings, the fall of bricks and plaster, until Vera Ketlinskaya found it difficult even to take a breath.

Army General (later Marshal) Nikolai N. Voronov, the country's top artillery specialist, returned to Leningrad in these days. Leningrad was his native city. Here he had been born, here he had spent his childhood before the Revolution, here he had grown to young manhood. Now he had been called back to aid the city in its hour of peril. Voronov was no stranger to war and siege. He had served in Spain during the Civil War. He had seen Guadalajara, Teruel and Barcelona. He had fought through the siege of University City and had lived in Madrid during the bombardment.

One day he climbed to the cupola of St. Isaac's. From a height of 260 feet he could look out on the city, could see the ARP posts and the AA guns mounted on the roofs of the tall buildings, the great gray warships of the Baltic Fleet brought into the wide Neva and moored as floating long-range batteries to fire back on the German siege guns. He could see the Red Army's ragged lines to the south and southwest and could make out the flash of the German guns as they trained in on Leningrad targets.

"Again and again," he recalled, "my thoughts returned to Madrid and what that city had survived. There also the enemy had closed in on all sides. But here it was all repeated on an even grander scale—the city was greater, the intensity of the battle, the size of the forces. Here everything was infinitely more complicated."

Complicated, it was, indeed. And it grew more complicated. One day Yelena Skryabina took a battered old *sumka*, or shopping bag. She put in it two or three bottles of very strong vodka which she had managed to buy after standing in line for hours at a small wooden street stall.

She also had a dozen packs of cigarettes, a pair of men's shoes and some women's socks. She went out into the country a few miles to see what kind of food she might get from the peasants. It was a terrifying experience. The peasants stood looking at her stolidly. She could not help remembering the days of 1918 or 1920 when the city residents had to go to the villages with their furs, their rings, their bracelets, their rugs, and haggle with the peasants for crusts of bread and sacks of potatoes. The same thing was happening all over again. She returned that evening, exhausted, with forty pounds of potatoes and two quarts of milk. "I don't know how long I can keep up this kind of trading," she wrote in her diary.

29 . Not All Were Brave

VSEVOLOD VISHNEVSKY HAD NOT BEEN IN LENINGRAD since returning from the inferno of Tallinn. Day and night he worked at Kronstadt composing pamphlets, writing dispatches for *Pravda* and *Red Star*, making speeches to the political workers and officers. Now on a fine, sunny day, September 11, he took a cutter across the choppy sound to Oranienbaum and a crowded train to Leningrad. An air alarm sounded and he could see fires and shells exploding in the direction of Ligovo (Uritsk), just south of the city, where the Germans were trying to smash through to the railroad line. Vishnevsky was pleased that the people on the train seemed relatively calm and that, despite bombs, shells and fires, the streetcars still ran and bootblacks manned their stands.

But not everything was going well. He found some open panic. Wild rumors circulated, stimulated by the absence of accurate communiqués. The communiqués of the Soviet Information Bureau were bland. Those with some grasp of the course of events sometimes could divine what was happening by identifying "Strongpoint N" (which had been lost) or the troops of the "Nth Army" (one of the Leningrad armies) or by a reference to a particular commander. It was a time when the OMS (One Major Says) News Agency flourished, not to mention the OBS (One Baba Says). "What's happened to the army around Volkhov?" people asked. "What about the railroad to Moscow?" They knew the railroad was cut. But the government had not officially said so. Not a word appeared in the press. Leningrad radio was silent. There was a rising feeling of uncertainty, of bewilderment over what was happening. It would not be the last time that Leningrad would feel shrouded by official secrecy from the swift progress of events which might decide her fate. Everyone knew the war was going badly—but how badly? How much worse than the communiqués admitted?[1]

[1] This problem persisted throughout the war. On January 24, 1944, Party propaganda agitators reporting on the mood of workers in the Paris Commune factory of Leningrad

Vsevolod Kochetov, a chronic alarmist, was convinced that if the Germans broke into Leningrad they would find it filled with informers and traitors ready to assist them. He remembered that in 1919 the White Guard General Yudenich had dreamed of hanging a Bolshevik to every lamp post in Petrograd. Now, Kochetov speculated in terror, there would not be enough lamp posts to meet the purposes of the Nazi execution squads. The Germans would have to put hundreds, possibly thousands, of gallows up in the Champs de Mars, Palace Square and along the embankments of the Neva. A chilling thought!

Kochetov knew what the Nazis were doing on the approaches to Leningrad, the areas which were already occupied. He had met a commissar named Semenov who had made his escape through the lines from a village near the front.

"There you see the true face of German Fascism," the commissar told him. "Orders, orders, orders. Threats, threats, threats."

Semenov showed him a proclamation he had torn from a village fence. It said:

No. 1 Red Army men will report to the military commandant within 24 hours. Otherwise they will be treated as partisans and shot.

No. 2. Each partisan will be immediately shot.

No. 3. Inhabitants aiding Red Army men or partisans will be immediately shot.

So it went, point by point, each ending: "will be immediately shot."

It would be the same, Kochetov felt certain, if the Nazis broke into Leningrad.

As for the spirit of the Leningraders, Kochetov saw among them and among his own journalist colleagues many whom he called cowards and panicmongers, people of little spirit who wanted by any means to escape the iron circle of blockade. He knew of one newspaperman who had wangled passage out by air and was hauled off the plane at the last minute by Maxim Gordon, an elderly *Izvestiya* correspondent. Nor was Kochetov impressed by the correspondents whom he encountered at Alexei Tolstoy's villa in Pushkin—the villa which now belonged to the Writers Union, the same in which Luknitsky had been living and working on the eve of the war.

Pushkin was crowded with writers and war correspondents. The division newspaper of the 1st People's Volunteers was being published on the presses of the local paper, having lost its portable press in a desperate escape attempt across the marshes after the collapse of the Luga line. The editorial offices were in House No. 4 on Proletarian Street—the Tolstoy villa. Every room

said there were three principal questions asked them by workers: Was there any Soviet populace remaining in areas being freed by the Red Army? What were Soviet military losses? Why didn't *Leningradskaya Pravda* publish maps showing the advances of the Red Army? (*900*, p. 212.)

of the villa was filled with newspapermen. In the 6th Military Encampment at the edge of town five thousand survivors of the 1st People's Volunteers were jammed into an old barracks. As a military unit it hardly had any existence, having lost the arms and equipment it had started with, together with two-thirds of its strength.

Vyacheslav Shishkov, author of the picaresque Siberian classic, *Grim River,* still lived and worked in Pushkin, although he was more and more worried about moving into Leningrad. Aleksandr Belyayev, one of Russia's leading writers of science fiction, had not left his house. He was critically ill.

Kochetov and his friend Mikhalev spent a night at the Tolstoy villa. Kochetov found it difficult to reconcile himself to the fact that a man like Tolstoy, of noble origin and Western, fastidious taste, should live and write in the Soviet Union. The luxury of the house and its furnishings offended him. Kochetov knew none of the writers and correspondents who were spending the night there, but he was invited to join them at a long table where champagne flowed freely—the gift of the local Party committee. He was not comfortable, and he did not like the way from time to time one of the writers would go to the door and listen to the sound of the firing which was coming closer to Pushkin. Somehow, he did not trust these people. In the morning Kochetov strolled around the lovely grounds. He went to the Catherine Palace and saw the hundreds of boxes in which its treasures had been packed for safekeeping. He visited the Alexandrovsky Palace where the last of the czars, Nicholas II, had lived. Here was the office where Nicholas worked. Kochetov thought it looked more like the office of a businessman than an emperor. Here was the imperial bedroom with its wall of icons. And the telephone, the direct wire to staff headquarters by which the Empress Alexandra communicated with her husband during the war, giving him the latest counsel which she had received from Rasputin. Kochetov walked out of the palace and into the park, where were buried heroes of the Revolutionary Civil War, past the Chinese Theater, the Hunters' Castle, the marble mausoleum. Never again was he to see many of these beautiful epitaphs to empire. The Nazis and destruction lay only hours away. Finally, with his fellow writers, Kochetov packed and left Pushkin by the Egyptian gate. He paused a moment to look at the granite and bronze monument to Pushkin. As far as the village of Bolshoye Kuzmino Pushkin's sad and gloomy visage followed them.

Now the Germans began to try some tricks. They dropped screaming, whistling bombs. They dropped booby traps, sometimes in the form of children's toys, fountain pens and cigarette lighters. And once some students named Mikhail Rubtsov, Konstantin Kruglov and Nadezhda Zabelina saw a big ball burst over the Narva Gates. It looked like a shower of leaflets, but when the youngsters reached the area, they found ruble notes scattered all over the ground together with ration cards. Did the trick work? It is hard to say. The authorities contended that all the counterfeit money and cards were collected and turned in.

But Dmitri Pavlov, who controlled the city's food supplies and had to deal with problems like those of forged ration cards, was deeply concerned.

"Egoists and crooks," Pavlov recalled, "tried by every means possible to obtain two, three or even more ration cards. For the sake of their stomachs they tried to obtain cards even if it cost the lives of their nearest and dearest."

The sharpers forged cards and worked rackets to get cards illegally or legally. They bribed house janitors to certify they were living in empty apartments. They applied for cards for dead relatives or imaginary persons. They stole cards. If the Germans dropped counterfeit cards in any numbers, chaos would ensue. The whole delicate rationing system would collapse. Steps would have to be taken quickly to thwart such tactics before the Nazis realized how vulnerable the system was.

The police reported to the Leningrad Command that the Germans were making more and more efforts to infiltrate agents into the city. There was a steady increase in circulation of dangerous and frightening rumors, many of which could directly be traced to Nazi sources. A man named Koltsov was picked up for circulating Finnish anti-Soviet leaflets in a beer hall. He was summarily shot. There were scores of cases of pilfering and juggling of books in the food-distribution system, and the black market in food, kerosene and soap rapidly expanded.

It was not easy to train citizens to stand fast and fight the frightening fires touched off by the Nazi incendiaries. People panicked at the sight of phosphorus bombs spreading rivers of fire over apartment roofs or inside factories. On September 11 four explosive bombs and hundreds of incendiaries fell on the great Northern Cable factory. In one shop a single fireman was trying to cope with raging fires while the workers huddled in terror against the wall. Finally, Party Secretary A. V. Kassirov came to the aid of the fireman and shamed the others into helping. The next day a group of workers applied for release from work. The factory had been badly damaged, windows blown out, shops riddled. One person had been killed and four injured. The factory director noted on the petition: "This is in the category of cowardice."

In these critical times there could be no sign of weakness. The poet Boris Likharev put it bluntly in the paper *On Guard of the Fatherland:* "We will be victorious at any price, whether we live or die—not one step backward. As for cowards and traitors—shoot them on the spot."

Special problems arose with the work battalions on fortifications. Many found themselves without food and shelter. Others were blasted out of their positions by Nazi bombing. Bewildered and frightened, many people left the construction sites and fled back into the city. Bands of Party agitators were sent to rally those who were branded deserters, panicmongers and whiners.

Every evening now Editor P. V. Zolotukhin of *Leningradskaya Pravda* made his way from his editorial offices at No. 57 Fontanka to Smolny, there to consult with Party Secretary Zhdanov and the other chiefs about the leading editorial, the play to be given stories and the wording of announcements. Often it was 2 or 3 A.M. before he telephoned back to the editorial offices, telling the weary staff that the paper could go as made up or ordering complete changes.

As times grew more tense, Zhdanov began to take on the task of writing or rewriting the principal editorials. He it was who wrote the editorial published September 16: "The enemy is at the gates . . . Each must firmly look the danger in the eye and declare that if today he does not fight bravely and selflessly in defense of the city then tomorrow he will lose his honor and freedom, his native home, and become a German slave." And as the times grew even more dangerous, it was Zhdanov who penned a savage call: "Mercilessly exterminate the Fascist beasts!"[2]

Entering Leningrad after several days in Kronstadt, playwright Shtein found a change in the streets. His papers were examined not just at the city limits. They were checked and rechecked every few blocks. There was a sentry post at every bridge, at important intersections, at the entrance of buildings. He saw workers' patrols on the streets, armed with rifles. They were rounding up those who could not prove their identity or occupation. Since the circle had begun to close around the city, the streets had been filled with wandering men in rumpled uniforms, some with insignia, some without. They were deserters, or malingerers, or just men who had lost their units. Some had been in the People's Volunteers. Some had been encircled and had slipped through the German lines and into the city. They were demoralized. Their eyes wandered. Shtein had seen them huddled at the entrances to apartment houses, going back to their homes. He had seen them in the beer halls, shouldering up to the head of the queues, demanding to be waited on first, as "military men."

Now this human debris was being gathered up. Some were sent to the firing squads, some to construction battalions. Others were put back into units and took their stand on the lines of the city's defenses. Military tribunals passed out the edicts—this man to be shot, this one to the front line, this to the barricades.

It was not easy to hold those lines. B. Rozenman had been wounded and in mid-September was going back to the front to rejoin the 168th Rifles, the Bondarev division, one of the finest defending Leningrad. Division headquarters, he understood, were somewhere near Moskovskaya Slavyanka. Leningrad was being heavily bombed as he and several officers made their way forward toward Pushkin. They met fewer and fewer persons as they got closer to the front. Alongside the road were signs of fresh bombardment. German planes periodically appeared overhead. Suddenly they saw a crowd

---

[2] Zhdanov's call, published in *Leningradskaya Pravda*, October 30, 1941, declared: "Only by mercilessly exterminating the Fascist bastards can we save our Motherland, save our wives and mothers, and save our children."

Air-raid barrage balloons over the Admiralty spire.

Evacuees assembling at railroad station. (*Sovfoto*)

Air-raid victims, Liteiny Prospekt, Leningrad. (Sovfoto)

German shell hit on Leningrad apartment building.

The Badayev warehouses, Leningrad's chief food storehouse, destroyed by Nazi incendiary bombs.

Drawing water from a hole in an ice-clad street. In the background, frozen streetcars are immobilized for the winter.

The famous "bronze horseman" equestrian statue of Peter the Great, sandbagged for protection.

Winter street. A woman pulls a sheet-wrapped corpse on a child's sled.

A woman draws a starvation-weakened man on a child's sled.

Leningrad in blockade. A woman listens to the radio, teapot on
the brick stove, with only a candle for light. (*Sovfoto*)

Coffins pile up outside Okhta Cemetery. Some dead are
simply wrapped in rags or clothing.

Corpses—one in sitting posture, one half covered with
snow—beside the Summer Gardens fence.

Tanya Savicheva, eleven-year-old Leningrad schoolgirl, and pages from her diary recording the death, one by one, of members of her family during the blockade winter and spring.

The Road of Life, the ice road for supplies across Lake Ladoga. (*Sovfoto*)

Girl traffic officer
on the Ladoga ice road.
(*Sovfoto*)

Survivors of the starvation winter, above and right. (*Sovfoto*)

Aleksei Lebedev, poet who died
on a Baltic submarine operation.

Olga Berggolts, Leningrad
poet and diarist.

Vera Inber, poet and diarist.

General B. V. Bychevsky, chief
of engineers, Leningrad front.

Marshal L. A. Govorov, Leningrad commander, talking with
Andrei Zhdanov, Leningrad Party chief.

Vsevolod Vishnevsky, Leningrad correspondent, with winter-clad tommy gunners.

The fortress of Oreshek at Shlisselburg, which held out
seventeen months against the Germans. (*Sovfoto*)

Reinforced-concrete gun emplacement, part of the Nazi siege
system around Leningrad. (*Sovfoto*)

Peterhof Palace, devastated by the Germans. (*Sovfoto*)

Piskarevsky Cemetery, where nearly one million victims of the Leningrad siege lie buried in common graves. (*Harrison E. Salisbury*)

of soldiers, obviously in panic. At the same moment a solidly built officer in a sun-faded jacket took his place in the center of the road and, pointing an automatic at the mob, shouted, "Halt!"

The soldiers halted.

"Where are you going, comrades?" the officer said. "Leningrad is behind us. Don't sully the honor of the Soviet soldier."

The soldiers were silent. A husky youngster with a week's stubble on his chin stepped out, cast an angry glance at the officer and said, "Go fight yourself. We've had enough. Come on, gang!"

No one budged to follow him.

"Turn back," the officer warned.

The youngster did not glance around. He strode forward with long steps. A shot rang out and he rolled to the ground.

"Those with weapons go to the left, those without to the right," the officer said crisply. Then he turned to Rozenman: "And you can help me." Rozenman tried to protest that he had to join his unit.

"Carry out the command," the officer snapped. Then stepping closer he whispered, "There are no soldiers on the front line. It's being held by artillerymen. Devil take you—can't you understand?"

Rozenman understood. He fought all day with the pick-up unit. At nightfall when the battle slackened, he went on to try to locate his own command.

A. Veresov was fighting near Ligovo (Uritsk). He never could remember which day of the battle it was—possibly the fourth, maybe the fifth. A flood of refugees was streaming down the highway from Ligovo toward Leningrad. Children crying in their mothers' arms. Women with glazed eyes, some with household goods strapped to their shoulders, dragging themselves along the broken road. And over the road shells fell. Methodically. Precise. The Germans had an artillery spotter in the Pishmach factory tower who through his binoculars could see the road as well as the palm of his hand. Soldiers dashed from their dugouts, grabbing youngsters and women, pulling them from the road, out of the line of fire. A herd of cattle, stirring up a cloud of dust, frightened by the flaming asphalt of the road (set afire by a shell), dashed out into a mined field. A fireman on his tower stuck to his post, which would totter in flames within the hour.

A scene of fright and devastation.

At the fork where the roads branched to Krasnoye Selo and Peterhof stood a sentry box. Officers halted the retreating soldiers—some in uniform, some without uniform, some with rifles, some without, all on the border of exhaustion. Among them appeared a sergeant in torn jacket and no cap, his hands muddy, his breeches wet to the knees. He stood on trembling legs and shouted, "They've conquered everything. The Germans will be here in a minute. I saw them myself. On motorcycles . . . Don't shoot. If we don't shoot, they won't hurt us. They'll go on past. . . ."

A crowd of troops surrounded the sergeant. The captain of the sentry post, a short man in the uniform of the Border Guards, quickly advanced. "Put yourself in order, Sergeant."

The sergeant's hands automatically went up to his open collar, but he dropped them and shouted, "What do you mean, order? Where is there any order? The Germans are at the Kirov factory. . . . And you talk about . . . order. We must save ourselves. Do you understand? Do you understand, now?"

The captain with a swift, silent movement ripped the triangles from the sergeant's epaulets, stepped back two paces and, not changing his voice, said to the soldiers, "Seize him."

The soldiers didn't understand. "But he's one of ours—"

"No," snapped the captain. "He is not one of ours. Carry out the order."

A moment later the soldiers had taken the sergeant aside. A single shot rang out. The captain paid no heed to the sound of the shot. He was too busy directing the retreating troops to collection points.

Late one evening Sayanov appeared at Smolny. He was delivering the draft of a new leaflet he had written, addressed to the German troops.

The long corridors were lighted by flickering electric bulbs, and for once Smolny was quiet and few people were scurrying about. Sayanov was talking with the Commandant of Smolny, Grishin, a man who had been there since Lenin's time, when a Major General came out of the office of the Chief of Staff. He knew Sayanov slightly.

"Where are you going?" he asked.

"Home," said Sayanov.

The General invited Sayanov to come with him "for a drive." He was in a great hurry. The two raced down the big wide staircase and out into the raw darkness of the September night.

Not until they had got into the car and were crossing the Liteiny Bridge did the General tell Sayanov where they were going—up to a "very dangerous place" in the front. A regiment was being assembled at the Kirov factory which was to follow the General up to the lines. They headed out into the suburbs. Soon they arrived at the Kirov factory, where they arranged for the troops to follow, and drove out the Peterhof Chaussée. An air alert sounded and searchlights scanned the near heavens. The AA guns barked. They heard planes overhead. The General's destination was Finskoye Koirovo, about twelve miles outside town. Somewhere near Kipen a sentry halted them. He was a Kirov worker, a member of a special battalion which had been sent to halt deserters and retreating soldiers and direct them to new units. The General talked a bit with the worker.

"What do you think?" he said. "Will we hold the city?" The worker said he thought the city would hold out. He remembered fighting for it in 1919. Then, he said, his commissar told him, "We can't retreat any farther. Next stop is Petrograd." "It's the same thing today," he said. The General went on through the night. At Finskoye Koirovo he met the commander, conferred with him for half an hour, and then returned to the car.

"I told him what was necessary," said the General. "Next stop Petrograd."

The car turned back and hummed down the Peterhof Chaussée. Sayanov was silent. So was the General. They met not one car, not one truck. They saw no one on the road. Not far from the Kirov factory the General halted to phone Smolny. He came back in five minutes. "Hurry," said the General. The car went a short distance, then halted. There was something wrong with the carburetor.

"Hurry up," the General said. "There's not a minute to lose. The Germans already have arrived at Ligovo."

"But our car passed through Ligovo not ten minutes ago," said the chauffeur.

"That doesn't mean anything," snapped the General. "It just means that we were the last car to come through Ligovo to Leningrad."

The General turned to Sayanov.

"Remember this night," he said. "Remember it. The most terrible battle for the city is now beginning."

"Will it be a siege?" Sayanov asked.

"Yes," said the General, "it will. It will be a siege."

The nine hundred days were beginning.

30 . *A Hard Nut to Crack*

DURING THE EARLY MORNING HOURS OF MAY 8, 1887, THE sound of carpenters' hammers could be heard in the courtyard of the ancient citadel of Oreshek. Oreshek was Peter the Great's "hard little nut," the fortress on an island at the point where the Neva flowed out of Lake Ladoga, the key to the water routes of Novgorod the Great, the ancient trade pathway from the land of the Varangians to the Black Sea and beyond.

Long before Moscow was more than a forest crossroads, a strongpoint had grown up at Oreshek. Who controlled Oreshek controlled the trade lines to the Orient—the rich flow of honey, of spices, of furs, of slaves, of precious gems, of perfume, of silks and of flax. As early as the fourteenth century the city of Novgorod the Great built a powerful Kremlin, a fortress, on Oreshek. For a hundred years before Peter, Oreshek had been held by the Swedes. After Peter wrested it back he rechristened it Shlisselburg, the "key city," and so it was now known. But two hundred years ago Shlisselburg had lost its role as a key fortress, and its grim casements had long been used as a state prison. Here Peter had incarcerated his former wife, Yevdotiya. Here Czarina Anna Ivanovna imprisoned her State Counselor Dmitri Golitsyn and the noble Dolgoruki brothers. Here Nicholas I sent half a dozen Decembrists, the brilliant but naïve young officers whose revolt in 1824 in Senate Square had shaken the foundations of autocratic Russia.

And here on this mild May morning carpenters were knocking into shape a great gallows with three gibbets that reached out, long and sinister, beyond the wooden platform. Behind a heavy iron grating in a stone-floored cell without light a young man waited for the dawn and the death which he knew it would bring. A half-hour before sunrise Aleksandr Ulyanov and four other young men were taken from their cells and marched to the courtyard. The sentence was read once again: death by hanging for their attempt on the life of Czar Alexander III. Each, as was carefully noted by State Counselor Dmitri Tolstoy, preserved his full calm. Each refused to see a priest.

The executions began. First, Vasily Generalov, Pakhomii Andreyushkin and Vasily Osipanov mounted the platform. A moment later their bodies swung out, lifeless and dangling. Aleksandr Ulyanov and Pyotr Shevyrev watched their comrades die, then mounted the scaffold and were hanged.

Since the October Revolution Oreshek had become a shrine. A marble plaque on the Royal Tower noted the names of the Revolutionary martyrs, first among them Aleksandr Ulyanov, elder brother of Vladimir Ilich Lenin.

Now in these strange September days of 1941 the sound of guns resounded nearer and nearer the old fortress.

The spearhead of the Nazi Sixteenth Army—the 122nd German Infantry, the 20th Motorized Division and units of the 12th Panzers—had been shouldering eastward since their breakthrough to the Neva banks on August 31. They had advanced north of Mga despite the fierce and repeated attacks of an NKVD rifle division, commanded by Colonel S. I. Donskov, and gradually pushed the NKVD troops back along the river road toward Shlisselburg. Three warships moved up the Neva, the gunboats *Strogy* and *Stroiny* and the cruiser *Maxim Gorky*, and laid down artillery support for the hard-pressed Soviet forces. It did no good.

On September 7 the Germans brought in three hundred planes to strafe the badly beaten Soviet forces. They fell back, some of the NKVD troops making their way to the north bank of the Neva and two regiments retiring into Shlisselburg. Other elements, including portions of a mountain brigade, retreated south of Sinyavino.

This movement left the river highway into Shlisselburg virtually clear. The Germans swept up the road and fought their way into the city.

On the morning of September 7 Party Secretary Andrei A. Zhdanov called a meeting in his Smolny office in an effort to save Shlisselburg and protect Leningrad's communications with "mainland" Russia. Urgent measures, he said, were being taken by the Leningrad Military Council to hold Shlisselburg. He ordered Admiral I. S. Isakov to take charge of transport facilities across Lake Ladoga and Inspector A. T. Karavayev of the Naval Political Administration was sent to the scene.

Karavayev arrived at Shlisselburg station—across the Neva River from the fortress—just after midnight September 8. Shlisselburg and the whole south bank of the Neva were in flames. Soot and sparks rained down on the Alekseyev factory and the 8th Power Station on the north bank.

The sound of machine-gun fire was clearly audible as the harassed NKVD troops sought to hold off the Germans in the Shlisselburg streets.

The wharf was filled with people, some refugees from Shlisselburg, others who had relatives there. An old woman ran up to Karavayev crying, "Help me! Help me! My son is on the other side and the Germans are already there."

Confusion was complete. No one was in charge. Only two small tugs were moving across the Neva, bringing out a handful of wounded.

Karavayev and other naval officers managed to restore partial order. The gunboat *Selenga* and the cutters *BKA-99* and *BKA-100* were supporting the NKVD troops. Under their cover Karavayev crossed the Neva and brought to the north bank several boatloads of women, children and wounded.

The NKVD regiments fell back through the streets and finally crossed to the north bank of the Neva by any means that came to hand. With the occupation of Shlisselburg the encirclement of Leningrad was complete. The only connection Leningrad now possessed with the "mainland" was across Lake Ladoga. Or by air.

Colonel B. V. Bychevsky was ordered to the north bank of the Neva to try to throw a pontoon bridge over the river by which a Russian counter-attack to recapture Shlisselburg might be mounted. Bychevsky looked across to the south bank of the Neva. Fires burned all along the highway to Shlisselburg. Smoke rose over the gothic towers of the fortress city. And through the flames he could see heavy Nazi traffic. The Germans were moving in force. On the northern, Soviet-held bank of the river, it was deathly quiet. Artillery firing points were not yet manned. The mortars were still coming up to the front.

He looked out the Neva estuary to the ancient fort of Oreshek. It lay near the entrance of the Neva 500 feet from the Shlisselburg wharves but somewhat closer to the Soviet-held shore. There it stood, the gloomy pile which had won the nickname the "Eternal Prison" because from its walls there had been no return. What was going on there Bychevsky had no idea. Probably, he thought, it was held by the Germans. But there was no sign of life, no sign of activity. Above the little islet he could see a circling German observation plane. Long since, Oreshek had lost its military significance. For years it had been an historic monument. The Lake Ladoga flotilla stored some small arms in the old casements where the Czar's prisoners once languished. But there had been no guns mounted in the fortress fenestrations since the time of Peter.

Unknown to Bychevsky—or to the Nazis—Oreshek was not deserted. A dozen sailors had been sent there to pack supplies belonging to the Ladoga fleet. When the Germans burst through to the Shlisselburg waterfront, the sailors were still in the subterranean ravelins. Now they had become silent and secret observers of the scene. They saw the German planes overhead. They could see the pontoon troops gathered by Bychevsky across the Neva near Sheremetyevka. From the solid watchtower of the old fort they looked over the harbor to where the Nazi troops were setting up posts on the waterfront, unloading Soviet supplies from the warehouses, and mustering Russian men and women to dig trenches and dugouts. Before their eyes the Germans erected a pillar in the center of Cathedral Square and, driving all citizens from the area, hanged four young workers from crossbeams.

Unable to restrain themselves, the sailors began to hunt through the jumble of old arms in the Oreshek cellars to see if any were serviceable. They found two cannon, long since discarded, neither with sights. One they mounted in the tower overlooking the city and the other on the fortress wall. Nikolai Konushkin, a youngster with some battery experience, directed the operation. He sighted the guns on a German firing point just across the water and gave the order: "Fire!"

It was never plain to the Russians why the Germans did not embark on cutters and seize the old fortress from the tiny group of defenders. Perhaps they thought it was heavily defended and not worth the price that would have to be paid. Perhaps they were too busy with other plans. Whatever it was, the Germans did not make the effort. Colonel Donskov sent in a reinforcement of NKVD troops, and a night or two later Captain Aleksei Morozov and a group of thirteen sailors of the Ladoga fleet were put ashore on Oreshek. Their task was to set up Battery No. 409—seven 45-mm cannon and six mounted machine guns—around the perimeter of the old fortress. They put in rifle-firing points and snipers' posts. By this time the Germans had begun to direct artillery fire at the ancient ten-foot walls of the fortress. But the firing points were installed. In the weeks and months to follow, the Germans would rain down thousands of tons of high explosive on Peter's "hard little nut." On one September day 250 heavy shells and thousands of mortars hammered at the old walls. It was not clear for a long time whether Oreshek had the strength to hold out. Not until November 7 did the Soviet command feel confident enough of its strength to unfurl the red flag over the fortress. Once the flag was flown, it kept on flying. Sixty thousand shells rained down on the fort. Six times the flag was shot down. Five hundred days later when the Red Army began its first effort to lift the Leningrad blockade, the red flag still flew over Oreshek.

Now the Germans stood at Shlisselburg. They stood along the Neva for fifteen miles. From the rapids at Porogi around the great bend, past Nevskaya Dubrovka and on to Shlisselburg the south bank of the river was theirs. Only the river and thirty or forty miles of wooded country stood between them and the Finnish lines; between the Germans and Hitler's prime objective, his basic order to von Leeb, to his commanders for Operation Barbarossa: junction with the Finns, the encirclement and extermination of Leningrad and then the massive sweep to the south to envelop Moscow.

The Germans stood in strength along the Neva now. Why did they not cross?

The answer is not apparent to Soviet scholars who have studied the battle with minute care.

The river is, of course, a formidable barrier. Starting at the Lake Ladoga entrance, it has a width of 400 yards and gradually broadens to 600 yards, then narrows to 250 yards and then to 175 yards where the river Mga joins it. The breadth is considerable. The Germans reached the river without pontoons or river-crossing equipment. Thanks to the foresight of Colonel

Bychevsky, the Neva bridges had been blown. The Nazis were not lucky enough to repeat their experiences of the early river crossings. Obviously, a crossing would not be easy.

Yet the question of why the Germans did not try is not answered.

Dmitri Shcheglov, the Leningrad writer who had joined a People's Volunteer unit, was dispatched with his battalion of Volunteers to the north bank of the Neva on August 31. They marched along the bank through a rainy night and on September 1 took up positions from the little village of Kuzminki (where Bychevsky had just destroyed the railroad bridge) through Peski to Nevskaya Dubrovka. They were spread over six or seven miles of river bank. Across the river they heard the constant sound of rifle and artillery fire in the days to come. On September 3 some villagers excitedly reported that they had seen a Nazi detachment cross the river in boats and land on a small island only about 100 feet from the Kuzminki shore. Shcheglov's Volunteer unit had no artillery. In fact, they had hardly any ammunition and only fifteen machine guns. There was an antiaircraft unit nearby, and they got the AA gunners to lay some fire onto the islet. Soon a squad of Nazis was seen hastily pulling away in a small boat. Later four bodies of Nazi soldiers were found on the island.

By September 5 the ill-armed Volunteers were reinforced by an understrength regiment of the 115th Division which had been pulled out of encirclement near Vyborg. This was a badly beaten-up unit, tired, grim, even more poorly armed than the Volunteers. They had lost all their guns and all their cannon and ammunition escaping the trap into which they had fallen. Their uniforms were torn, dirty and muddy. The men were so exhausted they could hardly stand. Shcheglov went to the staff headquarters, set up in a peasant hut at Plintovka. The Chief of Staff, Colonel Simonov, propped his head on a hand. His eyes were closed as though he were asleep. But he was not. He was listening to the discussion. Suddenly he sat bolt upright and started to talk:

"Why do you think we are here? Why did we have to give up Vyborg? Because the Finns concentrated against us 200,000 soldiers and officers, and on our side of the border there were only 50,000. They were able to do that and we still haven't learned anything! What's the result? They smashed three of our divisions. You have to know that. Don't hide your heads under your wings like ostriches! The Finns are at Terijoki. And they are moving on Beloostrov and the Sestra River. Right here the Germans are going to try to cross the Neva in order to join up with the Finns on the Karelian isthmus. And we are going to stop that operation. We have got to outdo them. Take the initiative in your hands. Is that clear?"

It was clear enough. What was not clear was what would halt the Nazis when they started to cross the river.

On September 7 Shcheglov and his battalion saw for the first time, from their foxholes on the banks of the Neva, the Germans in force. They were moving up the highway toward Shlisselburg. They saw troop trucks, heavy equipment and tanks. They could almost make out the expressions on the German faces. Communications units passed by, motorcycle detachments, perfectly visible between the sandy river bank and a line of workers' houses just beyond the Leningrad-Shlisselburg Chaussée.

"Why don't you open fire?" Shcheglov asked a young lieutenant at a machine-gun post.

"That is categorically forbidden," he replied.

"But you can see the enemy with your own eyes!" Shcheglov exclaimed. "He is getting ready to cross, devil take him!"

"I have less than a thousand cartridges for my machine gun," the lieutenant explained patiently. "And we have no bullets for our rifles. When we will get ammunition I don't know."

The Germans did not try to cross the river that day. Nor the next. Not until very late in the night of September 9 did the handful of Soviet troops on the Neva line get any artillery. That night twenty guns, straight from the gun works at the Kirov factory, arrived in a truck column. It was long after midnight. The night was deathly still. A full moon shone down. All that night Shcheglov went from post to post, distributing the guns. He found some commanders so tired he could hardly wake them. When they staggered up, hardly conscious, they could not understand what he was talking about when he warned that this very night the Germans might cross the river. It was dawn before the last gun was mounted. Would it be enough to halt the Germans?

Two days later Shcheglov and his units were still waiting. They knew the Germans were on the river across from them, but they had no notion of what was going on. They had lost all connection with Colonel Donskov and the NKVD troops that were defending Shlisselburg. What had happened to them and what had happened at Shlisselburg no one knew. On the night of the eleventh Shcheglov and a small unit slipped across the Neva to try and discover whether the Germans were preparing to attack. They found that Nazi tank columns were now returning from Shlisselburg, moving back in the Leningrad direction. That meant one thing: the Germans were not preparing to cross the Neva at this point. They must be mustering strength for a smash across somewhere closer to Leningrad, to the right of Shcheglov's position, possibly beyond Annenskoye village near the Mga River. The next morning they made contact with Donskov's NKVD units, which they found moving into positions on their left flank, having gradually reassembled after the fall of Shlisselburg and the crossing of the Neva.

The Germans, it appeared, had made a weak attempt to follow Donskov's troops across the river. But a small artillery unit commanded by Colonel F. A. Budanov had taken up a position across from Shlisselburg on September 7. Budanov's guns were able to cover the crossing by Donskov's troops and discourage the Germans from following over.

Among the Nazi forces on the south bank of the Neva was an SS division which had participated in the German parachute landing in Crete. It was ordered by von Leeb to carry out a crossing to the north bank of the Neva. Von Leeb is said to have ordered the crossing on September 9. If such an attack was tried, it apparently was weak and easily frustrated. No substantial accounts of any attempted river crossing have survived in the memoirs of officers and soldiers who were stationed along the Neva at that time, although many Soviet histories flatly assert that a Nazi attack was turned back. Why a determined German effort was not made is still a mystery.[1]

The mystery of the Neva deepens when examined from the German side. On August 31 Halder noted in his diary that the question of the "assault of Leningrad"—that is, of a frontal attack upon the city—was still being held open although Keitel's barbarous proposal that the Germans refuse to feed Leningrad's population after capitulation and, instead, that the people simply be driven from the city had been rejected because "it cannot be carried out in practice and therefore is wholly pointless."

Five days later Hitler again conferred with his staff. He now felt that the German objectives had been achieved and that Leningrad would become a "subsidiary theater of operations." The chief target was Shlisselburg—a decision which was obviously reflected in the drive of the Sixteenth Army up the south bank of the Neva to the old fortress city.

As for Leningrad, it was to be invested along what Hitler called "the outer siege line," and as much infantry "as possible" was to be put across the Neva in order to close a tight circle around the city from the east.

Once this was achieved, Reinhardt's armored corps could be released for the coming battle for Moscow. The junction with the Finnish Army was to be achieved through Lodeinoye Pole on the southeastern shores of Lake Ladoga.

The German opportunity to cross the Neva, join hands with the Finns

[1] One Soviet account asserts that the 115th Division and the Volunteer units to which Shcheglov was attached, together with students of a Border Guard academy, repulsed the Germans. (Shtein, *Znamya*, No. 6, June, 1964, pp. 145 *et seq.*; Sviridov, *op. cit.*, p. 153 *et seq.*) Pavlov (*op. cit.*, 2nd edition, p. 23) says the crossing was attempted on the night of September 9 between Porogi and Sheremetyevka but was frustrated with heavy losses by "workers battalions" on the right bank of the Neva. Presumably these are the battalions to which Shcheglov was attached. He mentions no such action. The Leningrad Naval Defense Staff reported that on September 9 the Germans attempted to cross the Neva between Porogi and Sheremetyevka but were beaten off by the 115th Infantry, the 4th Brigade of marines and workers battalions, supported by naval artillery on warships in the Neva. Hundreds of German bodies lined the Neva after the attack was repulsed (Panteleyev, pp. 156, 195). The official Leningrad history says the Germans attempted to cross but were hurled back by Soviet forces on the north bank aided by naval vessels in the Ivanovskoye rapids. (*Leningrad v VOV*, p. 147.) Kochetov says the Germans tried to break through at Porogi September 9. (*Oktyabr*, No. 6, June, 1965, p. 163.) What seems much more likely is the explanation of the authors of N.Z. (p. 152), who assert that the 39th Nazi Corps had no pontoons and that this forced the Germans temporarily to give up plans to cross the Neva. Small groups, these authorities say, tried to cross and were beaten back with heavy losses.

and seal off Leningrad completely from the outside world was missed. Had it been launched at any time during the first ten or twelve days of September, it could hardly have failed. There were not enough Soviet forces on the north bank of the Neva to offer more than light opposition. The guns were not in place. There was no ammunition. There were no tanks. The troops manning the thin line of hastily dug field works were either People's Volunteers or the remnants of divisions which had been so badly mauled they could have done little but offer token resistance.

Later on the Germans would try again to cross the Neva, to close the ring and cut off the Lake Ladoga communications route. But they would never have as good an opportunity as that which they missed during these early September days.

31 . Zhukov in Command

BY THE SECOND WEEK OF SEPTEMBER VON LEEB'S ARMY
Group Nord was driving on Leningrad for the kill. He had moved staff
headquarters up to Gatchina, and from this front-line observation post he
got a fine view of the city. All the grandiose architectural ensembles built
by Peter and Catherine and the later Romanovs lay spread before him like
a panorama—St. Isaac's, the Admiralty spire, the Fortress of Peter and Paul.
The dive-bombing and the great fires started by the 240-mm siege guns near
Tosno could be followed with clarity. Von Leeb felt victory within his
grasp. The Führer seemed pleased and graciously honored him with awards
and congratulations on his sixty-fifth birthday. The aging Field Marshal
had every reason to believe that he was on the verge of a success which
would crown his earlier achievements in breaking the Maginot Line and
occupying the Sudeten. Once Leningrad had been captured, he could look
forward to pleasant retirement on his East Prussian estates, basking in glory.
First, of course, he would participate in the envelopment and destruction
of Moscow. That should not take long. The role of Army Group Nord had
been clearly spelled out. It would wheel south after capturing Leningrad
and approach Moscow from the rear. With good luck the war would be
ended by mid-October at the latest—a bit behind schedule, but close enough.

Von Leeb had been concerned about the strength of the forces which
he had mustered against Leningrad in mid-August. But now with the
armored and air reinforcements which the Supreme Command had finally
(if belatedly in his view) given him, he felt that he could accomplish his
task.

He had at his disposal about twenty divisions. They comprised the
Twenty-sixth, Thirty-eighth, Fiftieth and Twenty-eighth armies and the
41st and 39th motorized corps. However, not all of these units were available for the final assault on Leningrad. Von Leeb had a long flank to the
south and southeast which had to be protected.

For the closing attack on Leningrad he was able to concentrate about eleven divisions, and he had been busily engaged in regrouping them during the first week of September. Now he had packed eight divisions, including five infantry, two Panzer and one motorized, into the narrow southwest approach to Leningrad, roughly from Ropsha to Kolpino, facing the special fortified regions which the Russians had created from Gatchina to Slutsk-Kolpino. Von Leeb had created a concentration of one division to each three miles of front. Slightly to the east he had positioned his other three divisions in the area from Yam-Izhorsk to Ladoga.

It was not too difficult for the harassed Leningrad Command to perceive von Leeb's intention. He proposed to smash into Leningrad from the southwest, plowing through the suburbs of Krasnoye Selo and Ligovo (Uritsk) in the direction of the Kirov factory. At the same time he hoped to break into the city from the southeast along the Leningrad-Moscow highway just beyond Izhorsk and Kolpino.

If it was easy to see what von Leeb intended, it was considerably more difficult to thwart him. The Soviet forces facing von Leeb's eight-division task force in the southwest were four weak divisions of the Eighth Army (backed up toward Oranienbaum), two broken divisions of the Forty-second Army, four divisions of the Fifty-fifth Army and the command reserves—two infantry divisions and a brigade of marines.

The numerical strength was about the same on each side. But the Nazi divisions were in infinitely better condition and close to full operational strength. They included two tank divisions. The Soviets had no tank divisions. The Germans also had complete control of the air.

Von Leeb launched his attack September 9. The Thirty-eighth Army and the 41st Motorized Corps attacked toward Krasnoye Selo after very strong air and artillery preparation. They were met by a People's Volunteer unit, the 3rd Guards, and in a day's heavy fighting pushed ahead a mile or two on a six-mile front. Baltic Fleet artillery joined the battle during the night and the next morning, shelling the Germans heavily and slowing them down, but by midday the Soviet lines began to crumble after von Leeb had thrown in the 1st Panzers from his 41st Motorized Corps.

Voroshilov was in a state that fluctuated from frenzy to despair. It was not only the Krasnoye Selo front which was crumbling. The Germans had begun their terrible air attacks on the city. The Badayev warehouses had gone up in flames. The capture of Shlisselburg had sealed the ring. For practical purposes the city had been in a state of siege for ten days, since the fall of Mga cut the last rail route. To the north the Finns pressed closer and closer to the outer suburbs. Inside the city Nazi long-range bombardment had shaken morale.

Nor was this all. The pressures upon Voroshilov and Zhdanov from Moscow had risen. Stalin's tongue on the VC line had grown sharper and sharper. He seemed to think Voroshilov was preparing to abandon Leningrad. And worse followed.

Voroshilov had tried to hold back the news of the fall of Mga. He thought he could recapture Mga before the Germans solidified their hold. But he had not. And Stalin had caught him out. Voroshilov had done the same with Shlisselburg. He simply could not bring himself to report its loss. But Stalin discovered what had happened and demanded explanations.

The world of the old revolutionary warrior seemed to be collapsing about him. Nothing he did could halt the Germans—or halt them for long. He had virtually no reserves left. On the shaky Forty-second Army front he threw in the 500th Rifle Regiment at Taitsy. But it was unable to occupy its assigned positions before falling back in wild disorder under air attack, abandoning the key Sparrow Heights to the Germans and opening their way to Krasnoye Selo and the vital Pulkovo Ridge. Voroshilov rushed up from Vasilevsky Island in Leningrad a brigade of marines, the 1st Brigade, commanded by Colonel T. M. Parafilo who had seen service in the Tallinn encirclement. Voroshilov ordered them into the breach at Krasnoye Selo.

The breach could hardly have been more dangerous. The Germans at 3 P.M., September 10, hurled at the little village of Payula two hundred tanks, including a number of flame-throwers. They burned out the concrete bunkers which the 3rd Volunteer Guards occupied.

The Baltic Fleet warships were ordered to pour fire into the area while the marines were being brought up.[1]

On the morning of the eleventh Colonel Bychevsky reported to Voroshilov at the field headquarters which the Marshal had established at Krasnoye Selo. Voroshilov seldom had a good word for Bychevsky. He had none this morning.

"Look here, Bychevsky," Voroshilov snarled, his pale blue eyes snapping fire, "why haven't the marines been supplied with entrenching tools? How are they supposed to protect themselves?"

Bychevsky knew that the marines had been rushed to the front. He had no idea why they had no trench shovels. Maybe they had never been issued any. Maybe the shovels had been supplied by the factory without carrying cases. He admitted to Voroshilov he just didn't know what had happened.

"You haven't any consideration for the troops," Voroshilov barked. "I'll give you half an hour. I don't care where you get them but get them and personally deliver them to the brigade."

Voroshilov was in no mood to be argued with. Bychevsky got the shovels. By the time he had them the marines were assembled for attack. They had taken up positions in the thin birch thickets, and Bychevsky could hardly see their long black cloaks beyond the underbrush. No Soviet outfit was more feared by the Nazi troops than the "black death"—the Red marines in their black wool capes. Around the marines roared the battle. The dust

[1] Karasev (p. 112) mistakenly calls it the 2nd Marines, others make it the 1st. (K. K. Kamalov, *Morskaya Pekhota v Boyakh Za Rodinu*, Moscow, 1966, p. 35.)

of exploding shells filled the air. High in the sky a dogfight was in progress between Nazi and Soviet fighters.

In front of the marines Bychevsky saw Voroshilov, his solid figure firmly planted. The wind carried Voroshilov's words down the ranks as the old commander called on them to fight for the Motherland, for the Party, for their sailor's honor. Many of the young sailors had thrown off their steel helmets. They stood, listening to Voroshilov, their blond hair tousled in the wind, their faces fresh, their chins grim. They stood quietly, concentrating on Voroshilov's words.

For a moment Voroshilov stood silently before them.

Then he said simply, "Let's go."

The youngsters began to move, slowly and steadily toward the German positions.

They shouted a quick "Hurrah!" Then they hurried on, overtaking the sixty-year-old Marshal.

Forward the troops went, Voroshilov at their head. They moved over the highway and drove the Nazis out of the village of Koltselevo. Again and again the Nazis counterattacked. Ten times the marines beat them off. But there were no reserves behind them. In the end they had to fall back. Within hours Krasnoye Selo was lost.

Word of Voroshilov's action spread quickly over the front by the soldiers' telegraph. Within a day or so the 109th Division heard it. General Dukhanov learned of it the next day. It entered into the legend of the Leningrad siege. Not everyone thought it just an heroic act by the aging commander. Not a few believed that Voroshilov, in despair at halting the Germans, had determined to die rather than suffer the disgrace of defeat— or the fateful penalty which Stalin might mete out to him.

Whatever the old commander's motivation, September 11 had not come to an end before he was removed as Leningrad's defense chief. The indictment: passivity in the face of the enemy.

Did Voroshilov know that he was being relieved of command when he marched out at the head of the black-clad marines? Perhaps not. But he may have had a premonition.

In his final report of September 11 to the Supreme Command, Voroshilov had replied to the indictment of failure to halt the Germans, of failure to grasp the initiative. The reasons, he felt, were clear. As early as August 13 he had reported to Moscow: "All our reserves, including aerodrome battalions and the headquarters security detachment, have been sent into action." And on August 27 he had said again: "Almost all our troops are committed to battle."

"For two months," Voroshilov wrote,

all our strength has been directed toward creating a strong shock group with which to seize the initiative from our enemy and go over to the offensive. It seemed that this would be possible through the formation of our four divisions of People's Volunteers, the rifle division of the NKVD and four infantry divisions sent from the Stavka.

Regrettably these divisions, formed at different times, completely untrained and weakly armed with automatic weapons, had of necessity to be thrown into the most threatened parts of the front.

This was in the second half of July at the time of the enemy's simultaneous blows at Petrozavodsk, Olonets and Ivanovskoye.

In the middle of August this was repeated on a bigger scale when the enemy simultaneously with the breaking of our front in the Novgorod direction cut off the Eighth Army in Estonia and went on the offensive in the Gatchina (Krasnogvardeisk) direction and on the Karelian isthmus.

In these conditions to talk of mounting a counteroffensive was impossible. The best Voroshilov had been able to do was to carry out local counterattacks.

Voroshilov's presentation was accurate. It was supported by Zhdanov and Secretary Kuznetsov. But it was not accepted by Stalin.

No full account of what happened on the night of September 11–12 has been made public. But it is probable that the culminating point in the indictment of Voroshilov was his failure to admit the loss of Shlisselburg.

Some time on the twelfth—possibly in the early morning hours, as this was Stalin's usual time for making important decisions—the Supreme Command in Moscow decided to send Marshal Zhukov into Leningrad.[2]

A day was spent by Zhukov in collecting a staff. One member was Army General Ivan I. Fedyuninsky, a first-class officer who had been on the western Ukrainian frontier commanding the 15th Rifle Corps when the war started. He had fought through the desperate summer campaigns in south and central Russia. He had just been called in by Marshal A. M. Vasilevsky, Deputy Chief of Staff, to take over the Thirty-second Army which was being formed for the reserve front. Hardly had he gotten to Vyazma to join the Thirty-second Army staff than he was summoned to Moscow. He flew back on September 12 and was instructed to be ready to go to Leningrad in the morning.

On the Li–2 transport which lifted off Moscow's Vnukovo airport early on the morning of September 13 with three fighters to protect it from German attack en route to Leningrad there were four generals: Zhukov, the toughest troubleshooter in the Red Army, the man who had been Chief of Staff at the war's outbreak, who had been thrown in at Yelnya on the Western Front when the going got rough and who was now facing the most difficult assignment in his career; General M. S. Khozin, a solid man of no special brilliance, who was to be Chief of Staff; General P. I. Kokorev; and Fedyuninsky.

Khozin knew Leningrad intimately. He had commanded the Leningrad

[2] The order relieving Voroshilov and naming Zhukov apparently was dated September 11. (*Istoriya VOVSS*, Vol. II, p. 257; Karasev, *op. cit.*, p. 5.)

Military District until the eve of the winter war with Finland, when he was transferred to the Ukraine. He not only knew Leningrad but was well acquainted with the Karelian isthmus. He was a bear of a man with a figure which one of his associates described as monumental. He moved slowly and spoke with great precision.

What Fedyuninsky was to do in Leningrad was not very clear—either to him or, apparently, to Zhukov.

"For the time being," Zhukov said, "you'll be my deputy. Then we'll see."

The flight to Leningrad was uneventful. Fedyuninsky looked about with interest as their cars sped from the airport to Smolny. The city seemed lovely. The weather was still sunny and warm. It was as though summer did not wish to leave the northern capital. But war's grip was easy to see. There were not many people in the great squares or avenues. Fedyuninsky noticed that the golden dome of St. Isaac's had been camouflaged a dirty gray. Under the red and orange leaves of the trees in the parks there were firing points and AA guns. Great silver balloons, which went up each evening at dusk to protect the city against low-flying German planes, nested on the ground in squares and open places. The sun sparkled on the gray waters of the Neva, and Fedyuninsky thought how natural it was for the Leningraders to love their beautiful city with such passion. He was surprised at the camouflage which had transformed Smolny. Under its daubing of paint and huge nets it looked like a park.[3]

Zhukov and his aides found Voroshilov, Zhdanov and Party Secretary Kuznetsov awaiting them at Smolny. The ceremonies were curt. After Zhukov had signed for the operational charts he went to the VC telephone and called Moscow. Marshal Vasilevsky was at the Moscow end of the line. Zhukov said, "I have taken over command. Report to the High Command that I propose to proceed more actively than my predecessor." That was all. Voroshilov did not talk to Moscow. He left the room without a word.

Voroshilov called to his office his chief commanders—Generals A. A. Novikov, V. P. Sviridov, N. A. Bolotnikov, P. P. Yevstigneyev, and Colonels I. N. Kovalev and Bychevsky. He gloomily shook each man's hand.

"Farewell, comrades," he said. "They have called me to headquarters. . . ." Voroshilov paused and then continued: "Well, I'm old and it has to be! This isn't the Civil War—it has to be fought in another way. . . . But don't doubt for a minute that we are going to smash those Fascist bastards right here. . . . Their tongues are already hanging out for our city, but they will choke on their own blood."

Within the hour Voroshilov and most of the staff which had been with him since he took over the Northwest Front had flown off to Moscow.

---

[3] L. Panteleyev thought the Smolny camouflage was silly and even stupid. He did not think the nets and the false towers, constructed of cardboard or plywood, fooled anyone. (Panteleyev, *Novy Mir*, No. 5, May, 1965, p. 163.)

Voroshilov, almost certainly, expected to be shot on his arrival in Moscow. This was the fate which Stalin meted out to generals who were relieved of command. That this was his expectation is strongly hinted by Dmitri V. Pavlov, the State Defense Committee's supply representative in Leningrad. In a tribute which emphasizes Voroshilov's personal bravery and the risk to which he subjected his life, Pavlov stresses the shock of Voroshilov's removal and the fact that Voroshilov did not know—nor did anyone—that he would ever again step foot in Leningrad.

Pavlov absolves Voroshilov of responsibility for the disasters which befell Leningrad from July to September. The fault lies elsewhere, he feels, and he urges the "deepest study and enlightenment" of this phase of the war.[4]

One villain he singles out—as does almost every Soviet writer—the criminally inept and vicious "police" general, G. I. Kulik. Kulik had been put in command of the Fifty-fourth Army with orders to prevent the breakthrough to Mga and, then, to recapture Mga. He failed miserably. In part, the fault was sheer military illiteracy. In part, it was tardiness, bureaucracy, dilatory movement. Kulik, in Pavlov's opinion (and that of many other commentators), could have saved the day. He lost it. But the legend of the "savior army," the Fifty-fourth, lived on for weeks in Leningrad. The besieged residents expected again and again that the Fifty-fourth Army would drive through the German lines and free them. It never did. Kulik was removed from command of the Fifty-fourth in late September. But the damage had been done.

The arrival of Zhukov and the change in command did nothing to lessen the threat to Leningrad. On the twelfth the Germans had taken Krasnoye Selo, Peterhof, Strelna and the Duderhof Heights. They pounded in at Ligovo (Uritsk) on the thirteenth and managed to occupy a series of villages on the edge of Leningrad—Konstantinovka, Sosnovka and Finskoye Koirovo.

From the cupola of the Pulkovo observatory the whole battlefield could be seen. Kochetov and Mikhalev climbed the tower. Shells were landing nearby, and they did not stay long. But through the smoke and dust they could see Ligovo, Krasnoye Selo, Pushkin and Pavlovsk. Great naval shells burst in the distance, throwing columns of earth fifty and one hundred feet into the air. They saw little clusters of German tanks, here three, there five. And behind the tanks straggled long black lines—these were the German infantrymen. A battalion of Russian artillery nearby was firing on the tanks and the German infantry. It was stationed in an open field, and the grass around the guns was aflame from shell bursts. The sound of shells and the echo of explosions was constant. Overhead there was the drone of Messerschmitts, Heinkels and Junkers.

---

[4] The wildest kind of rumors circulated in Leningrad over Voroshilov's removal. One story was that Stalin, personally, had come to Leningrad and ordered Voroshilov to surrender the city. Voroshilov, in anger, hit Stalin in the face. The story, of course, was apocryphal. (Konstantinov, *op. cit.*, p. 125.)

This was the night that Olga Berggolts stood guard duty with Nikolai Fomin, commandant of the "Tears of Socialism" building where she had lived so long. It was dead quiet on Ulitsa Rubinshtein, no traffic, not a vehicle moving. She could hear clearly the roar of distant cannon.

"The Germans have taken Strelna," Fomin said. "They have broken through to Red Putilov." He used the old name for the great Kirov works. It was a night of the full moon, about which the Nazis had warned, a night of wild rumors, including a persistent one that the Germans were about to use gas. The report about Red Putilov was correct. Nazi cycle detachments and light tanks had smashed through into Stachek Prospekt, right at the gates of the Putilov works, before being wiped out.

"The shame of it!" Fomin said suddenly. "The shame of it all . . . to let them in . . ."

Fomin clambered up to the rooftop. Below at the entrance to the "Tears of Socialism" building Olga Berggolts and the porteress stood at their posts, clutching gasoline-filled bottles to hurl at Nazi tanks if they broke through to Ulitsa Rubinshtein.

The Germans were smashing again and again and again at the weakened Forty-second Army. By the fifteenth they had concentrated their 1st, 58th and 291st infantry divisions and their 36th Motorized Division against the faltering Forty-second. The Forty-second had already been given the last reserve division at the disposition of the Leningrad Command—the 10th Rifle Division. But still it could not hold on.

On the thirteenth, or possibly the fourteenth, Dmitri Shcheglov, the writer-turned-Volunteer officer, telephoned Party Secretary Kuznetsov and asked to see him urgently. Shcheglov's unit of People's Volunteers was hold-ing a sector on the Neva and it had almost run out of ammunition. Kuznet-sov asked Shcheglov to come to Smolny immediately. Despite the tension Shcheglov found the ground floor of Smolny quiet. But on the third floor where Kuznetsov had his offices there was bustle and many uniforms. Shcheglov gave Kuznetsov a quick report. Kuznetsov nodded, took notes, thanked him for the report and promised to see to the munitions. As Shcheglov rose to leave, an officer came in and said he had very urgent news. "Already?" Kuznetsov asked. "Exactly," the officer said. "It's be-ginning."

"It" was the German storming of Leningrad.

Could any of the lines hold? Could the city be saved?

Zhukov had never been in a more foul mood—and he was not noted for easy temper.

Bychevsky was summoned to his presence on the fourteenth and gave him a general report on the fortifications. Zhukov listened in indifference, then suddenly interupted sharply: "Who are you?"

"Chief of the Engineering Corps of the front, Colonel Bychevsky."

"I asked you who you are," Zhukov snapped. "Where do you come from?"

His voice was angry, and his chin was thrust forward. His heavy, short figure loomed over the desk.

Bychevsky was baffled. He decided Zhukov wanted his biography and proceeded to outline his career briefly.

"You have taken Khrenov's place," Zhukov snapped. "O.K. And where is General Nazarov? I called for him."

"General Nazarov," Bychevsky explained, "worked in the staff of the Northwest Front Command and coordinated engineering matters between the two fronts. He has flown off with Marshal Voroshilov."

"Coordination . . . flying away," snapped Zhukov. "The hell with him. So go ahead and report."

When Bychevsky had reported, Zhukov, accidentally or not accidentally, brushed Bychevsky's papers on the floor. As Bychevsky picked them up, Zhukov glanced at them and asked about some locations for tanks. Bychevsky explained the tank groups were not real—they were mock-ups made by the Mariinsky Theater. He added that they had deceived the German reconnaissance.

"The fools!" Zhukov said. "Get another hundred of them tonight, and tomorrow morning put them in these two places near Srednyaya Rogatka— here and here."

Bychevsky said the theater workmen couldn't turn out a hundred fake tanks in one night.

Zhukov raised his head and looked Bychevsky up and down.

"If you don't do it, I'll have you court-martialed," he said. "Who's your commissar?"

"Colonel Mukha," Bychevsky said. (*Mukha* means "fly" in Russian.)

"Mukha," said Zhukov. "Very well, tell this Mukha that you'll go together before the tribunal if you don't carry out the order. I'll check upon you tomorrow myself."

Zhukov took the same tone with all the commanders. Colonel Korkodin, chief of operations, was packed off to Moscow after one brief talk with Zhukov. Two days after his arrival Zhukov fired Major General F. S. Ivanov, commander of the Forty-second Army, and within a week had removed the commander of the Eighth Army, Major General V. I. Shcherbakov and Commissar I. F. Chukhnov, the Eighth Army's Military Council member.

On the afternoon of the fifteenth Zhukov rushed Fedyuninsky out to the Pulkovo Heights, a two-hundred-foot ridge which overlooks Leningrad from the southwest. Here was located the famous Pulkovo astronomical observatory. The Pulkovo Heights were defended by the 5th Division of People's Volunteers, and their position had been gravely weakened by the loss of Krasnoye Selo.

The 708th Rifle Regiment and the 21st NKVD Division had been sent to reinforce the Pulkovo position, but the lines were not holding.

Fedyuninsky located the Forty-second Army staff in a reinforced concrete command post in the Pulkovo area. It was so close to the front that as

Fedyuninsky hurried down the trench to the command post he heard bullets whining overhead.

He found Ivanov sitting in the dugout, holding his head with both hands. Fedyuninsky had known Ivanov before the war when both were studying at the Academy of the General Staff. They had been in the same classes. Then Ivanov had become deputy commander of the Kiev Special Military District.

Fedyuninsky remembered Ivanov as an energetic, spirited, enthusiastic man. Now Ivanov sat tired, unshaven, hollow-cheeked, dejected. He expressed no surprise at seeing Fedyuninsky, although they had not met for several years. He asked, apparently out of politeness, "What brings you here? I thought you were commanding a corps in the southwest."

Fedyuninsky explained that he was deputy commander of the front and had come to learn the situation. He asked Ivanov to show him on the map where the lines were.

"I don't know where they are," Ivanov said, in despair. "I don't know anything. . . ."

"Haven't you any communications with your units?" Fedyuninsky asked.

"No," Ivanov replied. "The fighting has been heavy today. I don't know where they have gotten to. The communications have broken down."

Fedyuninsky questioned Ivanov's Chief of Staff and operations head. He quickly decided that only a miracle was keeping the Forty-second in action. He found that the Germans had occupied New and Old Panovo and had worked into Ligovo but apparently not yet in strength.

The worst of it was that between these positions and Leningrad there was little or nothing in the way of defense.

What to do? Before Fedyuninsky could think of anything a message called him back to Smolny. As he came out of the command post, machine-gun fire rattled strongly.

"I'm afraid I'll have to change my command post again," Ivanov said.

"No," said Fedyuninsky firmly. "You may not retire from here. That's an order by the deputy front commander."

"Well," Ivanov said sadly, "we'll try to hang on."

Back at Smolny, before Fedyuninsky could report, Zhukov said, "Don't bother to report. I know all about it already. While you were coming back, Ivanov changed his command post again. He is now in the cellar of a school across from the Kirov factory."

Zhukov was silent a moment, then spoke with decision: "Take over the Forty-second Army. And be quick about it."

Serious as was the moment Fedyuninsky couldn't help grinning. Zhukov noticed this.

"What are you snickering at?" he asked.

"It seems to me," Fedyuninsky said, "that you didn't express yourself quite accurately. How can you take over an army in such a condition? All I can do is take over the command."

Party Secretary A. A. Kuznetsov wrote out the order, assigning

Fedyuninsky to take Ivanov's place.[5] Zhukov and Zhdanov signed it and, with his chief of staff, Major General L. S. Berezinsky, Fedyuninsky hurried back to the front. He found Ivanov in the new command post in the basement of a school. The room was thick with tobacco smoke and a violent argument was in progress between Ivanov and the members of his Military Council, N. V. Solovyev and N. N. Klementyev, as to what to do next. Since they had no communications with their troops the whole argument was theoretical.

Fedyuninsky strode up to the table.

"I've been named commander of the army," he said. "The session of the Military Council is closed. You, Comrade Ivanov, have been called to Smolny."

To close the council was simple, Fedyuninsky thought.

But what to do next was not at all simple.

---

[5] The date is also given as September 16 (Barbashin, *op. cit.*, p. 70) and September 21 (*Istoriya VOVSS*, Vol. II, p. 90).

32 . *Blow Up the City!*

THE QUESTION OF WHAT TO DO NEXT BURNED IN THE
minds of everyone concerned with Leningrad's defense. It burned in the
mind of Andrei Zhdanov. It glowed in the angry eyes of Marshal Zhukov.
It flamed in the stout heart of Party Secretary Kuznetsov. And it curled and
circled through the crafty mind of Iosif Stalin.

But the motivations of these men were not necessarily the same. Zhdanov's
fate was tied to that of Leningrad. He must and would fight to the end
for the northern capital. Zhukov was the emergency commander, sent in at
the last moment to do the impossible. He would do it, sacrificing anything
and anyone to that end. Then he would go on to the next emergency. Party
Secretary Kuznetsov was bound to Zhdanov. He sank or was saved depending
on Leningrad's future. Stalin was something else again. His motives were
never clear, never simple, and he was surrounded in the Kremlin by men for
whom intrigue and plot and ambition were more important than any city or
any battle.

No one knew at this point whether Leningrad could or would be saved.
Some, certainly, thought that it should not be saved. But of this there was
no sign in the streets of the city, where youngsters appeared with pails of
whitewash and began to paint over the street signs and blank out the house
numbers. The city was preparing for street fighting, and if the Germans
broke in there was to be no aid from the signposts. The Nazis would, it
was hoped, lose themselves in the maze of avenues and buildings.

The city had been divided into six sectors for block-by-block defense,
taking into account the water barriers and bridges of the city. A special staff
for internal defense had been established. Street barricades were thrown
up—not merely paving blocks and timbers, but jungles of ferroconcrete,
railroad iron, steel tubing, capable of halting tanks and standing up under air
bombardment.

There were three main areas. The northern sector extended from the
Finnish Gulf to Murino, Vesely Poselok, Ruchyi Station and the metallurgical
factory. It was bordered on the east by the north bank of the Neva and the

Malaya Neva and included the Petrograd side and Aptekarsky island. The eastern sector adjoined the northern sector and extended to Rybatskoye. It included the city region on the north bank of the Neva. The southwestern sector covered the area from the Finnish Gulf to the south bank of the Neva.

The principal barrier around the city was the Circle Railroad. A second interior line was set up from the coaling docks to Alekseyevka, Avtovo, Slobodka, Alexandrovskoye, the village of Nikolayev, Farforovy Station, Volodarsky, and the Lomonosov factory.

To the south the defense region consisted of three sectors—the Kirov, Moscow and Volodarsky; to the north—the Coastal and the Vyborg; and to the southwest the Gatchina.

The city sewer department laid out an underground system through the great Leningrad conduits. Far below the pavement, safe from bombardment, communications lines and supply routes were set up through which ammunition and reinforcements could swiftly be rushed from one threatened area to another.

Special "extermination" points were built into manholes and sewer openings for directing fire at oncoming German tanks. In the ground floors of corner buildings ferroconcrete pillboxes were nested inside the structures, and supports were installed so that if the upper stories were wrecked strongpoints on the ground floor could continue to operate.

The bridges were plotted, and Colonel Bychevsky had special orders to be prepared to destroy them the moment they were threatened by German attack.

Every section of the city was directed to form new groups of Volunteers —150 in all, composed of 600 persons each. These got the designation of Workers Battalions.

Each Workers Battalion sector was defended by 8 reinforced machine-gun nests, 46 ordinary machine-gun points, 10 antitank positions, 2 76-mm gun posts and 13 mortar positions. Their barricades were specified to be 8 feet high and 12 feet thick. Each sector was to be protected with about 11.43 miles of barricades.

The task of coordinating construction of the city's defenses was placed in the hands of the NKVD, the internal police, on August 29. The police with their labor battalions had already been deeply involved. Now they had full responsibility, mobilizing not only prison labor, their own special construction forces, but the army of ordinary citizenry. More than 475,000 citizens, one-third of the city's able-bodied citizens, were put to work in ensuing months. The statistics of work accomplished and human beings engaged are staggering. In September a daily average of 99,540 persons worked on fortifications. In October the figure was 113,300. As late as January, 1942, 12,000 were still at work.[1]

---

[1] *900*, pp. 82–83. These figures may be slightly inflated. Other sources place the September 1 figure at 38,000, that of September 10 at 43,000, of September 20 at 66,000 and of October 1 at 90,000 (*Leningrad v VOV*, p. 79).

Everyone lent a hand. On September 3 the Military Council of the Leningrad Front mobilized 5,000 persons from each city region—a total of 80,000 persons for defense work within the city. They built 17,000 embrasures in buildings and houses, constructed 4,126 pillboxes and firing points and 17 miles of defensive barricades.

Even schoolchildren built fortifications. More than a thousand came from the Smolny region, 350 from the Moscow region. There was no end to the labor poured into this work by youngsters, by old men and women, by middle-aged spinsters and teen-age youths. More than 480 miles of antitank barriers were constructed, 17,874 miles of trench systems, and 420 miles of barbed-wire barricades. More than 5,000 wood-and-earth and concrete pill-boxes were set up.

The Yegorev factory turned out 1,750 steel "hedgehogs" to bar tanks from the city. It tested them by dropping 1½-ton blocks on the frames from a height of 25 feet. Not all of the hedgehogs passed the test. The same plant specialized in building "Voroshilov hotels" for the reception of the Nazis. These were steel-frame pillboxes in which antitank guns and artillery were installed.

Every effort was made to provide the newly formed Workers Battalions with weapons. But the shortages were intense. Old guns, flintlocks and muzzle-loaders, were taken from museum walls. Even so, in the Volodarsky region the Workers Battalions had only 772 rifles, 3 machine guns, 16 sub-machine guns and 3 mortars. In the Red Guard region there were 992 rifles, 15 machine guns and 2 mortars available.

Each factory had its fighting detachments. The Bolshevik factory battalion numbered 584 men, that of the factory named for Lenin 412, the Proletarian locomotive works 201, the October car works 356. In the Volodarsky region there were 3,500 workers in 5 battalions. By September 1 the city had 79 Workers Battalions with 40,000 fighters.

Another two People's Volunteer divisions and three mortar battalions were formed for internal city defense. Despite the shortage of arms, 4,000 rifles were found for an antiair corps, and some additional guns were distributed to factories for the defense of their grounds if the Germans broke through.

The city hoped to muster 26 rifle divisions and 6 tank battalions for the final battle, street by street. It had about 1,205 guns, or approximately 30 per mile of front, and 85 antiaircraft batteries. There were 50 antitank batteries.

The Party concentrated every ounce of strength on stiffening the fighting ranks of those defending Leningrad. On September 9, 300 experienced Party workers were sent to the front "at the disposition of the command." Three days later 3,000 Communists and Komsomols were mobilized to serve as front-line political officers. The next day 500 more were drafted to serve with the inner-line defenses.

A mass meeting of 2,500 youngsters was held September 14 at the Tauride Palace. Old workers who had fought the White Guards spoke. So did

Vsevolod Vishnevsky, who exclaimed: "Forward, comrades! Forward, youth! Forward, Leningraders! We will conquer!" The youngsters swore an oath to die before surrendering Leningrad, and hundreds marched straight from the assembly to the front. Rifles were passed out to them as they formed up outside the palace. Vishnevsky's speech was recorded and played to troops in the battle zone.

On September 15, fifty-two top Party leaders were sent from civilian posts to fighting duty. The calls for Communists to take front-line positions came, hour by hour. There was no time for preparation. Secretary A. A. Kuznetsov called in Party worker A. A. Trakhachev and said he must have 200 trained artillerymen in 24 hours. The next day the "artillerymen" went off to their units. Five hundred Communists were mobilized for combat political work on an hour's notice.

Controls on movement of population, already strict, had been tightened. Since August 24 all movement in the city between the hours of 10 P.M. and 5 A.M. had been forbidden. The highways leading into the city were barricaded. On September 18 three interior lines were set up on the south and southwest approaches to the city. Special Komandaturas prevented people from coming in or out of the city without full identification. The number of police in the city had been radically increased. There had been 36 police commands, with personnel of 352. Now the figure was 2,321. Special police posts had been set up in 1,250 institutions and factories and 80 special rooftop observation posts.

The Workers Battalions were placed on twenty-four-hour call. They slept in their factories or offices. The Military Council was trying to arm them with whatever came to hand—grenades, Molotov cocktails, reconditioned arms. Improvised antitank guns had been mounted on streetcar platforms, trucks and buses.

Machine-gun posts were set up in areas where German paratroops might drop—the Haymarket, Theater Square, Vorovsky, Commune, Trud, Vosstaniya, Plekhanov, the Champs de Mars, Palace Square, Isskustvo, Diktatur, Narva, Revolution, Leo Tolstoy squares, the park named for May 1, the Tauride Palace gardens, the Volkov Cemetery, Lenin Park, the Botanical Gardens, Chelyuskintsev Park and the Smolensk Cemetery. Similar precautions were taken on the outskirts of the city at such places as Porokhove, Rzhevka, Piskarevsky, Grazhdanka, Lesnoi and Kolomyagi.

As Red Army troops fell back into the city, they would take over command of the interior barriers now manned by NKVD troops.

In the ensuing street battles the workers' formations and all the general population were expected to take part. They would be commanded by the chief of each sector.

The task of the Baltic Fleet was to support the city with its naval guns and the guns mounted in land batteries. It was especially to guard against amphibious landings from the Gulf of Finland.

When Admiral Panteleyev came into Leningrad from Kronstadt after an absence of a week, he found the streets transformed—everywhere there were hedgehogs of railroad iron, concrete blocks and pillboxes. In the squares stood batteries of antiaircraft or antitank guns. Normal traffic had disappeared.

From the Neva most of the serviceable warships of the Baltic Fleet directed a ceaseless cannonade against the Germans in the suburbs.

The Germans now were within range of the guns of the cruiser *Gorky* and the battleship *October Revolution* (the former *Petropavlovsk*). The *Marat* was beginning to bring them under fire. As he returned to Kronstadt, passing through Avtovo, Panteleyev recognized the deep whine of 180-mm shells from the *Maxim Gorky,* which was stationed near the grain terminal of the commercial port. He heard, too, the guns of the *Marat,* which was at the entrance of the Sea Canal and was now opening up with its 12-inch guns.

The Germans had begun a propaganda drive, designed to create the impression that Leningrad was about to fall. Hitler congratulated von Leeb on his great success in the Leningrad campaign. General Jodl, Chief of Staff, flew to Helsinki to award Marshal Mannerheim the Iron Cross for the Finnish victories. He also promised to send the Finns 15,000 tons of wheat.

On September 6 the High Command of the Wehrmacht began to discuss the fall of Leningrad in its communiqués. "The encirclement of Leningrad is progressing," the communiqué said. A special press conference of foreign correspondents was called in Berlin. They were told that all the Soviet troops in the Leningrad area had been drawn into a noose and faced either starvation or extermination. The Germans had decided, it was said, not to storm the city simply for reasons of prestige. They had no desire to suffer unnecessary losses. If Leningrad did not surrender, it would suffer the fate of Warsaw and Rotterdam—total destruction by air and artillery bombardment.

The Germans appeared to believe their own propaganda. Hitler approved a directive dated September 6 for the mounting of his offensive against Moscow. It called for Army Group Nord to transfer not later than September 15 its Panzer and mechanized divisions and its dive bombers to the Moscow front.

Hitler insisted that von Leeb draw the tightest kind of circle around Leningrad. Secretly, the Führer instructed von Leeb that the city's capitulation was not to be accepted. The population was to die with the doomed city. Random shelling of civilian objectives was authorized. If the populace tried to escape the iron ring, they were to be shot down.

No hint of this brutal decision was made public.

Thousands of German leaflets rained down on Leningrad. Most residents feared even to pick them up lest they be seized and shot by the special "destroyer" battalions of workers, charged with maintaining internal defense. But by word of mouth the message of the leaflets spread. They were addressed to the women of Leningrad and they said: "Take every opportunity to convince your husbands, sons and friends of the senselessness of struggling against the German Army. Only by ending the battle of Leningrad can you save your lives." Leaflets directed to the Soviet troops proclaimed: "Beat the Political Commissars—throw a brick in their snouts."

Halder, always a skeptic where the operations of Army Group Nord were concerned, now reflected the optimism that was felt in the Fuehrer's Headquarters. On September 12 he made the entry:

"Leningrad: Very good progress. The enemy begins to soften on the front of Reinhardt's corps. It would appear that the population does not want to take a hand in defense. The Commander in Chief Nord [von Leeb] vehemently wants to keep Reinhardt's corps."

The next day, the thirteenth, he laconically noted that he had agreed to let von Leeb keep the armored corps for the continuance of the drive on Leningrad, and two days later he reported that the "assault on Leningrad had made good progress."

It had, indeed, made good progress. There was some truth in the German belief that not all Leningraders were prepared to defend their city to the last. One Soviet officer was convinced that the path into Leningrad lay practically open. Had the Nazis simply thrust forward, they would have brushed aside the weakening front-line units and won the day. Kochetov, who was quite ready to see the worst in his fellow citizens, was suffused in pessimism. According to his account Soviet secret police uncovered not only German spies, sympathizers and agents but individuals who were forming "fighting groups" which would lead an uprising in Leningrad to coincide with the culminating storm of the city by the Germans.

What about the city's ability to defend itself once the Germans broke in—if they broke in?

Kochetov, like the other Leningraders, could observe the hundreds of machine-gun posts, the antitank traps, the embrasures built into the buildings, the internal-defense preparations. The general view, he thought, was that there were "not too few, not too many" of these pillboxes. Were there enough? Could the city rely on them? That was the question. It is apparent from Kochetov that not everyone did. He insists that he and his friends did believe that the city's defenses would hold. Others had their doubts—among them Stalin, as was evident in Admiral Kuznetsov's curious discussion with him in the Kremlin September 13 about preparing the Baltic Fleet for destruction.

On the evening of the thirteenth Admiral Tributs returned to Kronstadt from his daily session at Smolny considerably earlier than usual. He had met the new front commander, Marshal Zhukov, and he had new orders. Admiral Panteleyev found Tributs unusually gloomy when he arrived at the Kronstadt staff dock on the Italian Pond across from the headquarters building. He felt immediately that something serious had happened. Tributs listened inattentively to the routine reports and then called his chief of operations, his chief of rear services, and Panteleyev into his office.

All knew that Leningrad was being prepared for street battle, that every house, every building, every square was to be defended. They knew of the staff of internal defense which had been formed, and they knew that every possible measure was being taken for saving the city.

The three officers waited with pencils and notebooks in hand for Tributs' orders.

"The situation at the front is critical," Tributs said. "A terrible battle is under way. Leningrad will be defended to the last possibility. *But everything is possible.* If the Fascists break into the city, troikas have been set up at all institutions and military objectives to destroy everything that might fall into the enemy's hands. All bridges, factories, institutions, are to be mined. If the enemy breaks into the city, he will die in its ruins."

A long pause followed. The Admiral wiped the perspiration from his brow and continued:

"The Stavka demands that not one ship, not one supply dump, not one cannon in Kronstadt fall into enemy hands. If the situation demands, all are to be destroyed. The staff and the rear services must immediately draft a plan for mining every ship, fort and warehouse. Before the ships are scuttled the personnel must be taken ashore, formed into ranks and marched to the front."

Tributs told his associates to carry out the orders immediately.[2] Panteleyev admitted that the announcement stunned him. "All kinds of unpleasant thoughts arose in my mind," he said.

The task of working up the plans, placing the mines, establishing the order in which crews would be removed from the doomed ships and of handling their actual destruction, was placed in the hands of what Panteleyev called "especially firm, dedicated Communists" for it was a matter which required great political strength. There had to be the most careful precautions to see that no catastrophes occurred such as the premature blowing up of some of the ships. While Panteleyev had no doubt about the steadfastness of the Communist organization in the fleet, nevertheless the strictest vigilance would be required of every Party man.

Late in the evening while the orders for scuttling were being typed up, General Mitrofan I. Moskalenko, chief of rear services, came into Panteleyev's office. He sat down on an old sofa, pushing aside an ashtray and a roll of maps, and waited for Panteleyev to get off the telephone.

"Tell me," Moskalenko said, "what does it take to get rid of this old divan? It must be a hundred years old. It's good for nothing but the rubbish heap."

The two men sat and talked about refurnishing the staff headquarters

[2] The formal order of the Leningrad Command apparently was dated September 15. (*Leningrad v VOV*, p. 155.)

while they waited for the typists to bring them their lists of military objectives, broken down into categories: "To be scuttled," "To be blown up," "To be set afire."

One sailor selected to assist in mining warehouses at the naval docks never forgot the hopeless gesture with which his commanding officer gave the squad its orders to place bombs under all the warehouses of the military port. Depth bombs. They were to be wired together so that a single thrust of the plunger would send the whole port up in one tremendous explosion.

The sailors went to work setting out the bombs while the port workers continued to move supplies in and out, keeping a fearful eye on the terrible business at hand.

The first intimation Colonel Bychevsky had that the destruction of the city was contemplated came when he was called back from the front late on the evening of September 15. He had worked all day in the Pulkovo region, where the situation was unbelievably serious. The Germans had cut the front of the Forty-second Army by reaching the Strelna-Leningrad highway, and two Nazi divisions were attacking toward Strelna and Volodarsky. The 21st NKVD Division under Colonel M. D. Panchenko had fallen back into Ligovo.

Bychevsky was received immediately by General Khozin, who asked, "Are the Leningrad bridges mined? Where are your plans and maps? Give me a report on all this in the morning."

To be called back in the evening when the reports weren't needed until morning didn't seem natural to Bychevsky. He knew Khozin well. He noted in Khozin's voice something that sounded like alarm. Bychevsky was deeply troubled.

In the morning of the sixteenth he was back at Khozin's office and laid before Khozin the plans which had been drafted for blowing up the Leningrad bridges. He pointed out how he would get electric power to detonate the explosives and the command arrangements for touching off the charges.

"Where are the explosives?" Khozin demanded.

"The Military Council thought it was not appropriate to put them under the bridges," Bychevsky replied.

Khozin ordered him to rework his plans and submit them within twenty-four hours, including the placing of charges in the galleries which already had been prepared under the bridges. Khozin asked for precise details on time, men and materials needed to put the plan into action.

It was apparent to Bychevsky that Khozin was speaking under orders. It seemed that the matter was not merely one of mining the bridges.

"What supplies of explosives do we have available?" Khozin asked.

"The supply in the city is limited to some tens of tons," Bychevsky said. "But the Party committee is taking measures to increase production. We are having serious difficulty with TNT, which is essential for antitank mines in the fighting zone."

"I am talking not about the operational area," Khozin said, "but about the operational rear."

What kind of "operational rear" did Khozin mean? Bychevsky decided to put the question.

"You are talking about the city of Leningrad, Comrade General?"

"Yes," said Khozin, "in a certain case."

The next day, the seventeenth, the "certain case" became clear. The Military Council ordered that forty tons of explosives from the army engineers' supplies be turned over to "regional troikas." The heads of the troikas were the first secretaries of the Party organizations in the Kirov, Moscow, Volodarsky and Lenin regions.

During the day the explosives were passed out to the troikas. They had orders to blow up every important object in their districts if the Germans broke into the city in strength.

Each regional troika issued a sealed packet to the subordinate troikas which had been set up in the big factories, institutions and buildings in its area. There were 141 of these lesser troikas. None of the lower echelons knew the exact contents of the sealed packet. They knew it was to be opened only if the Germans broke into the city in strength. Some, certainly, knew the contents more precisely—orders to blow up the buildings and march out to fight a final battle with the Nazis.

In each institution a close, armed, dedicated group of Communists was formed to carry out whatever order was given. These groups knew that one duty was to destroy the city by demolishing every large building, every bridge, every factory, every important objective within the limits of Leningrad.

At the Izhorsk factory, for example, which had continued to operate under Nazi shelling even though it was virtually on the front line, explosive charges and detonators were set under the cranes and presses. In the great petroleum reservoir a cylinder of hydrogen had been placed. At a signal the hydrogen could be released into the oil, touching off an explosion of tremendous force.

At the Kirov works the troika was headed by the regional Party Secretary Yefremov. He directed the placing of explosive charges under the blast furnaces, the rolling mills and the railroad viaduct under which the great KV tanks rolled as they emerged from the works and headed directly to the front just up the streetcar line at the seventh station stop from the factory.

The whole territory south of the Circle Railroad had been cleared of institutions and factories. Some twenty-one factories had been evacuated to the "rear" of the city—to the Vyborg and Petrograd sides and to Vasilevsky Island. All of these evacuated plants were ready to be blown up at the touch of the plunger. The Izhorsk plant—what could be moved of it—had been shipped out. More than 110,000 residents of the Narva, Moscow and

Neva Gates areas had been evacuated. This region was to be a no-man's land.

Would the signal be given?

The night of the sixteenth-seventeenth was the most alarming Leningrad had experienced, especially in the southern areas adjacent to the fiercest battles.

At 15 minutes to 11 P.M. G. F. Badayev, secretary of the Moscow region, called by telephone to all the directors of factories and big institutions in his region. This night, he warned, the Germans might break into the city from the south. He ordered the Workers Battalions, with all fighting equipment, to man the barricades.

Similar orders went to all factories and institutions in the Narva and Neva Gates regions.

"At thirty minutes past midnight we went into our positions," M. Strashenkov, a commander of a Workers Battalion at the Kirov works, jotted in his diary. "They are not far from the factory. Two pillboxes have been completed. One is half finished and a fourth hasn't been started."

All Communists, all Young Communists, all "non-Party activists" in the city were put on alarm and ordered to sleep at their posts.

The Workers Battalions at the great Elektrosila factory, the Bolshevik factory, the Izhorsk works, were on No. 1 Alert.

The threat to the Elektrosila plant became so great—the Germans were only about 2½ miles away—that all personnel were evacuated and a force of 1,100 workers occupied a perimeter defense system of pillboxes and trenches, in expectation of a Nazi breakthrough.

That morning the leading article in *Leningradskaya Pravda* was headlined: "Leningrad—To Be or Not to Be?"

Four days later, the night of the twentieth–twenty-first, Bychevsky was again called to Smolny in the early hours before dawn. He was handed an urgent order to prepare the central Leningrad rail system and all its approaches for destruction. He was appalled. Destruction of the rail network meant the end. He tried to get some explanation from General Khozin. Khozin coldly told him, "I'm occupied. Carry out the order." His only comfort was that his old friend General P. P. Yevstigneyev, chief of intelligence, didn't seem to think that the plan would have to be carried out.

Rumors and hints that Leningrad was being prepared for destruction raced through the city despite every effort to keep the enterprise secret. Too many knew. The plans were too alarming. Word spread. Aleksandr Rozen heard of it almost as soon as the orders were given. He lived in a big apartment house midway between the Leningrad Post Office and the Central Telegraph—two prime objectives of Nazi bombing, two buildings doomed to destruction. Not until years later when he read General Bychevsky's memoirs did he know the whole story—that orders had been given to destroy the whole rail network. "But what I had already learned that night was more than sufficient," he grimly noted.

Everyone waited. They waited for the signal to blow up the city. But it did not come.

Had the Germans broken in, Leningrad would have been destroyed.

That clearly was Stalin's intention: destroy the city of revolution and march out to final battle with the Nazis. This was the plan—if the lines did not hold.

Moscow had been burned to thwart Napoleon. An even more Dantesque catastrophe awaited Adolf Hitler if his jack-booted troops and his snub-snouted Panzers burst through the Narva Gates.

There would be no victory parade past the Winter Palace, no reviewing stand in Palace Square, no ceremonial banquet in the Hotel Astoria. All this—all that symbolized imperial Russia, all that had been created by Peter and Catherine, the Alexanders and the Nicholases,[3] all that had been built by Lenin's workers and those who had slaved for Stalin—all this was doomed to a twentieth-century Götterdämmerung. Hitler would have no chance to erase the hated cradle of Marxism from the earth. It would be erased by its creators.

---

[3] Perhaps not all of imperial Petersburg was doomed. Party Secretary Kuznetsov visited Peterhof September 8 to oversee the packing of its treasures. He categorically forbade that the buildings be mined. (Bychevsky, *op. cit.*, p. 83.) Machine-gun nests were set up on the roof of the Winter Palace to fire into Palace Square in case of a Nazi paratroop attempt. They were ordered removed in late September by the Leningrad Command. Similar installations at other historic sites were also removed in order not to give the Germans an excuse for attacking them. (S. Varshavsky, *Podvig Ermitazha*, Leningrad, 1965, p. 64.)

33 . *"They're Digging In!"*

THE STREETCAR TOOK THEM TO THE FRONT: LINE NO. 9, past the Narva Gates, where a firing position had been set up to command the broad sweep of Stachek Prospekt. Aleksandr Rozen rode the car out Stachek Prospekt. He had boarded it near the offices of his newspaper, *On Guard of the Fatherland*. Most of the passengers were soldiers. A machine gun was mounted in front. The red-painted trolley moved, then halted; moved and halted. A German air attack was in progress. Here and there Rozen saw a car stopped, burning, or a charred carcass, dead in the street— to stay there for months ahead, through the ice winter into the frigid spring, a skeleton, abandoned, pitiful.

Stachek Prospekt was filled with people. Here sprawled the Kirov works, the mightiest engineering establishment in Russia, with hundreds of shops and thousands of workers. Now it seemed that everyone in Leningrad capable of holding a gun was moving slowly toward the rambling buildings that lay behind wooden and wire-woven fences on either side of the broad avenue. Moving in the opposite direction was another throng—women and children, leaving the zone of fortifications from Avtovo to Forel Hospital, the no-man's land of hastily abandoned factories, apartment houses and build- ings, the area which was to be dynamited in a desperate effort to halt the Nazi Panzers. The women in shawls, string bags over their shoulders, milk tins and buckets in their hands, the children with cord-knotted bundles of bedding and clothes, moved slowly into and through the city toward the safer Petrograd and Vasilevsky Island districts. A shell fell beyond the Kirov Gates. Then came the deep roar of a Soviet gun, replying. The streetcar halted at the viaduct. Everyone sat silent, listening to the cursing of the motorman. Rozen watched stretcher bearers emerge from the passageway. A body lay under a blanket. All he could see were the man's high rubber boots, the kind that was hard to find.

As Rozen waited at the Kirov Gates for his pass to be checked, a 60-ton KV tank emerged from the passageway, wheeled majestically into Stachek

Prospekt and headed for the city limits. Just behind, racing to catch up, went the streetcar. The trolleycars ran as far as the Kotlyarov streetcar barns. There they halted and the conductor shouted, "All off. This is the front. End of the line." Beyond that you went by foot, picking your way through the military trucks, the barricades, the tank traps, the dugouts, the machine-gun nests, past the Krasnensk Cemetery and Forel Hospital to Sheremetyev Park. The trenches began there.

The front was about two and a half miles beyond the Kirov plant. It was ten miles from Palace Square.

Leningrad went to the front, as Olga Berggolts wrote, by "familiar streets that each remembered like a dream—here was the fence around our childhood home, here stood the great rustling maple. . . . I went to the front through the days of my childhood, along the streets where I ran to school."

On the night of the seventeenth of September, rather late, Party Secretary A. A. Kuznetsov and Colonel Bychevsky hurried through the silent, blacked-out city toward the front. Every window was dark. Here and there a vague blue light showed where a military vehicle was moving. The whole city—the whole densely populated eighty square miles—seemed in hiding, its very shape changed so that Bychevsky could hardly tell where he was, the shadows so deep, black and menacing. The weather was surly. Gone was golden September. Behind the blackened windows, thought Bychevsky, some are sleeping—probably children, for every adult was on guard, digging fortifications, feverishly working on this most fearsome of nights. The bombing had gone on until an hour or so ago. The glow of burning buildings gleamed in the long vistas.

Beyond the Kotlyarov streetcar barns they heard mortar blasts very close. Two big trucks sprawled in the highway, burning fiercely. A cobweb of shattered electric wires hung above the street. From here paths led off to Sheremetyev Park, where a machine-gun exchange was taking place. Ten tanks from the Kirov works had been set up in the park as stationary fire points. From the Sea Canal they could hear the deep roar of naval guns firing into the German positions just beyond Pulkovo.

They found Colonel M. D. Panchenko, commander of the 21st NKVD Division, in a dugout—the command post of his 14th Regiment just beyond Sheremetyev Park. They were practically at the edge of Ligovo—and the town was in the hands of the Germans. They could see this from the fires.

Panchenko, wearing a cotton-quilted Red Army jacket and steel helmet, an automatic rifle slung over his neck, stood, his head almost bumping the ceiling, leaning over a map with a kerosene lamp.

"Have you given up Ligovo?" Kuznetsov asked.

"We are holding on," Panchenko said, trying to make the best of the situation. "Rodionov has some strong groups in the town. They are still fighting."

"What does that mean?" asked Kuznetsov, nodding in the direction of a hot exchange of fire. "It sounds to me like your 'strong groups' have been cut off."

"They'll fight on," Panchenko said. "These are frontier guards!"

"Yeh," snapped Kuznetsov. "But where will they fight? Back of us? In Leningrad?"

Panchenko held his tongue.

"Have the Germans got the station at Ligovo, too?" Kuznetsov asked.

"Yes," Panchenko admitted. "I've just come back from there. I tried to get them out, but I didn't succeed. They have three tanks there and automatic weapons. We got up to the entrance but had to fall back. We'll try again in the morning."

Kuznetsov sank wearily onto a stool.

"Tell me this, Colonel," he rasped. "How does it happen that yesterday your division drove the Germans out of Ligovo and Staro-Panovo? Today you got an order to drive them farther. But, instead, this evening you abandon Ligovo to the Germans."

That morning, Panchenko explained, two of his regiments attacked from Staro-Panovo but were hit by fifty Nazi tanks. Before they knew it the Panzers had burst into Ligovo.

Kuznetsov ordered Panchenko to recover the town.

"I've already got that order from General Fedyuninsky of the Forty-second Army," Panchenko said. "He even threatened, 'If you don't carry out the order I'll have your head.'"

"And did you get the order that if you fall back from this line you'll also be minus a head?" Kuznetsov raged. "All the commanders know that!"

"I know," Panchenko gloomily replied. Then he began to name the officers who had been killed in the day's fighting.

Kuznetsov's anger died down. He rose to go. "Remember, Comrade Panchenko, the workers of the Kirov factory have gone to the barricades. That you must understand."

All the way back to Smolny Bychevsky sat silent. Neither he nor Kuznetsov spoke. Bychevsky never knew what Kuznetsov was thinking. But Bychevsky was filled with alarm for the fate of the 21st Division. It was not right that as a result of the day's "offensive" the division had been left without fortifications to spend the night in cold and mud before a big town. And back of it—the Kirov works. Who was to blame for this? Panchenko? Fedyuninsky? In some measure neither one nor the other. For the need of the moment was ceaseless counterattack. The enemy must not be given a moment's ease. Everything must be done even though it brought heavy losses.

Heavy losses there had been. Heavy losses lay ahead. The truth was that in Ligovo only a single building, the Klinovsky House, remained in Soviet hands. And it had changed hands several times. At 1:30 A.M. September 18 a file of troops headed by Lavrenti Tsiganov and Nikolai Tikhomirov cautiously went forward from a nearby trench to the house. Rockets cast an unearthly green light over the rubble. The upper stories of the Klinovsky House had been wrecked, but the soldiers found an old iron door leading to the cellar. The basement was packed with Soviet troops. A ring of firing points had been set up toward the German lines. On a long table lay loaves of bread, tobacco and piles of bullets. On a potbellied stove a teakettle was simmering. A fourteen-year-old youngster with a dog and an old man sat by the stove. They lived there.

Many of the soldiers in the basement were workers from the Kirov plant and the northern wharves. They worked by day, turning out the big KV tanks, and went into the trenches and barricades at night. "We are soldiers as much as you," said Vasily Mokhov, an old blacksmith from the Kirov works. He told of the command point in the subbasement in his factory from which the defense of the plant was directed. Last night the telephone had rung. A strange voice with a heavy accent said, "Leningrad? Very good. We will come tomorrow to visit the Winter Palace and the Hermitage."

"Who's calling?" the regional engineer asked.

"This is Ligovo," the German replied.

The Nazis had broken into Ligovo and the telephone lines had not been cut. Neither, it turned out, had the water mains. The Germans drank from the Leningrad water supply until someone thought of turning it off.

Some time between 3 and 4:30 A.M. the Germans launched another attack on Klinovsky House. The soldiers emerged from the cellar and fought from trenches. At 6:30 A.M. it grew light. From the shallow clay ditches the troops saw smoke curling up from the Pulkovo Heights. A wooden building was afire. From these heights—roughly 230 feet above sea level—all of Leningrad was visible. There lay the coal docks with their huge steel transporter cages. There the ships bunkered coal before long voyages. Now the port was empty and dead. Above the northern wharves towered a port crane—the one the Leningrad youngsters called the camel. To the right rose the twin towers of the Forel Hospital, now a divisional headquarters. Nearby was a streetcar blown from the rails by an aerial bomb. The asphalt of the paving had caught fire and the flames ran down the highway, casting clouds of black smoke toward the Avtovo quarter. Beyond it rose the old chimneys of the Kirov works and beyond them the inner city—the endless panorama of roofs, of chimneys, of cupolas.

All this, thought Tsiganov, the Germans now can see—the wharves, St. Isaac's, the Admiralty spire, the great Neva bridges, the houses, the streets, the squares. All of this was in the sights of the German guns. War had washed up to the edge of Leningrad.

Tsiganov looked toward the west—to the road to the Peterhof Palace. He could not believe his eyes. Germans. They fired and fell, fired and fell. They came closer and closer to the Klinovsky House. No artillery preparation. A silent, sudden attack. How many were there? The green devils crawled ahead . . . farther . . . farther. They rose and came forward at full height, no longer crawling. He heard them shouting.

"To the ready!" shouted the Soviet commander. "Grenades!"

Tsiganov got off two grenades. He could not throw a third. Over him a German suddenly appeared. He grabbed him by the throat and slowly choked him to death. The Germans were in the trenches now. No chance for grenades, too close for rifles. He pulled his bayonet and leaped on a German officer wearing a death's head helmet, plunging the bayonet in. . . .

The battle went on all morning. Another attack was mounted to recapture the Ligovo railroad station. It did not quite succeed.

At midmorning the troops, to their amazement, heard the sound of music. At a first-aid point a band had started to play. It struck up the soldier's favorite, "Katyusha." Some of the soldiers started to sing:

> Katyusha came to the shore,
> To the very highest bank.
> She came to sing a song
> For the one she loved,
> For the one whose letter she kept. . . .

In a lull the Russians heard from the German side a shout: "Play it again, Russ. Play it again!"

A new Russian attack started at 1:30. A young lieutenant named Anikeyev led his men out. He didn't shout, "For the Motherland! For Leningrad!" He said, "Let's go." Nobody said, "Hurrah!" They simply poured ahead into the German fire. In a half-hour's bloody engagement they drove the Germans from their second line of trenches beyond the Klinovsky House.

At 4:30 P.M. Tsiganov was sent back to Colonel Rodionov, commander of the regiment, with a message. Rodionov's headquarters were in Sheremetyev Park. After delivering his message Tsiganov got a present: an hour's sleep. About 6:30 P.M. he was aroused and sent on another errand to Captain Ivan Glutov, in charge of a sappers' detachment, stationed beside a dam and canal. Glutov had mined the dam. On a signal that the Germans had broken through, his duty was to blow up the dam, releasing the waters of the Finnish Gulf to flood the whole area from Ligovo to the Forel Hospital. This was what would happen if the lines broke at Klinovsky House.

Just after 9 P.M. Tsiganov felt the ground tremble under him. There was a roar like an express train. An earthquake? Had the dam been blown up? Against the red outlines of burning Ligovo he saw long arrows of flame against the heavens, roaring across the sky like meteors. They came from the region of the Forel Hospital and were headed for the center of the German position.

"There go our Katyushas!" Glutov shouted.

Katyushas they were—the rockets from multibarrel launchers, the most secret weapon in the Soviet arsenal launched on the most desperate of nights against the Germans beyond Klinovsky House.

At 11 P.M. the night of September 18 Colonel Panchenko wearily went back to Smolny to report to General Zhukov and the Leningrad Command. He brought what he tersely described as a report "about the fighting action of the division." The key to that report was that the Germans had been stopped.

No one really knew whether the Germans were stopped. It was better not to believe it. If they had been halted, blood had done it. The toll of lives taken in those September days could never be counted. A little stream ran past Klinovsky House. It ran red with soldiers' blood for days. The Katyushas? Perhaps. Nothing more frightening had been experienced in World War II than the Katyushas with their scream, their fiery trails, their thunderous impact, the mass that filled the air suddenly with fire and sound.[1]

Was it Zhukov's iron will?

He was terrible in those September days. There was no other word for it. He threatened commander after commander with the firing squad. He removed men right and left. And he insisted on one thing: Attack! Attack! Attack! This was the essence of his first orders on taking command. It made no difference how weak the unit. It made no difference if they had no weapons, no bullets, if they had been retreating for weeks. Attack! Those were his orders. Disobey and go before the tribunal.

Attack or be shot—a simple equation.

On September 17 Zhukov issued a general order to all commanders of all units in the Forty-second and Fifty-fifth armies. They were told that any withdrawal from the lines Ligovo-Pulkovo-Shushary-Kolpino would be considered the gravest crime against the Motherland. The penalty: to be shot.

In the early morning hours of September 18 Bychevsky was laboring on the Circle Railroad, transforming it into the inner defense line. Every fifty to a hundred yards he was installing gun positions, using equipment that had been salvaged from the ruins of the Gatchina and Vyborg fortified regions and thrown together in the Leningrad factories in the past few days. Artillerymen were calculating fields of fire. Ammunition was being brought up. There was no communications system thus far.

He had stationed sappers' groups at the big destruction points where mines had been planted under the intersections of the major highways, at the car barns at Kotlyarov, at the Port Station and Shosseinaya. Special commands were set up to deal with German tanks which broke through the city.

At 4 A.M. Zhukov's adjutant appeared and ordered him immediately to Smolny. As Bychevsky entered the reception room, he saw General Fedyuninsky and his Corps Commissar, N. N. Klementyev. Judging from their faces they had had a rough time.

Wet, covered with mud, tired, Bychevsky shuffled into Zhukov's office.

[1] Artillery Marshal N. N. Voronov credited mass artillery fire—field, coastal and naval —with halting the Germans. (Voronov, *Na Shluzhbe Voennoi*, Moscow, 1963, p. 189.)

The General was sitting with Zhdanov, leaning over a map.

"So," said Zhukov. "Here at last. Where have you been gadding about that we have to hunt you all night—snoozing, I suppose?"

Bychevsky said he'd been working on the fortification system.

"Does the commander of the Forty-second Army know about this system?"

"In the morning I'll give a map of it to General Berezinsky, his Chief of Staff. General Fedyuninsky himself will be with his troops."

Zhukov smashed his heavy fist on the table.

"I didn't ask you about drawing maps. I asked you whether the commander has been advised about the system. Can't you understand the Russian language?"

Bychevsky pointed out that Fedyuninsky was just outside in the reception room.

Zhukov flared up again.

"Do you ever think before you speak?" he said. "I don't need you to tell me he's here. Do you understand that if Antonov's division doesn't go into the defense lines along the Circle Railroad this very night, the Germans may break into the city?

"And if they do, I'll have you shot in front of Smolny as a traitor."

Zhdanov seemed uncomfortable. This was not his way of dealing with people. He never used rough language. Now he intervened.

"Comrade Bychevsky, how could you have failed to go to Fedyuninsky himself! He has just taken over the army. And Antonov's division, which must occupy the line, has just been formed. If the division moves up in daylight, it will be bombed. Do you understand what this is all about?"

The reason for the urgency finally dawned on Bychevsky. The Antonov division, the 6th People's Volunteers, had to get into position before daylight. He had not even known that the 6th Volunteers had been assigned to the Forty-second Army nor that they had been ordered into the lines behind Pulkovo before dawn.

Bychevsky asked to be permitted to show Fedyuninsky the new lines.

"Light dawns!" snapped Zhukov. "You better get your thinking cap on. If that division is not in position by 9 A.M., I'll have you shot."

Bychevsky made a hurried escape and met Fedyuninsky in the next room.

"Having trouble, Engineer?" Fedyuninsky said.

Bychevsky was in no mood for chaffing.

"Just a bit, Comrade General," he snapped. "The commander has promised to have me shot if the 6th Division is not in the Circle Railroad lines by morning. Let's go."

"Don't be angry, Engineer," Fedyuninsky smiled. "We've just been with Georgi Konstantinovich and we've got some promises, too."

The 6th Division got into place. But without much time to spare.

Aleksandr Rozen was with Fedyuninsky at his command post on the Pulkovo Heights. It had been an incredible time. All day long on the eighteenth the Germans had attacked. Now dusk was falling. The weak sun sank toward the west in a sea of clouds. A little rain began to fall, and the ground grew slippery. Fedyuninsky and his staff began to move toward a broken communications trench when the General suddenly halted and looked fixedly into the distance. It was growing dark, but he kept peering into the distance. A shell exploded. Some stretcher bearers came by. The Germans were bombing Leningrad through the clouds. Rozen edged up to Fedyuninsky in time to hear him say: "The 6th Division of Volunteers have occupied their defense lines on the Circle Railroad. That's the last line."

Zhukov demanded attacks, counterattacks, counteroffensives, from all the armies under his command. The Eighth Army was cut off from Leningrad when the Germans drove through to the Gulf of Finland, winning control of a tongue of land running from the Peterhof Palace on the west through Strelna to the Ligovo sector on the Leningrad outskirts.

Major General V. I. Shcherbakov, commander of the Eighth, was ordered by Zhukov to concentrate his forces, the 5th Brigade of marines, the 191st and 281st rifle divisions and the 2nd People's Volunteers, and carry out a counterattack on the Germans, centering on the village of Volodarsky in the direction of Krasnoye Selo. The idea was to hit the Germans from the rear while the 21st NKVD occupied them along the Pulkovo front. Zhukov transferred to Shcherbakov the 10th and 11th rifle divisions and the remains of the 3rd People's Volunteers from the Forty-second Army. He provided from the front reserves the 125th and 268th rifle divisions.

But the effort was beyond Shcherbakov. The divisions were mere decimals of their battle strength. They had been bled white and fought until they could not fight again. They had hardly any artillery. They had no shells for the cannon, no bullets for their rifles and few mines or hand grenades. Shcherbakov was compelled to report to Zhukov that he could not carry out the order. He had no strength for a counterattack. It was all he could do to hold the fading lines around Oranienbaum. Indeed, without the constant pounding of the Baltic Fleet cannon, those located on ships and the powerful coastal batteries at Krasnaya Gorka and Kronstadt, he could not have hung on.

Zhukov's reaction was predictable. He removed Shcherbakov and the Eighth Army's Military Council member I. F. Chukhnov. He put Major General T. I. Shevaldin in charge of the army as of September 24.[2]

General Dukhanov, the old veteran of the Leningrad front, was rushed

[2] A curious controversy has arisen in Soviet historiography about the Eighth Army and its orders to counterattack. The distinguished naval historians V. Achkasov and B. Veiner describe the counterattack as having been carried out. The authoritative *Bitva Za Leningrad* (Barbashin) suggests that it was carried out and gives the Eighth Army great credit for engaging and weakening the Germans. (Barbashin, *op. cit.*, pp. 70–71.) However, V. P. Sviridov, V. P. Yakutovich and V. Ye. Vasilenko cite chapter and verse of Shcherbakov's refusal to carry out the attack. (*Bitva Za Leningrad*, pp. 126 *et seq.*) And the authoritative A. Karasev and V. Kovalchuk agree with Sviridov and Co. (*Voyenno-Istoricheskii Zhurnal*, No. 1, January, 1964, p. 84.) The ouster of Shcherbakov September 24 suggests that Sviridov and Co. are right.

into the Eighth Army *place d'armes* to take over the 10th Rifle Division, which was fighting near Strelna. He got his orders September 17 and had to go by boat to Oranienbaum and then back along the coast by car to reach his troops.

He found a division in name only. Its biggest "regiment" numbered 180 men. This pitiful force was supposed to counterattack the German Panzers. Dukhanov managed to hold on, in part because the bridges at New Peterhof had been mined by Bychevsky's men and he blew them up in the face of the advancing Nazi tanks.

Then he was ordered by the new commander, General Shevaldin, to carry out a counteroffensive aimed at Strelna and Ligovo. An amphibious landing of marines was being attempted simultaneously. Dukhanov's men (now the 19th Corps) attacked and suffered heavy losses. The Germans were well dug in and couldn't be budged. Shevaldin—on Zhukov's orders—called Dukhanov.

"Not a step back!" said Shevaldin. "You must attack. All commanders, including division commanders, must lead the attack. All forward!"

Dukhanov started to protest, then swallowed.

"Yes, sir," he said. "I will tell the Chief of Staff to take over the corps and I will lead the attack."

"No," snapped Shevaldin. "You must direct the troops and take responsibility for their actions. Carry out the order."

Dukhanov slammed the receiver down. His Corps Commissar V. P. Mzhavanadze[3] said, "What's going on?" Dukhanov told him.

Mzhavanadze pulled on his greatcoat, grabbed his revolver and shouted, "Farewell." He led the 10th Division into action.

Dukhanov carried out his orders. Every commander, every political commissar went to the head of his unit and marched into battle. The attack halted the Germans, but did little more. The Russians didn't have the muscle to budge the Nazis.

"I could not then and I cannot today approve the measures for stiffening our troops which were taken by the Commander of the Eighth Army," Dukhanov wrote years later. "The corps was threatened with complete loss of leadership and might have suffered a frightful disaster."

But this was Zhukov's way: Attack. Attack. The commanders could carry out his orders. They could die in the attempt. Or be shot.

Fedyuninsky was fond of quoting an infantryman named Promichev who is said to have told his fellow soldiers, "Our principle is this: If you retreat, I will kill you. If I retreat without orders, you kill me. And Leningrad will not be surrendered." This was the Zhukov principle.

Zhukov applied the principle to all the armies. The Fifty-fourth, for example. This army had been created August 23 and sent into the Volkhov

---

[3] Mzhavanadze became First Secretary of the Communist Party of Georgia after Stalin's death and in 1957 was named a member of the Presidium (now Politburo) of the Soviet Communist Party.

region for the specific purpose of relieving pressure on the Leningrad front. It had been designed to prevent a whole series of events: It was to keep the Germans from enveloping Leningrad from the southeast. It was to protect the city from being cut off from Moscow. It was to hold open the routes to Lake Ladoga. It was to keep the Nazis from cutting through to Mga and Shlisselburg.

It had done none of these things. In fact, it had done virtually nothing. It was led by G. I. Kulik, the police general and toady of the notorious Beria. Zhukov had him fired on September 25 and sent his reliable and ponderous Chief of Staff, General Khozin, to take over the Fifty-fourth. The Forty-eighth Army had virtually disappeared under the weak and unreliable direction of Lieutenant General M. A. Antonyuk. Zhukov simply absorbed the Forty-eighth into the Leningrad front. There was little left to absorb.

Attack—or die.

The grim slogan echoed throughout Leningrad. Vsevolod Vishnevsky took it up: Death to cowards. Death to panicmongers. Death to rumor spreaders. To the tribunal with them. Discipline. Courage. Firmness.[4]

In the years to come there would be endless dispute over what stopped the Germans; and when they were halted.

Von Leeb had been under enormous pressure from Hitler to complete his assignment, to encircle Leningrad, to join forces with the Finns, to wipe out the Baltic Fleet. His forces were needed and needed badly on the Moscow front, where the Germans were closing in for the kill. But how could Hitler's grand strategy—the envelopment from the rear of Moscow, the enormous wheeling movement which was to carry Army Group Nord down behind the Russian lines at the very moment von Rundstedt attacked from the center—how could that be accomplished if von Leeb was still mired on the Leningrad front? It was a matter of timing, and time was running out. The nervous tension rose day by day. In the massive journal of Colonel General Halder the developments were noted as they were seen at the Führer's headquarters—and by himself.

Von Leeb had been instructed by Hitler September 5 to release his armor to the Moscow Group as quickly as possible. Because he was making good progress—or seemed to be—Halder with great reluctance let von Leeb keep the armor. He still had it on the twelfth. On the thirteenth Halder let him keep it "for the continuance of the drive." The Germans then thought Leningrad was almost in their grasp. Just a day or two and it would fall. Two days later, September 15, Halder was still hopeful. The assault was making good progress.

But two days later the Moscow front could wait no longer. The 6th Panzers were wheeled out of line. The shift of the main weight, the high-powered punch which had carried von Leeb up to the outskirts of Leningrad,

---

[4] A favorite slogan of these days was: "Leningrad is not afraid of death—death is afraid of Leningrad."

to Klinovsky House, had begun. The whole 41st Panzer Corps, the Hoeppner group, had been ordered to the Moscow front.

Zhukov had won. Leningrad had won. But no one knew this yet. Von Leeb was still trying frantically to grasp victory, to break into the city even though the parade of armor to the south was beginning. But success was doubtful.

Halder was gloomy. On the eighteenth he wrote in his journal:

> The ring around Leningrad has not yet been drawn as tightly as might be desired, and further progress after the departure of the 1st Panzers and 36th Motorized Division from the front is doubtful.
>
> There will be continuing drain on our forces before Leningrad where the enemy has concentrated large forces and great quantities of material and the situation will remain tight until such a time when Hunger takes effect as our ally.

That was the day the *Berliner Börsenzeitung* proclaimed: "The fate of Leningrad has been decided."

That was the day when von Leeb reported to the Supreme Command he had achieved a decisive breakthrough on the Leningrad front.

That was the day correspondents from Berlin wrote that the fall of Leningrad was expected within two weeks.

But already the pressure was beginning to lighten, although it did not seem that way at the front.[5]

In the early morning hours of September 21 Bychevsky sought out his old friend and reliable counselor, General P. P. Yevstigneyev, chief of intelligence for the Leningrad front. What was the real situation at the front? Was the pressure easing? Was it building up?

Late as was the hour and tense the moment, Bychevsky found Yevstigneyev quiet and peaceful. There was no shadow of concern on his face.

"What do you think, Pyotr Petrovich?" Bychevsky asked. "Are the Germans finally getting played out?"

Yevstigneyev considered the map on his desk for a moment. Then he raised his eyes.

"For the third day I've had reports from one intelligence group near Pskov," he said. "Lots of motorized infantry are moving from Leningrad toward Pskov. From there they are moving to Porkhov-Dno."

"Regrouping?"

"Possibly. Possibly. I got some confirmation of these data last night."

---

[5] A whole series of dates have been given by Soviet historians for the day the Leningrad front was stabilized. They range from September 18 (selected by only a few) to September 23, 25, 26, 29, and October 13. (Lieutenant General F. Lagunov, *Voyenno-Istoricheskii Zhurnal*, No. 12, December, 1964, p. 93.) Admiral Panteleyev heard from Leningrad on the evening of the nineteenth that the German attacks had been beaten off. (Panteleyev, *op. cit.*, p. 218.) "The front was stabilized September 19," says the authoritative *Leningrad v VOV* (p. 157).

Yevstigneyev fumbled through his papers. He looked like a scholar patiently studying some ancient Russian manuscript.

"I've reported to Zhukov," Yevstigneyev finally continued, "that all of this looks very much like a regrouping of troops away from Leningrad. From Gatchina the partisans also report that the Germans are loading tanks on railroad flatcars."

"That's fine!" Bychevsky explained.

"That's what I think," Yevstigneyev said. "I put together a report for Moscow. But Zhukov will have none of it. 'Provocations,' he says. 'That's what your agents are giving you. Find out who is behind this.' "

Yevstigneyev said he had heard from the Eighth Army on the Oranienbaum sector that they had recovered dead and wounded from the 291st and 58th German divisions. Zhukov was much interested because two days before these units had been in the line at Pulkovo.

Yevstigneyev concluded that the German frontal attack on Leningrad was, in fact, weakening.

Bychevsky observed that this was why Yevstigneyev seemed more relaxed.

"How can anyone relax at this time?" Yevstigneyev said. "It's just my professional manner."

That was the twenty-first. On the evening of the twenty-third Zhukov called in Yevstigneyev and asked whether he had sent his intelligence evaluation on to Moscow. Yevstigneyev had. Zhukov was relieved. Moscow had just reported the appearance of the 4th German Panzer group on the Kalinin front north of Moscow and wanted to know if Zhukov could confirm its departure from the Leningrad front.

The reports were true. The evidence from behind the lines and on the lines confirmed it. The Germans were beginning to pull troops out. Thank God, Colonel Bychevsky exclaimed to himself. Now he would not have to pull the plunger on the "hell machine," the central detonating fuse that would blow into the skies the Kirov works, the railroad viaducts, the bridges and all the great buildings of Leningrad.

A day or two later Yevstigneyev put together another report for Zhukov. He had information that the Germans had mobilized local residents to build permanent trenches and dugouts. In some instances the Russians were being shot after they had completed work on the installations. At Peterhof and other historic parks the Germans were chopping down the great pine and spruce groves for their command posts and heated quarters, installing stoves and moving in beds and good furniture.

"What is your conclusion?" Zhukov asked.

"It is evident that the tempo of the Fascist offensive is slowing down," Yevstigneyev said. "And even . . . it may be expected that the German Army is getting ready to winter on the outskirts of Leningrad."

He stopped there, biting his tongue as it was evident that Zhukov was still reluctant to jump to optimistic conclusions.

"The stupidest thing we can do," Zhukov snapped, "is to let the enemy dig in on our front where he wants to. All my orders about active defense and local attacks remain in force. In other words, we're the ones who will dig them into the earth. Is that clear?"

It was clear enough. So was the evidence of digging in. The word flew about Leningrad. Admiral I. S. Isakov went back to his quarters at the Astoria Hotel after listening to the exchange between Zhukov and Yevstigneyev. An elderly porter, long-bearded in traditional Russian style, asked, "Comrade Admiral, is it true what they say—that the Germans are digging in?"

"Maybe," the Admiral replied. "But if you want the truth, you'll have to ask Hitler's grandmother."

As he walked ahead, he heard the doorman saying to a policeman, "It's all clear. He means they are digging in but it's still a military secret."

But the evidence was almost too much for weary minds to comprehend.

Aleksandr Rozen had finally found the 70th Artillery, the outfit he had been with before the retreat into Leningrad. It was stationed now to the left of the Pulkovo lines near Shushary. He was asleep in a dugout with the regimental commander, Sergei Pudlutsky, when an aide awakened them. "Come quickly to the command post." The two men threw on their great-coats and went out. It was very early in the morning—a smoky, foggy morning. The smell of wet leaves was in the air. As they ran toward the command post, the sun broke fitfully through the clouds. At the command post they found a crowd gathered around the stereoptical observation instrument. Finally Rozen had his turn at the eyepiece. There swam into view German soldiers, apparently so close he could have touched them. They were hard at work with shovels and hammers, building dugouts and permanent trenches.

This was it. The offensive was over. The Germans were digging in for winter.

The twenty-first was the day at the Führer's headquarters that a special memorandum was submitted to Hitler by General Warlimont on the question of Leningrad. The frontal assault on the city, the Germans now knew, would not succeed. Indeed, it would not take place. What to do? Warlimont's thesis was headed: "On the Blockade of Leningrad."

> As a beginning we will blockade Leningrad (hermetically) and destroy the city, if possible, by artillery and air power. . . .
> When terror and hunger have done their work in the city, we can open a single gate and permit unarmed people to exit. . . .
> The rest of the "fortress garrison" can remain there through the winter. In the spring we will enter the city (not objecting if the Finns do this before us), sending all who remain alive into the depths of Russia, or take them as prisoners, raze Leningrad to the ground and turn the region north of the Neva over to Finland.

The next day a secret directive was issued, No. 1a 1601/41. It was headed: "The Future of the City of Petersburg."

It said:

1. The Führer has decided to raze the City of Petersburg from the face of the earth. After the defeat of Soviet Russia there will be not the slightest reason for the future existence of this large city. Finland has also advised us of its lack of interest in the further existence of this city immediately on her new frontiers.

2. The previous requests of the Navy for the preservation of the wharves, harbor and naval installations are known to the OKB. However, their fulfillment will not be possible in view of the general line with regard to Petersburg.

3. It is proposed to blockade the city closely and by means of artillery fire of all caliber and ceaseless bombardment from the air to raze it to the ground.

If this creates a situation in the city which produces calls for surrender, they will be refused. . . .[6]

The evidence of the men at the front was true. The Germans had halted. They had suffered terribly. Some Nazi divisions had lost up to two-thirds of their personnel.[7] But these were not to be compared to the ghost divisions which faced them—the Soviet outfits which had been wiped out, sometimes twice or three times over.

Zhukov had won the military battle of Leningrad. Within a week troops from Leningrad would be on their way to help stem the German tide before Moscow. The first of these troops, the 6th Guards Division, began to report to General D. D. Lelyushenko, hard pressed to hold his lines on the Mtsensk approaches to the capital, on October 5.

The next evening the telephone rang in Zhukov's offices in Smolny. It was Stalin. What did things look like in Leningrad? Zhukov said that the Nazi attacks had eased off, the Germans had gone over to the defense, and intelligence reports showed heavy movements of Nazi tanks and artillery away from Leningrad to the south, presumably in the Moscow direction.

Stalin received the report silently, then, after a pause, said that the Moscow situation was serious, particularly on the Western Front.

"Turn your command over to your deputy and come to Moscow," Stalin ordered.

Zhukov bade a hasty farewell to Zhdanov and his other Leningrad associates and telephoned General Fedyuninsky: "Have you forgotten that you're my deputy? Come immediately."

It was almost morning before Fedyuninsky got back to Smolny. "Take

[6] This order was reaffirmed in a secret decree of October 7, High Command Order No. 44 1675/41, in which the plans for the eradication of Leningrad were reaffirmed and it was again stated that the capitulation of neither Leningrad nor Moscow was to be accepted. (Barbashin, *op. cit.*, p. 77.)

[7] The German 1st, 58th and 93rd divisions had lost two-thirds of their personnel and material. The 121st and 269th were at about 40 percent strength. (Barbashin, *op. cit.*, p. 73.) The Russians estimated German casualties in the Leningrad campaign at 170,000 (*Ibid.*, p. 145); Pavlov says 190,000 to September 25 (Pavlov, *op. cit.*, 2nd edition, p. 28).

over command of the front," Zhukov said. "You know the situation. I've been called to Stavka."[8]

In the early morning hours Zhukov flew off to take over command of the Battle of Moscow. Now the real struggle would begin in Leningrad—the struggle with the allies whom the Germans had called to their side: Generals Hunger, Cold and Terror.

[8] Stalin's telephone call to Zhukov was produced by an incredible development. The attention of Stalin and his High Command had been riveted on the rapid Nazi drive toward Tula, southwest of Moscow. The night of October 4 and 5 had been the most alarming of the war. Communications between the Western Front and the Kremlin had been broken and Stalin had no notion of what was happening. As early as 9 A.M. on October 5 word came of a Nazi breakthrough on the central front, a scant hundred miles west of Moscow, toward Mozhaisk. The report first was dismissed as the product of "panic." At noon, however, a Soviet reconnaissance plane spotted a fifteen-mile-long Nazi armored column advancing rapidly on the Spas-Demensk highway toward Yukhnov. No one in Moscow could believe the Germans were so close, and there was no Soviet force to bar their sweep into the city. Two more reconnaissance planes were sent out. Only after each verified the sighting was the news reported to Stalin. His immediate order was to throw together a scratch force to hold up the Germans for five to seven days while reserves were brought up. Stalin then assembled his top echelon including Police Chief Beria. Beria called the reports a "provocation." He said his agents at the front, the so-called "special department," had reported nothing about a breakthrough. When others insisted that the air reports were correct, he responded with the words "Very well," pronounced with special emphasis. A short time later he summoned the responsible air officer, Colonel N. A. Sbytov, and put him in the hands of his chief of military counterintelligence, V. S. Abakumov, who threatened to turn Sbytov and the reconnaissance fliers over to a field tribunal for execution. The intelligence, however, was correct. It was in this crisis, with the Moscow line being held by infantry and artillery cadets and scattered forces taken from headquarters companies, that Stalin called in Zhukov. (K. F. Telegin, *Voprosy Istorii KPSS*, No. 9, September, 1966, pp. 102 *et seq.*) Fedyuninsky mistakenly dates this talk as of October 10. (Fedyuninsky, *Podnyatye Po Tvevoge*, Moscow, 1964, p. 60.) Zhukov in three versions says he turned over command to his Chief of Staff, General M. S. Khozin. In fact, the formal transfer of command from Zhukov to Fedyuninsky is dated October 10, but Zhukov had arrived in Moscow October 7. Khozin replaced Fedyuninsky as commander October 26, 1941. (Zhukov, *Voyenno-Istoricheskii Zhurnal*, No. 8, August, 1966, p. 56; A. M. Samsonov, *Proval Gitlerovskogo Nastupleniya na Moskvu*, Moscow, 1966, p. 18; A. A. Dobrodomov, *Bitva Za Moskvu*, Moscow, 1966, p. 56; Barbashin, *op. cit.*, p. 582.) K. F. Telegin, Political Commissar for the Moscow Military District, reports that Zhukov was called to Moscow on the evening of October 6. Zhukov says he arrived in Moscow on the evening of October 7 and conferred immediately with Stalin, who was ill with the grippe but working alone in his office. On October 10 Zhukov was named to command the Western Front. (K. F. Telegin, *Voprosy Istorii KPSS*, No. 9, September, 1966, p. 104; Zhukov in *Bitva Za Moskvu*, 2nd edition, Moscow, 1968, p. 64.)

34 . *The King's Fortress*

THE MORNING OF SEPTEMBER 23 DAWNED CLEAR, BRIGHT and crisp on the little island of Kotlin. Kotlin, a mile and three-quarters long by a half-mile wide, was better known as Kronstadt—home of the Baltic Fleet, the naval bastion of Leningrad, the "King's Fortress" or Kronstadt as Peter the Great christened it in 1710.

Today as on every day for three months Kronstadt awoke to war, grim, menacing, close. There was war all about the little island—war five miles across the sound on the Oranienbaum shore where naval guns at Krasnaya Gorka and Seraya Loshad were holding the Germans back, war in the anchorage where the great warships of the fleet poured molten lead and steel into the Nazi lines, war in the skies overhead where the German planes were attacking in greater and greater strength, war in the old streets and buildings of the naval town where German siege shells smashed down like triphammers.

That was the kind of morning it was. Admiral Panteleyev, a thoughtful man with a deep love of nature, noted in his diary that it was a "remarkably quiet, sunny morning in golden autumn." Long after, he was puzzled why he had used those words. But everything had become relative by that time.

He noticed that the German artillery fire seemed heavier than usual. The Germans were aiming for the naval factory and the ships in the anchorage. At the moment there was no air alert on, and a smoke screen had been laid to protect the ships and naval installations from the German fire.

The Baltic Fleet had suffered in its terrible exodus from Tallinn, but it was still a powerful force. Standing that day in the road at Kronstadt and in the Leningrad Harbor and the Neva were 2 battleships, 2 cruisers, 13 destroyers, 12 gunboats, 42 submarines, 6 coastal defense ships, 9 armed cutters, 68 trawlers and mine layers, 38 torpedo boats and 134 miscellaneous naval craft. The fleet had at its disposal 286 planes. Its coastal and shore batteries counted 400 guns. Before the year was over it would provide 83,746 sailors for shore combat, most of them in Leningrad. It was not a force to be trifled with.

Hitler had ordered the Baltic Fleet destroyed and Kronstadt razed. Within the week Nazi planes had showered the fortress and the fleet with leaflets saying: "Leningrad to the ground! Kronstadt to the sea!"

Hitler had launched his naval war in the east with one aim only: the extinction of the Baltic Fleet. Now he was not going to let it slip through his fingers. Even before the war Hitler told his commanders in May, 1941, that if the Soviet warships sought to intern themselves in Sweden the Nazi Army must prevent it. If the warships reached Swedish waters, Germany would demand that the Swedes surrender them.

Plan Barbarossa contained a special supplement called Warzburg. Under this, between June 10 and 20 the Germans had laid down a thick barrier of mines designed to keep the Baltic Fleet in Russian waters so it could be destroyed at leisure.

The Baltic Fleet, except for its submarines, had not moved from the Gulf of Finland, and Plan Warzburg had not effected its destruction. A new plan called Valkyrie was set afoot to destroy the main strength of the Baltic Fleet when it was driven out of Tallinn. This, too, had failed, although the Soviet losses at Tallinn were heavy.

Now with the Nazi ring being drawn close around Leningrad Hitler again feared that the Baltic Fleet might escape to Sweden. Two large naval forces had been concentrated by the Germans off the Aland Islands and at Libau. They were to destroy the Baltic Fleet if it tried to break out. The battleships *Tirpitz* and *Admiral Scheer*, the light cruisers *Nürnberg* and *Köln* and some smaller craft stood near the Aland Islands. At Libau were the cruisers *Emden* and *Leipzig*.

On September 6 Hitler issued Order No. 35, which said:

"In cooperation with the Finns mine barriers and artillery fire must be employed to blockade Kronstadt and prevent the fleet from entering the Baltic Sea."

The net was tight. But the Baltic Fleet was hardly passive. It mustered 338 large guns, either on warships, in coastal batteries or mounted on railroad carriages. These were guns of calibers of 100 or more. Among them were 78 guns of calibers from 180 to 406. The biggest was a 406-mm railroad cannon with a range of 45.6 kilometers (28 miles). It fired a shell weighing 1,108 kilograms (approximately 2,440 pounds).[1] The second largest was a 356-mm gun, also a railroad weapon. It fired 31.2 kilometers with a shell of 747.8 kilos. There was limited ammunition for these guns, and they were used rarely. The old battleship *Marat* had 305-mm guns in its main battery. They fired 29.4 kilometers and used 470.9-kilo shells. The work horses of the Baltic Fleet batteries were 108-mm, 132-mm and 130-mm guns with ranges of 37.8 to 25.5 kilometers.

The naval batteries had been integrated into the Leningrad defense system

---

[1] To convert figures from the metric system: 1 kilometer = .62137 mile; 1 kilogram = 2.2046 pounds.

September 4 by Vice Admiral I. I. Gren under plans which had been worked out by the Naval Commissar, Admiral Nikolai Kuznetsov, and the Army Artillery Marshal N. N. Voronov in early September.

Admiral Gren was one of the navy's leading artillery specialists. Like most artillery men he had a tin ear. Once he was attending a meeting at which Stalin savagely criticized the naval artillery plans. He sat silent, apparently unmoved by Stalin's words. Stalin was curious about this and asked who he was. Admiral Kuznetsov explained he had done much to develop Soviet naval gun power.

"In that case Comrade Gren should be promoted," said Stalin.

"At your service," responded Gren immediately.

Admiral Gren had set up his command post ashore and divided the fleet into three groups. The first, the Neva group, consisted of smaller craft— gunboats, mine sweepers, smaller destroyers. They were stationed in the Neva from Smolny east to the Izhorsk region. The second detachment, the Leningrad group, included the cruiser *October Revolution* (the former *Petropavlovsk), stationed at the coal wharves, the cruiser Maxim Gorky,* near the grain elevator, and some smaller warships scattered about the commercial docks. The third group was at the Kronstadt-Oranienbaum anchorage. This included the battleship *Marat* posted across from Strelna, the cruiser *Kirov* at Kronstadt, and a strong collection of other cruisers.

Since August 30 the naval guns had been defending Leningrad. That day the Neva squadron went into action against advancing Nazis in the Ivanov-skoye region of the river.

The next day heavy fleet batteries opened up at 1:45 P.M. against the Germans, probably in the Gatchina area. The Neva flotilla and the heavy Rzhevka polygon answered 28 calls for artillery fire and launched 340 shells from their 130-to-406-mm guns. The next day the 12-inch guns of the Krasnaya Gorka battery on the Oranienbaum plateau went into action against German armor.

Many naval guns were demounted and put to use on land. Two old 130-mm nine- and ten-gun batteries from the forty-year-old crusier *Aurora*, whose guns fired blanks on the Winter Palace that evening in November, 1917, and frightened the remaining Kerensky ministers into surrendering to Lenin's Bolsheviks, were placed in position on the Pulkovo Heights. Sixteen 130-mm two-gun railroad batteries went into action in late August. Another 55 batteries had been set up before the end of September, including 2 180-mm gun positions and 18 120-mm batteries equipped with guns demounted from warships.

The harder the battle raged, the stronger the naval guns resounded. When the Nazis broke through Krasnoye Selo and into Ligovo, the heavy guns of the cruisers *Gorky* and *Petropavlovsk* poured in their shells. The concentration of naval railroad artillery was so heavy in the Gatchina area that five batteries—Nos. 20, 21, 22, 23 and 24—fell into encirclement. Firing at open range against German tanks, all five fought their way back to the Soviet lines.

Battery No. 11, equipped with a 356-mm gun, firing a 1,500-pound shell, got off 568 rounds between September 9 and 25, knocking out 35 tanks, 12 artillery installations, a battalion of Nazi infantry and a train loaded with German troops and equipment. The Kronstadt guns laid down 358 barrages in September, delivering 9,368 shells.

By August 20 the navy had put into action 170 shore batteries, including 48 railroad guns. Six batteries were formed around 13 large guns taken out of the experimental naval artillery park. Leningrad factories worked twenty-four-hour shifts to complete heavy railroad carriages for new naval mountings. Battery No. 1109 was mounted on rails August 25 and at 11 A.M., August 26, went into action. Twenty-nine new railroad batteries with 70 guns were put into operation between August 1, 1941, and February 15, 1942, as well as 61 stationary batteries with 176 guns.

Almost half of the navy's fire power was concentrated along the Neva, backing up the sagging lines just south of the Leningrad city line.

Under intense naval bombardment, the Nazis began to throw in air power in an effort to knock out the fleet guns. Fleet air protection was weak. The fleet air fighter arm and its AA guns had been put under the Leningrad Air Defense Command. Admiral Tributs complained repeatedly that the warships strung out from the upper Neva to Kronstadt were poorly protected. The complaints went unheeded. The Leningrad Command was too busy. The truth was that Kronstadt and the warships had virtually no protection. So long as the Luftwaffe left the warships alone everything was fine.

Now trouble was beginning. For days Kronstadt had watched Leningrad being attacked. The horizon was red each night with the flames. The sound of the bombing, the rattle of the guns echoed over the narrow water barrier. Panteleyev watched the fires of September 8 from the Kronstadt ARP command post. Admiral Drozd watched from his command on the cruiser *Kirov*. The fleet and its shore batteries rained shells all night long on the Germans south of Peterhof and near Krasnoye Selo. By the thirteenth the naval arsenals began to run short of shells, so heavy was the rate of fire. But the need was no less. The guns fired on.

But Kronstadt's position was growing more difficult. The Germans now had land batteries at Ligovo, Strelna and New Peterhof. They began to shell the fortress and particularly the narrow water lane between Kronstadt and Oranienbaum.

Trouble for the fleet was piling up. The Nazis attacked the isolated naval garrisons on the Moonzund Peninsula on September 11 and Ösel Island off the Estonian coast on September 13. The garrisons were fighting desperately but were being driven back to Dagö Island.[2] The Baltic Fleet was too deeply

---

[2] They held out there until October 22, when they were evacuated to the Hangö base in Finland. (Achkasov, *op. cit.*, pp. 165 *et seq.*) The date of October 19 is given by Ad-

engaged to help. The garrisons had to fight it out for themselves.

Meanwhile, the fleet was given emergency orders by Zhukov to transfer two broken divisions of the dwindling Eighth Army from the Oranienbaum *place d'armes* to the main Leningrad front. The fleet commanders desperately tried to carry out the movement before the Germans brought Oranienbaum port under fire. There were rumors that the German fleet was on the move (it was; it had come out to prevent a suicide dash by the Baltic Fleet), and submarines were dispatched on intelligence missions. The Leningrad lines needed more and more support. The destroyer leader *Leningrad* and three mine layers were sent into the Neva. Four gunboats and the battleship *October Revolution* were positioned off Peterhof in the Sea Canal. So many sailors had been formed into marine detachments for shore duty (sixteen brigades) that the complements of ships afloat were down to one-third their normal rating.

And now the Germans began to find the range of the Baltic warships. On the sixteenth the first 150-mm shells hit the *Marat* and the *Petropavlovsk*, both stationed in the Sea Canal. The *Marat* took a shell through its deck. A 120-mm gun was knocked out and several sailors were killed or wounded. On the eighteenth the Germans concentrated on the *Maxim Gorky* and the *Petropavlovsk*. The *Gorky* was hit, but not seriously. The *Petropavlovsk*, unfinished and unable to move because its engines were not operative, was hit eight times and settled to the bottom.

On the twenty-first the Luftwaffe attacked the fleet. They hit the old battleship *October Revolution*, which was pounding Ligovo from the Sea Canal with its 12-inch guns. Panteleyev heard the explosion and saw the old ship enveloped in smoke and flames. Admiral Tributs ordered him to investigate what had happened. Panteleyev found a fire raging in the forecastle of the *October Revolution*, but it was continuing to fight. Control had not been lost, neither had power. The commander, Vice Admiral Mikhail Moskalenko, said that a flight of bombers had suddenly swooped out of the clouds and three bombs had hit the foredeck. Within the hour the battleship was being towed by a sea tug into the Kronstadt yards for repairs.

But this was only the beginning.

Life on Kronstadt was changing. On September 17 Vsevolod Vishnevsky had noted in his diary:

Saw the film *Masquerade*. Rain. Dark night. Went to bed at 2 A.M.

---

miral Kuznetsov for this move. (*Voprosy Istorii*, No. 8, August, 1965, p. 114). The Hangö garrison was gradually withdrawn to Kronstadt and Leningrad from late October to early December. The evacuation order was issued October 26, and the first 4,000 men arrived at Kronstadt November 4. In all, 16,000 men were removed, and the operation was completed by December 3. There were considerable losses of men and ships, due largely to magnetic mines. At the same time a small garrison of about 1,000 men was removed from the island of Hogland — an action which Admiral Panteleyev characterized as an "obvious mistake." (Panteleyev, *op. cit.*, pp. 266–272).

On the eighteenth he wrote:

> Worked in the library until 5:30 . . . 9 o'clock—concert. Cold wind from the north, fires at Peterhof.

On the nineteenth:

> Sunny day. Old woman at the gate said of the German planes, "They're black like crows." Heavy shelling of Kronstadt.

On the twentieth:

> Talk about last night's bomb. It was the first bombing in the center of Kronstadt since the war started. Leningrad doesn't answer on the direct telephone—for some reason.

And now on the twenty-first:

> Again air attacks on the ships and the center of Kronstadt. Base headquarters rocks. Firing. Bombs in the anchorage, attacks on our ships, explosions in the port . . . Another alarm . . . more attacks. Long firing . . .

The water system was knocked out. The electricity was cut. The hospital was hit. The fifth raid of the day was just finishing at 10 P.M. Tens of thousands of rounds had been fired by the antiaircraft guns. Five or six Nazi planes were claimed.[3] That night Vishnevsky put himself to sleep reading a cowboy-and-Indian story by Mayne Reid.

The Germans used 180 planes that day. Only five fighters were available to defend Kronstadt. Admiral Tributs angrily demanded better protection from the Leningrad Command. Nothing, they said, could be done.

Panteleyev was up most of the night of the 21st-22nd. The attacks had badly damaged the port city. Repair crews were trying to put the naval factory in order. Everyone was deadly tired. There had been many casualties. One young commander returned from his ship to find his house in ruins, his wife dead and two babies lying wounded in the wreckage.

It grew colder toward dawn. Panteleyev could see the flicker of flames toward Peterhof and along the southern borders of Leningrad. The heavy fleet guns were still firing, slowly, methodically. At 5:15 A.M. there was a new air alarm. The day dawned quiet and clear. Tributs ordered everyone alerted for air attacks—all the AA batteries and the tiny fighter force stationed on the Field of Bulls. At 8 A.M. the battleship *Marat* and the cruiser *Kirov* opened up against the Germans on the northern mainland. The Germans replied. Great columns of water flew up from the German shells falling in the harbor beside Petrovsky Park. The water splashed down on the linden trees and over the bronze figure of Peter the Great. These were heavy German guns, and they were firing at the ships anchored off Kronstadt and at the naval factory. Some shells fell in the naval city.

---

[3] Vishnevsky, *op. cit.*, Vol. 3, pp. 132 *et seq.* Panteleyev claims 10 (*op. cit.*, p. 227).

At 2 P.M. Vishnevsky went to lunch and then to the library. As usual he was poring over the history of past wars. This time it was the White General Yudenich and his unsuccessful attack on Petrograd. He had hardly sat down to read in the gloomy old reading room when the air alert sounded again. It was three o'clock. The AA guns opened on Nazi bombers attacking the naval factory and the warships in the Sea Canal. Bombs fell on one of the floating bases. When the all-clear sounded, a dangerous and difficult task began. Delayed-action bombs had fallen. They had to be found and de-activated. No bombs had yet hit fleet headquarters, but it was decided to move into the ARP underground headquarters on the edge of the town. The commanders were reluctant to leave the handsome white building with its magnificent view of the harbor and the shore—a building easily visible to the Germans at Peterhof. But the move was made. The next day the first shells fell on the staff headquarters.[4]

Vice Admiral Drozd was wounded during the twenty-second but not seriously. That night Vishnevsky noted in his journal:

Yesterday in the flights over Kronstadt there were 15, 40, 15 and 50 planes. It is clear that the enemy, meeting strong attacks from Kronstadt and the Baltic Fleet, is attempting to paralyze us. What next?

So it was that on the twenty-third the sun rose on a world which Pante-leyev somehow found fresh, remarkably quiet, sunny, the air bracing—a beautiful autumn day.

Vice Admiral Gren telephoned from Leningrad, as he did every morning, to report on the fleet batteries. He was in a good mood. The Germans had been firing heavily on the port area and on the cruiser *Maxim Gorky*. There had already been an air alert. It looked like a big day in the air. But the best news was that the front seemed to be stabilizing. The Germans had learned to respect the heavy fleet batteries.

Panteleyev reported this to Tributs, who was concerned about the little fighter force at the Field of Bulls. He sent Panteleyev to see how they were making out. The road to the field was very poor. Some shells fell, and as Panteleyev neared the field he saw the fighters taking off, one after another, all six of them. Another air raid.

A moment later the Germans appeared, flying straight out of the sun. They began bombing immediately—attacking the naval hospital and the naval factory. There were forty planes in the attack, one group after another. Panteleyev hurried back to the naval city. The streets were empty except for AA crews, first-aid detachments and military trucks. Everything looked grim and businesslike. At 11 A.M. when the guns began again, Panteleyev was in Petrovsky Park. It was the biggest raid yet. The guns fired crazily, and

[4] Vice Admiral Smirnov is highly critical of Admiral Tributs for his failure to pro-vide a secure bomb shelter for fleet headquarters before the outbreak of war. (Smirnov, *op. cit.*, p. 64.)

the ground shook under the explosions. He was standing near the Peter the Great statue under a large lime tree whose yellowed leaves shook with the explosions. To his amazement three or four youngsters were high in the tree watching the attack. He tried to get them down. They wouldn't come. Too dangerous, they said. Panteleyev looked at the statue of Peter facing the sea, his bronze eyes steady. On the fundament was inscribed: "To defend the fleet and its base to the last of life and strength is the highest duty."

Panteleyev could see a dozen JU-88's circling lazily over the battleship *Marat,* which stood in the main channel not far off Kronstadt. The bombs burst one ofter another . . . explosion . . . explosion . . . burst of flame.

Suddenly the whole foremast of the ship with its crossbars, heavy equipment, crosswalks, filled with scurrying sailors in their white uniforms, slipped away from the body of the *Marat* and slowly, slowly, slithered sideways into the water, sinking with an enormous explosion. The lower mast then rose up lazily, and the forward gun tower with its three 12-inch guns broke off and fell into the sea. The whole nose of the battleship vanished, including its first funnel. Panteleyev saw hundreds of sailors in the water. He heard their cries, louder than the whine of the AA shells.

He ordered all ambulance squads and every available boat, cutter and sloop to the aid of the *Marat.* The remainder of the ship, as if cut through by a knife, minus the forward part as far as the second tower, remained afloat. The ship settled to the bottom, but three of its towers remained intact.

Panteleyev made his way by cutter to the stricken battleship. He found its deck cleared and equipment stowed away. Only when he came to the second tower did he suddenly discover himself at the edge of the boat. Beyond this the warship simply had vanished. More than two hundred sailors, including Captain Ivanov, had been killed or wounded. Among the dead was Johann Zeltser, editor of the *Marat* newspaper and a Leningrad writer. He commanded the AA battery on the forward deck. A few days earlier he had written his wife Clara in Leningrad: "Perhaps I won't see you again. You can be sure I won't give my life cheaply. While I am conscious, I'll fight on. How I hate them! . . . I've sent you all the money I have. . . . You'll need it to bring up our children. I kiss you strongly, strongly—you and the children. . . ."

Within a matter of days the second, third and fourth gun towers of the *Marat* had been put back into action. But the damage at Kronstadt was not easy to cope with. Enormous craters scarred the streets. There were hunks of metal and piping where the bombs had smashed the mains. Here and there torrents of water gushed up like fountains. Flame and smoke covered the naval hospital and the naval factory. The bombing went on. The work went on. All through the night. It was long after midnight when Admiral Tributs called in the Air Defense Command. He wanted to know why the Nazi bombers had appeared over the fleet almost immediately after the air alert. The explanation was simple but tragic. The Germans had taken off from old Soviet fields nearby. They had flown first to Peterhof, then swiftly reversed course and appeared over Kronstadt in a minute or two. There had been 272 planes over Kronstadt that day. The damage to the hospital and naval works was grave. The mine layer *Oka* had been sunk. So had the *Grozny*. Two 200-pound bombs hit the *Kirov*. The *Minsk* had been sunk on a shallow footing. A transport and a submarine in drydock had been wrecked.

But the naval guns had not been halted. They went on firing. Some time during the night Panteleyev talked with Gren in Leningrad.

"Why do I see the sky aglow over Leningrad again?" Panteleyev asked.

"This was a record day," Gren replied. "There were eleven air alerts. One of them lasted seven hours. The Gostiny Dvor has been destroyed. But the warships haven't been damaged."

It was, it seemed clear, the worst day of the German air attack on Leningrad and on Kronstadt.

Aleksandr Shtein thought it was the culminating day of the German assault. The last two days had been a scene from Dante. He found the notebook of a German corporal, Hermann Fuchs, who had been killed in the fighting around Ligovo. It was brought back by a Soviet scout. In it he read:

> Yesterday and today here outside Petersburg it has been hell again. Yesterday we attacked a giant line of fortifications. Artillery fired the whole day without cease. The fire was so heavy you couldn't make out the bursts. Now again the hell has begun. In the harbor there are still one battleship and some cruisers. It is hard to describe the craters which their shells make. One burst 200 meters from me. I can say that I was thrown two meters into the air. I wanted to believe—and couldn't believe—that I was whole and not hurt. Because I could see the whole area covered with craters I knew that I was alive. All around me rolled parts of bodies—here a hand, there a leg, there a head.

During the endless raids of the afternoon and evening of September 23 Vishnevsky wandered into the dining hall of the Political Administration. It was empty. There was a bowl of kasha untouched on the table and an unopened bottle. The waitress looked at him with glazed eyes and said, "I don't want to die. I want to live. I have a daughter at home."

As Vishnevsky lay, trying to sleep, he could hear the bombs still falling, the guns still firing. The Baltic Fleet was still in action. It had gone through the worst day of the war, but it had not been destroyed. Hitler's orders to raze Kronstadt to the water had not been carried out. And the guns fired on.

Before he opened Mayne Reid and started to read once again, Vishnevsky noted in his diary: "There are some tendencies toward stabilizing the front."

35 . *Deus Conservat Omnia*

ABOVE THE IRON GATES OF THE SHEREMETYEV PALACE ON
the Fontanka embankment where Anna Akhmatova lived, the legend was
inscribed on an old coat of arms: *"Deus Conservat Omnia."* From her
window she looked out upon the palace courtyard, guarded by a great
maple whose branches reached toward her, rustling nervously through the
long winters and gently stirring during the soft daylight of the white nights.
Now the maple's scarlet and golden leaves had fallen, spattering the pavement with pastels that gradually turned to mud in the autumn rains. Now
it seemed to Anna Akhmatova that the naked black branches of the maple
reached out to her more urgently, calling to her, telling her to stay, to stay
in Petersburg.

Anna Akhmatova was the queen of Russian poetry. She was, perhaps, the
queen of Leningrad. Surely no one had more of the city in her life, in her
blood, in her experience—its fears, its hopes, its tragedies, its genius. She
was not Petersburg-born. But her parents had brought her to the northern
capital, to the gentle pleasure gardens of Tsarskoye Selo (Pushkin), when
she was a child. Her first memories were of "the green damp magnificence of
the parks, the meadows where my nurse used to take me for a walk, the
hippodrome where little dappled horses galloped, the old railroad station."
There she grew up, breathing the air of poets—of Pushkin, of Lermontov,
of Derzhavin, of Nekrasov, of Shelley. The princess, the queen-to-be—none
so mad, none so gay, so feminine, so passionate, so lyric, so romantic, so
urgent, so madcap—so Russian.

Before she was five she spoke French. She went to a girls' school, studied
law, studied literature, raced to Paris, fell in love with Modigliani (she didn't
know he was a genius, but she knew he had "a head like Antonius and eyes
that flashed gold"). She saw the Imperial Ballet of Diaghilev in its Paris
triumph. She saw Venice, Rome, Florence. She married a poet, the love of
her schoolgirl days in Tsarskoye, Nikolai Gumilev, a dark, brilliant, difficult
man. With him she founded a new school of poetry, a neoclassical movement

which they called Acmeism. Everything was possible, everything experienced. Her life was a poem of mirrored images, of galloping sleighs in white snows, of warm summer evenings in leafy parks, of boudoirs, of boulevards, of Paris, of golden stars. Of love. Of tragedy. These were, she later understood, the luminous lighthearted days, the hour before dawn. She did not know that shadows soon would pass at her window, terrifying, hiding behind lamp posts, changing the gold to drossy brass.

But tragedy's hand clutched early at her life. She saw it overhanging Petrograd in the war of the Kaiser and the Czar. She saw the "black cloud over mournful Russia." She saw her Petrograd transformed from a northern Venice to a "granite city of glory and misfortune." By the end of World War I Gumilev brought anguish and divorce to her. The tragedy deepened when he faced a Bolshevik firing squad in 1921 and was shot as a White Guard conspirator. The golden years of Tsarskoye Selo had ended. Now came the iron years of the Revolution's mills, grinding ever more harshly until the terror of Stalin's police closed in and swept away her son, Lev.

For seventeen months she stood with the other women in the prison lines of Leningrad, waiting for word of her son's fate, bringing him food, bringing him packages. Once a woman next in line, a woman whose lips were blue with cold or fear, asked her, "And this—can you write about it?"

"Yes," Anna Akhmatova replied, "I can."

The woman smiled a strange and secret smile.

Anna Akhmatova did, finally, write about those days:

> Would you like to see yourself now, you girl so full of
> laughter?
> The favorite of her friends,
> The gay sinner of Tsarskoye Selo?
> Would you like to see what's happened to your life?
> At the end of a queue of three hundred,
> You stand outside Kresty Prison,
> And your hot tears are burning holes in the New Year's ice.

By this time her son had been cast into exile, there to remain until Stalin's death in 1953.

In this September of 1941 Anna Akhmatova's life was taking another turn. She was leaving Petersburg, Petrograd, Leningrad. September was ending and she had to go, orders of the City Party. The plane—one of the few—was waiting. Already she had moved from the palace on the Fontanka to the building at No. 9 Griboyedov where so many writers had their home. Pavel Luknitsky dropped in to say good-bye. He found her ill and weak. She emerged from the dark little porter's house wearing a heavy coat and they talked together on a bench. Anna Akhmatova told how she had been sitting in a slit trench outside the Sheremetyev Palace during a raid. She was holding a youngster in her arms when she heard the "dragon's shriek" of falling bombs and then a "tremendous din, a crackle and a crunch." Three times the walls of the trench quivered and then grew quiet. How right it was, she said, that in their ancient myths the earth was always the mother, always indestructible. Only the earth could shrug at the terrors of bombardment. The first of the bombs fell next door in the former Catherine Institute, now a hospital. It did not explode. But two exploded in the Sheremetyev gardens, one at the corner of Zhukovsky and Liteiny and one in the house where the writer Nikolai Chukovsky lived. Fortunately he was at the front.

Anna Akhmatova confessed that the explosions left her crushed and feeble. A feeling of terror came over her as she looked at the women with their children wearily waiting in the bomb shelter during the raids—terror for what might happen to them, for what fate held.

The terror for the children of Leningrad did not leave her. From the desert oasis of Tashkent, to which she was evacuated in early October, she wrote in memory of Valya Smirnov, a little boy whom she might have held in her arms, a little boy who was killed by a German bomb:

> Knock on my door with your little fist and I'll open it. . . .
> I did not hear you moan.
> Bring me a little maple twig
> Or simply a handful of grass,
> As you brought last spring.
> And bring a handful of cold, pure Neva water
> And I'll wash away the traces of blood
> From your little·golden head. . . .

Deus Conservat Omnia. . . .
It was a time for God to come to the aid of the city beside the gray waters of the Neva. But He did not seem to hear. He did not hear the crunch of the bombs, the bark of the guns, the cries of the children with golden hair.

A. M. Dreving was on the rooftop of Leningrad's Public Library one late September day, a sunny day, a warm day. He stood with his fellow ARP workers when the guns began to go, scattering over the roof steel slivers of shrapnel. He watched a German plane sweeping up toward the library from the Summer Gardens. Bombs began to fall. One near the circus, another close to the Nevsky near Malaya Sadovaya. The plane headed straight for the library. He knew they usually carried four bombs. Would it hit the library? It did not. It fell a short distance away in the Catherine Gardens. Possibly it was one of the cluster which dropped about Anna Akhmatova as she sat in the slit trench with the little boy.

The big Erisman Hospital, of which Vera Inber's husband was the director, was located in what Leningraders called the "deep rear," Aptekarsky Island, one of the more remote parts of the city, lying on the north side of the Neva.

With the incendiaries the Germans dropped leaflets: "For the house-warning." Vera Inber worried because the grenadiers' barracks next to the hospital was used both by medical students as a dormitory and by the military as a storehouse for shells and ammunition. If these were touched off, there would be a dreadful tragedy. The shells were loaded and unloaded from freight trucks on the street outside or from barges in the Karpovka Creek. Beside the loading platform stood an AA battery. Unpleasant neighbors for a large hospital, overflowing with wounded, many of them critically hurt.

On a late September morning, just after ten o'clock, the air alert having just sounded, an enormous bomb fell beside the hospital's polyclinic, next to a fountain filled with cast-iron sculpture. It did not explode.

All day a sappers' detachment labored to defuse it. When the day ended, they had not yet succeeded. Streetcar traffic in the area was halted. The streets were cleared and the hospital surrounded by guards. The lying-in ward, adjacent to the bomb, was moved to other quarters.

It struck Vera Inber as curious that she had hardly felt the shock when the bomb struck the earth. It had seemed for a moment that someone had closed a heavy door at a distance. The building shook—nothing else.

The next day the sappers still worked on the bomb. Vera Inber sat with the wounded during a raid. She tried to read to them. No one was interested. The wounded were very nervous, helpless, trapped. They knew that if a bomb fell they could not save themselves.

On the third day the bomb still lay in the garden, sinking further into the earth. But the fuse had been taken off.

On the fifth day the bomb still lay there, and almost everyone in Leningrad had heard about it. Luknitsky knew it was only one of many delayed-action bombs which had been dropped and with which the demolition squads labored in sweat and danger. Yevgeniya Vasyutina heard a wild rumor that the great bomb had been filled with granulated sugar. It was said nine out of twelve bombs did not explode and that inside there were notes which read: "Save us if you can." She thought this was nonsense, and later she heard the truth—that the Erisman bomb weighed more than a ton and had penetrated nearly fifteen feet into the earth. No sugar.

Not until October 4 was the bomb hoisted out of the ground. Vera Inber and her husband went to see it—a monstrous thing painted blue with yellow speckles, a spiky snout and a blunt end. The huge object was carted off to a display of German war trophies. For days Vera Inber could not get it out of her mind. Finally she wrote a few lines about it for her poem "Pulkovo Meridian."

The atmosphere in the city grew more grim. Private telephone service had been disconnected; only public phone booths still worked. When Vera Inber heard a young woman's fresh voice say; "Until the end of the war the telephone is being disconnected," she wanted to say something, to protest, but it was useless. When she picked up the phone, it was silent and dead. Till the end of the war. Who knew when that might be?

Rumors . . . rumors . . . rumors . . . They grew with the disconnecting of the telephones. The government had cut off the phones because it feared the people, or to keep the enemy from spreading more rumors—that was the rumor. And the others: that all the house registers had been burned for fear they might fall into the hands of the Germans; that the police had destroyed their own records lest they be used against them; that the police had hidden their civilian clothes in cupboards, ready to try a quick getaway if worse came to worst.

There were hopeful rumors: that the Finns were being pushed back at Beloostrov and Sestroretsk; that Mga and Pushkin had been recaptured; that the troops on the northern bank of the Neva had broken the circle and made contact with a shock group pushing out from Volkhov. Unfortunately, as Luknitsky knew, when his photographer friend, he of the massive food reserve, passed on this news, none of it was true.

He knew that efforts were being made to break the encirclement—or would be. But he knew of no successes. What he did know was that there were spies in the city who spread false reports. He knew there were residents who were potential collaborators, who were ready to welcome the Germans.

There was, for instance, the friend of Yelena Skryabina's who announced he was confident that the Germans would break into the city—if not that day, then surely the next. "And," he concluded, "in any case if my expectations are not fulfilled, I have this." He drew a small revolver from his pocket. Madame Skryabina knew her friend was not alone, that there were many who awaited the Germans with impatience as "saviors."

It was not only Leningrad and its fate, Leningrad and its trials and hardships, which affected people's morale. It was the news from the other fronts. The fall of Kiev had been a terrible blow. Kiev was the mother of Russian cities, the founding capital.

The day that Kiev fell Vera Inber was sitting in a shelter with the correspondent, Anatoly Tarasenkov. He took from his pocket a letter he had just gotten from his wife in Moscow. She told how Marina Tsvetayeva, ill, suffering, evacuated to a miserable village in the Urals, separated from her son, had hanged herself, one more poet's life sacrificed to the Russian god of tragedy. It told of the death of their friend Margerita Aliger's husband. Outside, the noise of the guns and the bombs went on.

As the tempo of the German attack slackened at Leningrad, the storm rose around Moscow. Moscow fought for its life. Luknitsky felt that Moscow, like Leningrad, would hold out. He did not know why, but he felt it. Yet the news from Moscow was shocking. There had been panic. Probably not as frantic as Kochetov described it. As Kochetov told the story, thousands of little and middle-rank bureaucrats tried to flee the capital. They rushed out of Moscow along the highway toward the rear, toward Gorky. Workers detachments guarding the outskirts of the city intercepted them and pushed their automobiles into the canals. "This is hard to believe," Kochetov piously

added, "because we know of nothing like this happening here in Leningrad."
Vishnevsky heard there was panic among some artists in Moscow.

Luknitsky's version was less splashy, more accurate. There had been panic,
but it had fairly quickly been brought under control.[1]

In these days Luknitsky found people standing in lines for hours to get
300 grams (about ¾ of a pound) of bread, which was the ration of those
who were not production workers.

Many were going into the nearby countryside, looking for cabbage or
potatoes or beets. They found little. They stood in the queues through air-
raid alarms unless forced by the ARP squads or police to take shelter. Most
stores and even the movie houses continued to operate despite the alarms, but
many establishments had permanently shut their doors. Even the soft-drink
and fruit-juice stands had quit. About the only nonrationed products sometimes available were coffee and chicory.

One day Yevgeniya Vasyutina stood in line from ten in the morning to
three in the afternoon to get two kilos (five pounds) of beet sugar. Yelena
Skryabina blessed the good fortune that had enabled her to acquire twenty
or thirty pounds of coffee in August. Now it kept her family going. An old
Tatar servant turned up one day with four chocolate bars. Fortunately he

[1] The Moscow situation was so critical that Stalin put the city in a state of siege—that
is, under strict martial law. The action was taken between 10 and 11 P.M. on the evening
of October 19 at a meeting in Stalin's Kremlin office attended by most of the State
Defense Council members and A. S. Shcherbakov, the Moscow Party leader. Stalin called
in the Moscow commandant, Lieutenant General Pavel A. Artemev, and his commissar,
K. F. Telegin. For days Moscow had been disorganized by a wild flight of broken units
and refugees. Stalin asked Artemev what the situation was. Artemev said that it was
still alarming. He had taken steps to restore order. They had not been sufficient, and he
proposed proclamation of a state of siege. Stalin ordered Georgi Malenkov to write out
the decree. Then, irritated by Malenkov's slowness and wordiness, he snapped angrily
at him, tore the paper from his hands, and dictated to Shcherbakov a new proclamation,
which was promptly posted on the Moscow walls and broadcast over the radio. (K. F.
Telegin, *Voprosy Istorii KPSS*, No. 9, September, 1965, p. 104.) On October 16 the High
Command had been divided into two groups, a first echelon, the operational group,
headed by Marshal A. M. Vasilevsky, and a second, headed by Marshal B. M. Shaposhnikov. The second echelon was moved out of Moscow to an unnamed location from
which it could continue to direct the troops, even if Moscow fell or was encircled.
Both the Defense and Naval Commissariats were removed to Kuibyshev. General
S. M. Shtemenko directed the loading of the special headquarters train on the morning of October 17. The train left Moscow at 7 P.M. and arrived at the new headquarters the next morning. Shtemenko returned to Moscow by car on the night of
October 18. The High Command was working during evenings in the Byelorussian subway station because of the persistence and severity of German air attacks. It has been
widely rumored that Stalin left Moscow briefly at this time, but there is no confirmation in the memoirs. The Shaposhnikov group returned to Moscow in late December,
but a communications center was continued in the emergency locale for some time.
(Shtemenko, *op. cit.*, pp. 40–45; A. M. Vasilevsky, *Bitva Za Moskvu*, 2nd edition, Moscow,
1968, p. 20.) In his famous "secret speech" Khrushchev claimed that Stalin summoned
the Communist Party Central Committee to Moscow for a plenary session during
October, 1941. The members came to Moscow and waited several days, but the meeting
was never called. Whether the meeting and its postponement or cancellation were related
to the critical October days on the Moscow front Khrushchev never made clear.

was willing to take money for them. Usually, now, food was traded only for gold, jewels, furs or vodka.

Two days later Yelena Skryabina made an entry in her diary. The husband of an old friend had died on October 1. The cause: hunger. He lay down one evening to sleep. In the morning he was dead.

A week or so later Kochetov and his wife Vera were walking on the Nevsky near his newspaper office. In front of a pharmacy between the Yusupov Gardens and the Haymarket they saw an old man lying on the sidewalk, face down. His hat had fallen off and his long matted hair flowed over his shoulders like a wig. Kochetov turned the man over. The man protested feebly, "Don't bother, I beg of you." Kochetov tried without success to get the man to his feet. Then he went into the pharmacy and berated the middle-aged clerk for not doing something to help.

"What do you think, young man, that this is a first-aid station?" she said sourly. "Hunger is a terrible condition. Your old man has collapsed from hunger. And I might collapse any day myself—I'm getting more and more swollen."

Kochetov saw how puffed her legs were and realized that she looked very bad.

He next sought out a policeman. "It's just impossible," the officer said. Kochetov saw that he, too, was thin and hungry. He returned to the old man. First aid was no longer necessary. He was dead.

This was the first death from hunger which Kochetov had seen. It would not be the last.

The impact of Pavlov's rigid ration control fell most heavily on dependents and upon children. For the time being, workers and state employees got enough food to maintain their strength. But not the rest of the city—not those who were not making a direct and vital contribution to the war effort.

Nonworkers and children, as of October 1, received one-third of a loaf of poor-quality bread a day. For *the month* they got one pound of meat, a pound and a half of cereals or macaroni, three-quarters of a pound of sunflower-seed oil or butter and three pounds of pastry or confectionery. That was all. In addition to the slender bread distribution, they were expected to maintain life on a total of five and a quarter pounds of food a month—a little more than a pound a week. Moreover, almost immediately distribution of the nonbread items fell below schedule. Fish or canned good were substituted for meat. The "pastry" was so full of substitutes it had little nourishment. Candy might be substituted for oil or fat. As time went on, bread—such as it was—more and more often was the only food issued. A boy of sixteen and an infant of five got the same ration. The deaths which occurred in late September and October, surprising and shocking to the Leningraders who knew of them, occurred among people subjected to this radically reduced diet and who had no personal food reserves to fall back on.

Dmitri V. Pavlov, the energetic young civil servant who became Leningrad's food dictator September 8, drove relentlessly to muster every ounce of food for the city. The task was endless. He knew that, but he went ahead regardless. New ration cards were issued October 1 and rules were tightened.

The reissue brought the total down to 2,421,000, 97,000 less than in September, but still a very large number. Pavlov banned special rations of all kinds—there had been 70,000 special cards issued in September. Many had gone to children who had been evacuated, persons not living in Leningrad. Extra rations had been issued by factories to their office workers. All this came to a halt. Officials were warned they would be brought before military tribunals for violation of ration-card rules. One woman who worked in the printing shop where the cards were turned out was found with a hundred in her possession. She was shot. Armed guards were stationed in the print shop. A metal barrier was set up and not even the plant director was permitted in the area.

Precautions, Pavlov knew, were imperative. Every kind of device was being tried to obtain extra rations. Rackets sprang up. Swindlers painstakingly forged cards with ink and paper stolen from state supplies. In the dim light of flickering kerosene lanterns clerks could not detect forgeries.

Pavlov went further. He persuaded Zhdanov to issue a special decree October 10 which provided that every ration card in the city must be reregistered between October 12 and October 18. He feared that large numbers of forged ration cards might be introduced by the Germans.[2] It was an enormous task. Three thousand Party workers were enlisted to make the check. Thousands of man-hours were spent. Every citizen had to present his card and documentary proof that he was the individual to whom it was assigned. No food could be obtained after October 18 without cards stamped "reregistered." Cards not reregistered were confiscated after that date. Hard rules, but they cut bread ration cards by 88,000, meat cards by 97,000, cards for fats by 92,000. It was vital if Pavlov was to come anywhere near to fulfilling his job.

On the other side of the coin, Pavlov was gathering food from the most unexpected sources. He collected 2,352 tons of potatoes and vegetables from the suburban regions by September 20, often under German fire. Another 7,300 tons were brought in before the fields froze iron-hard. Eight thousand tons of malt were salvaged from the closed breweries and mixed with flour for bread. Five thousand tons of oats were seized from military warehouses. It went into bread. The horses starved or were slaughtered. Some were saved by substitute food—bundles of twigs, stewed in hot water and sprinkled with cottonseed cake and salt. Another horse-food substitute was made of compressed-cottonseed cake, peat shavings, flour dust, bone meal and salt. The horses didn't care much for it. A scientific team, headed by V. I. Sharkov of the Wood Products Institute, worked out a formula for edible

[2] In fact, in Pavlov's opinion, no forged ration cards were introduced by the Germans. (Personal communication, April 30, 1968.)

wood cellulose made from pine sawdust. In the middle of November it was added to the bread, and nearly 16,000 tons were consumed in the blockade days.

On September 15 Pavlov ordered bread baked according to the following formula: rye flour 52 percent, oats 30, barley 8, soya flour 5, malt 5. By October 20 the barley was exhausted. The formula was changed to: rye 63 percent, flax cake 4 percent, bran 4, oats 8, soya 4, malt 12, flour from moldy grain 5.

"The flavor of this bread was impaired," Pavlov conceded. "It reeked of mold and malt."

Food was brought in by barge and ship across Lake Ladoga. Zhdanov told the sailors the fate of Leningrad depended on them. Forty-nine barges were assigned to this service. Some were sunk with their grain cargoes, but 2,800 tons of grain, sprouting and not very appetizing, were salvaged from the lake bottom. That gave the bread its moldy flavor.

Yet Leningrad lived at the edge of disaster. On October 1 the city had on hand only a fifteen-to-twenty-day supply of flour—20,052 tons, to be precise.

The struggle to find substitute food never ended. A stock of cottonseed cake was found in the harbor. It had been destined to be burned in ships' furnaces. Such cake had never been used as human food before because it contained some poisons. However, Pavlov found that high-temperature treatment removed the poisonous essences. He added the cake—4,000 tons of it—to the food supplies. At first the cake made up only 3 percent of the bread formula, then it was raised to 10 percent.

"We are eating bread as heavy as cobblestones and bitter with cottonseed cake," Yevgeniya Vasyutina said. "This cottonseed cake ought to be given out on some kind of cattle ration."

Every nook and cranny was explored for food. A search of the warehouses of Kronstadt turned up 622 tons of rye flour, 435 tons of wheat, 3.6 tons of oats and 1.2 tons of cooking oil. In the Stepan Razin brewery a cellar full of grain was uncovered. By sweeping out warehouses, elevators and railroad cars 500 tons of flour were reclaimed. A recheck of supplies disclosed that flour reserves had been understated by 32,000 tons.

As October wore on, the shortages of food were felt more deeply. Sometimes, Yevgeniya Vasyutina went home and cried all evening. She was hungry and cold, and the news was too bad to think about. Feverish trading sprang up in the city. Vodka was No. 1 in trading goods. Next came bread, cigarettes, sugar and butter. People began to talk more and more about a new cut in the rations. Others said the rations would be lifted, that plentiful supplies were coming in over Lake Ladoga.

The mood of the city grew more grim. Luknitsky, nervous, worried about his elderly father, his cousins, his close friend Lyudmila, all more or less dependent on him, went to the Writers' House, just off the Neva embankment on Ulitsa Voinova. The last time he had been there with Vera Ketlinskaya it had been almost empty. That was three weeks ago. Now in mid-October it was overflowing with people. Only 130 meals could be served in the restaurant. That was all the food there was. Many writers went away hungry. An old translator hysterically cried that she would cut her throat with a razor that minute if she were not permitted to eat. Finally, she was quieted. But she got no food. Dinner consisted of watery soup with a little cabbage, two spoons of kasha, two bits of bread and a glass of tea with a piece of candy.

Luknitsky walked home along the Neva embankment. The *Petropavlovsk* spire was silhouetted against the sky. So were the formidable shapes of the Baltic warships standing guard, their guns elevated, their masts a fretwork against the darkening clouds.

Now another of the Nazis' allies moved into Leningrad: cold . . . winter . . . snow. . . . The first flakes fell at eleven in the morning on the fourteenth of October. The thermometer dropped. It was below freezing. "Ski day," the day the snow cover reached ten centimeters (about four inches), came October 31—an unprecedentedly early date. Always in Leningrad the first snow marked a holiday. This was the winter capital, the capital of snow and ice, the sparkling city of frost. But now the cold and snow brought forbidding thoughts. What about the water pipes? There was hardly any heat in the buildings. Most people got only a ration of 2.5 liters of kerosene in September. Now there was none. Nor would there be any until February. It was cold in the great stone buildings along the Neva. And it was growing colder. Luknitsky noticed ice on the sidewalks in the morning.

Autumn had ended, such an autumn as Leningrad had never known. Winter was setting in. Perhaps, he thought, it would help Russia—as it had against Napoleon. He did not then know how right he was. Winter would help Russia. But it would come near to destroying Leningrad.

He noticed a change in himself. He was constantly on the move between Leningrad and the front, now in Leningrad for four or five days, then at the front for a week. At the front he lived on army rations. The troops still were fed fairly normally—800 grams of bread, almost two pounds, a day, 150 grams of meat, 140 of cereals, 500 of vegetables and potatoes. For a day or two after coming back from the front he did not feel hungry. Then hunger overwhelmed him. From morning until late night he wanted to eat. The evening dab of cereal or macaroni did not satisfy him. He went to bed hungry and woke up hungry after five or six hours.

All over the city this was happening.

People grew thinner while you looked at them. And they grew more like beasts. Yelena Skryabina had a friend, Irina Klyueva, a beautiful, elegant, quiet woman, who adored her husband. Now she fought and even beat him. Why? Because he wanted to eat. Always. Constantly. Nothing satisfied him. As soon as she prepared food he threw himself on it. And she was hungry herself. Before October ended Irina Klyueva's husband had died of hunger. She did not even pretend to grieve.

Each person tried to make the ration go further. Yelena Skryabina's mother divided each piece of bread into three portions. She ate one in the morning, one at noon, one at night. Madame Skryabina ate her whole portion in the morning with her coffee. That gave her strength to stand in food queues for hours or hunt about the city for food. In the afternoon she usually felt so weak she had to lie down. She worried about her husband. He had a military rear-area ration, but it was not much better than that of the civilians. He got a cup of cereal with butter in the morning. But he saved it for their son, Yuri. The food queues grew so long that it was almost impossible to get into a store before the small supply was exhausted. Finally, her husband got their ration cards registered with a military facility where the family received eight bowls of soup and four bowls of cereal every ten days. By this time speculators were getting 60 rubles for a small loaf of bread, 300 rubles for a sack of potatoes and 1,200 rubles for a kilo of meat.

Yevgeniya Vasyutina sat at home like a troglodyte. There was no heat. She wore her greatcoat and felt boots, removing the boots only when she slept. But not the coat. She covered herself with the mattress and pillows, but when she rose her body was stiff and sore. She heated her tea and food on a tiny grill set between two bricks. Thin shavings provided the fuel. There was no electricity. A *burzhuika*, a little potbellied stove (the name *burzhuika* had come from their use by the "former people" during the cold and famine of Petrograd's 1919 and 1920), was beyond her dreams. More than anything in the world she just wanted a simple tea—tea with sugar and a roll. But this was impossible. She divided her ration of bread into three pieces, each the size of a chocolate bar. She put a little butter or oil on each. One she ate for breakfast, one for lunch, and the third she hid in her lamp shade, the one with a little dancing girl on it. She liked to spin the shade so that the dancer twirled in a rosy whirl. Now the electricity didn't work. No one would think, she devoutly believed, of looking there for food.

Hunger and cold had begun their harsh regime. Bombs and shells rained down. On only two days between September 12 and November 30 did the Nazis refrain from shelling Leningrad. The bombardment was continuous: in September 5,364 shells, 991 explosive bombs, 31,398 incendiaries; in October 7,590 shells, 801 explosive bombs, 59,926 incendiaries; in November 11,230 shells, 1,244 explosive bombs, 6,544 incendiaries; in December 5,970 shells, 259 bombs, 1,849 incendiaries. There were fires without number—more than 700 in October alone.

In these dreary fall months occurred 79 percent of the air raids which were to strike Leningrad during the whole of the war and 88 percent of the air-raid casualties.

The reports piled up in the City Records Office. One for October read:

Ulitsa Marat Dom 74. Two explosive bombs fell on two different wings. Under the wreckage of the ruined building were found the bodies of Engineer-Architect Zukov, 35; Ogurtsova 14, Ogurtsova 17, Tutina, 35, Potekhina, V., 17, Tsvetkov, 28. The body of Ye. V. Kunenkova, 60, was found in the opposite wing where she had been blown from a window by the explosive wave. Potekhina, V., was found under the wreckage of a two-story house; the girl was crying for help, and her father, being at the scene with the ARP team, started to pull away the wreckage. From under the obstruction came the cry: "Father, save me." But when the last timbers were pulled away, the girl had died of a wound in the forehead.

The Germans had charted the city for artillery. Firing point No. 736 was a school in Baburin Pereulok, No. 708 the Institute for Maternal Care, No. 192 the Pioneer Palace, No. 89 the Erisman Hospital, No. 295 the Gostiny Dvor, No. 9 the Hermitage, No. 757 an apartment house on Bolshaya Zelena Ulitsa, No. 99 the Nechayev Hospital, No. 187 the Red Fleet library. Smolny Institute, the NKVD headquarters on the Liteiny and the Admiralty were favorite targets. The Germans had the biggest guns in Europe trained on Leningrad—cannon from Skoda, from Krupp, from Schneider; railroad guns of calibers as high as 400 mm and 420 mm, firing shells of 800 and 900 kilos, over distances of 15,000, 28,000 and even 31,000 yards from six great artillery investments, circled about the city.

But life went on. Vera Ketlinskaya broadcast over Leningrad radio on October 19, marking the seventeenth week of war:

I was teaching my little son his first uncertain steps when the radio brought into our lives that new all-engulfing word—war. Now seventeen weeks have passed. War has changed the lives of each of us, in big things and little. I have put aside the book I was writing about happiness in order to write about struggle, about bravery, about unyielding stubborn resistance. My son sleeps in a bomb shelter and knows the sound of the air-raid sirens as well as the words "to walk" and "to eat." . . . There is no good news. Not yet. But we will wait. We will fight. . . .

The Philharmonic put on a concert in the big hall on October 25. Aleksandr Kamensky played Tchaikovsky. He did the Prater Waltz for an encore. The concert was given during the afternoon, and deep shadows filled the unheated hall. Spectators sat in their greatcoats. Many were military men.

Most of the famous old secondhand bookstores were still open. Ilya Glazunov[3] and his father visited their favorite, from time to time, at the corner of Bolshoi Prospekt and Vvedensky streets. Not much had changed since the war. Old men in overcoats, with chapped hands and gold-rimmed spectacles huddled together and peered at calf-bound volumes. There were stacks of a new edition of Dickens' *Great Expectations*. It had come off the press just before the blockade. Now all the copies were penned up in Leningrad. On the cover there was a drawing of a little boy, his hand held by a

---

[3] Glazunov is now a well-known Soviet painter of modernist tendencies.

middle-aged man, looking at a ship vanishing into the distance, far, far into the distance. It made a small boy dream.

The astronomer A. N. Deich undertook to rescue from the Pulkovo observatory whatever remained of the telescopic lenses, the scientific equipment, the valuable charts of the stars, the catalogues of the heavens, the remarkable library and archives. Battle had raged in and around the observatory buildings for weeks. The great dome of the main telescope site had been badly smashed, but Deich discovered that the central vaults in which most of the materials had been stored were still in Russian hands and apparently undamaged. He led an expedition to the observatory late in the night of October 13. The German lines were only a few hundred feet distant. Under cover of darkness the most valued observatory possessions, the incunabula among them, were removed. They had to be carried by hand for a quarter of a mile because the trucks could not mount the observatory hill.

Three nights later Professor N. N. Pavlov and a convoy of five trucks started for the observatory, also at night. They were spotted about a mile from the observatory and had to halt as the Germans brought them under fire. They took refuge in a ditch but finally were able to remove a full load of records and equipment. On their way out they again came under German fire.

One October night when the bombardment was particularly heavy Nikolai Tikhonov, the poet who was now a war correspondent, encountered a familiar figure in one of the lower corridors of Smolny—a stocky, handsome man, fiery, a great charmer of the ladies, with hair like King Lear and a beard like Jove—Professor Iosif Orbeli, director of the Hermitage.

Orbeli greeted Tikhonov with enthusiasm.

"You haven't, of course, forgotten the Nizami anniversary?" Orbeli said eagerly. Nizami was the national poet of Azerbaijan. His eight hundredth anniversary was October 19. Long before the war the Hermitage had made plans to mark the occasion. As Orbeli talked, Tikhonov could hear the crash of bombs, the bark of guns.

"Dear Iosif Abramovich," Tikhonov said. "You hear what's going on all around us. In these circumstances a celebration might not be very triumphant."

Bombs or no bombs, war or no war, Orbeli was determined to stage his meeting. He persuaded Tikhonov to speak. He persuaded the military authorities to release "for one day only" half a dozen leading Orientologists, serving on the Pulkovo or Kolpino lines. He promised that they would be back in the trenches before dawn.

Precisely as scheduled, the meeting was held at 2 P.M. on October 19 in the Hermitage and completed a few minutes before the customary late-afternoon alert. It was, Tikhonov later discovered, the only celebration in all Russia of the great poet's anniversary. Neither in Moscow nor in Baku was the day marked.

"People of light"—that was what Tikhonov called the people of Leningrad in these times.

But the light was flickering out for some—for a group of sailors who knifed a captain at the naval docks, stole a boat and tried to make their way to a Finnish port. They were caught. A cutter brought them back. The command was mustered out and the five men were lined up before an open ditch. One dropped to his knees, crying for his life. The order was given, a volley rang out and the five slowly fell into the ditch.

The light was dim for another group of sailors. They bought some *samogon*, moonshine, from a peasant and got drunk on duty. They were sent into a penalty battalion, where death would be their companion on mission after mission of the kind from which few return.

It was dim, too, for a buxom Russian girl with a strong face and rough hands. She wore a sailor's jacket and a short skirt. An ersatz sailor, the men at Kronstadt called her. They joked with her, tough sailor's jokes. She answered them back in kind. Jolly, tough, witless—so she seemed. One day she asked for the keys to the gun room. She said she'd forgotten to clean one of the guns. She unlocked the locker, took out a rifle, went to her bunk, kicked the boot off her right foot, hooked the trigger with her big toe and shot herself.

She could not go on longer. This was her second war. The first had begun in the late thirties when the "black crow" of the police had swept up to the jewelry store where she worked. All the clerks had been arrested. The manager, it seemed, had been stealing. What happened to him did not matter. What happened to Vera brought an end to her life. She was sent to an island, a prison where the men were on one side of a wall, the women on the other. Sometimes they beat the wall down. The men were like beasts. So were the women. Somehow, she had survived that. Now she wanted love, a home, children. And the man she loved did not love her. All around were war and death and suffering. It was too much. Why go on? She killed herself.

Hunger . . . cold . . . bullets . . . bombs . . . the allies of the Germans were hard at work in Leningrad.

Deus Conservat Omnia . . .

36 . *Seven Men Knew*

THE FIRST DAY OR TWO OR THREE WERE THE WORST. SO
Nikolai Chukovsky found. If a man had nothing but a slice of bread to eat,
he suffered terrible hunger pangs the first day. And the second. But gradually
the pain faded into quiet despondency, a gloom that had no ending, a weakness that advanced with frightening rapidity. What you did yesterday you
could not do today. You found yourself surrounded by obstacles too difficult
to overcome. The stairs were too steep to climb. The wood was too hard
to chop, the shelf too high to reach, the toilet too difficult to clean. Each
day the weakness grew. But awareness did not decline. You saw yourself
from a distance. You knew what was happening, but you could not halt it.
You saw your body changing, the legs wasting to toothpicks, the arms
vanishing, the breasts turning into empty bags. Skirts slipped from the hips,
trousers would not stay up. Strange bones appeared. Or the opposite—you
puffed up. You could no longer wear your shoes. Your neighbor had to
help you to your feet. Your cheeks looked as though they were bursting.
Your neck was too thick for your collar. But it was nothing except wind
and water. There was no strength in you. Some said it came from drinking
too much. Half of Leningrad was wasting away, the other half was swelling
from the water drunk to fill empty stomachs.

It was not true, Chukovsky felt, that you feared most your own death.
What was most terrible was to see the people around you dying. What you
feared was the inevitable process, the weakness that seized you, the terror
of dying alone by degrees in darkness, in cold and in hunger.

As Maria Razina, a Party worker, noted: "Leningraders live so badly it is
not possible to imagine anything worse—hunger, cold, and darkness in every
house with the fall of night."

October had been hungry, and it was stormy after the fourteenth and
snowy. The bombs and shells took their toll. In November the deaths began.
Not only the deaths from hunger. The elderly slipped quietly away of many
diseases. Younger people died of galloping consumption, of grippe. Any

disease finished you quickly. An ulcer was fatal. Half the food you ate was inedible. People began to stuff their stomachs with substitutes. They tore the wallpaper from the walls and scraped off the paste, which was supposed to have been made with potato flour. Some ate the paper. It had some nourishment, they thought, because it was made from wood. Later they chewed the plaster—just to fill their stomachs. Vera Inber visited her friend, Marietta, a pharmacologist at the Erisman Hospital where her husband worked. She noticed that the cages for the guinea pigs and rabbits that lined the corridor were all empty now. Only the smell remained. Outside the bomb shelter she saw a watchdog, Dinka. The dog, like most of those in Leningrad, was trained to go to the shelter when the air-raid siren sounded. But already dogs were becoming rare in the besieged city. You noticed those that remained. You thought about them.

Dystrophy and diarrhea appeared—the result of the inedible elements in the diet, the chaff in the bread, the sweepings, the plaster, the paste and the other indigestibles. A man's strength flowed right through him. Within a few hours he was dead. A certain order of starvation emerged. It was not the old who went first. It was the young, especially those fourteen to eighteen, who lived on the smallest rations. Men died before women. Healthy, strong people sank before chronic invalids. This was the direct result of the inequity in the rations. Young people twelve to fourteen received a dependent's ration, which was identical with the ration for children up to the age of twelve. As of October 1 this was only 200 grams, about a third of a loaf of bread a day—just half the ration of a worker. But vigorous, growing children needed as much food as a worker. This was why they died so swiftly. The ration for men and women was the same—400 grams of bread for workers, 200 for all other categories. But men led more vigorous lives. They needed more food. Without it they died more rapidly than the women. The monthly meat ration for children and young people was 400 grams, hardly a third of that for workers (1,500 grams). Young people got half the fats, a little more than half the cereals and three-quarters the sweets. Troops at the front received twice the worker's ration—800 grams of bread a day beginning October 1, 150 grams of meat a day, 80 grams of fish, 140 grams of cereal, 500 grams of potatoes and vegetables, 50 grams of fat and 35 grams of sugar.

"Today it is so simple to die," Yelena Skryabina noted in her diary. "You just begin to lose interest, then you lie on the bed and you never again get up."

She was concerned about her sixteen-year-old son, Dima. In August and September he chased from one end of the city to another in search of groceries, watching the war bulletin boards, playing with his friends. Now he was like an old man. He sat all day in his slippers beside the stove, pale-blue circles under his eyes. Unless he could be shaken from apathy he would die. Yelena Skryabina could find little to feed him. He got only a child's ration of 200 grams a day—a couple of slices of bread. Nothing for a growing boy. She tried to tempt him with such delicacies as she could contrive—a jellied pâté made by boiling old leather, soup thickened with cellulose.

It was no longer uncommon to see people collapse of hunger. Yelena Skryabina noticed a man walking slowly ahead of her in the street. As she overtook him, she glanced at his face, frighteningly blue. Death, she felt, must be hovering over him. She had not taken more than a few paces when she looked back. He tottered and dropped slowly to the sidewalk. When she reached him, he was dead.

There were wild rumors of plague and cholera—fortunately not true. But rats became bolder. They, too, were hungry. A sailor awoke with the feeling someone was staring at him. It was the yellow eyes of a great rat on the foot of his bed. The rise in dystrophy and scurvy astonished the doctors. Before November came to an end 18 percent of the hospital case load was starvation-related diseases. On November 20 the clinic at the Kirov factory issued twenty-eight sick reports for dystrophy. The next day the total was fifty. The Vyborg region registry bureau was unable to keep up with the demand for death certificates. By the end of November at least 11,085 Leningraders had died of starvation.[1]

Already the whispers had begun: In the markets some of the sausage was made not of pork but of human flesh. The militia, it was said, had evidence of this in their possession. Who could tell whether or not it was true? Better to take no chances. Yelena Skryabina's husband warned her not to let five-year-old Yuri play far from the house, even if he was with his nurse. Children, it was said, had disappeared. . . .

A whole new standard of values was arising. Women would trade a diamond ring for a few pounds of black bread so coarse it seemed to be baked of straw. When Luknitsky returned from the front, women waited outside the railroad station. They tugged at his shoulder, saying, "Soldier, wouldn't you like some wine?" They had a bottle or two of spirits to trade for bread, which was in better supply with the troops. Sometimes at the Writers' House there would be a bit of meat in the soup—horse meat.

Hunger brought other changes. Sex virtually disappeared. It was not only that physical sex traits vanished—menstruation halted, women's breasts shriveled, their faces sagged. The sex drive evaporated. Women made no effort to beautify themselves. Lipsticks were eaten as food in December and January. The grease was used for frying ersatz bread. Face powder was mixed into ersatz flour. The births dropped catastrophically in 1942 to only one-third the 1941 figure. In 1943 they dropped another 25 percent. The birth rate in 1940 was 25.1 per 1,000. In 1941 it was 18.3, in 1942 only 6.2.[2]

---

[1] By comparison, the autumn shelling of the city killed 681, wounded 2,269; bombing in September killed 566, wounded 3,853; in October killed 304, wounded 1,843; in November killed 522, wounded 2,505. The total of killed and wounded in three months' bombing and shelling was 12,533.

[2] In December, 1943, for the first time since the start of the blockade the birth rate exceeded the death rate. (*N.Z.*, p. 584.)

The wife of a friend of Pavel Luknitsky, Edik Orlova, gave birth to a child at a lying-in home on Vasilevsky Island, February 12. She was brought from her home at No. 9 Griboyedov Canal in a sled. She gave birth in darkness, lighted only by the flickering flames from a tin stove. Despite every effort the child died on the eleventh day.

Nikolai Chukovsky believed that hungry bodies conserved strength by eliminating the sex drive. Among starving people it was hard to tell men from women. They slept together for warmth, but their bodies aroused no sexual stimulation.

In late winter he took some workers from the fleet newspaper to a bath— a rare treat. The Leningrad baths closed in December and did not work for two or three months. Few workers had even had their clothes off for weeks, living and working in buildings where the temperature was near zero. As they prepared to go to the bath, clean clothing in hand, a question arose about Zoya, one of the typesetters. She appeared, ready to join her comrades at the bath. Chukovsky was embarrassed. Zoya certainly had every right to a bath, but what to do with her among a crowd of men? Nonetheless, they started off together. At the bathhouse there was a surprise. It was ladies' day! Zoya was the only one permitted to bathe. Now the shoe was on the other foot. Finally, Chukovsky appealed to the director and got permission for his sailors to bathe, too. The little band of men undressed and took their bath amid a crowd of women. There was not the slightest embarrassment. Chukovsky could not help thinking how his sailors would have reacted a few months before, surrounded by naked women. But here they were, all skin and bones, the women even more than the men. Neither men nor women gave it a thought. Zoya, instead of going into a corner by herself, joined the men. It seemed perfectly natural. They passed the soap back and forth, gossiped, soaked themselves, enjoyed the water and the warmth. There was no sign of sexual feeling on either side.

When rations began to increase, when starvation moderated, sex began to return to normal. The war gave rise to new forms of relations between men and women. "Front love" was what it was called in Leningrad—the love which sprang up between men and women, girls and boys, fighting in the lines together, serving in the AA crews, the love between the nurses and the men they cared for. Many of them had wives or husbands from whom they had long been separated. They did not know whether they would survive the war—or even the week. Chukovsky felt that "front love" commanded respect as a warm and necessary human relationship, one which was only natural in the unnatural conditions of the war and the siege.

Not everyone's nerves held up. One evening Luknitsky sat in the Writers' House at the table with Ernst Gollerbach, who began to explain that Hitler was bombing Leningrad in order to kill Gollerbach. He begged his companions not to blame him for the raids. "I would kill myself if it would stop the raids," he said, "but I am a Christian and it is not possible." After a few moments his companions realized that Gollerbach had gone out of his mind. What to do with the poor man? Could his wife care for him? To put him in an insane asylum was a death sentence. By this time the Writers' House had begun to give meals only in exchange for coupons. This meant a 50 percent cut in the ration of writers who had been eating there. When Luknitsky went home after such a miserable meal, he drank a glass or two of ersatz coffee without sugar or bread to try to quench his hunger.

Captain Ivan V. Travkin was a submarine commander. His submarine was stationed in the Neva and his family was in Leningrad. He got leave to visit them and found his wife, her body badly swollen, her eyes sunken in their sockets, hardly able to move. His daughter with puffy eyes—the first sign of dystrophy—sat on the bed muffled in bedclothes, eating soup made from library paste. His mother-in-law wandered about the dark, cold room mumbling, laughing and crying—she had lost her reason. The windows had been broken by bomb blasts and replaced by plywood. The walls were black with smoke from the little iron stove. There was a flickering kerosene lamp. Outside shells could be heard bursting. It was a typical Leningrad family on a typical Leningrad day.

Prices rose steadily on the black market. In early November a small loaf of black bread (if you could find one) sold for 60 rubles ($10), a sack of potatoes for 300 and a kilo of meat for 1,200.

The truth, as none knew better than Pavlov, was that time was running out for Leningrad. The Lake Ladoga shipping route had been less than a brilliant success. The little overladen boats left for Osinovets usually at night. The crossing took sixteen hours. German bombers watched like hawks. The boats often sank, either with the load of food being brought to Leningrad or with refugees being taken out.

The route had worked badly almost from the start. A military man, Major General Afanasy M. Shilov, had been put in charge. He ordered barges, overladen with grain and munitions, out onto the storm-tossed waters against the advice of their sailors. There were hideous losses. Shilov was called in by Andrei Zhdanov and warned that he would go before a military court (and face the firing squad) if he sent more ships out onto the lake against the will of the skippers.

Admiral A. T. Karavayev, who was present at the stormy meeting, thought Zhdanov looked seriously ill, pale and tired. He coughed and wheezed but never stopped smoking.

The pressure to get supplies into Leningrad was crushing. Two or three days later Zhdanov sent a telegram to Ladoga saying: "Bread is vanishing in Leningrad. Each 24 hours without shipments dooms the lives of thousands of Leningraders."

Leningrad in October had been using about 1,100 tons of flour a day. But in the first thirty days the Ladoga route brought in only 9,800 tons of food. Mountains of supplies piled up around Volkhov and Gostinopolye. More and more barges and ships were being sunk by Nazi planes, despite appeals to Zhdanov for better fighter cover.

The situation grew so critical that Mayor Popkov was sent to Novaya Ladoga October 13 to try and straighten out the mess. He arrived coincident with a savage German bombing of the docks and storage area. A meeting of those working on the shipping route was summoned and Popkov spoke in solemn terms:

"You know that the ration has been lowered for the third time in Leningrad. Workers are getting 400 grams, employees and children 200. It's not much. I remind you that a working man requires 2,000 calories. Four hundred grams of our bread gives a little more than 500 calories. . . . I'm not trying to persuade you of anything, but here is the situation: If for a few days grain is not brought across the lake, then the Leningraders will not receive a single gram of bread. The Military Council of the front and the fleet, the Party committee and the City Council have instructed me to tell you that the life of Leningrad is now in your hands."

This appeal had an effect. By herculean efforts the back of the logjam was broken and 5,000 tons of food were pushed over the lake to Osinovets. At the same time 12,000 tons of flour, 1,500 tons of cereals and 1,000 tons of meat were moved up from Gostinopolye to Novaya Ladoga to wait shipment to Leningrad. Then violent autumn storms hit and hampered shipments as much as did the Germans.

One of the worst disasters occurred November 4 when a German JU-88 attacked the gunboat *Konstruktor*, en route from Osinovets to Novaya Ladoga with decks loaded with refugees, mostly women and children. The captain dodged one bomb, then the ship was hit and sank with a loss of 204 persons, including 34 crew members.

Lake shipping came to an end with the formation of ice November 15 —except for a few final trips by Ladoga gunboats which managed to force their way through as late as November 30, bringing in another 800 tons of flour.

Total shipments by the lake had been 24,097 tons of grain and flour and 1,131 tons of meat and dairy products—a twenty-day supply in sixty-five days of shipping. Total freight brought into Leningrad was 51,324 tons— the difference being made up by munitions. In the same period about 10,000 tons of high-priority materials and 33,479 individuals were taken out over the lake. The blockade of Leningrad had occurred so suddenly and surprisingly that it trapped enormous shipments of industrial, military and artistic treasures, loaded in freight cars, unable to move from the Leningrad yards. A count of these goods after the blockade began found 1,900 cars loaded with art treasures, books, scientific apparatus and machinery. Another 227 cars were loaded with war supplies being sent out by the Defense Commissariat. In all, 282 trains of goods had been evacuated from Leningrad between June 29 and August 29, including 86 more or less complete factories. But the great Kirov works had not been sent out. It was only after the fall of Mga that Admiral I. S. Isakov was summoned to Smolny by Zhdanov and ordered to start to ship the Kirov machinery to the Urals—an operation which he attempted to carry out with the skimpy ship and port resources of Lake Ladoga plus what air transport could be commandeered. Again and again the Nazi air fleet struck at the Ladoga ships. By the end of the navigation period only 7 barges were left unsunk. Six small steamers and 24 barges had been lost.[3]

Leningrad began November with 15 days of flour on hand, 16 days of cereal, 30 days of sugar, 22 days of fats, almost no meat. What meat there was came in by air and that was not much.

"Everyone knew that food was scarce," Pavlov recorded, "since rations were being reduced. But the actual situation was known to only seven men."

Two confidential Party workers kept a record of deliveries of food to Leningrad. Only the inner circle of the Military Command and Pavlov knew the totals.

November 7 was approaching, the anniversary of the Bolshevik Revolution, the big Soviet holiday. This was the day when all Russia celebrated with feasts, wine, vodka, fat turkeys, suckling pigs, sturgeon in aspic, roasted hams, goose, sausages. It was a time of gaiety, merriment, family dinners, feasting, much drinking.

Not in 1941. Leningrad had cold, not warmth; darkness, not light. Everyone in Leningrad was hungry all the time now. November 7 was no exception. Pavlov had nothing in his storehouses to give the people. For the children he manged to find 200 grams—half a cup—of sour cream and 100 grams—a couple of tablespoons—of potato flour. Adults got five pickled tomatoes—some adults, that is; a few got a half-liter of wine and a handful of chocolates. A line of women was standing outside a store on Vasilevsky Island, waiting for the wine to be passed out, when a German shell hit. Bodies were blasted to bits. A passing Red Army man named Zakharov, just back from the front, was horrified to see the surviving women pick their way over the human wreckage and reform the queue, fearful that they might miss their allotment.

Yevgeniya Vasyutina traded 200 grams of cottonseed oil for a liter of kerosene and baked some flatcakes of pea flour for her holiday feast. She had four pieces of candy. Her factory closed early, at five o'clock. She sat

---

[3] Some Leningrad sources, including the authoritative *N.Z.*, give the figure of food shipments into Leningrad as 45,000 tons. This, D. V. Pavlov explains, is a figure which includes all shipments from September 1 through December 7. It includes freight reshipped from Shlisselburg after the arrival of the Nazis on the Neva at Ivanovskoye on August 29. Shipments into Leningrad included, in addition to food, 6,600 tons of gasoline, 508,000 shells and mines, 114,000 hand grenades and 3,000,000 bullets. (*N.Z.*, p. 207; Pavlov, *op. cit.*, 3rd edition, p. 124.) By airlift Leningrad received, from October 10 to December 25, 6,186 tons of high-priority freight and 47.3 tons of mail. The planes evacuated 50,099 persons and carried out 47.2 tons of mail and 1,016.7 tons of freight. (*Leningrad v VOV*, p. 225.)

down beside her radio loudspeaker. Stalin was supposed to speak. Music played until 10:30 P.M. Then an announcement: No speech that night; listen again at 6 A.M. She felt cheated as she went to sleep in the icy room.

The Germans had been preparing for November 7. For days leaflets rained down on the city: "Go to the baths. Put on your white dresses. Eat the funeral dishes. Lie down in your coffins and prepare for death. On November 7 the skies will be blue—blue with the explosion of German bombs."

It was not the first time the Germans had called on the women of Leningrad to wear their white dresses. In the terrible days of August when thousands worked on the fortifications outside the city the Nazi broadcasts had told them to wear white dresses—so the bombers could see and avoid attacking them. Hundreds of gullible babushkas put white scarves over their heads, white shawls over their shoulders, and were machine-gunned in the trenches, beautiful targets for low-flying Junkers.

The Leningrad Command was certain the Nazis planned a special observance on November 7. They now had a crack bomber echelon assigned to attack Leningrad, the Hindenburg Escadrille. In an effort to immobilize the German air arm over the November 7 holiday, the small Soviet Stormovik force carried out spoiling attacks on the nearby Nazi airdromes October 30 and again November 6. A night fighter patrol was set up over the city. On the night of November 4 there was a spectacular encounter. A young Soviet pilot named Aleksei Sevastyanov rammed his plane into a German Heinkel-11 bomber, which fell with a tremendous explosion in the Tauride Palace gardens in the center of the city. Both pilots came down by parachute. The Nazi flier was seized by a street crowd and almost lynched.

This did not weaken German determination to mark the November holiday in a special way. On the evening of November 6, as the radio was broadcasting Moscow's traditional ceremonial, the air-raid sirens sounded.

Vsevolod Vishnevsky and Anatoly Tarasenkov made their way through the barrage to the apartment of the mother of Orest Tsekhnovitser, the Dostoyevsky scholar who had been lost in the Tallinn disaster. The mother had sent Vishnevsky a letter, begging to know the fate of her son. Neither Vishnevsky nor Tarasenkov had ever met the mother. They found her in the typical flat of a Leningrad *intelligent*—book-lined, crowded with heavy furniture, cold and dark. The mother was gray but spirited. Tsekhnovitser's sister was there, old, worn and ugly. They insisted on hearing the whole tragic story. Then the mother told Vishnevsky that Tsekhnovitser's apartment had been commandeered by a police sergeant with the connivance of the building superintendent. Tsekhnovitser's valuable books had been sold. The women had been unable to get the police to oust the usurpers.

Vishnevsky carefully jotted down the details—the name of the police official (he was attached to the 35th Police Station), the address of the apartment, the superintendent's name—and promised to do what he could. A month later the policeman was given a seven-year term, the superintendent five years. Vishnevsky laconically noted in his diary: "Justice!"

The two correspondents left the apartment low in spirits. The air raid was still going on.

At Smolny the Leningrad High Command sat in the bomb shelter under the main building. Here they did much of their work. Here, in a common dormitory, slept most of the top generals and Party chiefs.

Now they were listening to the radio transmission of the Moscow ceremonial meeting which, they knew, was being held in the great Mayakov-sky Square station of the Moscow subway, one hundred feet below ground, safe from interruption by Nazi bombers. The reception was very bad.

Marshal Voronov telephoned Moscow and spoke with General N. D. Yakovlev, chief of the Artillery Administration, who had just come back from the Mayakovsky Square meeting.

"There's big news," Yakovlev shouted. The connection was so poor Voronov couldn't understand what the news was. He asked Yakovlev to spell it out by letters. Yakovlev spelled "P-A-R-A-D-E." Finally, Voronov got it. The traditional parade in Red Square would be held tomorrow, regardless of the war, regardless of the Nazi drive on Moscow, regardless of air attacks.

Voronov told Zhdanov the news. Zhdanov didn't believe it.

"They're just joking with you," the Party chief said. Then, he, too, called Moscow. It was true. Somehow it made Leningrad's troubles a bit easier to bear. And they were heavy. The Nazi air attack had not ceased. In a print shop, located in one of the old chambers of the Peter and Paul Fortress, workers of the newspaper *On Guard of the Fatherland* had been listening to the Moscow broadcast. A heavy bomb smashed through the ancient structure, killing thirteen of the fourteen men in the shop. The fourteenth man fled from the chamber, mad.

At the Finland freight station Ivan Kanashin was working with a large group of Young Communists to clear the freight jam. This was the station where food and supplies from Lake Ladoga arrived in Leningrad. It was also the collection point for refugees being sent out of the city via the Ladoga steamers. That night a crowd of women, children and elderly persons jammed the station awaiting a train to take them out of Leningrad, out of the iron circle of hunger, cold, fear and danger.

The evening started badly. A railroad bridge near Kushelevka was hit by a bomb, and movement of trains in and out of the station was halted while the damage was repaired. The jam increased.

A little later the air-raid sirens sounded. Around the station was a heavy concentration of antiaircraft guns. They began to bark. Then a blinding light appeared in the sky. The Nazis had dropped enormous flares on parachutes, which made the whole area lighter than day. Women and children huddled closer in terror. The bombs began to fall.

These were not ordinary high explosives. These were heavier than anything the Germans had used on Leningrad before—naval magnetic mines,

weighing a ton or more, with a diameter of nine or ten feet, attached to parachutes. Many were delayed-action weapons. The bomb disposal crews had
no experience with these weapons. They did not know that if they attacked
them with wrenches and metal hammers they were apt to set them off.

The heavy bombs smashed into the train yards, hurling loaded trains
from the rails, crushing cars already filled with women and children. Then
the Germans began to toss incendiary bombs into the smoking jumble.
Kanashin was in a car which stood next to a huge boiler. The boiler blew up
and knocked over the car. Only the heavy steel structure saved Kanashin
and his fellow workers from being crushed. The raid went on all night. In
the morning the freight station was strewn with the corpses of women and
children. There were enormous bomb holes everywhere. The cars were
twisted masses of metal. Two trainloads of heavily wounded had been in
the station. Now there was nothing but formless wreckage, piled high with
bodies.

Suddenly Kanashin heard a roar of voices. He saw a crowd of women approaching. They had in their hands a young Nazi flier who had been shot
down during the night. They brought him up to the mountain of bodies
which lay where the trains of the heavily wounded had been obliterated.
"Do you see what you did, you murderer?" they shouted. "Do you see?"

The next day Luknitsky was returning to Leningrad from the front in
Karelia. It was early morning, still dark. All night he had ridden in the
unheated car, filled with silent people. They were unable to enter the
Finland Station. The train halted two or three hundred yards away. The
station lay in ruins, the platforms smashed. Passengers picked their way
through a tiny service entrance. Tired and cold, with a heavy pack on his
back, Luknitsky made his way into the dismal deserted streets. He had to
walk from the Kirov Bridge all the way home. Streetcar No. 30 was not
running because a huge delayed-action bomb still lay in Wolf Street.

On the night of November 6 submarine *L-3* navigated without pilot, buoys
or lights from Kronstadt through the Sea Canal and up the Neva into
Leningrad. It was supposed to take up station at the Lieutenant Schmidt
embankment but couldn't get through the ice above the Institute of Mines.
It dropped anchor there and some crew members went ashore through
driving snow to see their families in Leningrad. German planes were overhead and fires swirled up in the city. Aboard the submarine the temperature
was 12 degrees above freezing. The steward laid a white cloth on the mess
table and produced some hot cocoa. The doctor found some wine in his
supplies, and the submariners celebrated the holiday with a little gaiety.
They were among the few.

Sergei Yezersky, a writer on *Leningradskaya Pravda*, jotted down his
impressions of that night:

> Midnight. The city is quiet and empty. The great streets and squares are
> dead. No lights. Only darkness. A cold wind whips the snow into little
> whirlwinds. The sound of artillery. Low clouds reflect the shelling.

Nearby an explosion. The Germans are shelling the city. At the intersections and the bridges—patrols. They challenge sternly: "Halt! Who goes
there?"

There was no celebration of the November 7 holiday. No parades. No
review in Palace Square. No great meeting at Smolny or the Tauride Palace.
A few red flags in the streets, on the Winter Palace and hung from windows.
No banners proclaiming the twenty-fourth anniversary of the Bolshevik
Revolution. The street radios blared out readings from Leo Tolstoy's
Sevastopol stories—tales of the heroic siege of the defenders of Sevastopol
during the Crimean War. Vishnevsky, ever on the search for something to
raise morale, thought the reading was marvelous. Zhdanov did not speak.
There were speeches on the radio by Mayor Popkov, the Leningrad front
commander Lieutenant General M. S. Khozin, the writer Nikolai Tikhonov
and a few others. *Leningradskaya Pravda* set the tone with its editorial: "We
will be cold—but we will survive; we will be hungry—but we will tighten
our belts; it will be hard—but we will hold out; we will hold out—until we
win." Nikolai Akimov gave Leningrad its only holiday premiere. He presented Gladkov's *Stepchildren of Glory*, a patriotic play about the war of
1812 at the Theater of Comedy. The cold, dark theater was half filled.

Cold and dark . . . those were the words most often used to describe
Leningrad on the twenty-fourth anniversary of the Revolution. Sayanov
walked down the Nevsky one early November day. Dusk had fallen. The
wind hurried the people along and swung the signs above the shops,
whirling the snow up in clouds, in and out of the doorways. It whistled
through the drainpipes. The people, dark and black, muffled in their winter
clothes, hastened along. They did not halt. They did not speak. Not far
away shells were falling. No one paid heed. They struggled across the Neva
bridges, past the granite embankments. Already there was ice on the river
where the warships stood and here and there a steaming hole beside the
shore. People had begun to bring water to their homes, where the pipes had
frozen.

It was a gray, granite city, and the wind was king. Sometimes people
found strange messages in their postboxes. Sheets of paper painfully initialed:
"Only God can save Leningrad. Pray to Heaven. The Time of the Apocalypse
has come. Christ is now in the peaks of the Caucasus." There were Old
Believers and Molokans, survivors of the sects of the forests, still in Leningrad,
and this was their message to their fellow Russians.

Time of the Apocalypse, indeed . . .

On November 8 the German 39th Motorized Corps under General
Schmidt captured Tikhvin, forty miles east of Volkhov, and severed the rail
connection between the Moscow mainland and the Ladoga supply route. On
that day Hitler spoke at Munich. He said: "Leningrad's hands are in the air.
It falls sooner or later. No one can free it. No one can break the ring.
Leningrad is doomed to die of famine."

It was true—or almost true. Leningrad had not surrendered, but it was doomed. Brass bands played over the German radio. Nazi commentators in broadcasts directed to Leningrad said over and over again: "Leningrad will be compelled to surrender without the blood of German soldiers being shed."

So it seemed. How could the city be fed? There were now panic and disarray in Leningrad. The news of Tikhvin's fall spread like the fierce wind on the Nevsky from person to person. The press, of course, said nothing. What food was left in the city? Very little—much less than the Leningraders knew. But seven men did know. They added up the total on November 9: flour for 7 days, cereals for 8, fats for 14, sugar for 22. No meat, not a ton in the reserves. On the other side of Lake Ladoga, now so stormy, so ice-filled that boats could hardly break their way across, there were 17 days' supply of flour, 10 days' of cereals, 3 days' of fats and 9 days' of meat.

Supply trains could get no closer to Leningrad than the tiny way station of Zaborye, 110 miles from Volkhov. From Zaborye to Ladoga not even a forest road connected the 220 miles. Could trucks struggle through that distance even if a road could be built? How long would it take? Would not the city starve first?

The answers to these questions were terrifying.

But only seven men in Leningrad knew how terrifying, Pavlov first among them.

There was no time to lose if the city was to be saved—*if the city could be saved*.

Emergency orders . . .

In Leningrad an immediate cut in military rations was instituted. The troops had been getting 800 grams of bread a day, plus hot soup and stew. Front-line troops were cut to 600 grams of bread and 125 grams of meat. Rear units got 400 grams of bread and 50 of meat.

To cut civilian rations further, Pavlov knew, would only doom the whole city to more rapid starvation. Civilians could not maintain themselves as it was. The hope was that the ice would quickly freeze on Lake Ladoga and food could be brought across the lake. The forecast was for lower temperatures.

Zhdanov and the Leningrad Defense Council gambled. They decided to hold the civilian ration at its present level. If the ice froze, it could be maintained. Each day their first concern was the thermometer. The temperature dropped, but the lake did not freeze. Five days passed. Supplies were near exhaustion. There was no alternative.

On November 13 the city's rations were cut again—to 300 grams (about ⅔ of a pound) of bread daily for factory workers. Everyone else was cut to 150 grams.

That reduced the daily consumption of flour to 622 tons. But Pavlov knew this level could be maintained for only a few days. He waited. He waited for the ice. It did not freeze, it was still thin. By November 20, time—and flour—

were running out. Again the ration was cut—brutally: to 250 grams for factory workers, 125 (two slices) for everyone else. Front-line troops got 500 grams, rear echelons 300.

That was the day that Director Zolotukhin of *Leningradskaya Pravda* came to Sergei Yezersky and asked him to write the editorial which brought the terrible news to Leningrad.

"To write the lead editorial," he recalled, "was always an honor. But what a difficult task this time!"

He went to his table in the section of the newspaper's cellar which was occupied by the literary department. It was a crowded corner, neither light nor dark, neither cold nor warm. The workers slept on couches, and if there wasn't room, they slept on the desks. There was always water on the concrete floor and they walked on wooden planking.

His editorial began:

> Bolsheviks never have kept anything from the people. They always tell the truth, harsh as it may be. So long as the blockade continues it is not possible to expect any improvement in the food situation. We must reduce the norms of rations in order to hold out as long as the enemy is not pushed back, as long as the circle of blockade is not broken. Difficult? Yes, difficult. But there is no choice. And this everyone must understand. . . .

The new norms brought daily consumption of flour down to 510 tons. Pavlov was now feeding something like 2,500,000 people on 30 carloads of flour a day.

It was incredible. He had cut the daily use of flour by about 75 percent. Here are the figures:

Beginning of blockade to September 11	2,100 tons
September 11–September 16	1,300
September 16–October 1	1,100
October 1–October 26	1,000
October 26–November 1	880
November 1–November 13	735
November 13–November 20	622
November 20–December 25	510

These rations doomed thousands to their deaths. By one estimate the cut doomed one-half the population of the city. Zhdanov knew this. So did Pavlov. They saw no alternative.

Zhdanov called in the leaders of the city's Young Communists. On these younger people would rest the main shock and burden of trying to pull the city through the tragedy which was unfolding.

"Factories are beginning to close down," he said. "There is no electricity, no water, no food. The fall of Tikhvin has put us into a second ring of encirclement. The task of tasks is to organize the life of the workers—to give them inspiration, courage, firmness in the face of all difficulties. This is your task."

On November 13 the bread formula had been changed again. Henceforth it was to contain 25 percent "edible" cellulose. Three hundred people were mobilized to collect "edible" pine and fir bark. Each region of the city was ordered to produce two to two-and-a-half tons of "edible" sawdust per day.

Terror began to live with people. Vera Inber and her husband were walking across Leo Tolstoy Square. There had been two air raids, and now the Germans were shelling the area. It was evening and the sidewalk was icy. Just outside a bakery they heard in the dusk a quavering voice: "Dearie . . . angel . . . help me."

It was an old woman who had fallen in the dark. Overhead the planes roared, the guns barked. She was alone. They helped her to her feet and started to go on. The old woman spoke again, "Darlings. I've lost my bread card. Do help me. I can't find it without you."

To her horror Vera Inber heard herself saying, "Find it yourself. We can't help."

But her husband, saying nothing, hunted on the icy ground and found the old woman's card. Then he and Vera Inber hurried down Petropavlovsk Street, and she wondered what had come over her.

To lose a ration card meant almost certain death. The niece of a friend of Luknitsky's was in a store when someone snatched her card and that of her mother. They were left without food until the end of the month. Luknitsky's friend gave them her card and tried to live on the watery soup of her hospital lunchroom. When he upbraided her, she angrily replied, "It's one thing when a grownup is hungry and another when it's a child."

In Yevgeniya Vasyutina's communal apartment her friend Zina's little daughter cried and cried. She was hungry. On the market you could trade 100 grams of sugar for a pound of cottonseed meal or a kilo of bread for a half-liter of vodka or a tin stove. Cats were beginning to get scarce. So were crows and sparrows. On November 26 Yelena Skryabina heard that 3,000 persons a day were dying in the city. That day, completely unexpectedly, an unknown Red Army man appeared at her door and handed her a pail of sauerkraut. It was manna from heaven.

The temperature was dropping. It was 15 below on November 11 and 20 below on the fourteenth. Luknitsky was sure the cold would beat the Germans. He did not realize it was likely to kill starving Leningrad first.

"November was the most alarming month of the whole blockade," the official historians of Leningrad concluded, "not only because of the difficulties but because of the uncertainties. War is war. And it was difficult to predict how events would develop around Leningrad. The Fascist command might again mount an offensive toward Svirstroi or toward Vologda. Such a possibility could not be excluded."

Vera Inber wrote in her diary for November 28:

The future of Leningrad is alarming. Not long ago Professor Z told me: "My daughter spent the whole evening in the cellar, looking for a cat." I was ready to congratulate her on such love for a cat when Z explained: "We eat them." Another time Z, a passionate hunter, said: "My life is finished when I have killed my last partridge. And it seems to me I have killed it."

As the plight of Leningrad worsened, the rumors flew. Toward the end of November everyone heard rumors that on the first of December no more bread would be issued. On that date adults would begin to receive cottonseed cake. Children would get hardtack. This was more than torn nerves could stand. Hundreds of people stormed the few food stores. On November 25 more than 2,000 persons pushed into the Vasilevsky Island department store. An enormous line appeared outside Milk Store No. 2 in the Smolny region, where soya milk was being issued. The queue did not disperse when air-raid sirens sounded. People patiently waited. Whatever they got would be better than what they could get after December 1.

"I've waited since 4 A.M.," one said. "I've not eaten all day." "I can't go home," another said. "My children are starving."

Shells fell in their midst. Some fell, killed and wounded. Others ran in terror. But half an hour later the survivors were back in line, waiting for the saleswomen, wrapped up like snow maidens, their fingers trembling with weakness and cold, to tear off the coupon and give them a husk of bread.

On December first, walking down Wolf Street, Vera Inber saw something she had never before seen—a corpse on a child's sled. Instead of being placed in a coffin the body had been tightly wrapped in a sheet, the knees and breast clearly outlined in the white swaddling cloth. A strange sight, like something out of the Bible or ancient Egypt. She did not know it would soon become a sight so common as not to attract a passing glance.

On December first the siege of Leningrad entered its ninety-second day. Ninety-one days had passed since the fall of Mga. Seven men knew the secret of Leningrad's destiny. It was so terrible they themselves could not believe the future which the black figures foretold.

PART IV

The Longest Winter

There are three of us in the room, but two
No longer breathe. They are dead.
I understand it all,
But why do I break the bread
In three pieces?

37 . *"When Will the Blockade Be Lifted?"*

INCREDIBLE AS IT SEEMED TO ADMIRAL PANTELEYEV, throughout October and into November the people of Leningrad assumed that almost any day the blockade would end. Even when the ration was cut, cut again and then again, friends said to Panteleyev: "Tell me, please, Yuri Aleksandrovich, when do they plan to lift the blockade?" With them there was no question of *can* the blockade be lifted; just a matter of timing, as though, Panteleyev thought, they were asking when the Red Arrow express was due to arrive from Moscow.

Panteleyev assured his friends that the siege would be broken very soon. But he knew that the truth was far different, that week by week the situation was growing worse, not better, and that, in fact, each effort to break the blockade had only deepened the plight of the city.

The first serious attempt to smash the German ring had been a desperate gamble in late September by Marshal Zhukov. He threw two divisions and a brigade of marines across the Neva River at a place called Nevskaya Dubrovka, northwest of Mga. The troops managed to win a toehold on the south side of the river but nothing more. Marshal Zhukov tried several other long shots, including amphibious landings around the Peterhof Palace. None worked. The Peterhof marines were wiped out almost to the last man.

But Moscow and Leningrad both knew that something had to be done. Stalin telegraphed Leningrad October 12 ordering a counteroffensive, and on October 15 Marshal N. N. Voronov arrived on the scene to make sure that the orders were carried out.

Voronov had been absent from his native city only about two weeks—just long enough to become involved in a dangerous row with Stalin's police chief, Lavrenti P. Beria. The dispute arose when Stalin questioned Voronov about an allocation of 50,000 rifles for Beria's police troops. Voronov said he didn't know why they were needed. Beria, a Georgian like Stalin, started making an explanation in Georgian. But Stalin was angry. He shut off Beria and cut the figure to 10,000 rifles. Beria blamed Voronov. "Just you wait," he said. "We'll tie your guts into knots!" On that note Voronov was delighted to go back to Leningrad, taking with him a small envelope in which, written on thin cigarette paper, were the Stavka plans for breaking the Leningrad blockade.

When Marshal Voronov arrived with the Stavka orders, General Ivan I. Fedyuninsky convened his Leningrad Military Council and decided to launch the offensive almost immediately—on October 20—with a simultaneous push by the Fifty-fourth and Fifty-fifth armies and the Neva Operating Group, a task force on the Neva River front. The High Command specified that almost all the mobile resources of the Leningrad front be thrown into the operation—eight rifle divisions, not less than 100 60-ton KV tanks, large-caliber artillery, all available rocket weapons or "Katyushas" and such air strength as could be assembled, including remnants of the Baltic Fleet air arm.

Actually, Fedyuninsky could mobilize only 63,000 men, 475 guns and 97 tanks (including 59 KV's). The Germans, he estimated, had a force of 54,000 men and 450 cannon.

Presumably for morale purposes, the Leningrad Command ordered all political commissars to take every possible step to "halt empty and harmful gossip" about the imminent arrival of new armies from the east which would liberate the city. "The city of Lenin is capable of liberating itself. We have everything we need: weapons and men."

This was brave but foolish talk.

The "liberating" attack was doomed from the start. Four days before the date set for the Red Army offensive the Nazis launched their own attack. General Rudolf Schmidt, commander of the 39th Motorized Corps, supported by the German 1st Army Corps, hit at the hinge of the Soviet Fourth and Fifty-second armies. Soon the Russians were reeling back in confusion. Within days they were fighting desperately to prevent the Germans from tightening the siege by forging a second circle around the city.

The Soviet Fourth and Fifty-second armies stood east and slightly south of Leningrad, guarding the rail line which approached Leningrad from the east through the junction point of Tikhvin. If General Schmidt captured Tikhvin, he would breach the only route by which the Russians could now bring food, fuel and ammunition to Lake Ladoga for transshipment to Leningrad. The capture of Tikhvin would seal the fate of Leningrad. The only alternative supply route would involve the 220-mile haul over primitive forest tracks to the Lake Ladoga ports. It was not credible, even by Russian standards, that sufficient supplies could be brought in by such means to maintain a city which still contained roughly three million persons, civilian and military.

The old rule of war that when one thing goes badly everything goes badly was striking Leningrad.

The promised Soviet offensive never really got going. The Germans had caught the Russians off balance, and the Soviet margin of superiority was too thin to produce a breakthrough.

There were, inevitably, other problems. General Fedyuninsky, new to the Leningrad Command and junior to several of his subordinate army commanders, asked Marshal A. M. Vasilevsky, Chief of Staff in Moscow, to be relieved. He pointed out that General Khozin, commander of the Fifty-fourth Army, was a lieutenant general whereas he was only a major general. Fedyuninsky had served under Khozin as a battalion commander when Khozin commanded a division.

Leningrad Party Secretary Zhdanov sought to persuade Marshal Voronov to take Fedyuninsky's job. Zhdanov had worked closely with Voronov, a Leningrader and a man of great military prestige and experience. Voronov, however, was wary. He knew the difficulties and dangers. He temporized. He pointed out that he was a Deputy Commissar of Defense, Chief of Red Army Artillery and the special representative of the High Command in Leningrad. If he asked for the Leningrad Command, Moscow might think he was trying to evade his responsibilities. It wasn't a convincing argument, but Zhdanov had to leave the decision up to Moscow. Moscow did the obvious. It sent Fedyuninsky to take over the Fifty-fourth Army and brought in Khozin, the Fifty-fourth Army chief, to take Fedyuninsky's job.

Voronov's role in these days was equivocal, to say the least.

"Never before in history," he wrote in his memoirs, "had Leningrad been in such a dangerous position. The honor of our generation depended on our saving her."

Yet he refused the Leningrad Command, and his principal efforts were directed not at saving the city from strangulation by the Germans but at shipping *out* of Leningrad guns, munitions and supplies for use on other fronts, particularly the Moscow front.

In his first conversation with Voronov on his arrival October 15, Zhdanov asked for more matériel and more munitions. Voronov replied that there were large quantities of military supplies in Leningrad and suggested the city should be able to boost its production to not less than a million shells of all calibers in November and even more in December. Meanwhile, he proposed to organize the shipment out of Leningrad of items needed elsewhere and in return would see about delivering powder and other products which Leningrad might need for shell production.

Under the influence of Voronov, Leningrad set a production quota of 1,722,000 shells and mines for December. (It was not, of course, fulfilled. By mid-December shell production dropped to zero.) Voronov actually shipped out of Leningrad 452 76-mm field guns, 120-mm mortars and 82-mm guns and 560 50-caliber machine guns. He advised Supreme Headquarters that he had on hand 50,000 shell casings for 76-mm armored shells and could send them out at the rate of 350 to 370 per plane. (He was using DC-3's for the most part or TB-3's.)[1] Moscow couldn't believe the figures at first. Later, they began to ask, "Can't you send more from Leningrad? Load up the planes quickly." He shipped 30,000 shell casings by mid-December.

Voronov's real task seems to have been to extract from Leningrad every last resource before final catastrophe befell the northern capital. Behind Voronov's assignment lay grim logic. The ring about Leningrad was tightening inexorably. Leningrad had won the great battle in September. But it well might perish in the smaller struggle of November.

In fact, one more Soviet army was now falling apart under the hammer of the Germans. The Fourth Army, commanded by Lieutenant General V. F. Yakovlev, was stationed in the dismal marshes along the Volkhov River, protecting the approaches to Budogoshch and Tikhvin on the lone rail link to Lake Ladoga. Neither Yakovlev nor his commanders had experience in fighting under such conditions. The roads were boggy tracks over porous soil. The weather was increasingly cold, with rain turning to sleet and snow. The troops were wet all day and wet all night.

Yakovlev gave ground slowly, but soon his forces were threatened with encirclement. He yielded Budogoshch on October 23 in the hope of saving Tikhvin, but General Schmidt outmaneuvered him.

The alarmed Supreme Command in Moscow ordered the 191st and 44th divisions airlifted from inside Leningrad to protect the approaches to Tikhvin.

But General Yakovlev fed his reserves into battle, one by one, without waiting to build up his strength. It was a fatal error. By November 6 the situation was hopeless. The Fourth Army had been cut into three segments. The central group, still under General Yakovlev's direct command, comprised the 44th and 191st divisions. They were falling back on Tikhvin.

There could be no thought among the bitter, weary Soviet troops of celebration of the November 7 holiday. Brief meetings were held in some units. Most were too busy fighting or trying to retreat through the endless marshes. On the morning of November 7 General G. Ye. Degtyarev, chief artillery officer, got a telephone call from General Yakovlev. "Obviously," Degtyarev commented, "it was not any holiday greetings."

The Nazis were breaking through the crumbling Soviet lines, directly threatening Tikhvin. The 44th Division had been cut in two. General Yakovlev encountered officers of the division, fleeing in confusion. He

---

[1] In the last six months of 1941 Leningrad produced 713 tanks, 480 armored cars, 58 armored trains, 2,405 field guns, 648 antitank guns, 10,000 machine guns, 3,000,000 shells, more than 80,000 bombs and rockets (*Leningrad v VOV*, p. 186). The October production quota (not fulfilled) was 1,425,000 shells, 800,000 mines (Karasev, *op. cit.*, p. 158). Karasev estimated that more than 1,000 guns were shipped by air from Leningrad for use by Moscow in the December, 1941, offensive (*ibid.*, p. 133). From October 31 to December 31, 11,614 Kirov plant workers, 6,000 workers of the Izhorsk factory and 8,590 wounded officers and men were evacuated from Leningrad by air (*ibid.*). As early as June three heavy naval batteries, including one from Battery K at Kronstadt, had been shipped to the Vyazma front. (Kuznetsov, *Oktyabr*, No. 8, August, 1968, p. 176.)

ordered them back to the lines and forbade any retreat. Then he personally set out to try and find some troops which might reinforce the front.

It was futile. That night the Military Council of the Fourth Army met at Berezovik, a village just north of Tikhvin. No longer could there be any doubt that the junction point would fall. General Degtyarev and a few others went into Tikhvin by the swampy back roads late at night in order to direct the removal of supplies. The oil depots already were burning, and the sound of detonations as sappers blew up the dumps was continuous. On November 8 General Schmidt's forces entered Tikhvin and the last rail link to Lake Ladoga was cut. All day on the ninth the Berlin radio blasted: "*Achtung! Achtung!* Tikhvin has fallen!"

A second chain of encirclement was taking shape around Leningrad. The Germans were so close to Gostinopolye, the transshipment base for Ladoga supplies, that they were able to bring the warehouses under artillery fire. The supplies caught fire, the shipping chief and his aide were killed, and the workers began to flee. They were halted at gunpoint by one of their fellows, a middle-aged soldier named Aleksei Fedorenko from Astrakhan. Fedorenko had fled with his companions but suddenly realized what he was doing. He got a grip on himself, pointed his gun at the others and terrorized them into going back and continuing to load food for Leningrad.

The peril caused Party Secretary Zhdanov to send one of his most trusted associates to the Tikhvin front—Terenti F. Shtykov, a Party secretary specializing in military and security matters. Shtykov was a native Leningrader. He was too young to have participated in the Revolution but had been a Young Communist and an ambitious factory worker in the Proletarian factory in Leningrad. He went to night school and in 1936 at the age of twenty-nine started to climb the Party ladder. Two years later he became a Leningrad regional Party secretary. From the start of the war he had been occupied with military questions. After the war he was to acquire a special distinction—the only close associate of Party Secretary Zhdanov, the only member of the Leningrad City and Party hierarchy, to survive the dreadful "Leningrad Affair," one of the most bloody of the special purges of the late Stalin era.

Now in these critical days he had been sent to assess the Tikhvin situation. It did not take him long to act. It was apparent that General Yakovlev had lost control of the situation. Shtykov went immediately to Sviritsa, the headquarters of General Meretskov who commanded the Seventh Special Army, defending the Svir River directly north and east of Tikhvin. The fall of Tikhvin threatened Meretskov's position. The two got in touch with Moscow on November 7 and talked first with Marshal A. M. Vasilevsky and then with Stalin. Stalin said he had no reserves at his disposal. He proposed that the command of the Fourth Army units adjacent to Meretskov's front be turned over to Meretskov. The command change was dated November 9, the day after the fall of Tikhvin. Meretskov immediately ordered his reserves forward toward the broken Fourth Army lines. He himself took a light plane and flew to Bolshoi Dvor, just east of Tikhvin where Fourth Army headquarters was said to be located. His plane came down at dusk, whirling up clouds of snow as it halted. At first glance the field appeared to be deserted. One of Meretskov's companions said, "Haven't our troops abandoned this field? I don't see either planes or people." Another added, "On what airfield have we landed?"

Meretskov was relieved to see an air force major approach his plane. The major said that he had been ordered to destroy the airfield and get out.

Meretskov gathered such troops as were present into a log hut on the edge of the field and gave them a pep talk. In a few days, he said, the Germans would be thrown out of Tikhvin. He saw some doubtful grimaces. The mood of the men was low. After the long retreat, the unsuccessful battles, the heavy casualties, they had lost hope of victory. He talked to the officers. Most of them had fallen back through Tikhvin. They could not explain why it had surrendered so quickly, and they did not know why it had not been defended. The explanation, Meretskov later became convinced, was the usual one. The divisions had been bled white. Most of them numbered no more than a thousand men. They had been cut off. They were out of ammunition. They had lost their arms. And General Yakovlev had lost control of them.

Meretskov's first task was to restore order and confidence. He began to call in Yakovlev's surviving commanders. Among them was General Degtyarev, Yakovlev's artillery chief, worn and dirty, just in from Tikhvin, where he stayed to the last, trying to get supplies out. Degtyarev was worried. He knew that Meretskov was stern and demanding. He did not relish having to go before the new commander in chief directly from fallen Tikhvin, for whose loss he regarded himself as guilty. Meretskov froze him with a long, searching look. The General was a heavy-set man of forty, with thick lips and cold gray eyes which narrowed as he gazed at Degtyarev.

"I want to ask you," Meretskov said, "why it was that during the retreat your artillery was not able to carry out its assignments."

Degtyarev's heart sank. He did not know whether Meretskov was aware that he was among the many Red Army officers who had been purged in 1938 and "rehabilitated" on the eve of World War II. But he recognized the familiar terms in which guilt was to be assigned. He braced his shoulders and said, "I am prepared to take the responsibility for the failures which we suffered at Tikhvin."

What Degtyarev meant, in the language of the Red Army, was that he was prepared to be shot. He stood silently. Meretskov got up, emerged from behind his desk and began to pace the room. He stared long and hard at Degtyarev. Then he sat down, picked up a pencil, put it down and said, "It is good that you are ready to take the responsibility. But the chief thing is not that. It is how we go on from here, in order not to repeat our mistakes."

Degtyarev could breathe again. He was not going before the firing squad.

The task ahead would not be easy. Already the Germans were turning north toward Volkhov. They were within a few miles of Volkhovstroi, site of the big power station serving the Leningrad region, a monument of the Revolution. It had been completed in 1926, the first unit in Lenin's program for the electrification of Russia.

The loss of Volkhov would put the seal to Leningrad's fate—if Tikhvin had not done so.

Volkhov was defended by the Fifty-fourth Army, which, since he had traded jobs wth General Khozin on October 26, was commanded by General Ivan Fedyuninsky, an energetic and able officer. With the fall of Tikhvin he had asked Leningrad for reinforcements and had been given one division—the 3rd Guards.

"We've nothing more to give you," Khozin said, "now or in the future."

As Fedyuninsky watched his right flank where the remnants of the Fourth Army, under Chief of Staff General Lyapin, were falling back, his concern mounted. Lyapin was, in Fedyuninsky's view, indecisive and unsound. He had set up his rear bases so far from the front that he was unable to maintain his supply lines.

Fedyuninsky sent a telegram to Supreme Headquarters November 10 asking that the remaining Fourth Army units under Lyapin's command be turned over to him. He added: "If this can still be done today, then the situation may be saved. If it is done tomorrow, then it will be too late. Volkhov will fall."

Fedyuninsky was directing his army from a command post in the forest, located in a dugout so small that it could accommodate no more than four or five persons at one time. As he awaited an answer to his telegram, Dmitri V. Pavlov, the Leningrad food chief, arrived with Captain V. S. Cherokov, commander of the Ladoga fleet.

Pavlov went right to the point.

"What do you think?" he asked. "Can we expect to hold Volkhov or should we begin to evacuate the stores? I want a frank answer."

Fedyuninsky told them about his telegram. As they sat there, he was called to the telegraph apparatus. A message in the clear was coming in. His request was granted. He was to take over the remaining Fourth Army troops, and the defense of Volkhov was placed on his shoulders. A confirming telegram came in late on the evening of November 11. The transfer was to take place at 6 A.M. the next day.

Fedyuninsky, Pavlov and Cherokov immediately started for the village of Plekhanovo, where General Lyapin had his headquarters. It was a big, peaceful settlement. Smoke was coming out of the chimneys and women were drawing water from the village well. A red dog came barking out of a barn. They spotted the headquarters hut by the telephone wires and an automobile which stood outside, carefully camouflaged with cut fir branches.

"Where is General Lyapin?" Fedyuninsky asked the duty officer.

"He is resting and ordered that he not be disturbed," the officer replied.

"Wake him up!" Fedyuninsky ordered. In due course General Lyapin appeared. He had taken his time about dressing. Fedyuninsky told him of the change of command. "By tonight I suggest that you get up to the front," he added.

Fedyuninsky's next step was to obtain permission to destroy the Volkhov Hydroelectric Plant, if necessary, to keep it from falling into German hands. He got the authorization November 12. Then he called in Major General Chekin of the engineering corps and ordered him to prepare the plant for destruction. Most of the power machinery had already been evacuated. The last shipment had gone out on November 5. Of ten turbines only two small ones remained—mostly to supply the little city of Volkhovstroi and the military command. Only twenty-six power station workers, headed by Director I. F. Zhemchuzhnikov, were still on hand. They had orders that if the Germans broke through they were to drain off the oil and run the turbines on dry bearings, destroying them. A detachment of sappers under the personal direction of Major General Chekin placed explosive charges under the power plant. General Chekin had orders not to detonate the charges without personal word from General Fedyuninsky. Fedyuninsky was determined that destruction would be carried out only as a last resort because of the historical association of the plant with Lenin and the Revolution.

The Germans were already within a few miles of the station. But Fedyuninsky thought he could save it. All of his forces had been categorically ordered not to retreat. The order was issued by Fedyuninsky and countersigned by his Military Council member V. A. Sychev and by G. Kh. Bumagin, a Leningrad Party secretary. Word was taken to each unit by political agitators and commissars. It meant one thing: any soldier or officer who retreated would be subject to summary court-martial and execution.

Fedyuninsky was dead serious. The 310th Infantry Division was the last unit holding the Germans back from the Volkhov station. Colonel Zamirovsky, an old friend from service together in the Far East, telephoned. The Germans were attacking his command post. What should he do? Obviously he expected Fedyuninsky to permit him to retreat. Fedyuninsky said, "Go on fighting. If you can't hold the enemy at a distance, then hold on in the command post."

"Yes, sir," Zamirovsky replied. Two hours later he called again. He had driven the Germans back half a mile.

"Good," Fedyuninsky said. "If you drive him back half a mile every two hours, your command post will be secure by dark. Good luck."

Fedyuninsky's hopes rose. But he suffered a blow from an unexpected quarter—a blinding toothache. He chewed tobacco. He put a hot water bottle on his cheek. He rinsed his mouth with vodka. Nothing helped. And there was no dentist at hand. Finally he called in a woman military doctor.

"Which tooth is it?" she asked. "You have three close together on the right side."

"How do I know?" Fedyuninsky wailed. "You can see how my cheek is swollen. Take them all out."

The woman shrugged, got out her instruments and yanked the three teeth. Fedyuninsky went back to the task of trying to save Volkhov.

November those in charge of Leningrad's fate came to remember as the most alarming of many alarming months. Each new communiqué of the Soviet Information Bureau was more depressing than the last. The Battle of Moscow raged on. No one knew whether the Soviet capital would hold out. And no one knew whether the second iron collar would remain around Leningrad's choking neck. Indeed, there were even more urgent fears. Would the Germans press on, sweep around the eastern shores of Ladoga, make contact with the Finns and drive east to Vologda, the junction point northeast of Moscow? Might not Moscow soon find itself cut off, just as Leningrad was? Such a possibility could not be excluded.

In this critical situation Mikhail I. Kalinin, the President of the Soviet Union, himself a Leningrader, an old Leningrad worker, an old Putilov worker, an ancient and respected figure—one of the few in the government —wrote a personal letter to the State Defense Committee, that is, to Stalin. He said:

> The difficulty and danger of the Leningrad situation have obviously increased. It seems essential to me that we must seek out and establish reliable routes for supplying Leningrad in winter conditions—by sledge, automobile and plane. The Germans obviously are driving for a distant goal, aiming for Vologda in order to cut us off from possible connections with America.

Kalinin proposed that a member of the State Defense Committee or some equally responsible figure work out practical measures to thwart the German objective.

Stalin, for once, was not deaf to a proposal by Kalinin.

"Your observations regarding Leningrad and Vologda," he replied, "are perfectly correct and timely. We will take all essential steps."

A special airlift was ordered on November 16 to bring not less than 200 tons of high-calorie foods daily into Leningrad, including 135 tons of concentrated cereals and soup, 20 tons of sausage and canned pork, 10 tons of dried milk and egg powder, 15 tons of butter and 20 tons of fats. The air force was ordered to provide 24 heavy transports and 10 heavy bombers to fly the food in. It was far from enough to save the city, and the quotas were seldom met. But it was a help.[2]

---

[2] From September 13 to December 31, 6,000 tons of high-priority freight, including 4,325 tons of food and 1,660 tons of arms and munitions, were flown into Leningrad (*N.Z.*, p. 256). From October 21 to December 31, 3,357 tons of high-calorie food were flown in. Some 64 planes had been assigned to the route, but only 20 or 22 were normally in condition to fly. They brought in 40 to 50 tons a day. (Karasev, *op. cit.*, pp. 132, 133.)

At Stalin's call the Supreme Command ordered an immediate offensive to relieve the pressure on Volkhov and free Tikhvin. What would be the result was far from clear. Meantime, Leningrad stood at the brink of catastrophe.

Party Secretary Zhdanov summoned the Leningrad Military Council to his Smolny office to explore what aid could be given the forthcoming operations. Lieutenant General M. S. Khozin, the front commander, was absent. He was spending almost all his time with the Fifty-second, Fourth and Fifty-fourth armies as they prepared their plans.

Zhdanov seemed very, very tired to Colonel Bychevsky, the chief of engineers. Zhdanov's asthma was much worse. His breath came in sharp, uneven gulps. His heavy face was puffed with fatigue and only his dark eyes glowed. He took a long Russian cigarette, creased its cardboard tube, lighted it, blew a ring of smoke and said, "The situation of Leningrad is very serious, and if we do not take steps, it will become critical. We must think of every way in which we can help the troops on the Volkhov front."

The discussion turned to the possibility of strengthening the Red Army foothold south of the Neva River at Nevskaya Dubrovka. Enormous efforts had gone into maintaining this position. The last light tanks in the Leningrad reserve had been put across the river the night before. Eight already had been destroyed by the Nazis, and the remaining six had been dug in as stationary firing points.

"To talk about an offensive from the *place d'armes* in such conditions borders on the senseless," the front's armored commander, General N. A. Bolotnikov, observed. "If you want to help the Fifty-fourth Army, then you need heavy tanks. Without them the infantry can do nothing. You can ask Bychevsky about trying to put KV tanks across. He hasn't any pontoons, and there is ice over almost the entire Neva."

Party Secretary Kuznetsov interjected nervously: "Are you proposing that we give up the *place d'armes* to the Germans?" Kuznetsov looked even more tired than Zhdanov. His face was hatchet-thin, his crooked nose pencil-sharp, his eyes fever-bright.

The discussion underlined the precariousness of Leningrad's position. To move tanks across the ice Bychevsky needed enormous quantities of wire netting. He thought he might find it somewhere in the city. But pontoons had to be produced by a factory. He asked Zhdanov to approve 5,000 kilowatts from the city power stations to power the machines. Zhdanov pulled a battered notebook from his pocket. "I can't give you 5,000," he said. "Maybe I can get 3,000." Bychevsky sighed so loudly Zhdanov raised his eyebrows. Bychevsky said his pontoon men were on a rear-echelon ration of 300 grams of bread a day. They didn't have the strength to carry on. Zhdanov promised to boost their ration to front-line levels, 500 grams a day, for the duration of the effort.

The strain was beginning to tell on Zhdanov and the other leaders as well.

These men, civilian and military commanders alike, worked normally eighteen, twenty or twenty-two hours a day. Most of them snatched a few moments' sleep, head down on a desk, or a cat nap on a couch in the office. They ate a little better than the general population. Zhdanov and his associates, like the front commanders, received a military ration: a pound or more of bread a day plus a bowl of meat or fish soup and possibly a little cereal or kasha. They had a lump or two of sugar to suck with their tea. They lost weight on this diet, but did not become emaciated, and none of the principal commanders or Party chiefs fell victim to dystrophy. But their physical strength was exhausted, their nerves were frayed, and most of them suffered permanent damage to their hearts and circulatory systems.

Zhdanov, more than some of the others, showed visible signs of fatigue, exhaustion and nervous debilitation. One November day he went to the front for a firsthand look at winter fighting conditions. He saw through the telescopic observation lenses that the Nazi troops around Shlisselburg had white winter camouflage coats and skis. The Red Army men were still wearing dark greatcoats and cotton-padded jackets. They had no skis.

Back at Smolny he summoned Lieutenant General Lagunov, chief of supply services, and asked why the Soviet troops were not yet equipped for winter. Lagunov said orders for winter camouflage capes had been given tardily, and they would not be ready for five or six days. There were few skis in the army warehouse. There were skis in the hands of civilian sports clubs, but it would take time to assemble them.

Lagunov was one of Zhdanov's best friends, an intelligent, precise, honest officer. But Zhdanov turned on him in towering rage. He charged Lagunov with lethargy and carelessness.

"I give you three days!" he shouted. "If in that time you haven't gotten the skis and capes—remember we are in a besieged fortress and the Defense Act is strictly applied to all violators."

In a word, Lagunov was to get the skis and capes within seventy-two hours or be shot. Fortunately, he fulfilled the order.

On November 24 the Supreme Command issued its directive calling for coordinated blows by three armies—the Fifty-fourth, the Fourth and the Fifty-second. The Fourth was to act first, followed by the Fifty-second on December 1 and the Fifty-fourth on December 3.

General Meretskov met with his Military Council on November 30. His face was ashen with fatigue. The VC high-security telephone from Moscow rang. Meretskov answered. "The Kremlin is calling," the operator said. General Degtyarev and his colleagues sat silently, listening and watching. Obviously a member of the State Defense Committee was talking. By Meretskov's answers it was apparent he was speaking of the terrible situation in Leningrad.

"I very well understand the situation of the defenders of Leningrad," they heard Meretskov say. "But it is not so easy for us either. At Tikhvin a fresh division of Germans has appeared, the 61st Infantry. The enemy still has a large superiority in strength."

Then they heard someone saying, "Wait a minute!"

Meretskov was silent. He nervously rubbed his prominent high forehead. It was clear to the listeners. He was waiting for Stalin. The members of the Military Council froze in their chairs.

Meretskov offered no more explanations. Now he listened, simply interjecting, "I understand. . . . I will take measures. . . . It will be done."

The talk was short. He hung up. Again he ran his hand over his brow. He went silently to the map, looked at it for a long time and then turned to the council, a grim smile on his lips.

"Well, that's the way it is," he said. "And you are offended when I put you on the griddle!" He walked back and forth from one end of the room to another. Then he spoke.

"We will join the troops within an hour. All of us."

Stalin was not toying. Three days later he sent a special commission to Meretskov's headquarters. It was headed by that ugliest of police bullies, G. I. Kulik, a lieutenant of Beria's.[3] Kulik was the police general who was personally responsible for much of the present difficulty. His ignorant and cowardly direction of the Fifty-fourth Army in September was credited by many Soviet military men with the major role in the Leningrad disaster. Marshal Voronov, for instance, put the blame on Kulik for the whole Leningrad encirclement. But Kulik still had the confidence of Stalin and Beria, and now he had been sent out to check the plans for the Tikhvin offensive.

Kulik cross-examined each of Meretskov's commanders in turn. Degtyarev outlined the artillery preparations, noting that the Germans had no shortage of ammunition. He conceded that the Fourth Army had a superiority over the Germans in number of guns.

Kulik attacked savagely: "With this superiority in artillery why haven't you cleared a way for the infantry into Tikhvin?"

Degtyarev tried to point out that his artillery concentration was only five or six guns per kilometer.

"You are sitting in your headquarters and you don't know what is going on with the troops!" Kulik shouted. "You should have been shot long ago. Tikhvin was lost because of you."

"It is hard to say how this might have finished for me," Degtyarev recalled

---

[3] Kulik served in Spain and was known there as "General No No" because the only Spanish he knew was "No." He used it on every occasion, appropriate or inappropriate. On his return to Moscow he was promoted and occupied a rank equivalent to that of marshal at the outbreak of war. He fell into encirclement on the Central Front but managed to make his way out and was sent south as a Stavka representative. He was reduced in rank for gross errors of conduct, but, in the words of Admiral Kuznetsov, this had little effect on him. (*Nakanune*, p. 244.) Voronov says he was demoted to major general for "failure to fulfill responsible assignments for the High Command in the first days of the war." (Voronov, *op. cit.*, p. 354.)

later. But Meretskov came to his defense, and Kulik finally subsided, muttering threats. Meretskov opened his offensive on the morning of December 5 with Kulik watching every move. There was one final row. Meretskov and Kulik tried to get more ammunition from Moscow. Moscow, just launching the historic offensive which was to drive Hitler back from the capital and administer his first serious defeat, said they needed all the shells they had themselves.

Fortunately, Meretskov's troops pushed forward savagely through the snow that drifted five and six feet deep and day by day fought closer to Tikhvin despite temperatures of 20 and 30 below zero. His drive was assisted by Fedyuninsky's Fifty-fourth Army, advancing from the north with the aid of KV 60-ton tanks which, incredibly, had been brought over the ice of Lake Ladoga. Their turrets had been demounted to reduce their weight.[4]

The final attack was marked by one oddity. The Germans announced over the radio that General Fedyuninsky had committed suicide. Party Secretary Zhdanov telephoned Fedyuninsky and wished him long years of life, and the next day a VC call came in from his wife in Sverdlovsk.

Mrs. Fedyuninsky hadn't heard about the rumor of her husband's suicide. But she was delighted to talk with him.

On December 8 Meretskov's Fourth Army fought into Tikhvin. By December 9 the city was firmly in Soviet hands again. It had been held by the Germans precisely one month. Its recapture on the seventieth day of the siege was the first real sign that the lines around Leningrad could be held, that the second ring could not be fastened about the northern capital, that the Nazi dream of striking to the east to Vologda and cutting off Moscow from the rear, from Siberia, from America, would be thwarted.

It coincided with a directive signed by Hitler December 8, No. 59, in which he ordered Army Group Nord to strengthen its control of the railroad and highway from Tikhvin and Volkhov to Kolchanovo in order to secure the possibility of joining hands with the Finns in Karelia.

Tikhvin was a real victory. Whether it would save Leningrad and its millions of people, now entering the skeletal world of starvation, of life without heat, without light, without transport, no one knew for certain.

On December 9 the Leningrad streetcar system, except for a few freight lines carrying ammunition, ceased operation. The ninety cars on the eight remaining routes halted. From now on Leningrad would walk with weak and tired feet on icy, drifted streets. "There is almost no electricity in the city," Director A. K. Kozlovsky of the Northern Cable factory wrote in his diary December 2. "Today there was none in our factory."

Pavel Luknitsky returned to Leningrad from the front on the night of December 8. He sat at his desk, writing in his diary at 11:30 P.M. on December 11:

---

[4] This detail, reported by Fedyuninsky himself, is probably in error. The KV's actually seem to have moved over the ice in January to assist a later offensive. (A. Saparov, *Doroga Zhizni*, p. 146.)

A dark night. In this room as in all the others in this house on Shchors Street and almost all the houses in Leningrad there is frost and unbroken darkness. Yes . . . Tikhvin has been liberated in the nick of time. Last night "changes in tram routes" were announced. But the trams have almost all ceased to run. *Leningradskaya Pravda* tonight came out in two pages instead of four. There is much new destruction. Snow drifts in the streets. People with exhausted faces walk slowly—dark shadows on the streets. And more and more coffins, roughly made, are pulled on sleds, by the stumbling, slipping, weak relatives of the dead. Worst of all—the darkness . . . hunger and cold and darkness . . .

Leningrad had won another victory. Would she survive it?

The Germans didn't think so. Colonel General Halder, the diarist of the Wehrmacht, jotted down under date of December 13: "The Commander of the army group is inclined to the view—after the failure of all attempts by the enemy to liquidate our foothold on the Neva—that we may expect the complete starvation of Leningrad."

38 . The Road of Life

ON THE EVENING OF NOVEMBER 19 CAPTAIN MIKHAIL Murov and his transport regiment were working on the defense lines at Pulkovo Heights, just outside Leningrad, installing new barbed wire on the approaches to the pillboxes.

Night falls by 3 P.M. in Leningrad in November, and it was long past sunset when Murov got orders to bring his drivers immediately to the Leningrad freight station for transportation to some unknown destination. Murov was puzzled. He didn't know where the railroad could take his troops in the blockaded city, but he began to move them into Leningrad. Most were People's Volunteers, and he permitted those who had families in the city to dash home for a moment on the way to the station.

The troops marched through the wind-swept streets. Hardly a soul was visible. There was no sound but the distant rattle of guns, no light, and even the moon was in a dark phase. The men tramped through the shadows of ruined buildings, here a gaping window, there a sagging roof. Under their tough felt boots was the crunch of broken glass. Trolleycars and buses stood motionless in the snow like frozen dinosaurs. Leningrad seemed an abandoned city. Some men managed to see their families and snatch a brief, often despairing moment with them. Some did not.

At the freight station they joined units already assembled and were loaded aboard heatless cars in which cardboard and plywood panels replaced broken windows. The train jerked to a start and crawled through the darkness. It was morning before the troops debarked at the bomb-cratered fishing village of Kokkorevo on the frozen shores of Lake Ladoga. There an officer put Murov in charge of a sledge battalion, part of a column which was about to move across Ladoga and bring back to Leningrad its first supplies by ice road.

The plan for the ice road had taken form as early as mid-October. The Leningrad Military Council ordered Lieutenant General F. N. Lagunov, chief of rear services, to begin preparations at that time after the success of the Nazi offensive under General Schmidt began to make it less and less likely that the circle around the city could be broken in the immediate future.

Lagunov was already engaged in improving the primitive Ladoga port facilities to increase the tonnage being carried across the capricious lake by the special Ladoga shipping flotilla. He had some twenty thousand workers building docks and warehouses at Osinovets and Kokkorevo on the Leningrad side and at Kobona, Lavrovo, Novaya Ladoga and Voibokalo on the eastern shore.

No one knew for certain whether an ice road could be built. Ladoga, or Lake Nevo as it was called in ancient times, was the biggest in Europe, although little known outside of Russia—125 miles long and nearly 80 miles across at its widest point. Its greatest depth was more than 700 feet, but in the southern part between Shlisselburg and Volkhov it was shallow, ranging from 60 to 150 feet deep.

Storms often swept the lake, particularly in autumn, when they might endure six or seven days. Lagunov could get little information about ice conditions. An observer who had spent thirty years tending a lighthouse on Sukho Island reported that he usually was cut off from the shore from the twentieth of October to the twentieth of January by alternately freezing and melting ice. The ice shifted and moved so often that it was too hazardous to attempt a crossing.

One Leningrad scientist worked out a formula on ice formation on the lake. At 23 degrees above zero 4 inches of ice would form in 64 hours; at 14 above 4 inches would form in 34 hours; at 5 above zero 4 inches in 23 hours. A foot of ice would be laid down in 24 days at 23 above. It would take 8 days to create a foot of ice at 5 above.

Four inches of ice could support a horse without a load. A horse pulling a sledge with a ton of freight required 7 inches of ice. A truck carrying a ton of freight needed 8 inches of ice.

Obviously, 8 inches of ice would be the required minimum for mass movement of supplies.

The inadequate statistics indicated that ice formation seldom began in the Shlisselburg gulf before November 19 and often not until early January. Once the ice formed, however, it usually reached a thickness of 3 to 5 feet —strong enough for almost any purpose.

The Russians had a good deal of experience in operating over ice. There had been ice offensives during the winter war with Finland, including an attack on Vyborg and a thirty-mile march over an ice road in the Ukhta area. Earlier, during the Civil War, trains had been operated on tracks laid across the Volga near Sviyazhsk, a crossing of about a mile. There had been an ice railroad across a corner of Lake Baikal when the Trans-Siberian was being built and one across the Kola River near Murmansk during World War I.

But none of these projects had the complexity—or the urgency—of the Ladoga route.

Ladoga had many special characteristics. For example, the level of the water varied enormously with the wind, and it might rise or fall from as much as a foot and a half to nearly four feet within a few hours—even in winter.

The projected route would be twenty to thirty miles long. It was linked at the Leningrad end to an old and poorly equipped branch railroad which in prewar days had been used for excursion traffic and little more. This line was thirty-five miles long and connected with five separate Leningrad depots.

The Leningrad Military Council on November 3 ordered that the road be put into operation over the lake as soon as the ice was hard enough. If the Ladoga ice road held a high priority before the fall of Tikhvin on November 8, it became vital after that date. There was no other possibility of providing Leningrad with the supplies for survival. To be sure, a few tons per day could be flown in, but this was not nearly enough for the defense forces, and the civilian population of more than 2,500,000 would die within a few weeks.

Nothing could be done while the lake was still unfrozen. But the fall of Tikhvin meant that a new land road must be built to Ladoga. The order for this route was issued by the Leningrad Military Council on November 8. It was to run from Novaya Ladoga through a series of unknown villages—Karpino, Yamskoye, Novinka, Yeremina Gora, Shugozero, Nikulskoye, Lakhta, Veliki Dvor and Serebryanskaya—to Zaborye. These peasant hamlets were so tiny they showed only on local maps. The road was to be finished within fifteen days, and the goal was to carry a minimum of 2,000 tons a day.[1]

This route led for 220 miles along the old Yaroslavl tract, one of the ancient forest routes of old Russia. It wound through tamarack swamps, cranberry or *klukva* bogs, lakes and dense timber. Much of the region was hardly inhabited; much was sheer wilderness. The notion that it might be possible to maintain a flow of supplies along so tortuous a road in the dead of Russian winter with its exhausting toll on trucks, sledges and men was wildly optimistic. Yet there was no alternative. Build the road or die.

Peasants, collective farmers, Red Army rear troops, anyone available was put to work on the highway. Meantime, aerial reconnaissance was carried out from November 8 to 10 to study ice formation, which, early as it was for Ladoga, had already begun. The fliers reported ice starting to form throughout the southern part of the lake except for one large open field

[1] Pavlov, *op. cit.*, 3rd edition, p. 135; Saparov, *op. cit.*, p. 43; Kharitonov, *Voyenno-Istoricheskii Zhurnal*, No. 11, November, 1966, p. 120. There is controversy as to the date the order for the road to Zaborye was issued. One account says the order was not approved until November 24 and that it was to be finished by November 30. (F. Lagunov, *Voyenno-Istoricheskii Zhurnal*, No. 12, December, 1964, p. 95.)

of water that cut right across the projected route. On the fifteenth a strong north wind set in. Observers reported that ice was strengthening rapidly throughout the southern area.

November 17 was gray, dark and bitter cold. The sun did not rise until well after 9 A.M. An hour earlier two reconnaissance groups had taken off across the young ice. One, headed by A. N. Stafeyev, tested the ice in the vicinity of Osinovets and Kokkorevo, the two ports on the Leningrad side. The other, led by Lieutenant Leonid N. Sokolov and including thirty men from the 88th Construction Battalion, moved out to check the route from Kokkorevo to the island of Zelenets and on to Kobona on the eastern shore. Each man wore white camouflage clothing and carried his own weapons and food. Each was equipped with ice tools, including axes and alpenstocks. They were roped together and some wore life belts. It was a hard struggle against the wind in the grim November day. They marked the route every one hundred yards with flagged stakes, to facilitate their return and to sight the future ice road. They found the ice averaging four inches thick—just about the minimum to support their movement.

The detachment had nearly reached mid-point when they encountered the first open water. They gingerly circled to the north and finally, after sloshing across a half-submerged ice field, they came out on firm ice again. One man, N. I. Astakhov, fell through, but was rescued. Hours went by. It was very slow going. On the shore Major A. S. Mozhayev waited nervously for their report. Finally Smolny called him. A report on the reconnaissance had been promised by 6 P.M. Where was it? Major Mozhayev gloomily said he was still waiting.

It was long after midnight before the reconnaissance group reached Kobona and 4 A.M. before Mozhayev was able to advise Party Secretary Zhdanov at Smolny that he had gotten a message from Sokolov, sent as they were nearing Kobona after a long detour to the north, expressing confidence that a route could be opened.

Major Mozhayev was unable to restrain himself. He mounted a gray mare and rode out across the ice, following the staked route of the advance party, and within four hours had arrived in Kobona, to the astonishment of his scouts. The ice was five to ten inches thick now, and the great *polynia* or open lake was rapidly shrinking. The temperature had dropped to about 8 degrees above zero.

On the nineteenth General Lagunov himself arrived at Kokkorevo. He took a local fisherman as a guide and moved off on the ice in a light M-1 scout car, following the flagged route. The car was not equipped for ice conditions; the wheels slipped and Lagunov had to travel slowly, paying close heed to cracks and ice trenches. But by late afternoon he was back in Leningrad and reporting in Smolny to Party Secretary Zhdanov that within a few days regular transport on the route would be possible. That evening after a sharp dispute between Zhdanov and Lagunov a decision was approved by the Leningrad Military Council to open the road immediately.

It was this decision which had brought the orders, transferring Captain Murov and his men from the Pulkovo Heights to the Ladoga shores. There beside the frozen lake Murov inspected the supply team with some apprehension. Half the men had had no previous experience with horses. Among them were scientists and even artists. As for the horses, they were rags and bones, so weak they could hardly pull the empty sleighs. Murov's only hope was that on the other side of the lake, at Kobona, there might be oats or hay. Of course, it was not certain that the horses would make it across the lake. Many had not been winter-shod. Fortunately, a box of cleats was found in one of the sledges and some of the horses were shod.

As the caravan waited to take off, an officer, probably a political commissar, came up to Murov and told him that the ration had been reduced again in Leningrad. It had been cut that day, the twentieth, to 250 grams of bread a day for workers and 125 grams for all other individuals. The ration for front-line troops had been cut to 600 grams of bread from 800 on November 8. Now it was cut again to 500. All other troops were cut to 300 grams, about half a loaf.

"There are supplies in the city for two more days," the commissar said. "After that there is nothing more. The ice is very young and not very strong. But we can't wait. Each hour is dear."

A few moments later the detachment started over the gray ice. There were 350 drivers. Intervals of thirty to thirty-five yards separated each sledge, and the column stretched over a distance of possibly five miles. Near the shore stood General Lagunov, watching the take-off. He commented to Murov that his men were too lightly dressed. It was true. The temperature stood at zero. The men did not have heavy snow jackets. But nothing could be done about it. The column moved on. At its head rode Sokolov on a thin but lively white horse. The lake spread out endless and drab. Soon the horses were covered with hoarfrost.

The column moved steadily until it reached Kilometer 9, where a wide crevasse appeared. After an hour's search the scouts directed the sledges to the south. Occasionally the ice cracked under the horses. The sun, never high on the horizon, was slipping under again by the time the column reached the island of Zelenets, where a halt was called for two hours' rest. A ration of 800 grams of bread—nearly a week's supply for an ordinary Leningrader—was doled out along with tea with sugar. But there was no forage. Some drivers shared their bread with the horses. It was midevening before the convoy reached Kobona. There, as the sledges were loaded with flour and food concentrates, more food was supplied the drivers, including hardtack, sugar, macaroni and cottonseed-oil cakes. But again there was nothing for the horses. Murov was in despair. This could be fatal. He did not think the animals would survive 20 to 30 miles back over the ice with loaded sledges. He remembered a trick of Civil War cavalry days and scraped back the snow, uncovering old grass for the horses. Many drivers gave their cottonseed-oil cakes to the horses.

In the dark early-morning hours the convoy reached the Leningrad side. The first few tons of food via ice road had arrived in Leningrad. Military Automobile Highway No. 101, the Road of Life, was open. It was the eighty-third day of the siege.

For several days most of the transport over the road was by horse sledge. In some places the ice was only seven or eight inches thick. General Lagunov assembled about 1,100 horses and sleighs. But he limited loads to 200 to 250 pounds during the initial phase. This was hardly a drop in the bucket compared with Leningrad's needs.

On the night of November 22 the first column of trucks, sixty in all, commanded by Major V. A. Porchunov, arrived on the western shore and on the twenty-third delivered thirty-three tons of flour to Leningrad. The next day only nineteen tons crossed the lake. Porchunov lost one 1½-ton truck and driver in the first crossing. Many trucks in the first days carried gasoline or kerosene to relieve Leningrad's desperate fuel shortage.

Though the ice road had been brought into being, it did not immediately promise to save Leningrad from starvation. On November 25 Leningrad received 70 tons of food; on November 26, 154 tons; on November 27, 126 tons; on November 28, 196 tons; and on November 29, 128 tons. On November 30 there was a thaw and only 62 tons crossed the lake. From November 23 to 30 the road delivered only 800 tons of flour—two days' supply at the barest starvation ration (Leningrad was now using only about 510 tons of flour a day). At this rate Leningrad would starve—only a bit more slowly. And in seven days forty trucks had gone to the bottom of the lake.

These shipments came from stores on hand at Novaya Ladoga. The forest haul over the rutted track from Zaborye did not get started until December 6, despite every effort of the peasants and Red Army men. When finished the road was so narrow in many places that trucks could not pass. The haul from railhead to the Leningrad side of the lake required ten to twenty days. Trucks took two weeks to make the round trip from Zaborye to Novaya Ladoga and back, averaging not more than twenty to twenty-five miles a day.

Party Secretary Zhdanov decided to send his fellow secretary, T. F. Shtykov, to Vologda, the control point for supplies to Ladoga. His task was to try to get food moving more rapidly. Shtykov arrived in Vologda November 25. The Vologda Party organization was providing substantial relief shipments of food to Leningrad. But the problem lay with forwarding food to the railhead at Zaborye and a secondary base at nearby Podborovye.

After Shtykov revealed how critical the situation was, the Vologda officials attempted to speed up shipments. The operation of the railroad had been hampered by lack of fuel. City and village residents were sent to the forests to cut wood. They brought it in by the sledgeload for the locomotives. Normal railroad operations through Vologda were suspended to route supply trains straight through to the railheads. Leningrad supply trains got special numbers. They were all in the "97" series. The moment a "97" train halted at a station for fueling or watering, rail workers dropped all tasks to speed it on its way.

There were enormous losses of trucks in the early days. The road was often shelled and strafed by the Nazis. Kilometer No. 9 was a special danger point. There were cracks in the ice and unexpected weak spots. So many machines were lost that Zhdanov called a Military Council meeting and asked Lagunov, "Don't you think that we will lose all our transport and find ourselves without trucks?"

Lagunov said he had made arrangements with Vice Admiral F. I. Krylov to raise the sunken machines as soon as the ice thickened.

Even heavier loss of machines occurred on the abominable forest road to Zaborye. In three days 350 trucks were abandoned in snowdrifts on the Novaya Ladoga–Yeremina Gora section. Two transport units lost 94 trucks, most of them running off the unmarked shoulders of the highway. The total losses on the ice and on the forest road were 1,004 machines. There was also the problem of maintenance. At one time, of 3,500 trucks engaged on the ice road 1,300 were out of service, awaiting repairs.

As the ice thickened, more and more trails were opened across the lake. By midwinter there were as many as sixty of these tracks with a total length of nearly a thousand miles.

But in December the route still worked slowly, slowly, slowly. It met neither the expectations of Zhdanov nor the needs of the city.

There was, however, the beginning of slight improvement from December 10 onward—and not because the trucks moved faster or ice conditions suddenly got better.

The improvement was due to the recapture of Tikhvin on December 9. On that day Leningrad had on hand nine or ten days' supply of flour, including all the remaining stores at Novaya Ladoga, on the eastern side of the lake. The bread being provided Leningrad was made almost entirely of "edible" cellulose, sawdust and flour sweepings. It did not support life. The death toll rose day by day. Leningrad required a minimum of 1,000 tons of supplies a day—not just food, but kerosene, gasoline, munitions.

Even if the Zaborye highway worked at maximum efficiency, not more than 600 or 700 tons a day could be expected.

The recapture of Tikhvin changed all this.

"Without exaggeration," wrote Dmitri Pavlov, the food chief, with characteristic understatement, "the defeat of the German Fascist troops at Tikhvin and the recapture of the Northern Railroad line up to Mga station saved from starvation thousands of people."

This put back into operation the Tikhvin-Volkhov railroad, the connections to Novaya Ladoga and, by the end of December, the line to Voibokalo. By December 25 the perilous, difficult, agonizing haul from Zaborye had been abandoned.[2]

Another help was the introduction on Lake Ladoga of the $1\frac{1}{2}$-ton GAZ-AA truck and soon thereafter of the 3-ton Zis-5. These trucks could move across the ice at speeds of twenty, thirty and even forty miles an hour. They cut transit time to a little more than an hour, reducing exposure to Nazi gunfire and making two or three trips a day possible for hardy drivers.

Service facilities were built on the ice—first-aid stations, traffic-control points, repair depots, snow-clearing detachments, bridge-layers (to put wooden crossings over weak points or crevasses). Soon there were 19,000 persons enrolled in the ice-road effort.

Party Secretary Zhdanov and Kuznetsov personally inspected the ice road, seeking some means of improving turnover. They imposed delivery norms ($2\frac{1}{4}$ tons a day for the GAZ-AA trucks), introduced a premium system, reorganized the direction of the supply system and were able to bring deliveries up to 700 tons by December 22 and to 800 tons by December 23.

This tiny improvement came very late. Death was stalking the Leningrad streets. The Party committee in the Central Kuibyshev District was struggling with a question which had no precedent—how to organize the trucking of bodies from the local hospital to the cemetery. Bodies were beginning to pile up in the courtyards by the hundred.

Party Secretary Kuznetsov had a bitter conversation one day with Major General P. A. Zaitsev at Smolny. Zaitsev was complaining that because of a lack of adequate support he had lost eight hundred men in three days' fighting. Kuznetsov gloomily observed: "Why do you think we are moving sappers out of the front lines? In order to dynamite mass graves in the cemeteries to bury civilians."

The December death toll was 53,000 persons, more or less—equal to that for the whole of 1940. The total was nearly five times that of the admittedly incomplete figure of 11,085 in November. Party members tottered into regional offices, put their cards on the desk and wandered off, mumbling, "Tomorrow I'll die. . . ."

One day Zhdanov called in General Mikhail Dukhanov. He had received a report of a dangerous outbreak of dysentery among youngsters in a boarding school. With typical Soviet bureaucratic suspicion he thought the school administration might be stealing food and depriving the children.

Dukhanov appeared at the school shortly after daybreak, hoping to catch the thieves at work. He watched the food checked out of the storehouse and into the kitchen, watched it cooked and examined the inventory. All was in order.

He stood by as the children ate breakfast—25 grams of bread and a mug

---

[2] In the opinion of Dmitri V. Pavlov the Zaborye road played no substantial role in supplying Leningrad. (Personal communication, April 30, 1968.)

of hot water with salt. He went to the dormitory. Youngsters who were strong enough put on their heavy jackets and went to the street where they were tearing down a wooden house for firewood. The others lounged listlessly on their beds.

For lunch they had 50 grams of bread and a pat of butter, a little soup made of frozen beets and some cereal which seemed to be mostly linseed-oil cake. General Dukhanov noticed that many children put part of their soup and cereal into jars. He thought they were saving it to eat later on. But he was mistaken. Soon those who were able to walk appeared in heavy clothes. They were going home to visit their relatives. Most of them clutched a glass or jar in which they were carrying food for a starving mother, brother or sister. General Dukhanov wanted to halt the youngsters and speak to them. But he suddenly realized there was nothing to say. He went back that evening and reported to Zhdanov that there was no stealing, just lack of food.

He asked Zhdanov if he had been right not to stop the children as they were leaving the school.

Zhdanov spoke slowly: "I would have done the same thing."

Then he turned and took up the telephone: "This is Zhdanov speaking. Within forty minutes put down a heavy barrage on the Nazi regiments of Majors Gnidin and Witte. What for? In order to inflict heavy casualties on the Fascists. Report to me when you have carried out the instructions."

Zhdanov hung up and turned back to General Dukhanov. "Go home and rest. Thank you for the report. We will evacuate those children immediately."

It was about this time that a ski detachment of sailors from the battleship *Marat* was sent on a night scouting expedition across the ice to reconnoiter the German gun positions around the Peterhof Palace. They found that the grandiose sculpture of Samson by Mikhail Kozlovsky which dominated the great cascade leading down to the sea was missing—it had been disassembled and shipped off to Germany.

When the sailors reported their discovery, the *Marat* was ordered to lay down a special barrage on the positions around Peterhof—in reprisal for the theft.

On the night of December 23 Zhdanov sat down with Party Secretary Shtykov, just back from Vologda, where he had been expediting movement of supplies.

"We'd like to increase the Leningrad ration from 125 grams," Zhdanov said. "Can you guarantee that the supplies will come in without interruption?"

It was a critical question. Shtykov considered a few moments, then replied slowly and solemnly, "I can."

There was on hand in Leningrad at that moment a little more than two days' supply of flour. The ice road had brought in only 16,449 tons of food since its start—an average of 361 tons a day. The next evening, the twenty-fourth, the Leningrad Military Council, at Zhdanov's initiative, ordered the first increase in the Leningrad ration—a miserable 100 grams (a slice of bread) for workers, and 75 grams for all others, including children.

It was, as Pavlov insisted twenty-five years later, a very daring and crucial act. There was no reserve in case of accident or interruption of the supply route. If something happened and the ration again had to be cut back, Pavlov could hardly bear to think of the dreadful consequences.

Zhdanov's act was a bold gamble. But he hoped that the deliveries by the ice road would continue to grow. And—although no Leningrad historian directly mentions the fact—the terrible toll of death within the city was already radically reducing the numbers of persons who had to be fed.

There was another reason for confidence on Zhdanov's part. He had just paid his first visit to Moscow since his return to Leningrad in the critical days of late June.

There had been a conference at the Kremlin—Stalin; Zhdanov; Marshal Boris M. Shaposhnikov, Chief of Staff; General Kirill Meretskov, commander of the newly created Volkhov front; General M. S. Khozin, commander of the Leningrad front; Lieutenant General G. G. Sokolov of the Twenty-sixth Army (soon transformed into the Second Shock Army); and Major General I. V. Galanin of the Fifty-ninth Army.

The conference was convened December 11 in the full flush of the recovery of Tikhvin, the recapture of Rostov and Marshal Zhukov's rapidly developing and successful offensive to drive the Nazis back from Moscow. Shaposhnikov described his plan for breaking the Leningrad blockade in which Meretskov with the Fourth, Fifty-second, Fifty-ninth and Twenty-sixth (Second Shock) armies was to play the principal role. The Fifty-ninth and Second Shock armies were just being re-formed. Shaposhnikov said Meretskov's task was to drive the Germans from the territory east of the Volkhov River, to cross the river and smash the divisions on the western shores. Then Meretskov would drive northwest and in cooperation with the Leningrad front destroy the German siege forces.

Optimism was high. Shaposhnikov emphasized the crisis in Leningrad and pointed out that it would not permit waiting for the full concentration of troops before beginning action. Zhdanov and General Khozin stressed the heavy toll of air and artillery bombardment in Leningrad and the rapidly rising toll of hunger and cold. People were dying in such numbers that every effort must be made quickly to liquidate the blockade.

It was agreed that the Volkhov front should continue the attack already under way. The offensive would be a rolling one and continue without pause until Leningrad had been liberated and the grip of Army Group Nord broken. The participants, filled with confidence, flew north from Moscow. For the first time since his reverses of the summer Zhdanov must have felt that fate was turning his way. With a bit of luck and hard fighting by three army groups—the Leningrad, the Volkhov and the Northwest—Leningrad should be freed. The city had suffered terribly, but a change seemed to lie just ahead.

The operative plans for the attack were transmitted to the Leningrad and Volkhov commanders on December 17. On the twentieth the offensive was to open. A very short term for preparation. But there was no time to waste, and Zhdanov and Meretskov did not wish to lose the momentum of the successful Tikhvin offensive.

It was under the influence of this heady prospect that Zhdanov took the risk of ordering the Christmas boost in the Leningrad ration.

Zhdanov's decision was communicated to Party workers on duty at Smolny at about 1 A.M. Christmas morning. It was the 116th day of the siege. The workers were asleep at their desks or catching a cat nap in the common dormitory in the cellar. They were routed out to spread the word to the various quarters of the city. The temperature was below zero, and wind swept snow through streets already piled high with drifts. The Party workers were in no better shape than their fellow citizens. "On my way to Vasilevsky Island," recalled N. M. Ribkovsky, a political instructor, "I had to stop and rest five times." Party representatives reached the bread stores before they opened at 6 A.M. and passed on news of the increase in ration. One party worker in the Vyborg region claimed that citizens queued up at the local bakery shouted "Hurrah!" An old railroad repairman named Petrov awakened his children. He reported that they cried when they heard they would be getting another morsel of bread.

The radio was not working on Christmas Day—because of the virtual absence of electric power. Only one power plant, the Red Oktyabr, was running. Perhaps for this reason, news of the increase in ration seems to have spread slowly through Leningrad. Many diaries of the period, even of such an energetic political optimist as Vsevolod Vishnevsky, fail to mention the event, or report it only a day or several days later.

On December 25 the musicologist Valerian Bogdanov-Berezovsky noted the ration increase in his diary. But he also mentioned more pressing matters. It was the end of the financial year and the funds of the Composers Union and Music Fund had been exhausted. "We are cut off from the Union of Composers and from the Central Music Fund," he wrote, "and don't even know to which city they have been evacuated (from Moscow). And they evidently don't know that there are composers and musicologists remaining in Leningrad or how many we are. I learned recently that the Committee for Artistic Affairs is in Tomsk and sent a telegram to its head, M. Khrapchenko, with a request that he establish connections with the Union and the Music Fund."

That day Bogdanov-Berezovsky visited a composer named Malkov on Plekhanov Street who lay ill in a little matchbox (but warm) room. He recorded the death of another composer, A. Budyakovsky, and added:

I am experiencing great difficulties in connection with the opening in the Astoria of a so-called *statsionar,* or feeding and medical station. The Union in the first drawing got three places. I have received many urgent requests. I have been especially disturbed by the call of L. Portov, who said several times in a pleading voice: "Please arrange it for me. Do it now. If you don't, within a week it will be too late. I'll not live." And in spite of this I could promise him only second place, together with F. Rubtsov and A. Peisin who are terribly weak, but in even worse condition is A. Rabinovich, long ill with tuberculosis, V. Deshevov, almost unable to move, and I. Miklashevsky. It is so difficult to choose. . . .

Vera Inber learned of the ration increase from her friend and hospital worker, Yevfrosinya Ivanovna, who went to the bakery to pick up her ration. On Tolstoy Square Yevfrosinya met a man who she decided was either drunk or crazy. He was crying, laughing and hitting himself on the head. Only when she arrived at the bakery and learned of the increase in ration did Yevfrosinya realize that the man was in ecstasy over the news.

A meeting was held in the dining room of the Writers' House on the evening of December 26. The writers slowly made their way through the drifts, past the corpses which had now begun to appear almost everywhere.

Vera Ketlinskaya made a speech. Soviet troops had broken two of the three circles around the city—the Tikhvin circle and the Voibokalo circle. Only Mga remained. That would be broken by New Year's Day. The boost in the ration was just the first swallow of spring. Enormous quantities of supplies were being concentrated within sixty miles of Leningrad—50,000 tons of cereals and macaroni, 42,000 tons of flour, 300 tons of meat. And much, much more. All of this would flood into the city once Mga was taken.

The writers, sitting like gray ghosts around the empty table, applauded weakly. Hope there was for life.

Hope there was. Zhdanov possessed it. A mass of supplies actually was being hurried to the perimeter. Anastas A. Mikoyan had arranged to move under the most urgent priorities 50,000 tons of flour and 12,000 tons of other food to Vologda, Tikhvin and the key distribution points for the Ladoga ice road. The Railroad Commissariat had been enlisted. Mikoyan and Zhdanov knew that Leningrad had less than five days' supply of flour on hand. The trains pounded north through the night from Zainsk, Rybinsk, Saratov. On the cars were scrawled in great letters *"Prodovolstviye dlya Leningrada"* ("Food for Leningrad"). The supplies poured into the ruined station and sidings of Tikhvin. They were loaded without cease upon trucks, which lumbered over the rutted roads north to Ladoga, out on the ice and on to the Leningrad shore.

The offensive of General I. I. Fedyuninsky, the drive of the Leningrad troops toward Tosno, was going so well that Zhdanov was confident that Mga would be liberated for the New Year's holiday.

To give the starving, freezing people hope, to help them to survive to the

New Year and the recapture of Mga, hundreds of meetings were held throughout the city—in the ice-festooned factories (hardly a plant was operating now—on December 19, 184 plants had been put on a one-, two- or three-day week); in the windowless government offices; in the apartment houses where burned small *burzhuiki*—makeshift stoves. The word was passed on to all: by January 1 Leningrad will be liberated; the circle will be broken; Mga will be retaken.

But Mga was not retaken. Even before New Year's Day it was suddenly plain to Zhdanov that his Christmas optimism had been ill-founded. The terrible truth was that the Soviet troops had neither the physical strength nor the munitions to dislodge the Nazis.

The Red Army men were weak and sick. A report as of January 10 showed 45 percent of the units of the Leningrad front and 63 percent of Fifty-fifth Army units understrength. There were 32 divisions on the front. Of these, 14 were only up to 30 percent of strength. Some infantry regiments were only at 17 to 21 percent of authorized manpower.

Nor was there any way to bolster their ranks. During the whole winter of 1941–42 the Leningrad front grew by only 25,000. From October 1 to May 1, 1942, about 17,000 or 18,000 men were sent to the front from rear and office assignments, 6,000 were obtained from construction units and 30,277 sailors were provided from the Baltic Fleet. Women were mobilized, largely for rear and ARP duties, but by June, 1942, there were 9,000 in the front lines. In the last three months of 1941 about 70,000 men were sent to the front by Leningrad—29,567 in October, 28,249 in November and 12,804 in December. In the ensuing six months Leningrad was able to mobilize 30,000 men for active Red Army duty, but only 8,000 of these were provided from December to March.

These replacements hardly matched the Red Army losses. From October, 1941, to April, 1942, 353,424 troops reported sick or wounded, an average of 50,000 a month or 1,700 a day. Half of these were ill, largely of dystrophy and other starvation ailments. More than 62,000 troops came down with dystrophy from November, 1941, to the end of spring. The number ill with scurvy reached 20,000 in April, 1942.[3] Deaths due to starvation diseases were 12,416, nearly 20 percent of troops on sick call, in the winter of 1942.

Men were too weak to fight or work. Yuri Loman, commissar for a truck unit, recalled that he had seen four men trying to load a mutton carcass, weighing possibly forty pounds. They did not have the strength to lift it. A. P. Lebedeva, head of the factory committee at the Krasnaya Treugolnik rubber plant, was at her desk when a middle-aged, gaunt man tottered in. She recognized him as a cutter in the shop. "Give me a bowl of soup," he said. "If you'll do that, I'll be back at work tomorrow." Lebedeva had no

---

[3] O. F. Suvenirov, in *Vtoraya Mirovaya Voina*, Vol. II. Moscow, 1966, pp. 159–166. Dmitri V. Pavlov mistakenly asserts that "no scurvy occurred during the whole of the war among Red Army troops." (Pavlov, *op. cit.*, 3rd edition, p. 103.)

food, but she poured him a mug of hot water. The worker drank it at a gulp, not realizing it was water. "Thanks for the soup, Lebedeva," he said. "Now, I'll go into the shop and start working."

Zhdanov's gamble was not paying off. Leningrad, incredibly, had slipped closer to utter disaster. The Military Council met in emergency session December 29. The previous day the ice road had delivered only 622 tons of freight, of which 462.2 tons were food. This was about half the essential minimum. To the horror of Zhdanov, General Khozin, Kuznetsov and Pavlov, deliveries dropped to 602 tons on December 29, of which only 431.9 tons were food.

The road of life might, it seemed, become the road of death.

On January 1, the 123rd day of the siege, the critical tabulation, known only to Zhdanov, Kuznetsov, Khozin, Pavlov and three others, showed that Leningrad's cupboard was bare. There was in the reserves: 980 tons of flour, 3 tons of grain, 82 tons of soy flour, 334 tons of cereals and macaroni, 624 tons of meat and sausage, 24 tons of fish, 16 tons of butter, 187 tons of vegetable oil, 102 tons of fat and 337 tons of sugar.

That was flour for less than two days. Never had Leningrad been so close to starvation.

The days were beginning of which Kuznetsov later was to say: "There was a time when we gave bread to no one. Not because we did not want to give it out but because we had none."

It was in these days that Filipp Sapozhnikov, a hard-working, bad-luck truck driver on the Ladoga ice road returned to his barracks, late once more as he had been almost every day with his truckload of flour. He found a notice posted on the bulletin board:

"Driver Sapozhnikov: Yesterday, thanks to you, 5,000 Leningrad women and children got no bread ration."[4]

It was true. The margin was that thin. One late truck, and thousands of Leningraders waited in vain before the bread shop and scores died.

The ice road was not working. In fact, it was critically close to failure. So was the sleazy one-track Irinovsky railroad which connected Ladoga with Leningrad. Under the impact of heavy traffic, lack of fuel, failing equipment, bad management, the weakness, illness and death of workers—from cold and starvation—shipments slowed and slowed again. By January 1 the branch was paralyzed. Not one train a day was getting through.

Director Kolpakov had started December with 57 of his 252 locomotives in service, of which 27 were switch engines. By the end of the month there were days when he had no more than 28 locomotives operating. He was getting only 92 hours' daily work from the engines—many of them were operating less than three hours a day. His staff was dissolving. From December, 1941, to February, 1942, he had 10,938 men and women on sick leave. Of these, 2,346 died, including 1,200 in January. The City Council

---

[4] One calculation was that each large truck carried 16,000 rations (Kharitonov, *op. cit.*, p. 37).

ordered 5,000 persons to help keep the railroad going by clearing away the snowdrifts. Not more than 400 or 500 were strong enough to report for duty, and many were too weak to lift a shovel. The railroad had been attacked 356 times by Nazi bombers, and much of the signal equipment, switches, sidings and terminals was badly damaged or out of use.

There was no more coal, and the city water supply which serviced the boilers had frozen. Machinists with picks and crowbars pried coal dust out of the frozen soil. There was plenty of dirt mixed with the dust, but this "fuel" was used to fire up the boilers. The average haul per locomotive in December was nineteen miles.

Once more the fate of Leningrad was in balance. Once more Zhdanov took strong measures. The railroad director was removed on charges of confusion and failure to organize his work. Probably he was shot.[5] Extra rations—125 grams of bread—were ordered for the railroad workers. The last few tons of coal in the city reserves were turned over. Woodcutting teams were sent to nearby forests to cut cordwood for the engines. Three top regional Party secretaries kept the pressure on. Even so, only 219 cars were loaded in January—a fraction of what was needed.

The great New Year's celebration which Zhdanov had promised Leningrad was not to be. True, some chauffeurs brought special gift parcels to Leningrad. Chauffeur Maksim Tverdokhleb was making his third trip over Ladoga on the day before New Year's. His normal load was thirty barrels of flour.

There was a sign in the loading shed: "Comrade Drivers! If you carry 200 pounds of flour above plan, you will fulfill the bread ration for thousands of Leningraders."

Tverdokhleb asked for his extra load. He was given a dozen wooden crates. He was surprised at their lightness. He thought they must be military supplies. Then he smelled a familiar but remarkable smell—tangerines! The cases were a gift from Georgia for the Leningrad children.

Zhdanov took desperate action. He put the Ladoga route under the iron command of Major General A. M. Shilov with I. V. Shikin, an experienced army political worker who had been prewar head of the big Gorky auto factory Party organization, as his chief aide. They were ordered to bring deliveries up to 1,200 tons a day and by any means necessary. Seven hundred Young Communists were sent to the ice road. Traffic control posts were established every 200 or 300 yards. Antiaircraft batteries guarded each kilometer of the route. The 7th Air Corps and the remaining fighters of the Baltic Fleet were assigned to ward off Nazi strafing planes. The short new Tikhvin-Volkhov-Voibokalo connection was put into use (at 5 A.M., January 1, 1942).

The temperature on the ice road ranged between 20 below zero and 40 below zero. The wind pressed endlessly from the north. The ice was

[5] Kolpakov was publicly excoriated by Leningrad's Mayor, Peter Popkov, January 13. (A. Dymshits, *Podvig Leningrada*, Moscow, 1960, p. 288.)

so solid that KV-60 tanks now could be—and were—moved to Fedyunin-sky's embattled army. But men froze to death in the cold, and trucks ground to a halt.

On January 5 Zhdanov addressed another appeal to the men of the ice road. He cast his message in fateful language. The road continues to work badly—very badly. It brings to Leningrad not more than one-third the freight needed for survival even on the scantiest level of existence.

"The supply of Leningrad and the front hangs by a thread," Zhdanov said. "The people and the troops are suffering unbelievable hardships.

"If the situation is quickly to be corrected, if the needs of Leningrad and the front are to be met, it all depends on you workers of the auto road—and on you only."

There was nothing more Zhdanov or the Party or the Leningrad Military Command could do. Now it depended upon the workers of the ice road.

Dulled, frozen, weak, often unable to keep to their feet, the people of Leningrad knew that survival hung in the balance. But they did not know by what a slender thread. They lived on hope, nourished by the December 25 ration increase, by the belief that Mga would be taken. They believed in the ice road, and it was at this time they first began to call it "the Road of Life."

Vera Inber was in a queue before a bakery one day. An old woman corrected a remark by her neighbor. "This is not black bread," the old woman said. "This is rye bread. It is Ladoga bread. It is the whitest of the white. It's holy bread, that's what." The old woman crossed herself and kissed the rough black loaf.

In her heatless flat Vera Inber fashioned the incident into a few lines for the poem with which she warmed herself in those arctic days, "Pulkovo Meridian." There were many in Leningrad who echoed the sentiment of the old woman. The bread was holy. They did not know that each coarse slice they ate might be their last.

"Never," wrote the authors of Leningrad's official history,

had Leningrad lived through such tragic days. . . . Rarely did smoke show in the factory chimneys. . . . The trams had halted and thousands of people made their way on foot through the deep drifts of the squares and the boulevards. . . . In the dark flats those who were not working warmed themselves for an hour or so before their *burzhuiki* and slept in their coats and scarfs, covered with their warmest things. . . .

In the evening the city sank into impenetrable darkness. Only the occasional flicker of fires and the red flash of exploding artillery shells lighted the gloom of the vast factories and apartment blocks. The great organism of the city was almost without life, and hunger more and more strongly made itself known.

Leningrad was dying.

39 ‧ *The City of Death*

ONE LATE NOVEMBER NIGHT A MIDDLE-AGED MAN, WORN
and tired, in officer's uniform, heavy wool greatcoat, fur collar and fur hat,
walked out of the Smolny grounds, past the sandbagged pillboxes, showed
his pass to the tommy gunners and turned into empty Tverskaya Ulitsa.

It was, he recalled later, like a scene out of Dante—the wastes of drifted
snow, the thin rays of the moon, almost obscured by scudding clouds, and
a silence so deep that each fall of his boots, each metallic squeak of leather
on frozen snow, echoed in his ears.

He was weary, and when the wind hit him, it stabbed into his lungs.
Snow sifted down on his fur hat and shoulders, and his feet seemed heavier
and heavier. The procession of squares and boulevards turned into a desert
of ice in which he was the only living being. He saw no homes, no people.
There was no sound but that of the wind, of his boots and of his heavy
breathing.

The city slowly, majestically, was freezing into death as the poet, Dmitri
Grigorovich, envisaged: ". . . the winter twilight of Petersburg sinking into
the black of night . . . and he alone . . . far, far from all, in the deep
shadows, the snowy emptiness and the swirling wind."

Presently he came to the bridge to the Summer Gardens and crossed
over. He could not always be certain that he was not suffering hallucinations,
but he thought he passed a woman, wearing a black cloak and black mask as
though going to a masquerade. He realized in a moment that the mask was
just the woolen face cloth with which so many Leningraders now protected
themselves from the cold and wind.

On a bench in the drifted park he saw a couple, a man and woman,
huddled together, resting, it seemed, from a long walk. He started toward
them and nearly plunged into a darkly outlined hole—an excavation. No.
A shell hole. He kept wondering about the two people sitting on the park
bench. They seemed to be asleep. Perhaps he, too, should sit for a moment.
As he went on, he glimpsed a man in the distance carrying a burden. The

man walked a bit, then rested, walked a bit and rested. The burden on his shoulder seemed to sparkle in the shifting light. As the man came nearer, it was clear that he was carrying a body. A woman, no doubt, possibly his daughter.

When he looked again, the figure with the burden had vanished as though it had never been there. A feeling of terror gripped the man, and he found himself reaching for his pistol and drawing it from the holster. He could not have told why. Presently he shuddered and walked on through the world of shadow, of cold, of snow and of wind.

The walker was Nikolai Tikhonov, born in Leningrad, one of Russia's best-known writers. He had not been in his native city when war broke out and had returned only in October as Leningrad began to descend into the white hell of starvation.

Tikhonov was living now at Smolny on the second floor in room No. 139. He shared these quarters with Vissarion Sayanov, Aleksandr Prokofyev and Boris Likharev, all of them poets.

Sometimes, they spent the night in room No. 139, reciting poems, dividing their tobacco, sharing their rations, pacing the corridors and arguing. As Boris Likharev wrote:

> In the nights of the blockade,
> How long it was to dawn!
> We divided the tobacco
> We got on the ration,
> And at midnight in the corridors
> Of Smolny strolled the poets
> Under the rumble of artillery,
> Writing proclamations to the troops.

Sometimes they gathered in the flat where Sayanov first heard the news of war and looked out to see the white sails of boats on the blue Neva. There they now huddled about a smoky makeshift stove, burning legs from the kitchen table, listening to the beat of the radio's metronome, which continued when no program was being broadcast, smoking "Golden Autumn" cigarettes (made of dried tree leaves), drinking hot tea or hot water, reading poetry and arguing about the war. Sometimes the talk and argument went on until dawn.

Other nights they gathered at Tikhonov's flat on the Petrograd side near the Tuchkov Bridge or at Prokofyev's apartment, also on the Petrograd side, near the Bourse Bridge. Wherever they met it was cold and dark. One late November morning Tikhonov returned to Smolny and told his comrades in room No. 139, "Last night I wrote a poem which touches the limits of frankness."

This was Tikhonov's great war poem, "Kirov Is with Us," a poem which his friend Prokofyev felt was minted from new metal: "In Leningrad's

nights of iron to the city came Kirov. . . ." It was a poem evoking the spirit
of the Leningrad leader whose assassination in 1934 had touched off Stalin's
most savage purge. It was a work, deeply inspirational, deeply evocative,
deeply patriotic. It caught the spirit of the great city as it struggled for its
life. Whether it struck a note which was likely to please Stalin was not so
clear. But in the agony of Leningrad Tikhonov's "Kirov Is with Us" became a legend.

The writers and the poets were luckier than ordinary Leningraders. They
could throw themselves into creative work and to some extent forget the
suffering which surrounded them.

The diary of Vsevolod Vishnevsky, the greatest optimist among them,
discloses how difficult this was.

On November 19 he made these entries:

> Last night we were thinking of the recent past . . . Strela . . . theaters
> . . . restaurants, . . . favorite dishes (it makes one's mouth water) . . .
> shashlik, in Kars style, Georgian soup, greens, greens . . . almonds, borsht,
> Kievsky cutlets, pies, champagne. . . . And in reality . . . today soup and
> cereal. Tomorrow soup and cereal. How boring.

The next day (November 20):

> Our military ration has been cut to 300 grams of bread. Monotonous
> food. We joke: It's better than the resort at Kislovodsk.

But the jokes were as thin as the breakfast gruel. The same day he entered
in his diary:

> Someone telephoned: The sailor-poet Lebedev has died. What talent! A
> romantic. He died on a submarine. For 12 years he served in the fleet.

It was true. Aleksei Lebedev was dead. Vera Petrovna could not believe
it. Even when she saw before her the yellow slip of paper from the Baltic
Fleet Command, saying, "Your husband, Lieutenant Aleksei Lebedev, died
in November, 1941, in battle for the socialist fatherland, true to his military
duty, heroically and bravely."

It could not be. There still was imprinted before her eyes the image of
Aleksei as he lay asleep in her lap beside the Baltic Sea on that distant
June 22 when an unknown girl came running to ask, "Haven't you heard
the radio? It's war!"

Vera Petrovna had not often seen Aleksei since that day. On October 26
she met him on the Neva embankment near the Liteiny Bridge. She
watched him approach, a long figure in a black-leather coat, black beard,
hands deep in his pockets. He saw her and his eyes lighted. They embraced.
And the next question was: "How are you getting on for food?"

He pulled out a couple of bars of chocolate, but she thrust them back
into his pockets, saying she had no place to keep them. In reality she was
afraid she'd start eating them if they stayed in her hands.

They had a few moments together and Alex read her a new poem:

> The cutter takes me to the ship
> Under the flaming clouds of scarlet,
> And I say "I love you,"
> For you are the best of all.

It was their last meeting.

Aleksei's mother got a letter: "Looking back at the city, so beautiful in its tragic colors in this gentle fall, I feel how good life is, how short it is, how senselessly war annihilates all that is good, all that humanity has achieved."

Then, one day in late November Vera Petrovna got a letter, too. Her heart rose. The notice was not true. Aleksei was alive. She looked at the date. November 11. It had been written two days before he went to sea on his last mission, a mission which she knew was to take him far in the rear of the Germans toward the Kiel Canal.

She opened the letter and read:

> Remember me, Ruth [her pet name], sometimes, for in a couple of hours I will already be far away and when I return—or if I shall return—I do not know. I am writing you and only you before I leave. You know that sometimes we may not speak for a long time but that then we even more strongly love one another. . . . I kiss you, my darling. Forgive me for the sorrow I have brought you. Do not forget me.
>
> YOUR ALEX

Lebedev put to sea as a lieutenant on the submarine *L-2*. The submarine was lost November 18 in the Baltic. Aleksei Lebedev was twenty-nine years old. His friends believed him one of the most talented of the Leningrad poets. The playwright Aleksandr Kron felt that his loss was sheer tragedy, not just an accident of war. The *L-2*, he was convinced, was poorly commanded. Kron, himself a naval man and a naval writer, knew submarine life. He knew how strong was the factor of morale, of training, of close-knit action and confidence in the command. A few days before his last voyage Lebedev confided to Kron that morale aboard the *L-2* was not good, that the commander imposed his orders from above, that the initiative of the crew was stifled.

"Who knows," said Kron, "perhaps in that circumstance lies the cause of the loss of the *L-2*."

On November 20, the day Leningrad's ration was cut to 125 grams of bread daily, the composer Valerian Bogdanov-Berezovsky noted that fact in his diary, observing that "the food situation is becoming more difficult."

He then proceeded to other matters—a recital at the Union of Composers by Boris Asafyev. The great hall of the union was darkened by metal screens over the balcony windows and was very cold. They used candles for light. There was no electricity. Fifteen members listened to Asafyev. All wore hats, heavy coats, overshoes.

Asafyev played "attractively and temperamentally and was childishly happy at the general reaction," Bogdanov-Berezovsky noted. There was a long discussion of his performance and by rare chance no air raid during the several hours of playing and talk.

Bogdanov-Berezovsky's next diary entry, for November 28, began: "Fourth day without warm food and only one tiny bread ration."

The questions of what happened, of how they had come to the brink of catastrophe, pressed urgently on the Leningraders. Pavel Luknitsky sat one cold evening in the Writers' House, listening to three young officers, convalescing from wounds, argue. A tank officer said he and his comrades had fought as best they could, but there had been mistakes at the top. Obviously, Russia hadn't been prepared. An engineer disagreed. Russia had not been surprised either politically or materially.

"Politically," snapped the tank officer, "maybe not. But matériel? What are you saying? Do you really think you can fight the Germans with T-26 tanks? Or a division of People's Volunteers armed with shovels—can they stop the German Panzers? Do you call a bottle of flaming gasoline a modern military weapon? And what about automatic rifles?"

The engineer cited the KV 60-ton tank. He had seen five in action at Izhorsk.

"Sure," snorted the tankist. "Five KV's. And if we'd had five hundred, where would the Germans be now?"

An aviator joined in the conversation, complaining that Soviet planes readily caught fire because their frames were made with magnesium instead of Duralumin. Soviet Duralumin, he said bitterly, had been provided to the Germans before June 22.

Frankly, he said, it was simply unbelievable that the Germans had captured Minsk, had swept through Byelorussia, the Ukraine, capturing Pskov and driving up to the very outskirts of Leningrad.

The three young men turned to Luknitsky for some explanation. He was deep in thought. So many of his countrymen had suffered disillusion. Now they knew the bitter truth. No one was going to save them—not Stalin, not the Red Army. Only themselves, only each man and each woman, fighting as he could, struggling as he could, just the simple men and women of Russia, of Leningrad, fighting in their ruined city, starving in the zero cold, fighting as long as they had strength . . .

These thoughts stayed in Luknitsky's mind as he came back to his flat. He learned of an incident that had happened the night before. A horse had fallen on the ice beside the house where his brother lived. In the morning only half the horse lay on the street. A policeman followed the tracks in the snow and found the missing half in a student dormitory. Horses were priceless. A soldier told of seeing one killed by a shell fragment. A score of people came running and within minutes had butchered the beast. He helped a girl cart home a horse's leg. It was too heavy for her to lift.[1]

Luknitsky recalled a talk he had had with his father about their dog Mishka. His father proposed giving the dog to a military unit because they could not feed it. Luknitsky objected: "Wait a minute, maybe it would be better to eat the dog ourselves." His father was appalled: "I would never under any circumstances eat our beloved dog." But after a few days his father said, "I've been talking with a man. He takes the head and feet of dogs and makes a good stew. . . ." And the two had looked at Mishka's sorrowful eyes, and each thought of how many tasty cutlets might be made from their faithful friend.

The problem of food worried Luknitsky more and more. He knew only too well the Germans were counting on starving them out. He knew that they must hold on until the Red Army tore loose the blockade. He tried to be bright and optimistic in public, to talk in easy confidence about the victory which was just around the corner. That, he felt, was his duty. But he was not blind. Speaking to himself, he had to ask: What will happen if the food situation is not improved? Even a man with the strongest spirit must have a minimum of calories to maintain strength. Hunger, general hunger, simply led to death.

There was rumor in the city of some move by the English or the Americans to save the city—a drive from Murmansk perhaps. But could it come in time, could it save Leningrad from starvation if Leningrad in the very next few days did not break the blockade?

He was not certain. His doubt was shared by his fellow citizens. And was Leningrad really doing all that could be done? He did not believe so. The battle to recapture Mga (he believed) was raging violently at that very moment. But not all of Leningrad's forces had been thrown into it. Everything should be committed to the battle—while Leningrad still had the strength to fight. At any price, at any sacrifice, the ring must be broken. Perhaps the cost would be tens of thousands of lives. But only thus could three million lives be saved.

Within ten days Mishka had been slaughtered by Luknitsky's brother with the aid of the porter. The first meal had been eaten—dog-leg stew. The intestines and one leg had gone to the porter as his share. Luknitsky had been at the front, but owing to bureaucratic red tape his ration was only two spoons of soup. He could hardly wait to partake of the tasty dog stew.

Luknitsky, a correspondent for Tass, a good Party man, kept his public front of confidence. Privately, his thoughts were pessimistic. He was not

[1] At the beginning of October the City Council had ordered all horses unfit for work to be delivered to the Kolomyagi and Porokhov slaughterhouses. Individual slaughter of horses was forbidden. The horses were slaughtered under veterinary observation, and the horse meat was used in the preparation of sausage according to the recipe: horse meat 75 percent, potato flour 12 percent, pork 11 percent, with saltpeter, black pepper and garlic added. (Pavlov, op. cit., 2nd edition, pp. 77-78.)

alone. In those days Aleksandr Dymshits, a writer serving on the Karelian front, occasionally came into Leningrad. He had a double task. In Leningrad he recorded broadcasts, telling of the bravery, fighting spirit and confidence of the men at the front. Once as he was going back to the front he heard his own voice on the loudspeaker. He was pleased how confident, how bold he sounded. Actually, like the others he was weak and worn. When he got to the front, he wrote stories for the army paper, telling the troops how strongly and well the people in Leningrad were fighting. Alas, he admitted to himself, the real situation bore little resemblance to the brave broadcasts. He spent his time in Leningrad exchanging news with his friends, learning who was dead, who had starved, who had been wounded. The Leningraders were like gray shadows, thin, tired and hungry. He was the same. They could hardly stand on their feet. A nightmare.

A nightmare, indeed. On the twenty-first of June Academician Orbeli had been concerned about the Hermitage expedition to Samarkand, preparing for the five hundredth anniversary of the Timurid poet, Alisher Navoi. Now the day of the anniversary, December 10, was at hand. On the ninth the last streetcars in Leningrad stopped. On December 10 *Leningradskaya Pravda* was published for the first time on a single sheet, two pages, instead of the usual four.

Vsevolod Rozhdestvensky, the poet who had entered the People's Volunteers in July, was still with his unit near the Obvodny Canal within the city. Rozhdestvensky had been on duty all night. He was sleeping heavily in a dugout when a sentry summoned him to the political officer, who handed him a pass. "You're wanted at the Hermitage. Be back by midnight." Rozhdestvensky was instructed to appear at the five hundredth anniversary celebration. Leningrad was starving, the city was near death, but Orbeli was going to hold the ceremony.

Rozhdestvensky walked all the way, past shattered apartment buildings and stores whose windows were boarded with plywood. He could hear from the direction of Pulkovo Heights the heavy thud of cannon, the thin whistle of shells, and the explosions in the city itself. The Germans were engaged in their daily bombardment.

He found the Nevsky virtually deserted. There were hummocks of snow in the street. Here and there a trolleycar stood frozen and battered. He walked past the Sadovaya, past the great Engineers Castle, past the Champs de Mars, studded with antiaircraft emplacements, to Palace Square and across the Winter Canal to the service entrance of the Hermitage, the very entrance where on the morning of June 22 employees had gathered for the "air-raid drill."

Now Orbeli stood here again, welcoming guests to the Navoi festival. The meeting was held in the State Council room of the former Czar, a great room with high ceiling and long windows giving onto the frozen Neva. It was cold, very cold, and Rozhdestvensky had difficulty in recognizing anyone among the bundled figures, their faces ravaged by cold, thin as hawks. But Orbeli was as always energetic, his long beard, now gray, flowing over his cotton-padded jacket. As he began to talk, his big dark eyes grew animated. He spoke of Leningrad's brave spirit, its unquenchable will, the humanism of Soviet science, the city's suffering, and the fact that Germany thought it a city of death.

At that moment there came a tremendous explosion. A shell had landed nearby.

"Don't be alarmed," Orbeli said, without change of voice. "Shall we remove the meeting to the shelter?" No one rose. "Very well," he said, "the meeting will go on."

Rozhdestvensky read his translations of Navoi. Another speaker was a young scholar, Nikolai Lebedev, specialist in Eastern literature. He was suffering from acute dystrophy. He knew what this meant. Already he was too ill to walk. His comrades had carried him to the hall. When his turn came, Orbeli asked him to remain seated while he read. His voice was so thin it hardly carried to the next row. Two days later a second Navoi session was held. Academician B. B. Piotrovsky read a paper on "Motifs of Ancient Eastern Myths in the Works of Alisher Navoi." Then Lebedev read excerpts from the poem "Seven Planets."

The effort exhausted him. He was carried down to his cot in the icy chambers under the Hermitage. There he collapsed and in his final weakness kept whispering verses from Navoi.

"When he lay already dead, covered with a flowered Turkmenian shawl, it seemed that he was still whispering his verses," a friend recalled.

The day after the Navoi festival Academician Sergei Zhebelev, seventy-four years old, slowly made his way through a new fall of heavy snow to the Hermitage. His great overshoes left enormous holes in the drifts at the door. He had come to thank Orbeli for the "holiday of science." Zhebelev was the last survivor among Orbeli's academic teachers.

"I am so glad," he told his onetime pupil, "that science continues to develop with us even under such difficult conditions. This is the way we scholars fight Fascism."

Zhebelev asked about his old friends at the Hermitage. They were working, Orbeli said. Natalia Flittner, a shawl around her shoulders, walked to all ends of the city to give lectures in hospitals, to military units. "They are all cold," Orbeli said, "all hungry, but they write and they work." Zhebelev asked about a friend, Valter, a librarian, and his wife, an antiquarian. Orbeli did not reply. He did not want to tell the old man that both had died in the underground vault only a few days earlier. Zhebelev began to talk of Yakov Smirnov, his close friend of university days, a man who had done much to save the Hermitage in the troubled times of Civil War. Smirnov had died at the age of eighty, in 1918, having continued his lectures up to three days before his death.

Finally, the two men embraced. Orbeli helped Zhebelev down the steps and through the heavy drifts around the entrance. He watched the old man as he slowly made his way along the embankment, wondering whether he would ever see him again.

That was December 13. December 29 was a terrible day at the Hermitage. There was heavy German shelling and one shell hit the wing of the Winter Palace near the kitchen courtyard. A second smashed the façade of the palace on the Admiralty side. A third crumpled the stone canopy over the granite Atlantae at the entrance to the Hermitage. That was the day Orbeli heard of the death of Zhebelev.

Some years after the war Orbeli wrote a brief essay which he called "About What I Thought During the Days and Nights of the Leningrad Blockade."

His thoughts were down-to-earth: of the thousands of treasures of the Hermitage which lay still in the chambers and cellars, subject to damage from German bombs and shells; of the safety of the priceless works of art sent to the Urals; of his native Armenia and the lands of the Caucasus where he spent his youth, and of the scholars of Leningrad and their dedication to science; of his last conversation with Zhebelev, "of his words, of all the thoughts which he then shared with me, of the great strength of the human spirit, the spirit of a man who in the course of his whole life fulfilled his duty unswervingly—the duty of a scholar, a teacher, a citizen."

The life of the Hermitage now descended to the subterranean chambers. Bomb Shelter No. 3, one of twelve in the great vaults under the palace, was the center of activity. Here people lived, worked, studied and died in darkness under the low ceilings. Here were their cots, row after row; here the plank tables where they huddled, swathed in greatcoats, a tiny "bat" light or candle stub flickering over the books of the scholars, the thin scratch of pens on yellow paper, the ink so close to freezing it had to be warmed by their breath. These were the catacombs—the center, such as it could be, of Leningrad's scholarly life. Here people worked until they died. Each day a few more were dead. With the civilian ration down to 125 grams a day (all the Hermitage was on this minimum ration), Orbeli had found one unexpected resource—the by-product of the interminable delay of the painters, the fierce wrangling in which he had been engaged at the time war broke out.

In preparation for the redecorating a quantity of linseed oil had been purchased for the Hermitage stores. There was also a large supply of paste. These products were edible. The linseed oil was used to fry bits of frozen potatoes, dug out of garden patches on the edge of the city. The paste was used to make a kind of "meat" jelly which became the stand-by of the Hermitage diet.

The chronicler of the catacombs was Aleksandr Nikolsky, chief architect of the Hermitage. Day by day Nikolsky kept a diary of Hermitage life. He and his wife Vera had moved to Bomb Shelter No. 3, having undergone a month and a day of continuous German air attack. On their first night, he noted, "we slept like stones under its uncrushable walls."

At first each morning the occupants of Bomb Shelter No. 3 would emerge —some to work in the Academy of Science, some in the Academy of Art, some in the Hermitage rooms. The older men and women, if they had nothing else to do (and there was no air raid), would go to the school cabinet and sit looking out the tall windows at the frozen Neva, across the river to the spire of the Peter and Paul Fortress.

There were two thousand people living in the cellars of the Hermitage.

To go from Bomb Shelter No. 2 to Bomb Shelter No. 3 one had to cross the vast Hall of Twenty Columns, emerging through the emergency door under an arched roof.

At night this route through the corridors and halls of the Hermitage was fantastic to the point of terror. There were no blackout curtains in the museum windows and lights were forbidden. On the floor of the great Hall of Twenty Columns there was a tiny light, but all around it was dark as a prison.

From the Hall of Twenty Columns you went into a smaller room that led to a chamber in which stood a vase of incredible size (the Kolyvan vase, eight feet tall and fifteen feet in diameter, weighing nineteen tons).

The darkness occasionally was lightened by a door opening; then all would again be black and you could see neither the floor, the ceiling, the columns nor even the vase.

Bomb Shelter No. 3 was located under the Italian Hall of the Hermitage. Nikolsky's cot and that of his wife were on the left side in the corner. Nearby lived the artist G. S. Vereisky. The Nikolskys shared their table with the Buts family. Buts was a bookkeeper at the Hermitage.

Nikolsky was an indefatigable artist. In late October he began sketching from life. Then as cold and darkness set in, he sketched the scenes of life in Bomb Shelter No. 3, Bomb Shelter No. 2, Bomb Shelter No. 5, from memory. There was no longer light to do so otherwise.

In late December Bomb Shelter No. 3 had its first *vernissage*. Nikolsky invited his friends to the corner where he lived. Here he spread his sketches on the bed and on the table. Crowding about in felt boots, cotton-padded jackets, so thin they could hardly stand, his comrades examined the sketches by the light of three altar candles. Here was the domed roof of Bomb Shelter No. 2 under the Hall of Twenty Columns, here Bomb Shelter No. 5 under the Egyptian Hall, here the Neva as seen from a Hermitage window, here the smashed interior of a Hermitage hall.

"To yield our city is impossible," Nikolsky noted in his diary. "Better die than give up. I am confident that soon the siege will be lifted, and I have already begun to think about a project for an arch of triumph with which to welcome the heroic troops who liberate Leningrad."

Nikolsky drafted plans for the Arch of Triumph and a Park of Victory, and after the war these were incorporated in a Victory Stadium and Park along the Baltic embankment.

During the Navoi festival Orbeli had not made his customary daily inspection of the Hermitage. Actually, his rheumatism was so bad, the pain so severe in the eternal cold, that it was almost impossible for him to get about. The pain lightened a bit during the Navoi meetings. Now it was back, stronger than ever.

Nonetheless, he determined to make his tour. He began on the second floor, walking from hall to hall. The palace mirrors reflected his stooped figure, his peasant's jacket, his fur hat. Here the windows were broken. Orbeli felt the walls—over them a coating of ice. The ceremonial rooms of the Winter Palace were even colder than those of the New Hermitage. One bomb had exploded in the courtyard of the theater across the Winter Canal from the Hermitage and the Winter Palace. There was plywood over some windows. Over some there was nothing. Orbeli went below to the halls of antique art. He walked through the Hall of Athens, the Hall of Hercules. These halls were not empty. Here there were many objects of art, removed from the more exposed upper chambers. He could hardly get through the Hall of Jupiter it was so crammed with packing cases. At the staircase he saw snow on the steps, knapsacks and packages—some Hermitage workers were still bringing objects of art from the Stieglitz Museum on the other side of the Champs de Mars for safekeeping in the Hermitage vaults.

Orbeli worked at his office as long as there was light from the windows on the Neva side. But in December this meant for only a few hours. It was deathly cold. His rheumatism grew worse.

One day he had a visitor, Captain A. V. Tripolsky, a famous submarine commander. Tripolsky had known Orbeli in the past, in fact, ever since his portrait had been hung in the Hermitage gallery of Heroes of the Soviet Union in 1940.

Orbeli greeted him warmly. He took off his glasses, put down his book, rose with difficulty (Tripolsky saw how crippled he was by rheumatism) and invited the captain to come below where it was warmer.

"It's too dark to work, anyway," Orbeli said. They crossed the Hall of Twenty Columns, Tripolsky following Orbeli blindly in the darkness. They made their way past the great Kolyvan vase, across the courtyard and down the staircase leading to Bomb Shelter No. 3. To the right was the shelter, to the left Orbeli's room. Orbeli lighted a candle and set it in a three-branch silver candlestick.

"My blockade office," he said proudly. There was a narrow cot, a table filled with books.

After leaving Orbeli, Tripolsky made his way straight to the Neva embankment. There, frozen in the ice, stood the *Polar Star,* once the Czar's private yacht, now a headquarters ship for the Baltic Fleet.

Tripolsky sought out the chief electrician.

"You know the Hermitage?" he asked.

"Naturally," he said. "It's right across from us."

Tripolsky explained its plight. They had no light, no electricity. Could the *Polar Star* help out by stringing a cable to the Hermitage?

"In a minute," said the electrician.

Within a few hours a cable had been laid across the ice and hooked up to the Hermitage. The sailors appeared in Orbeli's office, turned on the lamp and there was light. Orbeli clapped his hands like a small child. Then he sat down and lighted a cigarette. His leg was paining him badly. The sailors looked under his desk and found an electric heater which was not working. Soon they had it going.

"The ship gave its current to several of the rooms of the Hermitage," Nikolsky noted in his diary. "We have light. It is a priceless blessing."

It was a blessing, but a limited one. The *Polar Star* had fuel to power her dynamos—but not very much.

In the diary of V. V. Kalinin there is this notation of January 8 (the 130th day of the siege):

> I was in the city at the Hermitage. It is so melancholy there. They are so thin, their faces so white, bags under their eyes. They sit at their tables— in the cold by the weak light of a candle.
>
> In the bomb shelter the chief of guides, Sergei Reichardt, and his wife Kseniya have died. Sergei died January 6 among his beloved books, asking just before he died for one of his rare books to which he softly pressed his hand. Kseniya died today.
>
> I went to Orbeli in his little office in the arched cellar. It smelled raw and damp. An altar candle was burning. He seemed today particularly weak and nervous.

Possibly Orbeli's mood stemmed from the fact that on this day he had gotten two more requests, one from the Union of Architects, one from the Museum of Ethnography, each asking the same thing: "We request that the Hermitage prepare a coffin. . . ."

The great stock of packing materials which Orbeli had assembled to ship his treasures to safety was being put to new use. Almost alone in the city the Hermitage had a store of lumber, of packing boxes from which coffins could be made. This in early January was the principal task of the emaciated workers of the Hermitage—making coffins for their friends.

Now on this day for the first time Orbeli had to refuse a request for a coffin. The Hermitage carpenter had died, and there was no one with the strength to build one—not even for the Hermitage staff itself.

Henceforth when someone died at the Hermitage—and there were many deaths every day—the bodies were simply carried to the Vladimir corridor to lie there until, occasionally, a truck and army crew came and carted the bodies away.

Leningrad was, indeed, becoming a city of death.

40 . The Sleds of the Children

IN DECEMBER THEY BEGAN TO APPEAR—THE SLEDS OF THE children, painted bright red or yellow, narrow sleds with runners, sleds for sliding down hills in fur earlaps and a woolen muffler trailing behind, Christmas presents, small sleds, big enough for a boy taking a belly-flopper, or a boy and a girl clutching each other as they raced around the icy curves.

The children's sleds, suddenly they were everywhere—on the Nevsky, on the broad boulevards, moving toward Ulitsa Marat, toward the Nevskaya Lavra, toward Piskarevsky, toward the hospitals. The squeak, squeak, squeak of the runners sounded louder than the shelling. It deafened the ears. On the sleds were the ill, the dying, the dead.

In December Vladimir Konashevich, the artist, the illustrator of Pushkin and Lermontov, Hans Christian Andersen and Mark Twain, decided to write his memoirs. What else was there to do? He was starving and freezing. It was almost impossible to paint. He would write of his childhood in the last century in Moscow. It might drive out of his ears the squeaking of the sleds, the endless movement of the people in their coats of black wool as they drew the children's sleds along the icy sidewalks and dragged them through the streets.

There were no automobiles in the city. Only the people, pulling their burdens, the dead in coffins of unpainted wood, large and small, the ill clinging to the runners of the sleds, precariously balanced pails of water and bundles of wood. As Konashevich picked his way through the drifts, he thought more and more of his Moscow childhood, of the winter streets, the scenes of snow, the quiet, broken only by the sledges and the sleighs.

Not that he could drive the present from his consciousness. Try as he would, he could not drown out the cries of an old woman who lived in his communal apartment, who sat on a stool at her doorstep, thin, black, a hand extended, hoarsely whispering, "Bread . . . bread . . ." Every time he passed down the hall the hand went out and the voice croaked, "Bread . . . bread." Then the woman died.

Nothing now was more common than death in Leningrad. Luknitsky came back to his father's flat one night after a day at Smolny. He walked most of the way home to find that his aunt, Vera Nikolayevna, had died. She had gotten up that morning, complaining of a pain in her heart, sat down and lost consciousness. In a few hours she was dead. They put the body on a table in her room and closed the door. Now in the kitchen supper was being prepared, a small roast, cut from the remains of Mishka, the dog.

On December 29 Luknitsky noted in his diary that ten days earlier he had been told that six thousand persons a day were dying of starvation.[1] "Now, of course, many more," he observed. Six members of the Writers Union had died in the last two or three days—Lesnik, Kraisky, Valov, Varvara Naumova and two more. The aunt of M. Kozakov had lain in her flat dead for more than ten days. Kraisky died in the dining room of the Writers' House. He lay six days before they got around to moving the body out.

"To take someone who has died to the cemetery," Luknitsky said, "is an affair so laborious that it exhausts the last vestiges of strength in the survivors, and the living, fulfilling their duty to the dead, are brought to the brink of death themselves."

Luknitsky commented, as did all the Leningrad diarists, on the quiet of the city. It was the quiet of the grave. Automobiles rarely appeared—only frail people, slowly pulling the children's sleds. Not all the dead were in coffins. Many were simply swathed in a sheet, and when they were brought to the cemeteries, there was no one to dig a grave, no one to say a prayer. The body was just dumped. Not infrequently those who pulled the sled fell beside the corpse, themselves dead, without a sound, without a groan, without a cry.

Vera Inber discovered a terrifying spectacle at the back gate to the Erisman Hospital next to the dissection room. Here on the banks of the Karpovka Canal a mountain of corpses was growing. Each day eight to ten more bodies were added to the pile. The snow fell and covered them. Then new bodies were piled on top, some wrapped in rugs, some in curtains, some in sheets. Once she saw a very small body, obviously that of a child, tied in wrapping paper, bound with ordinary string. Sometimes, from under the snow an arm or a leg projected, strangely alive in the bright wrappings of the shrouds.

Vera Inber could not imagine what could be done about this. The dissection room itself was jammed with corpses. There were no trucks to take bodies to the cemetery, no strength for the task. There could be no registration of deaths under these conditions. The best that could be done was to give a simple body count to ZAGS (the city clerk).

---

[1] Incomplete data compiled at Smolny in January provided an estimate of 3,000 to 4,000 daily deaths. (*N.Z.*, p. 267.) Some Leningrad residents think the death rate rose to 10,000 a day at the worst time of the blockade. (Anatoly Darov, *Blokada*, New York, 1964, p. 145.)

The largest number of bodies were in the reception rooms. Many brought their dead to the hospital. Many tottered into the reception room and died. At the cemeteries long trenches were being dynamited for mass burials. Individual graves were almost impossible to obtain. Only for bread, the most precious of Leningrad commodities, would a gravedigger bury a corpse.

Leningrad's terrible winter—it was the coldest in modern times, with an average temperature in December of 9 above zero Fahrenheit (13 degrees below normal) and 4 degrees below zero in January (20 degrees below normal)—froze the ground like iron. The weakened Leningraders had no strength to hack out graves. Most corpses lay on the surface, gradually becoming buried under snow and ice.

Some were placed in common graves—actually long trenches, dynamited by army sappers—at the Volkov, Bolshaya Okhta, Serafimov, Bogoslovsky, Piskarevsky, Zhertva 9 Yanvarya, and the Tatar cemeteries. They were also buried in open squares on Golodai Island, at Vesely settlement and at the Glinozemsky factory. More than 662 common graves were dug in the winter of 1941–42, with a total length of 20,000 yards.

"I remember the picture exactly," recalled Y. I. Krasnovitsky, director of the Vulcan factory. "It was freezing cold. The bodies were frozen. They were hoisted onto trucks. They even gave a metallic ring. When I first went to the cemetery, every hair stood up on my head to see the mountain of corpses and the people, themselves hardly alive, throwing the bodies into trenches with expressionless faces."

The dead from the Kuibyshev, Dzerzhinsky, Red Guard and Vyborg sections were transported to Piskarevsky Cemetery. Steam shovels of Special Construction Administration No. 5 were ordered there. When they had completed their twenty-mile trip to Piskarevsky, the operators could hardly believe their eyes. They began to dig the trenches, trying not to look at the heap of bodies.

Returning from Lake Ladoga late at night, Vsevolod Kochetov saw the shovels at work. He thought they were working on new fortifications. The chauffeur corrected him.

"They are digging graves—don't you see the corpses?"

Kochetov looked more closely in the dim light. What he had thought were cords of wood were piles of corpses, some wrapped in blankets, shawls or sheets, some not.

"There are thousands," the chauffeur said. "I go past here every day, and every day they dig a new trench."

Even so, many bodies remained unburied or simply lay in open trenches. A Leningrader, jotting down his impressions in January, 1942, wrote:

> The nearer to the entrance to Piskarevsky I approached, the more bodies appeared on both sides of the road. Coming out of town where there were small one-story houses, I saw gardens and orchards and then an extraordinary formless heap. I came nearer. There were on both sides of the road

such enormous piles of bodies that two cars could not pass. A car could go only on one side and was unable to turn around. Through this narrow passage amidst the corpses, lying in the greatest disorder, we made our way to the cemetery.

The Leningrad authorities, almost powerless to act, nonetheless ordered on January 7 the observance of the "strictest sanitary norms" under threat of the "revolutionary tribunal"—in other words, death before the firing squad. Needless to say, the threat was meaningless.

"Never in the history of the world," comments the official Leningrad history of the blockade, "has there been an example of tragedy to equal that of starving Leningrad."

Every day more coffins both full and empty, appeared on the street. If they were empty, they slid from side to side on the sleds. One hit Vera Inber a glancing blow in the ankle. Usually two women pulled a sled. They put the straps over their shoulders—not because the corpses were so heavy, but because the women were so weak.

Once Vera Inber saw a corpse, that of a woman, on a sleigh. She was in a shroud, not a coffin, and those who had prepared her had carefully stuffed the shroud with shavings to give her breasts a more comely appearance. The professional touch made Vera Inber shudder. Someone probably had been paid, possibly in bread, to prepare this poor body—for what? Another time she saw two children's sleds pulled in tandem. On one was a coffin atop which, neatly arrayed, were a shovel and a crowbar. On the other was a load of wood. On the one death, on the other life.

You could see almost anything on a child's sled that winter in Leningrad: A brand-new chest of drawers being pulled by a starving woman, the chest to be broken up for kindling. Two women pulling a third, pregnant, hurrying to the hospital to give birth, yellow, thin, her face skeletal. Or two women pulling a man, his feet dragging behind him, shouting again and again, "Be careful. Be careful."

On a Sunday, walking from the gate of the Erisman Hospital to Leo Tolstoy Square, Vera Inber counted eight big and little sleds, each with a corpse, each wrapped in a different kind of shroud.

The very smell of the city was changing. No longer did you smell gasoline, tobacco, horses, dogs or cats. The healthy smell of people had vanished. Now the city smelled of raw snow and wet stone. White frost painted entry halls and staircases. And on the street one smelled the harsh and bitter odor of turpentine. This meant that a truck with bodies, bound for the cemetery, had just passed. Or one which had been to the cemetery coming back. The turpentine was used to drench the trucks and the corpses. The harsh smell lingered in the frosty air like the very scent of death.

In the charnel house that Leningrad was becoming the hospitals were worst of all. Yelena Skryabina, almost frantic with fear for her son Dima, who day by day was sinking into torpor, managed to get a job for him as a messenger in a hospital on the Petrograd side. For this he would receive one meal a day —a meat soup. This might save the youngster's life. The boy was so weak that he could hardly walk, and he returned from the hospital near collapse. It was jammed with bodies. There were bodies in the corridors, on the staircases, in the entryway. He could hardly get in and out of the building.

The streets were becoming places of inconceivable terror. Madame Skryabina's friend, Lyudmila, was hurrying home from work one night. A woman clutched at her arm, crying that she was too weak to take another step, she must have help. But Lyudmila herself could hardly stand. The woman's clutch was like iron. The two women slowly struggled until Lyudmila wrenched herself free, throwing the woman into a snowdrift, and ran down the street. She arrived home face white, eyes filled with terror, breath coming in gasps, saying again and again, "She is dying, she will die today."

Dmitri Moldavsky each day followed the same route. He went down Ulitsa Marat (more and more difficult to get through as bodies piled up at the morgue), down the Nevsky, across the bridge to the university. It took him three hours to walk this route with one halt. This was at a trolley-bus frozen in the ice at the corner of Nevsky Prospekt and the Griboyedov Canal, the very heart of the city. In this he stopped, unwound his scarf and rested while he counted to seventy-five. Then, difficult as it was to get up, he rose and continued his walk. He was never alone in the bus. There were always other passengers, the same passengers—three corpses. Who they were he did not know. Possibly others like himself who had paused a moment to rest and never got up again.

Once Moldavsky saw a woman fall in front of him on the Nevsky. She tried to rise but could not. She struggled and finally became still. He came up to her. Her face was black, her lips shriveled, her eyes open. Beside her lay a pair of red mittens, and he saw her fingers, white and thin as macaroni. Moldavsky and a woman passer-by tried vainly to put her on her feet. The victim opened her lips, muttering something that sounded like "soup." A Red Army man came along and the three of them got the woman up, but she fell again, dead.

"Well, we tried," the woman said.

"That's it!" said the soldier. "Let's go!"

Another time Moldavsky saw a man ahead of him, tottering down the Nevsky and nibbling at a crust of bread. A second man watched the man stagger along, bread in hand. "That's very good," said the second man. "A breakfast roll . . ."

He stood watching. Perhaps, thought Moldavsky, he is watching in case the man falls in hopes of getting the crust of bread.

People would do anything for food, for bread. In early December cemetery workers would provide a coffin and a grave for 300 rubles' worth of bread. Yevgeniya Vasyutina bought a little tin stove on December 10. She paid three days' bread ration for it—and the stove pipe was extra.

One day the wife of a friend came to Admiral Panteleyev. She and her family were starving. Panteleyev confessed he could do nothing to help. As she rose to go, she noticed his worn leather portfolio.

"Will you give me that?" she asked in despair.

He gave her the briefcase in puzzlement. A few days later he got a present from the woman. A dish of meat jelly and the nickel fittings for the portfolio. A note said she hadn't been able to make anything out of the nickel, but the jelly was the product of his briefcase.

By New Year's Day bread was selling at 600 rubles a kilogram in the black market. That was black bread, of course. There were half a dozen markets where packets of cigarettes, hunks of ersatz bread, jars of sour cabbage, dirty bits of rye bread, could be bought or traded for clothing, watches, jewelry or objects of art. But bread was so expensive that few Leningraders could dream of buying it. Vera Inber heard of one market where a friend had traded twenty-seven packets of ascorbic acid (Vitamin C) for a live dog. Her friend Marietta said judiciously, "That's a good trade—if it's a big dog."

Her friend Irina had an airdale terrier named Karma; she loved her dog like a human being. On December 1 the ration for service dogs ended. People began to eat their dogs. Vera Inber met Irina with the dog. "I'm taking him to the toxicologist to be put to sleep," she said. "But first I'll give him one last good meal. I have a crust of bread left. And what happens after that I don't want to know. But, of course, he'll be eaten. I know my co-workers have been waiting a long time for this."

Unfortunately, the toxicologist was so weak he bungled the injection. The poor dog cried like a human being before dying.

It was difficult even for the eternal optimist Vishnevsky to find reasons for meeting the New Year with hope. He was in the hospital recovering very slowly from a collapse. He had found himself there December 1, hardly knowing what had happened. By the end of December he was making fatuous diary entries: ("Today the temperature is 23 degrees below zero. In the country it is lower. Marvelous!") He had heard there was going to be an issue of cereals and macaroni for New Year's Day and that there would be special dining rooms for scientific workers. ("We are saving the intelligentsia!" he commented. The exclamation mark is Vishnevsky's.)

The Germans shelled Leningrad on the evening of December 31. At midnight Vishnevsky listened to the radio transmission of the Kremlin chimes. Then the naval guns of the ships on the Neva delivered a New Year's salvo to the German positions. The radio brought the Spassky chimes in Moscow, playing the Internationale. Two friends had come to be with him. They had a small glass of Malaga, recited some verses of Mayakovsky and Yesenin, and went to sleep.

Vera Inber had two celebrations. First at the Writers' House at 5 P.M., where an "Oral Almanac"—readings by writers and poets—was presented.

Vera Inber walked from Aptekarsky Island all the way to the Writers' House on Ulitsa Voinova. The temperature was well below zero. The streets were empty and ice-covered. She passed the trolley barn, from which cars no longer issued; the bakery, from which so little bread now came; shell-torn, snowdrifted autobuses; the Neva embankment, where stood two unfinished ships.

It was incredibly cold at the Writers' House. A few candles on the table gave light as Vera Inber read some stanzas from her new poem. This was "Pulkovo Meridian" (still untitled), her great war poem. When she got to the lines where she cursed Hitler and his Germany, she drew in her breath. Three times she started to speak. Each time she could not continue, gripped by emotion.

It was dark when she started home. Her husband had gone to get the day's bread ration and been caught by an air raid. Vera Inber was sick with worry before he returned.

At midnight they joined some doctors and drank their last bottle of sour Riesling. The party broke up when the receiving doctor telephoned. He reported that forty corpses were lying in the corridors and the long-unused baths. What should he do?

At midnight Luknitsky awakened his friend Lyudmila Fedorovna. They sat down to a New Year's feast—a bottle of champagne he had saved from before the war, 200 grams of almonds he had gotten at the Writers' Union and three pieces of dog meat which he had saved especially for the occasion.

This kind of scene was enacted all over Leningrad on New Year's eve. Yelizaveta Sharypina, a schoolteacher turned Party worker, lay in her frigid apartment. She had been lying there since the middle of December, all day in the dark, looking at the illuminated hands of her watch, and then, an hour before she expected her husband, she would light the tiny "bat." She didn't want him to think she lay all day in total darkness. Her children had been sent out of Leningrad, to somewhere in the Urals. She wanted to send them a New Year's card. But she was too weak to write. She lay in bed, thinking about caviar. She tried to stop, but she could not get the thought of caviar out of her mind. She even found herself running her tongue over her dry shriveled lips. Just a tiny, tiny piece of good Russian black bread and just two little drops of beluga caviar.

She lighted the little light, and presently Pavel came. "How are you, my little quarter?" he asked. He had called her his "better half." Now that she was so thin he called her his "quarter."

There was a surprise for New Year's: an hour or two of electric light. And another surprise: she had traded two dresses for a pound or two of sausage (better not to ask what kind) and a pound of horse meat. She and Pavel had saved their bread ration till evening, and she had put away five pieces of soya candy. They had a real New Year's feast.

Ilya Glazunov, the little boy who had been playing White and Red Russians in the country courtyard on June 22, was now in Leningrad, living in the gloomy big flat on Bolshoi Prospekt on the Petrograd side.

It was dark in the apartment, dark as a cave, Ilya thought. Outside there was a frosty sun. But within they no longer removed the curtains. Sometimes they heated up the little *burzhuika*—it had been in the flat since the days of the Civil War. There was no water. The plumbing had frozen. They drank melted snow.

Ilya would bring the snow from the courtyard in a saucepan. Once he returned to find his mother staring at the ceiling motionless. Ilya was terrified. He looked at her unseeing eyes and asked, "Are you sleeping?" "Don't worry," she replied softly. "I am not dead. I am just thinking about you and what you will do without me, being only eleven years old."

Ilya noticed that hunger made his head clearer. But he was weak. Sometimes there was a ringing in the ears. He moved from one mood to another with surprising lightness.

Bad as things were, his mother was determined that Ilya would have a New Year's tree. From somewhere came a fir branch. She put it in an old milk bottle and decorated it with little toys from past holidays. One candle was found. It was cut into four pieces. The grownups of the family made a grand entrance from the next room, dressed in shawls and scarfs, masks on their faces. The candles were lighted. There was a moment of silence. The candles flickered. Then all burst into tears. It was the last time Ilya and his family were together.

Death lay around the corner, and each death seemed more terrible to the little boy. The first to die was his father. He lay face up on his bed, wearing his coat, his fur cap pulled down on his forehead, and cried a high, piercing cry: "A-a-a-a." A note that never stopped, that froze the blood and made the hair rise on Ilya's head. His father lay and cried the strange high cry as Ilya's mother sat beside him, the little lamp in her hand, trembling and casting dark shadows on the wall, and the cries going on without end, his father rigid and staring without seeing at the ceiling. Fifteen minutes before he died Ilya's father fell silent. For nights thereafter Ilya awakened in terror of the cry and stifled his fears by burying his face in the woolen scarf which his mother wrapped about his head before he went to sleep.

"Hunger psychosis" was what the doctor called it. The doctor could hardly stand on his own feet. It was his last visit to the flat. He himself died a few days later.

Next came his grandmother. Ilya awoke one night, calling for her. She did not answer. He tried to look at her in the flickering light of the little lamp. She seemed to be staring at him, but her forehead was cold as granite. He tumbled into the bed where his mother lay, covered with blankets and her old winter coat.

"She's dead," he cried.

"Ah," said his mother, "it's easier for her than for us, my child. There's no escape from death. We'll all die. Don't be afraid."

In the stillness the boy heard the beat of the radio metronome, the distant crash of the German shells. All of Ilya's family died as the days went by. There were four rooms in the big old flat. In each lay a corpse. It was as cold in the apartment as on the street. Just one big icebox, the boy thought. And a good thing, for then the corpses did not smell. Once he went into the back room but fled in terror. A fat rat jumped toward him from the body of his Aunt Vera, dead these two weeks. The rat had been gnawing on her face.

His mother and his Aunt Asya decided to have his grandmother buried. They bargained with Shura, the portress. Once Shura had been round as jelly. Now she was a skeleton like everyone else. They wanted Shura to take 250 grams of bread and 100 rubles instead of the 350 grams of bread she asked. Eventually Shura agreed. Grandmother was carefully wrapped in a sheet, and in one corner was worked in thread her initials, "E. F." Shura put the mummy-like figure on Ilya's sled and started off for the Serafimov Cemetery.

A few days later Ilya was in the courtyard, gathering snow for the tea-kettle. Next door a truck had stopped and men were filling it with corpses, most of them just bones, covered with greenish-bluish skin. Some were clothed, some were in white underclothes, some in overcoats with their gas masks still over their shoulders (they had fallen dead, obviously, on the street). There were many bodies under the staircase. Ilya watched, shivering in the cold, and was about to leave when they lifted out another corpse, this one wrapped in a white sheet and resting on a child's sled. Ilya ran to get a closer glimpse. Yes. In the corner of the sheet were his grandmother's initials, "E. F."

Now there were only the two of them left—Ilya and his mother. One day a car arrived, sent by Ilya's uncle, to take the family to the military hospital. The uncle had no notion that his brother was already dead.

Ilya's mother was too weak to rise. Her eyes followed the men who stood with Ilya. "I'll soon be well," she said. "Then I'll join you."

Ilya could not understand why her eyes filled with tears.

"I'm crying," she whispered, "because we will be separated for a month. Not more, though. Only a month."

The strange man took Ilya by the hand. His mother gave him a little copper icon, one which had saved his grandfather's life from a Turkish bullet at the Battle of Shipka. "Take it for luck," his mother said. "Soon we'll be together."

In Leningrad now, as Zinaida Shishova wrote of a mother and her starving baby boy, they lived without radio, without light, warmed only by their own human breath:

> In our six-room apartment
> There live only the three of us—you and I
> And the wind blowing from the darkness. . . .
> No, excuse me. I am mistaken.

There is a fourth lying out on the balcony,
Waiting a week for the funeral.[2]

Real funerals were rare. Aleksandr Kron never forgot the burial of the father of Grisha Miroshnichenko. From somewhere a coffin was found and a small bus. Kron and two other Baltic Fleet correspondents, Anatoly Tarasenkov and Vasily Smirnov, had to carry the coffin from the fifth floor. But the body was so light that, weak as they were, it was no burden. The widow wanted her husband buried at the Okhta Cemetery. They drove past Smolny, across the bridge, and approached the cemetery over a road that was unbelievably torn up. A sharp wind drove in their faces, and they encountered a long line of people slowly dragging little sleds and corpses toward the cemetery. There were dozens of them, covered with rugs, curtains, towels. The gravediggers wanted to be paid in bread but were persuaded to take 250 rubles. Then the hole was too short for the coffin. It took an hour of hard work to make it long enough. Somewhere they found a little fir tree to put on the grave. The widow decided against a cross. So they took the handle of a shovel and set it at the head of the grave. They got back to their quarters, half frozen, started a small fire with some old newspapers and drank a little home-brew "Port wine-type."

Fewer and fewer people bothered to bury their dead. They did not have the means, nor the strength. If they did manage to get the body to the cemetery and return home, they often collapsed never to rise again. More and more often they took the body from the warmer room to a colder one and laid it on the floor. Little by little the houses of Leningrad filled up with dead. People no longer bothered to lock their doors. It took too much energy to get up if someone knocked. You could enter almost any house and any apartment, walk through the frozen rooms and see the dead, lying on the floor, lying on the beds, or in chairs around the stove where the fire had long since died away.

Sometimes the survivors took bodies to the street and laid them there for someone, they hoped, to bury. But the bodies were not necessarily buried. Passers-by might lift their hats slightly and go on past. Nikolai Chukovsky walked one day from Vasilevsky Island to the Petrograd side and back again. On the way he passed six bodies; on the way back, seven.

His offices were in a large building on Vasilevsky Island. Someone dropped

---

[2] Zinaida Shishova's poem "Blockade" is one of the most moving—some Soviet critics feel the *most* moving—work to be written in Leningrad during the blockade, an impression of the agony of the city as seen by a mother, trying vainly to save her infant son from death by starvation. Probably because of the realism and pathos of her lines the poem has never been published in full in the Soviet Union. It was read by Shishova at the Writers' House in Leningrad in late 1942. Excerpts from it are contained in *Poeziya V Boy*, a collection of war poems published by the Ministry of Defense in 1959. As the critic A. Abramov noted, even Shishova's name is hardly known to the present generation of Soviet readers and critics. (*Neva*, No. 6, June, 1965, p. 173.)

from an upper window the body of a young woman. It fell in the snow outside the archway leading to Chukovsky's office. Coming out of the courtyard, Chukovsky and his companions carefully made a new path that skirted the young woman's body as it lay sprawled in the snow. After four days the body disappeared and Chukovsky thought it had been picked up by a passing patrol. No longer did Chukovsky and his fellow workers gingerly skirt the spot. They walked straight ahead. Weeks passed. Slowly winter turned to spring. One warm sunny day Chukovsky came through the arch. The dirty snow was running off in rivulets and he saw to his horror a woman's hand emerging from the ice. No one had taken the body away. It had simply vanished under the snow. All winter long Chukovsky and his fellow editors had walked again and again over the frozen body.

A few days after New Year's Vera Inber ventured for the first time into the hospital reception room. She went into the shower rooms. The nude body of a male corpse lay on a stretcher. It was a mere skeleton. She found it hard to believe it had ever known human life. The eyes were open and the face was covered with post-mortem whiskers. The nose seemed to protrude remarkably. In the next room she found more stretchers on which corpses of men and women lay. In other rooms and in the corridors, on benches, on stretchers and simply on the floor, sat or lay living corpses— patients who were only a step from death. They sat or lay motionless hour by hour. Two nurses attended them, and the nurses, too, were more like corpses than humans. The patients were not being treated; they were simply being fed—an infinitesimal quantity. The disease from which they suffered was hunger.

A few nights later the dissection rooms burned. To the dissection laboratory had been brought many half-burned bodies from a factory which had caught fire. The corpses were still clothed in cotton-padded jackets, and in the jackets sparks had smoldered. No one noticed, and after smoldering for hours the sparks burst into flame, racing through the cotton and setting fire to the dry wood which had been collected for coffins.

The hospital fire command tried to pull the corpses out of the fire. They had no water. They tried to extinguish the fire with snow but failed. Hardly had the dissection rooms burned when a worse fire broke out on the other side of the Karpovka Canal, spreading to a gasoline tank and sending up flames higher than the hospital chimney.

Vsevolod Vishnevsky was released from the hospital on January 4 and walked again along the Liteiny Prospekt, along the frozen Neva, past the Admiralty with its spire, past the Winter Palace, past the Hermitage and the white wastes of the Champs de Mars. He hastened to jot down his impressions—of cold, stillness, snowdrifts, shadows, children hauling the bodies of their dead parents on sleds, parents hauling the bodies of their dead children on sleds, the Apraksin Palace, windows smashed in, the Passage department store, still open for business, selling Vologda lace, children's wooden toys, phonograph records, silk ribbons and children's stockings (but not needles or thread).

Vishnevsky noted the aspects of the people who passed him on the street —some pale white, some earthen gray, some puffed, some skeletal.

It was on one of these days that Dmitri Shcheglov came back to Leningrad by truck across Lake Ladoga. He was shocked to see people sitting in doorways, resting on icy steps, heads in their hands. Only when he came closer did he realize they were dead—starved and frozen. Past them walked the living, almost unnoticing.

Shcheglov met a friend: "Before me stood a blue-colored man with puffed cheeks. He looked like a ghost in a child's play. Only his eyes seemed to be alive."

This was Leningrad in January, 1942. As Nikolai Markevich, a correspondent for *Komsomolskaya Pravda* who was later killed in an airplane crash near Velikye Luki, noted in his diary for January 24, 1942:

> The city is dead. There is no electricity. Warm rooms are most rare. No streetcars. No water. Almost the only kind of transport is sleds . . . carrying corpses in plain coffins, covered with rags or half clothed. . . . Daily six to eight thousand die. . . . The city is dying as it has lived for the last half-year—clenching its teeth.

In the future museum of the Leningrad blockade, commented Secretary Ivanov of the Young Communists, the child's sled should have a place of honor.

41 . A New Kind of Crime

IT BEGAN AS WINTER SET IN, AND WITH EACH WEEK IT grew—what the pedantic clerks of the Leningrad militia or police department called "a new kind of crime," a kind which none of the many branches of the Soviet police had encountered before.

It was, in simplest terms, murder for food. It happened every day. A blow from behind and an old woman in a food queue fell dead, while a pale youth ran off with her *sumka*, or purse, and her ration card. The quick flash of a knife and a man walking away from a bakery fell in the snow as a dark figure vanished with the loaf of bread he had been carrying.

The Leningrad police, like all of Stalin's police, were well organized, well staffed even in these difficult days. But the new crimes were not, for the most part, being committed by hardened criminals (among whom the police had an efficient network of stool pigeons). The crimes were the acts of ordinary Soviet citizens, driven to murder and robbery by starvation, bombardment, cold, suffering. Some had wives or children at home, dying of dystrophy.

"It was characteristic," Militia Major A. T. Skilyagin wrote, "that many of these crimes were committed not by inveterate criminals, not by elements alien to our society, but simply by persons driven to desperation by hunger, bombing and shelling, persons whose psyches had been broken by the weight of their experiences."

As the winter wore on, roving gangs of murderers appeared on the streets of Leningrad. Sometimes they included deserters from the front, ex-Red Army men, desperate elements of every kind. They preyed on persons standing in queues, seizing their ration cards or their food; they descended on lone pedestrians, either by day or night; they carried out bold attacks on the bread shops and even commandeered trucks and sleds, bringing supplies to the bread shops. They entered flats, rifled them of valuables, and if an occupant raised a voice (often there was no one but the dead in the apartments), they hit him on the head and set fire to the flat to cover the traces.

447

Not all the criminals were Soviet citizens. There were German agents in Leningrad—it was no trick to slip them through the lines in the suburbs of the city. Sometimes the agents spread rumors, stirred up trouble in the bread queues, engaged in agitation, sometimes in sabotage.

The danger from within the city had been strongly in the minds of the Leningrad leadership since the outbreak of war. It had always been a pre-occupation of Stalin and his police chief, Beria. It played a significant role in the political maneuvering which handicapped Leningrad's defense in August and September. By winter Leningrad was crisscrossed with internal defense organizations, "destroyer" battalions of workers, special public order brigades of Young Communists. But as the blockade tightened, as starvation began to set in, as the "new kind of crime" appeared, none of this seemed to be enough.

On November 15 after the fall of Tikhvin confronted Zhdanov and his associates with the realization that the blockade might not quickly be lifted, that the suffering of the city might well carry beyond any parameters thus far conceived, that the spirit of Leningrad might break under the impact of these crushing blows, new steps were taken to defend the internal security of the city.

The Military Council of the Leningrad front established a special Administration for Internal Defense. This took a different form from the ill-fated effort by Zhdanov and Marshal Voroshilov to set up a Leningrad Council for Defense in August.

The new internal defense organization was to be independent and self-sufficient. It was designed to cope with any threat which might arise *within* Leningrad. It was comprised of workers battalions (often badly under-strength), several brigades of Baltic Fleet sailors, the city police department, such NKVD troops as were still available within Leningrad, the fire brigades, and odds and ends of artillery and machine-gun regiments. Five workers battalions were finally organized, numbering about 16,000 men. The total command as listed on paper by December, 1941, comprised about 37,000 men. The city was divided into six sectors, with fire points in many apartment houses.

Many workers detachments continued to stand duty in the great factories of the city, although by December they were frigid morgues in which hand-fuls of people tried to keep alive, huddled about tiny temporary stoves. The troops were available for any emergency, including, of course, internal disturbances or uprisings. They had one other task—to guard the approaches to the city over the ice, particularly from the direction of Peterhof. There were many small engagements fought on the ice, sometimes between iceboat patrols, scudding along at sixty miles an hour, but for the most part these were just scouting skirmishes.

The precautions were by no means unjustified. The regular police had been brutally weakened by forced drafts which had sent most of the NKVD units to the front. Many functions had been taken over by women. The regular police, like everyone in Leningrad, suffered from starvation, cold and physical weakness. Some reports suggest that the police, both regular and secret, almost ceased to function in late fall and winter, because of physical debilitation. Also, some Leningrad residents assert, the police were intimidated by the plight of the city and preferred not to show themselves too readily to the civilian population.

In the dangerous days of September the police had panicked. Some commandeered planes and got out of Leningrad. Day after day they burned their files, destroying Party lists, secret documents and even house registers, lest they be used by Nazi occupation authorities for compiling execution lists. The panic was not quite so compelling as in Moscow, where, in October, the sky was clouded for days by smoke from the burning files of the secret police, and citizens sometimes found their half-burned dossiers fluttering down from the NKVD furnace chimneys into the streets. But from September onward more and more Leningraders had demonstrated less and less fear of the police. They spoke more openly among themselves, heedless of who might hear or what might be reported about them.

Official accounts lay great stress on the physical weakness of the police. In December most units had only eight or ten men on duty, and these men had to work shifts of fourteen to sixteen or even eighteen to twenty hours daily. In January 166 police in Leningrad died of starvation and 1,600 were on sick call. In February the death toll rose to 212.[1]

The criminals with whom the police had to deal were far better armed than in peacetime. Often they had military rifles, sometimes submachine guns and almost always revolvers.

As the ration was cut and then cut again and again, not all Leningraders, as one Soviet source puts it tactfully, "received the news with bravery."

One January evening with the temperature at 20 below zero Maria Razina and Peter Yakushin, political workers in a large Leningrad apartment house, went to apartment No. 5 where an evacuated family was living. The mother was dead and three small children huddled about her. No ration cards could be found. Soon the owner of the flat, a man named Mark Schacht, returned and said he was making arrangements to take the youngsters to a children's home.

On a hunch Yakushin demanded that Schacht return the family's ration cards. He denied having them. Yakushin grabbed him by the throat and shouted, "Give me the cards, you bandit, or I'll kill you on the spot!"

Schacht suddenly produced the missing ration cards. Before Yakushin could summon a military tribunal (a squad of Red Army soldiers) to execute him, the landlord vanished.

[1] The size of the Leningrad police force can only be guessed at. In the summer of 1941 the police street patrol force (exclusive of traffic police and men in stationhouses) numbered 1,200. (Skilyagin, *Dela i Lyudi*, p. 247.)

Not all workers in the food distribution system could resist temptation. A grocery store director named Lokshina stole nearly 400 pounds of butter and 200 pounds of flour. She was shot. This was the fate of food criminals whenever they were uncovered. The chief of a Smolny region bread store named Akkonen and his assistant, a woman called Sredneva, cheated their customers of four or five grams of bread per ration. They sold the surplus, taking furs, objects of art and gold jewelry in exchange. They were summarily tried and shot.

As Party Secretary A. A. Kuznetsov put it bluntly in the spring of 1942, "I will tell you plainly that we shot people for stealing a loaf of bread."

In November *Leningradskaya Pravda* began to carry brief items, almost invariably on its back page, reporting the actions of military tribunals in cases of food crimes: three men shot for stealing food from a warehouse; two women shot for profiteering on the black market; five men shot for the theft of flour from a truck; six men shot for conspiring to divert food from the state system. Sometimes the defendants got twenty-five years in a labor camp. But not often. The usual penalty was shooting.

It was a rare day when *Leningradskaya Pravda* did not publish at least one such item, along with a theater listing or two (these vanished after January 10), a few notices of dissertations being defended, the daily communiqué of the Soviet Information Bureau, the press conferences of Solomon Lozovsky, the official government spokesman in Moscow, and an occasional dispatch by Vsevolod Kochetov, Nikolai Tikhonov or Vsevolod Rozhdestvensky.

The ordinary Leningrad city court was transformed, by order of the Leningrad Military Council, into a military court and the city procurator was made a military procurator. This put all persons accused of food crimes under military law. In practice it meant they went almost directly before the firing squad, with a minimum of formality and only the vaguest nod toward judicial process. A total of 3,500 Young Communists were directed into the stores and the rationing system, instructed by Party Secretary Zhdanov not to permit "even a suspicion" of dishonesty in food handling. The Young Communists carried out sudden raids on every link in food distribution and repeatedly uncovered irregularities. In one action in the Vyborg region twenty-three Young Communist units participated and exposed a whole network of food criminals. All were shot summarily.

The worst disaster which could befall a Leningrader was loss of his ration card. On June 22 Ivan Krutikov had been rowing on the lake at Pushkin when the war news broke. On December 15 he was in Leningrad, where his factory had been removed from Pushkin. He had suffered a concussion in a bombing raid and was weakened by scanty rations. On December 15 worse misfortune befell him. As he stood in a queue, a thief grabbed his ration card and fled. Krutikov gave chase but was able to run only a short distance. He saw the robber disappear and burst into tears at his helplessness. He didn't even have the breath to shout, "Stop thief!"

It was virtually impossible under the rigid rules established by Food Director D. V. Pavlov to get a substitute ration card. Prior to December a person who lost his card could apply to a regional bureau and get a new one. In October 4,800 substitute cards were issued. In November 13,000 persons got replacements. These figures seem to have been regarded as normal. But in December long lines began to form at the rationing bureaus. Before the alarmed Pavlov could halt the practice 24,000 cards had been given out. The people invariably claimed that they had lost their card during a bombardment or shelling or when their house burned down. Pavlov knew that many claims were legitimate. But he knew also that many persons must be claiming fraudulent losses in order to get a second ration. The power to issue substitute cards was withdrawn from regional offices. Hereafter new cards could be obtained only from the central office and only with irrefutable proof—testimony of eyewitnesses, supporting evidence from the building superintendent, the local Party worker, the police. For a time Zhdanov himself was the only man who was empowered to replace a lost ration card. It was impossible for the ordinary citizen to assemble the data required for issuance of a new card. Applications quickly dropped to zero for, in fact, if you lost your card you could not get another. The problem was solved, but at the cost of almost certain death for thousands of unfortunates who actually did lose their cards.

Thus Krutikov faced sixteen days without food—in other words, death. He had one hope. His factory was no longer operating due to lack of electric power, and he had applied for front-line duty in the army. On December 17 he got a notice to appear for induction and reported for medical examination. But the doctor rejected him, saying, "You have dystrophy in the full meaning of the word. We can't admit you until you have fed up a bit. Sorry not to be able to help you." At that time Krutikov weighed about eighty-four pounds, half his prewar weight. For four days he did not eat. Finally, his factory director suggested that he try to get readmission to a workers battalion in which he had formerly served.

It took Krutikov sixteen hours to walk four or five miles from his factory to the Narva Gates, where the workers battalion had its headquarters in the Gorky House of Culture. The temperature was 25 degrees below zero. He was so weak he had to rest every fifteen or twenty paces. Krutikov's old commander put him back on the rolls, with a ration of 250 grams of bread a day plus 100 to 120 grams of cereal and a bowl of hot water for breakfast. His life was saved.

Most were by no means so fortunate.

One night a mother, a pensioner, and her sixteen-year-old daughter, Lulya, appeared at Erisman Hospital. The daughter wore a cape and carried a fur muff. Both were in a state of hysteria. A confidence woman had made the daughter's acquaintance in a bread line and promised to get her a job with good meals in Military Hospital No. 21. At the beginning of February, she got the mother to lend her 45 rubles (all she had), took the pair's ration cards and led them through the blackout to Erisman Hospital for an "interview." In the complete darkness the mother and daughter heard their benefactor cry, "Follow me!" Then she vanished.

The two wept. The mother kept saying, "Lulya, you have put me into my grave—still living." The girl looked into space and mumbled, "What a night! What a night!" Vera Inber and her husband helped them to make out a report to the police. But what good it would do no one knew. They had no ration cards and it was only February 3. Four weeks without food: a death sentence.

Vsevolod Kochetov also lost his ration card but in a different way. He had gone with his wife Vera across Lake Ladoga to the Fifty-fourth Army front in late December. About January 12 he returned to Tikhvin to find that an urgent telegram from his editor, Zolotukhin, had been waiting several days for him, ordering him back to Leningrad. A whole week passed between the arrival of the telegram and Kochetov's return to Leningrad. He got back to find that Zolotukhin—with whom he had never hit it off—had put him up on charges of violation of military discipline. He was summarily discharged from *Leningradskaya Pravda* and expelled from the Communist Party. By coincidence (or possibly not by coincidence) Kochetov's best friend and wartime companion, Mikhalev, was given similar treatment for a slightly different offense—for using the newspaper car to transport a sick colleague across Lake Ladoga.

Kochetov eventually got his expulsion from the Party reversed. But he didn't get his job back, and he didn't get his ration card back. The ration card went with the job. Regardless of cause (and the only source for what happened is Kochetov, who never paints himself in anything but heroic colors), it was no snap being caught in Leningrad in midwinter of the blockade without a ration card. At one point he was reduced to buying 900 grams of lard at one ruble a gram—900 rubles—in the black market. Finally, the radio committee gave him a job, but it was several weeks before he got a ration card. He tramped five or ten miles a day in search of food, usually going to the front, to commanders whom he knew. Sometimes they let him share a bowl of soup. Sometimes they gave him a tin of canned meat, a half-loaf of black bread or a bit of sausage. Here and there around the city he stopped to look at bulletin boards and read the announcements posted there, handwritten on bits of yellow, white or blue paper: "Will remove corpses—for bread"; "Will buy or exchange valuables for records of Vertinsky and Leshchenko"; "For Sale: Complete works of Leonid Andreyev, Edgar Poe, Knut Hamsun"; "Lost: Little girl, seven years old, in red dress and fur hood. Anyone who has seen or met her . . ."

What could have happened to the little girl in the red dress and fur hood? Had she been on the way to the food store when an air raid struck and fallen victim to a random bomb? Was she a victim of the casual shelling of German long-range guns which went on day after day at any hour, sometimes in one street, sometimes another? Had she simply collapsed of hunger and died in the street as thousands did every day? Or was there a more sinister explanation? Anything could and did happen on the streets of starving Leningrad. The possibilities of tragedy were endless. More than one child had been killed for a ration card, even though theirs were of the lowest category. As early as November mothers and fathers had begun to keep their children off the streets because of rumors of cannibalism.

Both adults and children were turned into beasts by the privations. Yelizaveta Sharypina went to a store one day on Borodinsky Street. She saw an excited woman swearing at a youngster about ten years old and hitting him again and again. The child sat on the floor, oblivious of the blows, and greedily chewed a hunk of black bread, stuffing it into his mouth as rapidly as he could work his jaws. Around the woman and the child stood a circle of silent spectators.

Sharypina grabbed the woman and tried to make her halt.

"But he's a thief, a thief, a thief," the woman cried.

She had received her day's bread ration from the clerk and had let it sit for one moment on the counter. The youngster snatched the loaf, sat down on the floor and proceeded to devour it, heedless of blows, heedless of shouts, heedless of anything that went on around him.

When Sharypina tried to calm the woman, she broke into tears and sobbed that she had taken her only child to the morgue a few weeks before. Finally, Sharypina got the people in the bread store to contribute bits of their ration to the woman who had lost hers. She then questioned the ten-year-old. His father, he thought, was at the front. His mother had died of hunger. Two children remained, he and a younger brother. They were living in the cellar of a house which had been destroyed by a bomb. She asked why they hadn't gone to a children's home. He said they had to wait for their father. If they went to a home, they would be sent out of Leningrad and never see him again.

Even the stoutest heart began to wonder whether Leningrad could survive such a plight. Vera Inber, a woman of flaming courage who had deliberately come to Leningrad to share its fate with her physician husband, wrote in her diary for January 4:

> It seems to me that if in the course of ten days the blockade is not lifted the city will not hold out. Leningrad has taken the full brunt of this war. What is needed is that the Germans on the Leningrad front receive their due. . . . If only someone knew how Leningrad is suffering. The winter is still long. The cold is ferocious.

Three days later she wrote that everyone in Leningrad was saying that General Meretskov's troops would be in Leningrad by the tenth. "Well," she commented, "whether it is the tenth, the fifteenth or the twentieth or even the end of January, just let it happen."

The wildest rumors coursed through Leningrad. One was the legend of the "noble bandit." A young girl was attacked by a bandit gang on her way home late at night. She was compelled to hand over her fur coat, her wool dress, her new shoes. The bandits were about to leave her naked and freezing in the bitter night when one took off his leather jacket and threw it over her shoulders. The girl ran to her apartment and there, plunging her hand into the pocket of the jacket, pulled out a packet of money—5,000 rubles. Or, in another version, obviously influenced by the blockade, she put her hand in the pocket and drew out a loaf of bread and a large package of butter.

On January 12[2] Mayor Peter Popkov called a press conference at Smolny. The reporters thought he looked tired. His eyes were red and deeply shadowed, his face pale but freshly shaven. He did not rise to greet them, simply motioning to chairs at a long table covered with green baize. Without preliminaries he began to speak of the city's difficulties. His voice was hoarse, and he talked slowly without intonation. The city had been under siege for five months. There had been terrible problems with food. Now, he thought, the Ladoga road was solving them. "The enemy planned to stifle the city by hunger," he said. "This aim will be thwarted." But two things must be done. The food must be gotten into the city, and within the city a merciless struggle must be fought against robbers and "marauders," or pillagers as the officials called the organized gangs preying on Leningrad. "Robbers, speculators and marauders will be mercilessly punished by the laws of war," Popkov said.

The suffering grew worse.

On January 25 Party Secretary Kuznetsov got an urgent telephone call at Smolny from Power Station No. 5, the only plant still operating. The station had been limping along on daily shipments of 500 cubic meters of wood, delivered by the October Railroad. That day the last fuel had been exhausted. None came in by rail.

"Try to hold out a few hours," Kuznetsov begged. But there was no more fuel. The turbines turned slower and slower and finally halted. That deprived Leningrad's remaining water-pumping station of power. The pumps halted. No more water for the bread bakeries. Without water the bakers could not bake bread.

It may have been on this day that the City Soviet telephoned Power Station No. 2 and asked for 100 kilowatts of power. "We can't," came the answer. "We're sitting here by an oil lamp ourselves."

Leningrad was left with a total power production of 3,000 kilowatts, turned out by a small emergency turbine at Station No. 1.

At the Frunze regional bakery, one of eight still operating in the city, two fire department pumpers were brought in and kept the bakery going. In the

---

[2] The date is given incorrectly as January 17 by Chakovsky (pp. 62–63). The text of Popkov's remarks was published in *Leningradskaya Pravda* January 13.

Petrograd region the pipes quickly froze. A call was sent to the Young Communist headquarters:

"We must have 4,000 pails of water by evening for the bakery or there will be no bread tomorrow. We must have a minimum of 2,000 Young Communists because none of them can carry more than two pails; they don't have the strength."

The youngsters were somehow mobilized and formed a chain from the frozen banks of the Neva to the nearest bakery. They managed to provide enough water and then, on children's sleds, distributed the bread to the food shops.

By chance Vsevolod Vishnevsky made a speech before a thousand police workers the day after the power was cut off. He spoke in a large room at police headquarters and noted that it was in good order. There was light, although it was being "economized." He was told that the principal problem lay with the railroad, which was working so badly that 70,000 tons of food had piled up at Osinovets because it was impossible to bring it into Leningrad. If Vishnevsky found anything curious in the fact that with Leningrad bereft of light and heat the police force still was able to assemble in lighted, heated quarters, he made no notation of the fact. He did, however, make an oblique comment on the comparatively well-fed appearance of the NKVD.

When Vera Inber heard the news about cessation of power, she noted in her diary for January 25:

7 P.M. The situation is catastrophic. People now have fallen on the wooden fence around the hospital and are smashing it up for kindling. There is no water. If tomorrow the bakeries halt for even one day, what will happen? Today we hadn't even any soup—only cereal. There was coffee this morning, but there will be no more liquids. Our water supply: half a teakettle (we keep it on the warm stove), half a pan for washing and a quarter-bottle for tomorrow. That's all.

The next day she wrote:

I cried for the first time from grief and bitterness. I upset the cereal in the stove. Ilya swallowed a few spoonfuls mixed with ashes. No bread yet . . .

On the twenty-seventh she learned of the bucket brigade at the Neva which had been mustered to help the bakeries. There were enormous lines at the bread shops, but bread did appear toward evening and was slowly passed out. For practical purposes, however, Leningrad's bakeries in the depth of the famine winter were closed down for about forty-eight hours.

The fuel famine worsened despite every effort of Zhdanov, Kuznetsov and the others.

Leningrad had entered the blockade in no better shape for fuel than for food. On September 1 Leningrad had gasoline and oil reserves of 18 to 20 days, coal for 75 to 80 days. The Power Trust had 18 days' supply of wood, the bread bakeries 60 days'. By September 30 fuel oil was virtually exhausted and most factories were down to their last coal. The October 1 stock of wood was 118,851 cubic meters—about two weeks' supply. It had been 370,000 cubic meters a month earlier.

By mid-October power production had fallen to one-third prewar level. Young Communist battalions were beginning to be sent out to the suburban forests to chop wood.

The city in peacetime got 120 trainloads of fuel a day. Now it had three or four trains of firewood at best.[3]

The heating of buildings virtually ceased, although it was officially supposed to be maintained at 54 degrees Fahrenheit in apartments, 50 degrees in offices and 47 degrees in factories, as of November 17. In fact, by December there was no central heating whatever. The use of electricity for lighting was limited to Smolny, the General Staff building, police stations, Party offices, AA commands, post and telegraph offices, the fire department, courts and apartment house offices. Even the military were running out of fuel. By the end of November they were down to ten to eleven days of aviation gas and seven days' supply for the trucks.

By December 15 the director of Power Station No. 1 reported he was receiving only 150 to 350 tons of coal a day against a minimum use of 700 to 800. He was compelled to exhaust his emergency supplies and closed down. In the course of December most hospitals lost all their electricity, and in the forty which were dependent on electricity for heating, temperatures fell to 35 to 45 degrees. Laundries ceased to operate. So did public baths.

On December 10, 2,850 persons were sent out to cut wood. On December 12 another 1,400 were mobilized, mostly Young Communists. On December 24 it was decided to demolish wooden structures for fuel. Even so, only 20 percent of the December wood quota of 130,000 cubic meters was met. The bakeries got 18,000 cubic meters of wood from the demolition of 279 houses in January. In February they got another 17,000 cubic meters.

On January 1 the city authorities estimated fuel reserves at 73,000 tons of coal, a little more than a month's supply at minimum use. There were less than 2,000 tons of anthracite left in the city. The only sources of fuel now were the small forests around the city, a little peat that lay under frozen snow and ice along the north bank of the Neva and the wooden houses and buildings of Leningrad. Andrei Zhdanov authorized the demolition of almost any structure made of wood. He promised that after the war Leningrad would be rebuilt in new grandeur. Youngsters even tore away some wooden planks around the Bronze Horseman, the heroic statue of Peter the Great. On those that remained they scrawled, "He is not cold and we will be warmed."

The principal means of heating were the *burzhuiki* set up in apartments

---

[3] Pavlov, *op. cit.*, 2nd edition, p. 147. The figure is given as 36 trainloads by N. A. Manakov. (*Voprosy Istorii*, No. 5, May, 1967, p. 17.)

with a chimney that went out through the *fortochka*, the small ventilating window.

The result was inevitable: hundreds upon hundreds of fires, caused by the cranky, poorly installed, poorly attended makeshift stoves. From January 1 to March 10 there were 1,578 fires in Leningrad, caused by the estimated 135,000 *burzhuiki* in the city.

When the fuel supplies ran out at Power Station No. 5, the main water-pumping station got no power for thirty-six hours, the Southern and Petrograd stations got none for four days. The temperature was 30 degrees below zero. By the time the pumps came back, Leningrad's water system had been fatally frozen. So had the sewer system.

The city began to burn down. In January there were more than 250 serious fires and an average of nearly thirty a day of all kinds. Some were caused by German bombardment but most of them by the *burzhuiki*. They burned day after day. On January 12 there was a very bad series of fires, twenty in all. One of the worst was on the Nevsky, where the Gostiny Dvor, badly battered in the September bombing, burned again.

With his usual suspiciousness Vsevolod Vishnevsky thought that Nazi diversionists must be at work, although he conceded that the fires might be due to carelessness with the *burzhuiki*.

The sight of the Leningrad fires was chilling even to an insensitive observer like Vsevolod Kochetov. It terrified him to see a fire burn in a big building and return a day or two later to find it still burning, slowly eating away apartment after apartment, often with no one making any effort to extinguish it. The pipes were frozen, there was no fuel for the fire trucks, and most of the fire fighters were too sick or too weak to answer a call even if anyone had bothered to put one in. By December only 7 percent of the fire engines were still operative. In January in a typical fire command only eight of eighty fire fighters were able to report for duty.

One night Aleksandr Chakovsky was walking back to the Astoria Hotel from Smolny. A great fire was burning in the heart of the city, the sky was ablaze and rosy shadows played on the snow. As he approached, he found a large stone apartment house afire. There were no firemen about. But several women had formed a chain and were handing possessions out of the house— a baby in a perambulator, a samovar, a kerosene stove, a couch on which a figure lay wrapped in a blanket, possibly the mother of the baby.

Fedor Grachev, a doctor in charge of a large hospital on Vasilevsky Island, was walking through Theater Square, across from the Mariinsky Theater, one evening when he saw the glow of a huge fire on Decembrists Street. He turned into the street, soot falling in his face. The flames had attacked the three upper stories of a tall building at the corner of Decembrists Street and Maklin Prospekt, a building decorated with figures and scenes from Russian fairy tales. "The House of Fairy Tales" was what the Leningraders called it.

Tongues of fire licked out of the windows, casting a lurid light over the scene, and underfoot there was a carpet of broken glass. The heat of the fire was melting snow and ice, and this had attracted a crowd of people who patiently filled their pails and buckets with the precious water. No one made any attempt to put out the fire. In fact, no one paid any heed to it, except to take advantage of the rare source of easily obtainable water.

"Has it burned a long time?" Grachev asked a woman.

"Since morning," she said.

Grachev stopped long enough to warm himself and then went on.

In an effort to prevent soldiers passing through Leningrad from deserting to the ranks of the food bandits, heavy security detachments were thrown around the suburban railroad stations. Even so, a few men managed to slip away from almost every detachment.

It was at this point that the Leningrad Military Council, the City Party Committee and the City Council began to receive letters proposing that Leningrad be declared an "open city"—that is, as the Soviet historians note, that the front be opened and the Germans be permitted to occupy the city.

There are few references to the "open city" proposal in Soviet historical works. And in each case they draw upon the same documents in the Leningrad State Archives.

The Soviet historians seem convinced that the "open city" proposals came from resident Nazi agents within Leningrad. The "open city" proposal was first advanced, they contend, at the time of the September battles. They quote a Nazi agent as saying that the German plan was to stir up a revolt within Leningrad, simultaneous with the final attack on the city. Later on, the plan was changed and the Germans decided to provoke an uprising within the city, carry out a pogrom against Jews and Party commissars, and then invite the Germans into the city to restore order.[4]

Another Nazi agent (or perhaps the same one) is quoted as having said that with the deepening of the blockade the Germans hoped to touch off a "hunger revolt" in which bread shops and food stores would be attacked and women would then march out to the front lines and demand that the troops give up the siege and let the Germans enter the city.

The "agent's report" bears a striking resemblance to the events of February, 1917, when women in Petrograd, tired, angry and cold from standing day after day in the lengthening bread lines, began to demonstrate, touching off the revolution which brought down Czar Nicholas II.

The efforts of the German agents (if any) to produce in the leaden streets of Leningrad in January of 1942 a re-enactment of the events of 1917 did not succeed. But Andrei Zhdanov and the Leningrad leadership took the threat with grim seriousness despite their knowledge that Leningraders by this time hated the Germans with passion. (Desertions had long since ceased because the Russians had learned too much concerning Nazi treatment of prisoners and the occupied villages.)

[4] Kochetov heard of something like this in September.

The "open city" agitation obviously went a good deal further than letters to the Soviet authorities. It was a subject of conversation, if nothing more, among Soviet citizens. Special propaganda detachments were sent into many regions of the city to counteract this and other threatening or hostile moods of the populace.[5]

The city became quieter as its suffering grew. There were no Nazi bombing raids, less frequent shelling.

"The Hitlerites are confident," Yelizaveta Sharypina wrote, "that hunger will break the resistance of the Leningraders. Why waste bombs and shells?"

There came to her mind a line from a poem by Nekrasov:

> In the world there is a czar
> And that czar is without mercy—
> Hunger is what they call him.

[5] There is some reason to believe that the "open city" proposals did not, as the Soviet historians insist, originate with German agents. The basic account presented by A. V. Karasev in his authoritative *Leningradtsy v Gody Blokady* is followed almost word for word in the official war history of Leningrad, a sign that security considerations are involved. Karasev cites a Leningrad propaganda work, published in 1942, to explain the "open city" agitation, another source of doubt. There is no indication from German sources that such an "open city" maneuver was undertaken in January, 1942. The Nazi line then was to starve Leningrad into oblivion and to reject any "open city" proposal that might emanate from the Soviet side. (Karasev, pp. 120, 204, 205; *Leningrad v VOV*, p. 214.) The flat assertion by D. V. Pavlov that not one of the thousands of letters received by the Party committee during the blockade expressed any despondency, bitterness or opinions differing from those of the majority of the city's defenders is obviously inexact. (Pavlov, *op. cit.*, 2nd edition, p. 142.) A letter written by a professor from his deathbed at the Astoria Hotel in late January, 1942, to Andrei Zhdanov clearly indicates that many Leningraders blamed him and the Party for the city's plight. The professor went out of his way to exempt Zhdanov for responsibility for the Leningrad tragedy. The implication was clear that others, in contrast, did hold Zhdanov responsible. (P. L. Korzinkin, *V Redaktsiyu Ne Vernulsya*, Moscow, 1964, p. 264.)

42 . The City of Ice

WHEN THE WRITER LEV USPENSKY WENT TO RADIO HOUSE
one winter day, he was puzzled to find in the cold studio a curious wooden
device, a kind of short-handled rake without teeth, shaped like a letter
T. The director, Y. L. Babushkin, told him it was a support to enable him to
read at the microphone if he was too weak to stand.

"And you must read," the director said. "In thousands of apartments they
are awaiting your voice. Your voice may save them."

The wooden T was not just a gadget. Vladimir Volzhenin, the poet, had
collapsed in the studio from hunger after reading his verses to the Leningrad
public. He died a few days after being evacuated to Yaroslavl. Aleksandr
Yankevich, his face black, and breathing with difficulty, read Makarenko's
"Pedagogical Poem" over the radio, although he was so ill that Babushkin
quietly stood by to "double" in case Yankevich was unable to finish. Ivan
Lapshonkov sang a role in Rimsky-Korsakov's *Snow Maiden* for Radio
Leningrad. He was so frail he had to support himself with a cane. By nightfall he was dead. Vsevolod Rimsky-Korsakov, a nephew of the great composer, did fire-watching duty on the roof of the seven-story Radio House.
One January night he stood his post, as fires blazed up on the Leningrad
skyline, talking with a friend about the Victory Day which he was sure
would come. Before morning he was dead.

By January the life of Radio House centered in a long room on the fourth
floor that looked a bit like the steerage of an emigrant ship or, as Aleksandr
Kron thought, like a gypsy tent. There were cots and couches, office desks
and wooden packing boxes, stacks of newspapers, files, and always twenty or
thirty people—a youngster with a lock falling across his forehead bent over
a desk, patiently writing; a middle-aged woman with signs of tears on her
face, pecking at a typewriter; people sleeping where they had collapsed; a
five-year-old girl asleep with a doll clutched in her hand. There were two
small stoves in the room on which people cooked meals and heated water.
Here a thin girl with a white bodice and padded army jacket was washing

her long hair. Next to her a bleached blonde was reading sentimental verses. When the cold, bombardment and hunger were at their worst, microphones were set up in this room to spare weakened people the exertion of climbing the stairs. Anything to keep the radio going, to keep the rhythm of the city's pulse, the tick of the metronome sounding in the loudspeakers set up in the streets and in almost every apartment and office of the city.[1] Radio House was never hit by bombs, although adjacent buildings were badly damaged in September.

On January 8, 1942, the radio, in most areas of Leningrad, fell silent. There was no power for transmission. People from all ends of the city began to appear at Radio House, to ask what the matter was and when the station would be back on the air. An old man tottered in from Vasilevsky Island, a cane in each hand. "Look here," he said, "if something is needed, if it is a matter of courage—fine. Or even if it is a matter of cutting the ration. That we can take. But let the radio speak. Without that, life is too terrible. Without that, it is like lying in the grave. Exactly like that."

It was two days later, on January 10, that Olga Berggolts sat in the Radio Committee room (she thought it looked like a great long wagon). As always, it was filled with people, some working, some sleeping and one, a newspaperman named Pravdich, who seemed to be neither breathing nor moving. In the morning, as some had suspected hours earlier, it was discovered that he was dead.

Olga Berggolts remembered this evening as one of the happiest of her life. She and several colleagues, the artistic director of the Radio Committee, Y. L. Babushkin, the leader of the Literary Department, G. Makogonenko, among them, spent the night working on plans for a book they had decided to publish. It would be called "Leningrad Speaking . . ." It would tell the story of Leningrad, of its people, of its intelligentsia, in the struggle to overcome the Germans—the whole story, the Nazi attack, the suffering, the sacrifices and the ultimate victory. Of victory they had no doubt as they talked beside the tiny flickering lamp, shaded by a newspaper from their sleeping colleagues.

"Will we really live to see the day?" asked Babushkin. "You know I wildly want to live and see how it is all going to come out."

He smiled and laughed, his eyes sparkling with impatience, and Olga Berggolts quickly said, "Of course, you will live, Yasha. Naturally. We will all live."

But she saw that Babushkin was very weak. For a long time he had been bloated and green and could climb the stairs only with difficulty. He slept less and less and worked more and more. There was no way to get him to conserve his strength. He smiled at her reply, closing his eyes, and im-

[1] Only wired radio was in service in Leningrad. All ordinary receivers were confiscated on the second day of the war. Possession of a set or listening to a foreign broadcast was punishable by death.

mediately became very, very old. His friends did not believe Babushkin would survive the winter, but he did—only to be killed at the front, fighting as an infantryman in 1944 near Narva in the final battles to liquidate the Leningrad blockade.

But that night in January no one knew what the future held; everything went into the plan for the book: the gardens of the future city, the performance of Shostakovich's Seventh Symphony (no one knew that Shostakovich had already finished work on it, and, of course, the Radio Committee orchestra was almost nonexistent).

Not many mornings later Yasha Babushkin was dictating to Olga Berggolts the regular weekly report on the condition of the orchestra ("The first violin is dying, the drummer died on the way to work, the French horn is near death").

The radio, in the belief of those who worked on it and those who lived through the Leningrad blockade, was what kept the city alive when there was no food, no heat, no light and practically no hope.

"Not a theater, not a cinema was open," Olga Berggolts recalled. "Most Leningraders did not even have the strength to read at home. I think that never before nor ever in the future will people listen to poetry as did Leningrad in that winter—hungry, swollen and hardly living."

Aleksandr Kron, the naval writer, felt that the winter of 1941–42 blazed with intellectual incandescence. Never had people talked so much and so openly, never had they argued so strongly, as during long evenings around the little temporary stoves by the light of flickering lanterns. Even in the fleet Kron found sailors studying art, music and philosophy. Thousands of soldiers read *War and Peace*. On one submarine frozen in the Neva the whole command devoured Dostoyevsky's works in the course of the winter.

The book *Leningrad Speaking* never was published, but it kept the circle at Radio House alive. It captured their imagination. It made difficult days pass more swiftly. But it was never published. No explanation for this is offered by Olga Berggolts and her Radio Committee associates. Presumably it fell afoul of the same censorship, the same repressive bureaucracy, that affected so many projects launched with joy and hope in besieged Leningrad.

Vera Ketlinskaya and her friends of the Writers Union conceived the idea for a book to be called *One Day*—one day in the life of Leningrad under siege. Leonid Rakhmanov, V. Orlov and Yevgeny Ryss were among the writers who worked with her. They were imitating a scheme Maxim Gorky had proposed in the 1930's for a book—twenty-four hours in the life of the Soviet Union. It was Vera Ketlinskaya's idea to present twenty-four hours in the life of Leningrad, in all the regions of the city, the front, the rear, the factories, the ARP units, the fire brigade, the bakers, the scientific institutions, the artistic organizations. There would be a section on the High Command and one on the little sewing shops where they made cotton-padded jackets for the troops.

Every day writers came to the Writers Union offices in the old stone house on Ulitsa Voinova, their faces puffy with hunger and sleeplessness, and asked, "When will we be doing *One Day?* Let me know because I am ready to go anywhere you send me." But Ketlinskaya couldn't get clearance from the higher authorities. Once while she was talking by telephone to one of the Leningrad bosses Yevgeny Shvarts was in the office. He could not restrain himself. "Tell him that writers are dying without this work, that they cannot live without it."

Ketlinskaya knew this. Living in the cold, hungry, dark city, people held themselves together by the consciousness of being needed. They began to die when they had nothing to do. Nothing-to-do was more terrible than a bombing raid.

But try as she would she could not get permission for the book. She became convinced that though no one really opposed the book, no one wanted to take responsibility for approving it; the old Russian problem: bureaucracy. Finally, toward the end of December clearance came through. But by this time many of the writers were dead, the city was frozen and lifeless, and the writers still alive were almost too weak to work. The project was never carried out.

Rakhmanov called the failure of this project, which he blamed on "bureaucrats and reinsurers," sheer tragedy—not because the book would not be published but because collapse of the project brought down with it so many talented Leningrad writers, deprived of hope on which to live.

Rakhmanov had thrown his time and energy into the idea of *One Day in the Life of Leningrad.* He himself might not have survived had not another project been advanced just as *One Day* died. This was a new magazine, to be called *Literary Contemporary.* The magazine originally had been planned in the summer of 1941, but the editor, Filipp Knyazev, was killed in the fighting at Tallinn. Now Rakhmanov was named to head the magazine and by mid-January had material ready for his first two issues and was working on the third. But within a month he saw his latest dream go glimmering. At a moment when *Leningradskaya Pravda* was appearing in one single gray page, when old established magazines like *Krasnaya Nov* in Moscow had been suspended, no bureaucrat was going to approve the publication of a new, untested, uncertain journal.

But it would take more than censorship, more than bureaucracy, more than lack of paper, to stifle the spirit of Leningrad. Posters went up in the city—two or three, at any rate:

A Half-Year of the Great Fatherland War
January 11, 1942, Sunday
Literary-Artistic Morning
Beginning at 1:30 P.M.
Writers, Scientists, Composers, Artists—On the Fatherland War
Collection for the Defense Fund

Sunday, January 11, was sunny but very cold. The meeting was at the Academic Chapel at the Pevchesky Bridge, catty-cornered from the Winter Palace. It was as cold within the white, gold and red-velvet little hall as it was outside. The audience gathered slowly, wearing heavy coats, fur collars and felt boots. Probably not many recalled the occasion when Vladimir Mayakovsky had recited in the same hall years before. It was so hot that day that Mayakovsky had to pull off his jacket and sling it over the back of his chair.

To the platform slowly walked an elderly man in a coat that reached almost to his ankles. He began to talk in a weak voice that could hardly be heard. Slowly his voice began to strengthen. The speaker was Professor L. A. Ilyin, chief architect of Leningrad. He apologized for being late. He said that he had tried to save his strength by taking the shortest route in walking to the chapel on this cold Sunday, but Leningrad looked too beautiful in the sunshine and snow. He could not tear himself away from the marvelous boulevards and the grandiose architectural ensembles. As he talked on, Rakhmanov was struck by the thought that if the beauty of Leningrad could inspire such feeling, then truly the city was immortal. The city was immortal—but its people? Vsevolod Vishnevsky made a typical comment: "A beautiful city. I am happy that I am in Leningrad at my post and doing my job."

One February day Vissarion Sayanov was walking again on the Nevsky. Not much resemblance to those magic lines of Pushkin: "The sleighs race down the cold Neva [embankment], the girls' faces brighter than roses!" Steam was boiling up from a hole in the ice of the Fontanka where women were drawing water. It covered the trees in the Yusupov Palace gardens with frost. There was a line of women and old men with teakettles and pots. A soldier was pulling the water up with a pail on a rope.

At the Anichkov Bridge Sayanov encountered a man in a strange costume. Over his shoulders was draped a woman's fur cloak, a very wide one, as though it had been made for a giant. He wore *valenki* or felt boots on his feet and overshoes, wrapped in rags, over them. The man had a brush in his hands and an easel before him. Sayanov stopped to watch. It was a frosty day but sunny, and he could not but remember Professor Ilin's words: "I am happy that I can see the city in the snow with the sun shining on it, and in these difficult days how much I want to live. . . ."

The artist blew on his fingers and said quietly, "You must recognize your old acquaintance, comrade soldier."

The voice sounded familiar, but Sayanov did not recognize the strange artist.

"You don't know me," the man said.

"Vyacheslav!" Sayanov suddenly cried. "I never thought I would meet you on this day."

It was Vyacheslav Pakulin, a man with whom in the early 1920's, Sayanov had often engaged in violent arguments about the nature of the world and the kind of painting and poetry that should illuminate it. In those days, Sayanov recalled bitterly, each thought that he would be able to tell the truth about life through his own medium. How naïve! How distant from this frozen Nevsky Prospekt!

"One must paint more and talk less about art," said Pakulin, reading Sayanov's thoughts. "In the end an artist is judged only by his pictures."

"That's a one-sided view," Sayanov replied. "The personality of the artist is not to be separated from his creations."

Pakulin sighed. "It seems to me that I will never succeed in doing anything important in art. It is very hard."

A woman came by. She looked at the canvas, then at Pakulin and said, "I am also one of your admirers."

"Do you like this?" Pakulin said to Sayanov. "It seems to me that I have put my soul into this picture."

Sayanov looked again—the strange white sky, the soft violet clouds, the people walking on the Prospekt, the Anichkov Bridge without the Klodt horses.

"You understand," Pakulin said. "It is all strange. It is all alarming. But the sky is quiet as always."

"I understand," Sayanov said. He looked back at Pakulin as he went on his way. He would not live till spring. It was not possible. But Sayanov was mistaken. Pakulin lived for several years after the war, and when Sayanov went to the studio for the funeral, he saw many good pictures. But none of those painted during the war. For the official guardians of Soviet culture would not let the strange and terrible works of Pakulin in the time of the Leningrad blockade be shown publicly. Not for many years. They were too terrible, too alarming.

A film project to make a picture of Leningrad in battle fared no better than those for books and magazines. Vsevolod Vishnevsky was engaged to write the scenario in March of 1942. Several Soviet cameramen had shot thousands of feet of action, among them Yefim Uchitel, Andrei Pogorely and Yevgeny Shapiro. Directors Roman Karmen and Nikolai Komarovtsev were enlisted.

Vishnevsky was so moved by the sequences—the ruined observatory at Pulkovo; Academician Nikolsky sketching in the cellars of the Hermitage; an old woman falling, dropping a bowl of soup from her trembling hands; a winter scene at the Summer Gardens; a pair of hands grasping the great iron gates and gradually slipping until the body fell into a snowdrift; the sign on the courtyard gates: "Point for collecting bodies"; the composer, Boris Asafyev, sitting at a grand piano and playing with cold-stiffened fingers; the body of the elephant, Betty, lying in a pool of blood at the Zoo—that he cried like a child. He wrote seven different scripts for the film. None was ever published. Finally, on July 9, 1942, the picture,

Leningrad in Battle, appeared. It won a Stalin Prize. But thousands upon thousands of feet of the best sequences were not included. Nor have they been shown to this day. They remain in an archive of several hundred thousand feet of Soviet film which someday may show to the world the full measure of suffering which the war brought to Russia. A sequel to *Leningrad in Battle,* covering the events from May, 1942, to the liberation of the city in January, 1944, was also planned. Nikolai Tikhonov, the Leningrad poet and writer, was commissioned by the Leningrad Military Council to write the script. "It is a great pity," Tikhonov later commented, "that this picture, very strong in its contents, never saw the light. If it had been released for the screen, millions of spectators would have seen much that was unexpected, tragic and heroic."

Vera Ketlinskaya was one of Olga Berggolts' best friends. She had known "Olenka" for twenty years before the war—in fact, Ketlinskaya had first met her when Olenka's head was shaved like a young boy's, her hair cut off because of a children's disease. The two women were opposites in many ways. Olga Berggolts was certain that every bomb was aimed directly at her. She felt every blow which struck her friends and neighbors, often more deeply than they did. Vera Ketlinskaya walked about Leningrad, even during air raids and long-range shelling, confident that no bomb or shell would hit her. As the blockade went on, Olga and Vera drew closer and closer. Almost every night Olga telephoned from Radio House to the Writers' House: "Vera, you're alive?" Or if shelling was going on: "Is it in your neighborhood?" Sometimes, Vera would reply, "Not so far," and suddenly a terrific crash would come. Once as they were talking a shell hit the next apartment and Vera could not speak. She heard Olga on the telephone saying, "Vera, Vera—what's happened? Vera! Vera!"

Sometimes one or the other would get a present—a piece of frozen horse meat from the front, a packet of real coffee, or a pot of library paste from which they could make a wonderful jelly. They would invite each other to share such feasts.

One night Ketlinskaya telephoned Olga and told her that she had got a bottle of cod-liver oil and that she was going to make some "fantastic pancakes" out of dough, the basic ingredient of which was coffee grounds.

"I'll be right over," Olga Berggolts said.

It was two blocks from Radio House to Vera Ketlinskaya's flat. Ketlinskaya waited and waited. Olga did not appear. Finally, she arrived so shaken she could hardly talk. She had started out in the arctic night in streets that were completely dark. She felt her way along a path between high drifts, and as she passed Philharmonic Hall she slipped and fell heavily on something. The "something" was a corpse, half covered with snow. She lay stunned, weak, terrified, unable to rise. Suddenly, she heard her own voice, reading poetry. The voice came from the ether. It spoke quietly and simply. Olga Berggolts lay in terror. Was she resting on a frozen corpse or was it her own frozen body which she felt? She must be dead. Or perhaps she had lost her mind. She was gripped by such terror as never before had possessed her. On the periphery of consciousness she heard her voice halt and another begin to speak. It was the announcer for Radio Leningrad. What she was listening to was the radio loudspeaker at the corner before the Hotel Europa, transmitting a program she had recorded earlier in the day.

Gradually, Olga Berggolts regained control of herself. She sat beside Ketlinskaya and, feeding pages from old books into the *burzhuika*, they ate the "fantastic pancakes," wondering why in the past they had not liked fish oil.

Later in the siege an English correspondent, Alexander Werth, came to Leningrad. He asked Vera Ketlinskaya and some of her friends to tell him not *what* enabled them to survive but *how* they survived. This was the great question, and as years went by it became more and more difficult to answer.

In retrospect it seemed unbelievable to Vera Ketlinskaya that she had sat in her apartment in Leningrad in January, 1942, with the temperature so low that the ink froze in the inkwell and she had to tap out her thoughts on an unfamiliar typewriter. She was working on the first pages of her book *The Blockade*, writing of the death, in the novel, of Anna Konstantinova. Her own year-and-a-half-old son, Serezha, slept beside her under a pile of clothing, and in the next room lay her mother, dead of starvation, placed there on the floor three days ago, with no immediate prospect of getting her body buried. Vera Ketlinskaya did not cry as she wrote. She simply tried to make her fingers hit the strange typewriter. Pavel Luknitsky spent the evening of January 31 with her. The body of her mother still lay frozen and unburied in the next room. But such was the temper of the times that he recalled the evening with warmth. They talked "from the soul," in the Russian phrase, of the war, of the city, of the suffering, of the beauty and bravery of the epoch. They warmed themselves at the little iron stove, and Ketlinskaya read some lines from her new book.

Nikolai Chukovsky returned to Leningrad in late January from a brief visit to one of the airfields. He was walking along the Neva embankment when he saw a terrible sight. A dozen holes had been broken in the Neva ice, and hundreds of women, pails in hand, were moving toward the holes. Around each water hole he saw dozens of corpses, half covered with ice and snow. The women, making their way toward the water, had to wind around the bodies of the frozen dead. The granite steps leading down to the Neva were sheathed in ice, so thick it was almost impossible to climb up or down. The women slipped and fell, some never to rise again. Along the Palace Square, along the Nevsky, along Gorokhovaya, the line of women, pails in hand, stretched and stretched. On Gorokhovaya, icy with spilled water from hundreds of pails, Chukovsky became fearful lest he meet someone he knew, fearful lest the fright which he could not keep his face from displaying would show. At that moment he encountered Olga Berggolts, head and shoulders wrapped in a heavy shawl and face almost black with frost. Taken aback, Chukovsky sought for something innocuous to say. "Ah," he remarked, "how well you look, Olechka."

Olga Berggolts was pulling an empty child's sled.

"I've just come from the cemetery," she said. "I've taken my husband there."

Years passed and Chukovsky was certain that Olga Berggolts would never forgive him the stupidity of his remark.

Olga Berggolts' husband, Nikolai Molchanov, died January 29, 1942. His death was not a surprise. Olga's father, the doctor, Fedor Berggolts, had warned his daughter that her husband was doomed if they did not leave the city. Nikolai was a scholar, a specialist in literature and poetry. He had been exempted from military service because of his poor health and continued his literary work. He was planning after the war to publish a comparative examination of five poets—Pushkin, Lermontov, Nekrasov, Blok and Mayakovsky.

"You must get out. Absolutely. By any means," her father said. "In an ancient book it is written, 'Woe to those trapped in a city under siege.'"

That was in October. Olga had managed to get to her father's house a few hours before her grandmother died. The moment never left Olga's memory, the moment when her grandmother turned to her as explosions rocked the old wooden house (an air raid was in progress) and said, "Lyalechka, my first grandchild . . . you're a godless one, a Young Communist. But I am going to bless you just the same. You're not angry?"

"No, Grandma," Olga Berggolts replied.

The old lady gave her blessing and Olga kissed her hand, already growing cold. Then the grandmother asked about a second granddaughter, Maria, who was in Moscow.

"Which way is Moscow?" the grandmother asked. "On which side?"

They pointed to the wall. The old lady turned and with great effort raised her hand and made a small cross.

"Please, God," she said, "save your servant, Maria, and your beautiful capital, Moscow."

Then she sank back dying.

Now the prediction of Olga's father that Nikolai Molchanov could not survive the blockade had come true. Olga Berggolts wept for the death of her husband. It was the only time she wept during the blockade, for as she wrote in one of her verses, "The tears of the Leningraders are frozen." She wept when she took Nikolai's body on the child's sled and left it with the mountain of others at Piskarevsky Cemetery, and she wrote, in lines dedicated to Nikolai: "Really will there be a victory for me? What comfort will I find in it? Let me be. Let me be forgotten. I will live alone. . . ."

All during the days of the blockade Olga Berggolts carried in her pocket a piece of cardboard, slightly smaller than a postcard. It bore the words: "Propusk No. 23637. Permit to walk and drive in the city of Leningrad." This was her pass. It took her to every end of the city, by night and by day.

Now in these first days of February she started on a long walk, the longest she was ever to make. She was going to her father at the factory where he worked as resident physician, a distance of ten or twelve miles from Radio House in the center of the city to the Neva Gates and beyond. Olga Berggolts' comrades at Radio House had given her such supplies as they could spare—a child's milk bottle filled with a liquid resembling sweetened tea, and two cigarettes. She had her own day's ration of bread, 250 grams—all of this in a gas-mask bag.

She decided to eat bits of the bread as she went along in order to bolster her strength. She started out, walking slowly. The day was overcast and cold. The people whom she passed wore masks over their faces to protect against the wind—red, black, green or blue masks with peepholes cut out for their eyes.

Olga Berggolts had to walk all the way to the Lenin factory and then out the Shlisselburg highway. She even had to cross the Neva. Whether she would make it was not certain. She decided she would think only of the segments of her walk. First, to get to the Moscow Station. First, to walk down the Nevsky, counting one light pole after the other . . . one by one . . . one pole and then another—the stanchions where weakened victims of dystrophy held themselves up, then slowly sank for the last time to the ice and snow. One pole, then another. Now she had gotten to the Moscow Station. Now she could halt for a moment. Then, again out Staro Nevsky. From post to post. To the Alexander Nevsky Lavra. Here the bodies lay thick in the street. Here the trolley-buses stood, dead, empty. It seemed to her that they had come from a different life, a different century. The path here was in the center of the boulevard, a wide path, and Olga Berggolts heard behind her the squeak, squeak of a child's sled, a woman pulling a man wrapped in a blanket. The man was alive. Where could the woman be taking him? Olga Berggolts began to pass big barns, grain storage depots. She remembered the last time she had come this way, the day her grandmother died. Then the barns had been filled with grain, and even on the ground outside there had been mounds of rye and wheat. She could not stop thinking of grain, of the handfuls she had held in her hands in the threshing days as a child, of the smell of the rye fields. She had an overwhelming desire just to put a single grain into her mouth and taste its nutty flavor. Hunger overwhelmed her, and she almost reached into the gas mask and drew out her bread. But she said quietly to herself, "No. Only when I get to the Lenin factory. Then I'll sit down and swallow a little tea and eat some bread."

She went on, and it began to seem to her that the road was surprisingly short and quiet. Somehow she felt ready for death—or if not for death, just to sink down in the snow in the great drifts. Everything began to seem soft and tender. It was a mood, she later knew, which lay close to death, the mood in which people began to speak very quietly, very gently, to suffix all their nouns with "*chka*" or "*tsa*"—that is, to turn them into loving diminutives—"a little piece of bread," a "dear little drop of water."

Olga Berggolts came to a crossing of paths just as a woman, pulling a corpse in a small box on a sled, arrived at the same point. Each tried to let the other pass. Finally, Olga Berggolts stepped across the coffin and the two women sank in a snowdrift to rest a moment.

"You're from the city?" the woman asked.

"Yes."

"Long?"

"Quite a while—three hours, I think."

Olga Berggolts took one of her two cigarettes and lighted it. She had firmly determined not to smoke until she got to the Lenin factory. But now she smoked a bit and let her companion have a puff. Then she rose, telling herself she would not halt again until she reached the Lenin factory.

As she walked, she met more and more women pulling sleds with corpses, wrapped in sheets or blankets. At the Lenin factory she sat on a concrete bench in a small dispatcher's pavilion, constructed in Le Corbusier style, and accurately broke off a piece of bread. She ate it and then went on down the Shlisselburg Chaussée without looking to the right toward Palevsky, where five months ago her grandmother had died and where she had stood with her father and heard him warn that Nikolai could not survive the siege. She did not even think of that. All she felt was the cold, the hunger, the fatigue.

Now she was at the Neva, at the place where she must cross the frozen river. Dusk was falling, and over the river there hung a kind of lilac mist. It seemed farther than ever to her father's factory, although she could just glimpse it in the snow-filled distance and knew that to the left of the main shops was the old timbered building where he had his clinic.

There was one piece of bread left in her gas-mask bag, about 100 grams. "As soon as I get to Father's," she told herself, "we'll have a mug of hot water and eat this bread."

She walked out on the Neva. The path was very narrow and her steps grew uncertain. When she approached the other bank, she was in despair. It was like an ice mountain, leading up to heights that were cloaked in rosy-blue shadows. On her knees, starting to crawl up the ice, was a woman with a jug of water she had drawn from a hole in the ice.

"I can't climb that hill," Olga Berggolts heard herself say. The whole terrible journey had been in vain. She came up close to the ice mountain and saw that there were steps cut in the cliff. The woman with the water spoke to her: "Shall we try it?"

The two started up together, supporting each other by the shoulder, climbing on hands and knees, step by step, halting every two or three steps to rest.

"The doctor cut these steps," the woman said as they rested for the fourth time. "Thank God! It is a little easier when you are carrying water."

They reached the top and went on toward the factory, but when Olga Berggolts reached it, she halted in confusion. Somehow it all seemed strange, as if she had never been there before, a land of alien drifts of snow. Finally, she made her way into the building where she knew her father's clinic must be located. There was a little waiting room, to which a flicker of light came from a neighboring room. On a wooden bench lay a woman, wrapped in a padded jacket. It looked as though she were taking a nap while waiting for the next train. But she was not asleep. She was dead.

Olga Berggolts entered the next room. A man sat at a desk, his greenish-blue face lighted by a fat church candle, his gray hair tousled and his big blue eyes looking even bigger and bluer in the candlelight. She stood silently before him, and he raised his eyes and politely, very politely, asked, "Whom do you wish, citizen?"

She heard herself saying in a wooden voice, "I am looking for Dr. Berggolts."

"At your service," he replied. "What is the trouble?"

She looked at him. A strange feeling possessed her—not terror, but something touched with death, something numb.

He repeated, "What is the trouble?"

Finally she found her voice: "Papa! It's me. Lyalya."

For a moment her father said nothing. He instantly understood why she had come. He had known that Nikolai was in the hospital. He had known that he would not survive. But he said nothing. He rose, put his arm around her and said, "Now, come along, youngster. We'll have some tea. And we'll have something to eat, too."

The old doctor led his daughter into the next room. There by the light of two candles they sat beside a little stove, drank hot tea and ate pancakes made from old grain dredged from the cellars of a brewery. The doctor had two motherly aides, Matryusha and Aleksandra. They offered to give Olga Berggolts a hot bath. She refused uneasily but later found herself unable to resist Matryusha, who slipped off her heavy felt boots and bathed her cold, tired feet in warm water. She gave her father the single "coffin nail" cigarette. He inhaled lovingly, exclaiming, "What a rich life we are leading!"

Her father put her to bed in one cot and sat beside her on another. They talked a bit of old times, of the Countess Varvara, who had served with the doctor on a hospital train during World War I, who had saved his life and who had stayed behind in Russia, a romantic distant figure. Where was she now? Olga Berggolts asked. He did not know. What about the family at Palevsky—what about her Aunt Varya, what about Dunya, the old servant?

"They have all died of hunger," he said slowly, not taking his eyes off the candle. "Aunt Varya died on the way to the hospital, Avdotiya in her factory on the job. And the house was destroyed by a shell."

"That means no one lives there now?"

"No," he replied. "No one. Now it is just a snowdrift."

She was silent, then spoke again. "Papa," she said, "for my part I am no longer alive."

"Nonsense," he said sharply. "Of course, you are living. If you were not living, you would not be lying here and you could not have come here."

But, she thought, it really was not true. She did not want to live.

"Such foolishness!" her father said. "Take me. I want to live very much. I've even become a collector."

It was a psychosis, he said. He had started to collect postcards, buttons and rose seeds. Someone, he said, had promised to send him the seeds of a special rose, called "Glory of Peace." It was a fragrant, slow-blooming rose with golden tints and orange touches at the edge of the blossoms. Unfortunately, the wooden fence outside the clinic had been burned for fuel. But in the spring they would put up a new one, and beside it he would plant his roses. In two or three years they would bloom. Would she come and see them? Olga Berggolts heard herself saying that she would.

"Now," said her father, "sleep. Sleep is the best of all. And then you will see along my fence the new roses, Glory of Peace."

Before Olga Berggolts closed her eyes she looked at her father's hands lying under the flickering candlelight—the hands of a Russian doctor, a surgeon who had saved thousands and thousands of lives of soldiers and ordinary Russians, hands that had cut steps in the ice staircase, hands that would grow new flowers, never seen before on the earth.

"Yes," she thought, "I will see my father's roses. It will be just as he says."

43 . The Leningrad Apocalypse

THE HAYMARKET OR SENNAYA OCCUPIED THE HEART OF Leningrad. Some years earlier it had been named Peace Square, but no one called it that. The Haymarket it had been since the early days of "Piter," and the Haymarket it was in this winter of Leningrad's agony. But sometimes it was called the Hungry Market.

At one end of the Haymarket stood an old and undistinguished church and across from it a small barracks of early nineteenth-century architecture. The Haymarket was a square which opened out in the curving Sadovaya, the garden boulevard, one of the busiest shopping streets of pre-Bolshevik Russia. It had been a center of pushcart and stall trade, of peddlers, of *izvozchiki*, of coachmen and troikas, of flower girls and prostitutes, for two hundred years. Back of the Haymarket, in the tangle of streets between it and the imposing façade of St. Isaac's Square, extended a web of side streets, the region which Vsevolod Krestovsky memorialized in his classic *Petersburg Slums*. Here Fedor Dostoyevsky had lived. Here was the house of Mikhail Raskolnikov. Between Spassky and Demidov lanes rose the old building which had once been known as the noisy "Raspberry House." And at the corner of Tairov Street still stood the de Roberti house. These two had been the lowest dives in old Petersburg, notorious dens into which many a man walked never to emerge again alive. Nearby was the so-called Vyazemskaya Lavra, a haunt of thieves and criminals throughout the nineteenth century. Just beyond the Griboyedov Canal on Stolyarny Lane could be found the house in which Dostoyevsky himself lived when he was writing *Crime and Punishment*. It was a quarter similar to that in Maxim Gorky's *Lower Depths*. Here human life was cheap. The air was heavy with the fumes of cheap vodka, cheap *makhorka* or tobacco, cheap perfume, cheap whores, petty thieves, roguery, blackmail and murder.

All this, of course, had long since been put behind the Haymarket by the Revolution. No more prostitution. No more thievery. No more criminals. So it was said. Whether this had really been true before the war, before

Hitler's invasion, before Leningrad fell into blockade, was difficult to know. But now the Haymarket was once again what it had been in the past—the center for every kind of crime which could find a setting in the besieged city.

Before the war there had been in the Haymarket a great peasant market. This had been long closed, but as starvation deepened, trading for food began again in the Haymarket. By winter it had become the liveliest place in Leningrad. The market bore little resemblance to any other in the world. It was a market of exchange. Money, that is, paper rubles, had virtually no value. Bread was the common currency. Vodka held second place as a medium of exchange. For bread anything was for sale—women's bodies or men's lives. Nothing approached it in purchasing power, as the people of Leningrad learned, coming to the Haymarket with a gold watch, a diamond ring or a fur neckpiece. They could get a crust of bread for their valuables— but not much more, not nearly as much as they hoped. Yet why keep anything of value? What good are valuables if you are about to die?

Ordinary people found they had little in common with the traders who suddenly appeared in the Haymarket. These were figures straight from the pages of Dostoyevsky or Kuprin. They were the robbers, the thieves, the murderers, members of the bands which roved the streets of the city and who seemed to hold much of it in their power once night had fallen.

These were the cannibals and their allies—fat, oily, steely-eyed, calculating, the most terrible men and women of their day.

For cannibalism there was in Leningrad. You will look in vain in the published official histories for reports of the trade in human flesh. But the stain of the story slips in, here and there, in casual references, in the memoirs, in allusions in fiction, in what is not said as well as in what is said about the crimes-for-food committed in the city.

The history of anthropophagy goes deep into man's past. Suggestive traces of the practice have been found in fossil deposits as early as the Paleolithic period. Ancient chronicles suggest that cannibalism was no stranger to Russian soil, having been a custom of the Scythians, the mysterious peoples who inhabited the vast steppes before the rise of Kievan Russia. Among the nomadic tribal warriors who swept westward from the Asian heartlands it was not unknown and sometimes entered into myth, superstition and religion.

But commercial anthropophagy or cannibalism-for-profit is rare in the human experience.

Everything was for sale at the Haymarket. Here stone-faced men sold glasses filled with "Badayev earth"—plain dirt dug from the cellars of the Badayev warehouses into which tons of molten sugar had poured. After the great fire subsided, reclamation teams under Food Chief Pavlov pumped out molten sugar for days, but thousands of tons saturated the ashes and earth beneath the Badayev cellars. Alongside the official reclamation effort went forward unofficial digging ("on the left," in the Russian phrase). With the onset of winter the digging intensified. Men and women slipped into the Badayev site with picks and axes and hacked at the frozen soil. They sold earth from the first three feet of soil for 100 rubles a glass, that from deeper in the cellar for 50 rubles a glass. Some purchasers refined the sugar by melting it in a pan and running it through a linen cloth. More often it was simply mixed with flour or paste into a gummy confection, part earth, part paste or ersatz flour, part carbonized sugar. This was "candy" or "jelly" or "custard"—whatever the imaginative housewife decided to call it.

In the Haymarket people walked through the crowd as though in a dream. They were pale as ghosts and thin as shadows. Only here and there passed a man or woman with a face, full, rosy and somehow soft yet leathery. A shudder ran through the crowd. For these, it was said, were the cannibals. Dmitri Moldavsky met a man like that on the staircase of his apartment. The man had been to his mother's flat, where he traded four glasses of flour and a pound of gelatin powder for some clothing. The man had a pink face and splendid, widely spaced blue eyes. Moldavsky thought he would never forget the sight. Instinctively, he wanted to kill this man with the tender cheeks and the too, too bright eyes. He knew what he was.

Cannibals . . . Who were they? How many were they? It is not a subject which the survivors of Leningrad like to discuss. There were no cannibals, a professor recalls. Or rather, there were cannibals, but it only happened when people went crazy. There was a case of which he had heard, for instance, the case of a mother, crazed for food. She lost her mind, went completely mad, killed her daughter and butchered the body. She ground up the flesh and made meat patties. But this was not typical. It was the kind of insane aberration which might happen anywhere at any time. In fact, the professor recalled reading of a similar case before the war.

But rats and cats and mice and birds—that was different. No one could prove for certain that the rats abandoned the city of Leningrad in the winter of 1941–42. But there were many in Leningrad to testify that this was so. Rats had almost disappeared by the middle of January. Possibly they had frozen to death. But the men at the Leningrad front did not believe this. They believed that the Leningrad rats came up out of the frozen cellars, abandoned the bombed-out buildings and made their way by the tens of thousands to the front-line trenches. There food was more plentiful—not much more plentiful, but a bit more so. Certainly rats abounded at the front. The only comfort the starving Leningrad troops could take was that rats were more numerous in the German lines, where the food was better.

Not all the rats had left. Vsevolod Vishnevsky knew a Leningrad poetess, once a beauty. Now she was alone in Leningrad. She sat in her apartment, in a shawl, a karakul coat and heavy boots. Her room was large, filled with pictures, bric-a-brac and—cold. In the evenings she sat beside a small iron stove. Around her gathered a small company of rats, quiet, fearless. She permitted them to join her for their company's sake. They, too, wished to be warm. So she sat, night after night, alone, with the circle of rats. Perhaps they were waiting for her to grow weaker.

Rumors of cannibalism—yes. Leningrad had been swept by rumors since autumn, when people began to keep their children off the streets. There were reports that children were being kidnaped. Boys and girls were young, easy to seize, and their flesh, it was said, was more tender.

Whether the rumors were true no one really knew. Anything could be true in these times. There were other rumors—that officers at the front were living in luxury with special rations and champagne while the people in the city starved. This was not true. The front was starving like the rest of the city. But in these winter months the radio often did not work for lack of power. *Leningradskaya Pravda* continued to appear. It missed only one day, January 25, when the power went off and the ink froze in the presses. But often only a few copies were printed and there was no one to distribute them. No one had the strength to lift the bundles. The newspaper *Smena* did not appear between January 9 and February 5. In fact, all the printing plants in Leningrad had been shut down in December to save electricity except the Volodarsky publishing plant which printed *Leningradskaya Pravda*—and ration cards. Frequently the matrices from which *Pravda* was printed did not arrive in Leningrad. They were flown every day from Moscow. But sometimes the planes got lost. At other times the matrices simply vanished. No one knew where they went. No wonder that any kind of story was believed in the Leningrad of January and February. Life was so terrifying for each Leningrader that all other terrors were believable.

In these times people took a special attitude toward mice. Vera Inber and her husband, Dr. Strashun, had a mouse in their frigid apartment. They called her "Princess Myshkina." In the first days of January Princess Myshkina vanished. Apparently she had died. Vera Inber was surprised how much she missed the mouse, a little spot of life in a frozen world. A few days later she noted with delight in her diary that Princess Myshkina had appeared again. Vera Inber and her husband had had a feast—half a small raw onion, heavily salted and slightly pickled, their bread ration, three little tartlets and some Ararat port wine. After they went to bed she heard Princess Myshkina at work, picking at the crumbs like a bird. Then the mouse climbed the cream pitcher. It was empty, of course. At that point Vera Inber lighted a match. Summoning her last strength, Princess Myshkina leaped from the cream pitcher and vanished.

A mouse confronted one little Leningrad boy with a difficult moral problem. His grandmother had a tin box in which she put every extra scrap of bread and crackers. It was the family's "iron reserves." If all else failed—but only then—they would dig into the box. One day the boy was alone in the freezing flat. He heard a noise inside the tin can. He knew what this meant. A mouse was eating the iron reserves. He could not immediately decide what to do. Should he open the box and release the mouse? Should he open the box, kill the mouse and throw it away? Or should he kill the mouse and eat it? The last alternative was the one which most tempted him for, after all, the mouse had been consuming their food. But the thought of eating the mouse was repulsive. Finally, he took the lid from the box, shook it and let the mouse escape. After all, he thought, the mouse was as hungry as he, and how did he know whether it did not have as much right to live as he did?

Other Leningraders, starving though they were, nonetheless each night carefully put a saucer on the floor with a few crumbs from their miserly ration for a Prince Myshkin or Princess Myshkina.

There were, of course, no more birds in Leningrad. First to disappear were the crows, the black-and-gray northern European crows. They flew off to the German lines in November. Next to go were the gulls and the pigeons. Then the sparrows and starlings vanished. They died of cold and hunger just as the people did. Some said they had seen sparrows drop like stones while flying over the Neva, simply frozen to death in flight. An old ship worker, named Ilya Kroshin, recalled that when Petrograd was starving in 1920 the crows lived in the factory shops. "Now there are no crows," he observed sadly.

There was hardly a cat or a dog left in Leningrad by late December. They had all been eaten.[1] But the trauma was great when a man came to butcher an animal which had lived on his affection for years. One elderly artist strangled his pet cat and ate it, according to Vsevolod Vishnevsky. Later, he tried to hang himself, but the rope failed, he fell to the floor, breaking his leg, and froze to death. The smallest Leningrad children grew up not knowing what cats and dogs were. One of the most savage attacks directed at Anna Akhmatova in the postwar years was written by a Leningrad working girl who accused the great poetess of ignorance of Leningrad in the blockade years because, in a poem, she spoke of pigeons in the square before the Kazan Cathedral. There were no pigeons there, the girl asserted. They all had long since been eaten.

On January 1 a young man came to Yelena Skryabina and asked whether a large gray cat which belonged to a certain actress was still alive in her apartment building. He explained that the actress adored the cat. Unfortunately, Yelena Skryabina had to disillusion the young man. There was not a single creature alive in the building except people. All cats, dogs and other pets had been eaten. In fact, the son of the actress had led the hunt for stray dogs and cats and had been very energetic in killing pigeons and other birds.

Special patrols of front-line soldiers were detailed to move through the Leningrad streets, dealing with any kind of situation which might arise on the spot. Colonel B. Bychkov, a Leningrad police officer, kept a diary of the problems he encountered day by day. One of the most critical was the theft of ration cards at the beginning of each month. Anyone losing his card at the

---

[1] By February there were only five police dogs still in the service of the Leningrad police department. (*Dela i Lyudi*, p. 275.)

beginning of the month almost certainly would be dead before he could get a new card. The military patrols observed no judicial procedures in such crimes. They simply halted suspicious persons, searched them, and if stolen cards or unaccountable food supplies were found, they shot the person on the spot. Bychkov lectured the patrols on violations of legalities. But it seemed to make no difference. He probably did not mind too much himself. The patrols of front-line soldiers were the only real force for law and order in the city.

But no great effort was made to interfere with the grisly trade at the Haymarket. As early as November, according to some accounts, meat patties made from ground-up human flesh went on sale, although many Leningraders refused to believe that the meat was human. They insisted it was horse meat —or dog, or cat.

One Leningrader, walking through the world of ice late at night, came upon a bloody snowdrift into which had been hurled the heads of a man, a woman and a small girl, her blond hair still plaited in Russian braids. The bodies, he felt certain, had been carted off by the cannibals for butchering. No other explanation seemed to fit the presence of the human heads in the drift.

The evidence of butchery of corpses was widespread. Many a Leningrad woman, pulling a child's sled behind her, bringing the body of a husband or child to the vicinity of a cemetery, was appalled to see that fleshy parts had been cut from the corpses which lay about like scattered cordwood.

"In the worst period of the siege," a survivor noted, "Leningrad was in the power of the cannibals. God alone knows what terrible scenes went on behind the walls of the apartments."

He claimed to know of cases in which husbands ate their wives, wives ate their husbands and parents ate their children. In his own building a porter killed his wife and then thrust her severed head into a red-hot stove.

Not a few soldiers on duty in the front lines made occasional trips-without-leave back into the city to bring food to their starving families. Coming into Leningrad late at night, at an hour when there was hardly a patrol on the streets, these soldiers not infrequently fell victim to attacks by the cannibals. They were regarded as preferable victims since they had been better fed. The center of trade in flesh, as in every kind of food product, was the Haymarket. Starving men and women did not inquire too closely as to the nature of the cutlets—ground meat patties—which were offered for sale. Why should they? They knew that at best they must be made of horse meat, probably adulterated with cat meat or dog meat, possibly rat meat. They told themselves that, of course, there could be no human flesh mixed in. Indeed, it was not a question they were likely to put to the hard-eyed men or women who stood like rocks in their heavy boots and heavy coats, shrugging their shoulders at the possible purchasers. Take it or leave it. The prices were fantastic—300 or 400 rubles for a few patties. For some reason it was almost always meat patties which were offered, seldom sausage.

But if questions were not asked in the markets, there was terrible gossip in the queues where the women waited and waited for the bread shops to open. The talk was of children, how careful one must be with them, how the cannibals waited to seize them because their flesh was so much more tender. Women were said to be second choice. They were starving like the men, but, it was insisted, their bodies carried a little more fat and their flesh was more tasty.

In the Haymarket could be bought wood alcohol (it was said that if the alcohol was passed through six layers of linen it could be safely drunk), linseed oil which was used for frying blini or pancakes, occasional pieces of bacon fat or lard, hardtack from army stores, tooth powder which could be used for making pudding if mixed with a little starch or potato flour (it sold for 100 rubles a packet), and library paste in bars like chocolate.

There was usually bread for sale at the market, sometimes whole loaves. But the sellers displayed it gingerly and clutched the loaves tightly under their coats. They were not afraid of interference by the police, but they desperately feared the thieves and hungry robbers who might at any moment draw a Finnish knife or simply knock them over the head and flee with the bread.

There was more than one way in which the dead might help the living to survive. Again and again at Piskarevsky and Serafimov and the other great cemeteries the teams of sappers sent in from the front to dynamite graves noticed as they piled the corpses into mass graves that pieces were missing, usually the fat thighs or arms and shoulders. The flesh was being used as food. Grisly as was the practice of necro-butchery there was no actual law which forbade the disfigurement of corpses or which prohibited consumption of this flesh.

The dead also served the living through their ration cards. The cards were supposed to be invalid as soon as the holder died. There were strict penalties for not reporting deaths and turning in cards. In practice no one turned in a ration card. They were used to the end of the month. At that time the bonus to the living came to an end for everyone had to appear in person to get his card renewed.

Among the fantastic tales which circulated in Leningrad in the winter of 1941–42 was one that there existed "circles" or fraternities of eaters of human flesh. The circles were said to assemble for special feasts, attended only by members of their kind. These people were the dregs of the human hell which Leningrad had become. The real lower depths were those occupied by persons who insisted on eating only "fresh" human flesh, as distinguished from cadaver cuts. Whether these tales were literally true was not so important. What was important was that Leningraders believed them to be true, and this added the culminating horror to their existence.

Two friends of Anatoly Darov, a young man and his girl named Dmitri

480 . PART IV: The Longest Winter

and Tamara, visited the Haymarket in January of 1942. They had determined to buy a pair of *valenki* or heavy felt boots for a friend. By every
kind of economy Tamara had managed to put aside 600 grams of bread to
be traded for the boots.

The pair made their way to the Haymarket. Neither had visited it before.
At first they could find nothing but men's boots—policemen's or con-
ductors'. These were too big and crude. Finally, they saw a very tall man
who was extremely well dressed by blockade standards, wearing a fine fur
hat, a heavy sheepskin coat, beautiful gray boots. He had an impressive
beard and despite the starving times seemed to be filled with strength. In
his hands he held a single woman's boot, exactly the kind the young people
wanted.

They bargained for price. He asked a kilo (about 2 pounds) of bread for
the boots. The young man offered 600 grams (about 1½ pounds). The
giant examined the bread and finally agreed to take it. The other boot, he
said, was at his flat in the tangle of Dostoyevsky streets nearby. With some
trepidation the young man started off with the tall peddler. Tamara warned
him to be careful. "Better to be without *valenki* than without your head,"
she said, half-joking.

The two men entered a quiet lane and soon came to a good-sized building
which had not been damaged by either German gunfire or bombing. Dmitri
followed the tall man up the staircase. The man climbed easily, occasionally
looking back at Dmitri. As they neared the top floor, an uneasy feeling
seized Dmitri. There leaped into his mind the stories he had heard of the
cannibals and how they lured victims to their doom. The tall man looked
remarkably well fed. Dmitri continued up the stairs but told himself he
would be on guard, ready to flee at the slightest sign of danger.

At the top floor the man turned and said, "Wait for me here." He knocked
at the door, and someone inside asked, "Who is it?" "It's me," the man
responded. "With a live one."

Dmitri froze at the words. There was something sinister about them.
The door opened, and he saw a hairy red hand and a muglike face. From
the room came a strange, warm, heavy smell. A gust of wind in the hall
caught the door, and in the swaying candlelight Dmitri had a glimpse of
several great hunks of white meat, swinging from hooks on the ceiling.
From one hunk he saw dangling a human hand with long fingers and blue
veins.

At that moment the two men lunged toward Dmitri. He leaped down the
staircase and managed to reach the bottom ahead of his pursuers. To his
good fortune, there was a light military truck passing through the lane.

"Cannibals!" Dmitri shouted. Two soldiers jumped from the truck and
rushed into the building. A moment or two later two shots rang out. In
a few minutes the soldiers reappeared, one carrying a greatcoat and the
other a loaf of bread. The soldier with the greatcoat complained that it had

a tear in it. The other one said, "I found a piece of bread. Do you want it?"

Dmitri thanked the soldier. It was his bread, the 600 grams he had planned to trade for the *valenki*. The soldiers told him that they had found human hocks from five bodies hanging in the flat. Then they got back into their truck and were off to Lake Ladoga, where they were part of the Road of Life.

Nina Peltser, ballet star of the Musical Comedy Theater, had a less shattering adventure obtaining a pair of *valenki*. She was afraid that her talented feet would freeze in the Leningrad cold and decided to protect them with the warmest footwear in town—a pair of conductor's boots. She went to the chief of the Leningrad streetcar system and said, "Save my feet!" He found a heavy pair of men's felt boots, which she wore constantly, even donning them between numbers on the frigid stage of the Pushkin Theater, where she often performed that winter. She received only a worker's food ration, but admirers often brought her presents—a chocolate bar, a jar of fish paste or a tin of meat.

Police investigators in those months sometimes threatened to cast an obdurate suspect into the cell of the cannibals, "where they ate each other," if their victim did not confess to the crime of which the procurator had decided he was guilty. Whether, in fact, there was such a cell, whether the police actually permitted cannibals to feast on each other, is another matter. It is hardly likely. Yet the possibility was realistic enough for police investigators to use it as a blackmail threat.

More and more, Leningrad seemed to its residents to have become the city of the white apocalypse where humans fed on humans and the very water which they drank carried the sweet stench of human corpses. The water was now largely drawn from the ice holes in the Neva, the Fontanka and other canals. But the ice around the holes was strewn with the corpses of those who collapsed or froze to death while drawing water. And hundreds of bodies were dumped in the rivers and canals. No one who drank the water drawn from the Leningrad ice holes ever got the taste of it out of his mouth. It made no difference whether it was boiled or not (and often there was no fire and no fuel with which to boil the water and it was simply drunk raw from the river). Even when used for surrogate tea or coffee, the telltale flavor seemed to be there—faintly sweet, faintly moldy, tainted with the presence of death.

Through this city of the ice apocalypse Pavel Luknitsky walked in late January. He was so weak he could hardly keep to his feet. Two days before by actual count there had been thirteen unburied bodies in the writers' apartment house at No. 9 Griboyedov, including the body of one unknown man. Twelve members of the Writers Union had died of starvation—that he knew of—and twenty-four were on the verge of death. The widow of the poet Yevgeny Panfilov, with whom he had spoken at the Writers' House a few days earlier, her face looking like gray leather, her head wrapped in a scarf like a mummy, sitting in an armchair, motionless, hoping for some assistance, had just been found dead in her flat, her face gnawed off by hungry rats.

Luknitsky had gone to his old apartment on Borovaya Ulitsa for the first time since a bomb fell on the building in late autumn. He had a small sled and proposed to carry his literary papers and manuscripts to a place of safekeeping in the flat where he now lived on the Petrograd side. (Actually, he was so weak he simply brought them to the Writers' House at No. 18 Ulitsa Voinova.)

As he walked slowly through the streets, he thought of the heroic people who kept Leningrad alive—the Young Communist brigades who carried water from the Neva to the bakeries and brought half-dead people to the hospitals on their sleds, of the truck drivers transporting food over Lake Ladoga, of the people at Radio House who kept the radio going, of the handful of youngsters in the factories who turned out shells and bullets in arctic shops, of the thousands of people who each in his own way helped enable the city to survive.

And he thought, too, of the deadly criminals who attacked people for their ration cards, of the gangs of murderers and worse who roved the streets, and of the people who made their way through the city to their posts in these days of starvation, dying of hunger and risking attack from the bands of marauders who preyed on the weak in almost every street.

On the lips of the Leningraders who carried on in spite of every peril, he knew, was only one question, repeated again and again: "Will the Germans soon be driven off? Will the blockade soon be lifted?"

These thoughts filled his mind as he loaded on the sled his papers, which suddenly seemed almost more than he could drag. He made his way down the Borovaya. He passed a heavy sledge, heaped high with corpses, unbelievably thin, blue and terrifying—just skeletons with skin stretched tight and splotched with red and lilac-colored death marks. On the Zvenigorod he saw beside a house eight corpses, covered with rags or old clothes, lashed by ropes to small sleds, ready to be dragged to the cemetery. On Marat sprawled on his back was the corpse of an incredibly thin man, a fur hat falling from his head, and, two steps farther along, two women were emerging from a house. One with frantic face kept calling, "Lena, mine. Lena!" A third woman was muttering quietly, "Leonid Abramovich is dead and lying on the pavement."

On Vladimirsky Prospekt Luknitsky found his sled colliding with those of others passing him with corpses. One was a sled on which there were two corpses, the body of a woman with long hair trailing in the snow and that of a small girl, possibly ten years old. He passed carefully in order to avoid tangling the whitish-yellow hair of the corpse with the runners of his sled.

On the Volodarsky near the Liteiny Bridge he encountered a five-ton truck with a mountain of bodies. Farther on he met two old women who were conveying their corpses to the cemetery in style. They had hitched their sleds to an army sledge which was slowly pulled through the streets by a pair of starving horses. There he met the shadow of a man who carried nestled to his breast an incredibly thin dog—one of the rarest of city sights. The eyes of both the man and the dog were filled with hunger and terror, the dog's terror, no doubt, because he sensed his fate and the man's, perhaps, because he feared someone might rob him of the dog and he would not have the strength to defend his possession.

So Luknitsky walked through the city, passing hundreds of people, struggling to survive, pulling the corpses of their relatives toward hospitals or cemeteries, pulling their little sleds bearing pails of water.

Among the hundreds he met another kind as well—a man with a fat, self-satisfied face, well fed, with greedy eyes. Who was this man? Possibly, a food store worker, a speculator, an apartment house manager who stole the ration cards of the tenants as they died and with the aid of his mistress exchanged the miserable bread rations in the Haymarket for gold watches, for rich silks, for diamonds or old silver or golden rubles. The conversation of this man and his mistress would not be of survival, of how to live through their terrible times. On such things this man would merely spit. Was he a speculator? A murderer? A cannibal? There was little difference; each was trading on the lives of starving, dying people, each was living on the flesh of his fellows.

For such persons there was only one recourse. They must be shot.

Luknitsky met Red Army men, too. They were as thin and weak as the civilians. He passed two soldiers, half-carrying a third. Most of them, despite their weakness, tried to walk with a bold step.

"Such was the image of my own, unhappy, proud, besieged city," Luknitsky noted. "I am happy that I did not run away, that I share its fate, that I am a participant and a witness of all its misfortunes in these difficult, unprecedented months. And if I live, I will remember them—I will never forget my beloved Leningrad in the winter of 1941–42."

Daniel Leonidovich Andreyev, son of the great Leonid Andreyev, lived through the blockade in Leningrad. He wrote of the Leningrad apocalypse:

> We have known everything . . .
> That in Russian speech there is
> No word for that mad war winter . . .
> When the Hermitage shivered under bombs . . .
> Houses turned to frost and pipes burst with ice . . .
> The ration—100 grams . . . On the Nevsky corpses.
> And we learned, too, about cannibalism.
> We have known everything. . . .

44 . "T" Is for Tanya

IN THE CITY MUSEUM OF HISTORY IN LENINGRAD THERE
are a few torn pages of a child's notebook, ABC pages in the Russian alphabet: A, B, V, G, D and so on.

On them there are scrawled under the appropriate letters simple entries
in a child's hand:

> Z—Zhenya died 28 December, 12:30 in the morning, 1941.
> B—Babushka died 25 January, 3 o'clock, 1942.
> L—Leka died 17 March, 5 o'clock in the morning, 1942.
> D—Dedya Vasya died 13 April, 2 o'clock at night, 1942.
> D—Dedya Lesha, 10 May, 4 o'clock in the afternoon, 1942.
> M—Mama, 13 May, 7:30 A.M., 1942.
> S—Savichevs died. All died. Only Tanya remains.

The entries were made by Tanya Savicheva, an eleven-year-old schoolgirl.
They tell the story of her family during the Leningrad blockade. The
Savichevs lived in House No. 13, Second Line, Vasilevsky Island. The house
still stands, no signs of war to be found on its bland surface, and even the
building across the street, which was hit by bombs in 1941, gives no appearance of damage. All the wounds have been healed.

For years it was supposed that the entire Savichev family had died and
that after making her last entry Tanya, too, died. This was not quite correct. Like many Leningraders Tanya was evacuated in the spring of 1942.
She was sent to Children's Home No. 48 in the village of Shakhty in the
Gorky area, suffering from chronic dysentery. Efforts by doctors to save
her life failed, and she died in the summer of 1943.

Two members of the Savichev family survived the war. Both had been
out of Leningrad during the blockade. An older sister, Nina Nikolayevna
Pavlova, returned to Leningrad in 1944. Tanya's notations had been made
in her notebook. The sister found it when she came back to the apartment
on Vasilevsky Island, lying in a box with her mother's wedding dress. A
brother, Mikhail, also survived. When war broke out, he was at Gdov in

the nearby countryside and fought with the partisans.

The obliteration of the Savichev family was not unusual. This was what was happening to Leningrad in the winter of 1941–42. Not everyone died that winter. But the deaths went on in the months and years ahead as the privations of the blockade took their toll.

In the measured words of the official Leningrad historian:

> In world history there are no examples which in their tragedy equal the terrors of starving Leningrad. Each day survived in the besieged city was the equal of many months of ordinary life. It was terrible to see how from hour to hour there vanished the strength of those near and dear. Before the eyes of mothers their sons and daughters died, children were left without parents, a multitude of families were wiped out completely.

Party Secretary Zhdanov and his associates now knew the price that must be paid for the siege. Only the most radical measures would pull Leningrad through the winter, and how many would survive till spring was an open question. Hope that the offensive so boldly planned in Moscow by Stalin, Zhdanov and the generals in early December would liberate Leningrad was petering out. The attacks by the Fifty-fifth Army headed by General V. P. Sviridov on the Leningrad front, driving toward Tosno in an effort to unhinge the Germans at Mga, yielded meager results—and heavy losses. On January 13 General Meretskov of the Volkhov front and General Fedyuninsky's Fifty-fourth Army of the Leningrad front launched a simultaneous attack, hoping to free the rail and highway connections between Moscow and Leningrad. The battles went on all winter long.

"I will never forget," General Meretskov wrote, "the endless forests, the bogs, the water-logged peat fields, the potholed roads. The heavy battle with the enemy went on side by side with the equally heavy battle with the forces of nature."

General Fedyuninsky, whose Fifty-fourth Army fought through the winter in the same operations, spoke of the experience in almost identical terms: "If you asked me what was the most difficult time I would without hesitation reply: The worst time of all for me was at Pogost in the winter of 1942. The four months of constant bloodletting and, worst of all, unsuccessful fighting in the forests and marshy regions between Mga and Tikhvin remain a terrible memory for me."

The Russian attack developed slowly. There could be no hope of surprising the Germans. The Nazis were strongly dug in, and a more vigorous commander, Colonel General von Küchler, had replaced the aging von Leeb in early January. Just to move over the ground in the heavy snow required enormous expenditure of strength. Toward the end of January the Soviet Second Shock Army scored a small success, smashing through the main German defenses and capturing Myasny Bor in the direction of the Chudovo-Novgorod railroad.

Feverish efforts were made to achieve success in the winter offensive. Moscow had done everything—except provide the needed men and arms. Unsatisfied with the pace at which Meretskov was moving, Stalin sent one of his police generals, L. Z. Mekhlis, to the Volkhov front on December 24. The task of Mekhlis was to chivy and hurry the operation. The Fifty-ninth and Second Shock armies, according to the schedule of the General Staff, were to be ready for the jump-off by December 25. Actually, only one division was in place.

Delay followed delay. The date for the offensive was postponed to January 7, but by that time only five of the eight Fifty-ninth Army divisions had arrived and the Second Army was only half complete. There was no air support, and the Fifty-ninth Army had neither optical instruments nor means of communication with which to direct artillery fire. Meretskov sent an urgent telegram to Moscow, and Marshal N. N. Voronov appeared at Volkhov headquarters. The acid relations between police generals and regular army were shown in Mekhlis' greeting to Marshal Voronov: "Well, now the chief criminal has arrived, the one who sent us artillery which can't fire. Just watch how he tries to excuse himself." Voronov was able to help a bit but not too much, and January 7 found Meretskov still short of artillery, reserve supplies, fuel, forage for the horses and almost every kind of matériel. Nonetheless, the preliminary attacks were launched with expectable results. The commanders were not able to direct their troops, the Germans easily contained the infantry assaults, the whole movement was a disaster. Meretskov asked Moscow to let him delay the development of the operation by three days. On January 10 Stalin and Marshal Vasilevsky talked with him by direct wire. They expressed the frank opinion that the operation would not be ready even by January 11 and that it would be better to put it off another two or three days. "There's a Russian proverb," Stalin said. "Haste makes waste. It will be the same with you: hurry to the attack and not prepare it and you will waste people."

Meretskov regarded this as a serious reprimand, but he noted (many years later) that from the beginning there had been ceaseless haste and demands from Moscow to get the action under way. The Stavka had insisted by telephone and urgent directives to hurry in every possible way. Mekhlis had been sent in for no other purpose than to keep the pressure on.

Actually, the preparation should have taken at least fifteen to twenty days. But, of course, there was not a chance of getting that kind of time.

There was another serious problem. The Leningrad operation was designed as part of a triple winter offensive which was supposed, simultaneously, to lift the Leningrad siege and crush Army Group Nord, destroy and encircle Army Group Center on the Moscow front and defeat the southern German armies, liberating the Donbas and Crimea.

Meretskov, Fedyuninsky and the Leningrad commanders received a circular telegram from Stavka in Moscow dated January 10 which gave the aim of the operation as: "To drive them [the Germans] westward without pause, compelling them to exhaust their reserves even before spring, when we will have new and larger reserves and the Germans will not have large reserves, and thus secure the full defeat of the Hitler troops in 1942."

The task was far beyond Soviet capability. It represented almost as fatal a misreading of the situation as that which had possessed Stalin on the eve of the war.

There was another problem. The general in charge of the Second Shock Army, Lieutenant General G. G. Sokolov, was a police officer. He had previously been a Deputy Commissar of Internal Affairs. He had plunged into army affairs with great energy and aplomb, ready to promise anything. But he knew nothing about military matters and substituted clichés and dogma for military decisions. He had what Meretskov called "an original approach" to operational questions. Among the instructions which Sokolov issued to his troops were orders about when to eat (breakfast before dawn, dinner after sunset); the length of the marching pace (one arshin, a little less than a yard); the hours for marching (units of more than a company were not to march during the day; in general, all movements were to be made at night); the soldiers' attitude toward cold (they were not to fear it; if their ears or hands froze, they were to rub them with snow).

General Meretskov managed to get Sokolov removed on the eve of the offensive, replacing him with Lieutenant General N. K. Krykov.

None of these measures helped the winter offensive. It bogged down. On January 17 Chief of Staff Marshal A. M. Vasilevsky warned Meretskov that the "situation in Leningrad is exceptionally serious and it is necessary to take all steps to advance as quickly as possible."

Marshal Vasilevsky's words did not bring results. What was worse, in spite of repeated requests, Meretskov could not get the supplies he needed to feed his horses, fuel his trucks, provision his men and arm his guns. On January 28 General A. V. Khrulev, Deputy Commissar of Defense, arrived to try to speed up supplies.[1] This helped a little but not enough. The Second Shock Army ground to a halt and finally had to go on the defensive. The Stavka showered down telegrams, Meretskov was charged with indecisiveness and treading water. Meretskov complained in his turn about lack of

[1] During most of the war Army General A. V. Khrulev, a responsible, able, energetic officer, was in charge of Red Army rear services. But every session he had with Stalin was an ordeal in which front commanders and members of the State Defense Committee (Beria, Malenkov and others) sought to shift responsibility for errors, mistakes and deficiencies onto him. Stalin was well aware of Khrulev's competence. This did not prevent him from telephoning one day and exploding, "You are worse than an enemy! You work for Hitler!" Then he slammed down the receiver. Soon Khrulev's wife was arrested as a member of a "conspiratorial organization." Stalin continued to invite Khrulev to his dacha. The General was present at a drunken New Year's celebration at Blizhny ("The Near Place," the nickname for Stalin's villa on the Mozhaisk Chaussée) on New Year's 1944. But he was soon dismissed, presumably on Beria's provocation. (N. A. Antipenko, *Novy Mir*, No. 8, August, 1965, pp. 154-155.)

tanks, planes and shells, shortages of troops, inability to give his men relief after the incredible tasks of fighting in the cold, wet, miserable morass.

It was mid-February. Everyone was angry, depressed, blaming each other. Stalin sent Marshal Voroshilov to the Volkhov front to demand immediate action. Meretskov gathered his military council and offered a new plan, based on giving his men some rest, regrouping and bringing in reserves and new equipment, particularly artillery for the Second Shock Army. Voroshilov went from unit to unit trying to raise spirits. It did little good. The plain fact was that the men didn't have the strength. They were to remember the winter as the worst they had ever spent. Losses were great, results almost nil.

It was obvious in such circumstances that there would be no early response to the question on the lips of all Leningraders—"When will the blockade be lifted?"—and no early confirmation of the persisting rumors that the armies of Meretskov and Fedyuninsky were about to save the city.

Party Secretary Zhdanov turned to such resources as he had. One was the Communist youth. Their ranks had been savagely depleted like those of the Party itself.[2] Leningrad boasted 235,000 Komsomols in June, 1941. By January, 1942, only 48,000 remained. The rest had gone to the front, had been killed or transferred to urgent production tasks elsewhere. They were almost the only reserve of strength the city had.

The Young Communists were organized into service detachments. Their task was to go from apartment to apartment, to help the living, if possible, and to remove the dead. The first Young Communist units went into action in December, but it was only in January that their work achieved an organized character.

They themselves were little stronger than the rest of the Leningraders. A meeting was called at Smolny on January 30 by V. N. Ivanov, secretary of the Komsomol organization.

"There were no streetcars," one of those who attended recalled. "The meeting was called for noon. People started out at 8 A.M."

It was a long walk and they had to rest time and again.

Ivanov told them: "We are being put to a severe test by the Party and the country. We look forward with confidence. Through the difficulties and deprivation which Leningrad is experiencing in connection with the blockade we can see our coming victory. For this we are fighting and will fight to the last drop of blood."

The sights which met the eyes of the youth brigades in the frozen and bleak flats of Leningrad were almost beyond the power of a Dürer or a Hogarth to depict.

G. F. Badayev, secretary of the Moscow region of the Party, went to one frozen apartment. He heard the feeble cry of a child and turned his flashlight into a room. On a bed lay a dead woman, and beside her were two tiny children, hungry, dirty, frozen.

---

[2] In the first half of 1942 the Leningrad Party lost 15 percent of its membership by starvation. (*Leningrad v VOV*, p. 202.)

"How can we permit this?" he asked rhetorically. "Why did no one look in here sooner?"

It was a vain, pompous question.

Vissarion Sayanov met a young woman named Anna Ivanovna Shakova at a children's home. She had been wounded at the front and then took a job with a Komsomol brigade. One evening she went with a friend to an old house on Maly Prospekt. They entered a dark apartment and found a woman lying dead with an overcoat thrown over her body. On the bed there was a large bundle, wrapped in a tablecloth. Inside they found a nursing child, alive, whimpering and sucking on an empty nipple. They brought the baby to the nursery. No one in the apartment knew the child's name, all the neighbors were dead. "I told them to write down my name," Anna said. "Let him carry my name through the years." Before the winter ended she had taken in two more babies. She had a family of three and was not yet married.

In the great Kirov metallurgical plant there were about five thousand workers, still alive, still technically on the payroll, most of them living in the icy, shell-torn buildings, too weak to work, almost too weak to live.

After the blockade was lifted one of the girls, Anna Vasileyeva, a chubby, red-cheeked youngster, told of her life. She was a "Putilov girl," that is, her family for at least two generations had been workers in the Putilov, now the Kirov, plant. Her father and two brothers worked at the factory. The family lived in a house in a nearby suburb, close enough so they could walk to work.

When the war started, Anna, only fifteen, began to work at Kirov, too. When the Nazis swept almost to the Kirov gates in September, 1941, Anna's family had to abandon their house in the suburbs—it was in German-occupied territory. Then her father and one brother were killed by a German shell. The other brother went into the Red Army. Anna and her mother went to live in a flat in town. One day she came back from work to find her mother had been blinded by slivers of flying glass from a shell hit on a nearby apartment.

By January no work was being done at Kirov. No one was able to work. There was no power, no heat, no light. Several of the stronger girls, Anna among them, made up a brigade. Each day one or two started from Kirov with a child's sled. They visited three or four flats where their relatives lived—to see if they were alive, to remove any dead, to bring a little food, to light a fire or heat some water, whatever they could do. In late afternoon they would come back to the little room where their comrades huddled around a tin stove.

"Here is the way it was," she said. "The first thing you would do was to look around to see if everyone was there, if your friends were all alive."

It was the same each morning. When you awoke from your troubled, hungry, freezing sleep, you looked around the circle.

"Then," she said, "you'd notice someone sitting in a chair beside the stove. At first he would look all right. Then you'd look closer and see that he was sitting there dead. That was the way it was."

Anna Vasileyeva was seventeen. She had survived. No one else in her family had.

Yelizaveta Sharypina visited a flat on the Nevsky where a worker named Pruzhan was supposed to live. He had failed to show up for work. She made her way along a dark corridor. The first door was padlocked. The next door would not open. Finally, she found, an unlatched door and entered a dark room. There was a cold stove in the center and two iron beds. A man lay with his face to the wall on one bed, a woman, feeble but able to talk, on the other. Pruzhan, she said, was dead. His wife had died a few days before him. A daughter was at the store getting the bread ration. She herself was not ill, only weak. She had lost her bread card. "Obviously it is the end," she said quietly. Sharypina called a Young Communist team to see if the woman's life could, by some means, be saved.

At another apartment on Borodinsky Street Sharypina found the dying Stepanov family. The father had been out of work for three months. A few days before he seemed a bit better and sat by the window where a little sun came in. "Now it will be all right," he said. "We will live." A few moments later he toppled over dead. With the aid of a porter twelve-year-old Boris Stepanov had taken his father's body to the morgue. His mother, cloaked in a heavy coat, lay on her bed and stared into space. She had not said a word since her husband died. On a second bed lay sixteen-year-old Volodya. He did not speak. He chewed.

"What is he eating?" Madame Sharypina asked.

"He is not eating. There is nothing in his mouth," his brother Boris said. "He just chews and chews. He says he doesn't want to eat."

Despite Sharypina's efforts Boris and Volodya were dead within a few days. Only the shattered mother survived.

One February day Sharypina was walking slowly along Zagorodny Prospekt when she saw a child with a stick in his hand, a piece of blanket wrapped about his head. The child darted into the next courtyard and started digging at a mound of frozen garbage.

"What are you doing here?" she asked. The child, who appeared to be about seven years old, turned a pair of suspicious eyes on her and replied that he was looking for something for his sister Lena to eat. The night before, he said, he had found some cabbage stalks. Very good. Of course, they were frozen. Lena had eaten them and had given him a piece, too.

It was a typical Leningrad case—the father at the front, alive or dead no one knew, the mother long since taken to the hospital, alive or dead no one knew, the children living on frozen garbage heaps.

A doctor named Milova was called to Apartment No. 67 at 11/13 Borovaya Ulitsa one January day.

"The door to the apartment was open," she reported. "I found the room

I wanted and went in without knocking. My eyes met a frightful sight. A half-dark room. Frost on the walls. On the floor a frozen puddle. On a chair the corpse of a fourteen-year-old boy. In a child's cradle the second corpse of a tiny child. On the bed the dead mistress of the flat, K. K. Vandel. Beside her, rubbing the dead woman's breast with a towel, stood her oldest daughter Mikki. But life had gone, and it could not be brought back. In one day Mikki lost her mother, her son and her brother, all dead of hunger and cold. At the door, hardly able to stand from weakness, was her neighbor, Lizunova, looking without comprehension upon the scene. On the next day she died, too."

A teacher, A. N. Mironova, saved more than a hundred children in the winter of 1941–42. On January 28 she noted in her diary:

> To the 17th Line, House 38, Apartment No. 2 (on Vasilevsky Island) to get Yuri Stepanov, 9 years old. His mother was dead. The youngster slept day and night with his dead mother. ("How cold I got from mama," he said.) Yuri didn't want to come with me. He cried and shouted. A touching farewell with his mother ("Mama, what will happen to you without me?").

Another entry from Mironova's January diary:

> Prospekt Musorgsky 68, Apartment 30. Took a girl, Shura Sokolova, born 1931. Father at the front. Mother dead. Body of mother in the kitchen. Little girl dirty, scabs on her hands. Found her in a pile of dirty linen under the mattress.

V. N. Ivanov, secretary of the Komsomols, in a report on the winter of 1942 said, "I must tell you that nothing more terrible and difficult could have been possible. I worked under the weight of psychological trauma. I could not bear to see the people dropping around me. Human beings simply slipped away. They no longer could stand."

The Young Communists mustered 983 members for the service brigades, plus 500 to 600 additional young people enlisted in each region of the city. They visited 29,800 flats, provided medical aid to 8,450 persons and made daily visits to 10,350 starving persons—according to their official report. Another estimate puts the number of flats visited at 13,810 and the number of persons helped at 75,000.

Death, in a measure, was beginning to modify Leningrad's problems. The figures are not very accurate. All the Soviet authorities concede this. Probably 11,085 persons died in November of hunger. Nearly five times as many, 52,881, died in December. The figures for January and February are less precise. One of the most conservative authorities, A. V. Karasev, estimated deaths in January at 3,500 to 4,000 a day, or 108,500 to 124,000. Dmitri V. Pavlov, whose task it was to feed the survivors, puts the combined January-February death toll at 199,187. Pavlov's total is probably too low. The overburdened Leningrad Funeral Trust handled 9,219 bodies in November, 27,463 in December. The figures for January and February are missing.

Almost all these deaths were due to starvation-related diseases. By December dystrophy constituted 70 percent of the case load of clinics and hospitals and in January 85 percent. Most of these were men, and their death rate was about 85 percent. In February and March women constituted the majority of cases. One official report placed the death toll among those admitted to hospitals that winter at 30 to 35 percent. A more exact estimate places the dysentery death rate at 40.7 percent for the first quarter of 1942.

The disease and death statistics have no parallel in modern history.[3] Leningrad's death rate in 1941 was 32 percent over 1940. But for the year 1942 it was fifteen times greater than for 1940. In prewar years the death rate in Leningrad hospitals was 6 to 8 percent. In the fourth quarter of 1941 it rose to 28 percent and in the first quarter of 1942 to 44.3 percent and, for the whole year of 1942, to 24.4 percent. The death rate of all diseases jumped astronomically—typhus from 4 percent to 60 percent, dysentery from 10 to 50 percent, stomach-intestinal diseases from 4.5 to 54.3 percent. All kinds of surgery became more dangerous, with the over-all death rate rising five times. The incidence of heart disease was estimated at 40 percent in blockade residents over forty years of age.

In these conditions the number of mouths to be fed in Leningrad dropped radically, day by day. But they were still far greater than the resources available. The total of Leningrad residents for January—calculated on the basis of ration cards issued—was 2,282,000. The first-quarter figure is given as 2,116,000. The number of persons holding workers' food cards was about 800,000 (this meant 350 grams of bread daily after December 25). The number holding dependents' cards (200 grams after December 25) was at least 700,000. Children and nonworker employees also got 200 grams a day. It was in this category (which had received only 125 grams of bread daily from November 21 to December 25) that the heaviest death toll occurred.

It was obvious to Zhdanov that people on these rations could not survive. To try to save at least some elements of the population he ordered on December 27 the opening of what were called *statsionari*, convalescent centers, in which slightly better food would be given together with minimum nursing attention. These were designed to save such elite personnel as could be saved. In reality many persons arrived at the convalescent stations so ill and weak they promptly died. By January 9 it was estimated that about 9,000 persons were being thus treated. That day Zhdanov ordered a vast expansion of the *statsionari*, and on January 13 the city authorities authorized an increase in beds to 16,450.

[3] The incidence of ordinary contagious diseases dropped dramatically. In December, 1941, there were only 114 cases of typhoid fever compared with 143 a year earlier; 42 of typhus compared with 118; 93 of scarlet fever compared with 1,056; 211 of diphtheria compared with 728; 818 of whooping cough compared with 1,844. (Pavlov, *op. cit.*, 3rd edition, p. 145.)

One of the principal convalescent stations was at the Astoria Hotel, where 200 beds were set up, largely for scientists, writers, intelligentsia.

Nikolai Markevich, a *Red Fleet* correspondent, took a room at the Astoria January 30. He wrote: "The hotel is dead. Like the whole city there is neither water nor light. In the dark corridors rarely appears a figure, lighting his way with a 'bat,' a hand-generator flashlight or a simple match. The rooms are cold, the temperature not rising above 40 degrees. Writing these lines my hand is almost frozen."

The *statsionar* was just a drop in the bucket, as was evidenced by an appeal directed to the Leningrad Front Council on January 16 by the Writers Union:

> The situation of the Leningrad writers and their families has become extraordinarily critical. Recently 12 writers have starved to death. In hospitals now are more than 15 writers and many more are awaiting places. The widow of the writer Yevgeny Panfilov who died at the front has died of starvation in spite of our efforts to save her (our possibilities are very limited). She leaves three children. In the last few days we had to recall urgently from the front the poet, Ilya Avramenko, because of the critical situation of his wife and newborn child. In the families of writers there is a very heavy death toll. Suffice to say that in the family of the major Soviet poet, Nikolai Tikhonov, working now in the writing group of the Leningrad front, six persons have died. In the Writers' House at present lie a number of starving people who cannot walk and whom we do not have the strength to help.

The total of *statsionari* opened was 109, and 63,740 persons were helped by them in one way or another.

There was one slowly brightening spot. The Ladoga ice road, at long last, was beginning to work better. The urgent measures to improve the rail link from the lake to Leningrad had begun to take effect, and on January 11 the State Defense Committee ordered a rail line built from Voibokalo to the ice road. By February 10, thanks to a military construction crew, the link from Voibokalo to Kobona and Kosa was finished and the Ladoga truck haul was shortened by twenty miles.

In the first ten days of January the ice road delivered 10,300 tons of freight to Leningrad. In the second ten days the total more than doubled to 21,000 tons. For the first time, on January 18 the ice road teams exceeded their quota. For the first time since the start of the war, food was flowing into Leningrad faster than it was being eaten—in part because of better deliveries, in part because of the grievous decimation of the population.

Dmitri V. Pavlov, the food chief, breathed a bit easier. On January 20 he had nearly three weeks' food supplies in sight, either on hand in Leningrad, en route over the lake or at depots awaiting delivery. His chart showed these tonnages:

	Flour	Cereals	Meat	Fats	Sugar
On hand in Leningrad	2,106	326	243	94	226
At West Ladoga warehouses	2,553	690	855	130	740
En route across Ladoga	1,020	210	220	108	90
At Voibokalo-Zhikharevo	6,196	846	1,347	360	608
Totals	11,875	2,072	2,665	692	1,664
Days' supply at existing consumption rate	21	9	20	9	13

To be sure, he had only three or four days' supply of flour actually in Leningrad. But he could see daylight ahead. On January 24 he raised the rations for the second time—to 400 grams of bread daily for workers, 300 for ordinary employees, and 250 for dependents and children. On February 11 he raised rations again—to 500 grams for workers, 400 for employees and 300 for dependents and children.

These steps were taken against the background of a major decision by Zhdanov and the State Defense Committee: to evacuate from Leningrad over the ice road at least one-quarter of the remaining population—500,000 persons. The official order was issued January 22, and Aleksei Kosygin, the future Premier of the Soviet Union, was placed in charge of the task.[4]

Actually, the Leningrad front had ordered the evacuation of residents via the ice road as early as December 6 and had set a quota of 5,000 persons per day to be reached by December 20. But only 105,000 persons had been evacuated from Leningrad from August, 1941, to January 22, 1942, of which only 36,738 were native Leningraders—the others being refugees from the Baltic states.

Conditions on the ice road were so chaotic in December and early January that most persons who left the city had to make it on their own. Thousands died on the ice. From Kobona to Syasstroi throughout December and early January could be seen wrecked and abandoned cars and trucks in which elderly weak persons and feeble infants had frozen to death. There were no facilities for housing or feeding evacuees. The evacuation commission was so badly organized that hundreds of persons waited at evacuation points for days and then returned home. The evacuees often perished. The director of the Second Manual Training School tried to take his youngsters out of the city. They were confined to a frigid barracks at Ladoga for ten days, and the director eventually returned the survivors to Leningrad.

Under these conditions it was estimated that 36,118 persons had been evacuated via the Ladoga ice road up to January 22.

Now, it was hoped, all this could be changed. An echelon of several hundred buses was brought up from Moscow and stationed at Voibokalo. Evacuees were taken first to the Finland Station. There they were to be given a hot meal and 500 grams of bread. They were supposed to receive

[4] Most of the evacuees were sent to the Urals or to Central Asian cities. Some, however, were sent to the Caucasus and fell into German hands when the Nazis broke through to Maikop in the summer of 1942.

a kilo of bread when they took their places in the unheated train for transport to the Ladoga base at Borisova Griva. There they were placed in buses or open trucks and driven across the lake to Zhikharevo, Lavrovo and Kobona for entrainment to rear evacuation points. It was not supposed to take more than a couple of hours to cross Ladoga. There were warming points and first-aid stations at frequent intervals.

In reality, of course, it was many winter weeks before minimum conditions were met. The evacuees were so weak that it took hours to load them. An echelon arriving at Borisova Griva on January 23 took a day and a half to load, the people were so feeble. Not many survived the ordeal. But they could not have survived in Leningrad either.[5]

The death roll grew: the author of fantastic fiction, A. R. Belyayev, the poet A. P. Kraisky, the author of the novel *Hunger* (dealing with the Petrograd famine in the Civil War), S. A. Semenov, and the children's writer Ye. Ya. Danko. In all, forty-five writers perished. The losses in the Academy of Science included the antiquities specialist, S. A. Zhebelev; the Semitics specialist, P. K. Kokovtsov; the historians, B. L. Bugayevsky and P. S. Sadikov; 36 members of the Mining Institute, 8 from the Chemical Technical Institute, 7 from the Railroad Transportation Institute; 136 architects;[6] the artists, A. I. Savinov, V. Z. Zverev, N. A. Tyrsa, A. A. Uspensky, I. Ya. Bilibin (in all, 83 of the 225 artists in Leningrad); the composers, V. K. Tomilin, N. P. Fomin, B. G. Golts, Professor P. N. Sheffer and many others; 9 artists of the Maly Opera Theater and 29 of the Mariinsky; 44 workers of the Russian Museum (to February 13); 130 of the 560 Hermitage workers who remained in the city; hundreds of physicians, teachers, engineers, professors and students.

The list of brilliant, able, scholarly and artistic men and women who died with their beloved city ran into the thousands. Many of them were men like the distinguished physiologist, Aleksei A. Ukhtomsky. Ukhtomsky was sixty-six years old when the war broke out. He had just completed editing his lectures on the nervous system for the University of Leningrad publishing house and was planning in the 1941–42 academic year to offer a new course in physiology. With the onset of war he put aside these occupations and began to organize special research on traumatic shock and other problems connected with the war. His laboratory and institute were packed up and shipped to Elabuga in the Tatar Republic and Saratov, but he himself refused to go. His lifelong associate, Nadezhda Ivanovna Bobrovskaya, was critically ill; she had suffered a brain hemorrhage on June 6 and he was caring for her in his apartment. Moreover, his own health was extremely

[5] Even in the winter of 1941–42 people continued to be evacuated into Leningrad from surrounding regions. It was estimated that 55,000 persons were brought into the city during the winter, most of them ill-clothed, starving, with no place to live or means of survival. (Karasev, *op. cit.*, p. 186.)

[6] L. A. Ilyin, who spoke to the meeting at the Academic Chapel January 9 was killed by a shell fragment while walking on Nevsky Prospekt in December, 1942.

bad. He was suffering from chronic hypertension and was developing slight gangrene in his feet. Also, although few knew it, the first signs of cancer of the esophagus had appeared.

Nonetheless, he refused to be evacuated with his laboratory. Nadezhda Bobrovskaya died September 25, but Ukhtomsky still refused to go. There is not a single notation in his notebooks of any of his physical problems, although by October he could hardly swallow.

An old friend, A. I. Kolotilov, asked him why he did not leave Leningrad.

"I remain in Leningrad," he said, "in order to finish my work. I haven't long to live. I will die here. It's too late to leave."

The university organized a meeting on December 2 to mark the fiftieth anniversary of Lenin's graduation. It was held in the assembly hall. The electricity was working. From somewhere flowers had been produced for the platform. But the windows were broken, icy winds filled the chamber, and there were snowdrifts on the floor. Air-raid sirens sounded during the meeting, and there were occasional explosions of German shells.

Although he was now suffering from emphysema, although his toes were gangrenous and his cancer much worse, Ukhtomsky spoke with such vigor that participants counted his address one of his most striking.

Somehow Ukhtomsky managed to survive the winter, frequently giving lectures in the icebound university halls. He told his friends, "It's gloomy at home. It's more cheerful with people."

By the end of spring he was still alive and on June 27, despite his gangrene, his cancer, his emphysema and his hypertension, made his way on foot from his flat on the 16th Line of Vasilevsky Island to the Zoological Institute, where with half a dozen other academic colleagues he discussed the candidate dissertations of V. V. Kuznetsov and L. K. Mishchenko and acted as the official opponent of N. N. Malyshev, who was defending a doctoral thesis on the subject, "Materials on the Physics of Electrons." The presentation and defense of doctoral dissertations had gone on without pause in Leningrad, all through the terrible winter, in air-raid shelters, in cellars. There had been 847 defenses of dissertations in the first months of the war. In December the Leningrad Party Committee warned the academic community "not to permit any liberalization in evaluating the work of students" just because of the war and its hardships.

So the intellectual life of Leningrad went on; so the intellectuals kept to their laboratories and their libraries, dying by the hundreds but making no concession to the terrible enemies which threatened their existence.

To the end Professor Ukhtomsky continued to make notes, continued to talk with his students. Not until August 31, 1942, did he, like so many of his brave contemporaries, succumb. He was buried in the Volkov Cemetery. By this time Leningrad again observed the amenities. He had a grave and headstone of his own.

45 . The Ice Road to the Mainland

AT 3 A.M. ON FEBRUARY 2 PAVEL LUKNITSKY SAT AT THE typewriter in his freezing apartment at No. 9 Griboyedov Canal and tapped away on his diary. He was afraid to go to sleep lest he miss the ring of the telephone or the knock at the door he was expecting. He was waiting for a man named L. S. Shulgin from the Leningrad Tass office who would take him across Lake Ladoga to General Fedyuninsky's Fifty-fourth Army, to which he had just been assigned.

Luknitsky did not know it, but the assignment had been urgently arranged by his colleagues in the Writers Union who were fearful that unless he got out of Leningrad immediately he would die of starvation.[1]

For weeks Luknitsky had exhausted himself trying to help his fellow writers. Being a war correspondent, he was able to go in and out of Leningrad, and he had tried again and again to get permission to take a truck across Lake Ladoga on a foraging expedition to purchase provisions for the Leningrad writers. The difficulties were enormous. He had to get approval from half a dozen officials, and he needed someone to help buy the supplies. Unfortunately, he had become convinced that an honest man couldn't do the job, and he had no desire to go into partnership with a crook.

He had also been trying to persuade Smolny to send out of Leningrad some of the starving writers. And he had been seeking to evacuate his friend Lyudmila Fedorovna, who was at the point of death.

Finally, on January 20 he learned at Smolny of the impending plans for mass evacuation and with great difficulty succeeded in having twelve writers included in the first party to be sent out on January 22. He even got Lyudmila Fedorovna included in the first group of twelve. By this time he was so ill with grippe, so starved, he could hardly walk. But he had to go

[1] Luknitsky's assignment was arranged by Vera Ketlinskaya, secretary of the Writers Union, and N. D. Shumilov, a Party official at Smolny. Luknitsky learned the secret only eighteen years later when he found a notation to this effect in the unpublished papers of Vera Ketlinskaya. (Luknitsky, *op. cit.*, p. 700.)

back and forth between the Writers' House, his own apartment and Smolny to arrange for the evacuation tickets. They were supposed to be issued January 21 at 6 P.M. Some people had been waiting in line for them at Smolny since 2 A.M. At 7 P.M. the tickets still had not been issued because they had not been received from the printers. At 7:30 P.M. it was announced that instead of fifty buses for evacuation there would be only twenty-five. Only half of the people would be taken.

Luknitsky made thirty to forty telephone calls to Mayor Popkov and other officials and finally got the writers included in the smaller evacuation party. He then walked home in 30-below-zero weather, six to eight miles, in order to pack fifty pounds of luggage for Lyudmila Fedorovna and, after two and a half hours' sleep, brought her with the luggage on a sled to the embarkation point in the square opposite Smolny.

After hours of waiting in the cold the writers' group got away at 4 P.M. Luknitsky described eleven of those evacuated, including N. Vagner, S. Spassky and his wife, V. S. Valdman and her husband, as in "such condition that life hardly flickered in their bodies." The husband of Madame Valdman died in the bus. The twelfth person showed up in the cab of a truck overloaded with his possessions. He was healthy, insolent and gnawed unembarrassedly at a chicken bone. He pushed his way onto the bus, impudently stowing his bags and boxes over the heads of the feeble passengers.

As the convoy pulled out, 150 to 200 despairing persons watched. They had been promised places, but there was no room.

Luknitsky was so exhausted that he was hardly able to rise on January 23. But he had again to walk to the ends of the city, wait long hours at the military offices, obtain a new food order, stand in line in an unheated staff building where clerks worked without lights, and walk home skirting an enormous half-frozen lake (a water main had burst) which covered the squares opposite Dobrolyubov Prospekt and Dynamo Stadium, in which trucks were already being frozen for the remainder of winter. The next day he had a temperature of 102. He probably would have died that day had not an old friend, the chief of the regional air service, Korolev, taken him in hand, put him to bed in a warm room, given him a bath, 150 grams of vodka and a meal. He spent three days at the air base, and when he got back to the Writers' House, his associates had obtained his assignment to the Fifty-fourth Army.

It was for this reason that he sat in his freezing fifth-floor apartment, keeping himself awake by typing. He sat and sat. No one came. At 8:30 A.M., deathly tired, he tried to telephone, but the apparatus was not working. He pinned a note on his door saying: "Knock loud." Wrapping himself in his bedclothes, he sank back asleep. He had hardly closed his eyes when the Tass man, Shulgin, appeared. Hiding his typewriter behind the books in his study, and grabbing his knapsack, blanket roll, kettle, hand grenades and a candle stub, Luknitsky locked his apartment and hurried down the ice-treaded staircase to the street.

It was 9 A.M. Across the canal stood a 3-ton AMO truck, covered with a canvas top, camouflaged with white paint. The body was filled with boxes and people. It appeared that Shulgin, under the guise of taking a correspondent to the front, was evacuating from Leningrad all his close —and distant—relatives, including three half-crazy old aunts. There were, in all, fourteen persons in the truck, among them only two or three who were relatives of Tass men other than Shulgin.

It developed that the truck belonged to a tobacco factory where the chauffeur, Aleksandr Yakovlevich, worked. Shulgin had provided himself with a box of cigarettes and vodka and counted on acquiring gasoline en route from drivers of tank trucks coming across the lake. He planned to get his relatives out of Leningrad and return with a truckload of goods for sale in the black market.

The expedition started at 9:30. First, they had to get water for the radiator. Griboyedov Canal was frozen to the bottom, so they went to the Fontanka. While the chauffeur filled the radiator, Shulgin raced to a nearby house and picked up another relative.

The truck made its way through the drifted streets of Leningrad, past the sleds, the corpses, the long bread lines, past women lugging heavy pots and pails of water, and crossed the Neva by the Okhta Bridge, moving out Vsevolozhsky, meeting more and more military traffic, passing dozens of burned-out and abandoned carcasses of trucks. All trucks heading for the lake carried passengers, most of them people who had bribed the drivers. There were heated buses with *burzhuiki* and tin chimneys through the roof, canvas-covered trucks, and open trucks filled with exhausted people trying to keep out of the wind. There were even people clinging to the outside of gasoline tank trucks or lying one atop the other in the open trucks, wrapped like mummies, with telltale red and white frost marks on their cheeks, already half dead. Many refugees would not live to reach Lake Ladoga. There were some people slugging along on foot, pulling sleds with household goods. Here and there Luknitsky saw a man or woman collapsed in a drift, dead or dying while the survivors of the party huddled helpless around. No one had the strength to bury these victims. They simply removed the heavy clothing and any valuables, covered the body with snow and went on. As they neared the lake, they had to avoid the patrols—evacuation on foot was not permitted. Or they bribed the guards with cigarettes and tobacco to look the other way while they persuaded a chauffeur to take them across the lake. Everything depended on the chauffeurs. They were the lords of the lake, gods. They brought the food and fuel to Leningrad. The law was stern. For any kind of speculation or swindling they could be shot. But they had no fear. They demanded from the starving evacuees cigarettes or bread or a handful of flour.

The road was narrow, with hardly room to pass, and if a car got off the ruts, it was likely to land upside down in a ditch and the passengers would be left to try to make their way forward on foot with failing strength.

Luknitsky's truck moved slowly and finally halted altogether when a tie-up brought the column to a halt. They started again and arrived at Borisova Griva, the railroad station. Everywhere lay abandoned and broken-down trucks. At the station there were thousands of boxes of flour and a chain of hundreds, possibly thousands, of trucks, like a conveyor belt, bringing new loads to the station, unloading and then turning about for the return trip across the Ladoga to Zhikharevo. To the right of the road was a sign: "Bor. Griva from Leningrad—50 kilometers. From Lake 18." Luknitsky's truck halted for nearly two hours at Borisova Griva while the traffic was untangled. Luknitsky was fiercely hungry. A traffic officer took a quarter-loaf of bread from his pocket and held it ostentatiously in his hands, obviously wanting to trade it for a pack of cigarettes. Shulgin finally gave him twenty cigarettes and took the bread. He gave a piece to a three-year-old girl in the truck who was crying with hunger. Luknitsky got a morsel, and Shulgin ate the rest himself. Shulgin had a bottle of vodka, which he shared with the chauffeur and a friend. He did not offer a drink to Luknitsky. But Luknitsky had his own flask, so he took a slug without offering it to the others.

Finally, the column moved on, and Shulgin went to present a letter to the commissar of a truck company who was supposed to give them fuel and dinner. The commissar provided some cigarettes but refused to supply dinner. Instead, he offered four pieces of bread, about 350 grams. Shulgin took one piece and gave the others to Luknitsky, the chauffeur and his friend. One of Shulgin's aunts traded twenty cigarettes for a half-kettle of hot cereal. The truck went on. They reached Ladoga and saw ahead endless columns of trucks. Beside the road were antiaircraft batteries in shelters made of ice blocks. At 5:12 P.M. they started out on the ice, going full speed. The road was wide enough so that trucks could pass on either side. Everyone went full speed and the road extended into white infinity, a bit, thought Luknitsky, like the steppes of Kazakhstan. On either side there were high snow walls thrown up by the snow scrapers. At each kilometer stood a traffic officer in white camouflage cape with white and red traffic flags. The officers were protected from the wind by half-shelters made of ice blocks. Some had fires inside their ice blocks, stacks of wood and barrels of gasoline. At greater intervals there were repair shops, traffic centers and white-camouflaged antiaircraft posts. Here and there, half covered with ice and snow, lay the carcasses of broken or burned trucks.

As darkness fell, the traffic officers brought into play tiny green and white signal lights. Many trucks did not dim their lights, and the flash of headlights played over the snow and ice. Luknitsky's truck ran swiftly without lights and within an hour and a half had reached the eastern shore. The radiator was steaming, and Shulgin's friend got some water to fill it. The friend proudly showed Shulgin a small package. "Sweet butter!" he said. "I got it for five cigarettes." But it turned out to be a bar of household soap.

They had arrived at Lavrovo, but their goal was Zhikharevo. This took another hour and a half by moonlight. At Zhikharevo they expected a warm room, food and rest. They found chaos. There were thousands of persons wandering about the tiny war-beaten village. No one knew where there was a lunchroom, where documents could be obtained for the evacuation trains, when the train might be leaving, where you could stay overnight or even where to get warm.

Luknitsky finally located the evacuation office in a broken-down barracks. A long line waited while three men checked documents and issued coupons for the dining room.

Luknitsky discovered, however, that the coupons were only for those being officially evacuated. No provision for persons on military orders like himself or for Shulgin or the chauffeur or Shulgin's relatives. Somehow Shulgin got a meal ticket and then took his relatives to the station. A train was being loaded, but there was no room for the relatives, who became hysterical. They had no place to stay the night. The moon shone down and the thermometer stood at 20 below zero. Luknitsky eventually met the military commandant and got some dry rations for two days—750 grams of hardtack, 70 grams of granulated sugar and a packet of concentrated pea soup. But he needed hot food. Eventually, he stumbled on a kitchen where he could trade some dry rations for a bowl of hot wheat cereal. But there was no place to eat. The cereal was ladled out in an outdoor booth. So he sat down on the icy step of a barn and, half frozen, ate his cereal, holding his spoon with numb fingers, and downed the hot kasha with gulps of the icy wind. If only there had been some tea!

Somehow Shulgin got food for his relatives and, using the food coupons of two persons who had died, he got bread and dinner for himself. It was now almost 1 A.M., and Luknitsky had no place to sleep and had yet to find a place to get warm. There were hundreds like himself, wandering the wet, slippery, icy, rutted streets of the village—women and children, weak, collapsing, frozen.

There were, Luknitsky discovered, two persons in charge of the refugees —the commandant of the evacuation center, Semenov, and the chief of transfer, Streltsov. Both had been sent out by the Leningrad City Party, and they lived in room No. 6 of one of the barracks. Luknitsky spent the night on the floor of room No. 6, sleeping on a piece of plywood. The two men were working themselves to the bone. They slept two or three hours a night, on a wooden bench in their clothes, never undressing, trying to cope with the torrent of people who poured from the trucks day and night. They had no means of looking after the refugees. There was no hot water for tea, no plank beds, no mattresses, no lights, nothing but bare barracks with dirty floors. No doctors, no cleaning women, no personnel of any kind. All that was being done was to put people into trucks and deliver them to Zhikharevo.

That night the three-year-old girl who had come in Luknitsky's truck died. The wails of her mother filled the barracks. Then an engineer died, and his wife, composed and quiet, came to room No. 6 to find out what the formalities were. None, Semenov said. The body should be taken out of the barracks and put on the street with the other bodies. The wife didn't think she could move it. Perhaps, Semenov said, some of those in the barracks would help. If she wished, she could report the death to the police, giving them the name, the date and the address. The woman went back to the barracks, woke up some of those sleeping there and moved the corpse. Then another man died in the corridor. People just stepped over the body in the darkness.

Streltsov and Semenov had been sent out with the first evacuees January 22. The only word they had from Leningrad so far was that thirty cleaning women were being sent on foot. Why on foot and why from Leningrad there was no explanation. Nothing had been done to provide the evacuees with food for their trip.

Shulgin managed to get his relatives onto a warm, clean evacuation train, and the journey to take Luknitsky to the Fifty-fourth Army headquarters resumed. They drove through Voibokalo and Shum, only to find that General Fedyuninsky's headquarters were at Gorokhovets, twenty-two miles distant. Shulgin refused to take Luknitsky any further. However, after much argument Luknitsky managed to get to the village of Vloya, within Fifty-fourth Army territory. There he parted with Shulgin, who was in a feverish hurry to go to Volkhov, where he had "business" to transact before going back to Leningrad.

He told Luknitsky that he had never gone hungry during the blockade, that he had always managed to feed his relatives and that he looked forward to a time at the end of the war when the government would "re-examine its attitude toward private property and private trade." Never before or after, during the war did Luknitsky meet such a man.

There was little that was unusual about Luknitsky's trip across Ladoga. Not even the presence of Shulgin. The road attracted profiteers and black market operators. Sometimes speculators from Leningrad offered as much as 25,000 rubles a box for flour. Usually, the drivers refused the offers angrily. Sometimes the speculators were arrested and shot. Other drivers, however, engaged in black market dealings. A driver named Sergei Loginov found a friend and fellow Young Communist chauffeur who had turned off the ice road and was burying boxes of provisions in the snow. After an argument Loginov shot and killed the man.

Madame Skryabina made the Ladoga trip four days after Luknitsky. She took her seventy-four-year-old mother, so weak it did not seem possible that she would survive; a sixty-year-old nurse, with swollen feet, hardly able to walk; her son Dima, sixteen years old and suffering from an advanced case of dysentery, and her youngest child, Yuri, five years old.

Madame Skryabina rose early on February 6. She went to the bakery, got the day's rations, and when she got back to the communal flat, she found the former mistress of the apartment, Anastasiya Vladimirovna, had just died. There was nothing to do but to leave as planned. There were three trucks in the convoy and thirty people in the three cars. They waited three hours in the cold for one family, that of a hospital manager. Madame Skryabina was shocked at the appearance of this family—a wife, dressed as if for a ball, two healthy teen-age girls and another girl with a governess. Obviously, they had suffered little.

Finally, the caravan started out the Znamenskaya, past Kirochnaya, the Tauride Gardens, the Pedagogical Institute, Smolny, and through the suburban summer resort country toward Ladoga. Then the trouble started. Something went wrong with the truck. It halted on the ice, and dusk began to fall. The chauffeur worked for hours over the machine. Fortunately, there was a big drum of gasoline in the truck. They drew off some gas, lighted a fire and warmed themselves. But it was 10 P.M. when they got to the opposite shore. No one knew where to go, where the train was, when it would leave. The night was one long torment. The chauffeur found lodging in a peasant hut, but the evacuees stayed in the truck. By this time Dima was so weak that Madame Skryabina had to leave him in the hospital at Voibokalo. She took her two elderly companions and Yuri and tried to find a place in the crowded evacuation train. There were no seats, and they had to sit on their suitcases. As they sat, weary and forlorn, the hospital manager's wife brought out fried chicken, chocolate and powdered milk and fed her girls. Madame Skryabina had nothing but ersatz bread to give Yuri. She felt spasms in her throat, but not, she noted, "from hunger."

The train moved slowly through the night, stopping occasionally. At each stop someone would come along, knocking on the door with a hammer: "Have you any dead? Throw them out here!" But there was food at some of the long station stops—soup and cereal. The evacuees developed stomach complaints, probably because they were not used to eating. This went on for four days. Madame Skryabina decided she could go no farther. She would have to take her group from the train. They got off at Cherepovets. Her mother had collapsed. Also, Madame Skryabina hoped that she might get word from here of Dima in the hospital at Voibokalo. They got off and found themselves surrounded by snowdrifts. The townsfolk expressed surprise they had gotten off the train. Cherepovets was suffering a terrible food shortage. Madame Skryabina finally found a dirty little room, but it was not easy. Everyone was frightened of Leningraders. They were so hungry and so ill. She put her mother and the old nurse in a cold, filthy hospital. The women grew worse and worse. One day they told Madame Skryabina of the death during the night of a young engineer and his wife. The same day four students who had been brought in late at night were found dead in the hospital corridors where they had been laid. There was no food in the local

market except *klukva* (cranberries) picked in the local bogs. Madame Skryabina was able to obtain some potatoes from a peasant by trading a piece
of wool. On February 27 she found her mother dead in the hospital. She
could not get the body buried. No one bothered with that any more. They
simply piled the corpses at the cemetery gates.

In mid-March by a stroke of sheer luck (a tearful conversation at the
station with a soldier on a hospital train) she was reunited with her son
Dima and managed to join him on the train with Yuri and the old nurse
and leave Cherepovets. The family was saved. The train took them out
beyond Vologda and eventually to Gorky.

Slowly the evacuation improved as February progressed. The elapsed time
between Leningrad and Borisova Griva was cut to five or six hours, the
transfer from train to trucks and buses to one and a half to two hours, the
crossing of Ladoga to two to two and a half hours (although during snow-
storms it sometimes took seven hours). From January 22 to April 15, a total
of 554,186 persons were removed over Ladoga, including 35,713 wounded
Red Army men.

Late in February Vera Inber made the trip over Ladoga to General
Fedyuninsky's headquarters with a delegation. They rode in a truck which
had panel sides, a canvas top and an open end. They sat on wooden benches,
very uncomfortable, very cold, very exhausting. She hardly had the strength
to survive. A few days before in trying to walk across Leningrad to a poetry
reading before a naval detachment she had collapsed.

It took them only an hour and a half to cross Ladoga, but the whole trip
from Leningrad to Fedyuninsky's headquarters at Gorokhovets took thirteen
hours. On the eastern shore she saw goats, dogs and live chickens for the
first time in months. It was like a miracle. And she heard people singing.
No one in Leningrad had sung since the start of winter. People walked
briskly, breathed the sharp air deeply and blew out their frosty breaths.
Their cheeks were ruddy and glowing. Vera Inber and her companions
looked like pale, slow, whispering shadows.

At Zhikharevo she saw a terrible fire. Nazi bombers were attacking the
supply dumps and had hit a great kerosene tank and a train of coal cars.
She had never seen such flames—purple, crimson, yellow, and smoke so
black it weighted down the air.

To Vera Inber the Ladoga seemed a vast plain of ice, as covered with
snow as the North Pole—ice fences, ice enclosures, circular ice Eskimo
huts for the antiaircraft crews, ice bases on which the antiaircraft guns were
installed. Everything was snow. Everything was white.

Along the route were the skeletons of dead cars, the wrecked trucks and
machines sacrificed to the ceaseless flow of supplies. Day and night the
movement never halted, swift, ordered, relentless, despite Nazi planes,
despite the terrible *burya*, the Ladoga blizzards, despite the temperature
which fell to 30 and 40 below zero.

The Ladoga route had been brought into order. It was in constant flow, food and fuel pouring into Leningrad, people pouring out.

In a dugout Vera Inber sat with a division commander. It was so warm near the little iron stove that two or three birch shoots had pushed through the earthen walls and begun to sprout a few tender leaves. They drank a toast to the liberation of Leningrad, and the commissar said, "To live or not live—that is not the question. Our life belongs to Leningrad."

46 ◆ *Death, Death, Death*

PAVEL LUKNITSKY RETURNED TO LENINGRAD FROM THE Fifty-fourth Army on March 5, improved in health and spirits. He drove almost directly to his home. As he entered Cheboksarsky Pereulok, a woman walked toward him in the dusk, chanting a lament: "Death! Death! Death!"

As she came nearer, she stared at Luknitsky with unseeing eyes and continued her monologue. He heard her say, "Death by starvation will take us all. The soldiers will live a while longer. But we will die. We will die. We will die."

The woman passed him like a terrified spirit.

It was hardly an auspicious welcome, but Luknitsky threw over his shoulders his two big knapsacks, filled with food and supplies brought back from the "mainland," and climbed the five flights to his apartment. Everything was in order—except that the roof had been blasted off.

Death stalked Leningrad at winter's end.

The city was filled with corpses. They lay by the thousands on the streets, in the ice, in the snowdrifts, in the courtyards and cellars of the great apartment houses. The city and Party authorities were preparing to launch an enormous spring clean-up. But V. N. Ivanov, secretary of the Young Communists, was afraid of the psychological effect on his young boys and girls when they confronted the mountains of frozen, decayed and disintegrating bodies.

On one March night a sanitary brigade drove up to the courtyard "morgue" at the Hermitage and carted off forty-six bodies to the Piskarevsky Cemetery. There were corpses in the gardens of the Anichkov Palace, now the Palace of Pioneers, on the Fontanka and in the vaults of the Alexandrinsky Theater. There were twenty-four bodies in the Nikolsky Cathedral, awaiting delivery to a cemetery—one in a coffin, twenty-three wrapped in sheets and rags. Bodies had piled up in the hospitals. In many institutions the doctors and nursing personnel were too ill or weak to care for patients. There had been 6,500 doctors in Leningrad at the start of the war. By January 1 there were only 3,379 and by April 1 only 3,288. Leningrad lost 195 doctors from January 1 to March 15.

Illness was as widespread as death. In one big factory 55 percent of the workers were on sick call in January (mostly starving), 61 percent in February and 59 percent in March. On February 20 only 2,416 of 10,424 workers at the Kirov metallurgical works reported for duty—23 percent. The Kirov works lost 3,063 workers by death in 1942. Of 6,000 on the Kirov rolls in March and April, 2,300 died.

Scurvy was universal. Professor A. D. Bezzubov invented a process for extracting vitamin C from pine needles. Eight factories were put to work making pine-needle extract, and 16,200,000 doses were produced in 1942.

Even more critical threats appeared. Typhus broke out in a children's home at the corner of Mozhaisky Street and Zagorodny Prospekt in late February. The house was cordoned off. Only persons with medical clearance were permitted in and out. Fortunately, the epidemic was contained. Another case of suspected typhus appeared in the student dormitory at Erisman Hospital.

A special epidemiology committee was set up under Mayor Peter S. Popkov, and mass inoculation of the population was undertaken. By mid-March half a million Leningraders had been inoculated against typhus, typhoid and plague. More than four hundred disinfecting points were at work by April 10 and two thousand beds for contagious diseases were provided in children's homes.

The city was choked with filth. The lunchrooms and cafeterias where many Leningraders were fed were so dirty they defied imagination. Dishes and tableware had not been washed for weeks. Often food was served in tin cans. Dishes were shoved to the feeble customers without spoons or forks. They could eat with their fingers or lap it up like dogs. The City Party Committee, fearful of a general epidemic, ordered special measures to clean up all food dispensaries.

The people were as dirty as their eating halls. There had been no baths, showers or laundries in the city since the end of December. Now they began to reopen, and by the end of March twenty-five baths were operating—at least on paper. In the second quarter of 1942 thirty-two baths and a hundred laundries were reopened.

But the big task was to clean the city. Unless the corpses, filth and debris could be removed, Leningrad would perish in the epidemics of spring. The job started on March 8, International Women's Day, a traditional holiday, a day when every woman in Russia expects to get a present from every man who is close or dear to her—husband, brother, son, lover, father or friend.

This year it was a different kind of March 8. Several thousand women, spades and picks in hand, tackled the ice-clad streets. Vsevolod Vishnevsky made a typical note in his diary: "The city had a clean-up day. Cleaning up snow, streetcar routes, courtyards. People worked with enthusiasm. Belief in victory stirs them!"

That wasn't exactly how it seemed to Maria Razina. A concert had been arranged for the evening, but she and her friend Liza were so tired and weak they could hardly walk there. It was frigid in the meeting hall. There were speeches and reports. Through an open door they could see a table set for dinner. No one wanted to hear the concert. All they wanted was to eat. A shivering young woman in an evening dress sang "The Lark." Then the audience shouted, "Enough! Get dressed!" They trooped in to dinner—a piece of black bread, about 150 grams, two slices of sausage, a white roll and two apples. Later there was hot tea. They walked home beside the Neva. The snow was as high as a mountain. The two women agreed that the city must be cleaned and rapidly.

The job really got under way March 15 when more than 100,000 Leningraders turned out. Then on March 26 the City Council ordered all able-bodied Leningraders into the streets. Posters went up. The radio blared an appeal. On the first day 143,000 feeble, tottering men and women (mostly women) went into the streets. The next day there were 244,000; by March 31, 304,000; and by April 4, 318,000. Between March 27 and April 15, 12,000 courtyards were cleaned up, 3,000,000 square yards of streets were cleared and 1,000,000 tons of filth were removed.

Everyone went into the streets—old women, men hardly able to hold a shovel, children.

One of them was Hilma Stepanovna Hannalainen. She had worked all winter in the great Leningrad Public Library. The library never closed. In the basement the main catalogue had been set up adjacent to a small public reading room. Almost every day one or two hundred persons could be found there, sitting in fur hats and overcoats, huddled over books, reading by the light of small oil lamps. The librarians sent books to the hospitals. They answered a thousand questions put to them by the military and civil authorities: How could Leningrad make matches? How could flint and steel lighters be manufactured? What materials were needed for candles? Was there any way of making yeast, edible wood, artificial vitamins? How do you make soap? The librarians found recipes for candles in old works of the eighteenth century.

The library lost its light and heat January 26 and had to close the one reading room which had remained open. However, readers were permitted to use the director's room and one or two other small rooms where there were temporary stoves. In May a general reading room was opened again. The library lost 138 of its staff during the war, most of them in the winter of 1941–42.

One of those who worked day after day quietly and without complaint was Hilma Stepanovna. She was not alone. With her was her five-year-old son Edik. Edik was solemn, serious, strong, square-faced, silent, solid—very much like his mother. He came each day. While his mother was busy with the catalogue, moving between the aisles, Edik sat on a stool, swathed in heavy coat, felt boots, fur hat. He never spoke and his eyes never left his mother. If one wanted to know into which aisle Hilma had vanished, one had only to look at Edik. His eyes focused on the spot where she had disappeared and did not leave it until she reappeared.

When the call came to clean the streets, Hilma Stepanovna and the library workers answered it. They gathered in Stremyanny Lane. There was a mountainous heap of rubbish and at the bottom of it the very well-preserved body of a young man. It was frozen so hard that an iron crowbar hardly made a dent.

Standing to one side, his eyes on his mother, was Edik. He never moved despite the cold.

A few days after the mountain on Stremyanny Lane had been cleared away Hilma Stepanovna disappeared. So did Edik. At first it was said they had been evacuated to the rear. Then the truth slipped out.

They had been arrested as "enemies of the people"—this strong, solid woman and her strong, solid five-year-old. Despite the blockade, despite Leningrad's hardships, the vigilant secret police had not been inactive. They managed to send the mother and boy out of the besieged city to distant exile in Siberia. The reason was a conventional one in Stalin's Russia. Her husband had been an editor of a Karelo-Finnish paper who was executed at the time of the winter war with Finland, and his wife and son had been left behind in Leningrad. For reasons known only to themselves, the police at the end of the cruel winter of 1941–42 decided to send Hilma Stepanovna and the youngster into exile. Thus began a wandering life that lasted more than twenty years. In 1945 Hilma tried to return to Leningrad but was ordered out of the city on twenty-four hours' notice. She was permitted to live for a while in Estonia and then in Petrozavodsk. Not until 1964, nearly twenty-five years after her husband had been executed, was he formally "rehabilitated" by the Soviet authorities. Once again Hilma Stepanovna tried to return to Leningrad and once again she was refused permission to live in the city. She had lost her hearing in a bomb explosion during the Leningrad blockade and was completely deaf. In these conditions she found life very difficult.[1]

It was not only filth that had accumulated in Leningrad's streets. The life of the city had ground to a halt. It had been months since mail or telegrams had been delivered. Nikolai Mikhailovsky and Anatoly Tarasenkov went to the central post office one day to see if there was any mail for the fleet newspaper from the "mainland." They were halted at the door by an armed guard.

"What do you want?" the guard said angrily.

[1] Her case was taken up by the Young Communist magazine *Yunost* in 1965. After publishing an exposé the magazine directed an appeal to the Leningrad authorities to display some consideration for Hilma Stepanovna. Whether the appeal was heeded is not known. (*Yunost*, No. 5, May, 1965, pp. 97–99.)

"We are looking for our mail," they said.

"What kind of mail?" the guard asked in surprise.

"Ordinary mail."

"One of you can come along," he said, "and you can find out."

Tarasenkov came back shaken. The great hall of the main post office was filled with thousands of boxes of mail. There were post bags halfway to the ceiling—all in disorder, the building unheated, unlighted, no one at work.

By March the jam almost burst the building. There were 280,000 boxes of mail, unsorted, stacked in disorder in corridors and halls. Communist Youth brigades were sent to the post office to try to move the accumulation. The first mail and telegrams in months were delivered March 8—about sixty thousand pieces—but it was a year before the backlog was cleared up. Sometimes the youngsters who tried to deliver the mail were badly shaken. One young Komsomol girl took a letter to deliver. She found everyone dead in the apartment of the addressee. She went back to the post office. It was locked, and there was no one to tell her what to do.

A woman who had gotten no letters for a year came home one night to find her mailbox full. She started to read, beginning with the first letter from her husband. She read the letters, one by one. Then she opened the last letter and fainted. It was from her husband's commander, and it told of his death.

On April 11 Mayor Popkov signed an order directing the Streetcar Administration to establish normal operations on trolley routes No. 3, No. 7, No. 9, No. 10 and No. 12 at 6:30 A.M., April 15. (Routes No. 3 and No. 9 took you to the front.) The Streetcar Administration was not certain it could meet the directive, but by strenuous efforts 116 cars were sent out of the barns at 6 A.M. April 15. The sound of streetcar bells, the clatter of the cars over the rails, the sharp burst of sparks at the crossings, sent Leningrad wild. People cried on the Nevsky at the sight. "Really!" one exclaimed. "I rode the streetcar! I couldn't believe it. It seemed like I hadn't been on a tram for ten years."

A German prisoner, Corporal Falkenhorst, told his captors he had lost faith in Hitler when he heard the sound of streetcars in the Leningrad streets on the morning of April 15.

"The city again is lively," Vishnevsky wrote. "A Red Army unit, probably convalescents, came by with a band. So surprising, so strange, after Leningrad's quiet. Streetcars are moving, jammed with passengers. On Bolshoi Prospekt there is trade and exchange. Money will buy more than in winter. Many are selling clothing—of the dead."

Actually, black market prices had risen a little. A packet of cigarettes would buy 150 grams of bread—against 200 grams a bit earlier. Bread sold at 60 rubles for 100 grams. The speculators were calculating that soon the ice on Lake Ladoga would go out and that supplies would be short, at least for a time. People still posted notices on walls that they would trade mahogany beds and Bekker pianos for bread.

The tensions in Leningrad had not lightened. Vishnevsky felt the strain, heightened by what he called "intrigues and lack of understanding." He did not spell out what he meant, but he was having difficulty getting approval of a script for the *Leningrad in Battle* film, and Ivan (the Terrible) Rogov, the Navy Political Commissar, had come to town. Vishnevsky noted that "evidently there are deep nervous marks left from the literary dramas and wounds of 1930–1937–1938." What Vishnevsky was hinting was that the fatal quarrels, feuds and purges of the thirties had continued through the most horrible moments of the war.

Vera Inber found that winter's end brought most difficult times. She was deathly concerned about her husband, the physician Ilya Strashun. She had never seen such colors as appeared in his face—dust yellow with red spots. He was walking with a cane because he had a badly swollen foot. She feared he had been exposed to typhus in treating a student in the dormitory. The toll of death around her was rising more rapidly than ever—a good friend, Professor P.; the husband of Yevfrosinya Ivanovna; another friend named Dina Osipovna. She felt so exhausted. She was not afraid of bombs, shells or hunger but of spiritual exhaustion, of the limits of weariness at which you begin to hate things, sounds and objects. She worried that her nerves would give out and that she would be unable to write. She decided to sleep in another room, hers was so cold. She lay down on a divan. But she could not sleep. She kept thinking of a friend, now dead, who had slept there. At 1 A.M. she heard distant bombardment, but she got the feeling that it was actually an air raid and that she had not heard the alarm. In the strange room she fell into such terror as she had never experienced. She began to tremble. Finally, she woke up her husband. He said, "It's nonsense, dear." It did not seem so to her. She ran down to the shelter. It was locked. The night was bright as day—a full moon on the snow. She went back to her room and tried to read a French novel. Nothing worked. The panic went on the next day. Her strength was at the breaking point.

In this fateful atmosphere the first steps were being taken to put Leningrad back onto its feet. Party Secretary Kuznetsov called his regional Party chiefs, heads of factory units and directors of institutions to Smolny March 9. He told them the city must begin immediately to produce basic military supplies—shells, ammunition, mines. Power stations began to work again. New generators went into operation at the 5th and 1st Power Stations. Beginning March 20 the city got 550,000 kilowatt hours of power—more than three times the February rate.

The Party re-established its ties with the outer world. A delegation of partisans from the Leningrad region emerged from the marshes and forests. It was met at Kobona, on the eastern edge of Lake Ladoga, by Aleksei Kosygin, in charge of the Ladoga evacuation, Party Secretary Kuznetsov and other Leningrad officials. The partisans came into Leningrad for a meeting at Smolny with Zhdanov and the Leningrad Military Command. Delegations from Soviet cities began to arrive. A Moscow Young Communist group came in, headed by the Moscow City Young Communist chief, A. N. Shelepin, now a member of the Soviet Politburo.

The Chief of Artistic Affairs in Leningrad, B. I. Zagursky, was confined to his bed in a tiny room in the Bolshoi Drama Theater at the end of winter 1942. Nonetheless, he called in Karl I. Eliasberg, director of the Radio Committee orchestra. Eliasberg and his wife were suffering from dystrophy and were being treated in the *statsionar* on the seventh floor of the Astoria Hotel. Not since early December had there been a concert in Leningrad. Eliasberg brought with him a list of his orchestra members. Twenty-seven names were underlined in black pencil. They were dead. Most of the others were underlined in red. They were near death from dystrophy. Eight names were not underlined. They were available to play.

A few days later an announcement was made on the radio that a symphony orchestra was being formed. Volunteers were asked. Toward the end of March about thirty musicians gathered for rehearsal. These were all the able-bodied musicians in Leningrad.

The first concert was given April 5 in the Pushkin Drama Theater. (The Philharmonic Hall had been hit by a shell and was not yet repaired.) The performance started at 7 P.M., after the Musical Comedy Theater's presentation of *Silva* had finished.

Eliasberg appeared on the rostrum in a starched shirt and tail coat. Underneath he wore a cotton-padded jacket. He stood firm and tall, although he had to be helped to the theater. He had gone from the Astoria to his home on Vasilevsky Island to pick up the shirt and suit. A German artillery attack started. Had he not been given a lift by a Baltic Fleet commissar, he might not have made it. The concert was not long. The artists were too weak for a full presentation. They played Glazunov's Triumphal Overture, excerpts from *Swan Lake*, an aria sung by Nadezhda Velter, and concluded with the Overture to *Ruslan and Ludmilla*.

The Road of Life was coming to an end. Day by day with the advance of spring the ice became more spongy, the danger of breakthroughs more likely. Evacuation of refugees from Leningrad by the ice road was halted April 12 by Kosygin. He reported to the State Defense Committee that from January 22 to April 12 he had removed from Leningrad a total of 539,400 persons, including workers, employees, families and military personnel, 347,564; trade school pupils, 28,454; students, scientific workers, professors and teachers and their families, 42,319; orphans, 12,639; peasants from Karelia, 26,974; wounded, 40,986; plus 15,152 tons of valuable machinery and supplies.[2]

---

[2] *N.Z.*, pp. 340–341. Slightly differing totals are given by others. Karasev makes it 554,186 (p. 200). The same figure is given by *900* (p. 106). Pavlov makes it 514,069 (*op. cit.*, 3rd edition, p. 189.)

The ice road had continued to improve its performance. From November to April 24, when the last supplies came through, it delivered 356,109 tons of freight, including 271,106 tons of food. It built up in Leningrad reserves of flour for 58 days, cereals for 57 days, meat and fish for 140 days, sugar for 90 days, fats for 123 days.

The road delivered 52,934 tons in January, of which 42,588 tons were food. The average delivery was 1,708 tons a day. In February this was lifted to 86,041 tons, of which 67,198 tons were food. Average deliveries were 3,072 tons daily. In March a peak of 113,382 tons was reached, including 88,607 tons of food, a daily average of 3,660. The April total was 87,253 tons, including 57,588 tons of food, a daily average of 2,910 tons.

The road delivered 31,910 tons of military supplies and 37,717 tons of fuel.

The last supplies to come by ice road were onions. Three carloads arrived at the eastern base April 23. The road had been closed, but drivers worked through the twenty-third and twenty-fourth and managed to bring 65 tons of onions across the lake.

Leningrad got through the winter with no attention from the Luftwaffe. There had been no raids throughout January, February and March. However, the Nazi artillery had stayed active. In January 2,696 shells fell on Leningrad, in February 4,771, and in March 7,380. The bombardment killed 519 Leningraders and wounded 1,447.[3]

On April 15 Leningrad marked the 248th day of siege. The city had survived. But the cost had no equal in modern times. In March the Leningrad Funeral Trust buried 89,968 persons. In April the total rose to 102,497. Some of these burials were due to the clean-up, but the death rate was probably higher in April than in any other month of the blockade.

There now remained in Leningrad, with evacuation at an end, 1,100,000 persons.[4] The total of ration cards was 800,000 less than in January. When Leningrad's supply resources—the 58 days of flour, the 140 days of meat and fish—were calculated, it was on the basis of a population on April 15 only one-third what it had been when the blockade began August 30 with the loss of Mga.

More people had died in the Leningrad blockade than had ever died in a modern city—anywhere—anytime: more than ten times the number who died in Hiroshima.[5] By comparison with the great sieges of the past Leningrad was unique. The siege of Paris had lasted only 121 days, from

[3] The Germans resumed their air attacks on Leningrad in April. There were heavy actions April 4, 5, 14, 19, 20 and 23, directed primarily against the Baltic Fleet ships, still frozen in the Neva, and against Kronstadt and the heavy naval gun emplacements. (Panteleyev, *op. cit.*, pp. 309-315.) The attack of April 4 was the heaviest of the war. (*N.Z.*, p. 343.)

[4] Zhdanov used the same figure in July when proposing a further evacuation to bring the city's population down to a "military city" of 800,000. (Karasev, *op. cit.*, p. 254.)

[5] Deaths at Hiroshima August 6, 1945, were 78,150, with 13,983 missing and 37,426 wounded. In another tragedy of World War II, the Warsaw uprising, between 56,000 and 60,000 died.

September 19, 1870, to January 27, 1871. The total population, military and civilian, was on the order of one million. Noncombatant deaths from all causes in Paris during November, December and three weeks of January were only 30,236, about 16,000 higher than the number in the comparable period of the preceding year. The Parisians ate horses, mules, cats, dogs and possibly rats. There was a raid on the Paris zoo and a rhinoceros was killed and butchered. There were no authenticated instances of cannibalism. Food was scarce, but wine was plentiful.

In the great American siege, that of Vicksburg between May 18 and July 4, 1863, only 4,000 civilians were involved, although the Confederate military force was upwards of 30,000. About 2,500 persons were killed in the siege, including 119 women and children. No known deaths from starvation occurred. Horses, mules, dogs and kittens were eaten and possibly rats.

Leningrad exceeded the total Paris civil casualties on any two or three winter days. The Vicksburg casualties, military and civil, were exceeded in Leningrad by starvation deaths on any January, February, March or April day.

How many people died in the Leningrad blockade? Even with careful calculation the total may be inexact by several hundred thousand.

The most honest declaration was an official Soviet response to a Swedish official inquiry published in *Red Star*, the Soviet Army newspaper, June 28, 1964, which said: "No one knows exactly how many people died in Leningrad and the Leningrad area."

The original figure announced by the Soviet Government of deaths by starvation—civilian deaths by hunger in the city of Leningrad alone—was 632,253. An additional 16,747 persons were listed as killed by bombs and shells, providing a total of Leningrad civilian deaths of 649,000. To this were added deaths in nearby Pushkin and Peterhof, bringing the total of starvation deaths to 641,803 and of deaths from all war causes to 671,635. These figures were attested to by the Leningrad City Commission to Investigate Nazi Atrocities and were submitted at the Nuremberg Trials in 1946.

The Commission figures are incomplete in many respects. They do not cover many Leningrad areas, including Oranienbaum, Sestroretsk and the suburban parts of the blockade zone. Soviet sources no longer regard the Commission totals, which apparently were drawn up in May, 1944, as authoritative, although they were prepared by an elaborate apparatus of City and Regional Party officials, headed by Party Secretary Kuznetsov. A total of 6,445 local commissions carried out the task, and more than 31,000 persons took part. Individual lists of deaths were made up for each region. The regional lists carried 440,826 names, and a general city-wide list added 191,427 names, providing the basic Commission-reported total of 632,253.[6]

[6] The Commission report as published in the official Leningrad documentary compilation is dated "May, 1944," but the authoritative study of this document by V. M. Kovalchuk and G. L. Sobolev asserts it includes deaths reported to May, 1945. (*Voyenno-*

Impressive evidence has been compiled by Soviet scholars to demonstrate the incompleteness of the Commission's total. All official Leningrad statistics are necessarily inaccurate because of the terrible conditions of the winter of 1941–42. The official report of deaths for December, 53,000, may be fairly complete, but for January and February the figures are admittedly poor. Estimates of daily deaths in these months run from 3,500 to 4,000 a day[7] to 8,000. The only total available gives deaths for the period as 199,187. This is offered by Dmitri Pavlov. It represents deaths officially reported to authorities (probably in connection with the turning in of ration cards of the deceased). The number of unregistered deaths is known to be much higher. The Funeral Trust buried 89,968 bodies in March (it has no records for January and February), 102,497 in April and 53,562 in May. It continued to bury 4,000 to 5,000 bodies a month through the autumn of 1942, although by this time Leningrad's population had been cut by more than 75 percent. Thus mortality as a result of the blockade and starvation continued at a high rate through the whole year.

The Funeral Trust buried 460,000 bodies from November, 1941, to the end of 1942. In addition, it is estimated that private individuals, work teams of soldiers and others transported 228,263 bodies from morgues to cemeteries from December, 1941, through December, 1942.

No exact accounting of bodies delivered to cemeteries was possible in Leningrad during the winter months, when thousands of corpses lay in the streets and were picked up like cordwood, transported to Piskarevsky, Volkov, Tatar, Bolshaya Okhta, Serafimov, and Bogoslovsky cemeteries and to the large squares at Vesely Poselok (Jolly Village) and the Glinozemsky Zavod for burial in mass graves, dynamited in the frozen earth by military miners.

Leningrad had a civilian population of about 2,280,000 in January, 1942. By the close of evacuation via the ice road in April, 1942, the population was estimated at 1,100,000—a reduction of 1,180,000, of whom 440,000 had been evacuated via the ice road. Another 120,000 went to the front or were evacuated in May and June. This would indicate a minimum of deaths within the city of about 620,000 in the first half of 1942. Official statistics show that about 1,093,695 persons were buried and about 110,000 cremated from July, 1941, through July, 1942.

To take another approach. Leningrad had about 2,500,000 residents at the start of the blockade, including about 100,000 refugees. At the end of 1943

Istoricheskii Zhurnal, No. 12, December, 1965, p. 192.) The Commission was set up by decision of the Leningrad City and regional Party committees April 14, 1943. (Karasev, *op. cit.*, p. 12.) Among its members were Mayor Popkov, Chief Architect N. V. Baranov, Academicians A. A. Baikov, A. F. Ioffe, L. A. Orbeli, I. A. Orbeli, I. Ye. Grabar, A. V. Shchusev, and the writers, A. N. Tolstoy, N. S. Tikhonov, Vera Inber, Anna Akhmatova, Olga Forsh and Vsevolod Vishnevsky. (*Leningrad v VOV*, p. 690.)

[7] This is the estimate of two reliable and conservative Leningrad authorities. (Karasev, *op. cit.*, p. 184; N. D. Khudyakova, *Vsya Strana S Leningradom*, Leningrad, 1960, p. 57.)

as the 900 days were drawing to a close, Leningrad had a population of about 600,000—less than one-quarter the number of residents at the time Mga fell August 30, 1941.

The most careful calculation suggests that about 1,000,000 Leningraders were evacuated during the blockade: 33,479 by water across Ladoga in the fall of 1941; 35,114 by plane in November-December, 1941; 36,118 by the Ladoga ice road in December, 1941, and up to January 22, 1942; 440,000 by Ladoga from January 22 to April 15; 448,694 by Ladoga water transport from May to November, 1942; 15,000 during 1943. In addition, perhaps 100,000 Leningraders went to the front with the armed forces.

This suggests that not less than 800,000 persons died of starvation within Leningrad during the blockade.

But the 800,000 total does not include the thousands who died in the suburban regions and during evacuation. These totals were very large. For instance, at the tiny little station of Borisova Griva on Ladoga 2,200 persons died from January to April 15, 1942. The *Leningrad Encyclopedia* estimates deaths during evacuation at "tens of thousands."

What is the actual death total for Leningrad? Mikhail Dudin, a Leningrad poet who fought at Hangö and spent the whole of the siege within the lines at Leningrad, suggests that it was a minimum of 1,100,000. He offers this simple figure on the basis of 800,000 bodies estimated buried in mass graves at Piskarevsky Cemetery and 300,000 at Serafimov Cemetery. There is more than a little truth in the observation of the Leningrad poet, Sergei Davydov, regarding Piskarevsky: "Here lies half the city."

No official calculation includes a total for military deaths, and no official figures on these have been published. It is known, however, that 12,416 military deaths attributed to hunger diseases occurred in the winter of 1941–42. Over-all military deaths are likely to have ranged between 100,000 and 200,000 in the Leningrad fighting—possibly more.

One of the most careful Soviet specialists estimates the Leningrad starvation toll at "not less than a million," a conclusion shared by the present Leningrad Party leaders. *Pravda* on the twentieth anniversary of the lifting of the blockade declared that "the world has never known a similar mass extermination of a civilian population, such depths of human suffering and deprivation as fell to the lot of Leningraders."

Estimates of the Leningrad death toll as high as 2,000,000 have been made by some foreign students. These estimates are too high. A total for Leningrad and vicinity of something over 1,000,000 deaths attributable to hunger, and an over-all total of deaths, civilian and military, on the order of 1,300,000 to 1,500,000, seems reasonable.

It is germane, perhaps, to note that the Leningrad survivors of the blockade thought in January, 1944, that the starvation toll might be 2,000,000.[8]

The Soviet censors in 1944 refused to pass estimates stating the Leningrad death toll as 1,000,000 or 2,000,000. For nearly twenty years after

[8] This is what they told the author, who was present in Leningrad at the time.

the blockade they insisted the total was 632,253—not more, not less. Even today Dmitri V. Pavlov insists that new estimates, made by Soviet and foreign students, are incorrect. In a third edition of his magnificent *Leningrad v Blokade*, the best single source for many details of the siege, he incorporated an attack on the new totals. It is impossible, he insists, to remain silent in the face of assertions that a million or more people died in Leningrad. "Believe it or not," he insists, "there is no foundation for such serious conclusions." He insists that calculations based on the movement of Leningraders in and out of the city are unsound. He contends that the new estimates understate the number of Leningraders who entered military units (he puts the figure at not less than 200,000 rather than the 100,000 which Soviet authorities now use). He insists that the 632,253 calculation was accurate (he says it was completed in May, 1943, although the document is dated May, 1944, and other Soviet authorities contend it was not submitted until May, 1945).[9]

Pavlov concludes that "the life of the Leningraders was so grim that there is no need for historians or writers dealing with these events to strengthen the colors or deepen the shadows."

In this Pavlov is right. But the truth is that the Soviet Government from the beginning made a deliberate effort to lighten the shadows of the Leningrad blockade.

The death toll was minimized for political and security reasons. The Soviet Government for years deliberately understated the military and civilian death toll of World War II. The real totals were of such magnitude that Stalin, obviously, felt they would produce political repercussions inside the country. To the outside world a realistic statement of Soviet losses (total population losses are now estimated at well above 25 million lives) would have revealed the true weakness of Russia at the end of the war.

The Leningrad death toll had implications both for Stalin and for the Leningrad leadership, headed by Zhdanov. It raised the question of whether the key decisions were the right ones, whether all had been done that could have been done to spare the city its incredible trial. In these decisions the personal and political fortunes of all the Soviet leaders were intermingled.

Zhdanov declared in June, 1942, that there had been no line between the front and the rear in Leningrad, that everyone "lived with a single spirit—to do everything possible to defeat the enemy. Each Leningrader, man or woman, found his place in the struggle and with honor fulfilled his duty as a Soviet patriot."

This was not quite true, and it begged the question of whether the siege had to be endured, whether it could have been lifted, whether it could have been avoided. These were the questions for which the leadership might have to answer.

Whether Zhdanov was certain of the correctness of these decisions is

---

[9] Pavel Luknitsky comments that the official figures cannot account for all the deaths, particularly those who died during evacuation. (Luknitsky, *op. cit.*, p. 539.)

not clear. Not long before he died on August 31, 1948, he is said to have questioned himself and his acts, acknowledging that "people died like flies" as a result of his decisions but insisting that "history would not have forgiven me had I given up Leningrad."

Pavlov asked himself the same questions: Why did Leningrad remain in blockade for so long, and was everything done that could have been done to break the blockade? His conclusion was that the Soviet Command simply did not have the strength to do more than was done.

Meanwhile, "history" was corrected in the Soviet way. The sacrifice of Leningrad was understated; the death toll was minimized; the chance of political repercussions was reduced, at least for the time being.

Not until many years later was the inscription carved on the wall of the memorial at Piskarevsky Cemetery:

> Let no one forget; let nothing be forgotten!

For some years, at any rate, a determined effort was made to forget a very great deal that had happened during the siege of Leningrad.

PART V

Breaking the Iron Ring

The exploding bomb reminds us
Again of death,
But spring is stronger
And it is on our side. . . .

47 . Again, Spring

MAY DAY WAS A WORKING DAY IN LENINGRAD. FROM Moscow came the Party announcement that the traditional two-day holiday would be canceled. Everyone would work as usual for the war. No parade, no demonstrations, no bands. Just some speeches.

It was a beautiful day in Leningrad, sunny with an air of summer. On the streets Pavel Luknitsky noticed women, often in old army overcoats or workers' boots, with little bunches of the first spring flowers, marigolds, violets and dandelions, branches of spruce or pine or handfuls of green grass. Anything to provide a little chlorophyll, any source of vitamin C to combat the scurvy of winter.

The people were convalescent after their trials. They moved slowly in the warmth, letting the sun strike deep into their thin bodies, their pale faces, their wasted arms.

The politeness of Leningrad had begun to return. It had vanished during the terrible winter. Now Aleksandr Fadeyev watched a couple, a man and his wife, carefully, tenderly, supporting an older woman who walked with tottering feet and a rather embarrassed smile at her weakness. A Red Army man helped a little old lady onto a streetcar, lifting her from the pavement to the top step with one strong gesture. The old lady turned and said, "Thank you, son. Now you will go on living. Mark my word—no bullet will hit you."

On the walls appeared newly printed copies of *Leningradskaya Pravda* and of the Moscow papers. The presses were working again. A proclamation was pasted up by City Trade Chief Andreyenko, announcing extra rations for the holiday—issues of meat, cereal, dried peas, herring and sugar. Also vodka and beer. Notices offering to trade dresses, shoes, gold watches or sets of silverware for bread or food were still posted and black markets still operated. No longer did the cannibals stalk the Haymarket, but you could trade a watch for a kilo of bread or a woman's jacket for a glass of *klukva* or cranberries. There was even milk for exchange at a rate of a pint for 600 grams of bread.

Leningrad's streets were clean, but huge barricades of snow and filth stood along the banks of the Neva, the Moika and the Fontanka. The ice had moved out of the Neva, but not all the winter's toll had been liquidated.

May 1 was not just a pleasant sunny spring day in Leningrad. It was a day of very heavy German shelling. It went on from early morning until late at night. The Germans, it was clear, were celebrating May Day in their own way. Heavy shells fell in the square outside the Astoria Hotel and near the fleet headquarters. There were many casualties.

In the evening Fadeyev, Nikolai Tikhonov, Vsevolod Vishnevsky and Olga Berggolts spoke on the radio. Olga had just returned from Moscow. She had been flown out of Leningrad a few days after the calvary of her long walk to visit her father. A small plane took her low over the lines and over the endless wastes of snow and pine forest. She was amazed that from the air she saw no sign of fighting, no troops, no cannon, no war. In Moscow she was given a room in the Moskva Hotel, warm, comfortable, well lighted. She had what seemed like luxurious rations of food. But she did not feel comfortable. She belonged in Leningrad, not Moscow. A day or two after her arrival a man burst into her room, a Leningrad factory director. "Excuse me," he said. "I accidentally heard that you had just flown from Leningrad. I am also a Leningrader. Please tell me quickly— how is it, what's happening?" She told him of February in Leningrad, of the suffering. He nodded his head. "You understand?" he said. "That is life—there. I can't clearly express myself. There is hunger and death, but there is life, too." She told her Leningrad audience of hearing the first performance of Shostakovich's Leningrad Symphony in Moscow on March 29. When the symphony had concluded, she said, Shostakovich rose to acknowledge the ovation. "I looked at him," she said, "small, frail, with big glasses and thought, 'This man is stronger than Hitler.' " Vishnevsky noted in his diary that he was happy that his radio speech was heard by "millions of people and by my friends scattered by events throughout the land." He was happy, too, that Fadeyev mentioned him three times in his speech and "warmly."

After the broadcast Fadeyev walked up to the seventh floor of Radio House and looked out from a balcony. All around Radio House were wrecked buildings. But Radio House had not yet been hit. "It's a good bomb shelter," a young Radio House man said. "But it's a pity it's on the seventh floor."

Later in the evening Fadeyev and the others gathered in Olga Berggolts' room. Fadeyev asked the question which was on the lips of every visitor to Leningrad: "How did you live and work?"

"The chief thing," Olga Berggolts said, "was to forget about the hunger and to work and work and help your comrades to keep up their work. Work was the chief force of life. We did everything together. Everything we received we shared. The chief thing was to support those who were weaker."

She told of her husband's death and how her friends had helped her, and she showed Fadeyev a slip of paper on which was written in pencil: "Olya. I have brought you a piece of bread and I will bring some more. I love you so." A pale youngster sitting at the table had written the note. "You understand," Olga Berggolts said with deep feeling. "This was not a declaration of love!" It was something more than love, Fadeyev thought.

Someone provided a bottle of vodka. Glasses were found and a toast was proposed.

"What was the number of today's edition of the 'Radio News Chronicle'?" a Radio House worker asked. It was, it transpired, the 244th issue (May 1 was the 244th day of the Leningrad blockade).

"Well, the devil with it," the worker said. "Let's drink to the five hundredth issue."

They could not guess that nearly twice five hundred "Radio Chronicles" would go out into the ether before the Leningrad blockade ended.

It seemed to those who had survived the terrible winter that their ordeal must be drawing toward a close. The summer surely would bring a lifting of the siege.

Leningrad had a new front commander, a tall, handsome, reserved man who was not well known to the subordinate Leningrad commanders. He was Lieutenant General Leonid Aleksandrovich Govorov, an artillery officer. The late winter and early spring had turned the Leningrad Command into a comfortable, cozy group. Most of the time, the chief, Lieutenant General M. S. Khozin, had been across Ladoga, where the fighting continued, one grueling week after another. In Leningrad remained the newly promoted General Bychevsky, the fortifications specialist; Colonel (soon to be General) G. F. Odintsov, the new artillery chief; General S. D. Rybalchenko, a new air commander; and General A. B. Gvozdkov, operations officer. Major General D. N. Gusev, Khozin's deputy, ran the front. He was a pleasant officer with an open-door policy. He got on well with the generals and equally well with Party Secretary Zhdanov, who made most of the decisions. The generals and the Party secretaries, Zhdanov, Kuznetsov and Shtykov usually ate together at a common mess. They started each meal with a shot of "sauce" made from pine needles to ward off scurvy. Any time one of them returned from across Ladoga he brought a bunch of garlic which he shared with all—for the same purpose.

When word came in early April that General Govorov was being named to command Leningrad, no one knew him except Odintsov, who had taken courses under him in the Dzerzhinsky Artillery Academy in 1938. Odintsov could say little except that Govorov's character was in direct opposition to his name. Govorov stems from the word *"govoryat"* —"to talk." "Not even two words did he ever squeeze out," Odintsov said.

"And no one has ever seen him smile." About the only other thing that was known was that he was not a member of the Communist Party.[1]

Govorov was an experienced officer. Born in 1897, his military service began in the Czar's army in 1916, where he was enrolled in the Konstantinovsky Artillery School. He was impressed into Admiral Kolchak's White Russian Army but managed to desert with his battery and make his way to Tomsk, where he entered the Red Army. He rose steadily in the Red Army but in the late 1930's like many of his colleagues was caught up in the Stalin purges. His brief forced service with Kolchak was brought up against him, and he was removed from the General Staff Academy where he was a student. By a vagary of the Stalin era six months later he was named a professor at the Dzerzhinsky Artillery Academy. His career seemed to have turned the corner. But in the spring of 1941 Police Chief Beria again brought him up on charges relating to the Kolchak episode, and it was only the intervention of Marshal Timoshenko and Soviet President Mikhail Kalinin that saved him from exile or execution.

Although Govorov's name was little known in Leningrad, he had distinguished himself as one of Marshal Zhukov's right-hand men during the Battle of Moscow as commander of the Fifth Army. He it was who had recaptured Mozhaisk in mid-January, and he was inspecting the front lines of his Fifth Army sector near the Mozhaisk highway one early April morning when a call came from staff headquarters. He was wanted by 8 P.M. in Moscow. The road was slippery, and it was evening before Govorov arrived, so stiff he could hardly move—the effects of a recent operation. At Stavka he was told Stalin wanted to see him. His new assignment was Leningrad and, as always, there was a rush. Stalin ordered him to fly to Leningrad the next day.

Govorov was no stranger to Leningrad. He had gone there after finishing grade school to enter the Petrograd Polytechnic Institute. A few months later he was called to duty in the Czar's army. He thought of those times as he flew north to take over his new post. He knew that he had been picked for Leningrad because he was an artilleryman and only artillery (he believed) could protect the city so long as it was under siege. He flew over the northern reaches, now occupied by the Germans, still deep in the winter snow, over the pine and spruce forests, dark shadows on the land, over the villages and towns, burned and wrecked in the battles with the Nazis, and thought of Leningrad—how to hold the city, how to protect it, how it had managed to stand firm in the incredible days of autumn and winter, how it had halted the German armored divisions, how it had fought on despite hunger, cold and want. He thought again of his days as a Petersburg cadet and of the Petrograders he then knew, and suddenly this silent man exploded: "Brave lads!" His neigh-

[1] Govorov joined in July, 1942. He was admitted without going through the candidate stage. (N.Z., p. 345.)

bors on the plane looked at him in curiosity, but Govorov continued to peer out of the airplane window. They were nearing Leningrad now. He had seen no enemy fighters. He began to think about how to lift the siege, where to deliver the first blow.

The flight attendant came to his seat. "Leningrad soon. Very soon."

Govorov looked out the window. "But I don't see the city!"

"No," the attendant said. "We are landing at an airport outside the city. It is dusk already, and you will see no light from Leningrad. The city is completely blacked out."

Govorov's first meetings with his new colleagues were frosty. Bychevsky found him sitting at his desk, clenching his hands nervously, snatching an occasional glance at Bychevsky with unfriendly eyes, his face white, a little puffy, his mustache carefully trimmed, his dark hair shot with gray, carefully parted, a few large moles on his temples. Bychevsky reported on the state of fortifications. It was not a good report. The winter had been hard. Many trenches had fallen apart. Dugouts were filled with water. The troops had been too weak to repair the mine fields. The civilian population had done nothing since December. He had lost most of his specialized pontoon troops on the Nevskaya Dubrovka *place d'armes*. Govorov listened without an interruption or question. At the end he brought his fist down on his desk and uttered one word, quietly: "Loafer!"

Bychevsky had long since learned that engineers were more likely to get the stick than the carrot. But this was too much. "And do you know, Comrade Commander," he lashed out, "that we have on this front people who haven't the strength to pick up a stick? Do you know what dystrophy is?"

Bychevsky's words tumbled out. Govorov listened without comment. When Bychevsky finished, he got up, walked about the room and then said quietly in his deep base voice, "General, your nerves are upset. Go out and quiet down and then come back in half an hour. We have a lot of work to do."

"Loafer," it turned out, was a favorite epithet of Govorov's. It did not really mean what it sounded like. He had gotten the habit of using it when he was a young man, coaching students from well-to-do families. He used it on them. He had used it all his life.

From his first day in Leningrad Govorov turned his attention to artillery—to the counterbattery of the Leningrad guns against the German siege weapons which day after day so heavily shelled the city. Party Secretary Zhdanov had consulted the Leningrad Artillery Chief, General Odintsov, in late March about transforming the Leningrad batteries from a defensive to an offensive basis. So long as the batteries were defensive, responding only when the Germans fired, Zhdanov felt, the Nazis would, in time, destroy the city. He wanted to know how the Soviet guns could go on the offensive. Odintsov explained it was a matter of more guns, more planes to spot artillery fire, and many more shells. If they were to exterminate 10 to 12 batteries a month, it would take 15,000 shells a month. Now they were using 800 to 1,000. With Govorov's support, two air observation units were brought in and the shell quota was upped to 5,000 a month.

The Govorov principle was, as he once explained, "exceptionally accurate counterbattery blows against the enemy artillery." Govorov's guns did not wait for the Germans to open up. They systematically sought to destroy the Nazi firing points, one by one.[2]

Govorov took one radical decision. After examining the history of the costly *place d'armes* at Nevskaya Dubrovka he said briefly, "Nothing can be expected from that except a blood bath. We must quickly transfer the people to the right bank."

He won the agreement of Zhdanov to the evacuation and by April 27 had removed the 86th Infantry Division from the shell-pocked plot of ground to which it had clung since September, 1941. This action was not understood in Leningrad. Pride in the bloody triangle was high. Pavel Luknitsky was in despair when he learned of it on May 1. It was a great secret. But, as he heard it, the Germans had successfully stormed the foothold. The 86th Division had gone down fighting with the cry: "We will die before we surrender." Luknitsky shuddered to think of the blood that had been lost for the sector on the southern bank of the Neva and of the hopes they had had that it might be the wedge which would splinter the German front. Seven months the battle had gone on. Once there had been only six to nine miles that separated the Neva foothold from the Volkhov front.

The tragic event cast a pall over the May Day holiday for Luknitsky —that and the end of the Ladoga ice road. The ice went out on April 24. No connection at all with the mainland now except by air. When would it come back? How would Leningrad be supplied? He did not know that on April 2 there had been a meeting at the Kremlin with Anastas Mikoyan at which plans were approved for a pipeline under Ladoga which would supply Leningrad with fuel; that the engineers were hard at work on this; that the pipe had already been located in the now abandoned Izhorsk factory (only the factory director was still on duty, the warehouse keeper was killed in an air raid April 20, the day the Ladoga engineers located the pipe); that on June 19 the pipeline would go into service; and that a Ladoga shipping service would be operative by May 22.[3]

---

[2] The idea of "offensive" use of artillery against the German siege guns brought a tart comment from Marshal Voronov, chief of Soviet artillery. "There were people on the Leningrad front who, attracted to terminology, attempted to juggle concepts of the First World War in place of the accepted and legitimate concepts—extermination, destruction and suppression." (Voronov, *op. cit.*, p. 219.)

[3] The Ladoga shipping route proved very successful and efficient in 1942. By May 28 large-scale barge movements were under way. At the orders of State Defense Committee

"All night I have thought about it," Luknitsky said. "It makes 1

But if the liquidation of the Nevskaya Dubrovka foothold was
tragedy which Luknitsky believed, there was slowly building up
Leningrad front another disaster, the fruit of the terrible and indecisive
winter fighting.

Neither General Fedyuninsky, in charge of the Fifty-fourth Army,
nor General Meretskov, in charge of the Volkhov front, had been able
to make real progress, but Moscow had never relaxed its pressure to get
results. All winter long there had been High Command representatives
with Meretskov. During most of February and early March Marshal Voroshilov was assigned to him. In early March Voroshilov was recalled to
Moscow, but he returned to Meretskov's headquarters on March 9, and
he brought with him several companions. One was Georgi M. Malenkov,
making one of his increasingly frequent appearances at a fighting front.
Another was Lieutenant General A. A. Novikov, deputy air commander,
and a third was a brilliant new general whose star was rapidly rising,
Lieutenant General Andrei A. Vlasov. There had been a shake-up among
Meretskov's deputies, and Vlasov had been named by Moscow as deputy
commander of the Volkhov front. Vlasov, like Govorov, was a hero of
the Battle of Moscow. While Govorov and his Fifth Army were smashing the Germans at Mozhaisk, Vlasov and his Twentieth Army were retaking Volokolamsk. Both generals were young and vigorous. Both were
shown off to foreign correspondents, Vlasov just before Christmas, Govorov in mid-January. Among those who met Vlasov was Larry Lesueur,
a Columbia Broadcasting System correspondent, who thought the forty-
year-old Vlasov looked more like a teacher than a soldier and was impressed with his tall astrakhan hat with its crimson and gold crown and
his white felt boots. Eve Curie, who visited Russia as a correspondent,
was struck by Vlasov's professionalism. He considered each question strictly
from the military viewpoint. He spoke of Napoleon with deep respect
and thought it nonsense to compare Hitler with him. She was pleased to
find that he knew Charles de Gaulle's views on modern war and that he
respected General Guderian, against whom he had been fighting. Vlasov's
parting words to Eve Curie were "My blood belongs to my fatherland."

It was obvious that the introduction of this vigorous and successful
commander into the frozen bogs of the Leningrad hinterland was designed
to break the deadlock there. The fact that he was brought in under Malen-

---

representative Aleksei Kosygin, a major rebuilding and expansion of port facilities had
been carried out as well as preparation of large numbers of barges. During the 1942 navigation season, which closed November 25, 1942, the Ladoga route delivered 703,300 tons
of freight, including 350,000 tons of food, 99,200 tons of war supplies, 216,600 tons of
fuel, as well as horses, cows and sheep weighing 15,500 tons, and 41,500 tons of wood
(towed as rafts). The route moved out of Leningrad 270,000 tons of freight, including
162,100 tons of machinery. It evacuated 528,000 persons, including 448,700 civilians. It
carried to Leningrad 267,000 persons, including 250,000 troops. (V. Y. Neigoldberg,
Istoriya SSSR, No. 3, March, 1965, pp. 102 *et seq.*)

kov's auspices suggested, as well, that the appointment had a role in the endless game of military politics in which the Kremlin was engaged.

General Meretskov had no cause to find fault with his fast-moving new deputy. Vlasov did not attempt to take upon himself any responsibilities other than those given him by Meretskov.

During the remainder of the month there was a new effort to get things moving and particularly to improve the position of the Second Shock Army. This army had scored considerable advances beyond a point called Spasskaya Polist, midway between Novgorod and Chudovo in an area of tangled swamps, underbrush and tamarack bogs, roughly seventy-five miles southeast of Leningrad. Unfortunately, in penetrating into the German positions, it almost fell into encirclement. The Germans, seeing their opportunity, sent the 58th Nazi Infantry and the SS police division into action, and succeeded in cutting the Novgorod-Chudovo highway and railroad and closing the four-mile "throat" through which the communications and transport of the Second Shock Army was maintained. A week of fierce fighting ensued, back and forth, and finally the supply route was reopened and the encirclement of the Second Shock Army relieved, but only by the barest of margins. There is bitter argument between two Soviet generals as to whether the encirclement was really liquidated. General Meretskov contends that it was. General Khozin contends that it wasn't—that the Second Shock Army had only a corridor a mile to a mile and a half wide and that within ten days the Nazis choked it down again.

Whichever version is correct, events demonstrated that the position of the Second Shock Army was very shaky, very precarious. On April 9 the Germans attacked again and cut off the army. It was reduced to receiving supplies by plane and air drops. The situation was so difficult that Ivan V. Zuyev,[4] the Second Shock Army Political Commissar, held a meeting of all political workers, army procurators, military tribunals and members of the dread "special branch" of the secret police and ordered the "highest vigilance" against any German "agents." At this point the army commander, Lieutenant General N. K. Krykov, fell ill and had to be evacuated by plane. General Vlasov was sent in to replace him.[5]

The difficult situation was made more difficult by one of the erratic command changes which Stalin so often introduced. Stalin had been con-

[4] At the start of the war Zuyev was a political commissar in General Morozov's Eleventh Army headquarters at Kaunas, where he distinguished himself in leading units of the Eleventh Army out of the initial Nazi encirclement.

[5] There is uncertainty as to the precise date when Vlasov took command of the Second Shock Army. Luknitsky gives the date as March 6, obviously incorrect, since Vlasov did not arrive at Meretskov's headquarters until March 9. Meretskov says Vlasov took over the Second Shock Army a month and a half later. The formal command change apparently was April 16. (Luknitsky, *op. cit.*, Vol. II, p. 322; Meretskov, *Voyenno-Istoricheskii Zhurnal*, No. 12, January, 1965, pp. 66–67; Barbashin, *op. cit.*, p. 603.) Krykov was flown out April 16. (*Smert Komissara*, p. 102.)

tinuously dissatisfied at the failure of the efforts to lift Leningrad's blockade. He had sent one high emissary after another to get some action. Now he summoned the erstwhile Leningrad front commander, General Khozin, for a conference April 21. Khozin had repeatedly put blame for the failure of the deblockading efforts on lack of coordination between the sprawling units of the Leningrad (internal) and Volkhov (external) fronts. He repeated his complaints now and urged that the Stavka ensure close and effective collaboration. He presented his views to Stalin, Marshal Shaposhnikov, Marshal Vasilevsky and a number of Defense Council members, undoubtedly including Malenkov.[6] Unexpectedly, Khozin contends, Stalin proposed that the fronts be united and Khozin put in charge. Khozin describes the idea as having been as sudden to the others as to him. Because of the "colossal authority of Stalin," Khozin observed, no one thought of challenging the notion. An order was drafted to unite the two fronts as of midnight April 23 and put them under Khozin's command.

No one was more surprised than General Meretskov, the Volkhov front commander, at this decision. "I could not understand what the point was of this consolidation," he said. "In my view there was neither operative nor political nor any kind of advantage in it." He soon heard, however, that General Khozin had promised that if the two fronts were united he could lift the Leningrad blockade. In view of this, Meretskov thought it understandable that the Stavka had ordered the reorganization and strengthened the new front with the 6th Guards Rifle Corps and another rifle division. But he did think it odd that the Volkhov front commander, that is, himself, had not been consulted.

"I learned about the proceedings," he recalled, "on April 23 when General Khozin with the directive in his pocket and in a jolly mood appeared at the Volkhov staff headquarters."

Meretskov insists that he called Khozin's attention to the plight of the Second Shock Army but that "Khozin had his own opinion and didn't agree with me."

Meretskov went straight to Moscow, and there on April 24 he again raised the question of the Second Shock Army with Stalin and Malenkov.

"The Second Shock Army is practically stifling," Meretskov recalls saying. "It can't attack and it can't defend itself. Its communications are threatened by the German blows. If nothing is done, catastrophe is inevitable."

Meretskov proposed that the army be evacuated from the impenetrable marshes in which it was bogged down (especially dangerous with the heavy spring thaw which made every road and trail impassable) and brought back to the line of the Chudovo-Novgorod highway and railroad. He was listened to with patience and a promise of attention. He was then transferred to the Western Front to command the Thirty-third Army. Almost simultaneously the other top Leningrad commander, General Fedyunin-

[6] Malenkov seems to have had special responsibilities for the Leningrad front.

sky, was removed from the Fifty-fourth Army and sent to command the Fifth Army, neighboring the Thirty-third on the Western Front.

Khozin's story is that he gave first priority to the plight of the Second Army, which was virtually encircled and badly weakened by the winter of incredibly difficult fighting. Many units were down to 60 to 70 percent of rated strength. Tank brigades had no tanks and artillery no shells. The forests were so waterlogged it was impossible to move by truck or car. Even horses had difficulty getting around.

General Khozin got Stalin to agree that the Second Shock Army should go on the defensive in preparation for an effort to get out of the encirclement. There were at this time eleven infantry divisions, three cavalry divisions and five infantry brigades in encirclement. By May 4 the five cavalry brigades had forced their way out. Two infantry divisions and some smaller units broke out and joined the Fifty-ninth Army.

General Vlasov, with his Chief Commissar Ivan Zuyev, flew out of encirclement to consult with Khozin May 12. They returned to headquarters May 14 with plans for constructing a road through the wilderness along which it was hoped to move out the troops. But the idea did not get very far. The Germans had begun to build up their forces again, sensing that they were nearing the kill. The Bavarian Rifle Corps was brought in, and there were signs the Germans planned a simultaneous drive from Chudovo and Novgorod.

General Khozin had put the Fifty-ninth Army into action to try to lessen pressure on the Second, and Stalin agreed to lay aside the drive for lifting the Leningrad blockade while trying to save the Second Shock Army. Plans were laid for a simultaneous push June 5 by the Second and Fifty-ninth armies. But the Germans spotted the Soviet preparations and themselves went over to the offensive. Some Soviet troops forced their way out, but by June 6 the Germans had firmly closed the circle around parts of seven rifle divisions and six infantry brigades—altogether 18,000 or 20,000 men.

General Khozin did not try to conceal the disaster. He reported what had happened promptly to Moscow, and on June 8 General Meretskov was urgently brought back from the Central Front and again summoned to the Stavka. In the presence of virtually the whole High Command Stalin said: "We made a big mistake in combining the Volkhov and Leningrad fronts. General Khozin wanted to head the Volkhov operation, but he has done badly. He didn't carry out the orders of Stavka for the withdrawal of the Second Army. As a result the Germans have cut off the communications of the army and encircled it."

Stalin turned to Meretskov. "You, Comrade Meretskov, know the Volkhov front very well. So we are sending you with Marshal Vasilevsky to bring the Second Army out of encirclement even if you have to abandon the heavy artillery and equipment."

Meretskov flew into Malaya Vishera, where Khozin had his headquarters, before nightfall. He found a gloomy situation—the Second Army cut off completely, with hardly any supplies and no way to provide food or ammunition. There were no real reserves, but Meretskov gathered what troops he could and ordered a narrow attack on June 10 to try and create an escape corridor.

The effort was only partially successful. The Germans had mustered four infantry and an SS division to the north and about five divisions including an international legion to the south.

Meretskov attacked again and again, and Vlasov smashed from the inner side of the circle. About 6,000 men made their way out up to 8 P.M., June 22. Finally an all-out attack was ordered for June 23 into which Vlasov and his men were told to throw everything in a last effort. The attack was launched at 11:30 P.M., June 23. The Second Army drove toward the Fifty-ninth Army lines. The Fifty-ninth threw its strength into opening a corridor. Toward dawn (very early in these white nights) a narrow path was opened and the first men of the Second Army passed through. They kept on coming until about noon. Then the Germans closed the passage. At this point, according to Meretskov, General Vlasov lost control of the situation. He ordered his men to try to escape in small groups, individually and on their own. This disoriented them. Communications with Vlasov were now lost. Nevertheless, toward evening of the twenty-fourth the corridor was opened again and more men slipped through. But by 9:30 in the morning of the twenty-fifth it was closed again—this time finally.

Meretskov was personally directing the rescue operation, and on the morning of the twenty-fifth he was advised by some escaping officers that they had seen Vlasov and his senior officers on one of the back roads. Meretskov immediately directed a tank regiment and some mobile infantry, together with his adjutant, Captain M. G. Borod, to penetrate the region where Vlasov had been seen. They found no trace of him. Knowing that Vlasov had a radio receiver, they tried to reach him by wireless without result. Later, it was learned that Vlasov had divided his staff into three groups, which were supposed to come out about 11 P.M., June 24, in the region of the 46th Rifle Division. Unfortunately, none of them knew where the 46th command point was located. As they approached the Polist River, they came under strong German machine-gun fire. Vlasov apparently was not seen beyond this point. The Military Council and General Afanasyev, chief of communications, turned north. Two days later Afanasyev's group met a partisan unit and managed to make contact with a second partisan group which had a radio transmitter. With the aid of the transmitter General Afanasyev was able to communicate with Meretskov July 14. He was brought out by plane.

At some point V. N. Ivanov, secretary of the Young Communist organization in Leningrad, encountered Vlasov, but whether before or after the Polist River incident is not clear. Ivanov was dropped with some other young Communists, by parachute, behind the German lines. By mistake the pilot let them jump over a small village which was occupied by a Nazi SS unit. Ivanov was badly wounded and took refuge in a nearby forest, where he encountered Vlasov, in Soviet uniform, still holding out. Then they separated and trace of Vlasov was again lost.

After Afanasyev's rescue Meretskov telephoned Party Secretary Zhdanov, who ordered the partisan units to undertake a widespread search for General Vlasov and the other members of his staff. The partisans mobilized three groups and searched the regions around Poddubye for many miles but found no trace of Vlasov. A few of the command officers turned up. Colonel A. S. Rogov, chief of intelligence, got through the encirclement. He followed the route of the Military Council but came out a little behind them. For years the fate of Commissar Zuyev was unknown. Then, by chance, his grave was discovered near the 105th kilometer of the Chudovo railroad, near the Torfyanoye Station. Starving, wounded and weak, he had emerged at the railroad line and begged a bit of bread from some workers. One of them ran to tell the Germans. Before he could be seized Zuyev pulled out his service revolver and shot himself. About 9,322 men escaped encirclement; 8,000 to 10,000 were lost.

Vlasov did not shoot himself. Two days before Zhdanov ordered the partisans to search for him he surrendered to the Germans on July 12 and within a short time had placed himself at the service of the Nazi propaganda apparatus as the head of what became the Vlasovite movement, an organization of Russian soldiers and officers directed against the Soviet cause. He was the only Soviet general officer of prominence to defect, and his defection was always a prickly business in which he frequently would not play the Nazi game. But Vlasov's treachery became such a thing of awe and horror in wartime Russia that his name was hardly uttered.

Later, however, many Soviet writers sought to put the blame for the Second Shock Army's disaster on him. They suggested that he had been deliberately playing a double game. There is no evidence in the record of the desperate fight of the Second Shock Army to support such a view. General Khozin, who, of course, was himself deeply involved in the tragedy, concluded that the Soviet side simply did not have the strength to defeat the well-organized, well-reinforced German troops opposing them. The Germans were, he pointed out, "at the zenith of their power." At no time was the Supreme Command in Moscow able to send sufficient reserves to the Leningrad front to create a real breakthrough force.

This, rather than failures by part of the troops, bad generalship or incipient treachery by Vlasov, was the key. The Second Shock Army was in encirclement, almost inextricably bogged down in the marshes and confronted by powerful, well-led German forces before Vlasov flew in by

U-2 light reconnaissance plane in mid-April to take command. General Meretskov, not unnaturally, put much blame on Moscow for the absurd command change which ousted him in April only to bring him back in early June—a decision which played a part in the disaster. But nothing in Meretskov's conduct of the late winter–early spring operations gave hope that the fate of the Second Shock Army would have been different had he been left in charge. Vlasov's role was secondary, but his emergence at the head of the Vlasovite movement threw his actions and the whole question of the Second Shock Army into the lurid limbo of critical Soviet political issues. Everyone connected with the affair had to prove that the blame rested with Vlasov, that each had no connection with the traitor, that the fault lay with Vlasov and no one else. For twenty years there were only peripheral mentions of Vlasov in Soviet historiography, and even today the main thrust of the memoirs and studies is to establish that the individual commanders had nothing to do with Vlasov or the Kremlin's decisions in relation to him and the ill-fated Volkhov operations.

There is some substance to this. Vlasov's career until tragedy enmeshed him in the swamps of the ancient Novgorod tract bore telltale marks of Kremlin politics. The Volkhov-Leningrad front clearly fell within the responsibility of Georgi Malenkov, a sworn enemy then and later of Leningrad Party Boss Andrei Zhdanov. The role and fate of Malenkov's protégé, Vlasov, inevitably played a part in Kremlin politics.[7]

With the loss of the Second Shock Army one more hope for Leningrad went glimmering—the hope that spring or summer would bring an end to the blockade. In early June Party Secretary Zhdanov had gone to Moscow and bravely told the Supreme Soviet that the people of Leningrad stood as one, united, fighting for their city. This was true. But now on July 5 another kind of decision had to be made. The Leningrad Military Council that day ordered the transformation of Leningrad into a military city, with only the minimum population necessary to carry on the city's defense and essential services. The next day Zhdanov announced the decision: another 300,000 people must be removed by the Ladoga route. The city must be cut to the bare minimum—800,000 population, no more. It was July 6, the 340th day of the blockade. The city was holding out, but no one knew what summer would bring. The bright dreams of spring had faded. The Nazis were on the move once more. Soviet armies were falling back toward the Volga. The gains of winter in the north Caucasus had been lost. There were ominous signs of a new build-up at Leningrad. Hitler had issued directive No. 45 to General Lindemann of the Eighteenth Nazi Army and to Field Marshal von Küchler, now in command of Army Group Nord. They were

[7] Vlasov and his associate anti-Soviet officers fell into Russian hands at the end of the war. His execution along with that of some associates was announced August 2, 1946. (Alexander Dallin, *German Rule in Russia, 1941–1945*, London, 1957, p. 659.) Malenkov lost his post in the Party Secretariat about this time, possibly in connection with the Vlasov affair. However, his fall from favor was brief.

to set in motion preparations for the capture of Leningrad by the beginning of September. Heavy reinforcements both of men and artillery were being assigned to the task.

Leningrad could take no chances. The Germans were enormously powerful, and the momentum that would take them to Stalingrad and Maikop in the Caucasus was already visible. Despite all the sacrifices it might well take them into Leningrad itself.

It was at about this time that a young Leningrad soldier named Yevgeny Zhilo was making his way through the broken countryside just outside his native city. It was near dawn, and in the pale luminosity of the white night the sky was dipped in rosy pastels. Somewhere beyond the unseen horizon the sun was rising. He pushed through the clumps of lilac, his carbine tangling in the branches. For a moment he halted and buried his nose in the heavy perfume of the blossoms. In their rich fragrance, in the dew now sparkling in the sunshine, in the soft, strange quiet of the morning, there seemed nothing but the happiness and brightness of life. Standing there, a soldier for six brief months, tears sprang into his eyes. Remembering the experience twenty-five years later, Zhilo felt no sense of shame. He had cried not because he was a youngster but because it was the summer of 1942 and he was still there just beside Leningrad and he had forgotten nothing, nothing that had happened—the flickering lamp in the darkness of the room; the frosted window pane and the glare of the burning houses; the unthinkable silence of the great city; the sound of the steps of a passer-by, heard from such a distance that their approach became frightening. He remembered the starving children, little old men who knew everything, understood everything. He knew as he stood breathing in the rich scent of the lilacs that he would never see again the eyes of those nearest and dearest to him, those doomed to die with eyes wide-open, solemn and a little mad, those who stood already at the border of death.

He knew as he stood there with his carbine outside Leningrad on that sunny morning that what had happened around him had never happened in the history of the world and that no one would forget it nor would anything be forgotten—not for centuries upon centuries.

The young soldier stood in the clump of lilacs and cried and the tears ran down his face. Then he put his carbine over his shoulder again, brushed aside the lilacs, and shouldered forward toward the line of trenches, there to fight while he could.

So Leningrad entered the second summer of war.

48 . *Operation Iskra*

THE WHITE NIGHTS BROUGHT BACK TO LENINGRAD AN appearance of ease and relaxation. In the Summer Gardens fields of cabbages replaced grassy lawns. Between the antiaircraft batteries on the Champs de Mars sprouted potato patches. Here and there were small signs: "Dr. Kozin's garden," "Aleksandr Prokofyev's garden" and dozens like it. On the steps of the Kazan Cathedral a copper samovar bubbled and women drank tea made of some kind of herbs. Everyone rolled his own cigarettes with paper torn from strips of old *Pravdas*. They lighted them with magnifying glasses. No matches were needed so long as the sun shone.

There were flowers in the city—mignonettes, daisies, field roses. The streetcars were jammed. Only lines Nos. 12, 3, 7, 30, 10, 20 and 9 ran regularly. Often they stopped because of shelling. There were no buses, no taxis. Signs appeared on the streets: "In case of shelling this side is the most dangerous." Girls sold soda water at sidewalk stands, and a kvass wagon was parked on the Nevsky. Old fishermen tried their luck along the Fontanka and the Moika.

Death was more rare. Pavel Luknitsky walked through Leningrad one July day. He saw only two corpses—one on the Fontanka wrapped in a blanket on a wheelbarrow, the other in a coffin being pulled in a hand cart.

To be sure, people were thin and drawn. But they moved more swiftly, and many were ruddy from the summer sun. There were not many queues and, truth to say, not many people. The streets were empty. Too many had died, too many had been evacuated, and more were going all the time.

Everywhere people picked greens. Posted on the walls of buildings were check lists of edible wild plants. They recommended young nettles, dandelions, burdocks, goosefoot, rape, sorrel. One woman discovered a nettle patch outside the Catherine Gardens. She picked a panful and made a delicious summer soup. Never mind her nettle-burned hands.

There were still children in Leningrad. They ran and played. Sometimes it was "war," sometimes doctor-and-nurse with dystrophy victims. Sayanov encountered some youngsters who made their "patient" lie on a stove while they debated whether she should be evacuated or whether she could be cured by a special diet.

Luknitsky was sitting on a street bench one day, writing in his diary. An old woman (he knew instantly that she was really young and that only starvation and hardship made her look old) came up to him, carrying a portable phonograph in a red case, a black umbrella and a battered bag on her back. She tried to sell him the phonograph. She told him her husband was at the front, she had had no word from him, had been evacuated from her home and had no place to go with her child.

The Writers' House on Ulitsa Voinova was clean once more—no more bodies in the back rooms. Meals were served in the dining room by waitresses in neat uniforms—supper from three to five without ration coupons for members of the union: a full bowl of good barley soup, borsht, kasha and, for dessert, a kind of glucose or a chocolate bar.

No great problem now about looking after writers. Ilya Avramenko, the poet, and Luknitsky decided to evacuate all those not doing war work. They checked the prewar list of 300 members. There were 107 in the army, mostly on the Leningrad front; 33 had died of hunger, 11 had been killed at the front, and 6 had been arrested.

Of those arrested two, Lozin and Petrov, had been shot. Three had been put in prison on political charges. These included one whose name Luknitsky did not remember and another named Borisoglebsky. The third was Abramovich-Blek—the gallant, onetime officer in the Czar's navy who had jokingly promised in September, 1941, a place in his nonexistent barge on Lake Ladoga to "Lady Astor," the manager of the Astoria Hotel restaurant. Another writer, named Herman Matveyev, had been arrested for speculation. Already 53 writers had been evacuated. There remained about 30 in civilian status to be sent out.

What tragedy befell Abramovich-Blek is not clear. But a grim clue can be found in Vsevolod Vishnevsky's diary. Vishnevsky had "discovered" Abramovich-Blek as a writer, had sponsored his literary debut. On July 24, 1942, Vishnevsky noted:

> A certain B——k somewhere in an after-dinner conversation openly defended Fascist conceptions. . . . He was removed from the ship and taken into custody. Where do such types come from?

B——k, Vishnevsky insisted, secretly was hoping for Hitler's victory. Vishnevsky claimed he had seen a certain number of writers of the B——k type. They disguised themselves in Soviet colors, and their work was inevitably false and hypocritical.

Whether Vishnevsky believed his protégé was a traitor or whether he was covering his own tracks, there is no way of telling. The incident underlined the fact that the vigilance of the secret police had not slackened despite the heroism of the Leningraders.

Vissarion Sayanov decided to visit the composer Boris V. Asafyev. The wonderful old Leningrad bookstores were open again. Many book lovers had sold their libraries for bread. Many had died and left their books to be sold by their heirs; many were sold by thieves who ransacked empty apartments. Book trade was one of the few that thrived in Leningrad. (There was no basis for Vishnevsky's paranoid suspicion that saboteurs had burned up the total stock of new editions of *War and Peace* and Tolstoy's Sevastopol stories.)

Sayanov stopped in a bookshop on his way to Asafyev and picked up a pamphlet about a production of Tchaikovsky's *Queen of Spades* at the Mariinsky Theater, May 3, 1921. The author was Igor Glebov —the *nom de plume* of Asafyev. He opened the pages and was struck by a phrase: "From the beginning to the end of the opera the claws of death quietly and steadily draw the victim closer and closer."

He read on:

"The terrible design of the music of *The Queen of Spades* is to be found in its ceaseless beating into our brain of a feeling of the inevitability of death and, thus, delicately, frighteningly, moving us nearer and nearer to the terrible end."

Sayanov bought the book and presented it to Asafyev.

"How strange!" Asafyev said. "It's as though I had not written this, but someone else."

They came upon another sentence written by Asafyev twenty years before: "When spring came, there was no one in the world as happy as the people of this sovereign city."

Of this they had no doubt.

Sayanov was struck by his conversation with Asafyev. It dealt not with everyday living problems, food, rations, hunger. Asafyev had lived in the bomb shelter of the Pushkin Theater most of the winter. He had come to the margin of death. But he did not talk about his personal problems. He talked about the musical structure of the songs of the western Slavs and gave Sayanov a paper he had written on the opera *The Bronze Horseman*. Not a word about the terrible January days when Asafyev lay in his bed in the dark to conserve heat, light and strength, composing music in his mind and then, after daylight came, quickly writing down the notes while he still had the strength. In those days Asafyev wrote his whole autobiography in his mind, but it was many months before he was able to put it on paper.

Walking the streets of Leningrad, Luknitsky saw a group of women at the bridges over the canals and rivers, washing clothes or dishes. They looked healthy. Some had lipstick. Their clothing was not only washed but ironed.

On the Liteiny a hunchback set up a scales and did a rushing business. Everyone wanted to know how much weight he had lost during the winter. An old bootblack appeared at the corner of Sadovaya and Rakhov streets. He had to rest between shoeshines, he was so weak. A shine cost 5 rubles, a can of shoe polish the same. There were cigarettes for sale at street corners.

Prices in the black market were becoming stabilized: a quart of vodka, 1,500 rubles; 100 grams of bread, 40 rubles; a pack of cigarettes, 150 rubles; fish-cakes, 3 rubles. Musical comedy tickets were exchanged for two bread rations.

On the Nevsky the rubble of broken buildings had been carted away to be used in making bomb shelters and pillboxes. In the dental gaps made by destroyed buildings false fronts were erected. They were painted to resemble the building exteriors, windows and doors faithfully reproduced. Going quickly down the street it seemed undamaged. On the false front of a build-ing at the Nevsky and Morskaya the date "1942" appeared — whether to mark the date of destruction or pseudo reconstruction was not clear. A shell went through one onion tower of the "Church of the Blood" erected on the site of Alexander II's assassination. It was repaired with plywood, and no damage could be seen. The Engineers Castle took a direct hit (many persons were killed, for it was being used as a hospital), but from the outside it appeared whole.

The exterior appearances were deceptive. The city looked more peaceful. It seemed more peaceful. But in reality it still stood in deadly danger. And the danger was growing. To the south the German summer offensive was in full swing. Soviet troops had yielded Sevastopol and the Crimea. The Ger-mans were in motion across the broad waist of the South Russian steppes, driving toward the Volga. Nazi troops were thrusting deep into the Cau-casus.

Everywhere there were signs that they would soon try once again to take Leningrad. For more than a month German troop movements had been seen. Vishnevsky heard that German strength was 50 percent higher than in the spring. There were more and more reconnaissance flights. On July 10 Lieutenant General Leonid A. Govorov told the Leningrad commanders that a new test of strength was in the offing. Party Secretary Zhdanov warned that the Germans would again try to take the city by storm. With the oc-cupation of the Crimea, Hitler had ordered Manstein's Eleventh Army north for a new offensive against Leningrad. The 24th, 28th, 132nd and 170th infantry divisions of the Eleventh Army quickly appeared before Leningrad. They were followed by the 5th Mountain Division, the 61st Infantry and the 250th Spanish "Blue" Division. Vast quantities of heavy siege guns (in-cluding a 440-mm Big Bertha), many from the Skoda, Krupp and Schneider works, arrived. They had been successfully used by the Nazis in taking Sevastopol. By the end of July the Germans had massed twenty-one infantry and one tank division and one separate infantry brigade before Leningrad and at nearby Mga and Sinyavino.

In this atmosphere the Leningrad troops were once again ordered to take the offensive. The objective was to lift the siege—the fourth attempt. But there were other objectives: to lessen, if possible, the terrible German pres-sure in the south. The worst crisis of the war was at hand. Leningrad must, at any cost, prevent the Germans from shifting forces to the south and southwest.

The main responsibility of the new offensive was placed on General Meretskov's Volkhov command, which was stronger than the Neva Operating Group of General Govorov.

Steps were taken to boost Leningrad's morale. On July 25—Navy Day—for the first time German prisoners of war were paraded down the Nevsky, the only Germans to reach the heart of Leningrad. There were several thousand of them—unshaven, dirty, lousy, wearing jackets of ersatz wool. Many were plainly afraid of the crowds, mostly women who set up a shout: "Give them to us! Give them to us!" Troops and police held the women back. Here and there a child threw a stone or stick at the bedraggled Nazis. Not all, however, were cowed. Some sneered at the crowd, some laughed.

Vishnevsky noted discouragingly in his diary that some of these "whorehouse dregs" were the sons of workers, that many failed to bow under cross-examination, continuing to mouth Nazi slogans. Some, he said, burst into tears when told they would have to rebuild all that had been destroyed in Russia before being permitted to return to their homes.

At 7 P.M. on August 9 the doors of Philharmonic Hall opened. Again there were lights—some lights anyway—in the crystal chandeliers. Sunlight streamed through the great windows, repaired with plywood after the winter's bombing. Here was everyone in Leningrad: Vsevolod Vishnevsky and Vera Inber (by chance they met, walking in the greenhouse of the Botanical Gardens that afternoon, the one where the palms had frozen to death in the winter and where now, again, Victoria Regina lilies were beginning to bloom, where peonies were being cut and dark barberry branches were sending forth shoots); Lieutenant General Govorov, handsome in his uniform; Party Secretary Kuznetsov, dark, lean-faced but more at ease than during the winter months; and on the podium, Director Karl Eliasberg. Everyone was wearing his good black suit or her best silk dress, the most fashionable crowd the siege had seen. The score of the Seventh Symphony had been sent to Leningrad by plane in June, and rehearsals had gone on for more than six weeks.

The glory and majesty of the symphony were played against a crescendo of Leningrad's guns. General Friedrich Ferch, Chief of Staff of the Nazi Eighteenth Army, learning that his troops were listening to a radio broadcast of the symphony (it was carried by direct hook-up to all parts of the Soviet Union and by shortwave to Europe and North America), ordered cannon fire into the area of the Philharmonic Hall. But General Govorov, the counterbattery specialist, had foreseen this possibility. Soviet guns silenced the German batteries.[1]

---

[1] There is disagreement among Soviet witnesses on this. Yuri Alyanskii, who was present, contends no German shells fell in the city because of precautionary fire by Soviet batteries. (*Zvezda*, No. 11, November, 1961, p. 195.) V. M. Gankevich says Ferch

Generals Meretskov and Govorov, Admiral Tributs, and Party secretaries Zhdanov and Kuznetsov met August 21 near Tikhvin to agree on final plans for the new effort to lift the blockade. There was dispute between Leningrad and Volkhov, between Zhdanov and Govorov on one side and Meretskov on the other. Leningrad wanted to take the lead. Stalin supported Meretskov and insisted that "the basic weight of the proposed operation should lie on the Volkhov front."

Zhdanov sharply challenged Meretskov, insisting that Leningrad could lift the blockade by forcing the Neva with the Neva Operating Group. Meretskov and Stalin thought—correctly—that he was wrong.

Meretskov got more in reinforcements and arms than he had expected from Moscow in the light of the Stalingrad crisis. Stalin sent him 20,000 rifles and tommy guns, although he had asked for only 8,000 to 10,000. They were shipped by a roundabout route to deceive the Nazis about the coming offensive. The men were sent in closed railroad cars marked "fuel," "food," "hay." Tanks were sent on flatcars covered with hay.

The offensive failed. It rumbled on into October but never gave promise of breaking the German lines. Once again Leningrad troops forced the Neva River, sending three rifle divisions across in daylight September 8 in the face of terrible German fire. Govorov took the responsibility for the fiasco and proposed to try again. He especially trained some troops and brought in amphibious tanks. The new action started September 26. It went just as badly. Rain set in. Once again Govorov took the hard decision. He ordered the *place d'armes* liquidated and the troops withdrawn to the north bank of the Neva on October 8.

Meretskov had no better luck. His troops pushed forward a short distance, but by September 20 Manstein was counterattacking, trying to cut off the Soviet forward positions. The bad-luck Second Shock Army bogged down in the marshes. General Meretskov plunged into action to help extricate the 4th Guards Rifle Corps. Twice his personal car was destroyed by a direct hit. He got word that Stalin was urgently calling him on the VC high-security phone, but not until September 30 did he emerge from the marshes and put through the call.

"Why didn't you come to the direct wire?" Stalin demanded.

"I lost two machines," Meretskov replied. "But more than that I was

---

ordered his guns to fire but they were immediately silenced. (Gankevich, *op. cit.*, p. 80.) N. N. Zhdanov, then one of Leningrad's artillery specialists, says the Germans were kept from opening fire by Govorov's counterbattery barrage. (N. N. Zhdanov, *Ognevoi Shchit Leningrada*, Moscow, 1961, p. 76.) Neither Inber, Vishnevsky nor Bogdanov-Berezovsky mentions shelling. All were present. (Inber, *Izbranniye Proizvedeniya*, Vol. III Leningrad, 1958, pp. 347–348; Vishnevsky, *op. cit.*, p. 598; Bogdanov-Berezovsky, *V Gody Velikoi Otechestvennoi Voiny*, Leningrad, 1959, p. 146.) General Friedrich Ferch was convicted of war crimes and sentenced to twenty-five years in prison. In 1955 he was turned over to Western Germany and soon thereafter released. (*Istoriya VOVSS*, Vol. III, p. 128.)

afraid that if I left the command point of the corps, behind me would come dragging the staff of the corps and after them the staff of the units."

He reported he had extricated the surrounded troops. That was the end of the fourth effort to lift the Leningrad siege. It was October 6—the 402nd day of the siege. But the threat of a new German attack on Leningrad had been removed. Manstein had lost 60,000 men, killed or taken prisoner, 260 planes, 200 tanks and 600 guns and mortars. "Better be three times at Sevastopol than stay on here," men of the Manstein command said.

Yet somehow the mood of Leningrad was changing. The city was preparing for its second winter of war in a new spirit. The manager of the Astoria Hotel, a young woman named Galina Alekseyevna, mascara on her eyelashes, sang as she mounted the marble, circular staircase. "Why am I so happy?" she asked Pavel Luknitsky. "I really don't know. The city is being shelled, and I am singing. I never used to sing in the morning. I used to live quite well, but I cried all the time. The things I cried for! It makes me laugh to think of them. Now I've lost everyone. All my dear ones. I thought I couldn't survive that. But now I'm ready for anything. If I die, I die. I'm not afraid of death any more."

Luknitsky felt the same—except when he encountered the red tape of the army administration. He had a pass issued by the army in Moscow—it carried twenty stamps and signatures. And even this, often, would not persuade an army commander to give him a meal, a ration card or transportation.

What was changing the mood of the city was events. Party Secretary Kuznetsov spoke at Philharmonic Hall:

"The enemy recently created a large group of divisions which had been active on the Sevastopol front. But thanks to the Sinyavino [Volkhov] operation and the action of the troops of the Leningrad front, this group was smashed. And the time is not far distant when our troops will receive the order: Break the circle of blockade!"

He got a big ovation.

Now Leningrad prepared to celebrate the twenty-fifth anniversary of the October Revolution. No parade. The time for that was not yet. But there were holiday entertainments. Vishnevsky and two colleagues, Aleksandr Kron and Vsevolod Azarov, had written a musical comedy about the Baltic Fleet, not a very comical subject, in seventeen days. It was called *The Wide, Wide Sea*. Vishnevsky never had the remotest connection with music or comedy. In fact, he went to *Rose Marie* to see what a musical was like and burst into tears. *The Wide, Wide Sea* was written to orders—orders of the Baltic Fleet Political Administration. Vishnevsky had simply responded, "Yes, sir!" and then set about to discover what it was he was supposed to do. He flung himself into the project with such enthusiasm that he hardly noticed that nothing had come of an invitation Party Secretary Kuznetsov gave him on September 30 to go to the United States as *Pravda* correspondent, an invitation that was a by-product of Wendell Willkie's trip to Russia. Vishnevsky had plunged into that, too (he started to read Sinclair Lewis' *Babbitt* to prepare himself). But a few days later he was told the trip was off. He never knew why.

The usual preholiday reception was held at Smolny. Vishnevsky attended. So did the full Leningrad Party leadership—Zhdanov, Kuznetsov, the other Party secretaries, Lieutenant General Govorov. Vishnevsky was filled with emotion—twenty-five years of the Revolution, twenty-five years of Bolshevism. It had started in this very hall on the evening of November 8, 1917, when Lenin stepped to the platform and quietly said, "We will now proceed to construct the Socialist order." Vishnevsky tried to contain himself, but it was not easy. He looked at the honor guard—Baltic sailors with wide, bright faces—just like 1917. They listened to Stalin's speech. The news was good. Rommel had been defeated in the western desert. The chandeliers were bright with light (an underwater power cable across the depths of the Ladoga now linked Leningrad with the reactivated Volkhov power station), and the hall was all white and marble and gold. The crowd was mostly in uniform—70 percent of the Party was in the armed forces, 90 percent of the Young Communists.

Vishnevsky did not notice the adjutant who quietly walked up to General Govorov as he sat on the stage at the Assembly Hall. The officer whispered to Govorov, "There is a call for you." Govorov silently left the stage and hurried to the VC wire to Moscow. The conversation—with Stalin—could hardly have been more brief. The words which Stalin uttered were cryptic. He ordered Govorov to proceed with "War Game No. 5."

In his address to the nation that holiday eve Stalin had said that soon "there will be a holiday in our streets." He was referring to Stalingrad, where the Nazi offensive had one more week to run and the Soviet counter-offensive was only a fortnight distant. Soon, he was hinting, Russia would have something to celebrate. To Govorov the coded words meant that Leningrad would have something to celebrate as well.

"War Game No. 5" was a rather sophisticated code by Soviet standards. Dmitri Shcheglov listened one evening to a field telephone operator. "Jasmine" was calling "Rose." Rose reported to Jasmine in a code in which reconnaissance units were called "eyes," sailors were called "ribbons" (from the ribbon on their sailor hats), artillery was "black" (their uniform piping). The general was "the old man." The commander of the Eighth Army was "grandpa." Shells were cucumbers. Shcheglov wondered who was fooling whom.

As the war progressed, slightly more complex codes were employed. But not much. Stalin in April, 1943, was "Comrade Vasilyev," in May and August he was "Comrade Ivanov." Marshal Zhukov was "Konstantinov" in April, 1943, and "Yuryev" in May, 1943. In April, 1943, Marshal N. F. Vatunin was "Fedorov," Nikita S. Khrushchev was "Nikitin," and F. K. Korzhenevich was "Fedotov." In May, 1943, Marshal Rokossovsky was "Kostin."

Most code names derived from the commander's given name. Those for Stalin utilized the commonest of Russian surnames—something like calling him Mr. Smith or Mr. Jones.

Stalin tended to refer to his commanders by family name, contrary to the ordinary Russian habit of using given name and patronymic. In conversation, if Admiral Kuznetsov, for instance, referred to "Andrei Aleksandrovich" (meaning Zhdanov), Stalin would interject, although he very well knew who was meant: "Now which Andrei Aleksandrovich do you mean?" He made an exception for Marshal Shaposhnikov. Shaposhnikov could be called "Boris Mikhailovich" without any question from Stalin.

"War Game No. 5" was Govorov's instruction to proceed with plans for the offensive to lift the Leningrad blockade. Govorov went to his office, opened his safe and took out a fat folder. It had been his habit since he assumed the Leningrad Command to jot down endlessly ideas, plans, notations for the offensive. Now he locked himself in his office on the second floor of Smolny, told his adjutant to let no one in, even on the most urgent business, and began to select the documents he needed.

The November holiday meeting had almost concluded before Govorov returned to his place on the Smolny platform.

Soon a small group of Govorov's commanders, General Bychevsky, chief of engineers, General Georgi Odintsov, chief of artillery, and a few others set to work. This was to be effort No. 5 to break the blockade. And it was to be different. A preliminary draft went to Moscow November 17 and a more detailed plan November 22.

Leningrad was to have as much strength as Volkhov. There was to be a new army, the Sixty-seventh, led by General Dukhanov, one of the best commanders, a man under whom Govorov had once served before the war, when Dukhanov commanded the Leningrad Military District and Govorov was chief of an artillery regiment.

Govorov worked with intense concentration. He literally shut himself in his office, studying his charts and maps, pacing the floor from one end to another, drinking countless glasses of very hot, very strong tea. He was a little farsighted and used glasses for reading and for examining maps. He was a careful, studious man, painstaking about details. Once Vissarion Sayanov said to Govorov that in the early days of the war the Russians had fought bravely but seemed to lack skill in tactics and put too much weight on German military theory.

"Well," Govorov replied, "it seems that way not only to you but to anyone who understands military science. Of course, this is not the time to talk about that. But the time will come when all the mistakes that were committed at the beginning of the war will be discussed at the top of our lungs."

This time, if Govorov could help it, there would be no mistakes.

On the twenty-ninth of November he called in his commanders and laid out the general design of the offensive. The Neva would be forced on an eight-mile front from Nevskaya Dubrovka to Shlisselburg. The Volkhov front would thrust in the Sinyavino area to meet the Leningrad front. There would be a first echelon of four rifle divisions with a brigade of light tanks, a second echelon of three divisions and two brigades of heavy and medium tanks. The second echelon was to go into action within forty-eight hours of the start of the battle. The heavy tanks would cross immediately. There would be 2,000 guns—three times as many as in the disastrous attacks of 1941–42. Plans were to be ready within a month.

Formal orders for the offensive were issued by Stalin on December 8.[2] The objective: to end the blockade of Leningrad. The code for the operation: Iskra, the spark, a name long associated with the Revolution and with Petersburg-Petrograd-Leningrad, the name of the first Social Democratic newspaper, the one which Lenin edited before the break between the Mensheviks and the Bolsheviks.

General Govorov's opponent was Colonel General Lindemann, commander of the Eighteenth Army. Lindemann had more than twenty-five divisions at his disposal. He was well aware of the importance of the forthcoming battle. In an order to his troops he said: "As the source of the Bolshevik Revolution, as the city of Lenin, it is the second capital of the Soviet. Its liberation will constantly be one of the important goals of the Bolsheviks. For the Soviet regime the liberation of Leningrad would equal the defense of Moscow, the battle for Stalingrad."

Lindemann was right.

Govorov was determined to leave nothing to chance. For security all orders were handwritten and in only one copy. Units were prohibited from moving by day. Only small units could be moved through Leningrad and only by varying routes. The established routine of radio communications was maintained, and new units were forbidden the use of radio. No new intelligence operations were permitted, and artillery fire was deliberately dispersed.

Govorov met with the Sixty-seventh Army staff on Christmas Day. With him was Party Secretary Zhdanov, Party Secretary Ya. F. Kapustin, Party Secretary A. I. Makhanov and Mayor Peter Popkov and Marshal Voroshilov. Voroshilov had been assigned by Stalin as liaison between Moscow and Leningrad. The notorious Police General Mekhlis[3] had been assigned as

---

[2] *N.Z.*, p. 427. Barbashin gives the date as December 2. Moscow ordered preparations completed by December 31. (Barbashin, *op. cit.*, p. 237.)

[3] Admiral Kuznetsov, who heartily hated both Mekhlis and the other police general, G. I. Kulik, characterized Mekhlis as "a most unsuitable man for the role of representative of the center at the front. Possessed of wide authority, he always tried to supersede the commander and do everything his own way, but at the same time taking no responsibility for the outcome of the military operation." This trait was first noted during the winter war with Finland in 1939–40. Mekhlis was sent to the Ninth Soviet Army as Stalin's representative. Mekhlis removed dozens of officers and when the 44th Division fell into Finnish encirclement, demanded that its commander, A. I. Vinogradov, be shot.

Political Commissar to General Meretskov on the Volkhov front, and Party
Secretary Kuznetsov had been temporarily named Commissar of the Second
Shock Army on the Volkhov front in an attempt to keep that ill-fated army
from once again falling into encirclement.

Govorov ordered the Sixty-seventh Army to carry out a full simulation of
the forthcoming attack, an operation in which 128 hours of preparation were
invested.

The ice was still thin on the Neva, and General Bychevsky and his engineers kept searching for means of strengthening it so they could put T-34
tanks across the river. Major L. S. Barshai of the Leningrad Subway Construction Trust devised a wooden outrigger to which the tank treads would
be bolted. This enabled the weight to be distributed across the ice. It looked
promising. As Bychevsky showed a model to General Govorov, Marshal
Voroshilov walked in. He insisted on coming to a demonstration the next
day on the Neva near the Novo-Saratov settlement. Bychevsky was hardly
pleased when all the brass—Voroshilov, Govorov, Party Secretary Kuznetsov, General Odintsov and some others—turned up for the test.

The tank started out on the ice with turret open, at Govorov's insistence.
Behind it marched Voroshilov with Govorov at his side. The tank slithered
out on the ice. It had gone about 150 yards when the ice cracked in every
direction. Govorov yanked Voroshilov back from a yawning hole as the

---

Vinogradov was arrested but escaped execution. At the post-mortem on the Finnish war
held in April, 1940, Stalin told Mekhlis, according to Kuznetsov, "You, being right on the
spot, had the habit of depositing the command in your pocket and doing with it as you
pleased." Mekhlis took this as a compliment, Kuznetsov contends, and during World
War II continued to act in this style. In the first few months of war Mekhlis headed the
Army political propaganda organ and was described by an associate, Lev Kopilev, as "a
man remarkably energetic, remarkably vigorous and even more decisive but even less
competent, the master of varied but superficial knowledge and self-confident to the point
of willfulness." Mekhlis was removed from his post as Deputy Commissar of Defense,
reduced in rank and reprimanded by Stalin for his role in the Soviet loss of the Crimea in
the spring of 1942. Mekhlis, typically, sought to shift blame to the army and demanded
that a new general be appointed. Stalin accused him of wanting a "Hindenburg" to command the Soviet troops. Moscow had no Hindenburgs at its disposal, Stalin said, and
charged that Mekhlis was just trying to evade responsibility for his errors. He was formally reprimanded for crude interference in the functions of the front commander and
for giving orders which did not conform to the military situation. Mekhlis tried to im-
plicate Naval Commander A. S. Frolov of the Kerch naval base in the disaster and
threatened to have Frolov shot if Admiral Kuznetsov did not bring him up on summary
court-martial. Admiral Kuznetsov refused. Despite all this, Mekhlis was back in Stalin's
favor within a few months and was named Political Commissar to the Bryansk front in
1943, serving with General I. V. Boldin, one of the ablest Soviet commanders. Soviet
planes carried out an attack on advanced German positions on August 24, 1943. Mekhlis
became convinced the planes were attacking Soviet, not Nazi, lines. He ordered the
squadron grounded and sent before a military tribunal for execution. Only the intervention of an officer who had witnessed the successful air attack on the Nazi lines saved
the airmen. (Shtemenko, *op. cit.*, pp. 18, 50, 55; Kuznetsov, *Nakanune*, pp. 243–244;
VOVSS, p. 156; Lev Kopolev, in *Literaturnoye Nasledstvo Sovetskikh Pisatelei Na
Frontakh Velikoi Otechestvennoi Voiny*, Vol. I, p. 535; A. P. Teremov, *Pylayushchiye
Berega*, Moscow, 1965, p. 47.)

tank plunged under the water. A moment later tankist Mikhail Ivanov, wet, freezing but alive, bobbed up. Someone handed him a flask of vodka.

"Give him the Order of the Red Star," Voroshilov ordered. "And as for you, Bychevsky, we will have a conversation later."

Once again Bychevsky was in trouble. Fortunately, Govorov was not so disturbed. He ordered Bychevsky to continue his experiments.

It was a quiet New Year's in Leningrad. There were only 637,000 people left in the city—not a quarter of the number there a year before. Vera Inber had a party. Most of the Leningrad writers—all of them engaged in war work of some kind—came. So did many of the physicians at her husband's Erisman Hospital. There were cake and wine, vodka and caviar. Aleksandr Kron was there. So were Nikolai Chukovsky and Lev Uspensky. Vsevolod Vishnevsky came in late on the snowy, fresh evening. He had been broadcasting one of his blustery orations ("1943 will bring justice! This year will be *ours*! The blow is nearing. Forward, friends!"). Vera Inber had written out fortunes for each guest on bits of paper. Vishnevsky's said: "Don't think about the future; the future is thinking about you." He liked that.

Vera Inber's husband, Dr. Strashun, cut his finger opening a bottle. One of his colleagues bandaged it with the virtuosity born of treating thousands of more serious wounds. There was a radio speech by President Kalinin and a communiqué reporting enormous trophies and thousands of prisoners at Stalingrad. But Vera Inber was filled with disquiet. She had planned to put down on paper her achievements and her failures for 1942—and her hopes for the New Year. She didn't succeed. She didn't write anything. Her mood was low again. There was another air raid, and she was having trouble with the fifth chapter of "Pulkovo Meridian." Olga Berggolts spoke on the radio. She was more hopeful. She remembered New Year's of 1942. How much better things looked now. She read a poem which she called "The House-warming":

> Again winter. The snow flies . . .
> The enemy still at the city gates,
> But I call you to the housewarming.
> We'll meet the New Year with a party . . .
> We'll breathe warmth into the house
> Where death lived and darkness reigned
> Here will be life. . . .

Because of the weakness of the Neva ice, generals Govorov and Meretskov proposed to Moscow December 27 that the date for the offensive be set back to January 12. Stalin's reply came in on December 28. It read:

YEFREMOV, AFANASYEV, LEONIDOV:
The Stavka of the Supreme Command approves your proposal concerning the timing of preparations and beginning Operation Iskra.

"Yefremov" was the code name for Marshal Voroshilov, "Afanasyev" that of General Meretskov and "Leonidov" that of General Govorov.

The action began at 9:30 A.M. on January 12. More than 4,500 guns opened up on the Germans. The barrage lasted two hours twenty minutes on the Leningrad front, one hour forty-five minutes on the Volkhov front. It was not the familiar story of too little, too late or too weak. The unearthly roar of the multibarreled rockets, the Katyushas, shook the ice-clad earth.

At 11:42 A.M. a green rocket flashed over the Neva. General S. N. Borshchev, whose 268th Infantry Division was to lead the attack, suddenly froze. He saw his troops, mistaking the signal, start to push across the ice, not waiting for the Katyushas to complete their fire. It was too late to halt them. He could only watch in fear that turned to triumph as the men picked their way safely across the ice, their losses minimized by the sudden move.

General Dukhanov's divisions, the 268th led by General Borshchev and the 136th led by General N. P. Simonyak (one of the heroes of the fighting at Hangö), stormed across the Neva. They met heavy Nazi counterattacks, and the 268th was in serious trouble before the combined weight of the Soviet attack began to be felt. The Second Shock Army of Meretskov's Volkhov front pushed straight west toward a link-up with Dukhanov's forces.

Most of the Leningrad correspondents couldn't get permission to go to the front. Luknitsky had been at Dukhanov's command post but was ordered back to Leningrad on the evening of January 11. Orders had been given: "Not one correspondent is permitted here." Luknitsky raced back to Leningrad. It was not until 3 P.M. on January 13 that he and the others were permitted to join the attacking troops.

Sayanov joined the 86th Division pushing into Shlisselburg. It was late night, and the blue light of the moon shone down on the endless drifts which covered the low-lying land. On the edges of the snowy field he saw black shell holes torn in the earth. Everywhere sprawled a jumble of Nazi arms—cannon, machine guns, tommy guns, boxes of ammunition, shells, grenades, a box of iron crosses, cases of cognac, Goebbels' leaflets, tin cans, straw boots, broken cartons of cigarettes, stray wagon wheels. By morning, Sayanov thought, the wind will have dusted over the battlefield and it will disappear under the white powder. But now he could follow the course of the fighting. Here lay the body of a Russian soldier, a youth not more than twenty-three. Even in death he gripped his rifle firmly. He had been firing on the enemy to the last. A heap of expended cartridges lay beside him, his eye was still at the gunsight and his finger on the trigger. Someone had thrown a white camouflage cape over the boy and thrust a stick in the snowdrift with his helmet on it. There was a white paper glued to the helmet, probably the boy's name and possibly that of his family.

The battle raged on. From his headquarters at Novgorod three times Field Marshal von Küchler ordered the Shlisselburg garrison to hold out to the last man.

Rows broke out among the Soviet generals. Marshal Georgi Zhukov, hero of the Battle of Moscow, hero of Stalingrad, had been sent in to "coordinate" between the Volkhov front and Moscow.[4] He got on the VC high-security line to General Simonyak of the 136th Division. Why didn't Simonyak attack the Sinyavino Heights? The Nazi positions there were holding up the Second Shock Army.

"For the same reason the Second Army doesn't attack them," Simonyak replied. "The approach is through a marsh. The losses would be great and the results small."

"Tolstoyite! Passive resister!" shouted Zhukov. "Who are those cowards of yours? Who doesn't want to fight? Who needs to be ousted?"

Simonyak angrily replied that there were no cowards in the Sixty-seventh Army.

"Wise guy," snapped Zhukov. "I order you to attack the heights."

"Comrade Marshal," Simonyak rejoined. "My army is under the command of the Leningrad front commander, General Govorov. I take orders from him."

Zhukov hung up. Simonyak got no order to attack the Sinyavino Heights.

Steadily the Russians pushed ahead. By January 14 the distance separating the Leningrad and Volkhov troops was less than three miles. The confidence of Moscow in the outcome was demonstrated by Stalin's action in promoting Govorov on January 15 to the rank of colonel general. The next day the distance between the two fronts had dwindled to three-quarters of a mile. At midevening on January 17 General Govorov gave a final order: The gap between the two fronts was to be closed by any means. By this time Shlisselburg was almost surrounded. The 86th Division was attacking from the south, and the 34th Ski Brigade of Colonel Ya. F. Potekhin had circled around to the east. The end was near. The German commanders, desperately trying to keep an escape corridor open, ordered a counterattack at 9:30 A.M., January 18. It failed.

Within hours the units of the Leningrad and Volkhov fronts were joining hands—the basic blockade of Leningrad had been broken. The first meeting of Soviet troops came in the morning near Workers' Settlement No. 1, about five miles southeast of Shlisselburg. There at 9:30 A.M. Simonyak's 123rd Rifle Brigade met a unit of the 1240th Regiment of the 372nd Division from the Volkhov front.[5]

---

[4] Marshal Zhukov's name has vanished from most Soviet accounts of the battle. Marshal Meretskov, with whom Zhukov worked, has written several extensive versions without ever mentioning his name—another instance of Soviet military politics.

[5] General Dukhanov says the first meetings occurred at 11:30 A.M. and 11:45 A.M. at Workers' Settlements No. 1 and No. 5 respectively. (Dukhanov, *Zvezda*, No. 1, January, 1964, p. 156.) Gankevich says the meeting occurred at Settlement No. 1 at 10:30 and at No. 5 at 11:45 A.M. (Gankevich, *op. cit.*, p. 120.) Several Soviet sources, including *N.Z.*, treat the meeting at Settlement No. 5 as the first. Major Melkoyan of Leningrad's 123rd Rifles and Major Melnikov of Volkhov's 372nd drew up an "Act" to commemorate their meeting. They timed it at 9:30 A.M., signed the document and stamped it with the official stamps of the 123rd and 372nd divisions. (*Istoriya VOVSS*, Vol. III, pp. 138–139.)

It was dark before Shlisselburg fell. There had been fifteen thousand people in the old fortress city before the war. Only a few hundred were left. The rest had been shipped to Germany, died of hunger or had been executed by the Germans. Oreshek, the hard little nut, the fort which had held out for five hundred days, stood like a battered battleship just off the Shlisselburg piers. Sayanov spent a night at Oreshek, interviewing the defenders. Water trickled down the thick walls. The air was dank. A little oil lamp stood on the table. "It's very gloomy," Sayanov said. "It reminds me of one of the cells where they held the revolutionaries."

"It is," the commander replied.

All Leningrad was waiting. Each evening for days the people had waited for the "last-minute news at 11 P.M." Would the blockade be lifted? When?

All day on the eighteenth rumors ran through the city. Then just before 11 P.M. came the communiqué, read in the solemn tones of Yuri Levitan, Moscow's No. 1 announcer:

"Troops of the Leningrad and Volkhov fronts have joined together and at the same time have broken the blockade of Leningrad."[6]

Vera Inber had no night pass, but she had to get to Radio House. She had to, and she feared she would be too late. Radio House was a long way from Aptekarsky Island. But her fears were groundless. No passes were needed. Everyone was on the street. Leningrad radio stayed on the air until 3 A.M. For once there was no plan, no censor. People spoke. Music played. Poems were read. Speeches were made.

"This snowy moonlit night of January 18–19 will never vanish from the memory of those who experienced it," Vera Inber told the people of Leningrad. "Some of us are older and others are younger. All of us will experience happiness and grief in our lives. But this happiness, the happiness of liberated Leningrad, we will never forget."

Vsevolod Vishnevsky was at the command post of the fleet artillery when the communiqué came in. He promptly jotted in his diary: "Seventeen months of blockade, of torment, of expectation. But we held out! Now there is a holiday in our street!"

Pavel Luknitsky was in Shlisselburg. At three minutes to 1 A.M., January 19, less than two hours after the victory communiqué, he managed to get a direct military telegraph line to Moscow and sent off the first story to the Moscow press about the lifting of the blockade. A scoop.

Olga Berggolts wrote a poem:

> My dear ones, my far ones, have you heard?
> The cursed circle is broken. . . .

---

[6] The Germans lost 13,000 killed, 1,250 in prisoners, in the operation. General Fedyuninsky, General Meretskov's deputy, was seriously wounded by mortar fire January 20, and General Bolotnikov, Leningrad front armored commander, was killed January 22. (Fedyuninsky, *op. cit.*, pp. 140–142.)

But she warned:

> The blockade is not yet completely broken.
> Farewell, my loved ones. I am going
> To my ordinary, dangerous work
> In the name of the new life of Leningrad.

It was true. The flags went up in the streets, red flags everywhere. Girls danced down the pavement. They spoke to everyone. They threw their arms around soldiers. It made Vishnevsky think of the February Revolution. In the Radio House studios everyone kissed each other—Olga Berggolts, Boris Likharev, Yelena Vechtomova, Director Yasha Babushkin.

The siege had lasted 506 days. But, though the Germans had been pushed back, they still sat on Leningrad's doorstep. Their guns still raked the city.

On February 7 Pavel Luknitsky went to the Finland Station. Shell holes gaped. The train shed was a tangle of steel and girders. But the platform was decorated with red flags and bunting. At 10:09 A.M. a light locomotive, No. L-1208, pulling two passenger cars and a string of freight cars, chuffed into the station. It had come from the new line connecting Leningrad with the "mainland" via the new Shlisselburg bridge across the Neva and Volkhovstroi.[7] A band struck up. The crowd cheered. Mayor Popkov spoke. So did Party Secretary Kuznetsov. Just before noon the meeting ended and the train dispatcher shouted: "Train No. 719, Leningrad-Volkhovstroi, Engineer Fedorov, is prepared to depart!"

It was the 526th day of the blockade. Train service had begun again by an indirect, roundabout way, over temporary bridges and running a murderous corridor of Nazi artillery fire. The blockade was lifted, but only partially. Most Leningraders thought the full and final end of the siege was at hand. They were wrong. Many days, many weeks, many months, many lives lay between that February day and the ultimate freeing of the city.

---

[7] One version claims the train brought a load of food from Chelyabinsk. (*N.Z.*, p. 438.)

49 . *The 900 Days Go On*

NOT MUCH WAS CHANGED IN LENINGRAD BY THE JANUARY victory, not as much as the Leningrad survivors had hoped. Danger stayed at their sides. The hardships did not vanish, and the city lived in fear that its tenuous connection with the "mainland" might be broken at any moment.

That connection was maintained through what quickly came to be called "the corridor of death"—a narrow strip of territory at Shlisselburg where the German guns were only five hundred yards distant. At any moment Leningrad's link with the rest of Russia might be severed. In fact, only seventy-six trains managed to slip through the corridor of death in February, and the record in March was little better. Again and again heavy German artillery shells blasted the trackage into tangles of torn rails. The guns were mounted on the Sinyavino Heights in full view of the railroad tracks. In eleven months the Germans cut the railroad twelve hundred times. Often the trains could not make their way through for days. Usually passage was attempted at night, running blacked out without signal lights. Not until Special Engine Column No. 48, an elite military rail unit, was set up to handle operations through the corridor of death did service begin to improve. In the end 4,500,000 tons of freight were delivered to Leningrad in 1943, largely in the last months of the year. The cost in lives was heavy.

The danger which hung over the city lay in the fact that the Nazis hoped to close the narrow corridor and reimpose a full blockade. Not for a moment did this thought leave the minds of General Govorov and Party Secretary Zhdanov. The Germans, to compensate for being driven back a few miles, shelled Leningrad savagely. Not since September 4, 1941, when the first German long-range guns went into action at Tosno, had the shelling been so deadly.

There was no reason for Leningrad to relax. German strength had shown no sign of weakening, despite the great Russian victory at Stalingrad in January, 1943, in which the Nazi Sixth Army under Field Marshal von Paulus had been shattered with the loss of 300,000 German troops. The

Germans still stood on the Pulkovo Heights, where they could see with unaided eyes the Admiralty spire and the upward thrusting needle of the Peter and Paul Fortress. They held all Leningrad's environs, all the Baltic littoral, all the ancient lands of Novgorod, all Central Russia to within 130 miles of Moscow itself, all the rich lands of the Black Earth belt, all the Ukraine and the Black Sea's northern shores. Allied operations were moving ahead in Africa, but there was still no second front in Europe. Supplies from the United States to the Soviet Union were still only a trickle. The tide was slowly turning against Hitler, but this was hardly evident to the grim populace of Leningrad.

The city now bore little resemblance to the majestic capital of prewar 1941. It was more like that Petersburg of which Turgenev wrote: "... these empty, wide, gray streets, these gray-white, yellow-gray, gray-pink peeling plaster houses with their deep-set windows—that is our Northern Palmyra. Everything visible from all sides, everything clear, frighteningly sharp and clear, and all sadly sleeping." The city did not sleep, but it was empty. There were not many more people walking the streets of Leningrad than walked the streets of Turgenev's Petersburg in 1860 or 1870.

The people were somnambulant, numb from the terrible events which they had survived, uncertain of what lay ahead. The January victory affected their psychology more than their physical beings. The ration was increased to 700 grams of bread a day, almost a loaf and a half, on February 22. That was for workers in heavy industry. The ration for other workers was 600 grams, for employees 500 and for dependents and children 400. No one got fat. Supplies were uncertain. Meat and butter were seldom available. Not until well into 1943 did American canned butter, Spam, powdered eggs, powdered milk and sugar appear. Leningraders were grateful, although as they said, "Russian sugar is sweeter and Russian butter tastes better."

The city looked forward to celebrating May Day, 1943, as the first real holiday since the outbreak of war. But it was wet, cold, windy and snowy. The snow began in early morning and continued for hours—clinging, water-laden snow that turned the Champs de Mars, the Summer Gardens and the Smolny grounds into a fairyland of dark columns and snow-bowed branches. There was no parade in Palace Square, but factory workers were given the day off—their first free day since June 22, 1941, except for the winter of 1941–42 when hardly a factory operated for lack of fuel, lack of electricity and the illness and death of the working force. Food stores stayed open, and there was no time off for factories which were engaged in continuous operations, for power and water stations and communications facilities.

Red flags and bunting decorated the city, along with hundreds of badly painted portraits of Stalin and Zhdanov—more of Zhdanov than of Stalin. There were speeches on the radio. Mayor Peter Popkov spoke. So did Admiral Tributs, commander of the Baltic Fleet, and General Govorov.

Govorov declared that the winter offensive had smashed eight German divisions and cost the enemy 100,000 men. But he warned that German reserves were pouring in and "the storming of the city may occur at any moment."

The imminence of a new German attack was much in Soviet minds. Party Secretary Zhdanov met a few days later in Smolny with top Party workers. He demanded greater attention to AA defenses and workers battalions. He warned all that Leningrad "is a military city."

The warnings of Govorov and Zhdanov were hardly needed. The Germans delivered their own reminder on May Day. There had been heavy shelling of the city for several days, so heavy that the hearing in Vera Inber's right ear was affected. At 9 A.M. on May Day she was awakened by the rocking of her apartment building. Eight heavy shells, one after the other, landed in the vicinity. Probably, she thought, they were fired from railroad guns. Vishnevsky also attributed the shelling to railroad guns. Everyone in Leningrad had become a specialist in heavy armament by this time.

One shell hit a trolleycar on the Nevsky, killing almost all the passengers. Another hit the public library. The shelling went on all day at irregular intervals. Each time the German guns opened up, Soviet counterbattery fire suppressed them.

In the evening Vsevolod Vishnevsky, his wife and Vsevolod Azarov went for a walk in the brooding quiet. The flags fluttered in the occasional wind. They had a holiday meal—a few drinks of vodka, some soup with meat, rice pastries, fruit compote and tea. ("Luxury!" was Vishnevsky's comment.) Later he read Tolstoy's *Childhood and Youth*, drank a cup of coffee with his wife and talked about the psychology of citizens of a besieged city, the differences in feeling between those in the city and those in the trenches.

The threat of a new German frontal assault hung over Leningrad. The Nazis were still strong, and just ahead lay the terrible Battle of Kursk, possibly the bloodiest of the war. General Govorov was cautious as to what summer might bring. On June 3 he suggested that the "worst is behind us. In 1941 we stopped the Germans; in 1942 we didn't give them a yard; in 1943 we began to break the blockade, and it is our duty to carry the task to a victorious end."

He spoke these words at Smolny at a session of the Leningrad City Council attended by Party Secretaries Zhdanov and Kuznetsov as well as Admiral Tributs. The occasion was the presentation of the first medals "For the Defense of Leningrad." The medals were authorized for everyone who had survived the Leningrad siege. Mayor Peter Popkov handed them out. No. 40 went to Valerian Bogdanov-Berezovsky, the composer. He noted that they were handed out alphabetically. His initial being the second in the alphabet, he got a low number. Vsevolod Vishnevsky got No. 98. ("In the first hundred!" he commented.)

Vera Inber got her medal on June 8 along with other writers, intellectuals and scientists. She was so moved she was unable to say a word. "This little metal disk joins to itself all of Leningrad," she noted.[1]

The summer drifted along. The lilacs this year, Vera Inber noticed, were extraordinary. She could not remember their being so heavy, so fragrant, so numerous. Birdcherry was everywhere. Leningrad was supposed to average thirty-five cloudless days a year. It seemed as though a new record for sunshine might be set this summer. Despite severe difficulties some artistic and scientific institutions trickled back. The Bolshoi Drama Theater was permitted to come for a temporary visit at the end of March. It stayed on and in June was permitted to resume permanent operations. The Musical Comedy Theater put five new productions into rehearsal. The stadium reopened May 30 for a summer football season (won by the Dynamo Club). The second anniversary of war, June 22, the 661st day of the siege, passed almost without notice. Vishnevsky remarked in his diary that it was the summer solstice—eighteen hours and fifty-two minutes long. He spent most of the day arguing with members of the Military Council about his new play, *The Walls of Leningrad*. They wanted him to eliminate "negative characters." Vishnevsky told his critics, "I am sorry to see this bureaucratic cautiousness and calculation. Much is being forgotten and has been forgotten about the fall of 1941. This play is entirely authentic and taken from life."

The process of forgetting, as Vishnevsky was to learn, had only begun. Early in the year a new House of Scientists had been set up by the City Party organization. It set out to produce a book on the role of Leningrad scientists in the days of the war and blockade. The printer's proofs of this work still lie in the archives of the Leningrad Public Library. Its publication was never permitted.

Late July and August brought the worst shelling of the war to Leningrad. Never had Vera Inber experienced so terrifying a day as July 24. The Germans fired in short bursts. One shell hit an overloaded streetcar on the Liteiny Bridge. Vera Inber saw from her window an ordinary pickup truck arrive at the hospital filled with wounded. An hour later another truck arrived, filled with bodies. She saw an exposed shinbone poking out from under the canvas. The admitting director took one look at the truck's load and ordered it to the morgue. That evening Vera Inber talked with a surgeon. The summer's problems were bad, but those of the winter of 1942 had been worse. Then, he recalled, when he was doing an operation, the blood and pus froze on his hands, covering them like gloves. Now he had more wounded to care for, but primitive sanitary conditions had been restored to the hospital.

Vera Inber found the new shelling worse to endure than the trials of the

---

[1] A rumor went around Leningrad that only soldiers and "the specially chosen" would get medals. Vishnevsky wrote a story which was published in *Leningradskaya Pravda* July 4, emphasizing that all Leningraders who had been in the city during the siege would be so honored. (Vishnevsky, *Sobrannye Sochineniya*, Vol. 3, p. 246.)

winter of 1941–42. She began to be afraid—involuntarily afraid—of going out on the street. The whine of shells filled the air. "Already the first yellow leaves lie on the asphalt," she noted August 10. "Day after day the threatening monotone of whining shells. (Even right now.) I can't help it. I'm afraid to go on the street. And not only me. It is very hard." Even Vsevolod Vishnevsky found his optimism deserting him. His diary entries noted how tired he was, how difficult to keep up his spirits. "I feel tired and washed out," he wrote September 1. "It's from the blockade. We've got to break the blockade—completely—and we are falling behind."

The shelling was so heavy that the square in front of the Finland Station began to be called "the valley of death" and the Liteiny Bridge was christened "the devil's bridge." Extraordinary steps were ordered to reduce casualties. Trains were rerouted from the Finland Station to the Piskarevsky and Kushelevka stations. The Aurora and Molodezhny movie houses were closed. Changes were made in 132 streetcar stops, hours were revised for movies and theaters, special sandbagging was ordered at ninety stores and eight establishments were moved. In street after street new signs in white and blue paint went up: "Citizens: In case of shelling this side of the street is the most dangerous." The July, 1943, casualties were 210 killed and 921 wounded. There was serious reason to believe that the Germans had infiltrated agents who were giving their gunners corrections on their fire. Colonel N. N. Zhdanov was placed in charge of a special counterbattery offensive to try to bring the Nazi guns under control.

Rumors swept Leningrad that the war would be over September 15. Vishnevsky, typically, blamed the rumors on Nazi agents. An elderly writer told him that the poet Nikolai Tikhonov had predicted the war would last at least another year. What was Vishnevsky's opinion? Vishnevsky hedged. The war would go on through the winter, but it might be shortened "if our allies fight." (This was at the height of the Soviet campaign for a second front.) Vishnevsky's friend persisted. Was there any chance of the shelling coming to an end? Vishnevsky said, accurately, that there was no hope until the blockade was finally lifted. The German shelling remained at a very high level. In September, 11,394 shells fell in the city, 124 persons were killed, 468 wounded. For the first time since the start of the war the artillery barrage had become the chief concern of people. There were days when the life of the city was brought almost to a halt. Even so, Luknitsky noticed, the militia girls who had replaced regular police in directing traffic stayed on the job, calm, lively and jolly. Not infrequently they were wounded or killed by shell fragments. Another girl would promptly fill the spot. Men and women were better dressed, men mostly in uniform. But women looked much prettier, their summer clothes bright and attractive. Everyone again had a garden plot. In the Champs de Mars on benches surrounded by patches of potatoes and turnips, well-dressed (but callus-handed) ladies sat in the sunshine reading Shakespeare, the stories of Jack London or the newest issue of the literary journal *Oktyabr*. Nikolai Chukovsky believed that never in history had Leningrad been so beautiful as in the summer of 1943. The emptiness of the city emphasized for him its unbelievable beauty. Even the ruins seemed to possess an unearthly quality, particularly when the northern lights played across the sky and shed their curious flat colors on the gardens, courtyards and squares.

The city was still filled with empty apartments, but a commission had begun to inspect them, carefully noting the contents and attempting to ascertain whether the owner was dead, evacuated or serving at the front. People put carpets down on their floors, pictures back on the walls. A woman told Luknitsky, "I don't want to live any longer like a pig. I don't know whether I'll survive the next hour, but right now I am going to live like a human being." Schools slowly resumed—374 had opened before the end of the year—but industrial life barely flickered. Many plants produced only 5 or 10 percent of prewar output, and the number of factory workers was five times less than in 1940. Leningrad was still a front-line city.

In the worst days of blockade, in February, 1942, when the city lay dark, frozen, starving and near death, the City Council had set its surviving architects, among them Academician Nikolsky in the cellar of the Hermitage, to drafting plans for the future Leningrad—not just the reconstruction of Leningrad but what came to be called the Restoration, the Renaissance of the Northern Palmyra. Created by men working without light, without heat, with mittened hands, the plans gradually took shape—the dream of the new Leningrad, a city that would combine the old grandeur of imperial Petersburg with the new greatness of Soviet Leningrad. On January 19, 1943, the day after the breakthrough, the City Council ordered the plans put into action. At first, of course, only repairs could be considered (and in the summer of 1943 the German bombardment was destroying Leningrad more rapidly than it could be rebuilt). Indeed, in all of 1943 only eight buildings and 60,000 square feet of housing were rehabilitated. But on October 14 the City Council ordered ready by January 1 a complete architectural and technical design for a new Leningrad which would transform the city into a monument of contemporary technology, appearance and comfort.

People began to count on change, on better times. Vera Inber overheard a remark: "In such a time humor has to be kept on a leash." She wondered about that. So did others. Leningrad had begun to tell jokes—not very good jokes, but jokes. Vishnevsky scribbled them in his diary:

Two German soldiers talking:
Fritz: "How would you like to fight?"
Hans: "I'd like to be a German soldier with a Russian general, British arms and American rations."

"Why are you fighting?"
Hitler: "For living space."

Stalin: "Because we were attacked."
Churchill: "Who told you we are fighting?"

Vera Inber jotted down a couple of children's blockade remarks:

Child: "Mama, what's ham?"
The mother explained.
Child: "And has anyone ever tasted it?"

A little girl to her mother: "Mama, what's a giant and what kind of a ration does he get?"

Vissarion Sayanov put down some exchanges:

"Where are you from?"
"I'm a Leningrader from Tambov."

A front soldier: "Yesterday I suddenly saw a crow fly out of some bushes on the other bank. I thought there must be Germans there so I gave a shot and a wolf ran out."
"There are a lot of animals around."
"Yes, especially two-legged ones."

Leningrad was coming to itself again. As Vishnevsky put it: "The Germans now are just a hindrance. The people have begun to plan the future."

But there were other aspects of Soviet life, not so pleasant, that once again came to the fore: the sharp literary and political quarrels, the inner tensions which so often turned Soviet life into agony.

During the worst days almost all of this had vanished. Leningrad had become one family. Again and again the diarists of Leningrad, the survivors, spoke of this feeling. As seventeen-year-old Zina Vorozheikina, a student in the tenth grade, put it: "All of us Leningraders are one family, baptized by the monstrous blockade—one family, one in our grief, one in our experience, one in our hopes and expectations." Some even suggested that when the war ended Leningrad boys should marry only Leningrad girls—they had become a special breed, a special people.

But the blockade did not end the political and social processes of Soviet life. Vishnevsky noted that even so fine a woman as Vera Inber could not resist delicately "sticking a knife in the ribs" of her fellow poet, Olga Berggolts, for writing "minor, sad, old-fashioned" poems about the blockade.

In late October Olga Berggolts and Georgi Makogonenko, one of the Radio Leningrad staff who had sat up all through the night of January 12, 1942, outlining their projected book, *Leningrad Speaking*, presented to the Leningrad Writers Union a scenario for a film about the Leningrad siege. Vishnevsky found it observant, precise, sincere, pure. It was a story which centered about Young Communists who helped the people in their frozen, bleak, starvation-haunted flats during the winter of 1941–42.

"But," wondered Vishnevsky, "can the cinema convey the truth about Leningrad, about its people, about their spirit?"

The question was pertinent. The film, in fact, suffered the same fate as *Leningrad Speaking*. It never saw the light of day.

Vishnevsky himself was preoccupied with his play about the siege, *The Walls of Leningrad*. He had begun work on it late in 1942 and telegraphed his close friend Aleksandr Tairov, director of Moscow's Kamerny Theater,[2] January 2, 1943, that he was "writing a big play." He gave a first reading May 25, 1943, to a group of Baltic Fleet propaganda workers and the director of the Baltic Fleet Theater, L. Osipov.

On June 17 he read a new version to a group that included Nikolai Tikhonov, Vissarion Sayanov, Vera Inber, Aleksandr Zonin and some others. He capsulized their opinions for Tairov:

> Tikhonov: This is one of your strongest things . . . a saga of the sailors. . . .
> Inber: The play is remarkably strong and emotionally fulfilling. There will be difficulties. . . .
> L. Osipov (director of the Baltic Fleet Theater): Vsevolod Vishnevsky has given us a play, very close to us, very strong. . . .
> A. Zonin: The play is philosophical—the people are connected with the fate of their country, with history and not with sexual-personal themes.
> Pilyugin (director of the Bolshoi Drama Theater): It is an attractive work. Like all plays of Vishnevsky, it is difficult for the theater.

By mid-August the play was put into production by the Baltic Fleet Theater. In October the chief naval propaganda commissar, the fearsome Ivan (the Terrible) Rogov, asked Vishnevsky to play down one of his chief characters, Prince Belogorsky, a naval officer who had served under the Czar and was a member of the nobility. Rogov also wanted more "discipline and heroism."

At 6 P.M. on November 23 Vishnevsky appeared at the Vyborg House of Culture, where the play was to be performed. The cast gave him a present, a desk set and two candlesticks, made out of shell casings.

There was a full house—members of the Fleet Military Council, members of the City Council, girls from the AA batteries, sailors and friends of Vishnevsky's. The audience was excited. At the conclusion the curtain had to be raised eleven times in response to applause. The chief of the Leningrad Arts Committee, Boris Zagursky, congratulated Vishnevsky. Everything seemed fine. Then the director rushed to Vishnevsky pale and trembling: "The Military Council member forbids the play to be performed. In fact, he said, he strongly forbids it."

This was Vice Admiral N. K. Smirnov, and his complaint was simple: Too many negative characters; the portrait of the commissar was almost a burlesque, that of Prince Belogorsky dubious; regular officers played too small a role.

---

[2] Tairov's Kamerny Theater was suspended in 1950 after a long period of harassment by the literary dictators of the late Stalin era.

As Vishnevsky commented: "In their opinion the tragic days of September, 1941, should appear on the stage in ordinary colors, all 'cleaned up.' To show openly the trials, the trauma, the difficulties, and how they were overcome grates on their eyes and ears. Maybe this is understandable from the point of view of 1943. Maybe it is fully understandable (?)."

What Vishnevsky meant to convey by the question mark is not clear. But he went on to recall bitterly the fatal literary wars of the 1930's. Neither in his extended correspondence with Tairov nor in his bulging diary did he confide his innermost thoughts. Instead, he noted in his diary that he had placed an exact account of what had happened and of all the discussions in a special folder in his files. It remains there to this day, unpublished.

He struggled to control his feelings:

> I am thinking intensely about the general tasks of literature, about the difficulties of the work of writers, of how practically I can determine the fate of this play. Evidently what is needed now by the situation is not philosophical argument, not a tragic painting, but simple shock, agitational messages. I understand that, but it seemed to me that this time I had written an "optimistic" tragedy. I thought all evening, all night. I must save this work—the first important play about the defense of Leningrad. I must rework and revise it.

Unable to sleep, he picked up William Shirer's *Berlin Diary* and tried to read. But he could not keep his mind off his play. His telephone kept ringing, with people complimenting him, asking him when the premiere would be.

He decided to send a letter to one of the Leningrad Party secretaries, Makhanov, to enlist his support:

> I have written a play on a most difficult theme . . . about one of the most tragic moments in the history of the war—about the autumn of 1941 in Leningrad. . . . This production is part of my soul, part of my heart. You had a good reaction to the play and approved its appearance in *Zvezda* [the magazine]. Then came a sudden turnabout. Evidently on the stage the text sounded sharper and more tragic than in the reading. The army and the fleet are on the eve of the decisive offensive on the Leningrad front, and they need some other kind of play. . . .

Vishnevsky's appeal was fruitless. The verdict was simple: "The negative characters are clearly stronger than the positive. The former prince is a patriot and a hero. The commissar is a fool."

As Vishnevsky bitterly commented: "Really—haven't commissars ever been fools?"

The question was vain. The play was dead. Nothing Vishnevsky could do would revive it. Something worse was at hand. Leningrad did stand on the eve of liberation. The moment for which Vishnevsky had been waiting for nearly nine hundred days was near. But he was not to be there to witness it. On December 6 he was at the Party Bureau and got an outline of the forthcoming offensive. The news bolstered his shaken spirits. The next day he was summarily ordered to Moscow. No protest availed. He was not to see the end of the blockade. Orders were orders. Like a good soldier he made his preparations, typically noting in his diary: "Moscow! The heart of Russia, the center of the new world! I will have interviews and meetings. How has it changed in two and a half years? How will we find our home?"[3]

Preparations for the liberation of Leningrad had begun in September, 1943. All summer long fighting had gone on in an effort to wrest the Sinyavino Heights from the Germans. The Sixty-seventh Army attacked July 22 and was engaged until mid-September, but despite heavy losses the Russians could not dislodge the Germans. On the Central Front the Russians had defeated the Germans in the savage Battle of Kursk-Orel and had liberated Kharkov once again. German losses had been heavy, and the Soviet High Command was now planning with confidence for fall-winter offensives to drive the Nazis from central Russia and the Ukraine.

General Govorov held his first staff meeting to draw up plans for finally smashing the blockade on September 9. Two variants were drafted: Neva I and Neva II. Neva I was for use in the event the Germans, weakened on other fronts, withdrew on their own from the Leningrad area. The Stavka in Moscow warned General Govorov of this possibility, and Leningrad had similar intelligence of its own. The Germans had begun to set up defense posts at river crossings which would be used in a retreat. They were putting in mine fields and preparing to destroy bridges.

The principal effort, naturally, was devoted to Neva II. In its final version it called for a three-pronged offensive, driving from the Oranienbaum foothold, the Pulkovo Heights and in the direction of Novgorod (this attack to be carried out by General Meretskov's Volkhov front).

The offensive would not start until winter, when the ice was hard and troops could move more easily. The Leningrad Command had long since discovered that winter was the season which gave them a natural advantage over the Germans.

General Govorov carried out a detailed inspection of the Oranienbaum position in mid-October. It would be necessary to move large quantities of troops and guns into the area, and Govorov wanted to be certain that nothing went wrong. He then met at Smolny with Admiral Tributs, the top naval command, and Party Secretaries Zhdanov and Kuznetsov. The Baltic Fleet

---

[3] Vishnevsky and his wife left for Moscow December 9. He carried the manuscript of *The Walls of Leningrad* with him. His wife had made a scale drawing of the stage settings. Vishnevsky, against his violent protest, was compelled to take a medical examination and go to a convalescent home because of his "nervous condition." He did not leave Moscow to return to Leningrad until March 5, 1944. In the interval he revised and watered down *The Walls of Leningrad*. It was viewed by Rogov, the iron naval commissar, June 30, 1944, and finally publicly presented in Moscow August 21. The original version has never been published. (Anisimov, *Literaturnoye Nasledstvo Sovetskikh Pisatelei Na Frontakh Velikoi Otechestvennoi Voiny*, Vol. II, pp. 239–240; Vishnevsky, *Sobrannye Sochineniya*, Vol. III, pp. 458 et seq.)

had a major assignment—to shift secretly the Second Shock Army from Leningrad to Oranienbaum before ice hindered movement in the Neva River. It was no small task, involving 2 rifle corps, a tank brigade, 600 guns, mountains of shells and equipment. Beginning November 5, each night blacked-out caravans put out from the wharves at the Leningrad factory, Kanat, and from the naval base at Lisy Nos and landed on the Oranienbaum side without loss 30,000 troops, 47 tanks, 400 guns, 1,400 trucks, 3,000 horses and 10,000 tons of ammunition and supplies. After the ice froze, another 22,000 troops, 800 machines, 140 tanks and 380 guns were sent over.

The familiar arguments broke out between Leningrad and Moscow. Marshal Voronov was afraid that the Leningrad artillerists after three years of static defense might not be able to meet breakthrough conditions. He sent in some commanders who had distinguished themselves at Stalingrad and in the bloody summer battle at Kursk. Voronov was concerned about the Oranienbaum operation. He recommended that light artillery be employed, fearful that heavy guns could not be moved across the Gulf of Finland. He was reassured when General G. F. Odintsov, the Leningrad artillery chief, reported that 1,300 carloads of war materials had been landed on the Oranienbaum *place d'armes* and that, on the front as a whole, a concentration of 200 guns per kilometer had been achieved.

General Govorov urged Marshal Voronov to come to Leningrad for the offensive. "Leningrad is your native city," Govorov said. "Come and help us with the artillery."

This was not entirely without guile. Leningrad was trying to get more guns. Voronov was resisting. Finally, Party Secretary Zhdanov telephoned: "You are a Leningrader. You must be objective. You know our needs. We don't even have enough revolvers."

The argument grew sharp. Voronov declined to make more guns available. Zhdanov took the case to Stalin.[4] In the end 21,600 guns were provided for the Leningrad and Volkhov fronts, more than 600 antiaircraft guns, 1,500 Katyusha rocket guns, 1,475 tanks and self-propelled guns and 1,500 planes. It was probably the greatest concentration of fire power ever assembled— more than the Russians had massed at Stalingrad.

The Leningrad and Volkhov fronts had 1,241,000 officers and men. Op-

---

[4] The rows between Stalin, the Stavka, the Politburo and the generals grew more savage as the war advanced. Stalin intervened in the most trivial decisions. If an antiaircraft unit was to be moved, he would insist, "Who will take responsibility if the German planes attack this objective?" No one could guarantee anything in war and if, as was often the case, a man like Marshal Voronov assumed responsibility, Stalin could have his head if something went wrong. If Stalin gave an order, it did not mean that Malenkov or Beria would carry it out. One day Stalin ordered Malenkov and Beria to give Marshal Voronov 900 trucks for a sudden troop movement. Later Beria said, "I'll give you 400 machines and this conversation is finished!" Only when Voronov threatened to go back to Stalin did he get the 900 trucks. The common penalty with which Stalin threatened his associates and with which they threatened each other was death—execution by the firing squad. (Voronov, *Istoriya SSSR*, No. 3, March, 1965, pp. 9 *et seq.*)

posing them was Field Marshal von Küchler's Army Group Nord. Its strength was estimated at 741,000 men. He had 10,070 guns, 385 tanks and 370 planes, divided between the Eighteenth and Sixteenth armies.

Top Soviet commanders had been brought in to direct the principal armies. The Second Shock Army was commanded by the veteran Lieutenant General I. I. Fedyuninsky, who had repeatedly demonstrated his brilliance on the Leningrad front. The Forty-second Army, which was to drive over the Pulkovo Heights, was led by Colonel General I. I. Maslennikov.

One frosty, sunny morning in early January, 1944, General Govorov went to the Pulkovo Heights. No square meter of the Leningrad front had seen more fighting than this bloody hill, still dominated by the wrecked buildings of the Leningrad observatory. Today the front was quiet and sparkling brilliantly under its cover of snow. Govorov closely inspected the scene with his corps commander, Major General N. P. Simonyak. He visualized how it would be transformed in the first seconds of the crushing artillery barrage. He could not see the place where the Forty-second Army would meet with the Second Shock Army emerging from Oranienbaum. But he knew where it was. He knew how precisely timed the operation must be. The first objective was the recapture of Gatchina. Who held Gatchina controlled the front. Once Soviet troops had re-entered that battered town, the Germans must withdraw from Mga because they would have only one escape route left. Mga—soon it would be back in Russian hands again. Soon the terrible chapter of the Leningrad encirclement would unroll in the reverse direction. Govorov sighed. He could not think of Mga without a feeling of depression. "To Mga," he said frankly, "my heart has never been inclined."

He went back to his headquarters and called in his artillerymen once again. "On the tempo of our advance," he warned, "hangs the fate of Leningrad. If we are held up, Leningrad will be subjected to such a terrible shelling that it will be impossible to stand it—so many people will be killed, so many buildings demolished."

On January 11 a final meeting was held at Smolny. Every detail was checked. General Govorov said his men were fully ready. Long-range artillery had already begun methodically to destroy Nazi strongpoints. The air arm was carrying out intensive bombardment. There were 155,000 Communists and 115,000 Young Communists to stiffen the Leningrad front. The partisan forces in the rear of the Germans had been instructed to carry out simultaneous attacks and sabotage of rear bases, supplies and communications.

The operation was timed to start on the morning of January 14 from the Oranienbaum *place d'armes*. The attack from Pulkovo was to be launched January 15. The forces of General Meretskov were to attack January 14.

General Govorov flew in a light U-2 observation plane to the Oranienbaum sector to be present for the jump-off. During the night long-range bombers attacked German communications, railroads, command points. Heavy artillery at Pulkovo and Kolpino opened up to try and demolish the extraordinary reinforced steel-and-concrete firing points (often sunk two or three stories into the ground) which constituted the backbone of the Nazi defenses.

January 14 was the 867th day since the Germans had taken Mga, the 867th day that Leningrad had been cut off from normal communications with the "mainland," the 867th day of the siege.

The tension in Smolny was almost more than nerves could bear. They were waiting for word from the commander, from General Govorov with the Second Shock Army on the Oranienbaum *place d'armes*. But the front was drenched in fog. The reconnaissance planes of the Thirteenth Air Army of Lieutenant General S. D. Rybalchenko were unable to take off. There was no correction for artillery fire. Bombing planes were grounded.[5] General Govorov tried to return to Leningrad, but fog held him on the ground. Yet the Soviet forces had jumped off. The enormous concentration of guns on the *place d'armes* had laid down 104,000 shells on the Nazi lines in a one-hour-and-five-minute bombardment, not counting Katyusha rocket fire. The great cannon of the Baltic Fleet and the batteries at Kronstadt, Seraya Loshad and Krasnaya Gorka joined in.

The fog was so thick that General Bychevsky, the engineering chief who fought all through the Leningrad siege, was unable to see anything from the command post of General Maslennikov of the Forty-second Army at Pulkovo. But Bychevsky's sappers were delighted. They went on clearing a path through the mine fields, invisible to the Germans. General Govorov, unable to restrain his impatience, insisted on flying back to Leningrad over the violent objection of the air commander, General M. I. Samokhoin. Years later General Odintsov, who accompanied him, still remembered vividly how they circled and circled in the fog before locating the Leningrad airfield.

The Second Shock Army made progress, despite the fog. It advanced about two miles on a six-or-seven-mile front—not brilliant but not bad. It had still not emerged, however, from the roadless marshes and wastes that lay between it and its objectives. Snow began to fall.

The night of January 14–15 was sleepless at Smolny, at Blagodatny Lane, where the Forty-second Army had its headquarters, and in the mangled outskirts that stretched from shell-torn Sheremetyev Park to Pulkovo and Srednyaya Rogatka. The first echelon divisions were at forward positions, ready to attack.

Everyone in Leningrad knew what was happening. The roar of artillery, the crash of bombs filled the air. For three years Leningrad had awaited this day, this shaking of the earth, this roar in the heavens.

The artillery barrage for the Pulkovo attack was timed to begin at 9:30 A.M., January 15. It was to last one hundred minutes.

Just before that hour Party Secretary Zhdanov appeared at the artillery observation post of Colonel N. N. Zhdanov. He had told him the night

[5] Only 109 planes were able to participate in the preattack strike because of the bad weather. (Barbashin, *op. cit.*, p. 331.)

before: "We're of the same family [actually they merely shared a common name]. Tomorrow I would like to be at your command point. I hope you can arrange this."

Colonel Zhdanov was not delighted. His post was in the unfinished Palace of Soviets building, giving a good view from Ligovo to Pushkin. The Germans knew very well that there was an observation post in the building. They often showered it with fire. It would do Colonel Zhdanov no good if Party Secretary Zhdanov was killed at his post. He decided to take some precautions. He constructed a strongpoint on the ground floor, where he proposed to delay the Party Secretary for a few minutes, getting him to put on warm clothes before taking him up to the observation post by a rope lift that his soldiers had built into the unfinished elevator shaft. The delay, he calculated, would be sufficient to enable the Soviet barrage to start, after which he did not think the Germans would have time to bother with the observation post. His calculations proved correct. Zhdanov was delayed until the Soviet barrage was a few minutes under way. He was lifted up safely, watched the troops begin to move out to the German lines, and then was brought down to return to Smolny. In the course of the artillery preparation the Russians laid down 220,000 shells—not counting rocket shells—on the Nazi positions.[6] Three air wings bombed the Nazi trenches and forward installations. The storm of the German "circle of steel" which Colonel General Lindemann had assured his nervous troops could never be broken had begun. In the first day the Russians drove a wedge from one to nearly three miles deep into the Nazi lines on a three-mile front. General Maslennikov was not pleased with these results. He hurled epithets and threats at his commanders, particularly Generals N. A. Trushkin of the 109th infantry and I. I. Fadeyev of the 125th, although, in the opinion of General Bychevsky, the fault lay not with the troops but with the extremely strong German fire, which had not yet been suppressed.

Aleksei Panteleyev had been evacuated from Leningrad in June, 1942. On January 8, 1944, he boarded the train to return to Leningrad. It was a quiet, pleasant ride, marred only by a busybody typist returning to her Smolny job who gave the impression that Leningrad lay in ruins. ("You lived on Vasilevsky Island? Wait till you see it! Your house was on Basseinaya? Well, if you want to know, not one stone is left on top of another.") There was a tense moment going through the "corridor of death" at Shlisselburg, where the German guns were only a few hundred yards away. He ticked off the stations: Tikhvin . . . only the walls of the city were left . . . bullet holes everywhere . . . milk 60 rubles a pint, cranberries six rubles a glass. Volkhovstroi . . . no railroad station . . . piles of rubble. Budogoshch . . . forests . . . children on the station platform . . . no shell holes.

Panteleyev stayed at the Astoria. He was awakened early in the morning of the fifteenth by such thunder as he had never heard. It was the roar of thousands of cannon. It waxed and waned. It was so tremendous the chan-

[6] The Volkhov artillery preparation laid down 100,300 shells. (N.Z., p. 561.)

delier began to sway and plaster fell from the walls. There was no radio. His window looking out on St. Isaac's was frosted over. At 10 A.M. he went into the street. The thunder was titanic. The offensive had begun. He walked down the Nevsky. In a courtyard gate stood a young woman with a baby in her arms. The child was wrapped in a bright blue silk blanket and a white shawl—and, thought Panteleyev, over her head, high over her head, fly thousands of shells on their way to the German lines.

Panteleyev walked across the Anichkov Bridge. Here he had last seen Tanya Gurevich in September, 1941. She had been killed by the bomb which destroyed the Gostiny Dvor. Now on this January day he visited her sister, Rebekka Gurevich, in the Erisman Hospital. A young woman doctor at the hospital had been killed just three days earlier crossing Leo Tolstoy Square. And while Rebekka Gurevich was in the hospital, a shell exploded outside her apartment and filled it with splinters. He read in *Leningradskaya Pravda* the decision of the City Council to give back to the great boulevards and avenues of Leningrad their prerevolutionary names. The Nevsky (which had never been called anything else) lost its nominal name of 25th of October Street and became again the Nevsky. No longer would the signs on the Sadovaya read "3rd of July Street." And Suvorov, Izmailovsky, Bolshoy and all the other avenues returned to their original names. It could not, Panteleyev thought, have been done at a more appropriate moment.

The next day, the sixteenth, there was a thaw. Bad for the offensive; it slowed down the troops. The thaw continued during the night and the next day. There was rain. Panteleyev saw some pigeons outside the Nikolsky Cathedral. They were the same gentle Nikolsky pigeons which had always been there. But in February, 1942, when he had last been in the cathedral, there were no pigeons—only twenty-four bodies awaiting burial. He came to the building at the corner of Voznesensky and Yekaterinhofskaya, where the Agulyan confectionery store had been in the days of NEP in the early 1920's. He had lived in this building for eight years. Now it was a family tomb—the tomb of the Lebedev family. There had been two old aunts, a grandmother and Tanya, the daughter, a dear, extraordinarily talented person. Now all were dead. Tanya had been expelled from the Workers' Literary University when it was discovered that her father had been a clergyman. In the blockade the two aunts and the grandmother died. Panteleyev saw Tanya a day or two before her death. She would not eat. She handed Panteleyev a piece of fried leather. "You eat it, Aleksei Ivanovich. I don't need it. I am going to die anyway."

She wouldn't take the leather back. It stuck in Panteleyev's throat.

Another resident of the building was Grigory Belykh, Panteleyev's collaborator in the jolly satire, *The Republic of Shkid*. Belykh was an early victim of Stalin's. Why, no one knew. He died of tuberculosis in the prison hospital named for Dr. Gaaz in 1938. Even as he died in the prison hospital, Panteleyev thought, Belykh understood everything. Panteleyev and his friends wrote Stalin trying to get him released. The answer came after Belykh died. It was: No. Raya Belykh, Grigory's wife, starved to death in this building in 1942. Panteleyev had no idea where she was buried. Her daughter Tanya had been evacuated to a children's home, suffering from tuberculosis.

Panteleyev walked to the Kamenny Island, to the hospital where he had been taken in March, 1942, dying of dystrophy and cholera. There he had lain on a mattress on the floor for three days and nights—the mattress soaked with melting snow, the water in the carafe frozen, dark by day and dark by night, no electricity, no glass in the windows, no heat. How had he survived? Even now he could not say—possibly by sheer animal tenacity, possibly by the pitiful portions of food and the small attentions of the living corpses who served as nurses.

He spent the night of the eighteenth with his mother on Ulitsa Vosstaniya. Nearby there was a market where you could buy vodka for 300 to 350 rubles a pint, bread for 50 to 60 rubles a kilo, butter for 100 rubles for 100 grams and Belomor cigarettes for 30 rubles. A kitten cost 500 rubles. Everyone in town wanted one.

On the nineteenth the temperature dropped. The pace of the offensive picked up. When Panteleyev emerged into St. Isaac's Square, he saw before the great cathedral a Russian woman, on her knees, praying, crossing herself, bowing her forehead to the ground in the orthodox Russian manner. People passed with their sleds loaded with wood. She did not move. Finally, she rose and walked quickly away—perhaps to work at the nearby post office.

The offensive went on. Rebekka Gurevich said she had not eaten and had hardly slept, so many wounded were pouring in. "Soon Leningrad will be part of the mainland," one boy said as he awaited an amputation. The great warships on the Neva were silent. Possibly the Germans had been driven beyond their range.

At the Kuznetsky market Panteleyev found potatoes on sale at 65 rubles a kilo and felt boots for 3,500 rubles (the same kind the cannibals sold in the Haymarket two years earlier). There were also tobacco, cigarettes (only Belomors), flashlights, soap, meat, candy, milk and tangerines. Most of the sellers were war veterans, many of them crippled, many of them drunk, most of them quarrelsome. A rumor was going around the city that once the blockade was lifted all of Leningrad would be sent to rest homes for two months.

By January 22 reports said that the Germans were retreating in great disorder. Soviet troops were said to be having difficulty keeping up with them.

On January 27 at 8 P.M., over the sword point of the Admiralty, over the great dome of St. Isaac's, over the broad expanse of Palace Square, over the broken buildings of Pulkovo, the dilapidated machine shops of the Kirov works, the battered battleships still standing in the Neva, roared a shower of golden arrows, a flaming stream of red, white and blue rockets. It was a salute from 324 cannon marking the liberation of Leningrad, the end of the blockade, the victory of the armies of Generals Govorov and Meretskov. After 880 days the siege of Leningrad, the longest ever endured by a modern city, had come to an end.[7]

Panteleyev boarded his return train for Moscow two hours later. Truth to tell, he thought, the salute was not up to Moscow standards. Not enough guns. Too many were still firing on the Germans. But that did not make any difference. That evening he had shared a glass of vodka with Mikhail Arsentyevich, the janitor of his mother's old building on Ulitsa Vosstaniya. Before the war Mikhail Arsentyevich hadn't drunk. He'd gotten into the habit during the siege. Forty persons in that building had died of starvation. Almost all of them were taken away on a child's sled by the janitor. He took them to a kind of morgue set up in an old garage or stable. Gradually it filled with bodies. That was when he got into the habit of drinking.

Panteleyev leaned back in his compartment, writing in his notebook. At midnight the train halted at Malaya Vishera (where once the Second Shock Army and General Vlasov had headquarters). The car was carefully locked against "any internal enemies." One such Panteleyev heard on the platform in the darkness. He was an invalid, a demobilized sailor. He wanted to buy a pint of vodka and a pack of cigarettes in the buffet car. But he was not permitted on the Red Arrow.

"What did I fight for?" he shouted. "I fought for my country. And I can't buy a pack of cigarettes?"

Someone tried to quiet him, but as the train pulled out Panteleyev still heard him crying, shouting and tearing at his clothing.

Pavel Luknitsky was with the advancing troops at Rybatskoye on the evening of January 27. He had gone up through the ruined suburbs. Earlier he had stood outside the shell of Peterhof, had seen the arctic precipice which the great cascade of fountains had become, had seen the gaping hole where once Samson rested among the fountains, had stumbled through the dugouts and gun emplacements on the terraces leading down to the Baltic Sea. He and the poet Aleksandr Prokofyev stood beside the ruined cascade when Party Secretary A. A. Kuznetsov, Mayor Peter Popkov and other high officials and generals arrived to inspect the damage.

"We will not rebuild it," Popkov said. "We will level it all."

Luknitsky interjected: "No, Peter Sergeyevich. We must preserve it. For all time."

Many who saw the ruins agreed with Luknitsky that they should be preserved as an eternal reminder of German barbarity.[8]

Luknitsky was with the Soviet troops who entered Pushkin. The façade

---

[7] The length of the siege is sometimes calculated at 882 days (from August 28, 1941, when rail communications via Mga were cut) or at 872 days (from the fall of Shlisselburg, September 8, 1941). The 880 days is calculated from August 30, 1941, the date of the fall of Mga.

[8] A decision was made almost immediately to restore Peterhof and all the ruined imperial monuments. Years of labor and millions of rubles have gone into the effort, not yet completed.

of the great Catherine Palace was intact. But inside the building was a ruin. The great hall was gone. So was the amber room. The amber had vanished, along with it the parquet floor of amaranth, rosewood and mahogany. The Zubovsky wing had been turned into a barracks for the Spanish Blue Division. Under the great Cameron Gallery a 500-pound bomb had been placed. Fortunately, it had not gone off. The Half-Moon where Popov and his wife played piano duets had been smashed by shellfire. Just beyond the Half-Moon stood a great linden tree under which Konstantin Fedin and Popov had talked not long before the Germans entered Pushkin. As Luknitsky stood, dazed by the sight, a Red Army officer came up and directed his attention to four great hooks which swayed from a limb of the tree. "That's where the Nazis hanged their victims here in Pushkin," he said. "We cut down four bodies which we found there."

Vera Inber found it impossible to write about the end of the siege. On the night of January 27 she put down in her diary: "The greatest event in the life of Leningrad: full liberation from blockade. And I, a professional writer, have no words for it. I simply say: Leningrad is free. And that is all."

Olga Berggolts visited Peterhof and Pushkin. She wrote a brief poem:

> Again from the black dust, from the place
> Of death and ashes, will arise the garden as before.
> So it will be. I firmly believe in miracles.
> You gave me that belief, my Leningrad.

It was quiet in Leningrad now, Olga Berggolts noted. Only a few days ago, as recently as January 23, shells had fallen in the city. Now it was so still that it was hard to believe.

"In Leningrad it is quiet," she wrote.

And on the sunny side of the Nevsky, the "most dangerous side," children are walking. Children in our city now can peacefully walk on the sunny side. . . . And can quietly live in rooms letting on the sunny side. And can even sleep soundly at night, knowing that no one will kill them, and awake in the quiet, quiet sunrise alive and healthy.

She remembered how the workers of the old Putilov factory, the Kirov works, had said in September, 1941: "Soon death will be more afraid of us than we of death." Now, she thought, it was finally clear. It was not Leningrad which had been frightened by death. It was death which had been frightened by Leningrad.

The long ordeal, the ordeal of the nine hundred days, was over. Or so it seemed on the evening of January 27, 1944.

EPILOGUE

Oh, stones,
Be as firm as people!

EPILOGUE

50 . The Leningrad Affair

AT SIX IN THE EVENING ON APRIL 30, 1944, PAVEL LUKNITSKY made his way by streetcar to the Swan Canal and then on foot to Solyany Park. In one of the few buildings that still stood in the old "Salt Port" where nearly every house had been turned to a skeleton by German shells and bombs, an exhibition dedicated to the heroic defense of Leningrad was being opened.

In December, 1943, the Leningrad Front Military Council had given orders for the preparation of the exhibition. Most of the artists in Leningrad worked on the dioramas and panoramas. Outside the building on Market Street stood enormous German cannon, 406-mm siege guns, Tiger tanks, Panthers, Ferdinand self-propelled guns—the weaponry the Nazis brought to bear on the city. There were 14 rooms holding 60,000 exhibits, 24,000 square feet of floor space.

Luknitsky could not tear himself away. For four hours he went from room to room, reliving the blockade, day by day, week by week. Of course, he thought, as a Leningrader he knew much much more than was shown here, particularly about the deprivations. The horrors of starvation, for instance, were conveyed most delicately as contrasted with a vivid portrayal of the Ladoga Road of Life. The artists had somewhat romanticized the siege. They had not captured the simplicity and triviality of real life. The presentation was weak on literature, a few books of Nikolai Tikhonov, Vissarion Sayanov, Vera Inber, Olga Berggolts, Vsevolod Azarov and little more.

The exhibition moved Luknitsky strongly. The rooms were thronged with visitors and an orchestra played in the central hall. Nonetheless, he thought, for those like himself who had survived the blockade it presented only a weak shadow of reality.

Everyone in Leningrad crowded into the display rooms. They could not get enough of the experience of reliving the heroic and tragic days which they had survived.

When Vsevolod Vishnevsky visited Solyany Park, he was overwhelmed by the realization that the blockade days had now been put behind glass. That meant the worst was over, a whole chapter in his life had ended. What next? He felt nervous and upset. He had survived the blockade. Now he hungered for new aims, a new rhythm in his life.

Before Vera Inber and her husband, Dr. Ilya Strashun, left Leningrad that spring to return home to Moscow they, too, went to the exhibition. They exchanged few words as they walked about the display, which, Vera Inber thought, showed everything that had threatened Leningrad and everything that had saved it.[1]

Here she saw the very gun, a 154-mm cannon, which had fired on the Erisman Hospital (Objective No. 89 on the German artillery map). And here was "their" bomb—the evil monster which had fallen next to the hospital in September, 1941. She read the placard: "Weight 1,000 kilograms. Diameter 660 millimeters. Length 990 millimeters. Defused October 10, 1941, by Engineer-Captain N. G. Lopatin and Commander A. P. Ilinsky."

She and Dr. Strashun stood for a long time looking at the model of a Leningrad bread shop. The window was covered with a frosting of ice so thick you could only see through a narrow opening in its center. Within there stood a scales, on one side four small weights, on the other 125 grams of bread. Above the scales was listed the composition of the "bread":

Defective rye flour 50 percent
Salt 10 percent
Cottonseed cake 10 percent
Cellulose 15 percent
Soya flour, reclaimed flour dust, sawdust, 5 percent

These days were a time of creative work and enthusiasm for Leningrad writers. True, Vishnevsky had gone through agonies with his play, *The Walls of Leningrad*. But every writer who had spent the blockade in Leningrad was busy on an epic novel, a play or a great poem. Anna Akhmatova, the queen of Leningrad literature and princess of Russian poetry, had returned to her old quarters beside the Sheremetyev Palace gardens. She had spent the war in Tashkent, in Central Asia, and in Moscow, working and dreaming of her beloved northern capital.

Now she was back. On her breast she proudly wore the Medal for the Defense of Leningrad. It was awarded for her weeks in the city in the

[1] In 1946 the exhibition was transformed into a permanent Museum of the Defense of Leningrad under Director Major L. Rakov. Here were collected thousands of personal archives and trophies of the blockade—pictures, maps, models, photographs, panoramas outlining each stage of the siege, letters, diaries, personal materials on the commanders, the ordinary civilians, the soldiers and the political leaders who participated in the epic. One painting depicted the Izhorsk workers halting German tanks almost singlehanded at Kolpino. There was a list of twenty-two different dishes prepared in the winter of 1941–1942 out of pig skin. More than 150,000 visitors, including Soviet President Mikhail Kalinin, visited the museum in its first three months.

autumn of 1941 and for her patriotic poem, "Courage." Never had she seemed more cheerful, more at ease, more expansive. Pavel Luknitsky had last seen her in a bomb shelter as she was about to leave in the autumn of 1941, ill and depressed. Now she was a different woman.

Tomorrow, she told Luknitsky, was her birthday. "What are you going to give me—Cherbourg?" she joked. (The Allies were advancing in France.)

Luknitsky laughed. "Actually—Medvezhegorsk!" This was a town in the then Karelian Soviet republic where Soviet troops were rapidly moving forward.

The city was nearly back to peacetime. Or so it seemed to Luknitsky watching the girls in their short dresses, loading rubble from a ruined building on the Nevsky at Vosstaniya Square. He sat in the evening at the Buff Gardens on the Fontanka and drank beer. The garden was almost empty. But nearby two good-looking girls argued with a naval cadet whether they should go dancing or rowing. The work of restoring Palace Square was under way. They had begun to take the scaffolding down from the Alexander column. Soon the Klodt horses would be back on the Anichkov Bridge and the bronze horseman would emerge from his sandbox on the Senate Square.

The Renaissance of Leningrad was about to be undertaken. Its general outline had been presented by Party Secretary Zhdanov in a two-hour speech on April 11, 1944, at the first plenary session of the Leningrad City and Regional Party which had been held since the start of the war.

"Our task," said Zhdanov, "is not just reconstruction but the restoration of the city—not to restore it as it was, or simply to change its façade, but to create a city even more comfortable than it was."

Some notion of what was meant by the Renaissance of Leningrad was provided by the grandiose plans and sketches drafted by the city's architects and published in a handsome quarto volume under the direction of Chief Architect N. V. Baranov in 1943, a massive achievement for a city whose publishing facilities had not been restored.[2]

A vast square was to be created before the Smolny ensemble, and the whole area around the Finland Station was to be transformed into a vista honoring Lenin (to be depicted in the center atop the famous armored car from which he delivered his first address on his return to Petrograd in April, 1917). The city was to double in size to the south, southeast and west in order to provide direct access to the Baltic along the Gulf of Finland. The plans were based on a city population of 3,500,000, substantially above the prewar level of 3,193,000.

Everything was to be restored—everything historic and grandiose, that is. The Germans had destroyed 15,000,000 square feet of housing, depriving

[2] The volume presented comparisons of Leningrad with Washington and Paris and said that in planning the new city center of Leningrad the architects had incorporated the best features of the two capitals. The existing Leningrad center (Palace Square) was "far too small" in the opinion of the architects for the new role of the future city. (Baranov *et al., Leningrad,* Leningrad–Moscow, 1943.)

716,000 Leningraders of homes; 526 schools and children's institutions; 21 scientific institutions, 101 museums and other civic buildings, the Pulkovo observatory, the Botanical and Zoological institutes, much of the Leningrad University, 187 of the 300 eighteenth- and nineteenth-century buildings preserved by the government as historical monuments, 840 factories, 71 bridges—the catalogue ran on and on. Thirty-two shells and two bombs had hit the Hermitage alone. More than 300,000 square feet of rooms and 60,000 square feet of glass and windows had been damaged at the Hermitage. The total damage in Leningrad was estimated at 45 billion rubles.

Ilya Ehrenburg had a vision of the future which Leningrad saw for itself. He was present in Palace Square on July 8, 1945, when the Leningrad troops returned for their victory parade. The city looked forward to no mere cosmetic repair of the broken walls of the Engineers Castle, the crumbled cornices of the Hermitage. Leningrad, the eternal city, as Ehrenburg called it, was to be transformed. Already the Leningrad writers were arguing whether they should or needed to keep fresh the memory of the agony of the city. Ehrenburg thought it a pointless argument. It was not possible to forget what had been suffered, just as it was not possible to live only in those memories. While remembering its sacrifices Leningrad dreamed of new glories.

Ehrenburg, like so many others, thought that the ruins of the Peterhof and Pushkin palaces should be left as monuments of Nazi brutality. But for the city itself, of course, there would be a greater, a brighter life than ever.

He stood at Strelna one night and gazed out to the sea. He saw Russia once again setting out on a great journey. Petersburg had been envisioned as Russia's "window on Europe." That was far in the past. Long ago Russia, he thought, had become part of Europe, indivisible from the West. And if the young Decembrist officers had brought the idea of liberty back from the Seine to Petersburg's Senate Square then, now a new Russian generation had brought the idea of justice from the Neva to the squares of Paris.

"*We* have become the heart of Europe," said Ehrenburg, "the bearers of her tradition, the continuators of her boldness, her builders and her poets."

The new Leningrad was to be the symbol of this Russia, European and ecumenical.

A group of American correspondents visited the city in February, 1944, a few days after the siege was broken. They talked with Mayor Popkov, with Chief Architect Baranov, with Director Nikolai Puzerov of the Kirov works, with the survivors of the blockade. The correspondents saw the great architectural ensembles which had emerged from the drafting boards in the freezing days of 1941–42. They listened to the men and women of Leningrad talk quietly, confidently, earnestly, of how they would build their city anew.

Like Ehrenburg, the visitors caught the enthusiasm of the role which the northern capital hoped to play. Leningrad aspired to stand again as the window on the West or, as Ehrenburg suggested, as the gateway through which Russia, the new bearer and defender of Western culture, would emerge. There were some who thought that in the postwar metamorphosis of Russia Leningrad once again might become the capital city, might displace rude, peasant Moscow, might resume its role as the imperial city Peter planned.

It was a dream on a scale of magnificence worthy of the traditions of Peter, a dream which had been born in the depths of the hell which the people had survived.

Pushkin, in awe and pride and terror of Peter and his bronze horse, had written:

> Where are you flying, proud horse,
> And where will your hooves fall?

Where, indeed? Leningrad had survived without light, without heat, without bread, without water. It had, Ehrenburg felt, lived because of pride in the city, because of belief in Russia, because of the love of the people. Had there been in human existence an example more noble, more edifying? Petersburg, now Leningrad, symbolized the soul, the strength, the nature, the mission of Russia. It had its own style, its own spirit. A man came to Leningrad from the Urals or a woman from Tula. In a few years they were Leningraders.

So thought Ehrenburg. So thought many visitors. So thought the men and women of the city.

But there were other plans for Leningrad than those born in the city's agony. The plan for the Leningrad Renaissance was founded upon a decree of the State Defense Committee of March 29, 1944. This, naturally, gave priority to the restoration of heavy industry, to the rebuilding of the demolished machine shops, the specialized metallurgical crafts, the factories which were the bone and sinew of Russia's military and industrial capability.

Leningrad's population in January, 1944, had been estimated at only 560,000. Workers must be rushed back—never mind where to house them. Population must be rebuilt to one million by the end of the year. By July there were 725,000 in the city; by September, 920,000; by September, 1945, 1,240,000. Conditions of life and work became incredibly difficult.

The sums advanced for rehabilitation and restoration were niggardly. The 1945 capital construction budget was 398 million rubles, of which 200 million were for housing. This was about that of the peacetime 1940 budget. The appropriations for restoration of historic buildings were 39 million rubles in 1945, 60 million in 1946, 80 million in 1947 and 84 million in 1948.

Leningrad began to scale down its vision and cut the corners off its dreams. During the summer of 1945 meetings were held to discuss the plan for the city in the factories, in individual regions of the city, in meetings of writers, artists, scientists. The vast extensions to the south and to the east were "temporarily" postponed. Because destruction was so extensive, because suburban areas like Ligovo and Strelna had been demolished, not so much

land, it was said, would be required for housing and parks. Apartment buildings could be erected in areas where the wooden houses had been torn down
for firewood during the winter of 1941–42. The emphasis shifted to ordinary
housing, to the reconstruction of factories rather than imperial vistas and
Florentine plazas. About the only vestige of grandeur which seemed likely of
fulfillment was Academician Nikolsky's plan for a new Victory Stadium.[3]

Sometime in 1946 Party Secretary Kuznetsov and Mayor Popkov presented
to Moscow a new and revised plan for the development of the city, which
"reflected the experience and creative thought" of the city's architects,
production workers, technologists and scientific intelligentsia. It provided for
the "renaissance and further development of Leningrad as a great industrial
and cultural center of the country." The plan revived the original Leningrad
hope for a "wide front" along the Gulf of Finland, for expansion of the city
limits to incorporate broad areas to the south and to the east. Kuznetsov and
Popkov proposed that the Renaissance be carried out over a ten-year period,
presumably during the fourth and fifth Five-Year Plans.

More than fifteen years passed before another word was publicly expressed
concerning the Leningrad Renaissance. This was no accident.

Sometime (the exact date cannot be fixed) after the Leningrad Party plenary
in April, 1944, Zhdanov left Leningrad permanently to resume his career in
the Kremlin. Not for one moment during the war, during the nine hundred
days, had there been a moratorium in the secret political struggle within the
Kremlin. Indeed, every event in the Leningrad epic had a twofold significance: one in relation to the outer world of survival and another in the
morbid inner sphere of Stalinist politics. Every decision that preceded the
war and every event of the war itself played a role in the inner Kremlin
struggle. Zhdanov's fortunes suffered a precipitous decline at the outset of
the war (because of his culpability in the policies which led to the Nazi
attack) and in the early months when Leningrad's fate hung in the balance.
In the worst moments of August, September and October, 1941, Zhdanov's
fate as well as that of Leningrad was at stake in the critical battles. Had the
city fallen, Zhdanov's life would have been forfeit. Hardly a day passed in
which someone in the Kremlin, some high official, was not threatened with
execution or actually executed. This was the special quality of the epoch, the
flavor of the Stalinist-Leninist system, the medieval concentration of power,
the Florentine nature of Stalin's "court," the paranoid aura of Kremlin life.
Marshal Bulganin was not talking idly when he said once to Nikita
Khrushchev, "A man doesn't know when he is called to the Kremlin whether
he will emerge alive or not."

It was typical that even on Victory Day, May 7, 1945, Marshal Voronov
received a telephone call from Stalin. Artillery General Ivan Susloparov[4] had

---

[3] Completed in 1950. (Karasev, *Istoriya SSSR*, No. 3, 1961, p. 126.)

[4] Susloparov had been the Soviet military attaché in Paris at the outbreak of war and
had sent many intelligence reports back to Moscow in the spring of 1941 warning of Nazi
preparations for attack.

been present at the German capitulation at Rheims and in the presence of General Eisenhower had signed the protocol on behalf of the Soviet Union. What did Marshal Voronov mean by permitting his subordinate to sign a document of profound international significance without direct orders from Stalin? What kind of men did Voronov have in his artillery corps? (Stalin's call was the first news Voronov had of the Rheims ceremony and Susloparov's participation in it.) Stalin announced that he was ordering Susloparov immediately to Moscow "for strict punishment," which, in Stalin's words, meant the firing squad. Voronov hung up the telephone shaken. In the hour of victory one of his best men was going to the wall. For all he knew, he would be the next.

So it went. Murderous, suicidal politics came first, before everything. In this atmosphere the death of a man was nothing, the death of a million men little more than a problem in the mechanics of propaganda, the destruction of a great city a complicated but conceivable gambit in the unceasing game of power.

When Leningrad survived, when the Nazis failed to break through to the city, a new round opened in this deadly game. Slowly Zhdanov won back his position. His departure for Moscow in 1944 meant that the advantage was now passing to him. Quickly he moved ahead, profiting by the murderous hatreds which the war had generated within the Kremlin. From January 15 to 17, 1945, a Leningrad Party plenary was held. Zhdanov was "released" as Leningrad secretary in order to concentrate on his duties in the Central Committee in Moscow (and his chairmanship of the Finnish Control Commission). Party Secretary Kuznetsov was named Leningrad leader in Zhdanov's place. Within a few months Kuznetsov joined Zhdanov in Moscow in the Party Secretariat (supervising State Security organs—that is, Beria), and Mayor Popkov became the Leningrad Party chief. The year 1946 was a high-water mark for Zhdanov. His power was second only to Stalin's. His man Kuznetsov could boss, oversee and outplot Beria, and by mid-year Zhdanov had even driven Malenkov out of the Party Secretariat, possibly on a charge of collaboration with the traitor general, Vlasov, possibly by playing on other World War II intrigues. But the weapons Zhdanov employed cut two ways. He had inaugurated an era still known as the *Zhdanovshchina*, an era of mugwumpism in art and culture. The targets which had been selected almost certainly by Stalin were Anna Akhmatova, the classic purist of Russian poetry, and Mikhail Zoshchenko, the satirist, Leningraders both, true inheritors of the Leningrad tradition, the Petersburg spirit.[5]

[5] Zoshchenko was much impressed by the partisans of the Leningrad area. He wrote a cycle of thirty-two stories about their wartime achievements. The first ten were published by *Novy Mir* under the title "Never Let Us Forget." Their publication was suspended as a result of the Zhdanov attack, and the full cycle was not published until 1962. The topic of partisans was politically extremely sensitive because of behind-the-scenes quarrels between Beria and other Politburo members, including Zhdanov, over the direction of underground activities behind the Nazi lines. This may have been a factor in the suppression of the Zoshchenko stories. (*Istoriya Russkoi Sovetskoi Literatury*, Vol. II, Moscow, 1967, pp. 378–379.)

The blow fell in August, 1946. The writers of Leningrad were summoned to cast out of their circle the most brilliant of their number. Akhmatova, it was said, was a whore, Zoshchenko a pimp. The dream of a European ecumenical Leningrad went glimmering. Aleksandr Shtein met Yevgeny Shvarts on the day the Leningrad Union of Writers expelled Akhmatova and Zoshchenko. Neither Akhmatova nor Zoshchenko had been permitted to be present to defend themselves. No one had defended them. Shvarts, in ill health, shaken more profoundly than by any incident of the blockade, could not speak. There was nothing Shtein or Shvarts or anyone could say. Leningrad had survived the Nazis. Whether it would survive the Kremlin was not so clear.

As always in Russia, the writers and artists were the first victims of the savage political warfare.

One of Vera Ketlinskaya's best and oldest friends was Solomon Lozovsky, a salty old Bolshevik who acted as Soviet press spokesman early in the war. When she completed *The Blockade*, the novel on which she worked with cold-stiffened fingers as her mother's frozen body lay next door, she gave it to Lozovsky to read. Lozovsky was, in her view, "one of the most crystal-honest, ideologically sound, warmest and democratic of Communists." He was enthusiastic over her picture of Leningrad. Not so her editors. It was nearly three years before *The Blockade* was published. Lozovsky didn't recognize it. He asked, "Is this the same manuscript I read or another?"[6] Her novel, Ketlinskaya said, had been gone over with "cold steel and a hot iron." Everything "gloomy" or "terrible" or "negative" or "frightening" or "demoralizing" or "disquieting" had been taken out. Everything was left in the book—except the spirit of Leningrad.

The difficulties of Vera Ketlinskaya differed only in detail from those encountered by everyone who sought to write on the Leningrad theme. Olga Berggolts' Leningrad apartment became with the passage of the years a minor archive of the blockade. Here were collected her own manuscripts from the earliest days of the war, file after file marked simply "N.O." (*ne opublikovano*—not published). Among them was the manuscript of her play, *Born in Leningrad*, which no producer dared touch, fearful of the sharpness of her recollections, the genuineness of the human pain she portrayed.

The roll of Leningrad writers and novelists unable to publish or to com-

---

[6] Lozovsky vanished almost immediately after offering this opinion. He probably was arrested in late 1948 and was executed August 12, 1952, along with a number of Jewish intellectuals, presumably on the concocted charge that they were planning to set up a separate Jewish republic in the Crimea and detach it from the Soviet Union. The Crimea had been virtually cleansed of population by Stalin at the end of the war. He deported all the Crimean Tatars to Siberia on grounds that they collaborated with the Nazis. Whether the "affair" in which Lozovsky was caught up was connected with the others put forward in Stalin's last years, such as the Leningrad Affair and the so-called Doctors' Plot, is not known.

plete works on the Leningrad blockade included the novelist, Sergei Khmelnitsky (who Ketlinskaya thought might have produced the best novel of all had he lived), the playwright Leonid Rakhmanov, the novelist Yevgeny Ryss, and the novelist Nikolai Chukovsky (whose *Baltic Skies* suffered as severely in the hands of the censors as did Ketlinskaya's *The Blockade*).

Events acquired a momentum all their own. It is impossible to trace the moves and countermoves that so swiftly followed within the shadows of the Kremlin walls. Zhdanov did not succeed in destroying Malenkov. The latter beat his way back. By early summer 1948 it was Zhdanov who was losing ground. Stalin put the blame on Zhdanov for the breaking away of Marshal Tito from the Soviet bloc, the first crack in the monolith Russia had erected in postwar Eastern Europe.[7] In July and August, 1948, Malenkov's ascendancy was apparent. He it was who now signed the orders for Stalin's secretariat. On August 31, 1948, Zhdanov's death was announced.[8]

Now history swiftly began to run backward. One by one the figures of the Leningrad epic vanished: Secretary Kuznetsov, Mayor Popkov, all the other Party secretaries, the chiefs of the big Leningrad industries, and almost everyone who had been closely associated with Zhdanov, including N. A. Voznesensky, chief of the State Planning Commission; his brother, A. A. Voznesensky, rector of Leningrad University; M. I. Rodionov, chairman of the Council of Ministers of the Russian Federated Republic; Colonel General I. V. Shikin, head of the Red Army Political Directorate; and many, many more—possibly as many as two thousand in Leningrad alone.

Nor did the purge halt there. The career of Aleksei Kosygin, later to become Premier of the Soviet Union, hung in the balance. For several years no one, including himself, could say whether he would survive. Marshal Zhukov was banished to a minor command post in Odessa.

Nonpolitical people went down by the hundreds. Akhmatova came near to destruction. She was not arrested (although her son was), but she was deprived of a livelihood. She survived on the charity of her friends and her own iron courage.

In 1949, without notice or public announcement, the Museum of the Defense of Leningrad was closed. The director, Major Rakov, was arrested. The

[7] The blame actually lay with Stalin himself and with his police chief, Beria. It is probable that Beria and Malenkov persuaded Stalin that the fault lay with Zhdanov.

[8] The possibility that Zhdanov was poisoned or died of medical malpractice cannot be excluded. This charge was made in the so-called "Doctors' Plot" of January 13, 1953. Other supposed victims included his brother-in-law, Aleksandr Shcherbakov, who died in 1945, and General Govorov, the Leningrad commander, who was then still alive. There is reason to believe that in certain other cases where medical "murder" was charged by Stalin (specifically in the death of Maxim Gorky and Gorky's son) the deaths actually were criminally caused, but the instigator was not necessarily the person named in Stalin's indictment. Thus it cannot be excluded that a combination of Stalin, Malenkov and Beria or all three had a hand in Zhdanov's death. Stalin's daughter, Svetlana, points out that Zhdanov was known to be suffering from a bad heart condition. However, Stalin's *chef de cabinet*, Aleksandr Poskrebyshev, confirmed before his death that "we" (presumably meaning Stalin) did in fact employ poison in purges after 1940.

two guidebooks to the museum which he wrote were confiscated. The exhibits vanished into the maws of the secret police, whence many never emerged.[9] A new museum was opened in 1957. Here were collected some of the exhibits which once graced the earlier institution, but far from all. "It only to a minor degree reflects that heroic epoch which is so memorable to all people," in the view of Dmitri V. Pavlov, the food dictator of the blockade days.

The museum was not the only thing that vanished in 1949. The white-and-blue warnings which had graced the Nevsky and the Sadovaya, the ones which said, "Citizens: In case of shelling this side of the street is the most dangerous," had been preserved as a memento of the Nazi bombardment. One day in 1949 citizens walking on the Nevsky saw painters, brushes in hand, carefully painting over each warning notice. To some it seemed that not only were the notices being painted out but the memory of the nine hundred days.

All of this was done in the name of the Leningrad Affair. To this day no official explanation of the case has been made public, although its existence has been known since Nikita Khrushchev's "secret speech" of February 24–25, 1956.

The Leningrad Affair was a complex mechanism devised by Malenkov and Beria, with the close collaboration of Stalin himself and his *chef de cabinet*, General Poskrebyshev, to destroy the Leningrad Party organization and all officials of consequence who had been associated with Zhdanov. It took the same general form as the great purges of the 1930's, that is, it associated a large number of prominent Party figures and accused them of a bizarre series of charges involving conspiracy and treason.

The various purge scenarios of the Stalin epoch, beginning in the 1930's and continuing up to the time of Stalin's death, March 5, 1953, differed little in their general ingredients. The differences lay in the individuals. The plot or allegation was merely reconstructed to fit a particular historical epoch. The major difference between the early purges and those of the 1940's and early 1950's lay in the fact that Stalin publicized those of the 1930's very heavily. Those of the 1940's and early 1950's, except for the so-called "Doctors' Plot," which had only begun to be presented at the time of the dictator's death, were carried out in secret. The general public did not know their nature, although often there was widespread knowledge that some kind of purge was under way.

The Leningrad case was unusual in that not only was there no public mention of the "plot" in which so many high officials were exterminated, but

[9] After Stalin's death Major Rakov was released from concentration camp and began a new career as a playwright. He collaborated with I. Alem in writing a comedy called *The Most Dangerous Enemy*. (Shtein, *Znamya*, No. 4, April, 1964, p. 68.) Some manuscripts taken from the museum in 1949 were deposited in the archives of the Ministry of Defense, where presumably they repose as classified materials. But many items have never been found. (Karasev, *op. cit.*, p. 15.)

fantastic efforts were made to destroy the historical record of events in Leningrad so that future generations would be unable to ascertain what really had happened, particularly during the days of the war and especially during the nine hundred days.

Not only was the Museum of Leningrad's Defense closed, its archives seized and its director sent to Siberia. Not only were works of fiction suppressed or bowdlerized. The official records were concealed or sequestered. All the documents of the Council for the Defense of Leningrad, for example, were placed in the archives of the Ministry of Defense. No Soviet historian has had access to them, and they are still held under a high-security classification.[10] As early as December, 1941, commissions in the Kirov and other regions of Leningrad were set up to collect facts about the blockade, and in April, 1943, a special Party bureau began to prepare a chronicle of the blockade. It was never published. In January, 1944, Party Secretary Zhdanov ordered a collection of materials on the blockade published, including articles by himself, Secretary Kuznetsov, Secretary Y. F. Kapustin and Mayor Popkov. They were never published. The two-volume collection which appeared (and which is a bibliographic rarity today) contained little beyond newspaper clippings. Professor Orbeli was directed January 18, 1944, to prepare a work on the achievements of Leningrad science during the blockade. The volume listed 1,000 scientific discoveries and contained contributions by 480 authors. It was never published. Two proofs have been preserved, possibly by accident, one in the Academy of Science archives and one in the personal papers of the geologist, I. V. Danilovsky, in the Leningrad Public Library. A comprehensive work on the role of artists and intelligentsia in the war was prepared (printers' proofs still exist). Dmitri Shostakovich, the composers O. A. Yevlakhov and N. P. Budashkin, Ballerina Galina Ulanova and many others contributed articles. None of this material ever appeared in print.

The Leningrad epic was wiped out of public memory insofar as this was physically possible, and, as in Orwell's "memory hole," the building blocks of history, the public records, the statistics, the memoirs of what had happened, were destroyed or suppressed. Zhdanov's papers have never been published. No volume of his speeches exists. His personal archives (if they still exist) are unavailable, probably under security classification. Even the war-time files of the Leningrad newspapers are not publicly accessible, and references to blockade issues are rarely found in Soviet publications. The elaborate stenographic records which are a routine of official Soviet life are seldom cited, apparently having been suppressed or destroyed.

What were the charges in the Leningrad Affair? They may be deduced from the nature of the suppressions. The charges turned the heroism of

---

[10] Asked why no Soviet historian prior to himself had mentioned the existence of the Leningrad Council of Defense, D. V. Pavlov replied that "very few persons were aware of the facts." (Pavlov, personal communication, April 30, 1968.)

Leningrad inside out, presenting the Council for the Defense of Leningrad as part of a plot to deliver the city to the Germans. The Leningrad leadership was charged with planning to blow up the city and scuttle the Baltic Fleet. Treachery was alleged at many levels. In some way even the valiant stand of the Izhorsk workers at Kolpino became involved. It may have been contended that Zhdanov and the Leningrad group deliberately sought to involve Russia in war, hoping to procure her defeat and to set up a new non-Communist regime with the aid of the Nazis. At the end of the war, the conspirators were alleged to have taken steps looking to the seizure of power, the transfer of the capital from Moscow to Leningrad and the setting up of a new regime with the aid of foreign powers, specifically, in all probability, with British assistance.[11]

The fact that there was not one word of truth in the bizarre allegations made no difference. The charges were used to exterminate all Zhdanov's lieutenants and thousands of minor officials. They were shot or sent to prison camps.

Nothing in the chamber of Stalin's horrors equaled the Leningrad blockade and its epilogue, the Leningrad Affair. The blockade may have cost the lives of a million and a half people. The "affair" destroyed thousands of people who survived the most terrible days any modern city had ever known.

A quarter of a century later the great city on the Neva had not recovered from the wounds of war. The scars, physical and spiritual, could still be found. The deadly sequence of Stalinist events, beginning with the murder of Kirov, December 1, 1934, through the savage purges of the 1930's, the outbreak of war, the nine hundred days, the Leningrad Affair, left a mark nothing could erase. The dreams of a new gateway to Europe were not realized. Leningrad was the last great Russian city to be restored after World War II, far behind Moscow, Kiev, Odessa, Minsk and, of course, Stalingrad.

The passage of time did not diminish the political struggle over the Leningrad events. A volume of Leningrad memoirs, including some reminiscences originally set down in wartime and the years before 1948, was turned over to the printer in the summer of 1965. It was not cleared by the censorship for three years and when it finally reached the bookstores late in 1968 bore painful evidences of omission, revision and occasional falsification.[12] The time had

---

[11] There have long been vague rumors that part of the "plot" involved a project to conduct an international exposition or World Trade Fair at Leningrad.

[12] The volume contains a self-serving memoir by General Popov, the Leningrad commander at the outbreak of war, in which he obscures the fact that he did not return to Leningrad in time to participate in the initial military decisions. He reveals, however, that a prompt start on fortifications was hindered because no one would take responsibility for the politically sensitive action of mobilizing the civilian population. Only after a "painful" telephone conversation between Zhdanov and Stalin were the necessary orders issued. Popov's memoir makes clear that the Malenkov–Molotov mission to Leningrad in August–September, 1941, was in direct consequence of Zhdanov's setting up the ill-fated Council for the Defense of Leningrad (V. M. Kovalchuk, editor, *Oborona Leningrada*, Leningrad, 1968, p. 29).

not yet come when the people of Leningrad could freely tell their story in Russia.

But one thing was finally achieved. The blue and white signs reappeared on the Nevsky Prospekt in 1957. Once again the pedestrian was warned: "Citizens: In case of shelling this side of the street is the most dangerous." The signs are carefully touched up each spring. The Leningraders are very fond of them, very fond of their memories. They have etched on the wall beside the eternal flame at Piskarevsky the words of Olga Berggolts:

> Here lie the people of Leningrad,
> Here are the citizens—men, women and children—
> And beside them the soldiers of the Red Army
> Who gave their lives
> Defending you, Leningrad,
> Cradle of Revolution.
> We cannot number the noble
> Ones who lie beneath the eternal granite,
> But of those honored by this stone
> Let no one forget, let nothing be forgotten.

Stalin is dead. So are Zhdanov, Kuznetsov, Popkov, Govorov. So are Akhmatova, Zoshchenko, Shvarts, Chukovsky. A new generation has been born which does not know the names of Malenkov, Kulik, Mekhlis.

But the memory of the nine hundred days will always live.

Source Notes

The best sources for the Leningrad epic are the men and women who lived through the nine hundred days. The author began collecting accounts from the people of Leningrad on his first visit there, a few days after the blockade was lifted, January 27, 1944, when the events were vivid in the minds of all survivors. He has continued to collect them over the years. Especially since the death of Stalin an increasing flow of memoirs and literary treatments of the blockade has been published. The most valuable are those of Olga Berggolts, whose *Dnevnye Zvezdy* (*Day Stars*) has been heavily drawn upon; Vera Inber, a sensitive diarist; Vsevolod Vishnevsky, an insensitive diarist whose record is nonetheless fascinating; Pavel Luknitsky, a newspaperman and excellent reporter; Valerian Bogdanov-Berezovsky, musicologist, diarist and historian; Aleksei I. Panteleyev, who has an outstanding eye for detail; Vera Ketlinskaya, whose novel *The Blockade* despite Stalinist bowdlerizing presents a revealing picture of the siege; Vissarion Sayanov, a poet who spent the whole blockade in Leningrad; and Vsevolod Kochetov, a blundering, often unreliable newspaper correspondent whose recollections convey more than he is aware. Not all the diarists and writers remained in the Soviet Union. Among those now in the United States whose stories are memorable are Yelena Skryabina, Dmitri Konstantinov and Anatoly Darov.

One of the most painstaking accounts of life in Leningrad is that of the Hermitage Museum and its director, Iosif Orbeli, written by S. Varshavsky and B. Rest. These men have dedicated their lives to the Hermitage. They spent the whole siege in Leningrad. No single book conveys more of the suffering and heroism of the time than their *Podvig Ermitazha* (*Triumph of the Hermitage*). They, like many other writers, historians and ordinary Leningraders, have been tireless in assisting the author in the collection and verification of facts.

There are five major official works on the Leningrad siege. The first and most important book is that of Dmitri V. Pavlov, who was sent to Leningrad in September, 1941, to handle the city's food supplies. His book, *Leningrad v Blokade* (*Leningrad in Blockade*), published in 1958 and reissued in second and third editions, each containing additional information, is the classic source on the starvation winter. Many details of the Leningrad epic are still to be found only in Pavlov, and every Soviet writer on the subject since 1958 has based his work on Pavlov's. Almost equally useful is A. V. Karasev's *Leningradtsy v Gody Blokady* (*Leningraders in the Years of the Blockade*). Karasev is a painstaking professional historian who has searched the archives tirelessly. Many facts not available to Karasev when he published his book in 1959 are provided in *Na Zashchite Nevskoi Tverdyni* (*Defending the Neva Bastion*), a collective work produced under the auspices of the Leningrad Party organization in 1965. A fourth source is a collection of reports, decrees and official documents published under the title of *900 Geroicheskikh Dnei* (*900 Heroic Days*) in 1967. The fifth major source is *Leningrad v Velikoi Otechestvennoi Voine* (*Leningrad in the Great Fatherland War*), published in 1967 by the Institute of History of the Soviet Academy of Sciences as the fifth volume of a *History of Leningrad*.

On the military side there are five basic works:

Istoriya Velikoi Otechestvennoi Voiny Sovetskogo Soyuza 1941-1945 (History of the Great Fatherland War of the Soviet Union, 1941-1945), a six-volume general history of the war, issued in 1961, giving a detailed account of all military operations and an excellent summary of the state of preparedness—and unpreparedness—in 1941 on the eve of war; a shorter one-volume version by the same editors called *Velikaya Otechestvennaya Voina Sovetskogo Soyuza (The Great Fatherland War of the Soviet Union)*, which, interestingly enough, provides detail on Stalin's lapses and misevaluation of intelligence on the eve of war not included in the six-volume version; *Bitva Za Leningrad (The Battle for Leningrad)*, a collective work by I. P. Barbashin and others, which is illuminating when collated closely with the Leningrad section of the six-volume general history; a work of the same title, *Bitva Za Leningrad (Battle for Leningrad)*, by V. P. Sviridov and two others, an earlier and inferior history which is useful only for occasional details; and *Borba Za Sovetskuyu Pribaltiku V Velikoi Otechestvennoi Voine 1941-1945 (The Struggle for the Soviet Baltic in the Great Fatherland War 1941-1945)*, which reveals the disasters which overwhelmed Soviet forces in Leningrad's Baltic littoral in the first days of the war.

None of these histories is complete, and each seeks to suppress or overemphasize certain aspects of the Leningrad events. But by close comparison the general course of what happened can be established. A far more revealing source is the memoirs of the military participants, particularly those of Colonel (now General) B. V. Bychevsky, Chief of Army Engineers in Leningrad; Admiral V. A. Panteleyev, Chief of Staff of the Baltic Fleet; Major General Mikhail Dukhanov, Commander of the Sixty-seventh Army; Marshal Kirill A. Meretskov, one of the principal Leningrad commanders; General Ivan I. Fedyuninsky, another Leningrad commander; Admiral N. G. Kuznetsov, Naval Commissar. To these should be added the scores of individual memoirs and unit histories which pour in a steady stream from the presses of the Military Publishing House in Moscow.

Where possible, inquiries and questions have been put to individuals who played a role in the Leningrad epic, notably to Dmitri V. Pavlov. Interesting information on the events of June 21-22, 1941, was provided personally by Marshal Semyon Budyonny. The rare bound files of *Leningradskaya Pravda* for 1941-42, preserved in the archives of that newspaper, were examined in the offices of *Leningradskaya Pravda*, but so hastily that only general impressions could be gleaned.

The story of the breaking of the Leningrad blockade in January, 1944, was recounted to the author by many of the commanders who participated on the spot at that time. The plans for Leningrad's postwar Renaissance were outlined similarly at that time by Mayor Peter S. Popkov, later shot in the so-called Leningrad Affair in 1949, and by the city's chief architect, N. V. Baranov.

CHAPTER 1. THE WHITE NIGHTS

Detail for the description of Leningrad on June 21, 1941, was provided by many Leningrad residents, including S. Varshavsky, Dmitri Konstantinov, Vsevolod Kochetov, Aleksandr Kron, Aleksandr Shtein, Aleksandr Rozen, Olga Berggolts, Ivan Krutikov, Valerian Bogdanov-Berezovsky, Pavel Luknitsky, Olga Iordan, Vissarion Sayanov and Vera Ketlinskaya. The account of Orbeli comes from *Podvig Ermitazha* by Varshavsky and B. Rest. The Party plenum at Smolny June 21 is described in *Na Zashchite Nevskoi Tverdyni*, *Bitva Za Leningrad* (Sviridov *et al.*) and in *V Ognennom Koltse*.

CHAPTER 2. NOT ALL SLEPT

The description of General Kirill A. Meretskov is provided in his own *Nekolebimo, Kak Rossiya*. The story of Yuri Stasov is told in M. Ye. Sonkin, *Eto Bylo Na Baltike*.

Other sources: Admiral A. G. Golovko, *Vmeste s Flotom;* M. P. Pavlovskii, *Na Ostro-vakh;* I. I. Fedyuninsky, *Podnyatye Po Trevoge.* Panteleyev describes Tributs' activities in *Morskoi Front.* The account of Kuznetsov is drawn from his numerous versions, which often differ in detail.

CHAPTER 3. THE FATEFUL SATURDAY

Naval Commissar Kuznetsov's description is provided by himself. The story of the Soviet Embassy in Berlin, June 21-22, is given by Valentin Berezhkov, *S Diplomaticheskoi Missiyei v Berlin;* I. F. Filippov, *Zapiski o Tretiyem Reikhe;* and Raymond James Sontag, *Nazi-Soviet Relations, 1939-1941,* p. 353. Maisky's story is in his memoirs and in a bit more detail in *Novy Mir,* No. 12, December, 1965. The account of the Molotov-Schulen-burg meeting is based on Gustav Hilger and Alfred G. Meyer, *The Incompatible Allies,* with detail added from *Nazi-Soviet Relations, 1939-1941.* General I. V. Tyulenev's story is drawn from his *Cherez Tri Voiny.* The decision to set up the Moscow fighter command is from M. Gallai, *Novy Mir,* No. 9, September, 1966.

CHAPTER 4. THE NIGHT WEARS ON

Naval Commissar Kuznetsov and Admiral Panteleyev are the principal sources for this chapter, with detail from V. Achkasov and B. Veiner's work on the Baltic Fleet. The story of events at Sevastopol comes from I. I. Azarov, *Osazhdennaya Odessa;* Captain N. G. Rybalko, *Voyenno-Istoricheskii Zhurnal,* No. 6, June, 1963; N. P. Vyunenko, *Chernomorskii Flot v Velikoi Otechestvennoi Voine.* Marshal Voronov describes the night of June 21-22 in *Na Sluzhbe Voyennoi.* General Tyulenev is the source of Stalin's skepticism regarding Zhukov's reports of German bombing.

CHAPTER 5. DAWN, JUNE 22

The description of the military situation in Leningrad is drawn from General B. V. Bychevsky's *Gorod-Front* and *Na Zashchite Nevskoi Tverdyni.* Some detail is provided by *Istoriya Velikoi Otechestvennoi Voiny Sovetskogo Soyuza* and General Mikhail Dukhanov, *V Serdtse i v Pamyati.* The description of the Baltic Military District is provided by *Borba Za Sovetskuyu Pribaltiku,* with additions from Voronov. The description of General Sobennikov's Eighth Army comes from *Borba Za Sovetskuyu Pribaltiku* and *Bitva Za Leningrad* (Barbashin *et al.*). The description of events in the German Embassy in Moscow is based on Hilger, personal accounts by Dr. Gebhardt von Walther, then a secretary of the embassy and in 1967 German Ambassador to Moscow, and *Nazi-Soviet Relations;* that of the Soviet Embassy in Berlin, largely from Berezhkov's published work, amplified in personal correspondence.

CHAPTER 6. WHAT STALIN HEARD

The Kremlin military meeting is described by S. A. Kalinin, *Razmyshlyaya o Minu-vshem;* M. I. Kazakov, *Nad Kartoi Bylikh Srazhenii;* A. I. Yeremenko, *V Nachale Voiny* (Yeremenko's version is sharply challenged by V. Ivanov and K. Cheremukhin in *Voyenno-Istoricheskii Zhurnal,* No. 11, November, 1966); and Marshal Ivan Bagramyan, *Voyenno-Istoricheskii Zhurnal,* No. 1, January, 1967. One of the richest sources for data on Soviet intelligence concerning Nazi war preparations is the anonymous article, "*Sovetskiye Organy Gosudarstvennoi Bezopasnosti v Gody Velikoi Otechestvennoi Voiny,*" *Voprosy Istorii,* No. 5, May, 1965. Presumably this article was prepared by a high Soviet intelligence source. Others are: P. A. Zhilin, *Kak Fashistskaya Germaniya Gotovila Napadeniye na Sovetsky Soyuz;* Army General V. Ivanov, *Voyenno-Istoricheskii Zhurnal,* No. 6, June, 1965; Admiral Kuznetsov, *Nakanune;* Marshal A. Grechko, *Voyenno-Istoricheskii*

Zhurnal, No. 6, June, 1966; Berezhkov; numerous Soviet works on Richard Sorge, the Soviet master spy; A. M. Nekrich, *1941 22 Iuniya*; Hilger; and *Istoriya Velikoi Otechestvennoi Voiny S.S. 1941–1945*, Vol. I.

CHAPTER 7.   WHAT STALIN BELIEVED

Ilya Ehrenburg described his dealings with Stalin in his memoirs and added some details in personal conversation before his death. Zhilin is another source on the Kremlin. Sources on troop transfers include Kazakov; Bagramyan; A. M. Samsonov, *Velikaya Bitva pod Moskvoi*. Analyses of Stalin's conduct are provided by Nekrich, A. Zonin in *Prosolennye Gody*, and Admiral Kuznetsov. The Malenkov intervention of June 3 is reported in *Velikaya Otechestvennaya Voina Sovetskogo Soyuza*, p. 58, and by G. Kravchenko, *Voyenno-Istoricheskii Zhurnal*, No. 4, April, 1965. Maisky and Berezhkov describe the situation in London and Berlin. The Western frontier is described by Aleksandr Rozen in his historical novel, *Posledniye Dve Nedeli*; Bagramyan; L. M. Sandalov, *Trudniye Rubezhi*, and V. A. Grekov, *Bug v Ogne*. The reports on last-minute intelligence come from the *Voprosy Istorii*, May, 1965, study of state intelligence organs; *Istoriya Velikoi Otechestvennii Voiny S.S. 1941–1945*, Vol. I; and Admiral Kuznetsov. The movement of Nazi and Soviet troops to the frontier is assessed by P. Korodinov, *Voyenno-Istoricheskii Zhurnal*, No. 10, October, 1965; and Marshal Sergei Shtemenko in *Voyenno-Istoricheskii Zhurnal*, No. 6, June, 1966. The air force incident is reported by A. Yakovlev, *Tsel Zhizni*. Nekrich and Voronov describe Stalin on the eve of war. The rumors of a Russo-German deal were reported by Grigore Gafencu; von Hassell; Filippov; Gerhard L. Weinberg in *Germany and the Soviet Union, 1939–41*; Halder; and Angelo Rossi, *The Russo-German Alliance*. Stalin's suspiciousness and lack of plans are dealt with by Kuznetsov, Voronov, Tyulenev, Bagramyan and Nikita Khrushchev in his so-called "secret speech" of February, 1956, and on other occasions. Stalin's breakdown is described by Khrushchev, Maisky, Nekrich and others.

CHAPTER 8.   CLOUDLESS SKIES

Trofimov's story is contained in A. Dymshits, *Podvig Leningrada*; Glazunov in *Doroga k Tebe*; Gankevich in *Konets Gruppy 'Nord'*; Skryabina in *V Blokade*; Kanashin, *Poka Stuchit Serdtse*; Krutikov, *V Prifrontovykh Lesakh*; Konstantinov, *Ya Srazhalsya v Krasnoi Armii*; that of the Hermitage in Varshavsky and Rest, *Podvig Ermitazha*; the station scene in Ortenberg, *Na Ognennikh Rubezhakh*; Larin in Sozonkov, *Geroi Zemli Sovetskoi*; Kronstadt in Rudny, *Deistvuyushchii Flot*; Petrova's story in Konstantinov, *Zhenshchiny Goroda Lenina*; Sayanov in his *Leningradskii Dnevnik*; the story of Lebedev from the account of his wife, Vera Petrovna, *Zvezda*, No. 5, May, 1965; and Kochetov in *Oktyabr*, No. 1, January, 1964.

CHAPTER 9.   A MATTER OF DETAIL

This is largely based on standard German sources—Halder's diary; Guderian; Manstein; Restlinger, *The House Built on Sand*—Pavlenko, *Porazheniye Germanskogo Imperializma*; the two *Bitva Za Leningrad* books; Ortenberg, *Na Ognennikh Rubezhakh*; Pavlov and Meretskov.

CHAPTER 10.   ON THE DISTANT APPROACHES

Much of this chapter is based on the account in Orlov, *Borba Za Sovetskuyu Pribaltiku*; plus materials from Karasev; *Velikaya Otechestvennaya Voina Sovetskogo Soyuza*; the six-volume *Istoriya VOVSS*; and Barbashin, *Bitva Za Leningrad*. The Taurage incident is described by A. Ionin, *Zvezda*, No. 6, June, 1966. Detail on the Baltic Military District has been drawn from Chadayev, *Ekonomika SSSR v Period VOV;* Samsonov, *Vtoraya Mirovaya Voina; Leningrad v VOV;* and I. Boiko, *Voyenno-Istoricheskii Zhurnal,* No. 8, August, 1966. Thē figures on Soviet air losses come from Barbashin; A. M. Samsonov, *Stalingradskaya Bitva;* and A. S. Yakovlev, *Tsel Zhizni.* The description of General Morozov's headquarters is drawn from V. P. Agafonov, *Neman! Neman! Ya—Dunai!,* and Z. Kondrats, *IX Fort.* The description of Libau comes from V. Ye. Bystrov, *Geroi Podpolya;* R. Velevitnev, *Krepost bez Fortov;* and A. P. Kladt, *Istoriya SSSR,* No. 3, 1965. The report on Sobennikov is largely drawn from Orlov. The description of Pavlov's headquarters comes from I. V. Boldin, *Stranitsii Zhizni,* and Leonid Sandalov and Fedor A. Ostashenko in V. A. Grekov, *Bug v Ogne.*

CHAPTER 11. THE RED ARROW PULLS IN

The material on Meretskov and the purge of the Red Army comes from his memoirs; from *Pod Znamenem Ispanskoi Respubliki* (which he edited); *VOVSS;* S. A. Kalinin, *Razmyshlyaya o Minuvshem; Istoriya VOVSS;* A. V. Gorbatov, *Years Off My life;* B. V. Bychevsky, *Voyenno-Istoricheskii Zhurnal,* No. 9, September, 1963; I. Bagramyan, *Voyenno-Istoricheskii Zhurnal,* No. 1, January, 1967; A. M. Nekrich, *1941 22 Iunya;* N. N. Voronov, *Na Sluzhbe Voyennoi;* D. A. Morozov, *O Nikh Ne Upominalos v Svodkakh;* and Konstantin Simonov's novel, *Soldatami Ne Rozhdayutsya.* The prewar military situation is based on A. I. Yeremenko, *V· Nachale Voiny; VOVSS;* P. Yegorov, *Voyenno-Istoricheskii Zhurnal,* No. 5, May, 1967; Naval Commissar N. G. Kuznetsov, *Oktyabr,* No. 9, September, 1965; Meretskov; *Na Zashchite Nevskoi Tverdyni;* and Bychevsky, *Voyenno-Istoricheskii Zhurnal,* No. 1, January, 1964.

CHAPTER 12. EVEN THE DEAD

Olga Berggolts' description comes from her *Dnevnye Zvezdy,* with additional material from Yuri L. Alanskii, *Teatr v Kvadrate Obstrela.* The poem is from Berggolts' *Uzel.* The Konstantinov and Skryabina passages are from their memoirs. Dmitri Shcheglov's story is told in *V Opolchenii,* I. I. Kanashin's in *Poka Stuchit Serdtse,* the description of Leningrad from many sources and years of personal observation. The story of the Kirov repressions comes largely from *Ocherki Istorii Leningrada,* Vol. 4, and S. Kostyuchenko, *Istoriya Kirovskogo Zavoda.* The Akhmatova poem is from her *Rekviem.* The Orbeli description, of course, is provided by Varshavsky and Rest, *Zvezda,* No. 10, October, 1964. The description of events in Leningrad after Molotov's broadcast is based on Skryabina; Anatoly Darov's *Blokada;* Pavel Luknitsky, *Skvoz Vsyu Blokadu;* and *Na Zashchite Nevskoi Tverdyni.*

CHAPTER 13. THE DARK DAYS

The picture of Zhdanov is reconstructed from his public speeches, the impressions of Kuznetsov, *Oktyabr,* Nos. 9 and 11, September and November, 1965; Richard Lauterbach, *These Are the Russians;* Nikita Khrushchev's "secret speech"; M. I. Kazakov; *Na Zashchite Nevskoi Tverdyni;* and I. M. Maisky. The data on the Committee for State Defense are drawn from *Istoriya VOVSS* and Marshal Andrei Grechko, *Voyenno-Istoricheskii Zhurnal,* No. 6, June, 1966.

CHAPTER 14. ZHDANOV IN ACTION

The description of Leningrad's mobilization comes from *Leningrad v VOV;* A. Karasev and V. Kovalchuk, *Voyenno-Istoricheskii Zhurnal,* No. 1, January, 1964; *Na Zashchite Nevskoi Tverdyni;* Ilya Brazhin, *Neva,* No. 2, February, 1968; Pavlov; Karasev; A. Dymshits, *Podvig Leningrada;* Barbashin, *Bitva Za Leningrad;* V. Bogdanov-

Berezovsky, *V Gody Velikoi Otechestvennoi Voiny;* Yuri Alanskii, *Teatr v Kvadrate Obstrela;* Karasev, *Istoriya SSSR,* No. 3, 1961; N. N. Zhdanov, *Ognevoi Shchit Leningrada;* Bychevsky; Meretskov; and Varshavsky and Rest.

CHAPTER 15. THE WHITE SWANS

The chapter draws heavily upon Nikolai Mikhailovsky's *S Toboi Baltika* and his account in *Literaturnoye Nasledstvo Sovetskikh Pisatelei,* Vol. II; Vladimir Rudny; Aleksandr Zonin; and Admiral Y. A. Panteleyev, *Morskoi Front.* Details on conditions in the Baltic states are provided from V. Stanley Vardys, *Lithuania Under the Soviets;* A. A. Druzula, *V Dni Voiny;* Orlov; M. P. Pavlovskii, *Na Ostrovakh; Documents on German Foreign Policy,* Series D., Vols. VII and XIII; the anonymous article on Soviet intelligence, *Voprosy Istorii,* May, 1965; V. Achkasov, *Krasnoznamennyi Baltiiskii Flot;* Vsevolod Vishnevsky, *Sobrannye Sochinenii,* Vol. III.

CHAPTER 16. THE RED ARMY RETREATS

Among the principal sources are Mikhail Dukhanov, *V Serdtse i v Pamyati;* Barbashin; *Istoriya VOVSS;* Orlov; A. Kiselev, *Voyenno-Istoricheskii Zhurnal,* No. 6, June, 1966; D. D. Lelyushenko, *Zarya Pobedy;* Agafonov. The verdict on General Kuznetsov is that of the editors of *Istoriya VOVSS,* Vol. II, p. 29.

CHAPTER 17. THE FIRST DAYS

The portrait of Leningrad in the early days of war is a pastiche from many, many sources, among them Varshavsky and Rest; *Leningrad v VOV; Na Zashchite Nevskoi Tverdyni;* the collection *900 Dnei;* Olga Berggolts' *Dnevnye Zvezdy;* Bogdanov-Berezovsky, *V Gody VOV;* Madame Skryabina's diary; A. T. Skilyagin, *Dela i Lyudi;* Vera Ketlinskaya, *Neva,* No. 5, May, 1965; Vsevolod Kochetov, *Oktyabr,* No. 1, January, 1964; A. N. Vasilyev, *S Perom i Avtomatom;* Ilya Avramenko, *Den Poezii 1965;* L. Panteleyev, *Zhivye Pamyatniki;* Bychevsky; Barbashin; Meretskov; Pavlov; Karasev; *VOVSS;* S. Belyayev, *Narodnoye Opolcheniye Leningrada;* Lev Uspensky, *Zvezda,* No. 9, September, 1964; Shcheglov; Yuri Alanskii; S. Bubenshchikov, *V Ognennom Koltse;* V. Malkin, *Voyenno-Istoricheskii Zhurnal,* No. 1, January, 1964.

CHAPTER 18. THE LUGA LINE

The principal sources for the Luga battle are Bychevsky; Barbashin; Karasev; *Na Zashchite Nevskoi Tverdyni;* and General Dukhanov. Kochetov tells his story in *Oktyabr,* No. 1, January, 1964. Some detail on Kochetov is drawn from Vasilyev, *S Perom i Avtomatom.* Yeremenko describes the Western Front in *Na Zapadnom Napravlenii.* Material on the 2nd Volunteers is provided by Bubenshchikov's *V Ognennom Koltse.* The story of the 70th Guards is from N. S. Gudkova, *Mera Muzhestva;* and A. Rozen, *Zvezda,* No. 2, February, 1966.

CHAPTER 19. THE LUGA LINE CRUMBLES

The principal sources are Bychevsky; Barbashin; *Na Zashchite Nevskoi Tverdyni;* Kochetov, *Oktyabr,* No. 6, June, 1964; S. Belyayev, *Narodnoye Opolcheniye Leningrada;* and Karasev.

CHAPTER 20. THE ENEMY AT THE GATES

The description of Smolny is based on G. N. Karayev, *Po Mestam Boyevoi Slavy;* Pavlov; L. L. Shvetsov, *Smolninskii Raion;* and *Na Zashchite Nevskoi Tverdyni.* The crisis details are drawn from *Na Zashchite;* Belyayev; V. V. Stremilov, *Voprosy Istorii KPSS,* No. 5, May, 1959; *Leningrad v VOV;* Varshavsky and Rest; A. Shtein, *Znamya,* No. 4, April, 1964. The story of the Leningrad City Council of Defense comes from Pavlov; Karasev; A. E. Sukhnovalov, *Petrogradskaya Storona;* and *900 Geroicheskikh Dnei.* Other details are from Kochetov, Bychevsky, Luknitsky.

CHAPTER 21. STALIN ON THE PHONE

The Stalin description is based on Maisky; Barbashin; Kuznetsov; Voronov, *Istoriya SSSR,* No. 3, 1965; S. M. Shtemenko, *Voyenno-Istoricheskii Zhurnal,* No. 9, September, 1965; Robert Sherwood, *Roosevelt and Hopkins;* and Pavlov. The Stalin-Zhdanov-Voroshilov dispute is based on Pavlov, *Na Zashchite,* and V. Achkasov, *Voyenno-Istoricheskii Zhurnal,* No. 10, October, 1966. Details are added from P. Ponomarenko, *Voyenno-Istoricheskii Zhurnal,* No. 4, April, 1965; *Istoriya VOVSS,* Vol. I, p. 105; and T. Shtykov, writing in L. I. Ilin, *Khrabreishiye iz Khrabrykh.*

CHAPTER 22. THE TALLINN DISASTER

Sources on the Tallinn disaster are Mikhailovsky, Panteleyev, A. K. Tarasenkov, Vsevolod Vishnevsky (their diaries plus materials in *Literaturnoye Nasledstvo Sovetskikh Pisatelei,* Vol. II); A. Mushnikov, *Baltiitsy v Boyakh Za Leningrad;* V. Achkasov, *Voyenno-Istoricheskii Zhurnal,* No. 10, October, 1966; A. Zonin; K. K. Kamalov, *Morskaya Pekhota v Boyakh Za Rodinu;* N. Chukovsky, *Yunost,* No. 1, January, 1966; N. F. Mineyev, *Pervaya Pobeda;* Ya. Perechnev, *Na Strazhe Morskikh Gorizontov;* A. Shtein, *Znamya,* No. 4, April, 1965; and Orlov.

CHAPTER 23. THE RUSSIAN DUNKIRK

The principal source is Panteleyev. Others include Achkasov, *Voyenno-Istoricheskii Zhurnal,* No. 10, October, 1966; Vishnevsky; Mikhailovsky; M. Godenko's semifictional *Minnoye Polye;* Tarasenkov; P. L. Korzinkin, *V Redaktsiyu Ne Vernulsya;* A. Mushnikov; S. F. Yedelinskii, *Balticheskii Flot v VOV;* Kuznetsov, *Voprosy Istorii,* No. 8, August, 1965; Rudny; and Zonin.

CHAPTER 24. THE NORTHERN CRISIS

Most of this chapter comes from Panteleyev, Barbashin and Bychevsky. Details are added from *Leningrad v VOV;* Luknitsky; A. Dymshits, *Znamya,* No. 3, March, 1966; I. I. Kanashin, *Poka Stuchit Serdtse;* and A. Mushnikov.

CHAPTER 25. THE LAST DAYS OF SUMMER

Vera Inber's story is told in *Za Mnogo Let* and by Vera Ketlinskaya, *Neva,* No. 5, May, 1965; that of Shvarts in Ketlinskaya; Aleksandr Shtein, *Znamya,* No. 5, May, 1964; and S. Tsimbal, *My Znali Yevgeniya Shvartsa.* The picture of the city comes from *Leningrad v VOV;* Luknitsky; A. Rozen, *Zvezda,* Nos. 1 and 2, January and February, 1965; Shtein, *Znamya,* No. 6, June, 1964; Gankevich; Bogdanov-Berezovsky, *V Gody VOV;* Varshavsky and Rest; V. M. Barashenkov, *Istoriya Gosudarstvennoi Publichnoi Biblioteki;* and Karasev.

CHAPTER 26. WILL THE CITY BE ABANDONED?

The principal sources on the visit of the State Defense Committee group are *Na Zashchite;* Voronov; Kuznetsov, *Voprosy Istorii,* No. 8, August, 1965; Panteleyev; A. Mushnikov, *Baltiitsy v Boyakh Za Leningrad;* F. I. Sirota, *Voprosy Istorii,* No. 10,

October, 1956; Pavlov; Barbashin; Karasev; *Istoriya VOVSS.* The Nazi High Command controversy is reported by Halder. The Churchill-Stalin exchange is reported by Maisky and Winston Churchill, *The Second World War,* Vol. III, *The Grand Alliance.*

CHAPTER 27. THE CIRCLE CLOSED

Bychevsky is the principal source on Mga. His account of the Izhorsk battle is supplemented by detail from Sviridov, *Bitva Za Leningrad;* Barbashin; Chernenko's story in A. Dymshits, *Podvig Leningrada; Leningrad v VOV;* Vissarion Sayanov, *Leningradskii Dnevnik; 900 Dnei;* Bubenshchikov; and statistical detail from *900 Geroicheskikh Dnei.* The breakthrough to the Neva is described by Kochetov, *Oktyabr,* No. 11, November, 1965; Barbashin; *Na Zashchite Nevskoi Tverdyni;* Sviridov; Bychevsky; the taking of Shlisselburg by Gankevich, Bychevsky, Barbashin, *Na Zashchite.* Criticism is drawn from Dukhanov and Barbashin; the aftermath of Izhorsk from *900 Geroicheskikh Dnei;* Karasev; Ketlinskaya, *Neva,* No. 5, May, 1965; and Beilin, *Ryadom S Geroyami.* Shostakovich's story is from *900 Dnei;* Bogdanov-Berezovsky, *V Gody VOV;* and *Stranitsy Muzykalnoi Publisistiki;* Al Less, *Moskva,* No. 5, May, 1965; Olga Berggolts, *Literaturnaya Gazeta,* No. 56, May 9, 1965; A. N. Vasilyev, *S Perom i Avtomatom.* Other detail from G. G. Tigranov, *Leningradskaya Konservatoriya;* Panteleyev and Sayanov in B. M. Likharev, *Leningradskii Almanakh.*

CHAPTER 28. THE BLOOD-RED CLOUDS

Vera Inber's impressions are from her diary, *Izbrannye Proizvedeniya,* Vol. III; those of Luknitsky from his diary; Berggolts, *Dnevne Zvezdy;* Kochetov, *Oktyabr,* No. 6, June, 1964. Other sources: Bychevsky; Pavlov; *Podvig Leningrada;* Olga Iordan in *900 Dnei.* Statistics are from *900 Geroicheskikh Dnei; Na Zashchite;* Pavlov (who provides the detailed food estimates); Karasev; *Leningrad v VOV;* Varshavsky and Rest; S. Kostyuchenko, *Istoriya Kirovskogo Zavoda;* Panteleyev; N. N. Zhdanov, *Ognevoi Shchit Leningrada;* Bondarenko in *S Perem i Avtomatom;* Ketlinskaya, *Literaturnaya Gazeta,* No. 15, February 4, 1965; Voronov; and Skryabina.

CHAPTER 29. NOT ALL WERE BRAVE

Vishnevsky's observations are from his diary, *Sobranye Sochinenii,* Vol. III; Kochetov, *Oktyabr,* Nos. 6 and 11, June, November, 1964. Other detail from *Na Zashchite;* Pavlov; A. T. Skilyagin, *Dela i Lyudi; S Perom i Avtomatom; Leningrad v VOV;* Shtein, *Znamya,* No. 6, June, 1964; Rosenman in *Podvig Leningrada;* A. Veresov, *Neva,* No. 6, June, 1965; and Sayanov.

CHAPTER 30. A HARD NUT TO CRACK

The description of Oreshek is largely drawn from A. Veresov, *Neva,* No. 4, April, 1966. The story of the battle is based on Barbashin; Bychevsky; A. T. Karavayev, *Po Srochnomu Predpisaniyu; Podvig Leningrada,* pp. 428–429; A. I. Mankevich, *Krasnoznamennaya Ladozhskaya Flotiliya v VOV;* K. K. Kamalov, *Morskaya Pekhota v Boyakh Za Rodinu;* G. Odintsov, *Voyenno-Istoricheskii Zhurnal,* No. 12, December, 1964; Shcheglov; Kochetov, *Oktyabr,* No. 11, November, 1964; Gudkova, *Mera Muzhestva;* Shtein, *Znamya,* No. 6, June, 1964.

CHAPTER 31. ZHUKOV IN COMMAND

The military situation as Zhukov took command is best described in Barbashin, with detail from A. Saporov, *Doroga Zhizni;* Bychevsky; Karasev; Dukhanov; *Na Zashchite;* I. I. Fedyuninsky, *Podnyate Po Trevoge.* Bychevsky and the third edition of Pavlov are revealing on Voroshilov's displacement by Zhukov. Other detail from Kochetov, *Oktyabr*, No. 6, June, 1964; Berggolts; and Shcheglov.

CHAPTER 32.   BLOW UP THE CITY!

Plans for defense and destruction of Leningrad are described by *Na Zashchite;* Karasev; Bychevsky; Shcheglov; Barbashin; *900 Geroicheskikh Dnei;* Panteleyev; Konstantinov; Kochetov, *Oktyabr*, No. 11, November, 1964; Kuznetsov, *Voprosy Istorii*, No. 8, August, 1965; *Leningrad v VOV;* Godenko; A. Verezov, *Neva*, No. 6, June, 1965; Kostyuchenko; A. Rozen, *Zvezda*, No. 2, February, 1966.

CHAPTER 33.   "THEY'RE DIGGING IN!"

A. I. Veresov, *Neva*, No. 6, June, 1965, and in *Soldaty Sto Devyatoi*, presents vivid detail on the Pulkovo front, as does A. Rozen, *Zvezda*, No. 2, February, 1966. Other detail comes from Berggolts; *900 Dnei*; and much, of course, from Bychevsky; Barbashin; Dukhanov; Fedyuninsky; *Na Zashchite;* Vishnevsky; Kochetov; A. von Reinhardt's memoirs; *Leningrad v VOV;* I. Isakov, *Neva*, No. 3, March, 1967; *VOVSS;* and G. Zhukov, *Voyenno-Istoricheskii Zhurnal*, No. 8, August, 1966.

CHAPTER 34.   THE KING'S FORTRESS

The principal sources on Kronstadt are Panteleyev; Achkasov, *Voyenno-Istoricheskii Zhurnal*, No. 1, January, 1964; Karasev; Y. Perechnev, *Na Strazhe Morskikh Gorizontov;* Vishnevsky; and Shtein.

CHAPTER 35.   DEUS CONSERVAT OMNIA

Much material on Anna Akhmatova is drawn from her introduction to her *Stikhotvoreniya*, from her own *Rekviem* and from Luknitsky. Other sources: A. M. Dreving in Barashenkov; Inber's diary; Ye. Vasyutina, *Podvig Leningrada;* Konstantinov; Skryabina; Kochetov, *Gorod v Shineli;* Pavlov; *Leningrad v VOV; Na Zashchite;* T. V. Pokrovskaya, *Klimat Leningrada;* Vishnevsky; Barbashin; Ketlinskaya in *900 Dnei;* Glazunov; A. V. Koltsov, *Uchenye Leningrada v Gody Blokady;* Varshavsky and Rest; and Godenko.

CHAPTER 36.   SEVEN MEN KNEW

One of the most vivid descriptions of starvation is that of the late Nikolai Chukovsky, *Yunost*, No. 1, January, 1966. Others are provided by Maria Razina in *Podvig Leningrada;* Inber; Vishnevsky; Skryabina; Godenko; Karasev; I. V. Travkin, *V Vodakh Sedoi Baltiki;* and Luknitsky. Statistical data come from *Na Zashchite;* Karasev; *Leningrad v VOV;* Karavayev; Pavlov; V. Ya. Neigoldberg, *Istoriya SSSR*, No. 3, 1965. Detail from L. Panteleyev, *Neva*, No. 1, January, 1964; Berggolts; Sayanov; Kochetov; Tarasenkov in *Literaturnoye Nasledstvo*, Vol. II; Vishnevsky; Voronov; *S Perom i Avtomatom;* Kanashin; P. D. Grishchenko, *Moi Druzya Podvodniki;* Darov; Pavlov; Ortenberg.

CHAPTER 37.   "WHEN WILL THE BLOCKADE BE LIFTED?"

The principal sources are Panteleyev; *Na Zashchite;* Voronov; Barbashin; Fedyuninsky; G. Ye. Degtyarev, *Taran i Shchit;* Meretskov, *Nekolebimo, Kak Rossiya*, and *Voyenno-Istoricheskii Zhurnal*, No. 1, January, 1965; P. Yegorov, *Voyenno-Istoricheskii Zhurnal*, No. 5, May, 1967; Y. Alanskii, *Zvezda*, No. 11, November, 1966; Karasev; Saparov; G. A. Beresnev, *Ogni Sedogo Volkhova;* Sviridov; *900 Geroicheskikh Dnei; Leningrad v VOV;* and Luknitsky.

CHAPTER 38. THE ROAD OF LIFE

Curiously, there is no single satisfactory or dramatic account of the Ladoga ice road among the numerous Soviet sources. A. Saparov's *Doroga Zhizni* is weak and propagandistic, and A. D. Kharitonov's *Legendarnaya Ledovaya Trassa* is little more than a pamphlet. The chapter is based on M. Murov, *Zvezda*, No. 5, May, 1965; F. Lagunov, *Zvezda*, No. 1, January, 1964; Karasev; Pavlov; Kharitonov, *Voyenno-Istoricheskii Zhurnal*, No. 11, November, 1966; Y. Loman, *Neva*, No. 1, January, 1967; F. Lapukhov, *Neva*, No. 7, July, 1967; *Na Zashchite*; Dukhanov, *Zvezda*, No. 1, January, 1964 (some detail is omitted in his book version, *V Serdtse i v Pamyati*); *Leningrad v VOV*; Meretskov, *Voyenno-Istoricheskii Zhurnal*, No. 1, January, 1965; Bogdanov-Berezovsky; Inber; Luknitsky; Samsonov, *Vtoraya Mirovaya Voina*, Vol. II, pp. 159–166; *900 Geroicheskikh Dnei*.

CHAPTER 39. THE CITY OF DEATH

Nikolai Tikhonov's account comes from *Zvezda*, No. 1, January, 1964; with detail from D. Levonevskii, *Neva*, No. 2, February, 1966; Dmitri Moldavskii, *O Mikhaile Dudine*; Sayanov; Aleksandr Prokofyev, *Literaturnaya Gazeta*, June 22, 1965. Other sources: Vishnevsky; Vera Petrova, *Zvezda*, No. 5, May, 1965; *Leningrad v VOV*; detail on Lebedev from *Literaturnoye Nasledstvo*, Vol. II, and A. Kron in *Ryadom S Geroyami*. Other sources: Bogdanov-Berezovsky; Luknitsky; Sayanov; Aleksandr Dymshits, *Znamya*, No. 3, March, 1966; Vsevolod Rozhdestvensky, *Ogonok*, No. 5, May, 1964; *Podvig Ermitazha*; Orbeli in Ashot Arzumanyan, *Druzhba*; Yuri L. Alanskii; K. M. Yuzbashyan, *Akademik Iosif A. Orbeli*; Mikhailovsky, *S Toboi Baltika!*

CHAPTER 40. THE SLEDS OF THE CHILDREN

The Leningrad diarists are the principal sources for this chapter: V. Koneshevich, *Novy Mir*, Nos. 9 and 10, September and October, 1965; Luknitsky; Vera Inber; Vishnevsky; Skryabina; Dmitri Moldavskii in *Podvig Leningrada*; Panteleyev; Yelizaveta Sharypina, *V Dni Blokady*; Glazunov; and Shcheglov. The story of Zinaida Shishova comes from A. Abramov, *Neva*, No. 6, June, 1965; and the poem from V. Azarov's collection, *Poeziya v Boyu*. Other material is drawn from *Leningrad v VOV*; T. V. Pokrovskaya, *Klimat Leningrada*; *Na Zashchite*; Aleksandr Kron in *Talent i Muzhestvo*; Nikolai Chukovsky in *Ryadom s Geroyami*; and Nikolai Markevich in *V Redaktsiyu Ne Vernulsya*.

CHAPTER 41. A NEW KIND OF CRIME

Much detail comes from *Dela i Lyudi*, which, in large part, deals with the Leningrad police during the war. Material is drawn extensively from *Na Zashchite*; Karasev; Barbashin; Konstantinov; Darov; the Razina diary; Pavlov; Aleksandr Chakovsky; a hasty examination of *Leningradskaya Pravda* files for November, December, 1941, and the winter months of 1942; Ivan Krutikov, *V Prifrontovykh Lesakh*; Inber; Kochetov, *Oktyabr*, No. 5, May, 1965; Sharypina; L. Panteleyev, *Moskva*, No. 6, June, 1957. The description and text of Mayor Popkov's speech are from *S Perom i Avtomatom*, *Podvig Leningrada*, pp. 287–288, and Chakovsky. Other material is from Vishnevsky and Inber. *Leningrad v VOV*, *900 Dnei*, Pavlov, Karasev and *Na Zashchite* provide data on the bakeries and the power and fuel situation. *Podvig Leningrada*, pp. 115–116, contains data on the Leningrad fire department. The "open city" proposal is discussed by Karasev (pp. 120, 204, 205) and *Leningrad v VOV* (p. 214).

CHAPTER 42. THE CITY OF ICE

An excellent description of Radio Leningrad is provided by A. Polovnikov, *Neva*, No. 6, June, 1965; and by Yuri L. Alanskii, *Teatr v Kvadrate Obstrela*; in *S Perom i Avtomatom* by Olga Berggolts; and by Aleksandr Kron in *Ryadom s Geroyami*. Vera Ketlinskaya describes the writers in *Neva*, No. 5, May, 1965, and Leonid Rakhmanov adds detail in *Ryadom s Geroyami* and in *Moskva*, No. 6, June, 1957. Vishnevsky and Sayanov contribute vignettes. The story of the Leningrad film is told by Vishnevsky and V. Solovtsov in *S Perom i Avtomatom*. The story of Olga Berggolts and Ketlinskaya is told by Ketlinskaya, *Neva*, No. 5, May, 1965. Luknitsky describes Ketlinskaya, and Olga Berggolts tells the story of the walk to her father's in *Dnevnye Zvezdy*.

CHAPTER 43. THE LENINGRAD APOCALYPSE

Not all the sources of this chapter can be identified. Cannibalism is not a subject which Leningraders care to discuss publicly. Material is drawn from Kochetov, *Oktyabr*, No. 5, May, 1965; Berggolts; Moldavskii in *Podvig Leningrada;* Varshavsky and Rest; Vishnevsky; *900 Geroicheskikh Dnei;* Inber; Sayanov; Konstantinov; Alexander Werth, *Leningrad;* Skryabina; Darov; Alanskii; Luknitsky. The Andreyev poem has not been published in the Soviet Union, but a mimeograph copy is in the author's possession.

CHAPTER 44. "T" IS FOR TANYA

The Savichev notebook is in the Leningrad City Museum. The story of the family comes from *Literaturnaya Gazeta*, January 25, 1964. The winter campaign is described by Meretskov in his book and in *Voyenno-Istoricheskii Zhurnal*, No. 1, January, 1965; and by Fedyuninsky. Detail is provided in *VOVSS, Na Zashchite*. Anna Vasileyeva, the Kirov girl, was interviewed by the author, February 11, 1944. The Milova story is from Karasev, the Mironova diary from *Leningrad VOV*. The death estimates are from *Na Zashchite*, p. 264; Pavlov (3rd edition), p. 144; Karasev, pp. 184, 185; V. I. Dmitriyev, *Salut Leningrada*, p. 11; hospital deaths from *900 Geroicheskikh Dnei*, p. 342; and *Leningrad v VOV*, pp. 504 *et seq.* Ration card figures are from *Na Zashchite*, p. 284, and Karasev, p. 199. Markevich is published in *V Redaktsiyu Ne Vernulsya*, the writers' appeal in *Leningrad v VOV*. The ice road is described by Pavlov, *Na Zashchite*, and Karasev, and deaths are listed by *Leningrad v VOV;* Merkulov; G. A. Sobolev, *Uchenye Leningrada;* A. V. Kolstov, *Uchenye Leningrada;* and Sayanov.

CHAPTER 45. THE ICE ROAD TO THE MAINLAND

The stories come from Luknitsky, Saparov, Skryabina, *Leningrad v VOV*, and Inber.

CHAPTER 46. DEATH, DEATH, DEATH

The spring story is told by Luknitsky; Karasev; Yuri Alanskii; L. Panteleyev, *Novy Mir*, No. 5, May, 1965; *900 Geroicheskikh Dnei; Leningrad v VOV;* Inber; *Na Zashchite;* Vishnevsky; Razina in *Podvig Leningrada;* Mikhailovsky; Matvei Frolov, *Novy Mir*, No. 6, June, 1957; *S Perom i Avtomatom*. Statistics on Ladoga deliveries are from *Na Zashchite*, pp. 340–341. Death and burial figures are from Karasev, pp. 236–237; ration card and food estimates for April 15 from *Na Zashchite*, pp. 307, 340. The original official death figures are from *900 Geroicheskikh Dnei*, pp. 397–398; criticism from *Na Zashchite*, p. 336. The analysis of the death toll by V. M. Kovalchuk and G. L. Sobolev, published in *Voprosy Istorii*, No. 12, December, 1965, is the most important single piece of historical research done on the Leningrad tragedy. Mikhail Dudin's estimate appeared in *Literaturnaya Gazeta*, No. 39, March 27, 1960. The military losses are estimated by O. F. Suvenirov, *Vtoraya Mirovaya Voina*, Vol. II, p. 160. *Na Zashchite*, p. 336, estimates deaths at "not less than a million." Pavlov's criticism of the more recent death estimates is contained in the third edition of his book, pp. 148–149.

CHAPTER 47. AGAIN, SPRING

The portrait of Leningrad on May Day is from Luknitsky and A. Fadeyev, *Sobraniye Sochinenii*, Vol. III. The portrait of Govorov is from Bychevsky; A. Kiselev, *Voyenno-Istoricheskii Zhurnal*, No. 2, February, 1967; Sayanov; G. Odintsov, *Voyenno-Istoricheskii Zhurnal*, No. 12, December, 1964. The story of Vlasov is told by Meretskov, *Voyenno-Istoricheskii Zhurnal*, No. 1, January, 1965; Larry Lesueur, *Twelve Months That Shook the World;* Eve Curie, *Journey Among Warriors;* General M. Khozin, *Voyenno-Istoricheskii Zhurnal*, No. 2, February, 1965; Fedyuninsky; Boris Gusev, *Smert Komissara;* L. Panteleyev, *Novy Mir*, No. 5, May, 1965; Alexander Dallin, *German Rule in Russia*. Yevgeny Zhilo's lovely sketch is from *Zvezda*, No. 12, December, 1967.

CHAPTER 48. OPERATION ISKRA

The picture of Leningrad in summer is based on Luknitsky; *900 Dnei;* Sayanov; A. Shtein, *Znamya*, No. 6, June, 1964; and Vishnevsky. Military data come from Bychevsky; Barbashin; Meretskov, *Voprosy Istorii*, No. 10, October, 1965; *Na Zashchite*. The story of Vishnevsky's *The Wide, Wide Sea* is told by Shtein, *Znamya*, No. 6, June, 1964; Vishnevsky in his diary and in *Literaturnoye Nasledstvo*, Vol. II. Preparations for Iskra are drawn from Sayanov; Bychevsky, Barbashin, *Istoriya VOVSS*, Vol. III; code names from Shcheglov; G. Zhukov, *Voprosy Istorii*, No. 8, August, 1967; and Kuznetsov, *Nakanune*. The operation is described in V. M. Yarkhunov, *Cherez Nevu;* Bychevsky; Sayanov; *Leningrad v VOV;* Vishnevsky; Inber; Barbashin; S. N. Borshchev, *Oktyabr*, No. 1, January, 1968; Dukhanov, *Zvezda*, No. 1, January, 1964. Berggolts' poem is from *Izbrannoye*, Vol. II. The victory is described in the Vishnevsky diary, by Inber, *Literaturnoye Nasledstvo*, Vol. II, and Luknitsky.

CHAPTER 49. THE 900 DAYS GO ON

Much detail on Leningrad in 1943 is drawn from *Na Zashchite*, with additions from Karasev, *Istoriya SSSR*, No. 3, 1961; Vishnevsky; Inber; Bogdanov-Berezovsky; Luknitsky; Sayanov; *900 Geroicheskikh Dnei*. Vishnevsky's difficulties with *The Walls of Leningrad* are detailed in his diary and in his correspondence in *Literaturnoye Nasledstvo*, Vol. II. The military situation is from Bychevsky, *Voyenno-Istoricheskii Zhurnal*, No. 1, January, 1964; Barbashin; *Na Zashchite;* Voronov, *Istoriya SSSR*, No. 3, 1965; M. Streshinskii, *Neva*, No. 1, January, 1964; *VOVSS;* Sayanov; N. N. Zhdanov, *Ognevoi Shchit Leningrada;* Fedyuninsky, *Pravda*, January 26, 1964. The Leningrad description is from L. Panteleyev, *Novy Mir*, No. 5, May, 1965; Luknitsky and Berggolts, *Izbrannoye*, Vol. II.

CHAPTER 50. THE LENINGRAD AFFAIR

The description of the Leningrad exhibition is from Luknitsky; V. Makhlin, *Voyenno-Istoricheskii Zhurnal*, No. 1, January, 1964; Vishnevsky; Inber; Shtein, *Znamya*, No. 4, April, 1964; Karasev; and Pavlov, 3rd edition: Difficulties of writers are dealt with by Ketlinskaya, *Neva*, No. 5, May, 1965; Yuri Alanskii; Luknitsky. The conception of the Renaissance is based on Karasev, *Istoriya SSSR*, No. 3, 1961; *Leningrad v VOV;* the handsome wartime album of Leningrad plans prepared by N. V. Baranov and his associates. The Leningrad damage toll comes from *Leningrad v VOV*, pp. 687 *et seq.* Ilya Ehrenburg's essay is in *900 Dnei*. The plans for the future city were outlined by many officials and citizens during the writer's visit to Leningrad in February, 1944. Data on Zhdanov come from *Na Zashchite*, Khrushchev's "secret speech"; Shtein, *Znamya*, No. 5, May, 1964. Material on the Leningrad Affair is drawn from F. Kozlov, *Pravda*, October 14, 1952; Shtein; Karasev; Robert Conquest, *Power and Policy in the U.S.S.R.;* and Boris Nicolaevsky, *Power and the Soviet Elite*.

Bibliography

I. RUSSIAN SOURCES

BOOKS

ABISHEV, G., *Pod Znamenem Rodiny*. Moscow: 1967.
ACHKASOV, V., and B. VEINER, *Krasnoznamennyi Baltiiskii Flot v Velikoi Otechestvennoi Voine*. Moscow: 1957.
AGAFONOV, V. P., *Neman! Neman! Ya—Dunai!* Moscow: 1967.
AKHMATOVA, ANNA, *Beg Vremeni*. Moscow: 1965.
———, *Rekviem*. Munich: 1963.
———, *Stikhotvoreniya*. Moscow: 1961.
ALANSKII, YURI L., *Teatr v Kvadrate Obstrela*. Leningrad: 1967.
ANISIMOV, I. I., (editor) *Literaturnoye Nasledstvo Sovetkikh Pisatelei Na Frontakh Velikoi Otechestvennoi Voiny*, Vols. I-II. Moscow: 1966.
ANISIMOV, P. P., (editor) *Leningradskaya Promyshlennost za 50 Let*. Leningrad: 1967.
ANTIPENKO, N. A., *Na Glavnom Napravelenii*. Moscow: 1967.
ANTONOVA, L. V., *Kogda i Kak Postroyem Ermitazha*. Leningrad-Moscow: 1965.
ANTSIFEROV, N. P., *Prigorody Leningrada*. Moscow: 1946.
ARZUMANYAN, ASHOT, (editor) *Druzhba*. Moscow: 1957.
AVGUSTYNYUK, A., *V Ognennom Koltse*. Leningrad: 1948.
AVRAMENKO, ILYA, (editor) *Den Poezii 1965*. Moscow–Leningrad: 1965.
AVVAKUMOV, S. I., (editor) *Leningrad v VOVSS, Sbornik Dokumentov i Materialov*, Vol. I. Moscow: 1944; Vol. II: Leningrad, 1947.
———, *Ocherki Istorii Leningrada*, Vol. IV. Moscow–Leningrad: 1964.
AZAROV, I. I., *Osazhdennaya Odessa*. Moscow: 1962.
AZAROV, V., (editor) *Poeziya v Boyu*. Moscow: 1959.
AZAROV, VSEVOLOD, *Vsevolod Vitalyevich Vishnevskii*. Leningrad: 1966.
BADEYEV, N. A., Y. V. VARGANOV, and P. I. KUZNETSOV, *Geroi Sedoi Baltiki*. Leningrad: 1965.
BAKLANOV, GRIGORI, *Iul 41 goda*. Moscow: 1965.
BALYAZIN, V. N., *Shturm Kenigsberga*. Moscow: 1964.
BARANOV, N. V., (editor) *Leningrad*. Leningrad–Moscow: 1943.
BARASHENKOV, B. M., (editor) *Istoriya Gosudarstvennoi Publichnoi Biblioteki*. Leningrad: 1963.
BARBASHIN, I. P., *et al.*, *Bitva Za Leningrad 1941-1944*. Moscow: 1964.
BARBASHIN, I. P., and A. D. KHARITONOV, *Boeviye Deistviya Sovetskoi Armii Pod Tikhvinom v 1941 Godu*. Moscow: 1958.
BATOV, P. I., *V Pokhodakh i Boyakh*. Moscow: 1966.
BEILIN, A. M., (editor) *Dobroye Utro, Lyudi!* Leningrad: 1962.

BEILIN, A. M., *Ryadom s Geroyami.* Moscow–Leningrad: 1967.

BELOV, P. A., *Za Nami Moskva.* Moscow: 1963.

BELOVA, L. N., (editor) *Putevoditel po Leningradu.* Leningrad: 1957.

BELYAYEV, S., and P. KUZNETSOV, *Narodnoye Opolcheniye Leningrada.* Leningrad: 1957.

BERESNEV, G. A., and YU. P. GROMOV, *Ogni Sedogo Volkhova.* Leningrad: 1967.

BEREZHKOV, V., *S Diplomaticheskoi Missiyei v Berlin.* Moscow: 1966.

BERGGOLTS, OLGA, *Dnevnye Zvezdy.* Leningrad: 1960.

———, *Izbrannoye,* Vols. I–II. Leningrad: 1967.

———, *Uzel.* Moscow–Leningrad: 1965.

BERGGOLTS, O. F., V. N. DRUZHININ, A. L. DYMSHITS, A. G. ROZEN, and N. S. TIKHONOV, *900 Dnei,* 1st edition, Leningrad: 1957; 2nd edition (titled *Devyatsot Dnei*), Leningrad: 1962.

BEZYMENSKII, L., *Germanskiye Generaly s Gitlerom i Bez Nego.* Moscow: 1964.

BIRYUZOV, S. S., *Kogda Gremeli Pushki.* Moscow: 1962.

———, *Sovetskii Soldat Na Balkanakh.* Moscow: 1963.

———, *Surovye Gody.* Moscow: 1966.

BLOK, ALEKSANDR, *Gorod Moi.* Leningrad: 1957.

BOGATOV, M., and V. MERKURYEV, *Leningradskaya Artilleriya.* Moscow: 1946.

BOGDANOV-BEREZOVSKY, V., (editor) *Muzykalnaya Zhizn Leningrada.* Leningrad: 1961.

———, *V Gody Velikoi Otechestvennoi Voiny.* Leningrad: 1959.

———, *Stranitsy Muzykalnoi Publitsistiki.* Leningrad: 1963.

BOLDIN, I. V., *Stranitsy Zhizni.* Moscow: 1961.

BOLGARI, P., N. ZOTKIN, D. KORNIYENKO, M. LYUBCHIKOV, and A. LYAKHOVICH, *Chernomorskii flot.* Moscow: 1967.

BRODSKII, I. A., (editor) *Khudozhniki Leningrada v Gody Blokady.* Leningrad: 1965.

BUBENSHCHIKOV, S., (editor) *Nemetsko-fashistskii Okkupatsionnyi Rezhim.* Moscow: 1965.

———, *V Ognennom Koltse.* Moscow: 1963.

BUROV, A., and L. PEREPELOV, *Leningradskaya Aviatsiya.* Leningrad: 1947.

BYCHEVSKY, B. V., *Gorod-Front.* Moscow: 1963; 2nd edition, Leningrad: 1967.

BYSTROV, V. YE., (editor) *Geroi Podpolya.* Moscow: 1966.

CHADAYEV, YA. YE., *Ekonomika SSSR v Period Velikoi Otechestvennoi Voiny.* Moscow: 1965.

CHAKOVSKY, ALEKSANDR, *Eto Bylo v Leningrade.* Moscow: 1964.

CHERNOV, YURI, *Oni Oboronyali Moonzund.* Moscow: 1959.

———, *Meridiniay Baltiiskoi Slavy.* Moscow: 1968.

CHERNYAVSKII, YU. G., *Voina i Prodovolstviye.* Moscow: 1964.

CHUKOVSKII, NIKOLAI, *Baltiiskoye Nebo.* Moscow: 1955.

DALETSKII, P. L., (editor) *Priboi.* Leningrad: 1959.

DAROV, ANATOLY, *Blokada.* New York: 1964.

DAVYDOVSKAYA, S. A., (editor) *Berega Baltiki Pomnyat.* Moscow: 1966.

DEBORIN, G. A., *Vtoraya Mirovaya Voina.* Moscow: 1958.

DEGTYAREV, G. YE., *Taran i Shchit.* Moscow: 1966.

DEMENTYEV, A. G., (editor) *Istoriya Russkoi Sovetskoi Literatury,* Vol. II. Moscow: 1967.

DEMENTYEV, V. M., *Molodezh na Zashchite Leningrada.* Leningrad: 1961.

DENISOV, P. S., (editor) *Krakh "Severnogo Vala."* Leningrad: 1964.

DMITRIYEV, V. I., *Atakuyut Podvodniki.* Moscow: 1964.

———, *Salut Leningrada.* Moscow: 1959.

DOBRODOMOV, A. A., (editor) *Bitva Za Moskvu.* Moscow: 1966; 2nd edition, Moscow: 1968.

DOKUSOV, A. M., (editor) *Literaturnye Pamyatnye Mesta Leningrada.* Leningrad: 1959.

DRUZULA, A. A., *V Dni Voiny.* Riga: 1964.

DUDIN, MIKHAIL, *Izbrannoye,* Vols. I–II. Moscow–Leningrad: 1966.

DUDIN, M. A., and V. B. SOLOVYEV, *Radi Tvoyei Zhizni.* Leningrad: 1962.

DUKHANOV, MIKHAIL, *V Serdtse i v Pamyati.* Moscow–Leningrad: 1965.

DYMSHITS, A., (editor) *Podvig Leningrada.* Moscow: 1960.

FADEYEV, A., *Sobraniye Sochinenii,* Vol. III. Moscow: 1960.

FEDOROV, VLADIMIR, *Devyatsot Dnei Razvedchika.* Moscow: 1967.

FEDOROV, V. D., *Surove Trope.* Moscow: 1961.

FEDYUNINSKY, I. I., *Podnyatye Po Trevoge.* Moscow: 1964.

FILIPPOV, I. F., *Zapiski o Tretiyem Reikhe.* Moscow: 1966.

FILONOV, M. D., (editor) *Leningrad za 50 let.* Leningrad: 1967.

FLEROV, N., *Korabl imeni Revolutsii.* Moscow: 1967.

FOMICHENKO, I., *Velikaya Pobeda Krasnoi Armii pod Leningradom.* Leningrad: 1944.

GAGLOV, I. I., (editor) *Boitsy Leninskoi Gvardii.* Moscow: 1967.

GALKIN, A. A., *Germanskii Fashizm.* Moscow: 1967.

GANKEVICH, V. M., *Konets Gruppy "Nord."* Leningrad: 1965.

GERASIMOV, G. A., *Partizanskiye Kilometry.* Petrozavodsk: 1965.

GODENKO, M., *Minnoye Pole.* Moscow: 1965.

GODLEVSKII, G. F., N. M. GRECHANYUK, and V. M. KONONENKO, *Pokhody Boyevye.* Moscow: 1966.

GOLIKOV, F. I., *V Moskovskoi Bitve.* Moscow: 1967.

GOLOVKO, A. G., *Vmeste s Flotom.* Moscow: 1960.

GOLUBOVSKY, I. V., (editor) *Leningradskii Gosudarstvenny Akademichesky Ordena Lenina Maly Operny Teatr.* Leningrad: 1961.

GOLYAKOV, S., and V. PONIZOVSKII, *Rikhard Zorge.* Moscow: 1965.

GORBATENKO, D. D., *Ten Luftvaffe nad Yevropoi.* Moscow: 1967.

Gorod Velikogo Lenina. Leningrad: 1957.

GOROV, V., *Pered Grozoi.* Moscow: 1967.

GOVOROV, L. A., *V Boyakh za Gorod Lenina.* Leningrad: 1945.

GRACHEV, R., *Gde Tvoi Dom.* Moscow–Leningrad: 1967.

GRECHKO, A. A., *Bitva Za Kavkaz.* Moscow: 1967.

GREKOV, V. A., (editor) *Bug v Ogne.* Minsk: 1965.

GRINBERG, R. H., (editor) *Vozdushnye Puti.* New York: 1960.

GRISHCHENKO, P. D., *Moi Druzya Podvodniki.* Leningrad: 1966.

GRYAZNOV, B., *Dorogoi Soldata.* Leningrad: 1968.

GUDKOVA, N. S., (editor) *Mera Muzhestva.* Moscow: 1965.

GUSEV, BORIS, and DMITRI MAMLEYEV, *Smert Komissara.* Moscow: 1967.

GUSIN, I., *Orest Yevlakhov.* Leningrad: 1964.

ILIN, L. I., and N. F. NIKIFOROV, *Khrabreishiye iz Khrabrykh.* Leningrad: 1964.

INBER, VERA, *Izbrannye Proizvedeniya,* Vol. III. Leningrad: 1958.

——, *Stranitsy Dnei Perebiraya.* Moscow: 1967.

——, *Za Mnogo Let.* Moscow: 1964.

IVANOV, V. D., (editor) *50 Let Sovetskikh Vooruzhennykh Sil.* Moscow: 1967.

IVANOVA, Z. M., (editor) *Slovo o Komsomolii Leningrada.* Leningrad: 1965.

IVUSHKIN, N. B., *Za Vse v Otvete.* Moscow: 1965.

IZRAELYAN, V. L., and L. N. KUTAKOV, *Diplomatiya Agressorov.* Moscow: 1967.

KALESNIK, S. V., (editor) *Litva.* Moscow: 1967.

KALININ, N. V., *Eto v Serdtse Moyem Navsegda.* Moscow: 1967.

KALININ, S. A., *Razmyshlyaya o Minuvshem.* Moscow: 1963.

KAMALOV, K. K., *Morskaya Pekhota v Boyakh Za Rodinu.* Moscow: 1966.

KANASHIN, I. I., *Poka Stuchit Serdtse.* Leningrad: 1963.

KARASEV, A. V., *Leningradtsy v Gody Blokady.* Moscow: 1959.

KARASEV, A., and G. OSKIN, *50 Let Na Strazhe Rodiny.* Moscow: 1967.

KARAVAYEV, A. T., *Po Srochnomu Predpisaniyu.* Moscow: 1967.

KARAYEV, G. N., Y. I. YABLOCHKIN, and T. N. VOROBYEV, *Po Mestam Boyevoi Slavy.* Leningrad: 1963.

KARDIN, V., (editor) *Sovetskiye Poety, Pavshiye na Velikoi Otechestvennoi Voine.* Moscow–Leningrad: 1965.

KAZAKOV, M. I., *Nad Kartoi Bylikh Srazhenii.* Moscow: 1965.

KAZAKOV, V. I., *Na Perelome.* Moscow: 1962.

KETLINSKAYA, VERA, *Den Prozhityi Dvazhdy.* Moscow–Leningrad: 1964.

——, *V Osade.* Leningrad: 1960.

——, *Zrelost.* Moscow: 1967.

KHARITONOV, A. D., *Legendarnaya Ledovaya Trassa.* Moscow: 1965.

KHUDYAKOV, N. D., *Vsya Strana s Leningradom.* Leningrad: 1960.

——, *Za Zhizni Leningradtsev.* Leningrad: 1948.

KLIMENKO, B. N., (editor) *V Stroyu Bessmertnykh.* Tartu: 1964.

KLYATSKIN, S. M., (editor) *V Tylu Vraga.* Moscow: 1962.

KLYAVA, G. YA., (editor) *Ocherki Razvitya Gosudarstvennosti Sovetskikh Pribaltiiskikh Respublik, 1940–1965.* Tallinn: 1965.

KNYAZEV, S. P., M. P. STRESHINSKII, I. M. FRANTISHEV, N. P. SHEVERDALKIN, and YU. N. YABLOCHKIN, *Na Zashchite Nevskoi Tverdyni.* Leningrad: 1965.

KOCHETOV, VSEVOLOD, *Gorod v Shineli.* Moscow: 1967.

KOLESNIKOV, M., *Takim Byl Rikhard Zorge.* Moscow: 1965.

KOLTSOV, A. V., *Uchenye Leningrada v Gody Blokady.* Moscow–Leningrad: 1962.

KOMKOV, G. A., *Ideino-politicheskaya rabota KPSS v 1941–45.* Moscow: 1965.

KONDRATAS, Z., *IX Fort.* Vilnius: 1961.

KONSTANTINOV, D., *Ya Srazhalsya V Krasnoi Armii.* Buenos Aires: 1952.

KONSTANTINOV, A. P., (editor) *Zhenshchiny Goroda Lenina.* Leningrad: 1963.

KOROLKOV, YURI, *Chelovek dlya Kotorogo Ne Bylo Tain.* Moscow: 1965.

KORZH, V. Y., *Zapas Prochnosti.* Moscow: 1966.

KORZINKIN, P. L., and A. I. LANGFANG, (editors) *V Redaktsiyu Ne Vernulsya.* Moscow: 1964.

KOSOV, I. L., *19 Dnei v Brestskoi Kreposti.* Stalingrad: 1958.

KOSTYUCHENKO, S. I. KHRENOV, and YU. FEDOROV, *Istoriya Kirovskogo Zavoda 1917–1945.* Moscow: 1966.

KOVALCHUK, V. M., (editor) *900 Geroicheskikh Dnei.* Moscow–Leningrad: 1966.

——, *Ocherki Istorii Leningrada,* Vol. V, *Period Velikoi Otechestvennoi Voiny Sovetskogo Soyuza.* Leningrad: 1967.

KOZLOV, G. K., *V Lesakh Karelii.* Moscow: 1963.

KOZLOV, I. A., and V. S. SHLUMIN, *Severny flot.* Moscow: 1966.

KRASOVSKII, S. A., *Zhizn v Aviatsii.* Moscow: 1968.

KRON, ALEKSANDR, *Dom i Korabl.* Moscow: 1968.

KRUTIKOV, IVAN, *V Prifrontovykh Lesakh.* Leningrad: 1965.

KUZNETSOV, N. G., *Nakanune.* Moscow: 1966.

KUZNETSOV, P. I., (editor) *Krylatye Bogatyri.* Leningrad: 1965.

LELYUSHENKO, D. D., *Zarya Pobedy.* Moscow: 1966.

LEVSHIN, B. V., *Akademiya Nauk SSSR v Gody Velikoi Otechestvennoi Voiny.* Moscow: 1966.

LICHAK, N., (editor) *Front Bez Linii Fronta.* Moscow: 1965.

LIKHAREV, B. M. (editor) *Leningradskii Almanakh.* Leningrad: June, 1957.

LOKTIONOV, I. I., *Dunaiskaya Flotiliya v Velikoi Otechestvennoi Voine.* Moscow: 1962.

LORKISH, I. YA., *Nevidimye Boi.* Leningrad: 1967.

LOSHCHITS, M. F., *Geroi i Podvigi.* Moscow: 1965.

LUKNITSKY, PAVEL, *Leningrad Deistvuyet,* Vol. II. Moscow: 1964.

——, *Na Beregakh Nevy.* Moscow: 1961.

——, *Skvoz Vsyu Blokadu.* Moscow: 1964.

LUNEV, V., and V. SHILOV, *Nevskii Raion.* Leningrad: 1966.

MAISKY, I. M., *Vospominaniya Sovetskogo Posla: Voina 1939–45.* Moscow: 1965.

MANAKOV, N. A., *V Koltse Blokady*. Moscow: 1961.

MANKEVICH, A. I., *Boy u Ostrova Sukho*. Moscow: 1958.

————, *Krasnoznamennaya Ladozhskaya Flotiliya v Velikoi Otechestvennoi Voine*. Moscow: 1955.

MASHOVETS, V. I., (editor) *Atlas Leningradskoi Oblasti*. Moscow: 1967.

MAVRODIN, V. V., N. G. SLADKEVICH, and L. A. SHILOV, *Leningradskii Universitet*. Leningrad: 1957.

MERETSKOV, K. A., *Nekolebimo, Kak Rossiya*. Moscow: 1965.

MERKULOV, V. L., *Aleksei Alekseyevich Ukhtomsky*. Moscow–Leningrad: 1960.

MERTSALOV, A. N., *Zapadno-Germanskiye Istoriki i Memuaristy o Vtoroi Mirovoi Voine*. Moscow: 1967.

MESHCHERYAKOV, V. S., (editor) *Podvig Naroda*. Moscow: 1965.

MEYEROVICH, I. G., and YA. G. OKYULOV, *Meropriyatiya Leningradskoi Partiinoi Organizatsii po Snabzheniyu trudyashchikhsya v period blokady, 1941–42*. Leningrad: 1959.

MIKHAILOV, A. A., *Pulkovskoi Observatorii 125 let*. Moscow–Leningrad: 1966.

MIKHAILOVSKY, NIKOLAI, *Kogda Podnimayetsya Flag*. Moscow: 1966.

————, *S Toboi Baltika!* Moscow: 1964.

MINEYEV, N. F., *Pervaya Pobeda*. Moscow: 1966.

MOLDAVSKII, DMITRI, *O Mikhaile Dudine*. Leningrad: 1965.

MOROZOV, D. A., *O Nikh Ne Upominalos v Svodkakh*. Moscow: 1965.

MUNAYEV, N. A., *Vmeste s Flotom Boyevym*. Moscow: 1964.

MUSHNIKOV, A., *Baltiitsy v Boyakh Za Leningrad*. Moscow: 1955.

NEKRICH, A. M., *1941 22 Iyunya*. Moscow: 1965.

NEMIROV, N. G., (editor) *Vo Slavu Rodiny*. Moscow: 1961.

NEZHIKHOVSKII, R. A., *Reka Neva*. Leningrad: 1955.

NIKIFOROVA, ANTONINA, *Eto Ne Dolzhno Povtoritsya*. Moscow: 1958.

NIKOLAYEV, V., and V. ROMANOVSKII, *Morskiye Sapery*. Moscow: 1967.

NOVOPOLSKII, P., and M. IVIN, *Progulki po Leningradu*. Leningrad: 1959.

ORLOV, K. L., (editor) *Borba Za Sovetskuyu Pribaltiku v Velikoi Otechestvennoi Voine, 1941–1945*, Vols. I-II. Riga: 1966, 1967.

ORTENBERG, D., (editor) *Na Ognennikh Rubezhakh*. Moscow: 1965.

OVSYANKIN, V. A., (editor) *Istoriya Rabochego Klassa Leningrada*, Vols. I-II. Leningrad: 1962.

PANFILOV, A., *Geroicheskii Oreshok*. Moscow: 1958.

PANOV, N. N., *Severnomortsy*. Moscow: 1956.

PANTELEYEV, ALEKSEI I., *Izbrannoye*. Leningrad: 1967.

PANTELEYEV, L. (ALEKSEI I.), *Zhivye Pamyatniki*. Leningrad: 1966.

PANTELEYEV, YU. A., *Morskoi Front*. Moscow: 1965.

PAVLENKO, N. G., (editor) *Porazheniye Germanskogo Imperializma vo Vtoroi Mirovoi Voine*. Moscow: 1960.

————, *Sovershenno Sekretno! Tolko dlya Komandovaniya*. Moscow: 1967.

PAVLOV, D. V., *Leningrad v Blokade*. Moscow: 1958; 2nd edition, Moscow: 1961; 3rd edition, Moscow: 1967.

PAVLOVSKII, A., *Russkaya Sovetskaya Poeziya v Gody Velikoi Otechestvennoi Voiny*. Leningrad: 1967.

————, *Anna Akhmatova*. Leningrad: 1966.

PAVLOVSKII, M. P., *Na Ostrovakh*. Moscow: 1963.

PERECHNEV, YA., and YA. VINOGRADOV, *Na Strazhe Morskikh Gorizontov*. Moscow: 1967.

PEREDOLSKY, A. A., (editor) *Trudy Otdela Istorii Iskusstva i Antichnogo Mira*. Leningrad: 1945.

PETROV, G. F., *Piskarevskoye Kladbishche*. Leningrad: 1967.

PETROV, I. F., *Omskaya Partiinaya Organizatsiya v Pervy Period Velikoi Otechestvennoi Voiny*. Omsk: 1960.

PILYUSHIN, I., *U Sten Leningrada*. Moscow: 1965.

PIROGOV, P. P., *Vasilevskii Ostrov*. Leningrad: 1966.

PITERSKII, N. A., (editor) *Boyevoi Put Sovetskogo Voyenno-Morskogo Flota*. Moscow: 1967.

PLATONOV, V. V., *Eto Bylo Na Buge*. Moscow: 1966.

PLOTKIN, A., *Literatura i Voina*. Moscow–Leningrad: 1967.

POKROVSKAYA, T. V., and O. T. BYCHKOVA, *Klimat Leningrada i Yego Okrestnostei*. Leningrad: 1967.

POKROVSKII, B. A., (editor) *Yubilei Leningrada*. Leningrad: 1957.

POLYAKOV, U. A., (editor) *Eshelony Idut na Vostok*. Moscow: 1966.

POPEL, N. K., *V Tyazhkuyu Poru*. Moscow: 1959.

POSPELOV, P. N., (editor) *Istoriya Velikoi Otechestvennoi Voiny Sovetskogo Soyuza 1941–1945* (6 Vols.). Moscow: 1961.

———, *Velikaya Otechestvennaya Voina Sovetskogo Soyuza, 1941–1945* (Kratkaya Istoriya). Moscow: 1965.

POZDNYAKOV, O. A., *Izhortsy*. Leningrad: 1960.

REUTOV, G. N., *Pravda i Vymysel o Vtoroi Mirovoi Voine*. Moscow: 1967.

ROGINSKII, S. V., (editor) *SSSR v Velikoi Otechestvennoi Voine 1941–1945*. Moscow: 1964.

ROZEN, ALEKSANDR, *Posledniye Dve Nedeli*. Moscow–Leningrad: 1963.

ROZHDESTVENSKY, VSEVOLOD, *Golos Rodiny*. Leningrad: 1943.

———, *Izbrannoye*. Leningrad: 1965.

RUMYANTSEV, N. M., *Razgrom Vraga v Zapolyarye*. Moscow: 1963.

RUMYANTSEVA, N., *Fridrikh Zorge*. Moscow: 1966.

RUDNY, VLADIMIR, *Deistvuyushchii Flot*. Moscow: 1965.

SAKHAROVA, I., (editor) *Talent i Muzhestvo*. Moscow: 1967.

SAMSONOV, A. M., (editor) *Proval Gitlerovskogo Nastupleniya na Moskvu*. Moscow: 1966.

———, *Stalingradskaya Bitva*. Moscow: 1960. Second Edition, 1968.

———, *Velikaya Bitva pod Moskvoi*. Moscow: 1958.

———, *Vtoraya Mirovaya Voina* (3 Vols.). Moscow: 1966.

SANDALOV, L. M., *Perezhitoye*. Moscow: 1966.

———, *Trudnye Rubezhi*. Moscow: 1965.

SAPAROV, A., *Chetyre Tetradi*. Leningrad: 1962.

———, *Doroga Zhizni*. Leningrad: 1959.

SASHONKO, V. N., *Admiralteistvo*. Leningrad: 1965.

SAUSNITIS, K., (editor) *V Salaspilsskom Lagere Smerti*. Riga: 1964.

SAVIN, M. V., and V. I. SIDOROV, *Razgrom Nemtsev pod Leningradom*. Moscow: 1946.

SAYANOV, VISSARION, *Leningradskii Dnevnik*. Leningrad: 1958.

SEMENOV, V. P., (editor) *Rossiya; Polnoye Geograficheskoye Opisaniye*, Vol. XIII. St. Petersburg: 1900.

SHARYPINA, YELISAVETA, *V Dni Blokady*. Leningrad: 1966.

SHAUMYAN, L. S., (editor) *Leningrad, Entsiklopedicheskii Spravochnik*. Leningrad–Moscow: 1957.

SHCHEGLOV, DMITRI, *Tri Tire*. Moscow: 1967.

———, *V Opolchenii*. Moscow: 1960.

SHEVERDALKIN, P. R., *Geroicheskaya Borba Leningradskikh Partizan*. Leningrad: 1959.

SHLYAPIN, I. M., M. A. SHVAREV, and I. YA. FOMICHENKO, *Kommunisticheskaya Partiya v Period Velikoi Otechestvennoi Voiny*. Moscow: 1958.

SHTEIN, ALEKSANDR, *Povest o Tom Kak Voznikayut Syuzhety*. Moscow: 1965.

SHTEMENKO, S. M., *Generalny Shtab v Gody Voiny*. Moscow: 1968.

SHUTROV, S. F., *Krasnye Strely*. Moscow: 1963.

SHVETSOV, L. L., *Smolninskii Raion*. Leningrad: 1964.

SIMONOV, KONSTANTIN, *Kazhdy Den Dlinny*. Moscow: 1965.

——, *Soldatami Ne Rozhdayutsya.* Moscow: 1964.

SIROTA, F. I., *Leningrad Gorod-Geroi.* Leningrad: 1960.

SKILYAGIN, A. T., (editor) *Dela i Lyudi (Leningradskoi Militsii).* Leningrad: 1967.

SKRYABINA, YELENA, *V Blokade.* Iowa City: 1964.

SLADKEVICH, N. G., (editor) *Ocherki po Istorii Leningradskogo Universiteta.* Leningrad: 1962.

SLEPUKHIN, YURI, *Perekrestok.* Leningrad: 1965.

SLONIMSKII, M., *Kniga Vospominanii.* Moscow–Leningrad: 1966.

SMIRNOV, N. K., *Baltiiskaya Doblest.* Leningrad: 1966.

——, *Matrosy Zashchishchayut Rodinu.* Moscow: 1968.

SOBOLEV, G. A., *Uchenye Leningrada v Gody Velikoi Otechestvennoi Voiny.* Moscow–Leningrad: 1966.

SOKOLOVSKY, V. D., *Voyennaya Strategiya.* Moscow: 1968.

SONKIN, M. YE., (editor) *Eto Bylo Na Baltike.* Moscow: 1963.

SONKIN, M., and I. MAKSIMOV, *Morskiye Vorota Leningrada.* Leningrad: 1957.

SOZONKOV, S. G., (editor) *Geroi Zemli Sovetskoi.* Petrozavodsk: 1965.

STEPERMANIS, M., (editor) *Riga.* Riga: 1967.

SUKHNOVALOV, A. E., *Petrogradskaya Storona.* Leningrad: 1960.

SVIRIDOV, V. P., V. P. YAKUTOVICH, and V. YE. VASILENKO, *Bitva Za Leningrad.* Leningrad: 1962.

TAITS, R. M., T. A. YERMOLAYEV, and V. A. GORUNOV, *Korabelshchiki Narvskoi Zastavy.* Leningrad: 1967.

TELPULKHOVSKII, V., *Osnovnye Periody Velikoi Otechestvennoi Voiny.* Moscow: 1965.

——, *Velikaya Otechestvennaya Voina Sovetskogo Soyuza.* Moscow–Leningrad: 1959.

TEREKHOV, P. V., *Boyevye Deistviya Tankov Na Severo-Zapade v 1944.* Moscow: 1965.

——, *Pylayushchiye Berega.* Moscow: 1965.

TIGRANOV, G. G., (editor) *Leningradskaya Konservatoriya.* Moscow: 1962.

TORVALD, JURGEN, *Ocherki k Istorii Osvoboditelnogo Dvizheniya Narodov Rossii.* London, Ont.: 1965.

TRAVKIN, I. V., *V Vodakh Sedoi Baltiki.* Moscow: 1959.

TRIBUTS, V. F., *Podvodniki Baltiki Atakuyut.* Leningrad: 1963.

TSAMUMALI, A. N., (editor) *Na Beregakh Volkhova.* Leningrad: 1967.

TSIMBAL, S., (editor) *My Znali Yevgeniya Shvartsa.* Leningrad–Moscow: 1966.

TYULENEV, I. V., *Cherez Tri Voiny.* Moscow: 1960.

VALK, S. N., (editor) *Gorod Lenina v Dni Oktyabrya i Velikoi Otechestvennoi Voiny.* Moscow–Leningrad: 1964.

VARSHAVSKY, S., and B. REST, *Podvig Ermitazha.* Leningrad: 1965.

VAZHENTSEV, I., *Vo Glave Geroicheskogo Kollektiva.* Leningrad: 1959.

VASILYEV, A. N., and M. I. GORDON, (editors) *S Perom i Avtomatom.* Leningrad: 1964.

VEINER, B. A., *Severny flot v Velikoi Otechestvennoi Voine.* Moscow: 1964.

VELEVITNEV, R., and A. Los, *Krepost bez Fortov.* Moscow: 1966.

VERESOV, A. I., *Soldaty Sto Devyatoi.* Leningrad: 1963.

——, *Krepost "Oreshok."* Leningrad: 1967.

VILBASTE, G. and K. MUURISEPP, *Kadriorg.* Tallinn: 1967.

VISHNEVSKY, VSEVOLOD, *Sobrannye Sochinenya,* Vols. III–IV. Moscow: 1956.

VORONOV, N. N., *Na Sluzhbe Voyennoi.* Moscow: 1963.

VORONOV, N. N., (editor) *Pod Znamenem Ispanskoi Respubliki.* Moscow: 1965.

VOSKRESENSKII, M., *German Vedet Brigadu.* Leningrad: 1965.

VYUNENKO, N. P., *Chernomorskii Flot v Velikoi Otechestvennoi Voine.* Moscow: 1957.

YAKOVLEV, A. S., *Tsel Zhizni.* Moscow: 1966.

YARKHUNOV, V. M., *Cherez Nevu.* Moscow: 1960.

YEDELINSKII, S. F., *Baltiiskii Transportnyi Flot v Velikoi Otechestvennoi Voine.* Moscow: 1957.

——, *Balticheskii Flot v Velikoi Otechestvennoi Voine.* Leningrad: 1957.

YEFEBOVSKII, I. V., *Velikaya Otechestvennaya Voina Sovetskogo Soyuza, 1941–1945.* Moscow: 1965.
YELENIN, MARK, *Den Dlinoyu V Zhizn.* Leningrad: 1967.
YEREMENKO, A. I., *Na Zapadnom Napravlenii.* Moscow: 1959.
———, *V Nachale Voiny.* Moscow: 1964.
YEREMEYEV, A. M., *Glazami Druzei i Vragov.* Moscow: 1966.
YEROSHENKO, V. N., *Lider Tashkent.* Moscow: 1966.
YEVSTIGNEYEV, V. N., *70 Geroicheskikh Dnei.* Moscow: 1964.
YUNGA, YEVGENY, *Bessemertny Korabl.* Moscow: 1957.
YUZBASHYAN, K. N., *Akademik Iosif Abgarovich Orbeli.* Moscow: 1964.
ZAKHAROV, M. V., (editor) *50 Let Vooruzhennykh Sil SSSR.* Moscow: 1968.
ZAKHAROV, S. YE., M. N. ZAKHAROV, V. N. BAGROV, and M. P. KOTUKHOV, *Tikhookeansky flot.* Moscow: 1966.
ZAVARUKHIN, YU. I., (editor) *Gorodskoye Khozyaistvo i Stroitelstvo Leningrada za 50 let.* Leningrad: 1967.
ZHDANOV, N. N., *Ognevoi Shchit Leningrada.* Moscow: 1965.
ZHELEZNYKH, V. I., (editor) *Inzhenernye Voiska.* Moscow: 1958.
ZHIDILOV, YE. I., *My Otstaivali Sevastopol.* Moscow: 1963.
ZHILIN, P. A., *Kak Fashistskaya Germaniya Gotovila Napadeniye na Sovetsky Soyuz.* Moscow: 1966.
ZONIN, ALEKSANDR, *Prosolennye Gody.* Moscow: 1967.
ZUBAKOV, V. YE., *Nevskaya Tverdynya.* Moscow: 1960.
———, *Proryv Blokady Leningrada.* Moscow: 1963.

PERIODICALS

ABRAMOV, A., *"Cherez Ispytaniya K Pobede,"* Neva, No. 6, June, 1965.
ACHKASOV, V., *"Dunaiskaya Flotiliya v Velikoi Otechestvennoi Voine,"* Voyenno-Istoricheskii Zhurnal, No. 5, May, 1963.
———, *"Operatsiya po proryvu Krasnoznamennogo Baltiiskogo flota iz Tallina v Kronshtadt,"* Voyenno-Istoricheskii Zhurnal, No. 10, October, 1966.
———, *"Sryv planov Nemetsko-fashistskogo Komandovaniya po unichtozheniyu Krasnoznamennogo Baltiiskogo flota,"* Voyenno-Istoricheskii Zhurnal, No. 1, January, 1964.
ANDRIANOV, V., *"Vzaimodeistviya partizan c voiskami frontov v nastupatelnoi operatsii pod Leningradom i Novgorodom,"* Voyenno-Istoricheskii Zhurnal, No. 1, January, 1964.
ANFILOV, V. A., *"Nachalo Velikoi Otechestvennoi Voiny,"* review, Voyenno-Istoricheskii Zhurnal, No. 8, August, 1963.
ANTIPENKO, N., *"Pochetnaya sluzhba (Vospominaniya pogranichnika),"* Novy Mir, No. 12, December, 1966.
AVERIN, V., *"Chetvertaya bessmertnaya rota,"* Neva, No. 5, May, 1965.
AZAROV, VSEVOLOD, and ANDREI ZINACHEV, *"Zhivye, poite o nas! Geroicheskaya Byl,"* Znamya, No. 1, January, 1968.
BAGRAMYAN, I., *"Trudnoye Leto,"* Literaturnaya Gazeta, No. 47, April 17, 1965.
———, *"Zapiski nachalnika operativnogo otdela,"* Voyenno-Istoricheskii Zhurnal, Nos. 1–3, January–March, 1967.
BEREZHKOV, VALENTIN, *"Na Rubezhe Mira i Voiny,"* Novy Mir, No. 7, July, 1965.
BERGGOLTS, OLGA, *"Ot Imeni Leningradtsev,"* Literaturnaya Gazeta. No. 56, May 9, 1965.
———, *"Slovo Proshchaniya* (Anna Akhmatova)," Literaturnaya Rossiya, No. 11, March 11, 1966.
BLANK, S., and D. SHINBERG, *"Po Dnu Ladogi,"* Novy Mir, No. 2, February, 1968.
BOGDANOV-BEREZOVSKY, V., *"Zhivaya Legenda,"* Sovetskaya Muzyka, No. 5, 1965.

Boiko, I., "*Tyl Zapadnogo fronta v pervye dni Otechestvennoi Voiny,*" *Voyenno-Istoricheskii Zhurnal,* No. 8, August, 1966.

Borchenko, N., "*Geroicheskiye dela voinov MPVO,*" *Voyenno-Istoricheskii Zhurnal,* No. 4, April, 1968.

Borshchev, S. N., "*Proryv blokady,*" *Oktyabr,* No. 1, January, 1968.

Bragin, M., "*Ne Zabyvat Chas 'C,'*" *Novy Mir,* No. 9, September, 1965.

Brazhin, Ilya, "*Severnaya Tetrad,*" *Neva,* No. 2, February, 1958.

Bychevsky, B. V., "*Govorov,*" *Voyenno-Istoricheskii Zhurnal,* No. 9, September, 1963.

——, "*Pod Leningradom dvatsat let nàzad,*" *Voyenno-Istoricheskii Zhurnal,* No. 1, January, 1964.

Chukovsky, Kornei, "*Mikhail Zoshchenko,*" *Moskva,* No. 6, June, 1965.

Chukovsky, Nikolai, "*V Osade,*" *Yunost,* No. 1, January, 1966.

Deborin, G. A., and B. S. Telpukhovskii, "*V Ideinom plenu u falsifikatorov istorii* (A. M. Nekrich)," *Voprosy Istorii KPSS,* No. 9, September, 1967.

Dudin, Mikhail, "*Perekrestok Istorii,*" *Literaturnaya Gazeta,* No. 132, November 6, 1965.

——, "*Samaya Yarkaya Demokratiya Zemli,*" *Literaturnaya Gazeta,* December 5, 1964.

——, "*Voina i Diplomatiya,*" *Literaturnaya Rossiya,*" No. 19, May 7, 1965.

Dukhanov, Mikhail, "*Zapiski Komandarma 67,*" *Zvezda,* No. 1, January, 1964.

Dymshits, Aleksandr, "*Zvenya Pamyati,*" *Znamya,* No. 3, March, 1966.

Fadeyev, A., "*Leningrad,*" *Novy Mir,* No. 2, February, 1958.

Fedorov, G., "*Mera Otvestvennosti* (A. M. Nekrich, *1941 22 Iyunya*)," *Novy Mir,* No. 1, January, 1966.

Fedyuninsky, I., "*Velikii Podvig,*" *Pravda,* January 26, 1964.

Fidrovskii, A., "*Odin iz Gangutsev,*" *Neva,* No. 6, June, 1965.

Frolov, Matvei, "*Leningradtsy,*" *Novy Mir,* No. 6, June, 1957.

Gallai, M., "*Pervy boi my vyigrali,*" *Novy Mir,* No. 9, September, 1966.

Gerasimov, P., "*Dlya Sovetskikh soldat ne bylo nepreodolimykh pregrad,*" *Voyenno-Istoricheskii Zhurnal,* No. 7, July, 1967.

Glazunov, Ilya, "*Doroga k tebe,*" *Molodaya Gvardiya,* Nos. 10 and 12, October and December, 1965.

Golant, V., "*Ubitsa Leningradtsev Kukhler,*" *Neva,* No. 1, January, 1965.

Grachev, Fedor, "*V Te Dni na Vasilevskom,*" *Zvezda,* No. 2, February, 1960.

Grechko, A., "*25 let tomy Nazad,*" *Voyenno-Istoricheskii Zhurnal,* No. 6, June, 1966.

Grishchinskii, Konstantin, "*Geroi iz Legendy,*" *Literaturnaya Rossiya,* No. 19, April 23, 1965.

Gusev, A.,"*Svoya Diviziya,*" *Oktyabr,* No. 6, June, 1968.

Ionin, A., "*Pervye sutki,*" *Zvezda,* No. 6, June, 1966.

Isakov, I. "*Leningradskiye Rasskazy,*" *Neva,* No. 3, March, 1967.

Ivanov, V., and K. Cheremukhin, "*O Knige 'V Nachale Voiny,'*" *Voyenno-Istoricheskii Zhurnal,* No. 6, June, 1965.

Karasev, A., and V. Kovalchuk, "*Bitva za Leningrad,*" *Voyenno-Istoricheskii Zhurnal,* No. 1, January, 1964.

Karasev, A. V., "*Leningrad v blokade,*" (sources) *Istoricheskii Arkhiv,* No. 6, 1956.

——, "*Leningrad v period blokady,*" *Istoriya SSSR,* No. 2, 1957.

——, "*Leningrad v Period Velikoi Otechestvennoi Voiny i Sovetskaya Istoricheskaya Literatura,*" *Istoriya SSSR,* No. 3, 1960.

——, "*Vozrozhdeniye Goroda-Geroya,*" *Istoriya SSSR,* No. 3, 1961.

Kardashov, V. I., "*Pomoshch prifrontovykh raionov osazhdennomu Leningradu,*" *Istoriya SSSR,* No. 3, 1965.

Katukov, M., "*Podnyavshii Mech ot Mecha i Pogibnet,*" *Oktyabr,* No. 5, May, 1965.

Kazakov, M., "*Velikaya Pobeda pod Leningradom,*" *Voyenno-Istoricheskii Zhurnal,* No. 1, January 1964.

Ketlinskaya, Vera, "*Fevral 1965 Goda,*" *Literaturnaya Gazeta,* No. 15, February 4, 1965.

——, "*Ispytaniye dush,*" *Neva,* No. 5, May, 1965.

KHARITONOV, A., *"Legendarnaya Ledovaya trassa,"* Voyenno-Istoricheskii Zhurnal, No. 11, November, 1966.

KHOZIN, M., *"Ob Odnoi maloissledovannoi operatsii,"* Voyenno-Istoricheskii Zhurnal, No. 2, February, 1966.

KHRENKOV, D., *"Tanya Savicheva,"* Literaturnaya Gazeta, January 25, 1964.

KHVOSTOV, V., and A. GRYLEV, *"Nakanune Velikoi Otechestvennoi Voiny,"* Kommunist, No. 12, August, 1968.

KHRULEV, A., *"V Borbe za Leningrad,"* Voyenno-Istoricheskii Zhurnal, No. 11, November, 1962.

KISELEV, A., *"Na Sluzhbe Narodu (Leonid Govorov),"* Voyenno-Istoricheskii Zhurnal, No. 2, February, 1967.

——, *"Odin iz Talantliveishikh (I. D. Chernyakhovsky),"* Voyenno-Istoricheskii Zhurnal, No. 6, June, 1966.

KLODT, A. P., *"Geroi Pervykh Dnei Voiny,"* Istoriya SSSR, No. 3, 1965.

KLYATSKIN, S. M., *"Iz istorii Leningradskogo Partizanskogo Kraya,"* Voprosy Istorii, No. 7, July, 1958.

KOCHETOV, VSEVOLOD, *"Tak Nachinalos,"* Oktyabr, No. 1, January, 1964.

——, *"Vokrug Leningrada Stanovitsya Tesno,"* Oktyabr, No. 6, June, 1964.

——, *"V Koltse,"* Oktyabr, No. 11, November, 1964.

——, *"Zapisi Voyennikh Let,"* Oktyabr, No. 5, May, 1965.

KONASHEVICH, V., *"O Sebe i Svoyem Dele,"* Novy Mir, Nos. 9 and 10, September and October, 1965.

KONDRATOVICH, A., *"Nakanune Voiny,"* Novy Mir, No. 10, October, 1965.

KONEV, I., *"Nachalo Moskovskoi bitvy,"* Voyenno-Istoricheskii Zhurnal, No. 10, October, 1966.

KORKODINOV, P., *"Fakty i Mysli o Nachalnom Periode Velikoi Otechestvennoi Voiny,"* Voyenno-Istoricheskii Zhurnal, No. 10, October, 1965.

KOSTIN, A., *"Zapiski iz Smolnogo,"* Zvezda, Nos. 6 and 7, June and July, 1968.

KOSTYUCHENKO, S., I. KHRENOV, and YU. FEDOROV, *"Eto Bylo za Narvskoi Zastavoi,"* Neva, No. 11, November, 1964.

——, *"Sozdateli Groznikh Tankov,"* Zvezda, No. 5, May, 1965.

KOVALCHUK, V. M., and G. L. SOBOLEV, *"Leningradskii 'Rekviem,'"* Voprosy Istorii, No. 12, December, 1965.

KRANDIYEVSKAYA-TOLSTAYA, N., *"Iz Knigi 'V Osade,'"* Zvezda, No. 1, January, 1959.

KRAVCHENKO, G., *"Ekonomicheskaya Pobeda Sovetskogo Naroda v Velikoi Otechestvennoi Voiny,"* Voyenno-Istoricheskii Zhurnal, No. 4, April, 1965.

KRINITSYN, F., *"Oborona Moonzundskikh ostrovov v 1941 gody,"* Voyenno-Istoricheskii Zhurnal, No. 9, September, 1966.

KRON, ALEKSANDR, *"Aleksei Lebedev,"* Zvezda, No. 6, June, 1966.

——, *"Dom i Korabl,"* Zvezda, Nos. 7–9, July–September, 1964.

KUZNETSOV, N. G., *"Gody Voiny. Vtoraya Kniga Vospominanii,"* Oktyabr, No. 8, August, 1968.

——, *"Osazhdennyi Leningrad i Baltiiskii flot,"* Voprosy Istorii, No. 8, August, 1965.

——, *"Pered Velikim Ispytaniyem,"* Neva, No. 11, November, 1965.

——, *"Pered Voinoi,"* Oktyabr, Nos. 8, 9, and 11, August, September, and November, 1965.

——, *"Pervyi Nalet na Berlin,"* Literaturnaya Rossiya, No. 10, March 4, 1965.

——, *"Stranitsy Bylogo,"* Voprosy Istorii, No. 5, May, 1965.

——, *"Stranitsy Bylogo. Yalta-Potsdam,"* Voprosy Istorii, No. 4, April, 1965.

LAGUNOV, F., *"Po Ldu Ladogi,"* Zvezda, No. 1, January, 1964.

LAGUNOV, F., YU. LOMAN, and R. SOT, *"O Neketorykh Netochnostyakh v Rabotakh po Istorii Bitvu za Leningrad,"* Voyenno-Istoricheskii Zhurnal, No. 12, December, 1964.

LELYUSHENKO, D., "*Zarya Pobedy*," *Moskva*, No. 5, May, 1965.

Leningradskaya Pravda, June 1-21, 1941; October, 1941-March, 1942.

LESNYAK, T., "*Sovershenstvovaniye rukovodstva partizanskim dvyzheniyem*," *Voyenno-Istoricheskii Zhurnal*, No. 7, July, 1967.

LESS, AL., "*Semdesyat Pyat Minut*," *Moskva*, No. 5, May, 1965.

LEVONEVSKII, D., "*Na priklade vintovki (Stikhi voyennikh let Boris Likhareva)*," *Neva*, No. 2, February, 1966.

LEVSHIN, B. V., and G. L. SOBOLEV, "*Uchenye Leningrada v gody Velikoi Otechestvennoi voiny, 1941-45*," *Voprosy Istorii*, No. 3, March, 1967.

LOMAN, YU., and B. MOISEYEV, "*Doroga shla Cherez Ladogu*," *Neva*, No. 1, January, 1967.

LOPUKHOV, F., "*Dni Bolshikh Peremen*," *Neva*, No. 7, July, 1967.

LUGOVTSOV, N., "*Srazhayushchayasya Muza*," *Neva*, No. 6, June, 1966.

LYUDNIKOV, I., "*Pervye dni voiny*," *Voyenno-Istoricheskii Zhurnal*, No. 9, September, 1966.

MAISKY, I. M., "*Dni Ispytanii (22 Iyunya 1941 goda)*," *Novy Mir*, No. 12, December, 1965.

MALANDIN, K., "*Razvitiye Organizatsionnykh form sukhoputnykh voisk v Velikoi Otechestvennoi Voine*," *Voyenno-Istoricheskii Zhurnal*, No. 8, August, 1967.

MALKIN, B., and M. LIKHOMANOV, "*Ideino-politicheskaya rabota Leningradskoi partiinoi organizatsii v voiskakh*," *Voyenno-Istoricheskii Zhurnal*, No. 1, January, 1964.

MANAKOV, N. A., "*Ekonomika Leningrada v gody blokady*," *Voprosy Istorii*, No. 5, May, 1967.

MEBEL, B., "*Nastoyashchii Chelovek Uzhe V Pyat let Chelovek*," *Yunost*, No. 5, May, 1965.

MERETSKOV, K. A., "*Dorogami Srazhenii*," *Voprosy Istorii*, No. 10, October, 1965.

———, "*Dorogami Srazhenii. Kareliya-Zapolyarye-Norvegiya*," *Voprosy Istorii*, No. 12, December, 1965.

———, "*Dorogami Srazhenii. Pervii Dalnevostochnii*," *Voprosy Istorii*, No. 2, February, 1966.

———, "*Na Yugo-Vostochnikh Podstupakh K Leningradu*," *Voyenno-Istoricheskii Zhurnal*, No. 1, January, 1962.

———, "*Na Volkhovskikh Rubezhakh*," *Voyenno-Istoricheskii Zhurnal*, No. 1, January, 1965.

MIKHAILOVSKY, NIKOLAI, "*O Samom Pamyatnom*," *Zvezda*, No. 6, June, 1959; No. 2, February, 1960.

MOROZOV, V., "*Osvobozhdeniye Sovetskoi Pribaltiki*," *Voyenno-Istoricheskii Zhurnal*, No. 10, October, 1964.

MUROV, M., "*Na Sanyakh cherez Ladogu*," *Zvezda*, No. 5, May, 1965.

NEIGOLDBERG, V. YA., "*Ladozhskaya Vodnaya trassa v 1941-42*," *Istoriya SSSR*, No. 3, 1965.

ODINTSOV, G., "*Sovetskaya artilleriya v boyakh za Leningrad*," *Voyenno-Istoricheskii Zhurnal*, No. 12, December, 1964.

PANTELEYEV, L., "*V Dni Osady*," *Moskva*, No. 6, June, 1957.

PANTELEYEV, YU., "*Flangovyi Leningrada*," *Zvezda*, Nos. 5 and 6, May and June, 1965.

PERESYPKIN, I., "*Voiska svyazi v pervyi period Velikoi Otechestvennoi voiny*," *Voyenno-Istoricheskii Zhurnal*, No. 4, April, 1968.

PEREZHOGIN, V. A., "*42nd Armiya v Boyakh Za Leningrad*," *Istoricheskii Arkhiv*, No. 2, 1959.

PETROVA, VERA, "*I More yego ne Vernulo*," *Zvezda*, No. 5, May, 1965.

POLOVNIKOV, A., "*Otsyuda Peredachi Shli na Gorod*," *Neva*, No. 6, June, 1965.

PONOMARENKO, P., "*Borba Sovetskogo Naroda v Tylu Vraga*," *Voyenno-Istoricheskii Zhurnal*, No. 4, April, 1965.

POPOV, V., "*Lyudi, propravshiye smert*," *Zvezda*, No. 5, May, 1964.

PROKHORKOV, I., and V. TRUSOV, *"Reaktivnaya artilleriya v Velikoi Otechestvennoi Voine,"* *Voyenno-Istoricheskii Zhurnal,* No. 1, January, 1966.

PROKOFYEV, ALEKSANDR, *"Proidya Cherez Voinu,"* *Literaturnaya Gazeta,* June 22, 1965.

RAKHMANOV, LEONID, *"Dusha Goroda,"* *Moskva,* No. 6, June, 1957.

———, *"Rasskaz o Pozdno Priobretennom in Rano Poteryannom Druge* (Yevgeny Shvarts)," *Literaturnaya Rossiya,* No. 4, January 21, 1966.

ROMANOVSKII, V., *"Boi Na Podstupakh k Rige,"* *Voyenno-Istoricheskii Zhurnal,* No. 10, October, 1964.

ROZANOV, A., *"V Spore Nuzhny Argumenty* (M. Gallai)," *Novy Mir,* No. 7, July, 1967.

ROZEN, ALEKSANDR, *"Posledniye Dve Nedeli,"* *Zvezda,* No. 1, January, 1965.

———, *"Stranitsy Perezhitogo,"* *Zvezda,* No. 2, February, 1966.

ROZHDESTVENSKY, V., *"Pod Grokhot Kanonade,"* *Ogonok,* No. 5, May, 1964.

RYBALKO, N., *"V Pervyi den Voiny na Chernom More,"* *Voyenno-Istoricheskii Zhurnal,* No. 6, June, 1963.

SAPAROV, A., *"Metall i Tsvety,"* *Zvezda,* No. 1, January, 1964.

SAYANOV, VISSARION, *"Pamyatnye Gody,"* *Moskva,* No. 6, June, 1957.

SBYTOV, N., *"Vazhnyi vklad v istoriyu razvitiya otechestvennoi aviatsii,"* *Voyenno-Istoricheskii Zhurnal,* No. 10, October, 1967.

SHCHEDRIN, GRIGORII, *"Poslednii Pokhod 'Shch-421,' "* *Literaturnaya Rossiya,* No. 8, February 18, 1966.

SHELEST, I., *"Ispytaniye Zrelosti, zapiski letchika-ispytatelya,"* *Yunost,* No. 1, January, 1965.

SHESTERIN, F., *"Borba za gospodstvo v vozdukhe,"* *Voyenno-Istoricheskii Zhurnal,* No. 11, November, 1965.

SHESTINSKII, OLEG, *"Blokadnye Dni,"* *Zvezda,* No. 1, January, 1959.

SHTEIN, A., *"Povest o Tom, Kak Voznikayut Syuzhety,"* *Znamya,* Nos. 4–8, April–August, 1964.

SHTEMENKO, S. M., *"Sovetskii Genshtab i poslednyaya kampaniya voiny v Yevrope,"* *Voprosy Istorii,* No. 11, November, 1967.

———, *"Pered Udarom v Belorussii,"* *Voyenno-Istoricheskii Zhurnal,* No. 9, September, 1965.

SHUVALOV, N., *"Trudnyi Opyt (Iz Zapisok Narodnogo Opolchentsa),"* *Zvezda,* No. 2, February, 1967.

SIROTA, F. I., *"Voyenno-Organizatorskaya Rabota Leningradskoi Organizatsii VKP(b) v Pervyi Period Velikoi Otechestvennoi Voine,"* *Voprosy Istorii,* No. 10, October, 1956.

SMIRNOV, N., *"Leningrad Nastupayet,"* *Neva,* No. 1, January, 1968.

SOBOLEV, G. L., *"Dokumenty o Geroicheskoi Oborone Leningrada v 1941–1944,"* *Istoriya SSSR,* No. 2, 1967.

"Sovetskiye Organy Gosudarstvennoi Bezopasnosti v Godye Velikoi Otechestvennoi Voiny (Anonymous)" *Voprosy Istorii,* No. 5, May, 1965.

STAVITSKII, I. V., *"Rol Voyennykh Sovetov v Organizatsii partiino-politicheskoi raboty na frontakh Velikoi Otechestvennoi voiny,"* *Voprosy Istorii KPSS,* No. 2, February, 1968.

STEPANOV, B., *"V Narodnom Opolchenii,"* *Oktyabr,* No. 6, June, 1968.

STREMILOV, V. V., *"Leningradskaya Partinaya Organizatsiya v Period Blokady,"* *Voprosy Istorii KPSS,* No. 5, May, 1959.

STRESHINSKII, M., and I. FRANTISHEV, *"Znamya Gvardii,"* *Neva,* No. 1, January, 1964.

STRIZHKOV, YU. K., and V. A. CHERYAKOV, *"Sovetskiye Pogranichniki,"* *Istoricheskii Arkhiv,* No. 3, 1961.

SUKHIN, KONSTANTIN, *"Eto Bylo v te Dni,"* *Zvezda,* No. 1, January, 1964.

TARASENKOV, A. K., *"Dnevnik"* (excerpts), *Literaturnaya Gazeta,* January 23, 1964.

TELEGIN, K. F., *"Moskva-frontovoi gorod,"* *Voprosy Istorii KPSS,* No. 9, September, 1966.

TIKHONOV, N., *"Iz Blokadnykh Vremen,"* *Ogonek,* No. 5, January, 1964.

———, *"Iz Blokadnykh Vremen,"* *Zvezda,* No. 1, January, 1964.

TOGATOV, SERGEI, *"V Blokade i v Nastuplenii,"* Sever, No. 1, January, 1968.

TOLSTIKOV, V., *"Leninym v Serdtse,"* Pravda, January 27, 1964.

TRIBUTS, V., *"Baltiitsy v Reshayushchikh boyakh,"* Zvezda, No. 5, May, 1966.

URODKOV, S. A., *"Evakuatsiya Naseleniya za Leningrady v 1941–1942,"* Vestnik Leningradskogo Universiteta, Seriya Istorii, Yazika, Literatury, No. 8, 1958.

USPENSKY, LEV, *"U Lukomorya,"* Zvezda, No. 9, September, 1966.

VARSHAVSKY, S., and V. REST, *"Podvig Ermitazha,"* Zvezda, Nos. 10–12, October–December, 1964.

VASILEVSKY, A., *"Istodichesky Podvig Sovetskogo Naroda,"* Kommunist, No. 1, January, 1968.

VASILIEV, SERGEI, *"Nepovtorimoye, Geroicheskoye Vremya,"* Znamya, No. 2, February, 1966.

VERESOV, A., *"Na Etom Rubezhe,"* Neva, No. 6, June, 1965.

VINNITSKII, L., *"Tot Groznii Sentyabr,"* Leningradskaya Pravda, September 28, 1966.

VISHNEVSKY, VSEVOLOD, *"Proryv Blokady,"* Moskva, No. 2, February, 1958.

VOLKOV, F., *"Legendy i Deistvitelnost o Rikhard Zorge,"* Voyenno-Istoricheskii Zhurnal, No. 12, December, 1966.

VORONOV, G., YA. POTEKHIN, S. YENUKOV, and F. SMEKHOTVOROV, *"Obsuzhdeniye Knigi 'Bitva Za Leningrad,' "* Voyenno-Istoricheskii Zhurnal, No. 6, June, 1965.

VORONOV, N. N., *"Podvig Sovetskogo Naroda,"* Istoriya SSSR, Nos. 3–4, 1965.

———, *"Sokrushitelnye Zalpy,"* Oktyabr, No. 6, June, 1965.

VORONOV, YURI, *"Blokadnye Zapisi, stikhi,"* Znamya, No. 6, June, 1965.

YABLOCHKIN, YU. N., *"Pod Leningradom posle Kurskoi bitvy,"* Istoriya SSSR, No. 3, 1965.

YEGOROV, P., *"Dvadtsatiletiye Vyborgskoi i Svirsko-Petrozavodskoi Operatsii,"* Voyenno-Istoricheskii Zhurnal, No. 10, October, 1964.

———, *"Stranitsy bolshoi zhizni (K. A. Meretskov),"* Voyenno-Istoricheskii Zhurnal, No. 5, May, 1967.

ZHILO, YE., *"Vse Eto Bylo, Bylo, Bylo . . . ,"* Zvezda, No. 12, December, 1967.

ZHUKOV, G., *"Na Kurskoi Duge,"* Voyenno-Istoricheskii Zhurnal, Nos. 8 and 9, August and September, 1967.

———, *"V bitve za stolitsu,"* Voyenno-Istoricheskii Zhurnal, No. 8, August, 1966.

II. OTHER SOURCES

BAEDEKER, K., *La Russie.* Leipzig: 1902.

BOGDANOV-BEREZKOVSKY, VALERIAN, "Leningrad Composers in the Days of the Blockade," *International Literature,* No. 7, 1945.

BOURKE-WHITE, MARGARET, *Shooting the Russian War.* New York: Simon and Schuster, 1942.

CARELL, PAUL, *Hitler Moves East, 1941–1943.* Boston: Little, Brown, 1965.

CASSIDY, HENRY C., *Moscow Dateline.* Boston: Houghton Mifflin, 1943.

CHURCHILL, WINSTON, *The Second World War,* Vol. III, *The Grand Alliance.* Boston: Houghton, Mifflin, 1950.

CLARK, ALAN, *Barbarossa.* New York: Morrow, 1964.

CONQUEST, ROBERT, *Power and Policy in the U.S.S.R.* New York: St. Martin's Press, 1961.

———, *The Great Terror.* New York: Macmillan, 1968.

CURIE, EVE, *Journey Among Warriors.* New York: Doubleday, Doran, 1943.

DALLIN, ALEXANDER, *German Rule in Russia, 1941–1945.* London: Macmillan, 1957.

DALLIN, DAVID, *Soviet Espionage.* New Haven: Yale University Press, 1955.

DEAKIN, F. W., and G. R. STORRY, *The Case of Richard Sorge.* New York: Harper & Row, 1965.

Documents on German Foreign Policy, Series D, Vols. VII, XII, XIII. Washington: U.S. Government Printing Office, 1949.

ERICKSON, JOHN, *The Soviet High Command*. London: St. Martin's Press, 1962.

FISCHER, GEORGE, *Soviet Opposition to Stalin*. Cambridge: Harvard University Press, 1952.

GAFENCU, GRIGORE, *Prelude to the Russian Campaign*. London: Frederick Muller, 1945.

GARDER, MICHEL, *A History of the Soviet Army*. New York: Praeger, 1966.

GORBATOV, A. V., *Years Off My Life*. New York: Norton, 1965.

GOURE, LEON, *The Siege of Leningrad*. Stanford: Stanford University Press, 1962.

GUDERIAN, HEINZ, *Panzer Leader*. London: Michael Joseph, 1952.

HALDER, FRANZ, *The Halder Diary*, Arnold Lissance (editor), 7 vol. (mimeograph).

HASSELL, ULRICH VON, *The von Hassell Diaries, 1938–1944*. Garden City: Doubleday, 1947.

HILGER, GUSTAV, and ALFRED G. MEYER, *The Incompatible Allies*. New York: Macmillan, 1953.

HORNE, ALISTAIR, *The Fall of Paris*. London: Macmillan, 1965.

LAUTERBACH, RICHARD E., *These Are the Russians*. New York: Harper, 1945.

LESUEUR, LARRY, *Twelve Months That Changed the World*. New York: Knopf, 1943.

MANSTEIN, ERICH VON, *Lost Victories*. Chicago: Regnery, 1958.

NICOLAEVSKY, BORIS I., *Power and the Soviet Elite*. New York: Praeger, 1965.

RESTLINGER, GERALD, *The House Built on Sand*. New York: Viking Press, 1964.

ROBERTS, HENRY L., (editor) *The Anti-Stalin Campaign and International Communism*. New York: Columbia University Press, 1956.

ROSSI, A., *The Russo-German Alliance*. Boston: Beacon Press, 1951.

RUSH, MYRON, *Political Succession in the USSR*. New York: Columbia University Press, 1965.

SALISBURY, HARRISON E., *American in Russia*. New York: Harper, 1955.

———, *Russia on the Way*. New York: Macmillan, 1946.

SCHUMAN, FREDERICK L., *Soviet Politics at Home and Abroad*. New York: Knopf, 1946.

SHAPLEY, HARLOW, "Stars Over Russia," *Soviet Russia Today*, September, 1945.

SHERWOOD, ROBERT, *Roosevelt and Hopkins*. New York: Harper, 1950.

SKOMOROVSKY, BORIS, and E. G. MORRIS, *The Siege of Leningrad*. New York: Dutton, 1944.

SOKOLOVSKY, V. D., *Military Strategy*. New York: Praeger, 1963.

SONTAG, RAYMOND JAMES, (editor) *Nazi-Soviet Relations 1939–1941*. Washington: Department of State, 1948.

STAROSTIN, P., "They Were the First to Bomb Berlin," *Soviet Military Review*, No. 3, March, 1966.

STEVENS, EDMUND, *Russia Is No Riddle*. Cleveland: World, 1945.

TIKHONOV, NIKOLAI, *et al.*, *Heroic Leningrad*. Moscow: Foreign Languages Publishing House, 1945.

TOLSTOY, A., *et al.*, *We Carry On*. Moscow: Foreign Languages Publishing House, 1942.

VARDYS, V. STANLEY, (editor) *Lithuania Under the Soviets*. New York: Praeger, 1965.

WEINBERG, GERHARD L., *Germany and the Soviet Union, 1939–41*. London: E. J. Brill, 1954.

WERTH, ALEXANDER, *Leningrad*. New York: Knopf, 1944.

———, *Russia At War, 1941–1945*. New York: Dutton, 1964.

———, *The Year of Stalingrad*. New York: Knopf, 1947.

WOODWARD, DAVID, *The Russians at Sea*. New York: Praeger, 1965.

WUORINEN, JOHN H., *A History of Finland*. New York: Columbia University Press, 1965.

ZHUCHKOV, A., *Marshal Meretskov*, Information Bulletin, Embassy of U.S.S.R., March 30, 1946.